Finding Dr. Livingstone

Finding Dr. Livingstone

A HISTORY IN DOCUMENTS FROM THE HENRY MORTON STANLEY ARCHIVES

*Edited by Mathilde Leduc-Grimaldi
and James L. Newman*

Ohio University Press
Athens, Ohio

Published in association with RMCA

Ohio University Press, Athens, Ohio 45701
ohioswallow.com
© 2020 by Ohio University Press
All rights reserved

To obtain permission to quote, reprint, or otherwise reproduce or distribute material from Ohio University Press publications, please contact our rights and permissions department at (740) 593-1154 or (740) 593-4536 (fax).

Printed in the United States of America
Ohio University Press books are printed on acid-free paper ♾ ™

30 29 28 27 26 25 24 23 22 21 20   5 4 3 2 1

Frontispiece: "Mr. Stanley, in the dress he wore when he met Dr. Livingstone in Africa." Stereoscopic and Photographic Co. photograph. (S.A. 5155). The Stanley Archives (S.A.), property of the King Baudouin Foundation, are held in trust at the Royal Museum for Central Africa (Belgium).

Library of Congress Cataloging-in-Publication Data

Names: Leduc-Grimaldi, Mathilde, editor. | Newman, James L., editor. | Gryseels, Guido, writer of foreword. | Allard, D. (Dominique), writer of foreword. | Royal Museum for Central Africa, publisher.
Title: Finding Dr. Livingstone : a history in documents from the Henry Morton Stanley Archives / edited by Mathilde Leduc-Grimaldi and James L. Newman, forewords by Guido Gryseels and Dominique Allard.
Description: Athens, Ohio : Ohio University Press, published in association with RMCA, [2019] | Includes bibliographical references and index.
Identifiers: LCCN 2019032228 | ISBN 9780821423660 (hardcover) | ISBN 9780821446744 (pdf)
Subjects: LCSH: Stanley, Henry M. (Henry Morton), 1841-1904--Travel--Africa, Central--Sources. | Livingstone, David, 1813-1873--Sources. | Africa, Central--Discovery and exploration--Sources. | Africa, Central--Description and travel--Sources.
Classification: LCC DT351 .F56 2019 | DDC 916.70423--dcundefined
LC record available at https://lccn.loc.gov/2019032228

Contents

List of Illustrations	vii
Foreword (G. Gryseels, RMCA)	xi
Foreword (D. Allard, KBF)	xiii
Abbreviations and Editorial Notations	xv
Introduction	1

Documents

Journal S.A. 73, Excerpts (January 1871–May 1872)	17
Journal S.A. 7, Full Transcript (1871)	59
Journal S.A. 11, Full Transcript (10 November 1871–Unyanyembe, 8 May 1872)	182
Field Notebook S.A. 8, Full Transcript	296
Field Notebook S.A. 9, Full Transcript	345
Field Notebook S.A. 10, Full Transcript	391
Account Book of the *New York Herald* Expedition to Central Africa (S.A. 74), Full Transcript	424
Notebook S.A. 1, Excerpts for the Year 1871	439
Muster Roll of Soldiers Engaged for the *New York Herald* Central African Expedition (S.A. 74), Full Transcript	441
Journal S.A. 12 to Zanzibar, Excerpts (May 15–29, 1872)	449

Appendix

Contracts of Engagement of Employees for the Search for Livingstone	475
Contract of Selim Heshmesh (S.A. 4734)	475
Contract of Seedy Mubarak Bombay (S.A. 4744)	476
Contract of Abdel Kader, Bunder Salaàm, Celim (S.A. 4745)	476
Contract of W. L. Farquhar (S.A. 4746)	477
Contract of Saboori Mkuba, Saboori Mdogo, and Kombo (S.A. 4748)	478

Instructions to John W. Shaw (S.A. 2469)	479
Journal S.A. 4, Excerpts (1869)	480
Journal S.A. 5, Excerpts (1870)	482
Letter of Introduction from John MacGregor to David Livingstone (S.A. 480)	486
Letters from Francis R. Webb, American Consul in Zanzibar, to Stanley (S.A. 2598, 2654, 2655, 2657)	487
Letters from John Webb, American Consul in Zanzibar, to Stanley (S.A. 2658, 2659)	492
Letters from John Kirk, British Consul in Zanzibar, to Stanley (S.A. 2656, 2660)	495
Letters from Dr. Livingstone to Stanley (S.A. 477, 478, 479)	498
Letters from W. Oswell Livingstone to Stanley (S.A. 488)	506
Letters from the *New York Herald* Staff in London to Stanley	508
Finley Anderson (S.A. 2588, 2589)	508
Douglas A. Levien (S.A. 2626)	509
Letters from Stanley to J. Gordon Bennett (S.A. 6926, 6925)	511
List of Letters Carried by Stanley from Dr. Livingstone (S.A. 4754)	519
Contracts of African Soldiers with Uredi Manwa Sera as Captain to Serve Dr. Livingstone (S.A. 4749) and Contract of Mohammed bin Galfin (S.A. 4750)	521
Glossary of Kiswahili Words	525
Bibliography	527
Index	533

Illustrations

Maps

1. "Map of Part of Eastern Central Africa, shewing the routes and discoveries of Henry M. Stanley whilst in search of Dr. Livingstone 1871–1872"   xviii
2. The journey to find Livingstone, March–May 1871   329
3. The journey to find Livingstone, May–June 1871   330
4. The journey to find Livingstone, September–November 1871   331
5. Lake Tanganyika explorations and the start for Tabora, November 1871–January 1872   332

Plates

Main Characters and Contracts of Engagement   *Following page 42*

1. "James Gordon Bennett, Esq. Proprietor of the 'New York Herald'"
2. Henry Morton Stanley in Constantinople, 1870, setting out after Livingstone
3. Stanley in 1872, carte de visite photograph
4. David Livingstone, carte de visite photograph and signature
5. Contract of engagement of Seedy Mubarak Bombay for the Livingstone Expedition, Zanzibar, February 2, 1871
6. Contract of engagement of Bunder Salaam, Celim, and Abdel Kadir for the Livingstone Expedition, Zanzibar, February 3, 1871
7. Enlistment of Saboori Mkuba, Saboori Mdogo, and Kombo, September 17, 1871
8. "Selim, the interpreter"
9. Stanley with Selim and Kalulu, July 1872, Seychelles
10. "Portrait of Bombay and Mabruki"
11. "Portrait of Shaw and Farquhar"
12. "Some Characters": Chowpereh, Zaidi, Sarmini, Wadi Rehani, Manwa Sera, Majwara, Kirango, Wadi Baraka, photograph dated November 1877
13. "Three of the principal women": Bint Muscati, Zaidi's wife, Manwa Sera's wife

Journey to Lake Tanganyika and Encounters   *Following page 326*

    14. "Plan of Central Unyanyembe"

    15. Kalulu, carte de visite photograph

    16. Pencil sketch "Crossing the Rudewa"

    17. Pencil sketch "Mount Kibwe of Mukondokwa. Range opposite Kadetamari"

    18. "Mount Kibwe and Valley of the Mukandokwa River"

    19. Sketch of Lake Ugombo, dated April 9th

    20. "Lake and Peak of Ugombo"

    21. Pencil sketch of "Unamapokera, soldier of Mayomba"

    22. "Unamapokera"

    23. Pencil sketch of three headdresses

    24. Pencil sketch of "Ugogo warrior"

    25. "Ugogo man and woman"

    26. Pencil sketches of warriors and spears

    27. Pencil sketch "View before my tembe"

    28. "View in front of my tembe"

    29. "View of Kwihara"

With Livingstone   *Following page 452*

    30. "'Dr. Livingstone, I presume'"

    31. "Mr. Stanley, in the dress he wore when he met Dr. Livingstone in Africa"

    32. The page from Journal S.A. 7, November 10, Friday, 1871, when Stanley and Livingstone finally meet

    33. Entry from Journal S.A. 11 for November 11, 1871, expanding on Stanley's meeting with Livingstone.

    34. Sketch of Livingstone's head, November 16, 1871

    35. Ink and pencil map of Urundi

    36. Pencil sketch "View south of Cape Kazinga"

    37. Ink and pencil map, facing the page "stopped at Mukungu on night of 5th day–6th day Tuesday"

    38. Pencil sketch of tentative portraits of rowers

39. Pencil sketch of "Khamis negro of 20" and "On the sand, Selim an Arab boy"

40. Pencil map on the page "Dr Livingstone had no tent with him"

41. Pencil map on double page following that page

42. Notes calculating a "Giraffe weight" in "Livingstone's writing and figures" facing the page "22nd Monday"

43. "Livingstone's Prescription for Cure of Fever"

44. "Dr. Livingstone at work on his journal"

45. Sketch of the tent with Dr. Livingstone reading in front of it, and Stanley on the right

46. "Susi, the servant of Livingstone"

47. Pages from Journal S.A. 11 covering March 13, 1872, when Stanley and Livingstone parted

48. Double page of notes: "Rain. Rain ever since leaving [...] Wednesday [January] 31st"

49. Letter from David Livingstone to H. M. Stanley, Unyanyembe, March 14, 1872

50. Pencil sketch showing how a trunk or a canteen is organized, when packed

51a, b, c. Contract of African soldiers to proceed to Unyanyembe to serve Dr. David Livingstone, Zanzibar, May 21, 1872

52. "Manwa Sera. The Headman," photograph dated November 1877

53a, b. Telegram of congratulation, from George Hosmer, on behalf of J. Bennett Jr., to Henry M. Stanley, Aden, July 6, 1872

Foreword

RESEARCH AND INFORMATION dissemination on Central Africa, its past and present, have been the core activities of the Royal Museum for Central Africa (RMCA, Tervuren, Belgium) for 120 years now. Most of our researchers' and curators' work is typically anchored in today's Africa. Yet knowledge of the past and the protection and study of collections with considerable historical significance are key factors in understanding, coping with, building upon, and moving on from apparently remote periods to the present, which owes so much to them.

Over the past seventy years, the RMCA, with the support of the King Baudouin Foundation (KBF, Brussels, Belgium), succeeded in acquiring a huge set of Henry M. Stanley's private papers, photographs, and correspondence that still were in the possession of his heirs. Thanks to the care of successive RMCA curators Dr. Marcel Luwel, Dr. Philippe Marechal, and Mr. Maurits Wynants, those materials now comprise a valuable deposit at RMCA of more than seven thousand entries.

The Stanley Archives are an unparalleled source for research, encompassing an important part of the history of Africa and Europe in the last quarter of the nineteenth century. This treasure rightly spurs the interest of international scholars. It was essential to emphasize and address this feature of the collection. Both Emeritus Professor James L. Newman (University of Syracuse) and Dr. Mathilde Leduc-Grimaldi (RMCA) have been responsible for the complex, ongoing project of publishing the traveler's most important diaries and notebooks.

Ohio University Press and the RMCA decided to combine their efforts to achieve that goal. I am happy that this volume materializes this successful collaboration. The content of this volume considers Henry M. Stanley's travel in search of Dr. David Livingstone, the preparation for Stanley's journey, the "stop & go" instructions from his sponsor, the *New York Herald*, his meeting with the famous doctor on the shore of Lake Tanganyika, their three months together, and finally Stanley's return to Zanzibar.

This volume offers new data and new perspectives on Central Africa's precolonial era to students, scholars, and the general public. I am fully confident that this work provides new information and will encourage other researchers to further explore these archives.

Guido Gryseels, Director General, Royal Museum for Central Africa
Tervuren, July 4, 2018

Foreword

WHEN SOCIÉTÉ GÉNÉRALE de Belgique conducted the negotiations in 1982 for the purchase of the archives of Henry M. Stanley, everyone thought they had rescued the memory of this man, who is particularly emblematic of the nineteenth century. The historians at the Royal Museum for Central Africa in Tervuren were aware that swathes of documents were missing, but these were thought to have been irrevocably lost. Nevertheless, how was it possible that the meticulous work of Dolly Stanley after the death of her heroic husband could have omitted a number of especially important episodes in his life? The documents were not lost; they had only been mislaid. In 1999, during a house move, the unknown archives turned up in a hidden corner of the Stanley home at Furze Hill (Surrey). Acting at Tervuren's request, the King Baudouin Foundation deployed its Heritage Fund to purchase the documents and place them at the Museum alongside the other documents that had meanwhile been given to the Foundation by the companies in the Générale group. The Museum now had a single interlocutor owning the entire archive, and it was consequently able to make it available for use by historians throughout the world. Twenty years later, the King Baudouin Foundation is delighted to have been involved in this heritage process.

James L. Newman was one of the first to jump at the chance. Assisted by the late Maurits Wynants and then by Mathilde Leduc-Grimaldi, he followed Stanley's route from London to Istanbul, from Zanzibar to Matadi, and from Bombay to Brisbane, using the thousands of documents preserved in the Stanley Pavilion at Tervuren.

Today sees the publication of the long-expected book by James L. Newman and Mathilde Leduc-Grimaldi on the archives, travel diaries, and correspondence linked to Stanley's journey to Africa in 1870–72 in search of Livingstone. Everyone remembers from that journey the events of November 10, 1871, the day when the two men met and exchanged their historic words. Today the editors of this volume have given us the opportunity to travel alongside Stanley, hour by hour, on his two-year journey. This is an opportunity to understand the reference points used by Stanley in his own time, and the political and economic context in which he traveled.

Dominique Allard, Director for Philanthropy & Heritage, King Baudouin Foundation
Brussels, July 27, 2018

Abbreviations and Editorial Notations

FO: Foreign Office

HIFL: Henry M. Stanley, *How I Found Livingstone: Travels, Adventures, and Discoveries in Central Africa, including four months' residence with Dr Livingstone*, by Henry M. Stanley. (London: Sampson Low, Marston, Low & Searle, 1872)

IBG: Institute of British Geographers

KBF: King Baudouin Foundation

LJ: David Morton, *The Last Journals of David Livingstone in Central Africa, from 1865 to His Death*, 2 vols. (London: John Murray, 1874)

ms.: manuscript

no.: number

PRGS: *Proceedings of the Royal Geographical Society*

RGS: Royal Geographical Society

RMCA: Royal Museum for Central Africa

S.A.: The Stanley Archives. The number after S.A. refers to the Inventory (Peter Daerden and Maurits Wynants, *The Henry M. Stanley Archives*, 2005, www.africamuseum.be)

Skets: sketches

vol.: volume

<...>: word missing or undecipherable

[Page glued on the left side of the cover]: manuscript characteristics noted by the editors

Examples of reconstruction of the text:

To help in reading the notes, words whose beginning only has been written over the beginning of another word are expanded between brackets; for example:

'tkick' for 'thick' written over sk[ull] = written over the two first letters of skull.

'little' written over 'com[pass]': the word little is written over the first syllable of compass.

'co[mpanion]' written over 'wo[man?]': the two first letters of 'companion' are written over 'wo' which would most likely have been the beginning of 'woman.'

H. M. Stanley's, D. Livingstone's, and their correspondents' misspellings were left unchanged.

Format characteristics of these archival documents—written in ink, in pencil, and in ink over pencil; use of colored pencil; pages left blank; and pages taken widthwise—are noted in superscript font: [Ink], [Pencil], [Ink over pencil], [Blue pencil], [Page blank], [Page widthwise].

Finding Dr. Livingstone

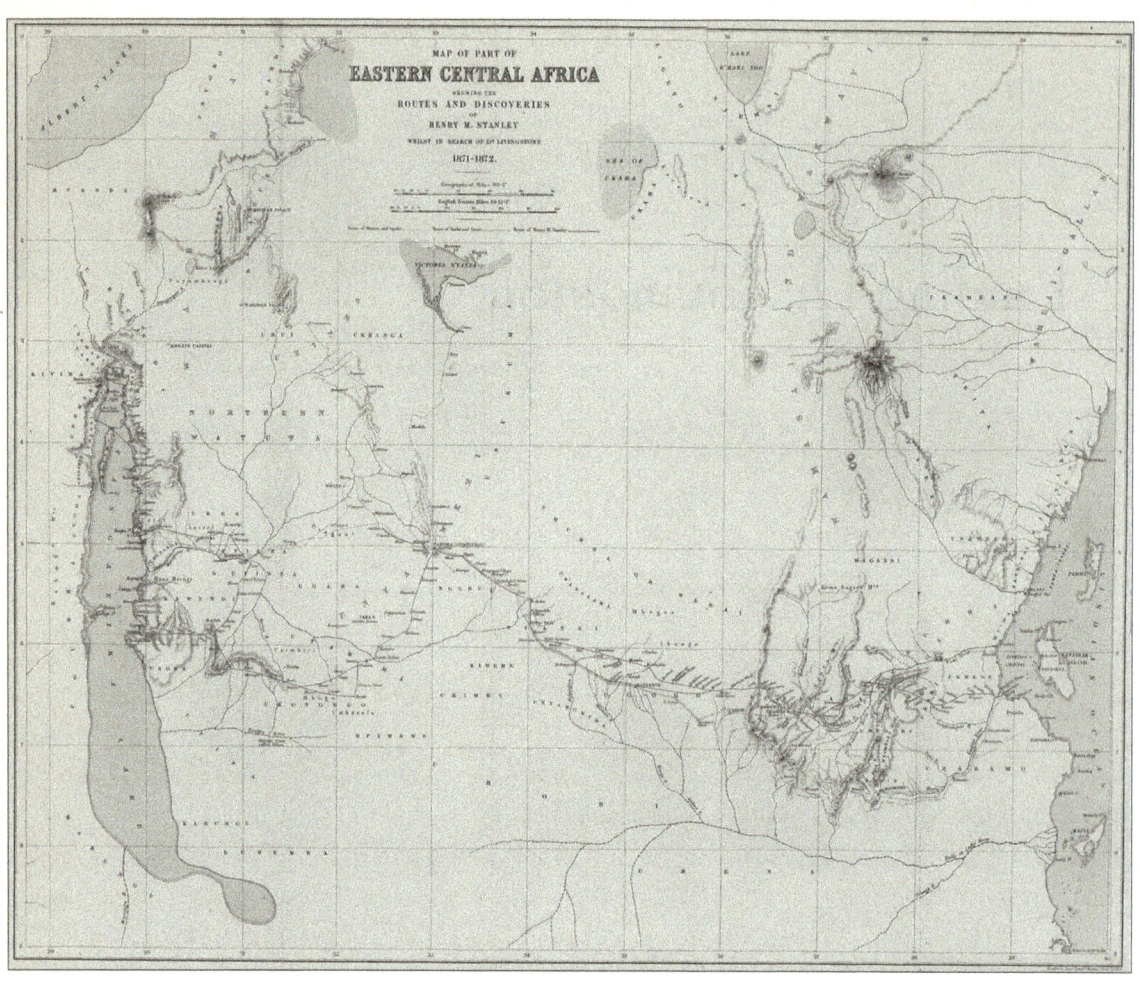

Map 1. "Map of Part of Eastern Central Africa, shewing the routes and discoveries of Henry M. Stanley whilst in search of Dr. Livingstone 1871–1872." From Henry M. Stanley, *How I Found Livingstone: Travels, Adventures and Discoveries in Central Africa* (London: Sampson Low, Marston, Low and Searle, 1872), facing page v.

Introduction

Mathilde Leduc-Grimaldi and James L. Newman

> I knew you would come out all right; I knew you would find the d...d old missionary, or his bones: and my only regret is that you did not bring him home, and chain him to a Scottish crag, with strict injunction to never hide himself again, not even though he may sometimes madly recall the charms of the dusky beauties of Unnne... and Uupann... Is that the way to spell them?
>
> —Edward King, journalist for the *Boston Journal*, to H. M. Stanley, September 14, 1872 (S.A. 2754)

This volume contains Henry Morton Stanley's diaries and field notebooks, along with relevant letters and accounts related to the *New York Herald* Expedition in search of Dr. David Livingstone. They are kept in the Stanley Archives (S.A.) at the Royal Museum for Central Africa (RMCA), and are the property of the King Baudouin Foundation (KBF).[1] We publish them to help conserve fragile documents and to offer researchers the opportunity to work with original manuscripts that have been scrupulously transcribed and thoroughly annotated.

These documents provide Stanley's views, thoughts, and perceptions on a variety of subjects as he prepares and carries out the expedition to find Dr. Livingstone. This volume does not provide a new history; nor does it attempt to scrutinize Stanley's mindset. The point of this work is to offer his day-to-day thoughts and actions contained in transcriptions of brittle and old papers, along with some annotation and context when needed. We hope our efforts will provide an invaluable source of information for curious readers and future researchers about an event that continues to capture attention.

---

1. For more about the story of the Stanley Archives at the Royal Museum for Central Africa, see Maurits Wynants, "The Trials and Tribulations of the Stanley Archives," in *Adventures of an American Traveller in Turkey*, ed. Mathilde Leduc-Grimaldi and James L. Newman (Tervuren, Belgium: RMCA, 2013), 15–27. The inventory of the Stanley Archives is online: https://www.africamuseum.be/research/collections_libraries/human_sciences/archives/stanley or https://www.africamuseum.be/docs/research/collections/archives/henry-morton-stanley.pdf.

A thorough and fair account of the expedition should not limit its sources to these archives, but rather should take into consideration oral history and other information available locally or scattered around the world (oral transcripts, memory studies in Africa, Livingstone's archives, and the like). Such extensive in-depth research was beyond the scope, time limits, and—to be frank—financial means of the editors and the institution backing this project. Our seemingly more modest objective has been to make these mostly unknown or unexploited private archives readily available to curious minds and scholars.

We have limited this volume to the story of the *New York Herald* Expedition proper, which ends with Stanley sailing back to Europe. His much-debated reception in England has been left aside. Interpretations can be found in the biographies of Stanley.

On January 6, 1871, the "Travelling Correspondent of the 'New York Herald,'" as Henry Morton Stanley titled himself in bold letters on the first page of his journal S.A. 7, landed at Zanzibar. Seventeen months, three notebooks, and two journals later, he embarked at Zanzibar on his way to England to tell the world about having reached Lake Tanganyika to meet with Dr. David Livingstone. The mission was the brainchild of James Gordon Bennett Jr., who had taken over management of the *New York Herald* from his father.[2] It began in 1868 when concern about Livingstone arose because no word about his whereabouts in Africa had been forthcoming for well over a year. Was he lost somewhere in the interior of Africa? Married to an African princess? Perhaps even dead? Then a rumor suddenly arose that Livingstone was on his way home via Zanzibar. At Bennett's urging, the *Herald*'s chief officer in London, Col. Finley Anderson, instructed Stanley to find out what he could about the doctor's status. To do so, Stanley first went to Suez, where an acquaintance of Livingstone gave him a letter of introduction. When nothing of substance could be had there, he tried his luck in Aden. Inquiries to the American consul Francis R. Webb in Zanzibar also failed to yield concrete evidence about Livingstone's return, other than to put the rumor to rest. Stanley thus abandoned the quest and took up several other reporting assignments for the *Herald*.

The project suddenly resurfaced when Stanley again met Bennett on March 25, 1869, in Paris.[3] There is nothing in his journals about a new mission to Africa, but it is clear from a letter to Stanley from Douglas A. Levien, the new chief officer of the *Herald* in London, that one had been set in motion. Dated November 29, 1869, it contained "a

---

2. On Gordon Bennett Sr. and Jr. see James L. Crouthamel, *Bennett's* New York Herald *and the Rise of the Popular Press* (Syracuse, NY: Syracuse University Press, 1989).

3. Letter from Finley Anderson, London, October 20, 1868: "Having received the joyful news that Dr. Livingstone is on his way home, from Africa via Zanzibar, the *New York Herald* desires you to proceed to Suez, or if practicable to Zanzibar, to meet him." Across the page, Stanley wrote "1st Search after Livingstone," Appendix, S.A. 2588.

letter of credit for £600" and his "best wishes" for Stanley's "great undertaking," that of finding Livingstone.[4]

Although at first Stanley considered such a mission "a regular wild-goose chase,"[5] the search for and the finding of Livingstone launched his career as journalist cum explorer. The journals and notebooks in which he reported his travels in detail became the sources for his ten dispatches to the *Herald*[6] and his book *How I Found Livingstone*, which remains iconic among travel narratives. Hints and advice in letters from the *Herald* executives Anderson, Levien, and George W. Hosmer, to whom Stanley reported, reveal that he did not have full freedom of speech in his writings. Moreover, Gordon Bennett Jr. was a much-feared boss who had sacked many correspondents.[7] As Stanley later told Livingstone, "I serve a hard taskmaster."[8] He also had to comply with the wishes of his book editor, Edward Marston, so as to suit the public's desire to read about dramatic events and heroes.

The diaries, field notebooks, and related letters provided herein let us view the uncensored Stanley recording what he saw, whom he met, how he felt and, most importantly, how he acted. In many ways the words are more vivid than those in published form, and they provide historians and other scholars with more meaningful evidence with which to evaluate Stanley as a person and the role he played in shaping the views of, and actions toward, Africa during the Imperial Age.

Presentation of Journals or Diaries, Field Notebooks, and Accounts of the Expedition

The number of documents dating back to Stanley's expeditions that have survived until now is remarkable, given that he had no home base and led a rather nomadic life. His "permanent" address was the *Herald* Office, care of the chief officer to whom and by whom letters and trunks were dispatched. Hotels, such as the Queen's and Langham in London, also served as addresses. Still, somehow Stanley seems to have kept virtually every piece of paper, be it a letter, invitation, telegram, or whatever could be of future

---

4. S.A. 2626.

5. S.A. 4, February 16, 1869.

6. See *Stanley's Despatches to the* New York Herald, *1871–1872, 1874–1877*, ed. Norman R. Bennett (Boston: Boston University Press, 1970), 3–123. Bennett published an eleventh text on pp. 123–26 that is kept at the Peabody Essex Museum, which he called Journal. It is not a dispatch to the *Herald*, but rather part of a notebook relating Stanley's last trek to Bagamoyo (April 29 to May 4, 1872).

7. Colonel Anderson was recalled to the United States and replaced by Douglas A. Levien on March 1, 1869. "This recall is as good as a dismissal," Stanley notes in his journal (S.A. 2).

8, S.A. 11, November 14, 1871.

use to him.[9] And he did so meticulously, as can be seen in a sketch of a trunk with compartments or drawers labeled "Lett's Diary, 1 ream foolscap, copying press, letter paper, envelopes, pens & pencils, ink," and a large compartment for "Written papers 4 by 12, 6 deep."[10]

Two full journals (S.A. 7, S.A. 11) and three pocket-sized field notebooks (S.A. 8, S.A. 9, S.A.10) are entirely dedicated to Stanley's travel during the *New York Herald* Expedition from his landing at Zanzibar to his departure from there (January 5, 1871–May 29, 1872). All five of those documents are reproduced here in full. In addition, excerpts from three other journals concerning Stanley's travel to Zanzibar and departure for England (S.A. 4, S.A. 5, S.A. 12) are included in the Appendix. The transcriptions in this volume open with excerpts from Journal S.A. 73 (which was compiled later and covers many years), containing some further useful information about the expedition in search of Livingstone.

The Royal Museum for Central Africa (RMCA) also has a well-preserved account book (S.A. 74) covering Stanley's missions from 1868 to 1879. It includes pages torn out of another account book, which is an original by Stanley of expenditures incurred during the search for Livingstone. The first page only is missing. Fortunately, the whole account of the *Herald* Expedition was transcribed later on (with some faulty readings of the original), and the copy provides the missing first page with expenditures on "Arms."

At the end of these detached pages, figures for the original muster roll of the expedition, an exceptional document with names, salaries, fines, and rewards of Africans enlisted in the expedition, are included.

Table 1 summarizes the archival materials dedicated to the *New York Herald* Expedition, all of which are transcribed in this volume, either in full or in excerpts that directly pertain to the search for Livingstone.

The three field notebooks served as the primary sources for Stanley's two journals. They contain notes jotted down in pencil on the spot in no apparent order and quite often not dated. He wrote from both ends of the notebooks, and thus one has to read backward and upside down for a time in order to connect the narrative. Some passages in pencil have been written over with black ink, with many letters dropped, an indication of haste. It is unclear whether Stanley intended that these passages in pencil should be left out when writing his journals.

None of the diaries or field notebooks is paginated. Dates, and occasionally Stanley's notation "continued," helped us correct the linking of the pages. Reconstruction of the

---

9. For example, see Hotel Bills at Bombay (Byculla Hotel), S.A. 4889, and receipts for passages from Bombay to Mauritius, S.A. 4891, and from Seychelles to Zanzibar, S.A. 4892.

10. See S.A. 10, sketch in pencil, last page; S.A. 9, pp. 103–4, two different sketches: "Writing tray for trunk, 30 inches long x 14 inches broad x 4 inches deep," with measurements of each compartment.

Table 1. Summary of the Stanley Archives dedicated in full or in part to the *New York Herald* Expedition*

Diary/Source Notebook	Field Notebook	No. of Pages	Size	Pencil	Ink	Ink over pencil	Skets/Maps	Remarks
1 *Notes & accounts		30	8 vo.	*	*			Few pages excised
4 *		90	8 vo.		*			"
5 *		75	8 vo.	*	*			"
7 *		160	8 vo.	*	*	*	*	"
8	*	140	15.5 x 4	*	*	*	*	
9	*	135	15 x 9	*	*	*	*	Binding damaged
10	*	129	15 x 9	*			*	

*Manuscripts S.A. 7, 8, 9, 10, and 11 and accounts S.A. 74 (*New York Herald* Expedition into Central Africa) have been transcribed in full. For S.A. 1, 4, 5, 12, and 73, only excerpts concerning the search for Livingstone have been transcribed.

field notebooks with damaged binding, some loose pages, and "non sequitur" notes was more difficult to interpret. To make the text more comprehensible to readers, we relied on matching broken words or lines at the ends of pages.

Reconstructing the intelligible order of the field notebooks was thus a puzzling task. For example, in a note in S.A. 8 (which is non paginated), Stanley mentions that the page that would be numbered 132 follows page 71, which is clear enough. Most of the time, however, he left no indication about connections: for example, page 108 ends with "he has heard from" and is followed, on page 107, with "the natives repeatedly." To ease the reading, pages are published in logical order.

Punctuation is often nonexistent, especially when lines end in the fold of the journal, or sometimes unorthodox. We have not bothered to make changes as long as the text is intelligible. Slips of the pen or misspellings are left uncorrected. Stanley made recurrent mistakes like "amunition" or "concieve/percieve" or let drop letters in his hastily jotted notes (narow, maket, pifering, quinne for quinine). He frequently switched from American to English orthography (honor/honour, color/colour). Even proper names have no fixed spelling (William Farquahar/Farquhar, Livingstone with or without a final *e*). The editorial task becomes more difficult still when transcribing names of his African encounters, villages, and porters. Stanley knew some Arabic and Swahili. He could understand and give orders. But when it comes to writing indigenous names, he more or less relied on an approximate American phonetic transcription with conflicting cultural interpretation (Bilali becomes Bill Ali), without always maintaining the same spelling all the way through his diaries. Standardized transcription of local names was a constant concern of geographical societies and congresses of the nineteenth century, to establish accurate routes of exploration and maps of Africa. It is interesting to

#	J	F	M	A	May	Jun	Jul	Aug	S	O	N	D	J	F	M	A	May
73	*	*	*	*	*	*	*	*	*	*	*	*	*	*	*	*	*
7	*	*	*	*	*	*	*	*	*	*	*	*					
8		*	*	*	*	*	*	*	*	*	*	*					
9										*	*	*					
10														*	*		
11											*	*	*	*	*	*	*
12																	*

Table 2. Months from January 5, 1871, to May 29, 1872, when field notebooks informed journals

note Livingstone's and Stanley's different spelling of the Rusizi/Lusize River. It is even more curious to find French spellings for profound (*profond*) or courier (*courrier*). Stanley said he was not fluent in French, but he probably had a good knowledge of the language, which may have come from his years in Louisiana, where French was still in use. In transcribing his idiosyncratic notes, we took care not to misrepresent the original writing of the traveler. Stanley's spelling peculiarities show his specific upbringing in some way and are part of his scribbling habits.

As can be seen in table 2, journals and notebooks overlap each other, especially for the months of November and December, when Stanley met Livingstone at Ujiji and then cruised with him on Lake Tanganyika to find out whether the Rusizi River linked the lake to the Nile watershed. It did not. The notes made were often as short as one word or a brief expression, such as "I am no short hand writer though I have a system of my own of abbreviating sentences which is intelligible to myself." Stanley went on to say that he refrained from taking too many notes, as "it occupies too much of the night to write them up" (S.A. 11, November 11, 1872, p. 10).

Journals and Notebooks: A Firsthand Perspective

African explorers of the Victorian Age "have proved immensely popular subjects for biographical studies."[11] With regard to Stanley, several earlier studies did consult some of the papers kept by the family at its Furze Hill estate in Pirbright, Surrey. By far, at that time, the best of the lot is Richard Hall's *Stanley: An Adventurer Explored* (1974). When the archives moved to RMCA, the documents were not immediately available to the public. In

---

11. Felix Driver, "Henry Morton Stanley and His Critics: Geography, Exploration and Empire," *Past and Present*, no. 133 (November 1991): 134–66.

1997 James L. Newman became the first researcher to gain access to them. Further visits resulted in his book *Imperial Footprints: Henry Morton Stanley's African Journeys*.

The Museum hired local historian and archivist Maurits Wynants in 1998 to re-catalogue the collection with a view to make it more accessible to scholars. His work, with the assistance of Peter Daerden, resulted in *The Inventory of the Henry M. Stanley Archives* in 2003.[12] Maurits Wynants had envisioned producing a series of publications based on the Archives, but his untimely passing left the project in abeyance. In 2010 the editors of this volume decided to begin a series of transcriptions to honor his memory. Three years later the first was issued—a manuscript by Stanley relating his travels in Turkey during 1866.[13] After its release they began transcribing the documents presented herein.

Finding Livingstone: A Synopsis

In *How I Found Livingstone*, Henry Morton Stanley claimed that on October 17, 1869, his boss, James Gordon Bennett, owner of the *New York Herald*, told him to "FIND LIVINGSTONE." A meeting between Stanley and Bennett did take place in October 1869, although on the 28th, not the 17th, and, indeed, instructions to search for Livingstone were given, but only after Stanley completed other assignments that would take him from the Suez Canal to India and possibly beyond.

On August 1, 1870, Stanley reached Bombay (Mumbai). After weeks there, mostly spent writing up his notes, he decided that the time had come to head for Africa, not knowing Livingstone's fate. To get there required Stanley first to board a ship bound for Mauritius, then to pick up another headed for the Seychelles, where he boarded a third that dropped him off at Zanzibar on January 6, 1871. Good news awaited: the doctor's whereabouts still remained a mystery.

A possible journalistic coup, thus, lay before him. But achieving it would require forming a caravan for a long march inland. Local Arabs familiar with the booming trades in ivory and slaves from inland regions provided information about the route and the necessary supplies. Stanley, however, had little money to cover the considerable costs of an expedition, and an expected bank deposit from the *Herald* had not arrived. To his great good fortune, the American consul Francis R. Webb agreed to guarantee Stanley's needed purchases and to safely store them. On February 5, four dhows filled to the brim left Zanzibar for Bagamoyo on the mainland, a favored place along the coast for hiring *wapagazi* (porters).

12. Online revised edition, 2005.
13. Leduc-Grimaldi and Newman, eds., *Adventures of an American Traveller in Turkey*.

The Men in the Shadow, the Wapagazi

Wapagazi were recruited under a written contract, with names, salaries, duration of the expedition, function (as boys, porters, or soldiers), and the promise to remain with the chief of the Expedition until the end of it, "to obey orders promptly and do all in their power to promote harmony, and the interests of the Expedition" (S.A. 4745, 4748, 4749). Several of them could be listed on the same contract signed or marked by all the parties. They received part of their annual salary upon signing the contract, thus giving them the opportunity to do business in the markets along the road. There was a strict hierarchy among them. Lacking soldiers during the episode of the war against Mirambo, Stanley offered some of his porters the opportunity to become soldiers for twice their original salary. Needless to say, they accepted.

On average porters toted sixty pounds on their heads, and Stanley knew exactly who was carrying what (S.A. 9). In addition, a porter might have to clear a path through low branches and thorny bush. Contingent on the difficulties of the terrain, access to water and markets, and their loads, they normally marched from 2 to 4 or 5 hours per day, but sometimes longer marches or "terekeza" up to 18 or 20 miles were required (S.A. 7, 9). The kirangozi woke up and grouped the muster, blew his horn to give the signal of the march, and showed the road, though Stanley noted that his kirangozi lost the road several times, so that he had to guide the caravan by himself. A caravan was not an army in marching order, and porters arrived in disarray at the end of the march. Stanley mentions several cases of desertion, and penalties for those caught included fines and chaining during a day or more. Unfortunately, a deserter alone was an easy prey for slavers.

The chief of the expedition, like the captain of a ship, had sole responsibility for the success of his expedition and thus had to oversee virtually everything: route, food, dangers, and physical condition of his employees. Accounts must be kept along with a logbook, and the camp secured, with the bales and arms accounted for. Fights or misconduct sometimes required intervention and esprit de corps must be maintained. Such constant effort led Stanley to regret that he had no "kidogo" (second in command) to assist him. The absence of a kidogo, besides the smaller figures given for the caravans in S.A. 7, could be an indication of a less numerous muster than Stanley reported in his printed narrative of the expedition.

Stanley certainly was a demanding master, but he knew the importance of rewards and kept a chart of those deserving of such, cloth being the usual payment (S.A. 74). He made special efforts to recruit skilled Swahili personnel: servants, cooks, tailors, carpenters, hunters, and above all, scouts and speakers of vernacular languages. Stanley preferred to hire professional carriers well known to European travelers from their previous travels, like Baruti the soldier and Mabruki Speke, both of whom had traveled with Burton and Speke, but unfortunately died during this expedition.

When back at Zanzibar in 1872, many of them signed a two-year contract with Livingstone, then later joined Stanley for his trans-African Expedition, and a few were still serving him in Congo in the 1880s.

From Bagamoyo to Tabora

A cholera epidemic had taken a large toll on life in the area, and only recently had able-bodied survivors begun to show up. In all, more than a month passed before enough men could be hired. Following advice from several locals, Stanley formed six smaller caravans designed to meet at Tabora, an important commercial center, some 430 miles away as the crow flies, but more than 500 miles on the ground. The first caravan left on February 18, the last one, with Stanley in charge, on March 22.

Right from the start Stanley faced one difficulty after another. Muddy riverbanks slowed the pace, especially of the pack animals, and the *masika*, or long rainy season, soon broke to make conditions worse. Thick stands of thorn bushes tore at clothes and skin, and an array of diseases afflicted man and beast alike. The first to go down were two horses given to Stanley by Arabs who wished him well: one died from worms, the other from horse sickness spread by bites from midges and gnats. Badly needed donkeys fell by the wayside on a regular basis due to disease and overwork, while regular bouts of dysentery plagued the porters, and several of them succumbed to smallpox. Stanley himself experienced two debilitating attacks of malaria, at the time mistakenly attributed to *miasma*, or "bad air." All along the way, porters deserted at every opportunity. Following caravan practices, Stanley responded by lashing those caught with a whip he carried. Such punishment did little good in halting the exodus, and the whippings would later be used against him as an illustration of his brutal nature.

Upon reaching Ugogo, about halfway to Tabora, Stanley fumed over numerous demands for *honga*, a customary payment to local African authorities for right of passage through their lands. It took hours, sometimes even a day or two, to reach an agreement about the amount of cloth and/or beads to be handed over. Beyond Ugogo, the caravan passed burned villages and abandoned fields, testimony to the horrors caused by the slave and ivory traders that recently visited the area.

After ninety-four days of travel, Stanley's caravan reached Tabora, where Arab traders welcomed him warmly, providing foods and comforts not seen for quite a while.

Pleasant quarters awaited in the nearby village of Kwihara. Despite the safe arrivals of the other caravans, only twenty-five men signed on to continue the journey. Hiring replacements thus became a top priority. The destination would be Ujiji, another trading town on the eastern shore of Lake Tanganyika, where rumors now suggested Livingstone either resided or would arrive soon. A serious obstacle, however, confronted Stanley: Mirambo, a local strong man, had assembled a highly disciplined army in an effort to secure the region's trade, and he now controlled the direct way from Tabora. No caravans could thus pass. To break Mirambo's blockade the Arabs prepared for what they thought would be a quick victory. Instead, the resulting battle turned into a disaster for them. Stanley had joined their ranks and almost certainly would have been killed or severely wounded, save for the quick action of his personal servant Selim Heshmy.

From Tabora to Ujiji, and the Meeting

The party endured days of sitting around, exacerbated by an attack on Tabora by Mirambo, this time aided by groups of Wangoni, offshoots of marauding warriors set off earlier by wars in southern Africa, who had been creating havoc in their northward-bound search for booty. As a result, Stanley decided that he needed to reach Ujiji via another route, one that would first head south to avoid conflict and then turn north at some point when conditions in that direction looked safer. The march began on September 20, despite Stanley suffering from another bout of malaria. It took them through uncharted territory, and porters began slipping away as before. This time Stanley tried using a neck chain that he had seen on passing slave caravans as a way to keep men in line. It had no more effect than the whip.

Stretches of the country were mostly uninhabited. A large woodland area harboring swarms of the tsetse that spread sleeping sickness kept people out, and beyond it others had fled or been killed by recent raids in search of slaves and ivory. Scarred bodies by the wayside revealed the presence of smallpox. Sensing precious time slipping away, Stanley ordered the men to turn north in hopes of reaching the Malagarasi River, the mouth of which lay just south of Ujiji. Thus began what Stanley labeled a "series of troubles." The most serious involved running short of food, to the point where starvation loomed. Good fortune, though, eventually came their way in the form of a village with ample provisions to sell. On November 1 they reached the Malagarasi. A passing caravan brought word about a white man spotted in Ujiji. Stanley thus decided to abandon the river route and take a more direct one overland. Now in populated country, onerous *honga* demands again had to be met.

On November 10 Ujiji finally came into view. Stanley saw a bearded, pale-looking man standing amidst a crowd and presumably uttered the words that would follow him the rest of his life and are parodied to this day: "Doctor Livingstone, I presume?" The answer was reportedly a simple "Yes."

Livingstone had a reputation for disliking intrusions on his privacy, even running away from would-be visitors, and thus Stanley worried about how he would be received. He needn't have, for the two men spent the remainder of the day in pleasant conversation, with the doctor thankful for the supplies Stanley brought with him. Further conversations deepened their relationship, and Livingstone even suggested that they join forces to "finish his discoveries" about the sources of the Nile. Stanley, still not seeing himself as an explorer and also not wanting to engage in what he thought an onerous distraction from his primary purpose of reporting on the encounter, balked at the idea but then agreed to a simpler plan that involved determining whether the Rusizi River flowed into or out of the northern end of Lake Tanganyika. Slowly making their way northward by boat, they found that the river flowed into the lake and therefore could not be part of the Nile drainage system.

Their Return and Parting at Kwihara

Upon returning to Ujiji, the two men confronted the question of what to do next. After evaluating the options, they decided to head for Kwihara, so that Livingstone could pick up supplies left for him there in anticipation of continued explorations. The journey began on December 27, following a circuitous and uncertain route designed to avoid areas where they might encounter conflicts. After fifty-four days, they finally reached their goal, with all in poor shape due to various illnesses and lack of food. Making matters worse, they found Livingstone's supplies in shambles, due to spoilage and theft. Stanley quickly went about finding replacements, but no porters could be found. Mirambo still held the upper hand in the region, and thus caravans of any kind had come to a stop, meaning no job opportunities existed. Stanley concluded that the only way to hire porters for Livingstone was to return to Bagamoyo. The thought of leaving the doctor pained Stanley to the core. Livingstone had become a beloved father figure, and when the time to leave came on March 14 Stanley recorded: "The regret I feel now is greater than any pains I have endured."

The small party he managed to pull together moved fast at the start, but on March 18 the *masika* rains broke earlier than usual, forcing them to ford rivers in high flood, a challenge made worse by a rare tornado that turned the countryside into a scene of devastation, a "howling waste" according to Stanley. On May 6, the exhausted men reached Bagamoyo. Upon hearing that Livingstone had been found, the Search and Rescue Mission sent out from England disbanded, leaving a large cache of goods up for purchase, and on May 27 fifty-seven men, none slaves, set off for Kwihara. His task completed, two days later Stanley boarded ship, headed for England.

Stanley's Diaries and Notebooks: More Than the Making of an Author?

As a correspondent for the *New York Herald,* Stanley's first duty was to send dispatches to the newspaper's offices in New York or London. He always followed the orders given and was quite anxious not to make a decision that the *Herald* could judge wrong or risky. As noted, Bennett regularly sacked people, and Stanley did not want to join them. As he recorded regarding the search for Livingstone, "I should say Bennett would never forgive me for running away from my duty to him. From what I know of him he would even begrudge the few days I must naturally stay here, & would say 'Your duty was to ask questions & note answers, obtain a formal acknowledgement that you had seen him, & hurry back to the Coast with the news.'"[14]

There is no doubt that the Livingstone assignment provided a golden opportunity not to be missed. Fame would come Stanley's way, with a best-selling book a possibility. As he noted, S.A. 7 was designed "to contain as much information respecting myself as may be condensed to the limits of the pages within."[15] He expanded upon this in *How I Found Livingstone* by remarking, "It must be remembered that I am writing a narrative of my own adventures and travels, and that until I meet Livingstone, I presume the greatest interest is attached to myself, my marches, my troubles, my thoughts, and my impressions."[16]

To solve both the material and financial issues of arranging his expedition, Stanley had to rely on himself for most things. Views about this are clear in S.A. 7, as are his concerns, including his inexperience as chief of the expedition, the lack of a valuable second in command, his bouts of illness, his knowledge of the country only from books, the secrecy of the whole operation, and finally having no precise budget from the *Herald*. In addition, Stanley felt highly insecure about having little in common with scientific travelers, or with literary tourists.[17] Plagued by such doubts and the fear that he

---

14. S.A. 11, 31.

15. The same expression appears at the end of Journal S.A. 5, December 31, 1870: "For further information about myself and Expedition, and daily incidents turn to Diary 1871."

16. *HIFL,* "Introductory," xxii.

17. On this distinction, see Felix Driver, *Geography Militant: Cultures of Exploration and Empire* (Oxford: Blackwell, 2001), 51–53.

might not succeed in his quest, this journal shows Stanley not as a triumphant hero, but rather more as a vulnerable human being struggling with self-doubt.

After having achieved his goal at Ujiji, Stanley's introspection sank into the background. As S.A. 11 shows, Livingstone, and Stanley's growing affection for him, became the center of attention. Their meeting and time spent together also sowed the seeds for Stanley to become a traveler and a man with a mission in life.

Documents

Journal S.A. 73, Excerpts (January 1871–May 1872)

[This journal is written in ink. It is not paginated.]
[Stanley transcribed these entries at a later date.]

1871

January

1 At sea on board Whaling Schooner "Falcon" Capt Josiah Richmond. New Bedford 126 tons. 19th day out. E Long 51°. N Lat. 4° 30'. 80 days from Bombay. 153 days since arriving in Bombay.

The Commission to find Livingstone was given to me Oct 28th 1869 verbally at the Grand Hotel in Paris.

3 We are 180 miles from Zanzibar

5 Sighted Pemba Island 15 m N of Zanzibar

6 Land at Zanzibar at last 159 days since reaching Bombay. Hospitably received by Capt F. R. Webb, U. S. Navy & Consul.

7 Nothing much to do. No letters from Bennett or his Agent & therefore no money. I can only read & stare, & lounge about like an habitué. Make acquaintance with Spalding Agent of rival house to Webbs.

8 Went with Consul Webb to see Sultan Burghash.

9 Am now busy at work. Think of going up Rufiji R. but Ludha Damji[1] nor Kirk[2] Eng Consul know anything of it. Was permitted to examine Capt Fraser's library on Africa.[3] Nothing about Rufiji. Webb has succeeded in getting me money from Tarya Topan 25 per cent discount. Have bought 2 boats for ascent of Rufiji.

Making tents & sails.

11 Paid 154 ½ dollars to Capt Richmond "Falcon" for passage from Seychelles.

---

1. Ludha Damji, a member of the Ismaili community, was the agent of the financier Jairam Shewji's firm in Zanzibar. See Padma Srinivasan, "Indian Traders in Zanzibar with Special Reference to Jairam Shewji (19th Century)," *Proceedings of the Indian History Congress* 61, part 2 (2000–2001): 146–47, https://www.jstor.org/stable/44144429.

2. John Kirk (1832–1922), companion explorer of David Livingstone during his second expedition, was acting as British consul in Zanzibar at this date.

3. Mentioned under January 10, 1871 (Journal S.A. 7).

14 At work every day. Nearly had a row with Webb. I had occasion to suspect dragoman Johari of dishonesty. He complained to Webb. Webb & his clerk Sparhawk very much offended, as they regard him as a paragon of honesty. My experience however with the Arab dragoman, the Turkish zaptieh, the Greek tout, the Persian Chappar-khan, the Hindi turjiman, compel me to doubt him. He asked in my presence the price of a Salter's balance and I heard it was $6. But Johari charged me $6.50. Then Johari is from Johanna Island, a fellow countryman of those who went with Livingstone & came back with that fearful tale of Livingstone's murder.

No letters from Bennett or his London Agent.

17 Had a talk with Dr John Kirk this morning. He gave me a very bad opinion of Livingstone. I am told he is hard to get along with, is cross and narrow minded. Has had no personal quarrel with him, but his companions, Bedingfield, Baines, & others have had reason to be dissatisfied. He thinks he ought to come home now, & allow a younger man to take his place. Livingstone takes no notes, nor keeps his journal methodically. He thinks Livingstone would run away if he heard any traveller was coming to him.

25 I find after questioning every one that the best road to the interior is the old caravan road to Unyanyembe, whence I shall try & strike straight for Ujiji. My object is to get to Tanganika Lake in order to inquire along its shores whither Livingstone went after reaching the Lake from Nyassa.

26 Am engaging men.

1871

February

1 22 men sign Engagement to accompany me into the interior

2 Paid Farquhar's Bill to Charley Zanzibar. Liquor & Beer $18.72 cts[4]

5 Left Zanzibar in dhow for Bagamoyo at 7 A.M. Reached Bagamoyo about sunset. At last I am on African soil. I have arranged with the Jemador Isa about house, when I am to prepare the Expedition.

18 Sent the 1st Caravan off into the interior 3 loads Cloth, 3 of Wire with letter of introduction from Sultan to Governor Said bin Salim at Unyanyembe.

21 Sent 2nd Caravan of 12 porters & 2 chiefs under 2 soldiers with 9 loads Cloth, 2 loads of Wire & 1 of Beads.

25 Despatched 3rd Caravan under Wm Farquhar with 8 donkeys, 11 Porters 3 Soldiers & Cook.

28 Despatched 4th Caravan.

---

4. See Farquhar's Bill to A. Charles, Zanzibar, from January 7 to February 2, 1871, S.A. 4893.

March[5]

4 At Bagamoyo. Despatched 5th Caravan

8 Rec.ed letter from Farquhar saying he was well, & preparing.

19 Went to Zanzibar for the last time to pay Bills to Soor Hadji Pallu,[6] my Broker.

21 Returned to Bagamoyo[7]

22 March to Kikoka 12 miles.

23 " " Rosaco 12 m.

24 " " Camp 8 ¾ m. Sent Shaw or Smith & Bombay back to Bagamoyo about the porters. They had not yet started from Shamba Gonera 2 ½ m from Bagamoyo.

25 Halt, to await return of Shaw & Bombay. Went out to hunt on horseback. Saw many tracks of antelope, hartebeest & elephant & zebra. Saw flock of guinea fowl only. Returned to camp unsuccessful. After breakfast went out with Selim Southward became lost amid the thickets. We struck into the depths of one of them into a tunnel caused by frequent wandering of game under overaching Euphorbia & acacia. The compass guided us back into Camp.

25 Rec.d letter from Webb Consul saying "Herald" agent has shamefully neglected me.

26 Visited by Natives of Kingaru, began trading for the first time with them. American sheeting & beads were bartered for Eggs, Millet & Indian Corn. A string of Khutu or brown beads bought 7 Eggs.

28 At Kingaru 12 miles. Shaw & Bombay to my great relief returned to Camp as we were starting

29 Halt at Kingaru. At 2 P.M. the Arab grey horse died. In the evening the second horse the bay died.

1871

April

1 Started in earnest.

3 The Porters of the 5th Caravan 27 in number left our Camp at Kingaru. We are to stay here in order to allow them a fair start from us.

4 Sheikh Thani & Khaif bin Asman came up with a small Caravan. They say that Mussoud carried some things to Unyanyembe for Livingstone some time ago.

6 March to Imbiki 15 m. Shaw however did not reach this place until 8 A. M. of the 7th. He has the little cart with him which has delayed his progress. 1 porter has absconded with 2 goats & 1 tent, & Uledi's stock of clothes.

---

5. 'March' in bold letters, written over 'February'.

6. Soor Hadji Palloo (*HIFL*). Sewa Haji Paroo, another businessman of the Ismaili community, like Ludha Damji and Taria Topan, managed his father's business, Haji Kanji & Co. See Christine E. Dobbin, *Asian Entrepreneurial Minorities: Conjoint Communities in the Making of the World-Economy 1570–1940* (London: Curzon, 1996), 120.

7. '21' written over '20'.

7 Good Friday[8] Khamis a porter has deserted. Halt.

8 March to Msuwa 10 m. A horrible time. Shaw did not reach us until midnight.

9 Owing to the tremendous strain of yesterday we have been obliged to halt again

10 March 6 miles. Met the first slave gang in chains bound for the coast. They appeared pretty contented.

11 Kisemo after a walk of 5 miles. A rather easy march but rain fell towards the latter part & made[9] walking heavy. Game abundant. Have seen 3 head personally.

12 Mussoudi on Ungerengeri 11 miles. We have left jungly lands & are now in open country. It resembles Park Land, without evidences of cultivation & arrangement.

Met Salim bin Rashid who gave news of Livingstone.[10] He met him in Ujiji a year ago. Lived next door to him. Described him as having a white beard & moustache & thin from illness. L was about to go to Marungu, & Manyema. Sent a letter to Mr Webb about this news.

13 Halt at Mussoudi because of scant supplies of food

14 March to Camp. Crossed the Ungerengeri R. a rapid & deep river. The cart gave us endless trouble, not even the strongest donkey though carrying 196 lbs weight on his back could draw it with only 225 lbs. Evidently this country is not adapted for carts.

April[11]

15 Mikesseh[12] 7 ½ miles

16 Ugallalla[13] Camp 7 ½ m. a heavy rain during night.

17 Muhalleh 11 ¼ miles. We are now hemmed in by hills, a welcome & agreeable change. Villages are built in a circle. We bartered a fathom of cloth for 15 measures of millet. We caught up with the 5th Caravan to-day

18 Ungerengeri near Simbamwenni 7 miles in 2 ¾ hours. The 5th Caravan had several on the sick list, but our cheery example had its influence.

19 Halt at this famous rendez vous to procure supplies. The last few marches have told on the donkeys fearfully. Have reduced their loads to 140 lbs. each. 3 donkeys belong to the 4th Caravan are dead. Country is flooded.

---

8. 'Good Friday' written in the margin.
9. 'the' crossed out.
10. According to *HIFL* (114), this meeting happened at Muhalleh.
11. 'April' in bold letters, written over 'March'.
12. Mikeseh (*HIFL*).
13. Ulagalla (*HIFL*).

20 Selim my boy from Jerusalem had a narrow escape from being shot by handling a double-barreled gun. He hung it on the tent pole peg on the trigger while loaded & was pointing the muzzle close to his breast. Tent was blown down & gun went off. A severe attack of ague attacked me. I discerned my old enemy at a distance observed his stealthy approach up the spine, along the ribs & to the shoulders & knew that when he reached the head, I should have to yield & rest. In the afternoon the fever with its insane visions, its loud brain throbs, and nausea came, & late in the night there was rest & sleep & dreams.

21 Halt. 5th Caravan marched, we go tomorrow.

Sarmine, Ferajji, & Hamadi the Kirangozi returned from their visit to Kiroka on a hunt after bamboos. They brought one back as thick as a girl's wrist.

1871

April

22 Halt. Rain incessantly. Ungerengeri is in flood & not fordable. The mountains about are in clouds. Food is dear – 2 fowls cost 1 fathom of cloth, while 4 were sold for the same quantity at Bagamoyo.

23 Simbo 5 miles. It cleared up this morning – we crossed a rickety & temporary bridge & then an easy march.

We tried for game but found none.

24 Camp 10 ¼ m W.N W.

Soon after leaving Simbo the rain poured in torrents.

This morning Bunder Salaam the cook was found guilty of pifering for the sixth time. He was punished & driven out of camp. The cart gave us infinite trouble. The mud was too tenacious. Bombay lost our new axe, the baggage tent, his own fine uniform & clothes & seemed to be utterly demented in consequence. Khamisi, a porter lay down in despair. Kaima could not bring his feet together. Cart did not reach us till midnight. Hyaenas prowl around camp.

25 Halt. No provisions in front. The donkeys were stampeded by an antelope. Saw two Kudu. Shot a moorhen & fat pigeon. A Caravan of Wanyamwezi came in from West. The neighborhood is now very lively – tomorrow it will be utterly desolate.

26 Halt

27 Halt

1871

April

28 Shaw with Mabruki – (Burton's "Bull Headed"[14] were sent off to hunt up the 3 soldiers yesterday commissioned to hunt up the thieving cook.

About 5 P.M. they returned bringing with them the absentees. They had a most melancholy account to give of themselves. Arriving at Simbamwenni on the track of two men who had been seen at this ferry, the Sultan caused them to be arrested & put them in chains. She[15] had also taken their guns & accouterments & suspecting the two men seen with Cook's donkey to have murdered him for the sake of his property she sent them in charge of a Swahili caravan to be judged & disposed of by Syed Bargash. The chiefs of the caravan got them set at liberty by stating that if not released I might return, and make trouble. Their freedom was given minus their guns & equipments.

The soldiers returned with the Cook's donkey, hat & spectacles & Malabar book on Religion.

29 Makata Plains. W by N. 6 ½ miles.

Started at 8 a.m. Men much demoralized after their lengthened halt. Shaw is sick of a fever also Selim & Zaidi the latter from small pox. Mud, mud, blackest mud. Had to cross 2 rivers. Camped E. side of Makata. Bought 200 lbs Hartebeest meat for 4 fathom of sheeting. Had a good feast. Passed a small village fortified after the style of Simbamwenni

1871

April

30 Camp on W. side of Makata River

It was a day's work to cross the Makata. Cut a path through 50 yds of jungle & then crossed the river 50 yds wide. Swam the donkeys across then built a bridge across the stream for the Escort & porters to carry the baggage. While we labored the rain poured in torrents and lashed us blind - & beat the road & plain into mortar-mud. To increase our ill-luck, Kingaru deserted. Despatched 2 soldiers after him who caught him in two hours.

Shaw still sick. Zaidi is down with small pox. Thus my small force is reduced. If I can only preserve my health, my courage I believe will be equal to the needs, but if I fall sick like the rest, it is doubtful whether we shall reach Unyanyembe.

---

14. No closing parenthesis.
15. 'He' corrected to 'She'.

The Search after Livingstone

1871

May

1 Camp in Valley of Makata. 9 m. W. N. W.

    One of the most dreadful days. The Makata plain during the rainy season turns out to be worse than reported. It was simply an extensive plain covered with 3 feet of water. The valley 45 miles[16] wide seems to be as level as a billiard table. We camped upon the only dry spot found in the whole expanse.

2 Rudewa R. 9 m. To day was similar to yesterday in our experience. The water however is now shallowing it is only about a foot deep.

3 Camp on banks of Rudewa. donkey lost with all our sugar & tea.

4 Rehenneko 7 ½ m. I am attacked with severe dysentery owing to four days mud & water – water armpit-deep.

5 Halt.

6 & 7 Halt.

8 March up Mountains of Usagara. 7 miles

9 Kiora 6 miles, on right bank of Mukondokwa.

    Caught up with Farquhar, sick of a dropsy – which I take to be the result of the 18 dollars worth of brandy consumed at Zanzibar. He is in a terrible state unable to stand. His legs appear quite Elephantine.

10 Halt

11 Camp on Mukondokwa Dist 11 m.

12 Madete. 6 miles. Have sent men back to try & find Shaw who is with the cart. I sent Chowpereh to him ordering him to pitch the cart & its loads into the bush. But Chowpereh on hearing what was in the note proposed to carry the cart on his head, & his chum Mabruki the Bull headed took the loads on his head. Finding that they were terribly long, I rode out at last to meet them & was astonished to find burly Chowpereh loaded with the cart, & Mabruki with the loads. The cart was there & then pitched into the bushes while Chowpereh – the ingrate cried out "See there goes the White Man's folly."

13 Discover Ugombo Lake March 6 miles. The Lake is 2 ¼ miles by 1 ½ m. Farquhar rode my donkey while I walked all the way. 2 donkeys died to-day.

14 Halt at Ugombo Lake. Farquhar I sent to Mpwapwa by hammock. Selim is very sick, Shaw down with fever. No end of calamities. In the night Shaw fired his rifle into my tent in the night. He is evidently half crazed.

---

16. 'miles' written over 'yds'.

April[17]

15 Halt at Ugombo Lake. Shot some grouse.

16 Matamombo 11 m. W N W. Donkey foal dies. Omar the dog brought from Bombay died from inflammation of bowels. The water is bitter – nitrous – at this place. Monkeys with exceedingly long tails seen here.

17 Mpwapwa 7 hours. A very long march made longer by difficulties. The Natives call this place Mbawbwa. It would be a capital site for a Mission, as the Natives are timid & amiable.

18 Halt. Met Abdulla bin Nasib with 500 tusks ivory bound to Zanzibar. He gave me some news of Livingstone. He is said to have gone West of Lake Tanganika a month's journey to a country called Unyema or Manyema. He had shot himself in the thigh while out hunting buffalo. There were many lakes West of Tanganika. Lake of Ujiji was very great. Lake Urua was very big. Bangueolo was very large, but Lake Manyema was great – great exceedingly great. This was the sum of Abdulla's report.

19 Halt. Saw cattle for the first time since leaving Coast.

20 Halt. I leave Farquhar behind at this place. He is not fit to travel, & I have no means of carrying him either to the Coast or with me. Leave supplies & servant with him & make arrangements with chief to look after him.

21 Kisokwé[18] 4 miles W N. W. Skirted Mpwapwa Mountains

22 Chunyu,[19] 1 ½ hour W. N. W.

23 Marenga Mkali or the Bitter (Nitrous) Water 8 ¾ m. Afternoon march 13 ¾ miles = 22 ½ miles. Saw Zebra Giraffe, Eland Antelope, rhinoceros, & florican.

24 Marenga Mkali wilderness 3rd march through it 10 miles. Reach Mvumi. Little Ugogo.

25 Mvumi. Great Ugogo 8 m.

26 Halt. Pay tribute to Chief. 18 ½ doti or 74 yds cloth mixed. 3 donkeys died. Hyaenas swarm.

27 Matamburu 8 miles Country populous

28 Halt. Paid 8 doti tribute.

29 Bihawana. 4 hours. Tribute 3 doti.

30 Kididimo Chief Mkata 2 hours.

31 Camp. Evening march 8 hours. 16 m.

---

17. 'April' instead of 'May'.
18. Kisokweh (*HIFL*).
19. Chunyo (*HIFL*, 121).

The Search after Livingstone

1871

June

1 March to Pembera Mperé.[20] 2 hours.

2 March to Mizanza. W by N. 5 ½ hours. Shaw says that these people must be "the genuine Ugogians".

An Arab was fined 9 doti for letting his donkey stray towards the millet fields.

3 Halt at Mizanza. The fever which has so peristently clung to me the last four days has yielded to four strong doses of Quinne.

4 Mukondoku 13 ½ m. W. N. W. Ugogo to the white traveller is just what Vanity Fair was to Christian.[21] It is an ordeal to train and discipline him. Paid 6 doti trib.

5 Halt at Mukondoku. Place very populous 30 villages

6 Halt "   "

7 Halt at Munieka 5 hours W by N. The Arabs & I having determined which road to take – one of them changed his mind at starting, but finally seeing no one followed him, he followed us.

8 Evening march to Mabunguru 20 miles. Plenty of water along this road. Curious huge rocks like those of Stonehenge.

9 Uyanzi country 8 miles

10 Kiti 4 ½ hours. W. N. W.

11 Msalalo. Chief Matumbi 15 miles or 6 ½ hours.

12 Ngaraiso. 3 ½ hours or 8 ¾ miles. Provisions Cheap.

13 Kussouri[22] 3 ½ hours. Great rocks Jiwe la Singa & Jiwe la Mkoa on our left.

14 Halt. Meet Sultan bin Mohamed's Caravan. I asked him to take Farquhar to Zanzibar. He promised to do so.

15 Mgongo Tembo. 3 ½ hours & 3 ½ hours. 17 ½ miles

June

16 Nqualah or Kwale[23] to Madedita 5 hours 12 ½ m. Met Hassan son of Said bin Salim. His news of Livingstone was that "His left shoulder was out of joint. That he was a very old man, beard nearly white – Has gone to Manyema with some Arabs a 3 months march, but he is now returning owing to a letter awaiting him at Ujiji. He has 15 bales of Cloth in store at Unyanyembe.

---

20. Pembera Pereh (*HIFL*).

21. Ironical reference to the Journey of Christian in *The Pilgrim's Progress from This World to That Which Is to Come*, by John Bunyan (1678).

22. Kusuri (*HIFL*).

23. Nghwhalah (*HIFL*).

17 Madedita to Tura 7 ½ miles. Plenty of honey & cheap.
18 Kwale R. 7 hours 17 ½ m.
19 Rubuga. A Zanzibari village. 18 ¾ miles
20 Halt. Visited to-day by Amir bin Sultan[24] who is going to Zanzibar. His news of Livingstone was "There is a White man – very old who came to Ujiji by the way of Lake Nyassa. After reaching Ujiji he went to Marungu and returned to Ujiji – then travelled to Manyema with some Arabs. There is a big Lake there – & it is said that he went to that country to see it. Lately a Caravan brought news to Ujiji that he had died, but the news may not be true. Inshal'ah." He had a strange idea respecting Victoria Nyanza. He says it is a salt Lake, & reaches nearly to the sea near Zanzibar, but the river running from it was fresh." He behaved exceedingly well to me.
21 Kigwa 5 hours 12 ½ miles
22 Shisa[25] – 7 hours 17 miles. My messenger returned from the Governor of Unyanyembe with offers of hospitality.
23 Arrive at Kwihara. Unyanyembe after 6 ¼ mile march. 94 days from Bagamoyo 525 miles from the Sea.
24 Halt. Am greeted by Said bin Salim, Amram bin Mussoud, Abdulla bin Juma, Sheikh bin Nasib.
25 Sick of the district fever the "Mukunguru"
26 Halt. The Sultan sons called to see me. Sick
27 Halt. Sick but prepare for my trip to Ujiji
28 Halt. Sick. I tried to write the Herald letter, but had to give it up.
29 Halt Sick abed
30 Halt.   "   "

The Search after Livingstone

Unyanyembe. 1871
July

1 John W. Shaw told me today that he had been at 4 levees of the Queen of England, that he had lost $10,000 - $5000 in the Metropolitan Horse Guards, & $5000 in the Waterworks. What Metropolitan Horse Guards or Waterworks he did not say, that he had studied Malay since he had been 7 years old. In relating a story of Lady Flora Hastings & the Lady of Bute the poor fellow shed tears for her[26] sad fate as though she had been his sister.

---
24. Amer bin Sultan (*HIFL*).
25. Shiza (*HIFL*).
26. 'her' written over 'their'.

   Halt

2 Halt

3 Halt

4 Halt. Wrote letter to "N Y Herald"[27]

5 Halt Khamis bin Abdallah[28] & Sheikh bin Nasib paid me a visit, Abdallah bin Juma & sons. Khamis is certainly one of the noblest looking[29] Semites I have ever seen. Sent my letter 1st to the "N. Y. Herald"

Engaged three new followers

6 Paid the ceremonious visit to Tabora – among the Arabs.

7 Very ill and abed.

8   "   "   all ablank

9   "   "   "

10   "   "   "

11   "   "   "

12   "   "   "

13   "   "   "

14 I recover my senses

15 Ill and abed.

16 "   "

17 "   "

18 "   " Said bin Selim sent me a present of a large black duck.

1871

July

19 Ill in Unyanyembe, and abed

20 "   "   Kirangozi for Ujiji is engaged and pledges his services by taking his advance.

21 Maganga came today. He says he will come again tomorrow.

22 Improving. 5 Wanyamwezi porters engaged, Sadala Saburi, Kombo, Baruti, Musa.

23 Sick abed. Am asked to join Arabs to open Ujiji Road.

24 "   "

25 Sick, but rise from bed. My 2nd Caravan arrives. The soldiers agree to serve for double pay as porters also for $5 per month. This is the first step I fancy to change the character of these men for all time. Sheikh Said bin Salim leads his Arabs to fight Mirambo. Amram bin Massoud however goes to Urori with 150 guns.

---

27. 'Wrote letter to "N Y Herald"' written with a clearer ink.
28. 'Abdallah' and 'Abdalla' have been transcribed 'Abdullah' in *HIFL*.
29. 'looking' added above the line.

26 We prepare to follow the Arabs to open the road, and if the Arabs succeed we will push on to Ujiji.

27 Said bin Salim & Arabs leave Mfuto to fight Mirambo

28 Had a great talk today with the wise & prudent Sheikh bin Nasib. He advised me to abandon my project because it was dangerous to march a caravan during wartime. I am therefore reduced to great straits. Am hesitating about which is best. No guide that is reliable can be engaged in a period of disturbance for the Kawendi Road, & the Mfuto road is closed by Mirambo. At 5 P.M. I resolved to start after the Arabs.

29 March to Zimbili 2 ¼ hours. Infinite trouble 3 soldiers sick of small pox, Wanyamwezi porters all absent. Shaw accompanied me.

30 Masonghi[30] 1 ½ hours. Mussoud son of Said bin Majid came to visit me & said the Arabs were waiting for me.

31 Eastern Mfuto 6 hours. Shaw has succumbed to illness.

30 rounds amunition served out to men.

The Search after Livingstone

1871

August

1 Central Mfuto ¾ of an hour's march

2 Halt. Our Arab General & Governor is sick.

3 Umanda. 6 hours. 15 miles

4 Zimbizo. Sultan Kolongo.

5 Halt. The Arab slaves killed 10 of Mirambo's people

6 Arab slaves go to fight. Capture a village. Kill Sultan & 5 men, & obtained much loot. But hearing a rumor that a large force of the Enemy was approaching they skedaddled. Another party found a young brigand asleep, brought him into Camp- & cut his throat before the gate of Zimbizo.
Mussoud son of Said bin Majid led 500 men against Mirambo' Capital & captured it. While the victors were looting it Mirambo reentered his capital by another gate & slaughtered over two-thirds of Mussoud's men. A panic overtakes everyone – and a general flight from Zimbizo begins at 3 P. M. back to Unyanyembe.

7 Retreat. Livingstone is now locked up West of the Tanganika. I am also to be locked up in Unyanyembe. Livingstone's loads 17 bales, 12 Boxes, 6 Beads – are in my storeroom at Unyanyembe with my own effects.

---

30. Masangi (*HIFL*).

8 Arrival at midnight of 7th at Mfuto after a headlong flight through the woods. The retreat has been most disastrous. Hundreds have perished through wounds & fright.

9 Return to Masanghi

10 Arrival at Kwihara – our own house in Unyanyembe.
   3 of my men have been killed & 1 died from dysentery.

11 Halt. Sick of a fever.
   Sheikh bin Nasib has called to comfort me.

12 Halt. Abdul Kader has broken my last tea-cup. The plan with my servants has been to drop my tea-cups two or three times in order to test their strength, like the monkeys did with the drum in order to find where the sound came from.

13 Sick of a fever.

14 Wrote letters to Zanzibar for medicine

15 Decide to send Manwa Sera, & Sarmine to Zanzibar to get medicine.

1871

August

16 A force of letter carriers return to Zanzibar with the news. My men are to be back on the 17th October. for 25 dollars each. 1050 miles for 50 dollars, in 60 days.

17 This is the second day of Shaw's fever, & the 7th of mine.

18 All hands engaged in stringing beads for the March to Ujiji. I feel so well that I am quite frisky now. We hear that Mirambo is advancing to attack our settlements here in Unyanyembe. I prepare my house for defence, pierce the walls, dig a well in courtyard, cut down trees & scrub in front.

19 Halt stringing beads & preparing for defence.

20 Halt. 1000 necklaces have been already strung. Arabs prepare to make a sally against Mirambo.

21 Halt. Busy on the defences of our house.

22 Halt. Mirambo attacked Tabora to-day. It is in view from the roof of our mud tembe. Khamis bin Abdalla & his kinsmen sallied out with their followers to fight him, and were slaughtered. Fugitives from Tabora have taken refuge with us.

23 We have passed an anxious day in Kwihara. I have now 50 armed men within my house & court.

24 Mirambo at dawn departed from Tabora inviting the lagging Arabs to follow him. Kwihara has returned to its former peace & quietness.

25 Halt. Visit my neighbour Sheikh bin Nasib. He is more dolorous than ever. But his 2 pounder is loaded with slugs ready. It is rumored that Mirambo intends visiting Kwihara next.

26 Halt. Councils of war are held each day. Meanwhile I am preparing for Ujiji independently of Arabs. Am purchasing guns at $5 each. This war will evidently last years.

27 Halt. No news today of Mirambo. Another council of war among the Arabs. I am continuing to string beads & resolve when all is ready to walk around Mirambo's territory.

28 Halt. Shaw got up & did a little work to day. I have been here about 2 months

29 Halt. Visit Said bin Hamed. He has a fine garden in Kwihara with manioc, onions, wheat, shallots, water melons, pomegranates & papaws. It is a sleepy country & a sleepy people, & Shaw has got a sleepy fever.

30 Halt. Shaw is too low down for any service

31 Halt. My prospects of departure from here do not improve. Shaw will not work, & nothing seems to advance.

The Search after Livingstone

Unyanyembe 1871

September

1 Halt in Unyanyembe. Visit Thani bin Abdalla at Maroro.

2 Halt. A visit from Sheikh bin Nasib who protests against my journey to Ujiji during such a troublous, distracted period

3 Halt. Asmani the Mgasiji soldier had occasion to open his load in which I saw by accident a package of letters addressed Dr Livingstone – Ujiji- Nov 1870. On the other side was written "Registered Letters." Asking Asmani about them I was told they had been given to his leader since dead at Bagamoyo, during the third month of their stay there last November. They arrived in Unyanyembe the middle of April this year where they have been ever since, & where they are likely to remain. I have today endeavored to induce Sheikh bin Nasib to let Livingstone's caravan go with me, but to no purpose as the Sheikh is convinced I shall never see Ujiji

4 Shaw has done the best day's work on the tent. Selim my Jerusalem lad has his fever regularly. Baruti is very ill with the small pox. The Wanyamwezi porters have all deserted and the Zanzibaris seem to be infected with the general fear.

5 Halt. Baruti has died. Uledi Speke, Uledi Khatalabu & Mabruk have also died of this terrible disease. I hear that Farquhar has died at Mpwapwa. The remaining men are dispirited at all the Evil rumors which poison our hearing.

7[31] Halt. Buried Baruti. Bought 3 boys from a slave gang seen perambulating about Kwihara. They are called Kalulu Bill Alli - & Majwara - I paid 60 dollars gold.

---

31. '7' written over '6'.

Bought a donkey for $10. He is called "Simba" or the "Lion". My Expedition now consists of 2 white men, 1 Arab boy, Selim. 1 Hindi, 29 Zanzibaris, & 3 slave boys – 36 souls. Three strong fellows have promised to engage as guides. I am in extremely good spirits to-night, at my prospects. Thank God!

8 Halt. Sheikh bin Nasib reports Mirambo has attacked Mfuto. Shaw is still very weak & sickly. Selim is one day well & down the next. Bought another donkey – for Shaw – for 36 yds cloth.

9 Halt. Mirambo was defeated at Mfuto. Shaw & Selim still sick.

10 Shaw is still very ill. Gave Shaw 1[32] grains of morphine as a sleeping powder. He slept well but acts today as though he was demented. What poor amusements Unyanyembe offers to an impatient mind.

Half a doz. croaking Arabs coming to regale my sickened senses with stories of wars, & battles never fought, of dead hundreds who never lived. Or gazing from my veranda at the eternal hills floating in a hazy atmosphere, of aged & dusky matrons passing to & from wells or markets with flapping hide robes, abed. Spindle legs adorned with clinking brass.

1871

Sept.

11 Halt. Shaw is sick & very weak. Sometimes I despair of his life. Yet it is incumbent on me to wait here for him until all danger is past. Mirambo is again reported to be coming.

12 Selim was punished to day for stealing & aggravating his offense by the most persistent lying. He was actually caught in the act.

Shaw drivels about the vices of mankind particularly of rich people. He deseved a better audience for his eloquence than I furnished him.

13 Halt. The Apostle of Africa Livingstone is always in my mind. Shaw has lost all spirit. Daydreaming is his sole enjoyment. Jumah suffers from rheumatism, Umgareza from ophthalmia, Zaidi from a stiff neck, Bill is crippled with an unknown disease, Ulimengo has inflamed lungs. Selim is constantly down with ague. I have only 17 effective men.

14 Selim is delirious today, Shaw still sick, and all my time is spent as a nurse. I engaged 2 porters & a soldier.

15 The third month of my stay in Unyanyembe & I am not gone yet. I reduced each load from 70 lbs to 50. I hope to be gone from here by the 20th inst.

16 Halt. We are almost ready for the march. Engaged 2 Soldiers and a porter, & 10 more talk of coming to me. I have now 40.

---

32. '1' written over '2'.

17 Halt. I gave a feast today to my 33 Soldiers. This feast consisted of a roast sheep, 15 fowls, 45 lbs Beef, 80 lbs Rice, 8 large loaves of Bread & 20 gallons of Pombe.

18 Halt.

19 Halt. Sick of fever.

20 **March**[33] to Mkwenkwe 3 miles S. W. Some more porters arrived last night & engaged themselves. Shaw consented to ride a donkey & try the road after infinite coaxing.

21 Sick of a fever & halt.

22 March to Inesuka. 2 hours. Ther. 108° Fah.

23   " " Kasekera, S. W. by S. Abdul Kader was discharged as he was useless. Mabruk Saleem attacked with violent diarrhoea, Zaidi with rheumatism. Shaw says he is getting worse.

24 March to Kigandu 2 ¾ hours S. & S. S. W. Asmani deserted.

25 Halt

26 Halt. I am obliged to send Shaw back to Unyanyembe as progress is impossible with him. Mabruk Saleem also sent back from diarhoea. At this rate Caravan will be reduced to nothing.

27 Ugunda. 7 hours. Shaw departed this morning borne in a hammock. Another soldier deserted last night. Great trouble to day with four sick men.

28 Benta 3 ¼ hours S by W.

29 Kikuru – 5 hours S W by S.

30 Halt.

The Search after Livingstone

1871

October

1 Reach Ziwani W by S. after 4 hours march thorny Forest & over plain thinly covered with scrub.

    The Ziwani means little pool. We found an old camp half consumed with fire which an hour's work sufficed to make habitable. The pool was so small that it was only 5 feet in diameter, but not to be despised. A magnificent Mkuyu sheltered nearly the whole camp. Its fruit resembles figs. The Zanzibaris ate it eagerly. Tsetse flies swarm, while there are plenty of elephants, antelope & guinea fowl in the vicinity.

2 Monday. March 6 ½ hours. W S. W. to Manyara.

    A long march under a hot sun through thin forest & plain with clumps of

---

33. 'March' written in large and bold characters.

jungle wherein the panga or tsetse fly swarms. Just as we entered the jungly plain saw a dead man victim to small pox. He probably belonged to one of Oseto's gang of bandits whose weapons are at the service of anyone who can afford to pay.

3 Halt. The market of Manyara is closed. To reopen it we were obliged to be very politic & Bombay was sent[34] presents of fine cloth. The effect was soon manifest. Provisions flowed in abundance to camp. Then the Mtemi condescended to pay us a visit, & the whole morning was spent in entertaining his Sultanship.

4 March to Gombe Creek 4 ¼ hours S by W & S. S. W. This river is one of the tributaries of the Malagarazi & is said to have its source near Khokoro.

5 Halt at Gombé Creek. Happy place, beautiful sport, 2 boars, 3 buffalo, 1 zebra, 1 bush buck, 1 jack rabbit, 2 antelope, 4 guinea fowl & 5 quail.

6 Halt. People wish to dry their meat.

7 Ziwani March W. 5h. 20m . Most troublous day. Mutiny & punishment after which the Expedition moved on in sullen mood.

8 March to Tongoni 1 ½ hour S. S. W. Buffalo gnats & tsetse are very troublesome, gazelle or antelope abundant in neighborhood.

9 March to Forest – S. 5 ¼ hours. Ruga Ruga & their doings in everybody's thought

10 March to Marefu 3 hours S. S. W.

11 March to Utendé 7 ¾ hours W by N.

12 Camp in jungle near Mtoni 4 hours W N W.

13 March to Mwaru. Sultan Kamirambo W N. W. 5 ¼ hours

14 "   " Mrera's 5 ½ hours. W by N ½ N.

15 Halt at Mrera's. Everybody fatigued.

16 Halt at   "   Caravan marches tomorrow if God is willing

17 March to Mtoni W by N. 4 ½ hours. This stream probably goes to the Rikwa.

18 March to Misonghi 4 ½ hours W.N.W.

1871

October

19 March to Mtoni for 6 hours. W by N direction

A long march through forest. Saw Sable Antelope for first time. Buffalo plentiful.

20 Friday March to Mpokwa in Utanda in 4 ¾ h.

On leaving camp saw hills in cones all round us. The natives are much disturbed by Simba, Chief of Kasera. Passed abandoned villages indicating hasty flight.

21 March to Mtoni for 3 hours N N W. up the marshy valley of Mpokwa. River drains

---

34. 'with' missing.

to Rungwa. Met a heavily armed native while out hunting. I was aiming at an antelope when I was surprised at seeing a man speeding away.

22 March to Mtamba R. W. by N. 4 ½ hours. Saw the big trees out of which it is said the Tanganika marines make their canoes. All the streams passed to-day drain N. to the Malagarazi. Shot a wild boar & a brace of ptarmigan, with Winchester Rifle. Lions roared all the night close to Camp.

23 Itaga in Rusawa Sultan Imrera. NNW. March 4 ½ h. District thickly populated.

24 Halt for well deserved rest.

25 March to Camp at base of Rusawa Mts 2 ½ h. N.N.E.

Made a strike Easterly to obtain a passage through the arc of mountains which closed us in to[35] W. & N. Crossed two or three small streams on whose banks grew wild date.

26 March to Mtoni N. N. E. & NNW. 4 hours.

Men to be disposed to be mutinous again. They do hate to move when once we have halted, but my face showed possibly that I was not in a mood to be trifled with. Happy people who have learned when it will be safe to break out. It saves great bother. Selim was flogged for eating Mbembu fruit. A small offence perhaps, but the fact is his bowels are out of order & this wild fruit starts his dysentery, then we have to carry & nurse him for a month or so. If a boy cannot take advice by words, we are bound to appeal to the scare of physical pain.

27 March to stream for 5 hours N ½ W. Camped on a site occupied once by Said bin Majid, when he was on his way to fight Mirambo for the murder of his son.

28 March to Camp in Forest for 6 hours N ½ E. Food is very scarce.

29 March to camp in jungle 5 ½ hours N by E. People most hungry, live on wild fruit.

30 March to Welled Nzogera 2 ½ hours N by East. We have obtained food, and people are happy. I gave them 6 days rations.

31 March to Camp in jungle 4 ¼ hours N by East.

The Search & finding of Livingstone

1871.

November.[36]

1 All Saints day. Wednesday. March N W. 2 ¾ h. Reached Kiala's on the Malagarazi R. Waited an hour to negotiate for the crossing then made camp. Spent 3 hours talking. Then I gave 13 doti to Nzogera 10 doti to Kiala, 2 doti for chiefs, 2 doti for Head men of ferry.

---

35. Word unclear.
36. Several changes of ink on the page.

2 Crossed Malagarazi R. at[37] Ihata Island. A day full of trouble, with natives & crocodiles. Lost my fine donkey Simba through one of the ferocious crocodiles.

3 Katalambula March N. N. W. 1 ¼ hour. Terrible days are these.

4 Kawanga NNW 5 hours. Reach Uhha. Met a caravan from Ujiji who had left there only five days ago. They say they saw a white man who had just come from a country to the West of the Lake. The White man was elderly, wore headdress & shoes. Paid tribute 12 doti

5 Sunday. Marched 1 hour to Lukomo. N N. W. Paid tribute 75 doti!

6 Kahirigi March 4 hours W N W. At dawn we were on the march silent & sad. Ujiji seemed to us as far as ever on account of these unconscionable rogues the Wahha who are perpetually mulcting us. We left the sleeping village at midnight & headed straight for the jungle to get rid of them.[38]

7 March 5 hours to Rusugi R.

8 March 4 ½ hours to Sunussi River W. N. W. March through bamboo jungle past Rugufu R. or rather swamp.

9 March to Niamtaga Village Ukaranga W by N ½ N. 9 ½ hours

We made ready last night for an entry into Ujiji in proper style. People immensely glad at the prospect of long rest in Ujiji. & we are all wondering who this white man at Ujiji is.

10[39] Arrived at Ujiji on Lake Tanganika, and discovered Dr David Livingstone who was supposed dead or lost![40]

After 6 hours March W. by S

11 Halt

12 Halt

13 Halt.

14 Halt. Sent letter off to John W. Shaw left behind at Unyanyembe to look after Livingstone's goods most carefully with other orders.[41]

15 Halt.

1871. November

November 15 [blank entry]

16 Embarked at dawn on our voyage to the North of the Lake. Went 12 m. Camped at Kigoma. Livingstone & I sleep in the same little tent. We propose to examine whether the river in Usige comes in or goes out of the Lake.

---

37. 'at' written over 'from'.
38. A line to indicate this sentence goes with the following day.
39. '10' written over '11'. This entry was most probably written on the 11th. Stanley almost forgot to write the event of the 10th.
40. Written in bold letters.
41. Letter to John W. Shaw, Ujiji, November 14, 1871, S.A. 2469.

17 Reached, Niasanga Tanganika Lake 12 m. Started at dawn.

18 Zassi Camp. 4 ½ hours rowing from Niasanga.

19 Nyabigma. We are now in Urundi. Nyabigma is a sandy island

20 Mukungu. Urundi – 4 hours rowing Last night was robbed of 1 bag of flour 500 cartridges of shotgun, & 1 Sounding Line. Bombay and Susi guardians of the boat were stupefied with sleep & look very penitent to day.

21 Mugeyo. Rowed to day 19 hours

22 Magala. 2 ½ hours rowing. Boatmen overpowered with fatigue. Fortunately the natives about here more amiable than those we passed yesterday.

23 Arrived at N. End of the Lake Tanganika in Usigé 3 ½ hours.
 The port of the village lies hidden among reeds where it is calm. Had a strong gale to-day.

24 Mukanigi,[42] Usige. 1 hour. N by E. Put up in Mokamba's village. Argued at night about politics with Livingstone. He is strong for Disraeli & I am as strong for Gladstone, but finding my fever increasing, I desisted & he fell to & nursed & coddled me.

25 Mukanigi. Halt. Am sick of a fever. The Doctor nurses me tenderly. Mokamba came to see us & after receiving his present of 10 doti & 5 fundo sent us 1 ox, 1 sheep & goat which is a fair return.

26 Mukanigi. Halt. Sick of fever. At dark we departed to Mugihawa[43] the district of Ruhinga the elder brother of Mokamba.[44] At 4 A.M. arrived having pulled from 7 P.M. to 4 A.M. 9 hours at 2 ½ miles

27 Monday. Mugihawa. Uringa. On awaking this morning found ourselves at head of lake in the Delta of the Rusizi.

28 Mugihawa. Exchanged presents with Ruhinga. Sent off our canoe for Mokamba & 8 riflemen. Met a most pious but rascally Coast man.

29 Mugihawa. Went out to hunt. Shot 2 fine geese, 1 ibis, 1 duck & a crane.

30 Thursday. Mugihawa. Paid our tribute to Ruhinga. It rained for the first time since I have been on the Tanganika.

1871

December

1 Livingstone told me to-day that his eldest son Robert served in the American Civil War under the name of Rupert Vincent in Co. H, 3rd New Hampshire Vol.[45] He

---

42. Written in bold letters.
43. Mugihewa (*HIFL*).
44. Mukamba (*HIFL*).
45. Co[mpany] H, 3rd New Hampshire Vol[unteers]. On Rupert Vincent, see John Murray, "Rupert Vincent, I Presume," *Crossfire*, no. 96 (August 2011), http://www.acwrt.org.uk/uk-heritage_The-Search-for-Robert-Livingstone.asp.

enlisted in Manchester N. H. for 3 years on the 6th October 1863.[46] Robert was born in S. Africa. Was 21 years old 5 ft. 7 in. in height. Dark Complexion. Hazel eyes. Dark Hair. Occupation Sailor. Was reported to be captured at Laurel Hill W Va. Oct 7, 1864.

2[47] Our canoe went over to Mukanigi to bring Mokamba. We have had an ox, 3 sheep & several pots of milk.

3 To day we churned our own milk & got about 3 lbs of good yellow butter which will be welcome for the Doctor's slapjacks. We also made several pounds of cheese. The Doctor took a series of observations for longitude by stars & lunars. While we were at it we looked into our hut and observed Selim's mouth under our honey bag.! Great fun.

4 Late in afternoon our canoe came back escorting Mokamba with 60 canoes.
5 I did not feel very well – therefore Livingstone went alone to Mokamba & carry with our farewell the parting gift. I had gone out in the morning to examine the bay lets at the head of the Lake, of which there are ten altogether

6 Still at Mugihawa but we propose going near the Lake Shore to sleep to night to get off early to-morrow morning. Livingstone took a series of obs for Longitude and his Latitude by star Acanaur,[48] was 3. 19° S Lat.
7 Kakumba, near Chigongo river & cape. From Mugihawa went round South to Katanjara[49] I[ds] and approached highland of Washi[50] near boundary line of Mokamba's country, and Uvira. Got beyond the extreme point reached by Burton & Speke in 1858. Halted at Kavimba to cook breakfast. Met a party of plundered Wajiji who had attempted to evade paying tribute

8 Came to "New York Herald" Islets 3.41 S. Lat in 5 hours.
9 Came to Luvumba. Basansi. At dawn set off as we had been visited twice during the night by would be robbers. We very near had a bloody fight to-day but Livingstone's unconquerable patience had the effect of quieting the drunken natives

10 Crossed the Lake in 17 ½ hours & came over to East side of Lake and we are coasting Urundi again.

    46. 'on the 6th October 1863' added above the line.
    47. Change of ink. Intermediate lines uneven.
    48. Acanaur *for* Achernar *or* Achenar, the brightest star in the constellation Eridanus, best observed from the Southern Hemisphere in November.
    49. Katangara (*HIFL*).
    50. Uashi (*HIFL*).

11 Arrived at Zassi River & Village after 7 hours pulling. S. Point of Muzimu I^d is direct West of Zassi

12 Reached Niasanga 3 hours. 7 ½ m. I feel very ill and Livingstone seeing my condition obligingly turned the canoe inshore, at this place. It was the fever induced by our residence in the Delta of the Rusizi.

13 Reached Ujiji at 1 P.M. after 7 hours. Got a letter from American Consul at Zanzibar dated June 11th.[51]

14 To day is resting day and visiting our Arab friends Muini Kheri,[52] Mohammed bin Sali, Muini, & Mohammed bin Gharib. Asked Muni Kheri for his canoe to take us as far as Tongwe.

15 I have comenced making saddle for Livingstone's donkey, & buying milch goats.

With Livingstone

1871

December

16 Ujiji. At work on Livingstone's saddle. He says he has finished all his despatches & he is now copying them into his journal. I expect we shall be off shortly to Unyanyembe in a few days now.

17 Had prayers (being Sunday) Livingstone spoke to Habay about Wajiji to take Muini Kheri's boat back from Tongwe. I showed "Rob Roy's" introduction of 1/68[53] to Livingstone to-day & he said he knew his mother well also his father or his sister & father I forget which. He gave me the story of the Kent, of which Macgregor's father was Commander.[54]

---

51. Could be the three-page letter from Francis R. Webb to Stanley, S.A. 2654 (see Appendix).
52. Moeni Kheri (*HIFL*).
53. See Appendix, Letter of Introduction from John MacGregor to David Livingstone (S.A. 480), Suez, November 16, 1868. Stanley had received a letter of introduction to Livingstone from the famous canoeist and sportsman John MacGregor while Stanley was on a prior *Herald* assignment to find out information on Livingstone's whereabouts or meet with him on a presumed return to Great Britain. Stanley's meeting with MacGregor is recorded on November 12, 1868 (Journal S.A. 73). In his book, MacGregor related his meeting with Stanley: "At Suez I met the foreign correspondent of the 'New York Herald,' who was waiting there to receive Dr. Livingstone, then expected every day. This active little Yankee had accompanied the armies of India, Sadowa, and Abyssinia, and had now 1000*l.* ready wherewith to telegraph to the American press every word he could get from the lips of the brave explorer. Such world-wide interest has this hero of Africa" (John MacGregor, *The Rob Roy on the Jordan, Nile, Red Sea, & Gennesareth, &c.: A Canoe Cruise in Palestine and Egypt, and the Waters of Damascus* [London: J. Murray, 1869], 42, note 6).
54. The *Kent* was an East Indiaman, one of the sailing ships carrying passengers and goods for the East India Company. The *Kent* ran twice from England to Bombay and China before being destroyed by a fire on her third trip, in 1825. John MacGregor's father, General Sir Duncan MacGregor, KCB (1787–1881), an officer in the 93rd Sutherland Highlanders, could not have been in command of the *Kent,* but he was on board with his young wife and his newborn son John ("Rob Roy") when the ship took fire and later exploded. Duncan MacGregor wrote *A Narrative of the Loss of the Kent East Indiaman in the Bay of Biscay on the 1st March, 1825* (Edinburgh, Glasgow, London, 1825).

18 Preparing for the road to Unyanyembe. Gave 4 days rations to the people. Promise to go soon after Christmas. Doctor says he will soon finish his letters home.

19 Sent 6 guns to be resteeled in the strikers. Determine upon going to Ngondo thence strike East for Imrera in Rusawa.

20 Heavy rain & thunder, & storm on the Lake. Was very sick last night from nettle rash or urticaria.

21 Busy writing all day. Wajiji ask 12 doti for an ox or slave in their market. Took a pencil sketch of Doctor while he was writing his jornal.

22 Fever

23 Fever

24 Fever

25 Am getting better after a severe attack. Tried to prepare a Christmas dinner but the cook Ferajji spoilt it. Our custard was burnt. Ferajji was reduced to porter's rank for spoiling the dinner of dinners.

26 To morrow we hope to leave Ujiji. Every body & every thing being ready. Why should we stop?

27 Departed from Ujiji & went to Ukaranga, after bidding[55] kindly farewell to our friends

28 Mouth of the Malagarazi.[56] Arrived 2 P.M. 18 miles from Ukaranga.

29 Kagongo.[57] At mouth of Malagarazi. Crossed Expedition to-day occupied 4 hours distance 3 m.

30 Kivoe.[58] Bears from Mviga 210°. Shot a crocodile at Mviga P^t. Started this morning from C. Kagongo, on rounding Mviga we came in sight of Kivoe.

31 Sunday. Sent out boat early to search for food. Got 4 days provisions. We had heard that for 6 days nothing could be obtained.

1872

January

1 Utongwe bears 190°.[59] Stopped at Sigunga for lunch. Arrived & camped at a retired spot at the mouth of a stream Uwelasia. Land party not come in.

2 Kabogo to P. Herembe 340°. Beyond Herembe passed a fine bay. Excellent site for a Mission or a military Station.

3 to 9 [Page Blank]

9 We embarked in our canoe, the main body marches overland along the shore of the Lake We have agreed to go down the Lake some distance, then cut across

---

55. 'after bidding' written above 'Bade' crossed out.
56. Change of ink.
57. Kagogo corrected to Kagongo (Kagungu, *HIFL*); 'n' was added in black ink, like the rest of the sentence.
58. From here to the end of the page, change to black ink.
59. 'bears 190°' added above the line.

country & strike our old road from Unyanyembe by which we avoid Mirambo's & his bandits.

10 to 31 [Page blank]

1872

February

1 to 9 [Page blank]

10 Received the long expected mails from Zanzibar. In a letter from Capt Webb, I am told "My latest advices from the U. S". reported that Mr Bennett had hesitated to pay your draft for $3750, and it was protested. So I was very anxious to hear from home but got nothing by the mail yesterday. However this morning on reading Tarya's letters from London, I find that his correspondents there had recieved the proceeds of the draft from mine in Salem.

The second letter dated Dec 23 1/71 was from Capt Webb's successor John F Webb. "Capt Webb before he sailed for home left with me a letter dated London Sept 25 which is as follows: I write to inform you that a change has been made in the "N. Y. Herald" Agency,[60] here, & that I am in charge while Mr Levien the former Agent has gone home. This you will understand may be of special interest in view of matters relating to the Expedition of Mr Stanley. Will you kindly make a note of the fact, that I am ready to cash here at any moment any draft that you or others at Zanzibar may cash for Mr Stanley or to order by telegraph, that the same be paid at Bombay or Alexandria." G. W Hosmer.

1872

February

11 to 17 [Page blank]

18th We arrived at Unyanyembe to day with Dr Livingstone, it being the 53rd day since we left Ujiji by our roundabout course & the 236th day since we left the Sea. Livingstone proposes to finish his correspondence before I start for the Coast. He is going to remain here & when he obtains some few trifles from Zanzibar, he will continue his travels and make what he calls a "feasible finish" to his long Explorations

19 to 28 [Page blank]

---

60. 'Agency' written over 'Office'.

1872

March

1 to 11 [Page blank]

12 The Arabs of Unyanyembe brought me 45 letters for Zanzibar

13 I sealed up Livingstone's Journal to day & wrote on it "Positively not to be opened" which he signed.

14 to 3 [Page blank]

1872

May

1 to 5 [Page blank]

6 Arrived at Bagamoyo on the Indian Ocean, having marched 525 miles in 35 days. We met Lieut Wm Henn, R.N who with Lieut Llewellyn Dawson R. N. W. Oswell Livingstone a son of the old traveller & the Revd Charles New was about to set out for the interior to do what I have done, as people had begun to think that I must be dead.

7 Crossed the Expedition over to Zanzibar, & was welcomed by John F Webb, Am. Consul. I[61] left Zanzibar last year March 23rd.

8 and 9 I find that Lieut Dawson had resigned at once upon the arrival of my courriers who brought my letters to Consul Webb, and is very annoyed at my having forestalled him. He says there is nothing left for him to do. Physically he is a splendid specimen of manhood, and exceedingly handsome. I am sorry he is pleased to be in a tantrum at my success.

10 It is rumored to day that Henn will also resign & that the Expedition will be taken up country by young Livingstone & New as an associate.

11 to 14 [Page blank]

15th Paid off the men of the Livingstone Search Expedition

1872

May

16 Begin to engage men to send up stores to Doctor Livingstone.

17 to 20 [Page blank]

21} Signed contract with Livingstone's men 57 in number before American Consul John Webb.

---

61. 'had' crossed out.

22} Paid 20 dollars advance to 56[62] men & 30 dollars to Mawa[63] Sera. Got 6 Nassick boys & 1 man called Salina = 64 men.[64]

23 and 24 [Page blank]

25 Lieut. Llewellyn Dawson left today per "Mary A. Way" for the Cape. He will thus avoid travelling home with me.[65]

Signed Engagement with Mohammed bin Galfin as Headman for Livingstone's Caravan.[66]

26 D[r] John Kirk called at American Consulate.

27 Sent 57 men across to Bagamoyo to take the stores he had mentioned he required to Livingstone. They are the best that could be obtained.

28 Chartered German Co. St[eamer] Africa about 500 tons to take us to Seychelles, to catch the French mail from Mauritius for Aden. The Price is 900 dollars.

29 Embarked to-day with Selim & Kalulu. Young Livingstone, Henn, New, and Capt Morgan whose ship was blown on the beach near the Sultan's house during the late hurricane.

30 and 31 [Page blank]

---

62. '6' written over '7'.
63. 'Mawa Sera' for 'Manwa Sera'.
64. See Appendix, S.A. 4749. The men agreed to work for the sum of thirty dollars per annum. Salina is mentioned as "supernumerary" and received $5 in advance. There is no indication of payment to the 6 Nassick boys.
65. The barque *Mary A. Way* was expected to leave on Tuesday, May 21. Stanley and Dawson did not get along well: "I should have proceeded by the same route [*via* Bombay], but though I do not grudge Mr. Stanley well-earned success, it would be distasteful to me, if not to both of us, to travel in company." (Lieut. Dawson's Official Report to the Secretary of the R.G.S., Zanzibar, May 19, 1872, *PRGS* 16, no. 5 [1871–72]: 419–21.)
66. See Appendix, S.A. 4750. Mohammed bin Galfin was engaged in the capacity of Ras Kafilah (chief of caravan) with the salary of $500 per annum, and received $100 in advance.

Main Characters and Contracts of Engagement

Plate 1. "James Gordon Bennett, Esq. Proprietor of the 'New York Herald.'"
From Henry M. Stanley, *How I Found Livingstone: Travels, Adventures and Discoveries in Central Africa* (London: Sampson Low, Marston, Low and Searle, 1872), facing page xv. Titles of the engravings from *HIFL* are as in the original edition (and not from the present editors).

Plate 2. Henry Morton Stanley in Constantinople, 1870, setting out after Livingstone. (Photo Album "Stanley," S.A. 5153)

The Stanley Archives (S.A.), property of the King Baudouin Foundation, are held in trust at the Royal Museum for Central Africa (Belgium).

Plate 3. Stanley in 1872, carte de visite photograph, 8.5 x 6.1 cm; three-quarter view, mounted on card with ink inscription "Henry M. Stanley." (S.A. 5159)

Plates 4a and b. David Livingstone (signature of David Livingstone on the back), carte de visite photograph, The London Stereoscopic and Photographic Company. (S.A. 5178)

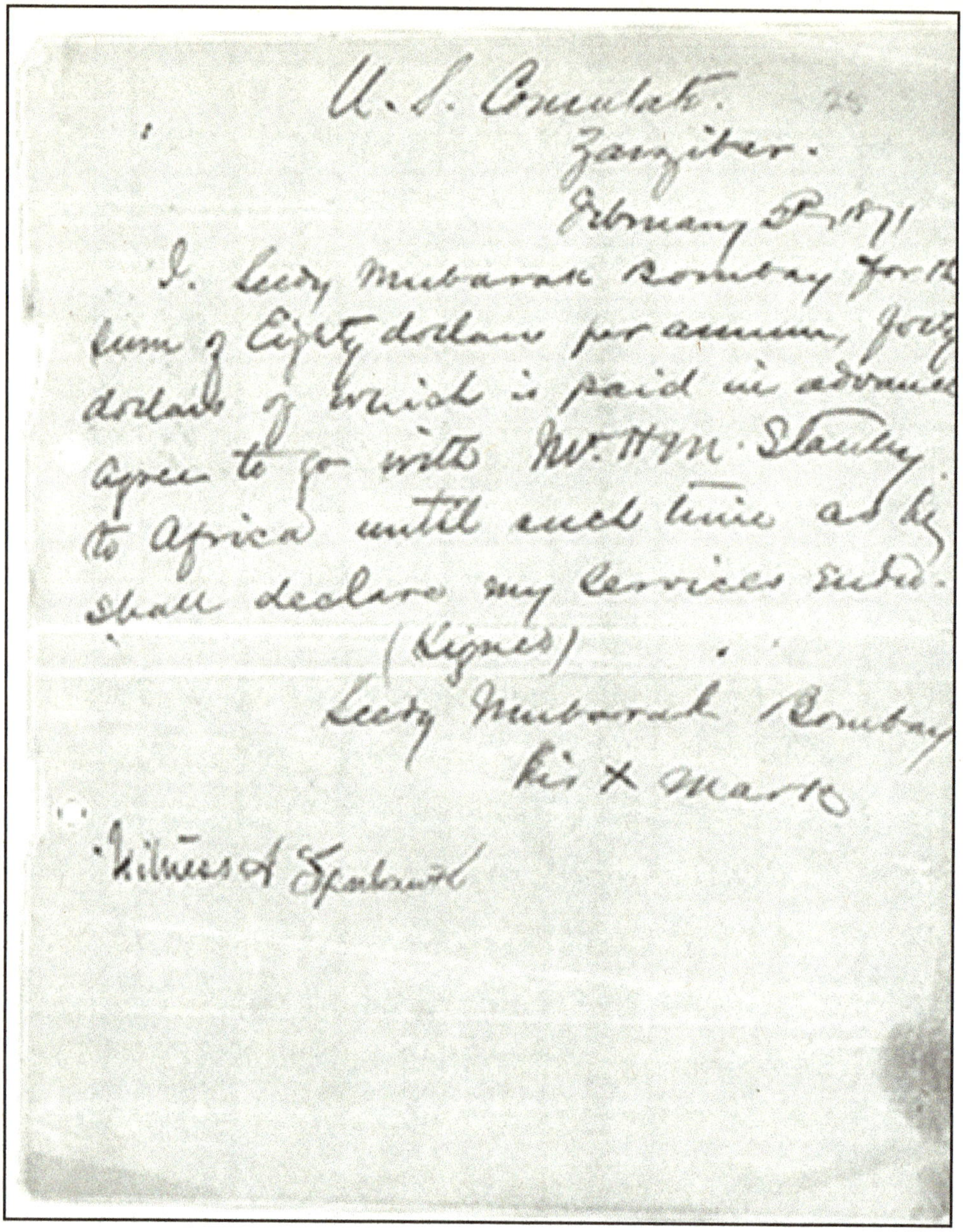

Plate 5. Contract of engagement of Seedy Mubarak Bombay for the Livingstone Expedition; with countersignature of A. Sparhawk, U.S. Consulate, Zanzibar, February 2, 1871. (S.A. 4744)

(Facing page)
Plate 6. Contract of engagement of Bunder Salaam, Celim, and Abdel Kadir for the Livingstone Expedition, with countersignature of Francis R. Webb, U.S. Consulate, Zanzibar, February 3, 1871. (S.A. 4745)

U.S. Consulate Zanzibar.
February 1st 1871

We the undersigned agree to accompany Mr. H. M. Stanley of New York during his Expedition to Africa, and to remain with him until such time as he shall declare his Expedition terminated for wages to the amount of Ten and Nine dollars respectively, and promise to obey orders promptly and do all in our power to promote harmony and the interests of the Expedition — failing which we agree to abide the consequences.

Butler
Abdel x Kadir   his Gilion x mark
Valet
or
General Help
Cook

Signed in my presence at Zanzibar this 3 day of February A.D. 1871
Francis R. Webb
U. S. Consul

Bunder Salaam $20.
Selim   15.

Witness to payment
Francis R. Webb
U. S. Consul

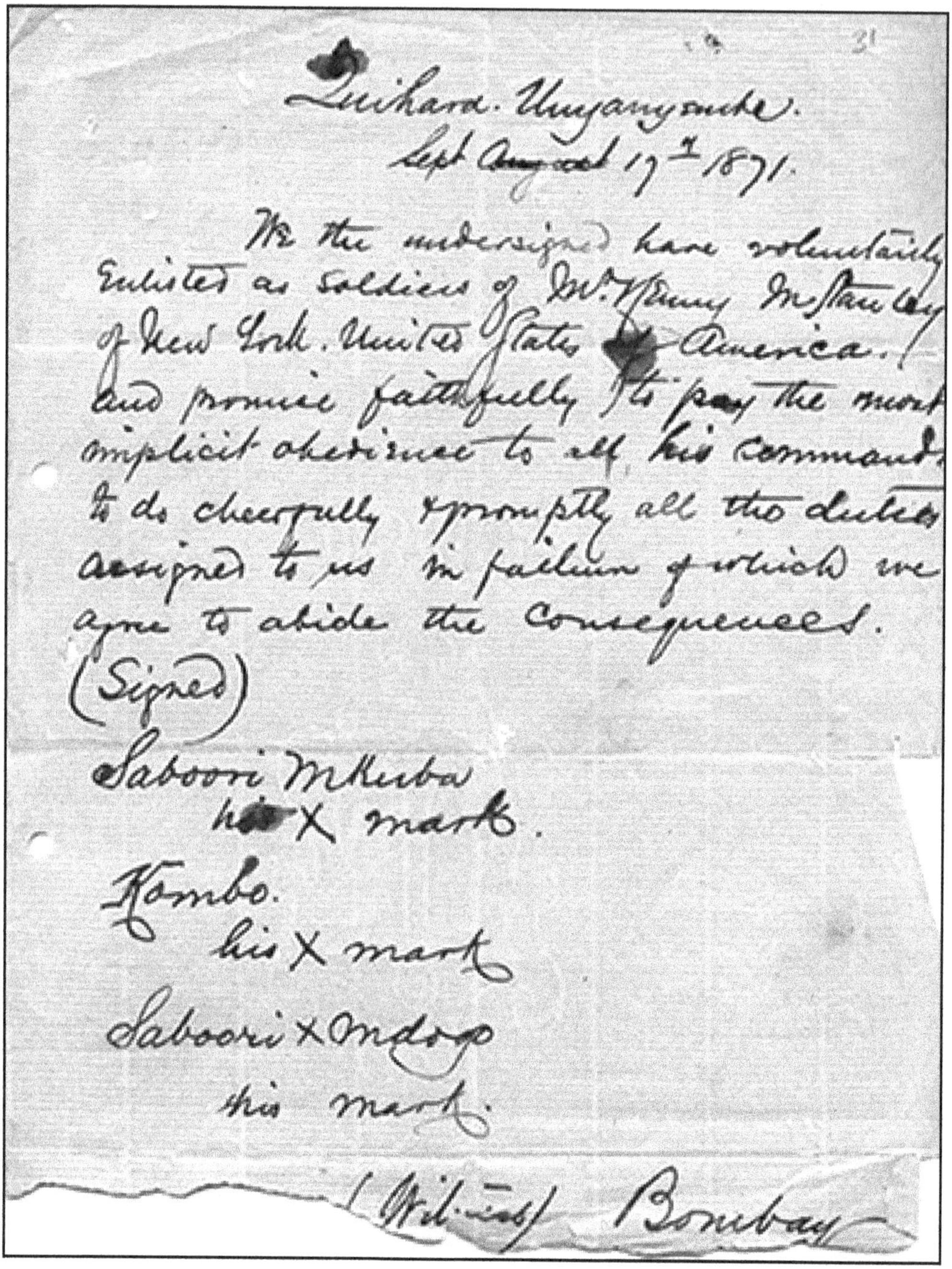

> Quihara. Unyanyembe.
> ~~Sept~~ August 17th 1871.
>
> We the undersigned have voluntarily enlisted as soldiers of Mr. Henry M. Stanley of New York. United States of America. and promise faithfully to pay the most implicit obedience to all his commands, to do cheerfully & promptly all the duties assigned to us in failure of which we agree to abide the consequences.
>
> (Signed)
>
> Saboori Mkuba
>   his X mark.
>
> Kombo.
>   his X mark.
>
> Saboori X Mdogo
>   his mark.
>
> Witness Bombay

Plate 7. Enlistment of Saboori Mkuba, Saboori Mdogo, and Kombo, September 17, 1871. (S.A. 4748)

(Facing page)
Plate 8. "Selim, the interpreter." (*HIFL*, facing 352)

SELIM, THE INTERPRETER.

Plate 9. Stanley with Selim and Kalulu, July 1872, Seychelles. (S.A. 5236)

Plate 10. "Portrait of Bombay and Mabruki." (*HIFL*, 69)

Plate 11. "Portrait of Shaw and Farquhar." (*HIFL*, 121)

(Facing page)
Plate 12. "Some characters. 1. Chowpereh. Engaged in four of my expeditions 1871–84. 2. Zaidi. Saved from the cataract. 3. Sarmini the Detective of the camp. 4.Wadi Rehani. The Treasurer. 5. Manwa Sera. The Headman. 6. A headman. 10. Majwara. He attended Livingstone at his death. 7. Kirango. First struck at Bumbireh. 8 The guide. 9. Wadi Baraka. The humourist at Bumbireh." Captions are as given originally by H. M. Stanley. These pictures date from 1877 or after, and were taken at the end of the Trans-African Expedition. Many of the Trans-African Expedition members were Zanzibaris who had accompanied Stanley in his search for Dr. Livingstone to Lake Tanganyika, went back to the Coast with him, and reengaged in the caravan of supplies for Livingstone. (Photo Album "Congo," S.A. 5154)

Some Characters

1. Chowpereh.   engaged in four of my expeditions 1871–84
2. Zaidi   Saved from the Cataract
3. Sarmini   The detective of the camp.
4. Wadi Rehani. The Treasurer
5. Manwa Sera. The Headman
6.   A headman
10. Majwara.   He attended Livingstone at his death.
7. Kirango.   First struck at Bumbireh.
8.   The guide
9. Wadi Baraka. The humourist at Bumbireh.

Plate 13. "Three of the principal women. 1. Bint Muscati, who died the day she reached home after the Expe[dition]. 2. Zaidi's wife. 3. Manwa Sera's wife." (Photo Album "Congo," S.A. 5154)

Journal S.A. 7, Full Transcript (1871)

[Inserted: Loose pages of Appendix to Lett's Diary for 1871 containing a special "address to our subscribers…"]

[Left page torn in half, in pencil] Stanley
[Figures crossed out]

Henry M Stanley[1]
Travelling correspondent of the "New York Herald". 1871.
This book was purchased in Bombay, store of MacKer Vining & Co. It is intended to contain as much information respecting myself as may be condensed to the limits of the pages within. Henry MS.

Letter paper 8 ½[2]

My Russian Friends[3]

Miss E. Farquhar
10 Henderson Place
Ferry Road
Bormington
Edinburgh

[Right page]

Descriptive order for bookseller

---

1. Henry M. Stanley's signature.
2. Written obliquely at the bottom of the page. Verso page: blank. On the following recto and verso pages (in print): Lett's Diary, or Bills due book, and an almanac, for 1871. Colonial Edition. Birthdays of the Royal Family. Holidays at Public Offices in Australasia and India. Eclipses. Sovereigns of Europe. Colonial Official Passage Allowances. Jewish Kalendar. Following pages have been torn off.
3. Written at the upper part of the verso page. The rest of the page is blank, except for Miss E. Farquhar's address written at the bottom.

Arabs, Hindoos, Parsees

Margharsh bin Said[4]	Sultan of Zanzibar
Ladha Damji[5]	Collector of Customs
Taria Topeen[6]	Merchant

January 1 Sunday, 1871

[Ink] At sea, on board whaling schooner "Falcon".
Capt Josiah Richmond New Bedford, 126 Tons, bound from the isle of Mahe, Seychelles, to Zanzibar. 19th day out. Calms, squally weather & contending against the currents serve to lengthen the voyage. Longitude 51°, Lat 4° 30'

  Explanation. On the 13th of October 1870[7] I left Bombay in the Bark "Polly" for Mauritius, accompanied by my Boy Selim[8] of Jerusalem who is to act as my interpreter with the Arabs, and one young black & tan pup then 2 months old, called Omar.[9] My intention was to proceed to Zanzibar E. coast of Africa, and then if my money which I expected from the "New York Herald" Agent (Douglas A. Levien, 14 Cambridge Square, Hyde Park, London) had arrived care of Dr Kirk, or Consul Webb,[10] as directed, I would go to the interior to Lake Tanganyika, Victoria N'Yanza, Albert N'Yanza, in search of Doctor David Livingstone the Great Traveller, for this was my commission from James Gordon Bennett Jr. given to me verbally at the Grand Hotel, Paris, Oct. 28th, 1869.

---

  4. His name should be rendered as Barghash bin Said, ruler of Zanzibar from 1870 to 1888. In *How I Found Livingstone*, Stanley adopted "Syed Burghash," used by the English consul John Kirk in his letters to Lord Granville.
  5. Ludha (*HIFL*).
  6. Tarya Topan (*HIFL*), one of the wealthiest businessmen in Zanzibar, was able to finance the caravan trade to the interior of Central Africa. He advanced the money for the expedition when funds from the *Herald*, which Stanley expected to be on deposit in Zanzibar, were not there. (See this diary, January 12, 1871, and Journal S.A. 11, February 14, 1872.) On Taria Topan, see Padma Srinivasan, "Indian Traders in Zanzibar with Special Reference to Jairam Shewji (19th Century)," *Proceedings of the Indian History Congress* 61, part 2 (2000–2001): 1142–48, and Christine Dobbin, *Asian Entrepreneurial Minorities: Conjoint Communities in the Making of the World-Economy 1570–1940* (London: Curzon, 1996), chap. 5, p. 117.
  7. '1870' added above the line.
  8. See Appendix, S.A. 4734, agreement between Selim Heshmesh, Jacob Heshmesh, and H. M. Stanley, January 20, 1870, Jerusalem.
  9. For the details of this nearly four-month journey from Bombay to Zanzibar, see Appendix, Journal S.A. 5.
  10. Francis Ropes Webb (1833–1892), of Salem, Massachusetts, was the American consul in Zanzibar. He befriended Stanley and backed the loan provided by Tarya Topan. Cf. Peter Duignan and L. H. Gann, *The United States and Africa: A History* (New York: Cambridge University Press, 1983), 141. Stanley had applied to him when sent to Aden by Gordon Bennett in 1868 to inquire into rumors about Livingstone's return to Europe. See Appendix, S.A. 2598, Letter from Francis R. Webb, American Consul in Zanzibar, to Stanley, Zanzibar, December 26, 1868.

On my arrival at Mauritius no vessel proceeding direct to Zanzibar, I sailed for the Seychelles Nov. 21st 1870, per Schooner "Romp" with Wm Lawrence Farquahar,[11] late mate of the "Polly" whom I engaged as my Navigator Assistant through Africa, and the Arab boy Selim, and my dog "Omar". We arrived at Mahe 9th December. On the 14th December last we sailed from Mahe for Zanzibar per Brigantine "Falcon" as above stated.

January 2 Monday, 1871

On board the "Falcon". <u>At sea</u>
Sailors are as is well known difficult to please. This is proverbial. Yet I hardly imagined that a sailor any more than a man of any other profession could be so blind as not to appreciate a benefit, and a good position promising good pay, plenty of change & easy work. My head man, and assistant Farquahar is a sailor, intelligent after a fashion, and understands his business as first mate very well so far as I can judge, but he is no exception to the rule above stated. He has been remarkably sulky since he has been on board, taciturn, and reserved with me, and apparently unwilling to work, no matter how trivial the job. My boy Selim wanted some clothes very badly and I purchased from Captain Richmond some Twill stuff enough to supply him with a pair of serviceable Turkish Bags. Upon asking Farquahar to make a pair for him, he raised a great many objections. Quoting his words, he did nit[12] see what the h-ll[13] such things were for, it was only a d—d barbarous nation which wear such things. It was in this snorting, growling dissatisfied spirit that he went to work at last upon them. After being finished, I hinted to him that there was another pair to be made. He answered he had done enough for one day,[14] his back ached, besides he was no sailor.[15] This was the second time within 40 days that he had worked. I feel assured he does not intend to go with me, otherwise common sense would tell him that this was not the way to work with one with whom he intended to travel through Africa.

---

11. Stanley often misspelled Farquhar's surname. See Farquhar's signature on his contract of engagement for the Livingstone Expedition in the Appendix, S.A. 4746, and Letter to Stanley from Farquhar's father inquiring about his son, July 31, 1872, S.A. 2675.
12. Slip of pen for 'not'.
13. Stanley very seldom included profanity in his writing, even in a personal journal.
14. 'and' crossed out.
15. A slip of pen for 'tailor'?

January 3, Tuesday, 1871

On board the "Falcon". At sea

We were at work yesterday and to day upon my African hand cart. The cooper M^r. Daw has almost finished it, and so far has made a respectable job of it. In order to suit the foot paths of Central Africa I had an axle (iron) made in Mahe, Seychelles, but 16 inches from wheel to wheel. It is this upon which Mr Daw has constructed for me a cart. According to opinions of practical men, the cart will be strong enough to bear 500 lbs weight on rough or yielding road. If it will prove true to these prognostications, it will save me 8 porters or pagasis whose average burdens are between 60 & 70 lbs.

Capt Richmond has also made me a very good scabbard for a Persian sword which I bought in Tiflis, whose former rough case had undergone considerable damage. While the captain was making a new scabbard, and making handles for my chisels, I set to work to make a[16] hilt for the scimetar. The cooper however is about to set a whalebone hilt for it.

While we were thus busying ourselves, over these trivial but necessary things having constantly in view my African tour, my man Farquhar who engaged himself to me for £5 per month held himself aloof, and had not the grace to offer to lend his services however they might be wanted.[17] But not being as he says, either a tailor, cooper, cartmaker, joiner, or scabbard maker he had more sense I presume than to offer his unskilful services.

At 12 M[18] we were 180 miles from Zanzibar, and are going 8 P.M. 5 knots West ½ S.

January 4 Wednesday, 1871

On board the "Falcon". At sea

The Cooper Mr Daw hailing from New Bedford finished my hand-cart to-day, and from what it appears to be now, I have not the least doubt but that it will prove extremely useful to me. He then commenced to work to make a whalebone hilt for my Persian Sword.

Tomorrow we expect to see land. Ah, I wish that I could fly to Zanzibar and procure my letters, which I suppose to contain my instructions, and money for the

---

16. 'sword' crossed out.

17. In spite of Stanley's second thoughts (see Appendix, Journal S.A. 5, on December 22, 1870, "My man W.L. Farquhar is intensely lazy…", and December 28, "Mr Farquhar's conduct became so unbearable…"), the engagement of Farquhar was put in writing at Zanzibar on February 1, 1871, and countersigned by the American consul on February 3, 1871 (S.A. 4746). Stanley provided another side of Farquhar's character in *HIFL* (27): "Farquhar was a capital navigator and excellent mathematician; was strong, energetic, and clever."

18. 12 M for 12 meridian, an oft-used designation at the time for noon.

prosecution of my work. But (as there are so many disappointments, inaccuracies, and inattention in this life) supposing my letters had not arrived! Supposing Douglas A Levien Herald Agent (14, Cambridge Square Hyde Park, London) did not send me the money! Or suppose he did not send enough the sum I demanded £600! Then in that case the Expedition will be a failure! In that case my long voyage and the great expenditure I have already risked will have been for nought! In that case I shall believe myself truly unfortunate, and not only I, but also the "Herald" in having such a careless man as agent in London.[19]

Supposing Livingstone already heard from as gone down the Nile, or having met with Baker, or had come to Zanzibar, and left for home! Ah, then in that case I had better go home too or continue my voyage to China as ordered by M^r. J. G. Bennett Jr. My long imprisonment at Sea, on shipboard I shall not readily forget nor the expenditure this long voyage has incurred.

January 5 Thursday 1871

On board the "Falcon". Off Pemba Island E. Africa
Sighted Pemba Island (15 miles north of the northernmost point of Zanzibar Island) about 11. A.M. About 3 p. m. saw it from deck, low, clothed with dense forests of cocoanut trees. It appears to be about 40 miles long. The current, East of it is very strong, probably a knot and a half. The Captain expects to see Zanzibar Island about 9 p.m. and in that case will cruise about till morning, when he will bear down for the town which is on the western side of the island, weather & wind favoring.

About 4.30 p. m. we had a "row" on board. It commenced with a wordy exchange between a young Englishman called Cockney, and a Swede – "Gus" – of a rather acrimonious nature which terminated as such disputes generally do in blows between them. Mr Berry, a peevish nervous & fretty person thought it his duty to estop the "row", by punishing the belligerents. Done in a brutal way as nervous & fretty persons generally do with his fists. While he was befisting "Gus" with bitter temper, the Captain came on the deck. Before the Captain could arrive at the scene the mate had sprung towards Cockney and the Captain seeing which way the annimus went sprung upon Cockney with the speed of a flying Ariel and vigor of Heenan.[20] Cockney cried off when the Captain & Mate directed their vengeance upon Gus, who had to receive a second dose with Spartan fortitude, this time almost

---

19. Stanley had not much confidence in the "Herald folks," but he resented the *Herald*'s neglect as a stab in the back (see Appendix, Letter from Stanley to J. Gordon Bennett, Zanzibar, January 17, 1871, S.A. 6926, pp. 1–4). And he did not forget to recall this "Herald" failure when announcing the success of his mission (Appendix, Letter from Stanley to J. Gordon Bennett, Zanzibar, May 18, 1872, S.A. 6925, p. 2.)
20. John Camel Heenan (1834–1873), famous American bare-knuckle boxing champion.

overpowering, for Berry struck Gus a villainous blow on the head with a[21] belaying Pin. Results, loss of temper on all sides, and of blood to Gus. At night all was well.

January 6 Friday, 1871

Zanzibar

During the night Capt Richmond stood off & far Zanzibar Island not daring a too near approach to the sound, where he had once got ashore. At day light this morning we were five miles North East of the Island, altered our course & steered West rounding the Northern point of Zanzibar Island, the high lands of main Africa looming as a lengthy[22] shadow through the grey of dawn. About 10 A. M. we were steering south with a strong puff of the North-East trades which commence during December, pushing us swiftly through the dark sap green waters of the straits. Zanzibar Island lay but one mile on our port side, one of the fairest gems of Natures Creation. To me so strong was my agreable disappointment it appeared as if it had but unveiled its head from the foam of the Ocean, and risen to view decked for an universal gala-day in a spick & span suit of green of the richest quality. And dropping smiles I mean to say that of all islands I have seen Zanzibar is the most perfect for the comfort of man. It is a low island but it is not flat there are gentle elevations cropping here & there above the languid but graceful heads of the cocoa trees, and there are depressions where a cool gloom seems possible from the richness & depth of the leafy jungles which surround them. With the exception of the thin line of sand over which the sap green water rolled itself with a constant murmur.

January 7 Saturday, 1871

Zanzibar

To day I had not much to do. Mr Webb is busy all day as Agent for his house.[23] I could but read and stare, and lounge about like an established habitue. In the evening went over to Spalding's house over the way, and had the usual slow confab of persons getting acquainted. The Americans are very enterprising

---

21. 'a' written over 'his'.
22. 'lengthy' added above the line.
23. In *Zanzibar: City, Island, and Coast* (London: Tinsley Brothers, 1872), Richard F. Burton devoted a chapter, "Ethnology of Zanzibar," to the foreign residents. Though it was written more than twelve years before its publication, we find the same names as in Stanley's narrative: "The principal American houses are those of Messrs Bertram & Co represented by Capt. Mansfield, Mr Ropes and Mr Webb, Messrs Rufus Green & Co, also of Salem, have three agents, Messrs Winn, Spalding, and Wilkins. Lastly, there is Mr Samuel Masury, of Salem" (318). On commerce between The United States and Zanzibar, see Jeremy Prestholdt, "Mirroring Modernity: On Consumerism in Cosmopolitan Zanzibar," *Transforming Cultures eJournal* 4, no. 2 (November 2009), http://epress.lib.uts.edu.au/journals/TfC.

I do not[24] think sufficient credit for good temper, humanity & forbearance has been given to human nature. I begin to think that we too much given to disparage the human race men are not so black[25] natured, as they are painted.

January 8 Sunday, 1871

Zanzibar
After breakfast 10.30 A. M., the Consul and I went to see the Sultan. Before the front[26] door of his palace were drawn up about a company of strong limbed Arabs armed with scimetars. Sultan, Ladha Damji, & Taria Topeen were standing on the Front steps. As they saw us advancing the Sultan came forward shook hands with the Consul then with myself. Passed between the Guards with our hats off. Sultan waving us forward at every few steps. We had to mount some narrow & high steps. Consul in advance hat in his hand ascending sideways, keeping the corner of his[27] eyes on every motion of the Sultan, I imitating him as I best could. As we had to ascend a very lofty flight it was very fatiguing mode of ascent, and the Consul no doubt seeing my impatience, or ignorance of the Etiquette whispered, "Don't turn your back to him". On all the landings we had to turn our fronts to him, expectantly upon which the Sultan with a wave of his hand[28] would urge us on.

The reception room was[29] long & narrow, timbers of the ceiling painted dark green, walls whitewashed, furnitured with just 12 semi-gilt chairs.

Conversation began with
To the Consul "Are you well?
A.[nswer]. Yes, quite well, thank you. How is his Highness.
Highness. Quite well.
To me. Are you well.

January 9 Monday, 1871

Zanzibar
I have been from this Monday to Sunday the 15th inst. very busy at work on my tents, boats, sails & tools, repairing, purchasing, arranging, and have not had time to write my diary diurrally[30] as I had commenced. Nor indeed has there been any cause why I should, nothing having transpired necessitating a memo.

24. 'do not' added above the line.
25. 'black' written over 'vile'.
26. 'Before' written over 'after'; 'front' written over 'first'?
27. 'his' written over 'your'.
28. 'of his hand' added above the line.
29. 'a' crossed out.
30. 'diurrally', ms, for 'diurnally'.

The week commenced with my going to Ladha Damji the Collector of Customs at this port ($ 400,000 per year) to receive information respecting the Lufiji[31] River, up which stream I intend to go. He[32] could not tell me nothing further but that it was a river[33] – he believed of[34] considerable size – that he had dhows trading up it for eight tides – which may mean thirty or forty miles up – that he was told it ran a good way inland, that there were people who used bark canoes. This much old Ladha had gleaned from Banians residing in those districts & from his Arab Captains. He had never been there himself and he did not think it worth his while to go up.

Dr John Kirk companion of Livingstone whom I next visited, knew no more, he had never been on that river he thought of going some time, was pretty

January 10 Tuesday, 1871

At Zanzibar

sure it was a large river. Captain Fraser Agent-Lloyds Surveyor. Merchant & Sugar[35] planter, and Cocoa-nut raiser we found also at home with a very fine collection of books upon Africa in the room.[36] Not one book said anything about the Lufiji except from report. Arab traders had told a few travellers, that there was such a stream.

It is this river that I intend to ascend, as far as the longitude of Zungo-Mero at least; as far as the head waters the Ziwa Lake if possible, thence to the Tanganyika. I have purchased two rowing boats, one from Consul Webb, the other from Mr Morse clerck to Spalding & Co.[37] To convey a horse, and five or six donkeys I shall have to engage a lighter or purchase one. A lighter is very deep, and may probably give me some trouble. However I will try it, and if upon reaching south of Zungo-Mero, I shall find it impossible to travel on it, I can then strike northward for Zungo-Mero.

My men have been hard at work on the tent and sails.

On Saturday the 14th I thought there was going to be a tempest at this house unwittingly occasioned by myself. I had reason to supect the dragoman of this consulate of cheating me, and charged

---

31. Due to pronunciation differences, writers sometimes used Lufiji instead of the correct Rufiji.
32. 'had' crossed out.
33. 'river' written over unintelligible word.
34. 'some' crossed out.
35. 'Sugar' written over 'Cocoa'.
36. Captain H. A. Fraser was a former officer of the East India Company merchant navy, and resident businessman at Zanzibar. He published "Zanzibar and the Slave Trade" in *The East African Slave Trade, and the Measures Proposed for Its Extinction, as Viewed by Residents in Zanzibar*, by Captain H. A. Fraser, the Right Rev. Bishop Tozer, and James Christie, M.D. (London: Harrison, 1871).
37. About Morse, see *Stanley's Despatches to the* New York Herald, ed. Norman R. Bennett (Boston: Boston University Press, 1970), 9, note 30.

January 11 Wednesday, 1871

At Zanzibar

him with it, upon which he went straight to Mr Webb & informed him that I had[38] charged him with cheating me. Mr Webb thought it well to appear very much offended, as also his clerk a Sparrowhawk[39] from Boston. Nile travellers will remember doubtless how they regarded their respective dragomans as so many paragons of honesty, & so will Syrian tourists, how during 3 ½ years of Eastern travel I have not met the Arab dragoman, the Turkish zaptieh, the Greek,[40] the Persian chappar, the Hindi.[41] Educated after[42] the manner of their forefathers, born on their father's soil, that did not regard the pale-faced traveller from Europe, infidel that he is, as a person who was to pay higher for the things of this life than one of their own[43] color, as a person who was indescribably verdant, as one who was to be cheated in every way, from the hour of his coming into their country, to the last moment of his departure.

Mr Webb believes he has an honest servant, because he has entrusted him with $70.000. I who took this man to a shop, and demanded the price of a Salters spring Balance, and when told by this man that it was $ 6, knew very well when this same honest man came next day & said it was $ 6.50, that I was being fleeced as usual by the dragoman of the

January 12 Thursday, 1871

Consulate.

Further, this same honest man is of Johanna,[44] proverbial for the duplicity and pilfering propensities of its people.[45] Think of Moosa, Livingstone's man. Read Young's account of them. Ask the ship Captains who have visited Johanna. But every man has a right to his opinions, and has the liberty to express them. If Mr Webb thinks Johari[46] honest as the broad sunlight, and thinks it his duty to defend him from

---

38. 'had' added above the line.
39. Very likely Augustus Sparhawk, who witnessed the agreement between Mubarak Bombay and H. M. Stanley at the U.S. Consulate, Zanzibar, February 2, 1871 (see Appendix, S.A. 4744). Sparhawk later joined Stanley, who was then serving King Leopold II in Congo.
40. This word is followed by a blank, as Stanley failed to identify the proper occupations of "the Greek."
41. A blank after 'Hindi'.
42. 'after' written over 'in'.
43. 'own' added above the line.
44. One of the Comoro Islands: Anjouan.
45. An opinion shared with Burton: "Among Eastern impostors the Comoro, especially the Johanna men, are facilè principes: the singular scoundrels have completely mastered the knack of cajoling Europeans—no Syrian Dragoman can do it better" (Burton, *Zanzibar,* 341).
46. Johari bin Saif. See Bennett, *Stanley's Despatches,* 5, note 10.

the aspersion of dishonesty even to insulting a guest, of course Mr Webb has a perfect right, but I am sorry that it should have been so, -for I had begun to think that Mr Webb was an exception to this rule, being so practically[47]-minded, & so large-eyed in other things.

The letters I expected from my Agent have not arrived. I should be very sorry if it were not that Mr Francis R. Webb, has been kind enough to use his influence to obtain the requir[ed] sum for the Expedition from Taria Topin.[48]

January 13 Friday, 1871 [Page blank]

January 14, 15, 16, 1871 [Page blank]

January 17 Tuesday, 1871

Had a talk with Dr Kirk this evening. He gives me a very bad impression of Livingstone. I am told he is a hard man to get along with, is cross & narrow minded. Has had no personal quarrel with him, but he has had always trouble with his companions. He thinks he ought to come home now and permit a younger man go in his place. L. takes no notes nor journal.[49] Kirk thinks that Livingstone would run away.

January 18, 19, 20, 21, 22, 23, 24, 25, 26, 27, 28, 29, 30, 31 [Page blank]

February 1, 2, 3, 4 [Page blank]

February 5 Sunday, 1871

Left Zanzibar at 7 A.M. in Dhow for Bagomoyo

February 6, 7, 8, 9, 10, 11, 12, 13, 14, 15, 16, 17 [Page blank]

---

47. 'practically' written above unintelligible word crossed out.
48. See Appendix, Letter from Stanley to J. Gordon Bennett, January 17, 1871, S.A. 6926, p. 11.
49. This stunning assertion does not appear in the relation of Stanley's visit to Kirk (ibid., pp. 5–7), though Kirk did not spare Livingstone when describing him to Stanley.

February 18 Saturday, 1871

Sent 1st Caravan off carrying 3 loads cloth 3 loads of wire under charge of 3 soldiers bearing letter of introduction from the Sultan of Zanzibar to his governor Sayed bin Salim in Unyamyembe[50].[51]

February 19, 20 [Page blank]

February 21 Tuesday, 1871

Sent 2nd Caravan of 12 Pagazis and 2 chiefs under 2 Soldiers to Unyanyembe with 9 Loads of Cloth, 2 Loads of Wire, 1 Load of Beads.

February 22, 23, 24 [Page blank]

February 25 Saturday, 1871

Sent Farquahar off to Shamba Gonera with the third Caravan – consisting of 8 Donkeys, 11 Pagazis, 3 Soldiers & 1 Cook.[52]

February 26, 27, 28 [Page blank]

March 1, 2, 3, 4, 5, 6, 7 [Page blank]

March 8 Wednesday, 1871

[Ink] **Received answer from Farquhar to letter sent to him by Sarmine[53] that he was well.**

---

50. Unyanyembe was an area covering part of western Tanzania, occupied by the Wanyamwezi. About organization of peoples, conflicts, and trade in Unyanyembe, see Tony Waters, "Social Organization and Social Status in Nineteenth and Twentieth Century Rukwa, Tanzania," *African Studies Quarterly* 11, no. 1 (Fall 2009): 57–93, in particular 61–66, http://africa.ufl.edu/asq/v11/v11i1a3.htm.

51. Figures given by Stanley for the composition of these first three caravans are much lower than those in *HIFL*, 68. Inconsistencies concerning the composition of the caravans when comparing this Journal first with Stanley's despatches to the *New York Herald*, then with his book, are notable.

52. Information about the composition and organization of the caravans at the launching of the expedition are quite confused. In this Journal (May 9, 1871), Farquhar is said to be in charge of the fourth caravan, but in his first despatch to the *Herald* (Bennett, *Stanley's Despatches,* 12) Stanley says the fifth caravan was under "the Scotchman who acted as my first mate," i.e., W. Farquhar. Besides, though Stanley asserts in *HIFL* (68) that two more caravans (the fourth and the fifth) left the Coast on March 11 and 21, his diary is surprisingly blank on these dates.

53. Sarmian (*HIFL*).

March 9, 10, 11, 12, 13, 14, 15, 16, 17, 18 [Page blank]

March 19 Sunday, 1871

[Pencil] Zanzibar for the last time to pay my bills to Soor Hadji Palloo[54].[55]

March 20, 21, 1871 [Page blank]

March 22 Wednesday, 1871

[Pencil] Stopped at Kikoka this day owing to delays of Bombay[56] in bringing the last store of provisions bought in Zanzibar. Hamadi left.

    Kikoka is the extreme corner of Uzaramo.

March 23 Thursday, 1871

[Ink] 12 miles

[Pencil] Left Kikoka at 7. 20 A.M., arrived at Rosâco[57] 12, distance 12 miles. Rosaco is the 1st place we come in Mkwere. Course W. by North

March 24 Friday, 1871

[Ink] 10 miles

[Pencil] Left Rosaco 8.30 A.M., arrived at camp 12 m. distance at 2 ½ miles per hour distance 8 ¾ miles.

Sent Smith[58] & Bombay back to Bagomoyo about the Pagazis. They had as yet not started from Shamba Gonera.

---

54. See Account Book of the *New York Herald* Expedition into Central Africa (S.A. 74), "Miscellaneous": "To Soor Hadji Palloo for procuring 66 pagazis, & supplying them with cloth $738."

55. When Stanley left Zanzibar on that day, rather precise news from Dr. Livingstone had arrived ten days earlier at Zanzibar through two letters from Arab merchants at Ujiji, one from Sherif Basheikh bin Ahmed to Dr. Kirk dated November 15, 1870, and another from Said bin Majid to Ludha Damji. Both said Livingstone was journeying in Manyema in company of Mohamed bin Gharib, with the intention of returning to Ujiji, but was destitute and helpless. Dr. Kirk immediately sent this information to Lord Granville on March 10, 1871 (National Archives, Kew, FO 84/1344, No. 25, Fol. 204–207), which the Foreign Office received on May 5. A copy was sent to Sir R. Murchison the same day (RGS-IBG Collections, DL4/12/2), and published in the *Proceedings of the RGS* 15, no. 3 (1870–71): 206. But it seems that Dr. Kirk kept it undisclosed at Zanzibar.

56. About Bombay's agreement "to go with Mr. H. M. Stanley to Africa," see Appendix, S.A. 4744, contract between Seedy Mubarak Bombay and H. M. Stanley, U. S. Consulate, Zanzibar, February 2, 1871.

57. The circumflex accent (^) in Rosâco never appears further in the manuscript.

58. About John Smith's agreement "to enter the services of Mr. H. M. Stanley," see S.A. 4747, U.S. Consulate, Zanzibar, February 3, 1871. But after having been sent back to Bagamoyo with Bombay, he was not mentioned again. A detailed account of Smith's expenses up to February 1 is given on pp. 5–6 of notebook S.A. 1; again in Account Book of the *New York Herald* Expedition to Central Africa, S.A. 74.

March 25 Saturday, 1871

[Ink] In Camp.

Halted at the Camp this day to wait the return of Smith & Bombay from their vengeful excursion to Bagomoyo against our irrepressible ally Soor Hadji Palloo. In the morning went north on horseback for a hunt, saw many tracks of antelope[59] hartebeest, elephant, and zebra. Saw nothing however but a flock of Guinea fowl which took a sudden flight eastward before we were aware of their presence. Consequently returned to Camp miserably unsuccessful.

After breakfast I went out again with Selim southward of the Unyanyembe road and after a mile march over the tall grass of the verdant plain lost ourselves amid the thickets which bounded the plain south. We struck into the depths of one of them through which under a tunnel caused by the thick overarching branches of euphorbia & acacia giraffe whose unyielding thorny branches punished us[60] terribly, a footpath used by the wild animals of the forest led.

By following this path we were led so far into the jungle that had it not been for my pocket compass we should inevitably have been lost. Even with the compass it took two good hours before we reached the open glades, of its outskirts.

Continued on Page 41. Long account Book.[61]

March 26 Sunday, 1871

[Ink] In Camp

Today we were visited by the natives of Kingaroo, and were – a novelty to us, initiated into the mysteries of trading American sheeting and red beads (sami-sami[62], for eggs, matama[63] grain, and Indian corn. For 7 eggs, a comely woman demanded a khete[64] and a half of the red beads. Before concluding the bargain the custom of chaffering which obtains through out Africa came to my mind, and I accordingly tried its virtue. Opening the Bag containing 2 frasilah of sami-sami, after painstaking efforts I succeeded in extracting a khete which I presented with a most demure look to the comely aborigine whose glowing bosom were more exposed to the male eye[65] than that of the bold Empress of France at the Inauguration of the Suez Canal.

---

59. 'antelope' written above 'deer' crossed out.
60. 'unmercifully' crossed out.
61. The entry March 25 is supposedly continued on p. 41 of a "long account book," which so far has not been found. This bottom line is written in paler ink.
62. Second bracket missing in the ms.
63. Matama (for Swahili Mtama) = sorghum.
64. One khete is a length of threaded beads measured from index finger tip to wrist. 10 khete make one fundo, measured from round the thumb to the elbow bone. Those measures vary from one country to another, and may be half-size in the interior of Central Africa. (From Richard Burton, *The Lake Regions of Central Africa*, 2 vols. [London: Longman, 1860], Appendix, 424.)
65. 'even more to' crossed out.

Here take a khete, said I.

Ugh, ugh with a look of contempt[66] and a shrug of the left shoulder at the poverty of the offer.

No! then take your eggs.

The wide eyes opened wider, and thought made the face more serious.

March 27 Monday, 1871 [Page blank]

March 28 Tuesday, 1871

[Ink] Kingaroo 12 miles

Smith & Bombay to my great relief returned to camp as we were about to start for Kingaroo a small village situated about 4 miles off. They had accomplished their errand in a most perfect manner. For just behind them were the long looked for pagazis. Leaving them to follow us at their leisure my caravan moved off, and reached Kingaroo about 12 m. having started 9.30 A.M. The land was more broken on this march and the first real difficulty with jungle was experienced here. For the road through it seemed like a narow excavation, through which the loaded donkeys & pagazis had to struggle. Also for the first time rocks appeared across the route, and the soil changed from that of sand, to a rich dark loam wherein swarmed all manner of noxious insects. The first species of these that attracted our attention was a black ant an inch in length, which emitted a stench similar to the prairie skunk. Indeed I had my gun ready to shoot the animal so certain was I that the nauseous odor proceeded from it, but not[67] finding it I bent down to examine more closely a huge black ant which just then darted across the path, and it was then my sicken nostrils detected the cause of the effluvia.

March 29 Wednesday, 1871

Today we stopped at our camp in order to permit the 26 pagazis to be one day ahead of us, as they are much afraid of the Musungu.[68] The Arabs have made it a habit to impress on the minds of the Wanyamwezi that Europeans use the stick very often.[69] I am not sure but that the Hindi Soor Hadji Palloo has been one of the party, that I might not find out how cheaply he obtained pagazis.

---

66. 'at' crossed out.
67. 'not' added above the line.
68. Musungu is a common word for white man in Kiswahili.
69. About Nyamwezi and Arab traders on the caravan route from Bagamoyo to Tabora and Ujiji, cf. Karin Pallaver, "Nyamwezi Participation in Nineteenth Century East African Long-Distance Trade: Some Evidence from Missionary Sources," *Africa: Rivista trimestrale di studi e documentazione dell'Istituto italiano per l'Africa e l'Oriente* 61, nos. 3–4 (September–December 2006): 513–31, http://www.jstor.org/stable/40761872. See in particular 513–20.

At 2.30, my grey horse the present from the Sultan, Said Bargash died, not from the effects of fly-bites, but from worms. I had him opened, and on examining his stomach, found one half[70] it black with disease, while on the other half were 25 loathsome worms eating[71] into his stomach coating like leeches, while his entrails, and excrement were perfectly alive with long white worms. We buried the poor Horse in the little opening before the village of Kingaroo.

March 30, 31, 1871 [Page blank]

April 1 Saturday, 1871

Started in earnest[72]

April 2, 1871 [Page blank]

April 3 Monday, 1871

[Pencil] Filled the canister with sugar 4 lbs.
Pagazis of the 5th Caravan 27 in number left our camp at Kingaroo, we are to stop here 2 days more in order to give the pagazis a good start.

April 4 Tuesday, 1871

[Ink] Sheik Thany[73] and Sheik Khaif bin Asman came with a small caravan. They say that an Arab named Moussoud took Livingstone's things to Unyanyembe.[74] We have very nearly finished our canvas tent. After to-morrow we expect to leave for Kiroka. Zingomero[75] is three days march or 75 miles south of Simbawenneh.[76] Simbawenneh is at the extreme southern extremity of Usegura. At Kiroka the Arabs told me we could obtain first class bamboo poles.

---

70. 'of' missing.
71. 'eating' added above the line.
72. According to Stanley's first despatch to the *New York Herald* from Kwihara, July 4, 1871 (Bennett, *Stanley's Despatches,* 13), this is when the sixth (and last) caravan left Bagamoyo.
73. Sheikh Thani (*HIFL*).
74. The Arab mentioned here could be Amram bin Moussoud (or Mussood in *HIFL*), who visited Stanley in Unyanyembe on June 24, 1871. These goods (probably the second load the RGS meant for Livingstone) arrived at Unyanyembe but could not be dispatched further because of Mirambo's war. They were stored there with those left by Stanley before starting for Ujiji. (Cf. August 7, in this diary.)
75. 'Zingomero' here in one word.
76. Simbamwenni (*HIFL*).

April 5 Wednesday, 1871 [Page blank]

April 6 Thursday, 1871

Imbiki 15
With sanguine hearts we left the ill-omened hollow & Mtone Bank of Kingaroo, for a long march to Imbiki, which Arabs said was 7 hours off. I with the head of my caravan arrived at 2 P.M. having started at eight, thus at the steady rate of 2 ½ miles an hour would make the march 15 miles. Shaw however did not arrive with the cart until next morning at 8 A.M. thus compelling us to halt once more. My soldiers seemed to have become completely demolazed[77] from their long detention at Kingaroo. 1 pagazi ran away with 2 goats, 1 soldiers tent, and Uledi's stock of beads & clothes that he had bought with the advance money I gave him.

April 7 Friday, 1871

Halt.
We waited to day for Shaw & the cart with the soldiers, and had a halt in consequence. Received a present of 3 chickens from the chief of the village for which in accordance with custom I gave him a shukkeh[78] of American sheeting. Khamisi the pagazi having deserted, I was driven to do away with another load of boat boards in order to be able to proceed.

April 8 Saturday, 1871

Msuwa. 10 miles
A most horrible march of 10 miles through a continuous jungle with the exception of breathing intervals. Jagged stumps, hawser thick climbers, great & tall calabash, and a number of acacia horrida acacia giraffe, & poisonous plants which emitted a most horrible, pungent & acrid odor.
Did not arrive in camp until 5 P.M. though we had started 7.30 A.M. Shaw had trouble with the cart, did not arrive until midnight.

April 9 Sunday, 1871

A halt.
Owing to the tremendous strain the poor donkeys were subjected to yesterday, & the soldiers also needed rest greatly, for it had been one continuous labor of putting on

---
77. 'demolazed', ms., for 'demoralized'.
78. A shukka is a measure equivalent to two yards of cloth (*HIFL*, 721).

loads & watching them, ropes, chains, mats, canvas saddles all needed repair as the donkeys had forced their way through the jungle.

Uledi & Feraggi[79] not returned, but heard of them from the companion of Sheikh Thani.

April 10 Monday, 1871

[Pencil] Camp. West by South Course. 6 miles.
We had a short march to day owing to fears that the jungle would prove too much for the donkeys. There was only one stiff bit however but the Kirangosi declared Kisemo too far. Once out of the jungle a magnificent & soul inspiring country expands into long rolling swells capped by gigantic calabash, ebony acacia. 1 Mtone close to Msuwa. Mishense[80] are bad people we heard several times on the road.
Saw a slave gang chained on their road to the Coast. They looked comfortable.

April 11 Tuesday, 1871

[Ink] Kisemo 5 miles
But little difficulty was experienced on this march owing principally to its shortness. Towards the latter part a heavy rain fell which gave the cart and drivers great trouble. A little stream runs behind the village in a South Easterly direction and falls probably into the Kingani. Game is abundant the natives on the other side though I for one have but seen but 2 deer & 1 hartebeest since leaving the Bagomoyo side of the Kingani. A little incident happened here. Shaw wanted to clear a space for his little tent, and in doing so lifted a stone to throw it[81] out of the way. The chief ran up, took up the stone quickly & set it back again, and setting his foot upon it warned the ignorant Musungu that it was Uganga or Medicine, & that it must not be moved. I begged him to lift it up, upon doing which he disclosed a stick driven deeply in which he said was "Uganga". The belles of this village exhibited a large amount of finery, such as a spiral coil of wire reaching from the wrist to the elbow joint, the same from their angles to their knees. Necklaces[82] of beads of various colors from the neck to the navel, & their[83] hispid heads revealed their[84] various tastes.

---

79. Ferajji (*HIFL*).
80. 'Mshenzi' is the singular in Kiswahili for an uncouth, savage person; Stanley should have written 'Washenzi' for the plural.
81. 'it' added above the line.
82. 'Necklaces' preceded by 'bracelets' crossed out.
83. Inkspot on this word, may be 'hair' crossed out.
84. 'their' added above the line.

April 12 Wednesday, 1871

Moussoudi in Ungerengeri[85] 11 miles

Happily for our patient donkeys we have left the jungle paths, and tread the free open road running through a country as deliciously beautiful as any the sun shines upon. Happily for ourselves also, for we have no more the care, of the packs & the anxiety about reaching camp before night. The packs once set on firmly on the backs of such good donkeys they arrive in camp without a single displacement, or giving cause to one impatient word. Were the road to Unyanyembe like this, I should consider it as comfortable as crossing over to Staten Island for a Sunday holiday, or[86] travelling to Central Park by horse-car, that I might rejoice in its beauty, &[87] dream in its arbors. Take away the gravelled path, the Lakes & Ponds, the Museums within the trellised arbors, the kiosk, the well-dressed visitors in short all evidences of civilized culture, and what would remain of Central Park with its refreshing lawns & gentle hollows & grove-clad swells[88] would give those who have seen Central Park a fair illustration of what the march between Kisemo & Moussoudi presented.[89]

Met Salim bin Rasheed who gave news of Livingstone having met him at Ujiji a year ago, lived next door to him. L had a white beard & moustache was very thin from sickness, was about going to Marungu & Maniema[90].[91]

– Sent a letter to Mr Webb by Sheick Salim bin Rasheed.

April 13 Thursday, 1871

Halt at Moussoudi

We halted this day because[92] the poverty of the people prevented us from procuring the needful daily supply of grain. They had Indian corn unshucked which required a day before it was in a fit condition to eat. Moussoudi stands in a well cultivated valley neighboured by several villages of equal size, population & wealth. The swift and brawling little river of Ungerengeri has cut a circuitous line through it, and after[93] seeking an outlet at its southern extremity turns along an Eastern course which it continues to Kisemo whence it abruptly seeks the south & soon[94] finds its infinity in the Kingani.

---

85. Mussoudi in Ungerengeri (*HIFL*). Stanley corrected his first spelling of Unkerengere, by writing g over k and i over the last e.
86. Part of a word crossed out.
87. 'revel' crossed out. This is one of many examples of Stanley editing his own journal.
88. 'of grove-clad hills' crossed out, and 'grove-clad' added above the line, before 'swells'.
89. Most of this comparison passed into *HIFL*, 110.
90. The correct spelling should be Manyema.
91. In *HIFL*, Stanley placed this meeting with Salim bin Rashid some days later at Muhalleh (*HIFL*, 114).
92. 'of' crossed out.
93. 'after' added above the line.
94. 'soon' added above the line.

Among[95] the curious vegetation which is found in and contiguous to this valley is the lordly Mparamusi – a tree so exactly like the stately chenars in the Char Bagh of Ispahan that I had welcomed it as an old friend until a closer examination dispelled the illusion. It is a strange and noble tree nevertheless with a wealth of foliage around its lofty head so vividly green that the eye rests with rapture, as it discerns it towering above all.

April 14 Friday, 1871

Camp 11 miles. from 8.30 to 1 P.M.
Left Moussoudi, crossed the Ungerengeri and took a N. W. course. The river is rapid and deep when it is sluggish it is about 15[96] yards broad at the ford. It is banked with a rich black loam deposits from its inundation, which nourishes a rank growth of tiger grass, reeds, a few banana plants the fruit of which the natives take particular care to monopolize expecting to receive shukkas[97] of merikani by their sale. On leaving the western bank we had another mile of the valley with its excessive moist soil, and enormous grass, after which we gained the uncultivated parts – an open forest of tamarind & tamarisk, mparamusi, and other tall trees,[98] between which everywhere flourished nutritious grass for cattle. At the ninth[99] mile of the march after the[100] ascent of a[101] considerable slope we began a steep descent which terminated in a deep but dry gulley, or mtoni, as all gulleys and rivers are called. On the other side we had to regain the elevation we had lost. And a similar country opened into view until we found a newly made boma with well built huts of grass near a pool of water which we at once occupied as a halting place for the night. The cart gave us considerable trouble, not even the strongest donkey which usually carried on its back 196 lbs weight could draw it with only 225 lbs. This second difficulty occasioned us to discard another load of provisions, chains, handy articles which we found to be superfluous.

April 15 Saturday, 1871

Mikeseh 7 ½ miles. 7 A.M. to 10 A.M.
We made an early start so as to reach Mikeseh early. By 8.30 we were ascending the southern slope of the Northernmost[102] cone of Kira.

---

95. 'other cur' crossed out.
96. '15' written over '30'? Stanley decided on 20 (*HIFL*, 111).
97. 'skukkas' corrected in 'shukkas'.
98. 'in' crossed out.
99. 'ninth' written above 'sixth' crossed out.
100. 'after the' written above 'we had ascended' crossed out.
101. 'a' added above the line.
102. 'Northernmost' written above 'first' crossed out.

Ukwere ends at Kisemo. Okami[103] commences and extends to Kira Peak. Udoe southern extremity commences at Kira Peak to Ugalalla – 8 miles from Mikeseh – Usegura commences & goes to Simbawenni. Simbawenni was formerly a portion of the territory of the Wakami but the Wasegura came & conquered it, since which it became Simbawenni & belongs to the Wasegura. Udoe stretches South[104] of Mikesh[105] 1 day's march to a man with empty hands, when he comes to the Ruvu River, on the other side is Khutu.

At the western[106] foot of Kira Peak is a well cultivated little valley of Kiwrima. A large[107] Pond supplies the villagers with an abundance of water. After ascending the Kira slope we find ourselves in Udoe.

April 16 Sunday, 1871

Ugalalla[108] Camp. 7 ½ miles
A heavy rain visted[109] us during the night compelled to start late from Mikeseh to allow the tents to dry, and to collect matama for our tramp through the wilderness. Uruguru commences directly South of Simbawenni, and stretches across the Mgeta to Mvuha. <u>South</u>-East of it is Ukwenni, South East of Ukwenni is Kirangawana. We cross the Mrima to the Kingani across the river is Uzaramo as far as Rosaco, thence is Ukwere as far as Kisemo, thence is Ukami as far as the Kira Peak, thence is Udoe as far as Ulagalla thence is Useguru as far as M'kata, thence is Usagara

April 17 Monday, 1871

Muhalleh 11 ¼ miles, 6.30 A.M. to[110] 11 A.M.
We were hemmed in with mountains on to day's march, the change was welcome & agreeable. Because when tired of looking into the depths of the forest with its deep woods, its strange trees & plants the scores of flowers of varied hue which relieved the vivid greenness of foliage & grass we had but to lift the head to observe the sinuous spine of the Uruguru Mountains but five or six miles off parallel with the road, & mentally report upon its outline, its spurs, & projections, its chasms, its bulging rocks, and above all the dark green woods which clothed them from their highest summit to

---

103. Ukami (*HIFL*, 110).
104. Actually north of Mikeseh.
105. 'Mikesh' without e, end of the line.
106. 'western' added above the line.
107. 'large' added above the line.
108. Ulagalla (*HIFL*).
109. 'visted', ms., for 'visited'.
110. 'to' added above the line.

their base. And a pleasing occupation it was when not looking after the mundane task, of observing the donkey's packs, or the pace of the careful stepping pagazis, to wat[ch][111] the vapors play about the mountain[112] summits, to see them fold[113] into crowns, dissolve, gather together into a tremulous cloud that threatened rain and sail away before the brightening sun.[114]

    Villages built in a circle, and a walled fence, or prickly mimosa bushes surround them. Chief brings present of matama, or Indian corn with a chicken or two, and a few eggs not always fresh. The return present is given next morning before marching, according to the gift, 5 measures or 15[115] lbs to a shukka of Merikani or Kaniki.

We caught up with the 5th caravan to day Kingaru the chief.[116] We did not stop at Muhalleh.

April 18 Tuesday, 1871

Ungerengeri near Simbawenni. 7 miles 2 ¾ hours.

Left Muhalleh in a shower, and though the 5th caravan had several on the sick list and would fain have lingered out of consideration for their invalids, yet our cheery example had it influence, & they finally set off in advance so that we presented quite an imposing caravan as we[117] marched past the fortified walls of Simbawenni with[118] the banner of the 5th red & white and the American flag in the centre. Our National flag for the first time in these regions attracted general attention, and we could plainly see a couple of armed warriors pointing at its distinctive features, as the wind toyed with its folds.

    Simbawenni 2nd (daughter of the 1st) very punctually sent her seedy ambassador after the tribute, but a few words – about my caravans having paid already, and that it was out of reason that I should have to pay over again, satisfied the envoy who returned to report such to her[119] Highness.

Moto is the greatest chief of Useguwa occupying the most northern part, while Simbawenni retains paramount rule over the southern part.

---

111. Paper scratched.
112. 'mountain' added above the line.
113. 'out' crossed out.
114. This paragraph was integrated, almost word for word, in *HIFL*, 113–14.
115. '15' written over '10'?
116. One word unreadable after 'Kingaru' on the bottom line; 'the chief' is a tentative restitution.
117. 'advanced' crossed out.
118. 'banners' crossed out.
119. 'Imperial mistress' crossed out.

April 19 Wednesday, 1871

Halt.

This is a great rendez vous for Halts, for the purpose of procuring supplies for the up march, to reorganize your packs, &c. We needed it very much – the last five days steady marching without rest told on the donkeys fearfully – their backs having become literally raw, besides having thinned from insufficient food. As several of them carried nearly 200 lbs weight, I determined to reduce the loads to the maximum of 140 lbs, instead of 200 lbs as heretofore. The reports I daily received of the flooding of the country around Makata, and the loss of 3 donkeys out of 8[120] belonging to the 4th caravan made me naturally anxious that[121] mine should go through without stoppage. For I was so loaded that had 3 donkeys died out of my caravan I should be under the neceessity of halting a long time to obtain carriage.

April 20 Thursday, 1871

Halt.

Selim broke the trigger of my gun & almost occasioned his own death, by hanging the double barreled smooth bore on an iron peg that ran through the pole of my tent, while it was full cock.[122] Last night tent-pole gave way under a rain squall, gun fell down, and went off one oz ¼ bullet flying close to his body, while he was lying close to the door of the tent inside.

To day at 11 A.M. my old Enemy the Ague attacked me. I discerned him at a distance while he was climbing up the spine[123] & ribs and up to my shoulders, and I knew that when he reached the head I should have to give up & rest. So I surrendered at once & the fever in the afternoon came with its insane visions, its frenetic brain throbs & dire sickness, and late in the night there was rest,[124] sleep & sweet dreams.

April 21 Friday, 1871

Halt.

5th caravan left, we go to morrow if all is well.

Timely medicine saved me from another attack this morning, so as soon as my strength was restored with some sago gruel, my journal attracted my attention & I wrote.

---

120. 'of Farquarh' crossed out.
121. 'mine' written over the first letters of 'my caravan', the last letters 'avan' crossed out.
122. Selim was fined £1 for this damage (Notebook S.A. 1).
123. 'the spine' written above 'spinal' crossed out; word after 'spinal' crossed out.
124. 'and' crossed out.

Sarmine, Ferajji & the Kirangozi returned from their visit to Kiroka on a hunt after bamboo tent pole, with a cane as thick as a girl's wrist about a fifth of the size required.

April 22 Saturday, 1871

Halt.
Because of incessant rain, & the rise of the Ungerengeri, which is not fordable[125] during the Masika season. The mountains about seem to be eternally covered by the heavy clouds which distill the showers. The sun appears to be but a pale image of itself. It is a thorough London rain, a miserable[126] drizzle giving all men a gloomy dissatisfied appearance. On the Eastern side the rain – though crops of holcus & Indian corn thrive astonishingly – has rendered the black earth a soft,[127] quagmire. Armies of black, & white ants infest it. Enormous centipede like worms, of all colors trail their lengths on the[128] shrubs & plants, clinging to the under branches of dwarf trees are the honey combed nests of yellow headed wasps, beetles as large as mice roll their dung-balls over the ground. It is a hot-bed of malaria, unpleasant to look at, an abomination to memory.

Food is[129] very scarce[130] in the neighbourhood, or the Wasegura are more extortionate than their brother races tribes[131] further East. 2 chickens cost a shukka of Mericani, 4 can[132] be bought at Bagomoyo. 5 scant[133] measures of corn cost a shukka, 10 full measures were purchased at Kingaroo in Ukwere. When I think[134] of the broad valley of Ungerengeri teeming with such corn that a Georgia or an Arkansas planter would have envied watered by two wide mountain streams, nourished by incessant[135] rains, &[136] mist & dew, I imagine the dearness of food at my camp arose from greed.

---

125. 'at any season' crossed out.
126. 'but' crossed out.
127. 'slipper' crossed out.
128. 'the' added above the line.
129. 'is' written over 'was'.
130. 'scarce' written above 'dear' crossed out.
131. 'races' added above the line, 'tribes' may be crossed out.
132. 'can' written above 'might' crossed out; 'have' crossed out, 'been' changed into 'be'.
133. 'scant' added above the line.
134. 'think' written above 'cast my eyes' crossed out; 'of' written over 'over'.
135. 'incessant' added above the line.
136. '&' may be crossed out.

April 23 Sunday, 1871

Simbo. N by W. & W-N.W. 5 miles 11 A.M. to 1 P.M.
It cleared up this morning and the sun revisited the gloomy valley which gave us a chance to cross the deep & rapid Ungerengeri. Our camp being but half a mile off soldiers & pagazis were roused up at five to convey the baggage over a[137] bridge which was of the most temporary kind, the plan of which could only have emanated from the brain of an ignorant Washense. Even for Pagazis it must have proved anything but comfortable to walk. Only a tight rope performer could have carried a load with ease. Indeed it can not be called walking over an African bridge, it is more of a hop from land to the stout limb of a tree which has been thrown[138] across and lashed to a few neighbours of similar ruggedness, then a skip to another limb, finally a long jump on land. With 70 lbs weight of cloth on his back the Pagazi finds it no easy task. However without an accident we had our goods conveyed across to the western bank. The donkeys were hauled one by one through the river whether they would or not. This little performance[139] of crossing cost us 5 full hours, though energy, abuse & fury enough were expended for an army.

From the western bank to our camp at Simbo was an easy march of 5 miles. Bamboo at Simbo rocky, quartze ground. Water is abundant, grass plentiful. Boma pretty fair. No game though I tried plenty of tracks.

April 24 Monday, 1871

Camp 10 ¼ miles W N W.
No sooner had we left Simbo than the clouds dropped rain in torrents, wetting everybody & everything save what was covered by waterproof Bags.

In the morning Bunder Salaam Cook[140] was found guilty of pilfering for the sixth.[141] This time in such a gross manner that the talking spent on him had been in vain. I therefore ordered Shaw to administer a sound dozen to him, & to drive him donkey & pack out of camp saying I would have no such incorrigible thieves in my camp. I did not intend that he should actually be sent adrift at the mercy of every Mshense who might think him worth robbing. But not thinking that he would be bold enough to return to Simbawenni by himself I did not give any one order to see that he followed us. We arrived in camp, but he did not. The cart gave us a great deal

---

137. 'temporary' crossed out.
138. 'thrown' added above the line.
139. 'aided' crossed out.
140. See Appendix, contract of engagement for Bunder Salaàm, Abdel Kader, and Celim, signed on February 3, 1871 (S.A. 4745).
141. 'For the fifth time', Stanley tells in *HIFL*, 126.

of trouble on account of the mud, & every one more or less tumbled into the ditch of difficulties though the march was only 10 ¼ miles. Bombay lost our new axe, the property or baggage tent – his fine uniform & cloths & powder in fact everything – & seemed to have entirely lost his wits. Khamisi – pagazi lay down in despair Farjalla pegged out. Kamna could not bring one foot together. Cart did not arrive until midnight. Hyaenas close to camp.

April 25 Tuesday, 1871

Halt
This morning ordered a halt. No provisions in front at Makata. Sent back four soldiers, one to hunt up Bombay's loss 3 to Ungerengeri to buy provision. Tent & articles not found. The soldiers were also ordered & they had a donkey with them to bring the cook back by force if necessary.

On sending the donkeys out to graze early, one of them espied a deer, which gave them a regular stampeder. I thought it might have been a carnivorous beast and so ran up with my smooth-bore to meet him. What was my surprise to see a deer jump up almost under my feet. Subsequently saw Koodoo (2) missed them Shot a moor-hen & fat pigeon.

A caravan of Wanyamwezi carrying ivory camped close to us – so that the place which yesterday gave no signs of having been inhabited presents quite a busy scene now.

April 26 Wednesday, 1871

Halt.

April 27 Thursday, 1871

Halt.

April 28 Friday, 1871

Halt.
 Shaw with Mabruki were sent back to find out what became of the 3 soldiers I sent in search of the cook. About 5 P.M. they returned[142] bringing with them the absentees. They had a most melancholy account to give of themselves. Arriving at Simbawenni

---

142. On [?]… Word under an inkspot.

on the track of two men who had been seen by the people of the ferry, they were put in chain & the Sultana of Simbawenni had robbed them of their guns & accoutrements, & suspecting the two men found with the Cook's donkey to have murdered him for the sake of his property she sent them in charge of a Swahili caravan to be judged & disposed of by Syed Barghash. The masters of the caravan obtained the release of my soldiers by intimating to her that if they were not set at liberty, I should come after them, and make a fuss. But their freedom was given minus their guns & equipments. The soldiers returned with the Cook's donkey, hat & spectacles & Malabar[143] book on Religion.[144]

April 29 Saturday, 1871

Makata. W by N. 6 ½ miles.
Started at eight A.M. Soldiers much demoralized from their long stay. Shaw sick of the fever – also Selim & Zaidee. Mud, mud & vexation of crossing, 2 Rivers. Camped about 50 yds this side of the Makata. Bought half a hartebeest 200 lbs meat for 2 doti of sheeting, had a good feast. Passed a small village fortified after the manner of the people of Simbawenni.

April 30 Sunday, 1871

Camp on Makata West ¼ a mile.
It was a day's work to cross this stream of Makata. Cut our way through 50 feet of jungle & then crossed a stream 50 yards wide owing to its inundation. After swimming the donkeys had to construct a bridge across the rapid stream for the soldiers & pagazis to carry the luggage. As we were working down poured the rain in torrents, beating the road & the entire plain into mortar-mud. To cap our discomforts, Kingaru soldier deserted. Despatched 2 soldiers after him who within half an hour caught him. Paid 2 doti & 11 khete of beads to the Fundi of Makata village for arresting him. Shaw still sick, and shows a new phase of character under the infliction a phaze[145] none of the pleasantest. Zaidee[146] soldier sick of the smallpox, & thus my force is being gradually reduced. If I only preserve my health I know my courage will keep me up under it all, but I fall sick, & seriously God knows when we shall get to Unyanyembe.

---

143. In Malabar print (*HIFL*, 133).
144. The incident is more complex. See Stanley's relation in *HIFL*, 130–34. Stanley seems uneasy when justifying Bunder Salaam's punishment and absconding as though his responsibility were involved. A letter from the American consul F. Webb gives some more details about this incident, which was reported to the Sultan of Zanzibar. See Appendix, Letter from Francis R. Webb, American Consul in Zanzibar, to Stanley, Zanzibar, June 11, 1871, S.A. 2654.
145. Both words 'phase' are written 'phaze'.
146. Zaidi (*HIFL*).

May 1 Monday, 1871

Camp in Valley of Makata W. N. W.

9 miles 7.30 to 12 M.

One of the most dreaded of days. Before starting from Bagomoyo I heard ominous rumors respecting the Valley of the Makata, but no one seemed to know where it lay. They said during the masika season it was horrible, and our experience of today verified the statement to the last letter. It was simply one <u>vast</u> lake, a small Tanganyika – but fortunately not so deep, being but 3 feet at the deepest part. The cause of this extensive surface of water over so large a valley is very evident. The valley throughout its length & breadth of 45[147] miles being as level as a billiard table. It might be called a prairie, but the Usagara & Usegura ranges folding it in, on the[148] Western & Eastern horizons, makes it[149] a large valley. We arrived at camp pretty nearly exhausted, & found a boma on the only dry spot found throughout the march, where we nested like Noah's dove. The Palm covers the valley.

May 2 Tuesday, 1871

Rudewa River. West & NW. 7.30 to 11.45 A.M.

at 2 ¼ miles per hour. 9 miles & 1/8th

Today was but a second edition of yesterday, but as we drew nearer the Usagara Mountain which rose 10 miles to the westward the waters were abating though deep in all the depressions.

May 3 Wednesday, 1871

[Ink] Camp in Makata on banks of Rudewa 4 miles. West by S

[Pencil] Donkey lost with all our sugar and tea.

May 4 Thursday, 1871

[Ink over pencil] Rehenneko 7 ½ miles. Course S.W.

Sick with severe attack of dysentery.

May 5 Friday, 1871

[Ink over pencil] Halt.

---

147. '45' written over '35'.
148. 'Eastern' crossed out.
149. 'makes' written over 'gives it'.

May 6 Saturday, 1871

[Ink over pencil] Halt

May 7 Sunday, 1871

[Ink over pencil] Halt

May 8 Monday, 1871

[Ink over pencil] Camp   3 ½ hours at 2 miles   7 miles
Course W by S.[150]
We ascend the Mountains of Usagara

May 9 Tuesday, 1871

[Ink] <u>Time 7.45. to 11.15. A.M.</u>
[Ink over pencil] Kiora 6 miles. Course West S. W. on Mukondokwa right bank. River very crooked, caught up with Farquahar.

[Ink] This was a road across[151] an intricate jumble of cones jostling against each other, which led us up the hill & down again repeatedly, still[152] it was a descent through gradual ending finally in the ravine-like valley of the Mukondokwa, a[153] rapid brown[154] stream averaging, so far as we saw it about 40 feet in breadth.
Malaria, miasma and other diseases resulting from black mud, river deposits, overflows and redundant vegetation springing up spontaneously[155] with the power and vitality of Jonah's gourd[156] to choke others already in existence, swept up & down its[157] winding length by[158] rushing winds, and pent in by the overhanging crowns of the lofty mountain walls on either side, made the passage of it a real calamity. Men, donkeys & dogs of the Caravan felt it. We travelled along the left bank of the river until we came to Missonghi crossed the river-deepest part, but thigh deep, and travelling a half a mile further came to a miserably small village called Kiora, where amidst the dry muck, & fly heaps, filthy children, lay in bed in tent Farquhar who led the 4th Caravan.

---

150. 'W by S' written over 'C. W by S.'
151. 'across' written above 'through' crossed out.
152. 'still' preceded by 'untill' crossed out.
153. 'stream' crossed out.
154. 'brown' added above the line.
155. 'like' crossed out.
156. Biblical reference to Jonah 4:5–11.
157. 'its' written over 'in'?
158. 'by' written over 'and'.

May 10 Wednesday, 1871

[Ink over pencil] Halt

May 11 Thursday, 1871

[Pencil] 51 days from Bagomoyo[159]

[Ink over pencil] Camp on Mukondokwa course for 2 hours on 4[160] miles West, 2.50[161] West by N ½ N.

Started 7.15 A.M. Camp 12.10 M. Dist. 10 m.

May 12 Friday, 1871

[Pencil] 52

[Ink] Madete. Course W by N. ½ N. 11 A.M. to 2 P.M. @ 2 miles = 6 miles.

At 5 A.M. even until 8 A.M. Shaw had not come in with the cart, though there were but 11 saddles, & 1 load on it. I sent Chowpereh back to Shaw with the following written on a paper slip, "You will upon receipt of this order pitch the cart into the nearest ravine river, or gulley, also all the saddles except 3 which you will place upon one of the men's heads, Farquarhar's bed put upon Sarmine, and come along for God's sake, we must not starve here[162]" In about an hour's time came Sarmine much fatigued with Farquhar's pack on his head, stating that the "Bana Mdogo"[163] had not yet crossed the river which news was rather startling, and unexpected after the efforts made to relieve him. Finding no better way to hurry the laggard crowd than to go myself, I called for my donkey, and rode to the river. On the way there, I met Mabruki staggering under a load of saddles, just behind, and lo sturdy Chowpereh with the cart on his head, wheels shafts body axle & all – he having found that carrying it was a[164] much better way[165] than drawing it behind. It was such a damper to my experiment that the cart was then & there taken into the tall weeds, & left there standing out of the way lest the Washense should say "See the Musungu's folly". Shaw[166] was riding at agait which seemed to leave it doubtful, whether he or the animal felt most sleepy.

---

159. From here, Stanley wrote the number of days from Bagamoyo. He would stop counting at Shisa, one day before arriving at Unanyembe.
160. '4' written in ink over '3' in pencil.
161. 'H' written in pencil above '2' in ink; 'M' written in pencil above '50' in ink.
162. 'here' added above the line.
163. 'Bana Mdogo' for 'Bwana Mdogo': little master (*HIFL*).
164. 'carrying it was a' written above 'way a' crossed out.
165. 'of carrying' crossed out.
166. 'Shaw' preceded by 'M'' crossed out.

May 13 Saturday, 1871

[Pencil] 53

[Ink] Ugombo Lake W by N ½ N. 6 miles 6.45 A.M. to 9.45 A.M.

Ascending a long hill, we descended it coming into view of the beautiful little lake of Ugombo.[167] The lake is about half[168] the size of Anchangi[169] in Abyssinia, is 2 miles ¼ long by a mile & a half in width at its widest part. We travelled its extreme length in one hour and a half. Black Swans,[170] Fish Eagles. Hawks, Pelican, Ibis Sacra, Florican, Duck, Crane, Owls Pigeons, Small Toucan, Hippopotami, Crocodiles, Guinea Fowl, Grouse, Wood-Cock[171] infest its waters, Wild Boar, Kudu, Small deer & Buffalo. Jacko tried to desert. Shot pigeons, & ate Wild Boar. Farquhar rode my donkey I walked all the way. Two donkeys died today.

[Pencil] Hyrax squatted in a clump of thick grass on the slope of a humpy hill facing the Lake.

May 14 Sunday, 1871

[Pencil] 54

Halt at Ugombo Lake.

I was surprised to find Jacko had deserted with one of my carbines. Ordered a halt. Sent three soldiers in pursuit, Uledi, Chompereh, and Mabruk Saleem, as well as to bring posho,[172] and return with the cart, since from here to Unyanyembe we are told the road is excellent. Farquhar being useless and very much in the way I sent with Mabruki Speke to Umpapaw[173] on my riding donkey. I also sent a gorah of domestics[174] to purchase a cow. Selim is very sick, with the kunguru, and is so much reduced by it that he is as weak as a child. Shaw got down with fever in the evening, and there seems to be no end of calamities. Towards night Jacko returned, with the statement that he had been asleep from sheer fatigue. Had he not given me so much trouble, I might have had sympathy for him, but now I am obliged to punish him, owing to circumstances. Kiboko made terrible noise last night.

---

167. "A grey sheet of water lying directly at the foot of the hill.... The view was neither beautiful nor pretty, but what I should call refreshing," says Stanley in *HIFL*, 153.

168. 'half' added above the line.

169. Lake Ashangi.

170. 'Black Swans' added above the line.

171. 'Guinea Fowl, Grouse, Wood-Cock' added above the line.

172. 'Posho' often for 'posha': daily rations for porters. Cf. *A Standard English-Swahili Dictionary* (Oxford University Press, 1992).

173. Correct spelling: Mpwapwa.

174. The "domestics" is a certain type of cotton cloth from Massachusetts, the main center of production being Salem, which explains its connection with Zanzibar. A gorah is equivalent to 7 1/2 doti of Merikani or 30 yards; a gorah of domestics could be slightly different.

May 15 Monday, 1871

[Pencil] 55

Halt at Ugombo Lake.
Shot some grouse, filled cartridges.

May 16 Tuesday, 1871

[Pencil] 56

[Ink] **Matamombo**
Mtoni, 11 miles. Time from 8.30 A.M. to 2.30 P. M. 6 hours. Course W.N W. Donkey foal died early in the morning. Within 15 minutes of our camp, the dog "Omar" faithful companion of mine from Bombay & guardian of my tent, died from inflammation of the bowels, brought on from excessive dysentery which attacked him as well as many of my men during the transit of the Makata Valley.

Water uncommonly bad at this place. Encountered on the road two skulls of rhinoceros. Robeho[175] Mts on our left far away.

[Pencil] Monkeys with exceedingly long tails found at Matamombo

May 17 Wednesday, 1871

[Pencil] 57

[Ink] Mpapaw[176] 7 hours. 7.15 A.M. to 2.15 P.M. @ 1 ¾ miles per hour 12 ¼ . Course N. by W ½ W.

A very long march made longer to me by my difficulties with the cart, being obliged owing to Shaw's illness to stop behind with it. A plain covered with grass parched to the color of stubble, followed by a 6 mile jungle of acacia horrida Kolquall[177] saplings, whose leaves had the Autumn brownness. Rubeho Mountains flanked obliquely our left – the Mpapaw lay on our right – to a deep bend of which our course directed. Far away behind S.S.E. could be seen the tall peak of Ugombo purpling, then fading[178] into dim blueness, as we increased the distance. Contrasting with the Autumnal aspect of the plain we traversed were the slopes of Mpapaw fresh & springlike, from which the rills of Umpapaw flowed clear and sweet.

[Pencil] This place is called by the natives Mbambwa and so is the opposite range to Rubeho, [Ink] by the Arabs Mpwapwa ,

---

175. Rubeho (*HIFL*).
176. Capital M written over 'Um'…
177. Kolqual. One of the vernacular names for *Euphorbia abyssinica*. E. Bein, B. Habte, A. Jaber, A. Birnie Bo Tengnas, *Useful Trees and Shrubs in Eritrea* (Nairobi: Regional Soil Conservation Unit, 1996).
178. 'dimly' crossed out.

May 18 Thursday, 1871

[Pencil] 58

Halt.

  Found Sheikh Thani & his caravan also Abdullah bin Nasib with a host of native satellites who revolved around the great man and his 500 frasilah of ivory which he was taking to Zanzibar. Abdullah said he had some donkeys & cows he would sell me. Cows I had no use for, donkeys I would buy 4 if he would be kind enough to sell.

  Abdullah gave me some information respecting Livingstone. L. had gone to Maniema which was a month's march from Ujiji. He had shot himself in the thigh while out hunting buffalo. As soon as he got well he would return to Ujiji. There were many Lakes there. Lake Ujiji was very great,[179] Lake Uruva was very great also,[180] Lake Banguelo was great, but Lake Maniema was great[181] great, exceedingly great. This was the sum of Abdullah's report.

May 19 Friday, 1871

[Pencil] 59

[Ink] Halt.

Was very fortunate to day in securing pagazis 12. Wanyamuezi were engaged in a very short time at the rate of from 9 to 12 doti per head. My soldiers were thus relieved from carrying[182] loads, and could attend to the property while at camp & on the march much better.

  The Mbamba, a lofty and noble species of sycamore flourishes here, while the tamarind hitherto dwarfish & weakly assumes[183] gigantic dimensions[184] with a parachute like crown of leafy branches whose umbrage[185] would[186] shelter a full regiment[187] from noonday heats.

  Matama, Muhallaka – or beans, Hindee – or Indian Corn, Cucumbers, Melons, the Abyssinian Teff pea-nuts[188] are grown here.

  And for the first time since leaving Bagomoyo the sight of cattle grazing on the verdant grass of the mountain slopes recalls[189] memories of delicious milk &

---

179. 'great' written over 'big'.
180. 'but' crossed out.
181. 'greater' modified into 'great'.
182. 'their' crossed out.
183. 'the' crossed out.
184. 'of' crossed out.
185. 'whose umbrage' written above 'that' crossed out.
186. 'embrace' crossed out.
187. 'in the shadow' crossed out.
188. Teff is a grain, not a nut. Traditionally used to make bread in Ethiopia.
189. 'the delici' crossed out.

butter, beef, & fat, ghee & such homely edibles, & luxuries. A gourd full of milk; what would we not give for it[190]? Or a pound of good fresh butter? Or a rump steak, a roast rump, or beef soup? And a pound of beef[191] fat, or ghee; to what uses could we not put them to? Could we not fry our lean scraggy goat meat, and so have a little gravy? Could we not have some fritters, & pancakes, slapjacks & what not. Chickens, eggs,[192] even slop mush were improved for a little fat or ghee? And so we feeding on these thoughts we are actually wrought frenetically esurient[193] by the time we have camped. With ravenous appetites sharpened by the sight of[194]

May 20 Saturday, 1871

[Pencil] 60

Halt

green slopes, and a healthier atmosphere we offer princely prices for milk, butter, eggs, ghee, or beef. Few of these things however[195] could be got. The people kindled at the sound of such wealth of cloth & beads, but the article milk was scarce, not more than two quarts could be procured.

The white ants or the termites usurp the place of the red ants, these latter not being seen here. The black species were also scarce, while the earwigs were abundant, and claimed our paramount attention because of their extreme obtrusiveness, constantly assailing our heads & ears.

At this place I was compelled to leave Farquhar, who had ever since his engagement proved a bad investment. At Mauritius, Seychelles & Zanzibar he had disgraced his employer by being normally[196] inebriated, his sober moments being only in the morning before commencing another course.[197] On board ship he was inveterately lazy & insolent. When asked to sew a pair of pants for the boy Selim, he replied his back was broken from excessive work, though this was the first task required from him during[198] six weeks. In the work of preparing for the journey into Africa, he was useless, he was neither tailor, sailmaker, carpenter, or anything else that I required, his work was begrudlingly given, small & purposeless always. When dispatched at the head of the 4th Caravan[199] completely furnished with all necessary things, my

---

190. 'it' written over 'one'.
191. 'beef' added above the line.
192. 'Our' preceding 'Chickens' and 'eggs' crossed out.
193. Hungry, greedy.
194. Continued under May 20, 1871, after 'Halt'.
195. 'could' written above 'can' crossed out.
196. 'drunk' crossed out.
197. About Farquhar's consumption of brandy, wine & beer, see the Bill of expenses spent by Farquhar to A. Charles at Zanzibar, S.A. 4893.
198. 'during' written above 'in' crossed out.
199. On February 25, 1871, Farquhar was said to be leading the 3rd caravan.

knowledge of his character compelled[200] me to admonish him frequently upon the course he should adopt in extreme cases. But when I found him camped in the filthy village of Kiora, my opinion of him[201] low as it was, was much exceeded by his despicable appearance.

May 21 Sunday, 1871

[Ink] 61 days

Kisokweh. W.N.W. 4 miles. 2 hours[202]

Skirted the Mpapaw Mountains, following its folds in many places. Opens & curves in deep amphitheatral recesses, with bearded pyramidal knolls scattered here, and there outside the line. Through fields of Bajri[203] & matama, the mountain skirts are populous small square tembes are frequent, at their foot & on the slopes.

May 22 Monday, 1871

[Pencil] 62

Choonio[204] 1 ½ hour, N. W. by W.

Continued our route along the skirts of the Mpapaw Mountains, crossing two or 3 spurs of the range that stood isolated from the range. Passing through a small gap which separates the last of these outlying spurs we came in sight of Choonio tembe, and the Khambi of the caravans lying[205] below with the district of Marenga Mkali spread like a map before us – blue mountains running North & South bounding the view. Dark & gloomy was the view except where the bleached grass lay in circlets surrounded by the gloomy colored shrubs. These grassy patches appeared like sandy[206] amidst the picture.

    In the maritime region the feather tribe was numerous & and[207] in great variety. We were gladdened by the sound of the strange notes, many of which were singularly harmonious. But in this region all species save white eagles & toucans & turtle doves have left us. Guinea fowl are abundant near water.

[Pencil] **An addition**

---

200. 'compelled' written over 'caused'.
201. 'had been' crossed out.
202. 'h' of hours, written over '½'.
203. Bajri is a name for pearl millet in parts of India.
204. 'Chunio' crossed out for 'Chunyo', and both crossed out. Stanley kept the spelling 'Chunyo' in HIFL.
205. 'at the foot of' crossed out.
206. Word unintelligible.
207. '& and', ms.

May 23 Tuesday, 1871

[Pencil] 63
[Ink] Marenga Mkhali [Pencil] 3 ½ hours at 2 ½ mile an hour= 8 ¾ miles [Ink] 1st march
[Ink] 2nd march
[Pencil] from 12 M to 5.30 P. M. at 2 ½ miles an hour 13 ¾ miles
Zebra, Giraffe, Eland antelope, rhinoceros. Florikan.

May 24 Wednesday, 1871

[Pencil] 64
[Ink] Marenga Mkhali. [Pencil] Third march 4.20 A. M. to 8.30 A.M. Arrival at [Ink] Mvumi. Little Ugogo. [Pencil] 4 hours 10 minutes at 2 ½ hours per miles. 10 miles. Course W. ½ South.

May 25 Thursday, 1871

[Pencil] 65
[Ink] Mvumi in Great Ugogo.
[Pencil] 4 hours . 2 miles. 8 miles.
Course W. W

[Ink] Operations

May 26 Friday, 1871

[Pencil] 66
[Pencil] Halt at[208] [Ink] Mvumi
[Pencil] Paid 18 ½ doti mixed cloths Muhongo and 1 Fundo of beads
         6 ½ doti[209] for bullocks
         3   "   for food
3 donkeys died, hyenas swarmed, in the morning crows, pert, saucy, tricky as ever in swarms.

Ugogo very dear – having arrived, caravans hurry through. The mode of trade is similar to that of Abyssinia.

---

208. One word crossed out.
209. One doti (or two shukkas) measures four yards (Bennett, *Stanley's Despatches*, 10).

May 27, 1871

[Pencil] 67

[Ink] Matamburu-Matambulu

[Pencil] Chalamaganza

Course W. by South 4 hours. 2 miles. 8 miles

This morning looked & saw all[210] my donkeys, nearly cleared out by the hyaenaes.
[Ink] Country very populous – villages – square & low lie scattered over – the clayey colored plateau. As soon as we camp, the natives crowd to see[211] and wonder, in as fantastic a costume, as any wild Indian of our plains delighted in. Their shields are elongated and painted in broad lines of white black, and ochre. Their bodies are smeared over with a compound of ghee, and ochre, which relieves greatly the Egyptian blackness of their bodies. They are stout, fleshy people, probably because they live well, on butter, milk, beef luxuries denied to the unhappy people of the lowlands. They are comely also I have seen girls & young lads among them exceedingly handsome & well formed. But[212] very few have those thick lips, low brows; and generally hideous countenances which characterize the Negroids of the Western Coast. Their countenances are open & have a candid expression,[213] the features well defined, and their dress seems to consist of whatever cloth shukka doti, tobe,[214] goat skin, sheep, or calf they possess.

May 28 Sunday, 1871

[Pencil] 68 days

[Ink] Halt at Matamburu, Matambulu, or Matômburu – as the Arabs contrive to be contrary always. Paid our Mahongo to the Sultan this morning which through the[215] policy of the Arab Sheikh amounted to but 8 doti, consisting of 1 Sohari Ulyah, 2 doti Kaniki Ulyah, 2 doti Merikani, 1 Barsati, 1 Dabwani, 1 Rehani.

    Engaged 2 Pagazis more at 6 doti each as far as Tula.[216]

[Five lines left blank]

This evening after the horn had sounded the signal for the morrow's march, Sheikh Thani's Kirangozi stood up to speak before the camp 300 strong. Listen Ye[217] Kiran-

---

210. 'all' written above 'both' crossed out.
211. 'see' written over 'hear'.
212. 'But' preceded by 'But look as often as I would' crossed out.
213. '& have a candid expression' added above the line.
214. A length of cloth. A tobe in Abyssinia was said by Burton to equal a doti (Burton, *Lake Regions*, 1:151).
215. 'the' written over 'his'.
216. For 'Tura'.
217. 'Ye' added above the line.

gozis.[218] Listen Wanyamuezi. The journey is to morrow. The road is bad, bad. The Wagogo who steal the Masters cloth, and murder the pagazi lie hidden in the jungles. The Wagogo have been to your camp, & know our road. Wanyamuezi keep your eyes open. Keep close together – lag not behind. Kirangozis, walk slow, that the weak may keep up with the strong. Take two rests on the journey to enable the sick to travel with you. Do you hear my words Wanyamuezi? (A loud shout Yes). Do you understand? Yes.

May 29 Monday, 1871

[Pencil] 69

[Pencil] 8. 5. 9. m.

Bihawana. West by N. 4 hours

Chief Mukatika. 3 doti Mahogo

Heard that my fifth caravan had been attacked by Wagogo. Waganga had driven them off. Killed two, recovered 1 bale of cloth, 1 bag of beads lost.

Today was through a continuous jugle & over hills. Crossed several sandy water cour[se]. Thorns prevalent.

May 30 Tuesday, 1871

[Pencil] 70

[Pencil] Kididimo, chief Mkata. 2 hours. W.N.W.

[Ink] A flat elongated lying between 2 lengthy low hill spines dotted thickly with the dark[219] forms of the mighty baobab.

The Sultan of this place, one of the miserablest & bleakest in aspect. Even the Wagogo's faces seemed to have contracted bleak hue[220] from the general bleakness that looked out from all things. The water had the flavor of warm horse urine & mud, and the two donkeys sickened & died in less than an hour from its effect. Man suffered belly-ache, nausea, and an unconscionable irritability, and accordingly cursed the place and its imbecile ruler most heartily. The climax came however when Bombay[221] appeared to[222] reveal the remarkable fact that the Sultan's head had suddenly increased to enormous dimensions, -in his phrase – 'Got very big now he hear one big Musungu come!' which dimensions could not be reduced unless the Musungu paid 10 doti as tribute.

---

218. See a similar harangue to the pagazis when the journey enters Ugogo in Burton, *Lake Regions*, 1:250.
219. '& mighty' crossed out.
220. Last letters 'ness' of bleakness crossed out; 'hue' added above the line.
221. 'came' crossed out.
222. 'appeared to' added above the line.

May 31 Wednesday, 1871

[Pencil] 71

[Pencil] Tirikeza[223] W. 8[224] hours

[Ink] Starting at dawn we made a two hours march to some pools favorite haunts of herds of elephants and other large animals. The water was wholesome & sweet. The young forest & dry streamlet beds overshadowed by mimosa[225] contiguous to the water[226] afforded excellent retreats while[227] the caravans prepared for the fatigue of a long afternoon march. At Meridian, our thirsts quenched, gourds refilled, stomachs fortified we emerged from the cool shades to brave its white heat. Our path ran its serpentine course, through bits of bleached[228] grass stubble, thickets of black thorn, which[229] emitted odor as rank as a filthy stable, clumps of mimosas, colonies of baobab, through a country abounding in game[230] which were[231] as safe from our rifles as if we had been on the Indian Ocean. For 6 hours we labored on thus, taking five minute rests every two hours,[232] seeing nought, save a few yards around of bush or clear space – a circle of glossy sky flecked by a few fleeting clouds – hearing nought save the din of the caravan's march or the notes of the feathered inhabitants of the forest. At sunset we camped. On[233] mustering the people one of my pagazis was found absent: a sick man suffering from acute[234] dysentery. No one would volunteer to go after him, not even his brother alone. So he was left to perish, no one caring to undergo the terrible task of such a long march.

June 1 Thursday, 1871

[Pencil] 72

[Ink] Nyambwa.

[Ink over pencil] Pembera Pereh [Pencil] course W. 2 hours.

[Pencil under Pembera Pereh] name of Sultan

---

223. Four different spellings can be found in the diary—tirikesa, tirekesa, terekeza, terekesa—for a long and quick march.
224. Stanley wrote 6 originally, which was the time of the terekeza; he then added the two hours march of the morning and changed 6 to 8 accordingly. '8 hours' was kept in *HIFL*.
225. 'overshadowed by mimosa' added above the line.
226. 'to the water' added above the line.
227. 'pagazis' crossed out.
228. 'bleached' added above the line, and crossed out before 'thickets'.
229. 'which' preceded by 'emitt' crossed out.
230. 'but' crossed out.
231. 'which were' added above the line
232. 'and arrived' crossed out.
233. 'On' added above the line.
234. 'acute' written above 'chronic' crossed out.

[Ink] Two hours from the jungle camp brought us to this place. It has good water, but a wicked old man for a ruler. We seem to have entered another Ugogo, for the inhabitants are wilder, and approach more to my ideas of perfect savagery than any other I know. My sailor overseer who had a way of his own of expressing himself at all times "delivered[235] himself after this fashion "Well, I declare, these must be the genuine Agogians[236] for they stare; – Stare! My God there is no hend to their staring. I'm almost tempted to slap'em in the face!" So insolent were some of these rowdies that I picked out the rowdiest of them & administered to him a thrashing which educed from his tribe all their native power of vituperation and abuse, in expressing which they were peculiar; they vented a chorus of Hi-Hi-ogh-ogh, -and a jerking hah, uttered in a skill[237] crescendo tone. They paced backwards & forwards uttering to themselves questions, "Are we Wagogos to be beaten by this Musungu? A Mgogo[238] is not used to be beaten with[239] a stick." But whenever I made a motion toward them with my donkey whip the mighty Drawcansirs[240] found it convenient to move to respectable distances from the irritated Musungu.

Achmet fined 9 1st class doti for letting his donkeys stray towards the Matama.[241]

June 2 Friday, 1871

[Pencil] 73

[Pencil] Mizanza 5 ½ hours [Pencil, in very small letters, above hours] 2 ¼[242] W. by N.

Perfect flat. Saline pond.

Shaw says of those people, Well I declare these must be the genuine Ugogians, for they stare: –Stare! My God, there is no hend to their staring. I'm almost tempted to slap'em in the face sometimes.

[Ink] Sultan. Small old man decrepit with age, the very type of an old[243] Savage clad in a greasy barsati came to see me. As he entered the tent, by absence of mind natural to one in his position & age astonishmend[244] by[245] the interior of the tent with its

---

235. 'delivered' preceded by 'Well I' crossed out.
236. From Greek, *agogè*, a reference to military education for boys at Sparta.
237. 'skill', ms., for 'skilled'.
238. "A Mgogo is a Mgwana (a free man)" (*HIFL*, 187). In Kiswahili a free man is *mwungwana*.
239. 'with' written above 'by' crossed out.
240. Drawcansir: a daring braggart. One of the characters of *The Rehearsal*, a play by George Villiers, Duke of Buckingham.
241. Achmet is Sheikh Hamed, elected guide of the united caravans while traveling through Ugogo. About the fine of 9 doti of first-class cloth, see the full story in *HIFL*, 189–90.,
242. 2¼ is probably the caravan's speed per hour, and the calculation at the end of the page, the number of miles of the march.
243. 'barbarian' crossed out.
244. 'astonishmend', ms. Stanley probably meant to write 'astonished'.
245. 'by' written over 'at'.

lofty[246] apex, and symmetical arrangement the greasy barsati his only & sole apparel fell to the ground at his feet

[Ink, a calculation] 5 ½ x 2 ¼ = 11 [rest] 1

June 3 Saturday, 1871

[Ink] 74

Halt at Mizanza.

  We were obliged to make a halt today much to my delight, for I knew then that the fever which had so persistently attacked me for the last 14 days, must succumb to four strong doses of Quininae sulphas. I was confined to bed during the heat of the day perspiring profusely between blankets, towards night I got up devoutly thankful that the fever had left me.

  At night, Ulimengo one of the Wanguana[247] soldiers shot a couple of hyaena which were feasting on one of my donkeys[248] with my Jocelyn carbine. Shaw had never seen one before though they had troubled his night dreams often before. Selim the Arab boy, whose ears had been startled out of[249] slumber by their nocturnal ululations, was also gratified at the sight – and declared them to be very like, the pictures he had seen of such.

June 4 Sunday, 1871

[Ink] 75

Swarura[250]

Mukonduku[251] 13 ½ [252] – 6 ½ hours. Course W. first ½ hour – then N. W.[253] skirting the mountain bank which lay a N. W. course across the great saline[254] plain that stretches from Kanyenye to the Masai land.

Ugogo is to the white traveller what Vanity Fair was to Christian & his friends.[255] It is an ordeal to prove of what stuff he is made of. He will be tempted a score of times each day to draw a bead with his rifle on some of the yelping, taunting savages who

---

  246. 'dome' crossed out.
  247. Wanguana (or Wangwana) are freed slaves active in trade. See Field Notebook S.A. 10, March 24, 1872.
  248. 'which were ... donkeys' added above the line.
  249. 'out of' written above 'at' crossed out.
  250. Swarura spelled Swaruru (*HIFL*, 203) is the name of Mukundoka's Sultan.
  251. Mukondoku (*HIFL*).
  252. '13' written over '12. ½ seems' crossed out.
  253. 'along' crossed out.
  254. 'saline' added above the line.
  255. Christian is the main character of *The Pilgrim's Progress from This World to That Which Is to Come*, by John Bunyan (1678). Vanity Fair is an obliged stopping place for Christian in his pilgrimage, as Ugogo is for Stanley.

prank alongside of him – rush up to his face, shouting Hi, What a man! And who quiz at each & every portion of his apparel. Such an outburst of anger would be bitterly regretted afterwards, because it would be bitterly resented by the Sultan with whom reconciliation must be made upon such terms as his kindled avarice may dictate. Any hesitation to pay would be followed by a declaration of hostilities, and the desertion of every pagazi, Mgwana, & Myanwezi.

    3 Doti were paid as honga to the first village in the district of Mukondoku, which has for its lord a brother of him who rules at Mukonduku Proper.

June 5 Monday, 1871

[Ink] 76

Halt at Mukonduku
6 Doti Mahongo
Very populous. 30 villages, determe[256] upon avoiding Kiweeh and making a tirikeza to avoid its exacting Sultan.
[Several lines left blank]
"To your tembes[257] Wagogo, why do you come to trouble the strangers. To your tembes I say. Haste or the Mtemi[258] will punish you. Every Mgogo found in the traveller's Khambi without meal to sell or something else, shall pay to the Mtemi cloth or cows. Away with you! These words were addressed at this place to several hundred Wagogo who crowded every space & made a furor such as only exultant & insolent Savages could make by the chief sent by the Sultan at Thani's request.
Wahumba, Greeks of East Africa, small heads[259]
Wahehe, Romans of   "   "   bearded.

June 6 Tuesday, 1871

[Ink] 77

Halt. at Mukonduku

June 7 Wednesday, 1871

[Ink] 78

Manieka
Camp near Munika.[260] W. by ½ N. 5 hours.

---

256. 'determe', ms., for 'determine'.
257. 'tembes' is written over another word (tents?).
258. About the role of the 'Mtemi', see Field Notebook S.A. 10, April 12, 1872.
259. *HIFL*, 195.
260. Manieka, Munika: Stanley decided for Munieka in *HIFL*.

The caravans had quite a scene shortly after, starting from the Khambi of Mukonduku. It had been decided after several goings backward & forward from my tent to the Arabs, which lasted until 10 P.M. that we should take the Munika road and from thence make a terekeza to Kiti's village of ------------[261] but Achmet ever troublesome & fidgety after starting from Camp allowed himself to be swayed by lazy inclined pagazis, who beguiled themselves & their employer with extremely dolorous information that had no foundation in fact about the long road & a double terekeza which led to Kiti. After travelling a mile on the Kiti road Achmet suddenly resolved to take the Kiweeh road by which if we had followed him, we should have been subjected to a heavy mahongo. I had taken pains to acquire exact information about the several roads viz – the Simbo, the Kiti, and Kiweeh, and of all Kiti was my choice. My pagazis had already started after Achmet's, but the cry – Return – the White Man's Caravan, recalled them, & after they were collected together I addressed them, and said that Wasungu were not in the habit of changing their minds like the breath of the wind, and that as I had said that we should go to Kiti, to Kiti we should go whether the Arabs want or not. This[262] little firmness[263] on my part took effect on Sheikh Thani, who said that as we had started to Kiti it would be folly to return to take the road to Kiweeh. These words were conveyed to Achmet's ears & to the Arab servants in charge of small caravans, & they in like manner returned.

Good water in stony basins, clear as crystal cool as ice.

June 8 Thursday, 1871

[Ink] 79

Terekeza, to Mabunguru Mtoni, and camp distance[264] 20 miles. Course [pencil] W. 8 hours [Ink] time

2 ½ x 8 = 20.4

Mabunguru Nullah runs South westerly. Sources of it from[265] the mountains which bound inhabited Ugogo[266], good clear water in stony basins, the water had worn the hard basalt and granite boulders, greatly, & had excavated deep basins which in the dry season served as reservoirs.

---

261. Stanley left a blank space.
262. 'resolution' crossed out.
263. 'had on' crossed out.
264. '20' written over '10'? Under is another figure in pencil (16 ?). It seems that given the length of the march (8 hours) and the average speed of the caravan (2 ½ mile per hour) Stanley estimated the distance to be 20 miles (in ink). However, in *HIFL*, 203, he noted that they had a difficult terrain, steep, rugged, and thorny, for the first two hours, which could explain the other figure in pencil.
265. 'from' written over a word unintelligible.
266. 'U' of Ugogo written over 'Wa' of 'Wagogo'.

Plenty of water on this road – jungle thick, but in some places becomes a thin forest. Rocks, huge & curious – as those of Stonehenge – or the fantastic boulders visible between Avila & the Escurial in Spain.

In the afternoon march struck the Kiweeh road, the cultivated district of which was plainly visible from the ridge spine along which we were travelling

June 9 Friday, 1871

[Ink] 80

Uyanzi

[Pencil] 2 hours. W. Village of [Ink] Unyambogi

6[267] miles

Rose up at 1 a.m. to continue the terekeza. Thermometer 53°. As none of us seemed to know the road, we raised no objections against this unusual proceeding, but followed Achmet's Kirangozi meekly enough. But we were rather astonished to find that we had reached a village where there was plenty of "Entertainment for man & beast", at 3 a.m. Laid down to grumble at Achmet's folly, and slept until morning. In the morning Achmet wished Thani and myself to proceed. Thani demurred preferred to leave it to me. I vetoed the whole thing as sheer nonsense.

June 10 Saturday, 1871

[Ink] 81

[Pencil] Kiti 4 ½ hours W. N. W.

[Ink] We found Achmet, the irrepressible Arab who would be a Ceasar among his fellows. Now sadly disconsolate, weeping for runaway servants who had absconded with several fanciful dishdashash[268] – long silvered sleeve kaftans, & jackets, bales of cloth, pots & huge copper rice & pilau dishes – "Shall I leave Sheikh Thani behind", said he to Selim when asked why he did not proceed. Later he went away himself in search of his slaves, and during his absence a favorite slave died of the small pox, resulting I really believe from the effects of that raw[269] mornings terekeza, against which we had all vetoed, but to no use.

---

267. A very small 3 above 6 is linked by a line to the 2 (of 2 hours), 6 (miles) being the result of the multiplication. Thus Stanley estimated the speed of this march at 3 miles per hour, which was faster than the average of 2 ½ mph. "The pagazi, almost naked, walked quickly in order to keep warm," Stanley notes in *HIFL*, 208.

268. For 'dishdashas'. A dishdasha is a long tunique, ankle length, for men.

269. 'raw' added above the line.

June 11 Sunday, 1871

[Ink] 82 [Pencil] 2 ½

[Ink] Msalalo, Sultan Matumbi, 13[270] miles, 6 ½ hours. W by North ½ North. Achmet arrived at camp late last night from an unsuccessful search after his runaways, only to hear that a favorite slave had died. This morning he started early, determined to reach Ngaraeswa but the long march to Msalalo proved too much for his tired pagazis.

The country continued its magnificent swells – or waves – the highest ridge rising not more than from 15 to 20 feet above the general level of the land. Thin jungle, sometimes opening into cleared areas.

Wakimbu very industrious people, fence their cultivated fields carefully with the impenetrable thorn, showing considerable skill in doing so. Drive forked poles into the ground at distance of ten feet from each[271] these forked tops rest rails. The thorn bushes are piled thickly against these rails, thus forming an impenetrable fence.

Near their villages the people have been polite enough to construct curious signs to inform caravans that their villages are near, signs easily read by tired pagazis and serve to reinvigorate them.[272] two forked trees on each side of the road sustain a rail low enough to compel pagazis to bend low to pass under or in the shape of a tall pole on which wisps of dry grass have been tied.[273]

June 12 Monday, 1871

[Ink] 83 [Pencil] 2 ½ 3 ½ 7 ½ 1 ¼ [274]

[Ink] Weldo Ngaraiso[275] 3 ½ hours, 8 ¾ miles
Flourishing little place provisions as cheap again as at Kiti. Procured a beef for 3 doti, 3 Frasilah of Sweet Potatoes for 3 cubits of Merikani. Pagazi ran away taking with him his cloth & his comrades bow.
[Pencil] Passed Ngraiso[276] – uncle or Kirurumo

---

270. '5' in pencil, written over '3' in ink. Stanley probably corrected the distance of the march according to the speed of 2 ½ miles per hour, which is in the upper margin.

271. Ink spot followed by an unintelligible word.

272. Small sketch on the line of two vertical poles and one horizontal.

273. Probably signs to mark the correct path. See Stephen J. Rockel, "A Nation of Porters: The Nyamwezi and the Labour Market in Nineteenth-Century Tanzania," *Journal of African History* 41, no. 2 (2000): 184.

274. Again these figures must be the calculation of the distance: 2 ½ x 3 ½ – 7 ½ .1 ¼.

275. For Welled Ngaraiso? In *HIFL*, 208, this stop is wrongly dated June 15.

276. For Ngaraiso.

June 13 Tuesday, 1871

[Ink] 84

Kusouri[277] 3 ½ hours. 8 ¾ miles.
Great rocks. Jiwe[278] la Mkoa, & Jiwe la Singa, on our left the latter in sight of the village of Kusouri. Kusouri so called by the Arabs is called Kunsuli[279] by the villagers. This is however but one instance out of many where the Arabs have misnamed, or corrupted the names of villages districts & countries.

Kirurumo[280] which we passed is now a thriving place, with several thriving neighbours around it. As we passed it, the inhabitants came out to greet the Musungu whose advent had been heralded by his loud-mouthed caravans.

A little further on we came across a large Khambi[281] occupied by Sultan bin Mohammed – an Omani Arab of high pedigree, who as soon as he was notified of my approach came out to welcome me & invite me to his Khambi. As his harem lodged in his tent of course I was not invited in, but a carpet had been spread a few yards off on which I was invited to seat myself. After the usual questions about health, the news of the road, the latest from Zanzibar & Oman, he asked me if I had much cloth with me. As indeed I had but half a bale left of Pamba – Posho – or Food Cloth left I could unblushingly reply in the negative, but a few minutes later much to my confusion the same reply was given by Achmet, who had come in after me, and who had with more than the over-politeness of a Frenchman made pretensions to kiss hands & expressed

June 14 Wednesday, 1871

[Pencil] 85. [Ink] Halt at Kusouri

[Pencil] Halt. Had

the greatest anxiety to know if Sultan bin Mohammed and his grown up son who sat by were well, quite well quite, quite well. Sultan bin Mohammed after exchanging word for word with the polite Achmet, asked him if he had much cloth with him. "Very few indeed said he, when I well knew he had 50 bales of cloth with him." Upon making enquiries from honest Thani I was made aware that very few Arabs gave any other answer, though on their return to the coast their over-anxiety to purchase ivory at Tanganyika and Karagwah compelled mostly all to ask the same questions of outward bound caravans.

---

277. Kusuri (*HIFL*).
278. Jiweh (*HIFL*). Jiwe means "rock."
279. Konsuli (*HIFL*).
280. Preceded by 'Early in the mor' crossed out.
281. A Khambi is a camping place.

Sultan bin Mohammed made me a present of about a bushel of fine white Unyanyembe rice, which I hardly cared to accept after the negative reply I gave him about the cloth. He also requested me to permit him to convey any letters or little parcels for me to Zanzibar –a service I was glad to accept, and offered to take Farquhar the white invalid left at Mpwapwa back to Zanzibar.

Halt

Had a visit from a party of elephant hunters under the leader-ship of a former Sultan – or chief of Bagomoyo, who have squatted at Jiwe la Singa. Though they brought nothing as a present the quondam Sultan did not fail to beg for Paper, Curry & Soap – these things I could very ill spare – as the Makata Swamp had made such stock but small.

Sheikh Thani came up with his caravan, having lost a slave another victim to small pox.

June 15 Thursday, 1871

[Ink] 86

Mgongo Tembo, & Mtoni. Terekeza.

3 ½ hours + 3 ½ hours 7 + 2 ½ miles 17 ½

We were obliged to leave Sheikh Thani & his sickened caravan behind as he said he would have to stop 4 days at Kusuri.

Mgongo Thembo[282] we found burnt, withered poles alone remaining of a once prosperous settlement. Elephant and rhinoceros bones hung up in sport by the pagazis of caravans indicated the road to a Khambi where we stopped to lunch on Maweri[283] bread & honey, & tea.

A cluster of palm trees standing on the Easter bank of a tiny gulley where water was found, revived my recollections of Egypt.

Pagazis wished to camp here but after a full hours stormy debate upon the different beauties of what the several parties desired – my commands had to be given in decided tones for the Terekeza. 3 ½ hours later we arrived at the Nquala Mtoni where we found an abundance of good water in the deepest[284] depressions of the river bed.

---

282. 'Thembo', ms., for 'Tembo'. *Tembo* means "elephant"; *Mgongo Tembo* = Elephant's back.
283. Maweri, a cereal common in East Africa, belongs to the genus *Panicum*. Stanley gives several equivalents in *HIFL* such as millet, or sesame.
284. 'deepest' added above the line.

June 16 Friday, 1871

[Ink] 87

Nquala Mtoni to Madedita

5 hours 2 ½ = 12 ½ miles

Starting at sunrise we met an hour's march from the Mtoni Hassan son of Syed bin Salim, governor of Unyanyembe who gave me news of my caravans & with the courtesy of one Arab presented me with a goat & 60 lbs of very fine rice.

He was very anxious to know why I came to the country – was sure I was come to buy ivory, or visit the silver mines of Marungu or being an American to purchase slaves. Anew Livingstone was to this effect: " He is a very old man with a beard nearly quite white, has the left shoulder out of joint by a wild beast, went to Maniema with some Arabs, which is 3 months march but is now returning owing to a letter waiting him at Ujiji which Arabs informed him was there. Has 15 bales of cloth at Unyanyembe not yet despatched to Ujiji.

   Tetse[285], called Chufwa by the Wanguana stung us all to frenzy.

   Found one small pool of good water at Madedita.

June 17 Saturday, 1871

[Ink] 88

Madedita to Middle Tura. 3 hours 7 ½ miles

Plenty of honey & cheap. Milk scarce, 1 gallon – 1 shukka.

A short two hours brought us to Tura in Unyamwezi, a small village to which we all swarmed, making free with honey water, & making ourselves for a comfortable rest, of half an hour. The first view presented from this small village is as distinct & different as though Mgunda Mkali was 500 miles off.

Low, but vast swells denuded of trees. Here we found Nondo, a runaway of Speke's boarding at the village.

   Half an hour afterwards we passed the banana plant. An hour from Tura village, we came to Central Tura. Vast fields of Maweri – Matama, millet, & Indian Corn stacked & stored on the flat tembes.

   A caravan of travellers from Ubanirama[286] west of Uhumbo travelled with us from Nquala Mtoni, giving us frequent lifts – here left us. Many are known by two tatooed lines extending downwards from the eyes – chip[287] two front teeth of the

---

  285. For 'tsetse'.
  286. Ubanarama (*HIFL*)
  287. 'the' crossed out.

upper row. Wear brass spring loin coils to hold their leather aprons up. Ear ornaments are small brass rings, their necks are coiled with Nob & brass wire.[288]
Carry knives on the right arm above the elbow.

[Enclosed an article on bananas & plantains]

June 18 Sunday, 1871

[Ink] 89

Ngwhalah Mtoni 7 hours, miles 17 ½
Nghwhala
Forest teeming with honey. Wakimbu of Tura very bad people. Three camps visited in one night. At one a thief was shot dead.[289]

  I have no Kidogo[290] with me to press me to the afternoon march. At all times it is myself that has been compelled to roust the men from their Khambi huts for the tirekeza, always it was I that had to argue for its utility and necessity. Indeed the task before me was one that required the correspondent's best energies. Were it possible that I should have been delayed 134 days on the road, I should I think I left the caravan & gone alone or with a few choice fellows.

  Terekeza. Arrived late in the evening the stars out. An hour from Western Tura, there are two large ponds[291] situated in the middle of a small mbuga[292] – or an opening in the forest denuded of trees, where caravans supply themselves with water previous to making the Terekeza. Five hours from hence brings the traveller through a forest of Ukongo & thorn to the Nghwhalah –called Kwalê by Burton – where he can revel in plenty of water.

June 19 Monday, 1871

[Ink] 90

Rubuga. Wanguana village 7 ¼ hours = 18 ¾ miles[293]
Started early – though every-body was grumbling, and many were footsore. Abdul Kader[294] declared that he was dying that he was dead. He would kiss my feet & thank

---

288. 'Nob', ms.; '& brass wire' added under 'nob' at the end of the page. The last sentence 'carry … elbow' was written in smaller characters and added in the space left at the bottom of the page.
289. 'shot dead' added above the line.
290. 'Kidogo' means 'small'. Here, Stanley has no second to help him.
291. 'where caravans' crossed out.
292. A small depression of heavy clay soil supporting grass-like vegetation.
293. As often, Stanley estimates the speed at 2½ miles per hour. The calculation is under 7¼.
294. Abdul Kader or Abdel Kadir (see his contract of engagement, Appendix, S.A. 4745).

God & me if he would but be permitted to[295] go anywhere to die in peace. When he received a gracious permission to depart[296] to the jungle, & leave his bones, he informed me he did not wish to leave me there, but after arrival in Unyanyembe, which[297] proved his readiness to take advantage of my protection, & partake of the bountiful rations I served out to my men, as far as Unyanyembe, & his disinclination to brave the dangers of the Rubuga jungle[298] alone. Abdul Kader was therefore briefly informed that since all my donkeys died but two[299] & that as all the pagazis & soldiers carried loads & there remained but one small load 35 lbs weight, he should have to convey it to Unyanyembe, or should go the jungle.

A Long march – but the Kirangozi had received a scolding, and he had declared to me that neither Sarboko, or any one else should have to tell him what he should do, or what he should not do, but that he would make.

June 20 Tuesday, 1871

[Ink] 91

Halt

Visited to-day by the old Sheikh Amir bin Sultan & his son Selim bin Mahmoud who were returning to Zanzibar after a ten years residence in Unyanyembe.

About Livingstone he gave me the following information. "There is a Musungu a very old man who came to Ujiji by the way of Lake Nyassa. After[300] arriving at Ujiji shortly after he went to Marungu, and returned to Ujiji. About a year ago he crossed over to Tanganyika, and accompanied some Arabs to Lake Maniema which is a very great Lake, much larger I am told than Tanganyika. Lately a caravan coming from Ukonongo[301] brought the news to Unyanyembe that he was dead, but I do not know that the news is true. The caravan may have been misinformed."

This old man had a strange idea respecting Lake Victoria N'Yanza. He said the water of it was salt, & that it came from the sea near Zanzibar, but though the water was salt, the river running from it was fresh."
He was very hospitable, sent in to my tent a glorious dish of cooked rice & excellent[302] chicken curry. Later he gave me a bag of rice, & a goat.

---

295. 'he would but be permitted to' written above 'let him' crossed out.
296. 'depart' written over 'go'.
297. 'showed' crossed out.
298. 'by him' crossed out.
299. 'and as I was' crossed out.
300. 'returning' crossed out.
301. 'tol' crossed out.
302. 'curried' crossed out.

June 21 Wednesday, 1871

[Ink] 92

Kigwa 5 hours. Miles 12 ½

From Rubuga I sent Sarmeen & Baraka to[303] notify the Magnates of Unyanyembe that the Musungu would soon be there.

    Travelled through a forest sloping gently westward, put up at a small village one out the few left intact by . . .[304] Sultan of Unyanyembe, when he visited the Kigwa & Rubuga district with his vengeance. Plantain plants.

June 22 Thursday, 1871[305]

Shisa[306] 7 hours. Miles 17 ½

3 ½ hours took us through Kigwa to the Mtoni the boundary between Kigwa & Unyanyembe through a forest sloping westerly.

    At the Mtoni we cross over and are in Unyanyembe – country bears a different aspect – very picturesque at times

    1 ½ hour to Mai Shamba – or spring water, pass through a short defile and behold Unyanyembe's beautiful outline in truth

    Leave Ugundo where Speke stopped to our left & half an hour afterwards enter the village of Mai Shisa.

    Music & dancing from the girls – a wandering musician from Uganda with a harp not unlike that pictured in the Harper's tomb discovered by Belzoni at Thebes.[307]

    Am treated with pombe, which is a poor kind of Boston ale in taste, and milk & water in color.

    Give a bullock to my men for a[308] farewell banquet.

    Sarmeen returned from Syed bin Salim with hospitable information, & that all the caravans were at his house but one – which was the second.

June 23 Friday, 1871

Unyanyembe 2 ½ hours. Miles 6 ¼

---

    303. 'inform' crossed out.
    304. Space left blank.
    305. From this date, no more numbers in the upper margin.
    306. Shiza (*HIFL*).
    307. Harper's Tomb, named after the bas-relief representing two blind harpers, is part of the complex structure of the Ramesses III tomb (Valley of the Kings). It was visited by the archeologist and traveler G. B. Belzoni (1778–1823), author of *Narrative of the Operations and Recent Discoveries… in Egypt and Nubia*, 2 vols. (London: Murray, 1820).
    308. 'last' crossed out.

June 24 Saturday, 1871

[Operation in the date margin]
Halt
Syed bin Salim, Amram bin Moussoud, Abdullah bin Jumah, Sheikh bin Nasib, called[309] to see me.[310] Later Syed bin Salim gave me a bit of an account respecting his life with Burton.

June 25 Sunday, 1871

[Ink] Halt. [Pencil] Unyanyembe
[Ink] Sick of the Mukunguru[311]

June 26 Monday, 1871

Halt
Son of the Sultan came to see me, and on departure asked me if I would like a present of ivory.

June 27 Tuesday, 1871

Halt
Sick with Mukunguru
Loaded cartridges. Separated bales, and prepared for my trip to Ujiji. Shaw's posho, and Abdul Kader's were set aside.[312]

June 28 Wednesday, 1871

Halt
Mukunguru attack
To-day I tried to write up, but it was a mere attempt.

---

309. 'called' preceded by a line left blank.
310. Stanley set up in Kwihara, one of the villages forming Unyanyembe (Cf. *HIFL*, 311). These Arab merchants' tembes were in Tabora. Amram bin Moussoud had his tembe burned when Mirambo set fire to Tabora (August 22, 1871).
311. Mukunguru was notorious for malaria and thus was often used as a synonym.
312. Did Stanley already have in mind parting from Shaw and Abdul Kader? Three months later Abdul Kader was discharged and Shaw, who could not make it farther than Kigandu, had to be transported back to Kwihara.

June 29 Thursday, 1871

Halt.

June 30 Friday, 1871

Halt.

July 1 Saturday, 1871

[Ink] Halt.
[Pencil] Shaw
From the age of 7, or 8 years he had been studying Malay
Lost $10 000. – $5000 Metropolitan Horse Guards $5000 waterworks (what Metr. H. G. and W-W, I do not know[313]
In relating the tale of Lady Flora Hastings, & the Lady of Bute, the poor fellow silently dropped tears for her sad fate as if she has been his sister.
Been at 4 levees of the Queen of England

July 2 Sunday, 1871

[Ink] Halt

July 3 Monday, 1871

[Pencil] Halt

July 4 Tuesday

[Pencil] Halt

July 5 Wednesday, 1871

[Pencil] Halt
Khamis bin Abdulaah & Sheikh bin Nasib Abduldah bin Jumah & sons paid me a vist
Got 3 pagazis
Sent letter to the "Herald"[314]

    313. What Metr[opolitan] H[orse] G[uards] & W[ater]-W[orks] I do not know. Closing bracket missing.

    314. First despatch to the *New York Herald* dated July 4, 1871, from Kwihara, district of Unyanyembe, and published without Stanley's name, December 22, 1871 (Bennett, *Stanley's Despatches*, 3–23). Stanley did

July 6 Thursday, 1871

[Pencil] Paid a visit to Tabora[315]

July 7 Friday, 1871

[Pencil] Sick in bed

July 8 Saturday, 1871

[Pencil] Sick in bed

July 9 Sunday, 1871

[Pencil] Sick in bed

July 10 Monday, 1871

[Pencil] Start for Ujiji
Sick in bed
This place is in 6° S. 33 E.
So[uth] to latitude of Greenwich that is in 52° N and the 6 degrees South makes 58°. Makes 65° to Cairo from Unyanyembe, on a 2 ½ point course.[316]

[Pencil] Drop them down two or three times in order to see where the sound came from like the monkey did with the drum

July 11 Tuesday, 1871

[Pencil] Sick in bed

July 12 Wednesday, 1871

[Pencil] Sick in bed

---

not number his despatches, but it may be assumed there was no other despatch sent to the New York Herald before this one, since Stanley recounts his mission from his arrival at Zanzibar.

315. About Tabora and surrounding villages, see Karin Pallaver, *Un'altra Zanzibar: Schiavitù, colonialismo e urbanizzazione a Tabora (1840–1916)* (Milan: Franco Angeli, 2010).

316. From 'This place' to '2 ½ point course', writen in pencil and crossed out.

July 13 Thursday, 1871

[Pencil] Sick in bed

July 14 Friday, 1871

[Pencil] Sick

[Ink] I recover my senses

July 15 Saturday, 1871

[Pencil] Sick

July 16 Sunday

[Pencil] Sick

July 17 Monday, 1871

[Pencil] Sick

July 18 Tuesday, 1871

[Pencil] Sick

Said bin Salim sent me a large black duck

July 19 Wednesday, 1871

[Pencil] Sick

July 20 Thursday, 1871

[Pencil] Sick in bed

Kirangozi takes his cloth.

July 21 Friday, 1871

[Pencil] Sick in bed

Maganga[317] came today, tomorrow says he will come

July 22 Saturday, 1871

[Pencil] Sick in bed but slightly better
5 Wangwana Pagazis engaged.
Sadala, Saboori, Combo,[318] Baruti, Mareo[319]

July 23 Sunday, 1871

[Pencil] Sick in bed.

July 24 Monday, 1871

[Pencil] Sick in bed.

July 25 Tuesday, 1871

[Pencil] Sick, but risen from bed

Caravan 2nd arrived after 6 months absence.[320] Soldiers made pagazis at 5 doti each to Ujiji. Sheikh Said bin Salim & Arabs leave Unyanyembe to fight Mirambo[321]
Amram bin Moossud starts with 150 guns to fight Warori

---

317. *Maganga*: a traditional doctor. Mganga is also the name of a Nyamwezi whom Stanley recruited at Kwihara (September 1, 1871), "a good and excellent pagazi" (S.A. 74). Was he also acting as a diviner? (See the role of the *mganga*, Rockel, "A Nation of Porters," 184.)

318. See Appendix, S.A. 4748, Enlistment of three soldiers, Saboori Mkuba, Saboori Mdogo, and Kombo, at Quihara (Kwihara, roughly 2 miles from Tabora), Unyanyembe, Sept. [August, crossed out] 17th 1871. Since Stanley was sick in bed, the contract could have been drawn later. Or had he lost all notion of time?

319. Most likely Marero.

320. The 2nd caravan had left for Unyanyembe on February 21, 1871.

321. Causes of the war against Mirambo are summed up in Kirk's letter of September 22, 1871, to Lord Granville: "The Arab colony of the Interior whose center is Unyanyembe has for some time been led by a set of avaricious unprincipled men, whose acts of extortion both on natives and the poorer Arabs have for some time back been complained of to Seyd Burgash who is impotent to interfere at such a distance so long as things go well for the Arabs" (National Archives, Kew, FO 84/1344, N°96, Fol. 477–480). Upon instruction from Lord Granville, Lord Enfield sent a copy of this report to Sir Henry Rawlinson "for information of the Royal Geographical Society" (RGS-IBG Collections, DL4/15/2).

About Mirambo, see Norman R. Bennett, *Mirambo of Tanzania, ca. 1840–1884* (New York: Oxford University Press, 1971).

July 26 Wednesday, 1871

[Pencil] Preparing for the morrow's march

July 27 Thursday, 1871

[Pencil] Sheikh Said bin Salim and Arabs leave Camp for Mfuto to war with Mirambo
[Three lines left blank]
[Pencil] Watusi – pastoral people – wear hides tanned – have an objection to cloth about theirs limbs – heavy weights of thin copper wire about their ancles reaching half way up the lower legs on some.
like the Wahumbu[322] in their houses.
Did not start owing to Fundi's delay returning with my $150 gun, which he was reparing.
Have made all my soldiers pagazis, but experience a difficulty in getting a guide to take me on the Kawendi road, the Mfuto road being closed owing to the war.
A Sultan of Wiogo came to beg Cloth from me & to see the wonderful shooting gun.

July 28 Friday, 1871

[Pencil] An old Unyanwezi came with a sheep fattailed as an exchange for some medicine to stop chronic dysentery. As I did not wish to break his confidence in the powers of the Muzungu, I said that I had no medicine for his disease.
Mabruki son of Ferous hired to day for Ujiji for 5 doti.
Had a great talk to day with Sheikh bin Nasib. He advised me not to go because it was dangerous to march a caravan during war-time. I am therefore reduced to great strait, do not know which way to go. No one can be hired to act as a Kirangozi during war time, on the Kawendi road – and the Mfuto road is closed by Mirambo.
At 5 P.M. made up our minds in nothing else offering to start tomorrow for Zimbili, then the next day march to Mfuto, thence storing the goods at an Arab's house wait the events which must make themselves evident before many days.

July 29 Saturday, 1871

[Pencil] Ujiji I hope to reach
March to Zimbili 2 ¼ hours 4 ½ miles

---

322. Wahumba (*HIFL*). Stanley notes that Wahumba "live in plastered (cow-dung) cone huts, shaped like the Tartar tents of Tukestan" (*HIFL*, 195).

Infinite trouble of a start – 3 soldiers sick. Wamyamezi[323] all absent. Bombay inutile as at Makata. The dread of Mirambo has much to do with it. The Wanguana forgot the bullock bin Nasib gave us in their great fear. The tailor Abdul Kader was left behind as an useless man. Shaw was taken to fight Mirambo.

Bin Nasib & friends came out to bid us farewell.

Southwest of Mount Zimbili an admirable place for a robber's roost lies the village of Zimbili chief Bom-boma

July 30 Sunday, 1871

[Pencil] Masanghi[324] 1 ½ hours, 3 miles
Bullock came. Kirangozi also with one pagazi who had strayed away.
The son of Said bin Majid, Mussoud[325] bin Said called on me, & said the Arabs were waiting for me, asked me if I had any words for them.

July 31 Monday, 1871

[Pencil] Eastern Mfuto. 6 hours.
Shaw gave out. Powder, Balls & Flints distributed to soldiers 30 rounds each.

August 1 Tuesday, 1871

[Pencil] Eastern[326] Mfuto, ¾ of an hour

August 2 Wednesday, 1871

[Pencil] Halt
Sheikh Said sick

August 3 Thursday, 1871

[Pencil] Umanda 6 hours, 2 ½   15 miles[327]

---

323. As is in ms.
324. Masangi (*HIFL*).
325. Is called Soud bin Sayd bin Majid (*HIFL*, 278).
326. 'Eastern' written above 'Central' crossed out.
327. '3¹/' written under '6' in the middle of the page.

August 4 Friday, 1871

[Pencil] Zimbizi. Sultan Kolongo
Unyanyembe is the California & Pike's Peak of the Arabs. Prospecting not for gold but for ivory.

August 5 Saturday, 1871

[Pencil] Halt
Arab slaves killed 10 men.

August 6 Sunday, 1871

[Pencil] Halt. [Ink] & retreat.
[Pencil] Arab slaves go to fight, capture 1 village. Kill Sultan & 5 men. They make slaves, but upon a voice being heard in the forest as they were bringing them to Zimbizo, the 500 brave slaves armed with muskets deserted slaves – ivory, & in short ingloriously skedaddled.

A small party went out towards the low, woody[328] hills in short distanse north of Zimbizo, found youthful thief probably 18 years old – asleep – They sprung on him, drew his head back, and cut his head off with a knife, as they do with a goat or sheep.

Another party went out a couple of miles south to attack a strong boma. After vigorous firing they captured it with precious stores of ivory & slaves. While they were inside, a large force of Mirambo appeared in front & rear, hiding themselves in the grass. Ensued a general skedaddling in which many lost their lives.
Soud bin Said
Nasim bin Moussoud
Mohammed bin "
Said bin Abid

August 7 Monday, 1871

[Ink] Retreat.[329]
[Pencil] * 17 cloth, 12 boxes, 6 beads[330]
Livingstone is now locked up with small means of escape. I am also locked up in Unyanyembe & cannot go to Ujiji until this war with Mirambo is settled. Livingstone

---

328. 'woody' added above the line.
329. 'Retreat' written in ink over 'Halt' in pencil.
330. These words must be read after Livingstone cannot get his goods.

cannot get his goods*.[331] They are stored up with mine in the tembe I lived in at Unyanyembe. He cannot return to Zanzibar, and the road to the Nile is blocked up for him with his small party. He might possibly reach it by traveling northwards through Urudu[332] thence through Ruanda, Karagwah, Uganda, Unyoro Ubari to Gondokoro, but he has no men, nor the opportunities & means to get them for an escort. Pagazis he cannot obtain, for the sources whence such in supply could be drawn are shut up. It is an erroneous supposition to imagine that Livingstone any more than any other white man can travel through this part of[333] Africa without a strong escort, and a durable supply of the marketable cloth & beads. When he[334] was coming[335] from Nyassa Lake, towards the Tanganyika,[336] the very same time that the world thought him murdered[337] he was met by an Said bin Omar's bound to Ulamba[338] caravan with whom were two of Speke's Faithfuls (who afterwads proved as faithful to me) with 4 men – with an Arab caravan belonging to Mohammed bin Ghalib.[339] Mohammed bin Ghalib coming from Urungu met Livingstone at Kwachi cumbi[340] country, and together they travelled to Maniema. Maniema is 40 days steady march from the North of Nyassa. (Six years ago) Livingstone tried to engage Speke's men.[341] Livingstone was walking, he was dressed in American Sheeting. He had lost all his cloth in the Lake Livemba or Luemba[342] while attempting to cross it in a boat. He had hired[343] three canoes on its banks in one he put his cloth & two soldiers, in another he put two small boxes & two soldiers he himself went into another with two[344] fishermen, (Luemba is in the country of Uemba.[345]

---

331. John Kirk drew the same conclusion in his report to Lord Granville dated September 22, 1871: "Such is the constant state of things in Central Africa, the road to Ujiji will now be shut for a time, & when we may again hear of Dr Livingstone is most uncertain" (National Archives, Kew, FO 84/1344, fol. 477–480, despatch no. 96, here at fol. 477r–478r). The document reached the Foreign Office on December 4, and a copy was sent to the RGS the same day (RGS-IBG Collections, DL4/15/1 B).
332. Urudu has been replaced by Urundi in *HIFL*.
333. 'the country' crossed out.
334. 'came' crossed out.
335. 'was coming' written above 'came' crossed out.
336. 'towards the Tanganyika' added above the line.
337. 'Ulimengo' crossed out.
338. 'Said bin Omar's bound to Ulamba' written above 'Arab' crossed out.
339. Mohamed bin Ghalib and Mohamed bin Gharib are one and same person.
340. Kwa-chi-Kumbi (*HIFL*, 291).
341. 'Returned to Mfuto' was first written in pencil on this page and can be read under. Livingstone tried to engage Speke's men. (Six years ago) was added in the short space left at the end of the preceding line. Stanley probably wrote this page later than August 7. In *HIFL*, this story is reported under August 12.
342. 'or Luemba' added above the line.
343. 'hired' written under 'found' crossed out.
344. One word crossed out. 'Wasiwa'?
345. Bracket missing.

August 8 Tuesday, 1871

[Pencil] Halt Mfuto

August 9 Wednesday, 1871

[Pencil] Return to Masangi

August 10 Thursday, 1871

[Pencil] Return to Unyanyembe
3 soldiers murdered
1 died from dysentery

August 11 Friday, 1871

[Pencil] Halt. Sick of fever.
Sheikh bin Nassib called to see me

August 12 Saturday, 1871

[Pencil] Halt
Abdul Kader broke the last China cup.

August 13 Sunday, 1871

[Pencil] Halt
Commenced to take Bombay's medicine

August 14 Monday, 1871

[Pencil] Halt
Wrote Letters to Zanzibar

August 15 Tuesday, 1871

[Pencil] Halt
Decide upon sending my own soldiers to Zanzibar.

August 16 Wednesday, 1871

[Pencil] Halt

Sarmeen & Uredi[346] taking letter for 'Herald', 3 for Webb-Consul[347] 1, for Dr Christie, 1 for Dossabhoy Merwanjee & Co.,[348] and proceed to Tabora

August 17 Thursday, 1871

[Ink] Halt. This morning my soldiers Sarmeen and Uredi in company with 10[349] slaves belonging to different Arabs start on their courier errand to Zanzibar. My soldiers have received 6 letters to carry,[350] a packet containing $30 in gold which is to pay for the medicines, $5 to spend for themselves & $5 to purchase cloth for the return march. They are to be back by the 17th October of this year for which they are to receive as present $25 dollars each. They will have walked 1050 miles in 60 days

August 18 Friday, 1871

[Pencil] Halt.

This is the second day of Shaw lying down.

August 19 Saturday, 1871

[Ink] Halt

Soldiers are employed in stringing beads

Rojab & Uliwengo I put in prison for repeated absence without leave from the tembe.

To day I feel so well that I am able to walk about quite lively, and enjoy returning health.

---

346. For 'Uledi'.

347. Stanley's letters to the Consul Webb were dated June 23, and August 14 & 15, 1871. Sarmeen and Uredi handed Stanley's letters to the American consul on September 21, 1871, who sent the carriers back with his answer and a box of medicines, on September 25. See Appendix, S.A. 2657.

Consul Webb passed some information to Consul Kirk who reported to Lord Granville immediately (September 22, 1871, p. 1): "Naturally the letters written by Mr Stanley, an American gentleman, who was on the spot are the most circumstantial & reliable. I am indebted to Mr Webb, the American consul here for some details related in those letters which will no doubt be published in full elsewhere" (RGS-IBG Collections, DL4/15/1 B).

Consul Webb answered Stanley's letters on September 25, and advised him against mingling with Arab wars, but Stanley had already left Kwihara.

348. Dossabhoy Merwanjee was one of the principal Parsee families in Bombay. Their house of commerce was actively engaged in American trade (Taylor Bayard, *A Visit to India, China, and Japan in the year 1853* [New York: Putnam; London: Sampson Low, 1855], 39). Before leaving Bombay, Stanley left three trunks at Dossabhoy Merwanjee & Co. (October 11, 1870, S.A. 73).

349. 'others' crossed out.

350. 'in' crossed out?

> We hear Mirambo is coming

Arabs with their slaves have therefore left for Mfuto to guard the powder left there by the redoubtable Sheikh Said bin Saleem the commander in chief of the Arab settlements of Unyanyembe.

August 20 Sunday, 1871

[Pencil] Ujiji
[Ink] Halt
Soldiers are employed in stringing beads.

August 21 Monday, 1871

[Pencil] Halt. 100 Fundo of Beads finished strung this day. Arabs are preparing for another sally against Mirambo.
[22 lines further] 150[351]

August 22 Tuesday, 1871

[Pencil] Halt.
Mirambo with his allies the Watuta attacked Tabora today. Sheikh Khamis bin Abdullah, Mohammed bin Abdullah, Ibrahim Rasheed killed with several of their slaves, and hired soldiers. Several of Mirambo's men as well as the Watuta fell victims to the vengeance of the Arabs. It was a sorry scene to witness from our excited valley of Quihara[352] almost the whole of Tabora in flames, & to see the hundreds of people arounding into Quihara from Tabora. Finding that my people were willing to stand by me I made preparations for defence by boring in the stout clay walls of the tembe loopholes for muskets. They were made so quickly & so well that my people got quite brave & Wanguana refugees with guns, seeing the excellent state of our defences, volunteered to fight under me. As the more the merriest, I very gladly received them so that by night I had 150[353] stout fellows in my court yard all well armed awaiting attack. To morrow all say we in Quihara shall be attacked. In case of our defences being broken through, I have made small preparation of retreat[354] through the jungle

---

351. Is it the total of the strings of beads? Or the total of Stanley's forces as said on the next page?
352. Kwihara (*HIFL*).
353. Number hard to read: Stanley wrote 130, then 5 over 3, but going over 0, seems to have added another 0 between 5 and 0.
354. 'of retreat' written over 'to return', then changed into 'of returning'.

towards[355] Urori, thence proceed to Ujiji[356] But by God's help we will try the merits of a stout resistance first. If that fails we will try to make good our retreat.

August 23 Wednesday, 1871

[Ink] Halt.

We have passed a very anxious day, all in the valley of Quihara. Our eyes were constantly directed over the saddle which connects two hills separating Quihara from the plain of Tabora. Over this saddle we could see Tabora still flaming and people coming over it towards Quihara and others passing over towards Tabora. Three tembes only stood out the storm of fire with which Mirambo visited once happy and prosperous Tabora. Speke's house, and Burton's friend Snay[357] bin Amir's, were among the burnt houses. Mokrima[358] & Amram bin Moussoud's were also included among those destroyed. Sultan bin Ali, Salim bin Sayf, & Said bin Habeeb were not burnt – the Arabs prefering to stand the fire of Mirambo's people rather than surrender their wealth & houses to certain destruction. All we in Quihara could do was to prepare as well as possible to resist the invader. My tembe was brought to as perfect a state of defense, as its style & means would permit. Provisions & water were also procured to last five or six days. I have now about 150[359] armed men, the half of them volunteer refugees. The tembe could hold 60 more men, which would make the garrison sufficient to defeat all attempts at capture. Bullets, powder, flints & cartridges there are enough for a steady fight of 2 weeks. The Arabs my neighbours, endeavor to seem brave, but it is evident they are almost despairing.

August 24 Thursday, 1871

[Ink] Halt.

Mirambo at dawn deported himself from the boma of Kazima, leaving the lagging Arabs to pursue him at their pleasure. Yesterday the Arabs surrounded his boma but refrained from attacking because Mirambo asked for a day's grace to eat the beef he had stolen from them inviting them to come this morning. Thus Quihara was restored to its former peaceful aspect, the people no longer thronged its narrow limits, in fear & despair.[360] Khamis bin Abdullah, Khamis his little adopted son, Sayf bin Ali

---

355. 'through the jungle' written over some unintelligible words; 'towards' is written over 'possible'.
356. 'thence proceed to Ujiji' added above the line.
357. Sny bin Amir (*HIFL*).
358. Spelling uncertain.
359. '150' written over 'forty'.
360. This sentence is found under August 26 (*HIFL*, 298).

& Mohammed bin Rasheed it seems had led their slaves to the attack but when they commenced firing the worthless slaves ran away, leaving their masters to their fate. Mirambo's people surrounded them. Sheikh Khamis first received a bullet which broke his leg & turning to retreat was assisted by young Khamis and a slave, who took hold of each arm. These were first speared then the stout Sheikh and his friends. As soon as they were dead they were mutilated in the manner of medicine making Africans, the skin of the forehead, the beard & skin, the fore part of the nose, the fat over the stomach & abdomen, the genital organs, and lastly a bit from each heel. Each Arab was thus mutilated & the flesh thus taken is well[361] boiled and is then[362] called medicine which is mixed up with their dish of goat & rice & eaten. Their arms are thus strengthened, and their lives ensured against the Arab bullets.
[Pencil] Wilyankuru, Ugowa, Usanghi, (Usayengi) after Ugalla
Uyowa – Mirambo's country.

August 25 Friday, 1871

[Ink] Halt.

Visited Sheikh bin Nasib who is my neighbour to-day and was astonished to find how despairing he looked, like Sheikh bin Salim of yesterday. They have nothing to say, listen to one's voice more like dying men, than men alive possessing all the requisite means of defence & offense. It is true that Mirambo has made good his retreat with what ivory, cloth, beads & cattle they secured in their bold[363] raid upon Unyanyembe.

A rumor is current that he has merely gone to secure his booty after which he will return to Unyanyembe. And make a raid upon the valley of Quihara in which I live. In which case I shall have the satisfaction of testing the merits of my breech loaders upon Mirambo's Ruga-Ruga (thieves) & plundering Watuta.[364]

Sheikh bin Nasib has a two pounder duly loaded with ball and grape, small slugs of iron, an old Portuguese piece which did service against the Arabs when they invaded Zanzibar.

---

361. 'well' added above the line.
362. 'then' added above the line.
363. 'bold' above the line.
364. Gangs of Watuta (Ngoni) acted independently of Mirambo's troops, and Arab chiefs sought their alliance, in vain. (See this journal, August 26, 1871).

August 26 Saturday, 1871

[Ink] Halt.

The Arabs hold councils of war now-a-days, battle-meetings, of which they are very fond, but extremely slow to act upon. They were about to make friends with the Watuta but Mirambo was ahead of them. They had talked of invading Mirambo's territory the second time, but Mirambo invaded Unyanyembe with spear & fire, bringing death to many a household,[365] & killing their chief man. The Arabs spend their hours in talking, and allow the days to pass by without an effort made to open the Ujiji road. Indeed many of the influential Arabs talk of returning back to Zanzibar with what few Wanyamuezi will be bold enough to take the road during war time. I have lost all respect for them. One Thani bin Abdullah quartered to the South of Marora a mile or so deserted his tembe strong as a fort with 100 slaves and fled to Sheikh Said bin Salim in Cwcuru,[366] Mkasiwa's boma.

Meanwhile with poor success however, perceiving the impossibility of getting Wanyamuezi to proceed to the Tanganyika I am purchasing guns at 5 doti each, and enlisting soldiers to increase the number to 50 men[367] with which I shall be able to travel anywhere despite war. It is an expensive proceeding, but the only way open to act, unless I return.

August 27 Sunday 1871

[Ink] Halt.

No news today of Mirambo. Councils of war are still held but nothing has been agreed upon. Sheikh bin Nasib called on me towards night, but except on small philosophy he has nothing to say.

To-day soldiers strung beads 40 fundo – 3 fundo each – and I am preparing for the flying caravan to Ujiji by an extreme southern road viz that of Kawendi despite Arab protestations.

August 28 Monday, 1871

[Ink] Halt

Shaw got up to day for little work.

Alas! All my fine spun ideas of proceeding by boat over Victoria N'Yanza thence down the Nile have been totally demolished & scattered by this war with this

---

365. These lines are included word for word in *HIFL* (298), but under August 27.
366. Kwikuru (*HIFL*).
367. 'after' crossed out.

black Bonaparte. Already I have been here over 2 months, and there is every prospect that I shall be 2 months longer because the Arabs take such a long time to make up their minds, to arrive at a decisive conclusion. Advice is plenty but no one has any decision. Their star is dead in Khamis bin Abdullah yet none of the influential Arabs lament him. The lesser people idolized him, & bewail the misfortunes of the Arabs now that he is dead.

Their arms are of the miserablest description, yet when they see my guns they are in raptures & wish to buy some like them immediately. Yet I know of an American joiner in Zanzibar who had some of the same guns months upon months at their houses, and were returned as unsaleable being too dear or too complicated for them.

August 29 Tuesday, 1871

[Ink] Halt.
Visited Said bin Hamed one of the richest Arabs in the Valley of Quihara. He has a fine large garden containing Muhogo, Onions, wheat, shallots, water-melons, Pomegranates – and a luscious fruit called by the Wasawahahili[368] – Mapapy, it is a large water melon kind of fruit growing on a curious tree with spiky leaves in tiers-like. Inside this fruit is like a mush-melon but much sweeter.
Lemons, Limes – and a fruit called suffurjal by the Arabs of Muscat, it much resembles an orange, not yet ripened. The wheat ripens about October. Sow but just sufficient for a few sweet cakes and Halwa, & now & then a piece of sweet bread. Rice or pilaf being the staple food.

Unsuccessful as yet about soldiers which makes me almost despair of ever being able to move from here. It is such a drowsy, sleepy, slow country. Arabs, Wangwana, Wanyamwezi all are alike oblivious of the flight of time, that to-morrow means sometime within a month if ever. To one live American it is almost maddening.

My man Shaw seems to have caught this sleepy fever, for he is unable, or will not work.

August 30 Wednesday, 1871

[Ink] Halt.

I cannot get Shaw to stir himself. I have petted him, & cooked little luxuries for him, and yet for the life of me I cannot get him to work more than a couple of hours while I am straining every nerve to get another caravan ready for a start. I have

---

368. Wasawahili (*HIFL*).

worked at the tent myself in order to encourage him, and bear the constant lamentations about his infirmities, though his presence is most unlovely, & unlovable he makes it more so by exaggerating whatever complaint he suffers from, by breathing as if he was about to gasp his last breath, and in a pantomimic way goes through the performance of a man suffering the severest bodily sickness. While I know it proceeds from nothing else than a little sick ennui. If I had recourse to the stick I could cure him in less than ten minutes of all this annoying by-play.

I bought a pipe from a Nyamwezi for 1 doti.

I was promised 5 men including a guide to the Tanganyika Lake just about dark, which if the promise is worth anything, is certainly a God-send. Of course the road is the Kawendi road the one that I wished to go for the last six weeks, but permitted myself to be over-ruled by the Arabs.

August 31 Thursday, 1871

[Ink] Halt.

My prospects of departure from this vale of sorrow & procrastination do[369] not improve a bit. Nothing of all I desired have I been able to get. Neither soldiers, pagazis, or slaves.

Shaw will not work nothing seems to advance towards completion, and there is always so much to be done.

I have promised Thani bin Abdullah if I feel well to-morrow to visit his tembe, near Maroro.

September 1 Friday, 1871

[Ink] Halt.

Visited Thani bin Abdullah to-day in his boma isolated in a narrow valley between running out of Maroro. In a poor position for defence but happily secluded in times of peace, abundance of water & wood close by, and stone to build if he had a mind to do but as he says, We do not come here to live we but come for money, then we return.

The Arabs seem to have strong objections to my departure for the Tanganyika. Whenever I mention the subject, they immediately declare the thing to be simply impracticable, the roads are all closed. I must wait until the war is ended, or else return. Yet while Thani bin Abdullah was advising his guest upon the impossibility of travelling, another guest was on the burza but 2 feet from him who was about to venture on the morrow on the same road which he so strenuously urged as impracticable, and

---

369. Stanley wrote 'does' first, then crossed out 'es'.

when that guest was about to depart he was heard to say to him "Good bye, should you chance to meet any of my people on the road, help them if they need it, and give them my salaams.".

Mirambo according to Thani lost 200 men in the attack upon Tabora while the Arabs lost but 13 men, 5 Arabs & 8 slaves. Mirambo took 280 ivory tusks & 60 cows & bullocks.

September 2 Saturday, 1871

[Ink] Halt.

Something I ate at Thani bin Abdullah's yesterday disagreed with me, for at midnight I suffered agonies until relieved by a hearty vomit.

Livingstone's soldier Asmani who is now in charge of the caravan for him informed Sheikh bin Nasib that he wished to accompany me by the Ukonongo & Ufipa road to the Tanganyika. In consequence of which I was honored by a visit from the Sheikh who at once protested against the folly of travelling while this war was still in progress. I told him that I knew I risked something by going, but that I must try it or return, & to return after spending so much money was out of the question with my work unfinished. That the war with Mirambo would not be finished before six months if so soon, & that if I waited 6 months I would not be better off, but to wait 6 months was impossible. Sheikh bin Nasib retired very much excited against the people who had given me such[370] information about the Ukonongo road, and promising to give his last word either to-morrow, or the next day.

September 3 Sunday, 1871

[Ink] Halt.

Nothing very particular to-day except that towards night Asmani the Mgasija soldier, in charge of Livingstone's caravan had occasion to open his tent in which I saw a package of letters or papers addressed:
"Dr. Livingstone", Nov. 1870, Ujiji
On the reverse side were the words "Registered Letters". Asking of Asmani about them, he said they were given to his friend (then leader, since dead) to take to Ujiji[371] last November after which they went to Bagomoyo where they remained getting pagazis until the 14th day of the third month of their stay there when they left. They

---
370. 'such' added above the line.
371. 'to del' crossed out.

arrived in Unyanyembe about the middle of April where they have been ever since, and are likely to remain since the Arabs Sheikh bin Nasib & Said bin Salim are the Agents in this business. I have endeavored to induce Sheikh bin Nasib to let the caravan of Livingstone go under my charge to Ujiji but all to no purpose as he declares it is his formed belief that I shall never see Ujiji if I travel at this dangerous season.

The Mgasija soldier has very faithfully seconded me in my efforts.

September 4 Monday, 1871

[Ink] Halt.

Shaw has done the best day's work yet on the tent. Selim has the Mukunguru every other day regularely. My force is being gradually[372] increasing Umgareza is blind. Baruti has the small pox very badly. Shaw & Selim are sick all the time. Bill-Alli[373] has a strange complaint rear-ward. Sadala is at home in Maroro ailing. My Wanguana pagazis never visit me, all my Wanyamuezi have deserted me long ago. The latter will not depart anywhere, not even to Bagomoyo & the Coast during war times, and it seems that the Wanguana have been infected with this idea for after a month I have not succeeded in engaging one new soldier.

September 5 Tuesday, 1871

[Ink] Halt

To night I feel very much dispirited. Baruti one of my best soldiers & one of Speke's Faithfuls has just died of the small pox. Uledi Speke, Uledi Khatalaboo & Mabruk have already died at the fatal attack upon Wilyankuru. Farquahar my superintendent died at Mpwapwa & Jacko the Carpenter God knows where he has gone too, or what has become of him. My ears have been poisoned to-day with reports of the bad state of the road I am about to travel, but in fact it is every day the same story. "The roads are bad", "all the roads are closed". You will be robbed". The Washense are at war against each other & each man has made himself a "Ruga-Ruga" or thief". My people are becoming dispirited, they imbibe the fears of those by whom they are surrounded.

---

372. 'reduced instead of' crossed out. In *HIFL*, Stanley developed the word "increasing" which here may appear conflicting with the enumeration of sick soldiers, by adding after "increasing": "though some of my old soldiers are falling off" (302).

373. Bilali (*HIFL*).

September 6 Wednesday, 1871

[Ink] Halt.

At about 7 A.M. we buried Baruti the soldier a few yards west of the tembe where I live. The grave was made about 4 ½ feet deep & 3[374] feet wide as neat as any sexton could make it. At the bottom a narrow shallow trench was excavated on the eastern side into which Baruti was put lying on his side with his face turned towards Mecca. The body was wrapped in a doti and a half of new American Sheeting, after it was put in its last resting place a sloping[375] roof[376] of sticks his mat, and cloth were placed over neatly in order to prevent the earth from falling on the body. The grave was then filled, soldiers laughing merrily. On the top into a small hole excavated with the hand[377] directly over the head water was poured lest he might feel thirsty on his journey to Paradise, & water was sprinkled all about & the gourd then broken. This ceremony completed the soldiers commenced repeating rapidly the Fathah after which they left the grave of their dead comrade to think no-more of him.

[Inside a circle] For slave boys 10 & 12 years old Arabs demand $25- to $40 in gold, for grown up men from $15 to $30, for women from $20 to $100, from[378] Unyamuezi donkeys from 5 to 40 doti of cloth, for Zanzibar donkeys from $30 to $200 in gold.

September 7 Thursday, 1871

[Ink] Halt.

Bought a little boy slave about 10 years old named Dugum Ali[379] for $20 in gold from an Arab to carry one of my hunting guns which would have required a soldier.

Bought a donkey for 10 doti or $10 dollars engaged 4 soldiers which increases my force to 29 soldiers altogether. The Expedition now numbers 2 white men, 1 Arab boy, 1 Hindi, 29 natives,[380] 1 slave boy total 36[381] souls, exclusive of 2 slave women.

---

374. '& 3' written over 'but'.
375. 'sloping' added above the line.
376. 'ing' of 'roofing' crossed out.
377. 'water' was crossed out.
378. Probable slip of the pen for 'for'.
379. Ndugu M'hali (*HIFL*). This little boy was to be renamed Kalulu (*HIFL*, 303). According to the price paid for him (20% less than the price for a boy of ten), he must have been very young, as his Swahili surname let it guess, Kalulu, being a Swahili term for the young of the blue-buck antelope (*HIFL*, 303). The antelope *perpusilla* belonged to the *Neotragus Pygmaeus* genus, and was very small (Cf. Ph. L. Sclater & O. Thomas, *The Book of Antelopes* (London, 1896–97), 2:62. But Stanley says nothing in his journal about the mock christening he described in *HIFL*. There is just one other mention of Kalulu in this diary (December 13th, 1871). Kalulu was left with the main body of the Expedition, while Stanley and Livingstone were exploring Lake Tanganyika.
380. Stanley first wrote 'total 33', then crossed out 'total 3' and wrote '1' over the second '3' of '33'.
381. Stanley first wrote '34', then wrote '6' over '4' in large character with another ink. If the total of '36' is accepted, the two slave women are included in the total.

Three men have promised to go with me as guides to the Tanganyika also I have been promised four more Wanguana to act as pagazis, so that I am in extremely good spirits to night. I shall be soon able to start Thank God.

Today we had quite an alarm great firing was heard about Tabora about 2 P.M. The Quihara people were seen flying in all directions to ascertain the cause which was soon reported to be the arrival of Sultan Kitambi to visit.
Mkasiwa Sultan of Unyamyembe, others said the Arabs were drunk with medicine.

September 8 Friday, 1871

[Ink] Halt.

Towards night Sheikh bin Nasib received a letter that Mirambo had attacked Mfuto with a large force of Washense, and accordingly despatched messengers to inform the principal men of Quihara myself among the number to be ready, for to-morrow or the day after Mirambo would probably enter the valley of Quihara.

We are progressing slowly with our preparations for the journey to Tanganyika by the Ukonongo road. Shaw is still very weak & sickly and utterly unfit in his present state to travel. Selim still continues to suffer from the attacks of the Mukunguru. Another donkey was bought to day for 9 doti making the number four. I made a cot to day for the journey, upon a model I invented during my sleepless hours which I passed last night.

September 9 Saturday, 1871

[Ink] Halt.
Mirambo was defeated with severe loss yesterday in his attack upon Mfuto. He was successful in an assault upon a small Wanyamuezi village, but when he attempted to storm Mfuto he was repulsed with the loss of three auxiliary sultans and many men. Upon[382] withdrawing his forces from the attack the inhabitants sallied out and chased[383] him to the forest which divides his territory from Mkasiwa's, where he was utterly routed, Mirambo ingloriously flying from the field. Three heads of the sultan[384] will, it is said be brought to Quihara to-morrow, to exhibit to Mkasiwa.

My new cot, which I propose to take with me on my journey weighs 24 lbs altogether, which makes a difference of 26 lbs in favor of the new over the old.

Selim still continues to be sick, and so does M^r. Shaw.

---

382. 'Upon' added above the line.
383. 'them' crossed out.
384. 's' for the plural of Sultan in the fold?

September 10 Sunday, 1871

[Ink] Halt.

I have been besides working hard all day endeavoring to purchase a boy slave to carry one of my guns, but the prices demanded for one 12 years old was, as I consider it, enormous, so I did not buy one. The price asked was for one $30 in American Sheeting at $6 per gorah or 7 ½ doti, for another was asked $60, which however was reduced to $45.

Shaw is still very ill. Last night I gave him 1[385] grain of morphine as a sleeping powder, he slept well but as[386] acted to day like one deprived of his senses. The last three days work of his was nil – required to be undone.

What poor amusement did Unyanyembe furnish a fretting impatient mind like mine. Half a dozen croaking Arabs coming to regale my sickening senses with stories of wars that existed not, of battles never fought, of dead hundreds who never have lived. Or gazing from my barzani at the same hills floating in vague atmosphere, of aged & dusky Cynthias[387] striding with a flippaty-flop of their besmirked[388] hide robes, about their spindled & brass adorned legs.

September 11 Monday, 1871

[Ink] Halt.

Busy all day on the tent. Shaw is so sick & weak that he can absolutely, do nothing. Sometimes I despair of his life and in such a case as his it is incumbent on me to wait here for him until all danger is past, and he is sufficiently strong to travel.

The soldiers amuse themselves every night in dancing & music, every night it is the same wild inharmonious music nothing equal to the Somal[389] or the Abyssinian, but is a tune which is in favor from South of Somali Land to the Mozambique, and stretches west beyond the Tanganyika. The Wanyamuezi are infinitely superior. They are able to improvize upon great occasions thus the war song against Mirambo has obtained great popularity with all the people who claim Mkasiwa for Sultan.

Mirambo was talked of to-night as being en-route here by some Watusi shepherds. All have been warned of his coming, and are prepared to give him[390] warm reception.

---

385. '1' written over '2'; 's' of 'grains' crossed out.
386. Slip of pen for 'has'.
387. 'Cynthias' may be crossed out.
388. For 'besmirched'.
389. For 'Somali'.
390. 'a' crossed out.

September 12 Tuesday, 1871

[Ink] Halt.

Mirambo did not come after all. The Watusi shepherds whose fears got the better of them reported falsely. It is the story of the boy & the wolf over again.

Hard at work as ever, on the tent, though I hope that to morrow will see it finished. Then there are water bottles to make & to tar, for our transit throught[391] the several long forests which[392] we have to traverse on the new route through Ukonongo.

Selim was well flogged to day for stealing the sugar, and aggravating the offense by the most obstinate lying. He had prepared a very nice dish of sweet milk & sugar when caught in the act.

Shaw is a sentimental driveller with a large share of the principles of Joseph Surface[393] imbued within him, was able at time to kindle into a[394] eloquent rant about the vices of mankind – particularly of rich people, his philippics on this topic[395] deserved a better audience than I furnished him.

September 13 Wednesday, 1871

[Ink] Halt.

The "Apostle of Africa" – Livingstone is always in my mind, and as day after day passes without starting to find him I find myself subject to fits of depression. Indeed I have many things to depress me. Shaw is sick stubbornly so, he is a spiritless man totally devoid of the commendable ambition to do a good thing of whatever nature it may be. By disclosing to him the purpose of the Expedition I thought to interest him, to stir him into action, but no, he seems to be plunged in apathy. Daydreaming is his sole[396] enjoyment from which like the hankering after opium with a confirmed[397] opium-eater it seems impossible to rouse him. Besides him, I have six others Jumah with rheumatism in the legs, Umgareza from ophthalmia, Zaidi from a stiff neck, Bill-alli a disease unknown, Ulimengo, inflamed lungs, Selim constant ague & fever. This number from 24[398] gives me only 17 effective men, which is totally inadequate for an Expedition which may last four, five or even six months.

---

391. 'throught', ms., for 'through'.
392. 'will' crossed out.
393. Joseph Surface, described by Richard B. Sheridan in *The School for Scandal* as a liar and fortune-hunter.
394. ms.
395. 'were, though' crossed out.
396. 'sole' written above 'only' crossed out.
397. 'confirmed' written above 'normal' crossed out.
398. 'men' crossed out.

Shaw is "self-absorbed" – has an oddity quite the reverse of Jack Bunsby,[399] instead of looking towards the furthest distance, he regards the ground at his feet, with a look which seems to say, there is something wrong somewhere, and I am trying to find out where it can be and how to rectify it.

September 14 Thursday, 1871

[Ink] Halt.

Selim is delirious from constant fevers. Shaw is sick, and these two occupy most of my time. I am turned into a regular nurse for I have no one to assist me in attending upon them. If I try to instruct Abdul Kader in the art of being useful, his head is so befogged with the villainous fumes of Unyamuezi tobacco that he wanders bewildered about breaking things & upsetting cooked dishes, until I[400] get so exasperated that my peace is destroyed for a full hour. If I ask Feraggi our now formally constituted cook to help his thick wooden head fails to grasp an idea, so I am compelled to stand over him, and play the part of chef.

To-day I engaged two pagazis, and a soldier, but I have been deceived so often by similar engagements that I am doubtful whether they are sincere or not. The cloth has been cut 6½ doti to one, and 7 ½ to the other.

September 15 Friday, 1871

[Ink] Halt.

The third month of my stay in Unyannyembe is almost ended, and I am not gone yet, but I hope to be gone before the 23rd inst.

All last night until 9 this morning my soldiers danced & sung to the manes of their dead comrades whose bones now bleach in the forest[401] of Wilyankuru. Two or three huge pots – containing about 6 gallons each – of pombe failed to satisfy the raging thirst which the vigorous exercice they were engaged in created, so early this morning I was called upon to contribute a shukka for another potful of the potent liquor.

Today I was busy in selecting the loads for each soldier. In order to lighten their labor as much as possible I reduced each load of 70 lbs to 50 lbs so that I hope we will be able to travel pretty comfortably. I have two or three men still very sick and it is almost useless to expect that they will be able to carry anything, but I am in hopes that other men may be engaged to take their places before the actual day of departure, which now seems drawing near rapidly.

---

399. Jack Bunsby, a character in *Dombey and Son* by Dickens.
400. 'am compelled' crossed out.
401. Plural crossed out.

September 16 Saturday, 1871

[Ink] Halt

We have almost finished our work. On the fifth day from this we leave, God willing, we engaged two soldiers & 3 pagazis and 10 more talk of[402] coming, but I shall not put myself out of the way at all for their coming or going. My number is complete to 40 souls, & really I have no need of any more, still if they come I can make use of them.

To morrow a feast is given to the soldiers to celebrate our departure from this forbidding country.

September 17 Sunday, 1871

[Ink] Halt.

I gave a feast to day to my 33 soldiers, consisting of 1 whole Sheep, 15 Chickens, 45 lbs of Beef, 80 lbs of Rice, 8 large loaves of Bread, made of Corn Meal, Eggs, butter & sweet milk. A dance then followed & 20 gallons of Pombe were then distrited[403], to the intense delight of the guzzling loving Africans.[404]

September 18 Monday, 1871

[Ink] Halt.

September 19 Tuesday, 1871

[Ink] Halt.
Sick from Mukunguru.

September 20 Wednesday, 1871

[Ink] March to Mkwenkwe. 1 ½ hour. 3 miles S.W.[405]

Leaving the windy[406] valley of Quihara, and striking south in a short half hour we are in view of scenery totally different from that my eyes were accustomed to while residing at Quihara.

---

402. One word unintelligible crossed out.

403. 'distrited', ms., for 'distributed'. Stanley rightly wrote 'distributed', but his ink was very pale. So he wrote the last syllable (-ted) again over the two last (-buted), with darker ink.

404. In *HIFL* Stanley inflates the amount of goods served at the banquet: two bullocks instead of 45 lbs of beef, three sheep instead of one, 120 lbs of rice instead of 80, 20 large loaves of bread ... but he adds that the men invited their friends and neighbors, and about 100 women and children (*HIFL*, 307).

405. Before leaving Kwihara Stanley wrote two despatches to the *New York Herald* dated September 20 and 21, 1871, in which the war with Mirambo and Stanley's role are detailed. The *New York Herald* published them only in August 1872.

406. 'plain' crossed out.

My newly enlisted pagazis & soldiers give me considerable trouble. They required to be petted, yet having arrived at camp they all leave en-masse without so much as "by your leave, Sir" to have one more[407] debauch! My donkey herd also followed suit & found their way back to the grassy hollows of the valley wherein they had luxuriated so long.

September 21 Thursday, 1871

[Pencil] 2
[Pencil] Halt, from Mukunguru

September 22 Friday, 1871

[Pencil] 3
[Ink] March to Inesuka 2 hours.
Matama fields. Hills agreeably rising around us. Filthy village. Thermometer in the tent 108° Fahrenheit.
[Pencil] Imbiki apple.

September 23 Saturday, 1871

[Ink] March to Kasagera,[408] or Kasagala 3 hours. S.W. by S.
Forest. Abdul Kader discharged this morning. After seven months trial of him my patience was utterly worn out. I paid him off with 12 doti first-class Merikani equal to $13, having already paid him as advance $10 in gold.
    Mabruk Saleem attacked with violent diarrhoea, & Zaidi with rheumatism give a deal of trouble to poor old Bombay who is obliged during Shaw's sickness to bring up the rear.
[Pencil] Vetches placed in long hollow sheaves of grass.
    Absentees return from fani[409] at the Coast, great rejoicings, lu-luing & drumming. Dressed in new cloth Kaniki & Amerikani.

September 24 Sunday, 1871

[Ink] March to Kigandu 2 ¾ hours. S. & S.S.W.
Forest. During the night Asmani one of the soldiers engaged in Zanzibar deserted taking his gun with him. Bombay & 3 soldiers despatched in pursuit. When I gave the

---

407. 'bout at' crossed out.
408. Kasegera (*HIFL*).
409. Reading uncertain. Could be a Swahili word "fani" meaning successful [journey]?

orders to march there were no less than seven loads untaken, the bearers of whom were sick. Even a slave hired as a soldier but yesterday swore he could not stir. The slave was instantly put in chains, and the other soldiers, but one who was really sick flogged to their duties.

Emerging from the forest and ascending a gentle ridge where there was a huge rock standing as guardian over the miles of forest, we now spread out in view on either hand of us.

Arriving at Kigandu we were briefly informed we could not enter, because one time during the memory of those living one Mgwana shot a Mnyamwezi of that village through the thigh. Still, if we paid 2 doti as tribute to the daughter of the Sultan Mkasiwa who was Mtemi of the village, we might, but we declined and sought quarters at a little village about a mile to the north where we were far more comfortable than we could possibly have been at the larger village.[410]

September 25 Monday, 1871

[Pencil] Halt.

The view which the eye hurries to embrace as the traveller ascends some ridge higher than another is one of the most disheartening that can be conceived. Away, one beyond another stand[411] the lengthy rectilinear ridges clad in the same garb of color.[412] Woods, woods, woods, forests, leafy branches green and sere – then an ocean the color of it[413] being lost as it recedes beyond ken of vision. The horizon all around shows the same scene, a sky dropping into the depths of the forest, some tree top higher than the rest conspicuous in its outlines against the lucid sky. On no one point does the eye rest with pleasure, it has viewed the same outlines, forest, horizon, day after day, week after week, and again like Noah's dove from wandering over[414] a world without a halting place it returns wearied with the search.

Asmani found & put in chains. All returned well.

[Ink] Humboldt in his "Views of Nature" says[415] that "all formations are common to every quarter of the globe and assume the like forms". He referred to the physical aspect of the Earth. Following his bold statement, I declare that in[416] the

---

410. This description is quite different from that in *HIFL*, 320: "As we would not pay toll, we were compelled to camp in a ruined, rat-infested boma ..."
411. 'stand' added above the line.
412. 'stretch' crossed out.
413. 'of it' added above the line.
414. 'the' crossed out.
415. Stanley was indeed traveling with a library, though it is unclear exactly which books he had. He bought "books on Africa" at Bombay, on October 11, 1870.
416. 'in' added above the line.

physiology[417] of the races there is but little difference. Features of white Americans residing in New York I have seen in black in Africa, the same in Turkey Persia. Spain Fra Jacinto I have seen in Africa, J. C. Heenan I have seen in Africa, with the same herculean form.

September 26 Tuesday, 1871

[Pencil] Halt.

[Ink] I have been obliged to make arrangements for the transportation of Shaw back to Quihara. It seems useless to strive against fate. On the road he seemed like one bound to my back as a punishment inflicted on me for some sin. For three months he has been worse than useless, and to day he told me he was getting worse. Under such circumstances it was best he should return for should he fall sick as I was hurrying home from Ujiji he must be left behind, with no white man to return for him.

Another soldier Mabruk Saleem having fallen sick – expectorating blood, I must leave behind. At this rate the caravan recruited after such expense & trouble will soon be reduced again.

I saw a Mganga's stores of medicine with which he makes his arrows against the wild game plentiful. Eye of zebra, web of Ostrich feather, bit of dry moss, dry dung & bark of tree, bit of nose of buffalo, bit of lip of zebra, altogether 18 ingredients. His arrow heads were all kept together with this medicine in a small kivindo[418] or box.

September 27 Wednesday, 1871

[Ink] Ugunda. S by W. & S. S. W. 7 hours. Forest. 2 watering places. Uninteresting.

Shaw departed this morning borne on the shoulders of 2 stout pagazis. Another soldier deserted last night, the new man Dasturi enlisted at Mkwekwe, though he was in chains.

Infinite trouble to-day from three or four, Kuddam, Zaidi, Asmani & Chanda.

Ugunda is a very large village probably contains 1000 souls. But though they are secure here from the war with Mirambo, yet they express as much dread as if Mirambo was but a few miles off neighbour to them. I could not enlist a soul as pagazi to Ufipa or Ukonongo. There are also reports of wars ahead.

---

417. 'physiological' altered into physiology.
418. a pot in which a potter keeps his tools (cf. *A Standard English-Swahili Dictionary* [London: Oxford University Press, 1992]).

September 28 Thursday, 1871

[Ink] Benta. S. & S. by W. 3 ¼ hours.
The route was principally after traversing the[419] cultivated grounds which led past the village of Kisari where there was the proprietor of a caravan <u>intending</u> to travel to Kawendi when he should have succeeded in procuring pagazis (a very dubious task) through a dim jungle of black jacks then a forest of the most sombre color. All the grass & low shrubs had been burnt & the trees appeared as if dead. Arrived at the small & clean village of Benta a good strong boma – clear water – no goats – no matama. Indian corn & vetches had usurped all other grains.

  Corn stored on the flat[420] roofs outside in great boxes made of bark. Some of these boxes are very capacious, the largest I have seen was at this village, & was 7 feet in diameter & 10 feet high.

September 29 Friday, 1871

[Ink] Kikuro.[421] 5 hours. S. W. by South.
Forest, and extensive sun-cracked mbugas or plains overgrown by black jacks, saw two trees joined together, both forming one large tree. Ant hills very numerous & large.

  Mukunguru is very plentiful & violent in these extensive & flat forests owing to an[422] imperfect drainage of such a vast flat area. In the view of it there is nothing very offensive to the sight. Numbers of trees lie about in the last stages of decay, and working away with might and main are numberless insects of various species to clear the Earth of the malarious influences. Impalpably however the poison of the dead & corrupting vegetation is inhaled into the system with as fatal result, as that which is said to arise from the vicinity of the Upas tree. The first evil result experienced from the presence of malaria is confined bowels, and an oppressive languor excessive drowsiness,[423] a constant disposition to yawn.[424] The tongue has a sickly yellow hue, colored almost to blackeness. Even the teeth assume a yellow color, & become coated with an offensive matter. The eyes sparkle with a lustre which is an unmistakeable symptom of the incipient fever, which shortly will rage through the system, and lay the sufferer prostrate, quivering with the agony. This fever is sometimes preceded by a violent[425]

---

419. 'mat' crossed out.
420. 'flat' added above the line.
421. Stanley first wrote Kikuru and kept this spelling in *HIFL*.
422. 'an' added above the line.
423. 'with' crossed out.
424. 'Even in mid-day' crossed out.
425. Sentence incomplete—it continues on September 30, 1871.

September 30 Saturday, 1871

[Ink] Halt

[Pencil] Salt obtained at a small village Wananghombeh to the East, fine pure. Salt also at Ugunda.

[Ink] What a vast amount of good could a living soul brimful with the[426] philanthropical feelings of a John Howard[427] do to this long benighted land and people! By first of all confining himself to the specific duties of a real practical man, whose mind was bent on doing practical good to suffering human beings. Then if his mind[428]

[Continuation of the previous day]

shaking fit during which period blankets may be heaped on the patient with but little amelioration of the chilliness which he feels.

This ague is then succeeded by an unusually severe headache with excessive pains about the loins & spinal column, spreading over the shoulder blades, and running up the nape of the neck, find a lodgment in the back & front of the head. Usually this fever is not preceded by an ague, the patient is at once seized with excessive heat, throbbing temples, and the loin and spinal aches, a raging thirst takes possession of him, the brain becomes crowded with strange fancies, which sometimes assume most hideous shapes. Before the darkened vision of the sufferer float in a seething atmosphere figures of created & uncreated reptiles which are metamphorased[429] every instant into stranger shapes & designs growing every instant more confused, more complicated, more hideous & terrible, until the sufferer unable to bear longer the distracting scene with an effort opens his eyes, & dissolves it, only to glide again unconsciously into another dream-land where another unreal inferno is dioramically revealed.

October 1 Sunday, 1871

[Ink] Ziwani. W. by S. & S.S.W. 4 hours.
Forest, and thinly clad Mbuga.

[Continuation of the previous day]

---

426. 'with the' written above 'of' crossed out.
427. Probably the British philanthropist (1726–1790) who dedicated his life to reforming English prisons.
428. Sentence incomplete—it continues on October 1, 1871.
429. 'metamphorased', ms., for 'metamorphosed'.

was resolved upon their conversion, he would find pliable souls ready to receive a doctrine which would first sound so strange to them. Even[430] the simple duties[431] of teaching them to supply themselves with good and pure water, of instructing them in the art of building better houses, for living in, better bomas for defense, by supplying them with better tools for their agricultural & domestic wants, would be reciprocated finally by their willingness to listen to the words of salvation. The Wanyamuezi being naturally docile & quiet people offer ---

---

[Ink] Wanyamuezi mothers carry their children over the buttocks so bountifully provided for them by nature the young like simians cling to them.

Arrived at the Ziwani, or little pool, we found an old khambi half burnt which an hour's work sufficed to rebuild thoroughly & render it perfect almost for defense. The Ziwani was a little pool indeed being a small circular pit – 5 feet in diameter, but[432] not to be despised for its superior water compared to the rush grown marsh that formerly bore the name of Ziwa, or pool. A magnificent Mkuyu Sycamore sheltered the whole khambi which was certainly 400 feet in circumference. Its fruit is very like a fig in appearance. The Wangwana ate them eagerly. Tsetse, antelope, elephants & Guinea fowls plenty.

October 2 Monday, 1871

[Ink] Maniara[433] 6 ½ hours. W.S.W.

A long march under a hot sun through a forest & plain with clumps of jungle wherein the fierce tsetse – or panga fly swarmed. Just as we entered the jungly plain saw a dead man, a victim to that fearful scourge of Africa – the small pox. He was one of Oseto's gang of Ruga-Rugas whose bows and spears are at the hire of any man who can afford to pay them, and need their services. They were returning from a raid on[434] Mbogo's territory in Ukonongo. No village permitted them to enter its boma, outside of Unyanyembe to whose ruler they now belonged.

Soon after leaving the Mbuga we emerged from the forest that separated it from the cultivated fields of Maniara. Arriving before the village we were told we could not enter but might camp at the khambi whose ruined huts appeared very uncomfortable after such a long march. When the Kirangozi was sent with the cloth

---

430. 'in' crossed out.
431. 'duties' written above 'facts' crossed out.
432. 'contain' crossed out.
433. Manyara (*HIFL*).
434. 'Ukonongo' crossed out.

to buy posho or provisions for the transit of the long wilderness before us he was told by the people that the Mtemi had strictly prohibited them from selling. The Sultan was visited by Bombay with a present of[435] a Kitambi[436] or cloth, but he was sulky & refused to accept it, saying that we must wait until to-morrow, that nothing could be done this day. As entreaties were no avail the caravan went supperless to bed and in very bad humor with each other & the world. Njara's croaking words came to their minds, and there was a prospect of a general decamp.

October 3 Tuesday, 1871

[Ink] A <u>Halt</u>, in consequence of the market of Maniara being closed. It was necessary to remove this prohibition, and be most politic with the surly sultan whose knowledge of Mirambo's policy might induce him to imitate the redoubtable chief of Uyowa.[437] Soon after dawn, Bombay was dispatched with a magnificent present of a broad shukka of crimson Joho, a most royal Dabwani, being of the finest that is manufactured, and specially reserved against such incidental cases, as was now presented, besides these were sent a doti of the best Kaniki for his chief man, and a handsome barsati for his wife. The effect of the present thus sent was soon made manifest in the abundance of provender – beans, vetches, rice, matama, and Indian corn that came to camp, and in the appearance of the Mtemi himself who came in best state accompanied by a large escort of musketeers, & spearmen to visit the first[438] Musungu who ever travelled on this road. Behind the escort came a munificent present, fully equal in value to that sent, consisting of several large gourds of honey, fowls, and enough vetches & beans to supply my 50 soldiers with food for four days. The whole morning was spent with this state visit, and in amusing his sultanship, which was highly successful. Very enthusiastic, as each wonderful thing was exhibited & explained, clasped my hand in ecstasy & shook hands with his chiefs. Arabs he said were miserable people compared with the Wasungu.

October 4 Wednesday, 1871

[Ink] Gombe Creek or Mtoni 4 h. 15 m. S by W, & S.S.W.
Mbuga with small clumps of jungle around which flocked the great game for which Africa is famous, such as zebra, buffalo, kuru, niamera, giraffe, wild boar, stein-bok, antelope we were entering upon the famous hunting ground between Bagomoyo & the Tanganyika, which should be called & spelt Tanganika.[439]

---

435. 'of a kitambi or cloth' added above the line.
436. A length of piece of cloth.
437. Uyoweh *(HIFL)*.
438. 'first' added above the line.
439. Spelling without y. See Stanley's note in *HIFL*, 25: "It will be seen that I differ from Capt. Burton in the spelling of this word, as I deem the letter "y" superfluous."

Last night Hamdallah one of my kirangozi deserted after[440] costing me no less than 22 doti. He had eaten 15 doti within 14 days. Maniara the friendly Sultan assisted us in the search throughout the village but he was not found.

Arrived at the Khambi we found ourselves near a large pool or a depression in the course of the sometime creek – full of water wherein the Silurus fish swarmed.

We had eight Wakonongo with us who were proficient in the art of finding honey, so that by night the people were pretty well-fed with buffalo, & boar meat, Guinea fowl & quail, Silurus fish & wild honey, while water was abundant and sweet though slightly muddy. I thought it such a happy place that I ordered a halt for the morrow to enjoy one good day's sport & feed.

The Gombe is one of the effluents of the Malagarazi, and is said to commence near Khokoro.

October 5 Thursday

[Ink] Halt at Gombe Creek.

Happy place, bountiful sport & feed. 2 boars, 3 buffaloes, 1 zebra, 1 kuru, 1 rabbit, 2 antelope,[441] 4 Guinea fowls, 5 quail. Kuru an enormous animal, boar at first sight strike one as somewhat resembling a lion.

October 6 Friday, 1871

[Ink] Halt.

The people wished to dry their meat, so after much entreaty on their part I ordered a halt for this day also, on the condition that it be made up on the road. Saw 3 great herds of zebra, and kuru as well as gazelle and the huge reddish deer.

October 7 Saturday, 1871

[Ink] Ziwani 5 hours & 20 minutes. West course.

A most troublous day. We had but left camp three quarters of an hour following the course of the Gombe when we came to a large lake-like part of the Creek where the Kiboko & the Crocodile sported in the broad water. The kirangozi listening to the complaints of the lazy Wanguana soldiers begged me to stop until the after-noon's when we should make a terekeza or an after-noon's march and reach the Ziwani about dark. As such a course was out of the question after two days halt, & feasting on meat, and it was not yet 7 A.M. of course, I immediately refused. Bombay had already soon after leaving camp with his natural forgetfulness forgotten to tie the

---

440. 'after' added above the line.
441. '2 antelope' added above the line.

saddle bags on the pack donkey the consequence of which was that when the intractable animal took to a run the saddle bags fell to the ground, and four days corn[442] provisions for three donkeys were spilt, & now when I heard him seconding the proposition of the kirangozi the pent up wrath was poured on his head, and as he did not seem to mind words, he was put in chains & made to carry a 60 lbs load on his head, which he found to be an extremely heavy load before reaching camp. Soon after striking into the forest kirangozi halted, Bombay got head wig,[443] caravan put down load, a general disposition to be violent & mutinous Bombay had the stick, Ambari was pitched into in fisticuff fastened, kirangozi brought to his sense at the muzzle of a buckshot loaded double barrel.

No water at Ziwa,[444] was finally procured from Tongoni.

October 8 Sunday

[Ink] Tongoni 1 h. 30 m. S.S.W.

We arrived upon a scene where the Ruga Rugas of Mirambo played once a cruel part the two villages which formerly stood here were attacked, taken and committed to the flames, and the kindly people of the little territory of Ukamba, slaughtered like sheep. The largest herds of buffalo as yet seen now drink[445] of the small pond which furnished the villages with water.

<u>Iron ore</u> crops out of the ground in large lumps close to the water,[446] as well as at the Ziwani of yesterday.

<u>Wild fruit</u> is abundant between Maniara and Mrera, the wood apple, & lemon, a plum-like fruit also is very plentiful but not eaten. Honey bird was first heard on this march, its note is a harsh chirrup. Wanyamuezi very successful in finding honey the attention they pay to its cries. They procure a fire by rubbing a hard stick in the palm of the hand, with its end resting upon[447] a flat piece of firewood.[448] A fire is as quickly made in this manner as quickly as with our fire glass.

Buffalo gnats & tsetse are very troublesome. Gazelle and buffalo plentiful in this vicinity.

---

442. 'corn' added above the line.
443. An insect of the order Dermaptera that invades human ears.
444. One word unintelligible: 'at last'?
445. 'the water' crossed out.
446. 'the presence of' crossed out.
447. 'another' crossed out.
448. 'When' crossed out.

October 9 Monday, 1871

[Ink] Camp in forest. 5h. 15 minutes. South.

Starting at a little before 2 P.M. with the sun glaring hotly above us we arrived at our Khambi in the Forest about dark. This was a terekeza – or an afternoon march, because we were to camp where there was no[449] water. The People of the Mrima[450] & Central Africa generally travel through countries where more or less water is procured every day, but it happens sometimes as at Marenga Mkhali, & one or two places in Mgunda[451] Mkali that long marches have to be made where no water can be got. At such times they resort to what is[452] called a terekeza previously filling their gourds which however seldom last the march out, as they recklessly drink their supply without thought of the after thirsty hour that must transpire before they reach water.

Selim was always a poor hand on a terekeza. It did not matter how much water he carried, it would always fail him before reaching camp. And his complaints were[453] afterwards grievous. The Wanguana stole each other water on the[454] evening of such a day and a chorus of loud squabbles would invariably close the day.

On these evenings during war time the Ruga-Ruga obtains a prominent place in everybody's thought & conversation, they are held in such dread by the timid Arabs & Wangwana.

October 10 Tuesday, 1871

[Ink] Marefu or Marevo. 3 hours. S.S.W. & South.

Continuing our march throught the long narow mbuga or plain traversed yesterday a three hours march brought us[455] within view of the boma of Marefu. We sent a deputation of Wanyamuezi to inform the Sultan that the caravan was coming which was received very graciously with a permission to pass by & camp close to the village. The villagers were out in full force to stare the Muzungu out of countenance. Encamped in this place was the Peace Commission of the Arabs to the King of the Watuta bearing presents to him, headed by Old Hassan the Mseguhha. It had started before us 12 days, and though we had been delayed many days on the route

---

449. 'no' added above the line.
450. Coastal area of Tanzania.
451. Magunda (HIFL).
452. 'is' written above 'are' crossed out.
453. One word unintelligible crossed out.
454. 'the' written above 'such an' crossed out.
455. 'to the [word?]' crossed out.

for the[456] various reasons already explained yet here they were with very little prospect of ever reaching the Watuta for Hassan was already talking of returning to Unyanyembe.

Sultan received a present of a doti, and sent a present back to me in return of matama & fowls, & as my gift was utterly unexpected, his delight was unbounded.

October 11 Wednesday, 1871

[Ink] Utende 7 hours ¾. W. by N.
Made a most determined march in order to avoid sleeping in the jungle infested by the Ruga-Ruga. Rhinoceros & elephant abounded but though we saw a dozen trails we were not fortunate enough to see any of these large animals.
The men treated themselves to ripe mpundu as we now & then halted for rest.[457] These trees very much resemble the pear tree, and the fruit might be called the forest peach from its resemblance to it. In Mbogo further South this fruit is abundant. With culture it might be made a favorite fruit, as a real ripe mpundu is not to be despised. On a single tree I saw as much as would produce 40 or 50 bushels.

Selim is ill, and seems to be affected with the same disease as Shaw, has a weakness in the legs, and sprawls & trembles most painfully when walking. (Ptarmigan and Guinea fowl abound near this village)[458]

Arriving at a hill, the first we had seen[459] since leaving Kigandu, we were in view of a scene that might be called animated compared with the eternal forest & jungle through which we had travelled since leaving Unyanyembe. At our feet stood the village of Utende, and from it sloped a forest for miles & miles bounded by[460] a hilly ridge[461] running North West.

The Sultan was very surly & returned no thanks nor allowed himself to be seen, for the two doti I sent him. Famine prevailing him he could present me with no more than a quarter bushel of sweet pea.

October 12 Thursday, 1871

[Ink] Mtoni. Camp in Jungle near Mtoni. 4 hours. W.N.W.
An hour after leaving our Khambi we had to fight with a fire which roared through the thin forest like volleys of small arms. The grass being so high & dry it

---

456. 'the' added above the line.
457. Mpundu: *Strychnos innocua*. http://www.fao.org/forestry/25323-096344a3de335832e8f363c3ac5184a66.pdf.
458. Sentence in brackets added between two lines.
459. 'before' crossed out.
460. 'by' added above the line.
461. 'on the North W' crossed out.

burned before the East wind like powder, and we had to run for about a mile every man for himself. The powder carriers were in such trepidation that they had to be watched lest in their fright they would drop their loads & desert. Happily no accident occurred, and all arrived safe at the Mtoni which consisted of one pool 40 yards long by ten wide, of excellent water near by which we made our khambi.

A little before camping we saw a herd of nimba (horned animals, reddish skins). By the quantity of bois de vache[462] buffalo must be plentiful here – as well as elephant & rhinoceros. Birds large with bags under their bills to catch flies, storks, pelicans, eagles, hawks, green & blue birds with harsh screams.

Course of the Mtoni North West.

October 13 Friday, 1871

[Ink] Mwaru. Sultan Camirambo. W.N.W. 5 h. 15 m.

Marched through the once flourishing country over which Camirambo[463] ruled. Village after village was passed destroyed by Mkasiwa in his warfare against Manwa Sera and his adherents. Niongo the brother of Manwa Sera has lately been fighting against Mbogo but we hear that he has been defeated and is retreating towards Northern Ukonongo, through which we are now travelling. The[464] fields are no longer cultivated but are overgrown with corn under brush which in this rich land soon usurps the place of grain if left one season untilled. After marching 10 miles we commenced the ascent of the hilly ridge visible from the hill behind the village of Utende – and felt and saw the influence of the Tanganika even here, in the tall rank grasses & thick jungle which reminded us somewhat of the jungles of Ukwere on the Mrima.

This is a plateau similar to that we ascended when emerging from Ugogo we entered the Mgunda Mkali. Quartz, iron ore, syenite, boulders conglomerate.

Camirambo now contents himself with a small village buried in the forest & situate[465] half a mile north of a small pool, of excellent water near where we camped. Heard from Caravan of Mohammed an Arab, from Ufipa, that Livingstone had gone to Urua.

---

462. *Bois de vache* (dried buffalo dung used for fire wood on the Great Plains) is derived from the French "bouse de vache" (cow dung), which Stanley used more properly in *HIFL*, 357. "Bois de vache" was still in use in Mississippi Valley French in the nineteenth century (cf. J. F. McDermott, *A Glossary of Mississippi Valley French, 1673–1850* [St. Louis: Washington University Studies, 1941]). Stanley may have learned the expression when roaming Missouri and Mississippi.
463. Ka-mirambo (*HIFL*).
464. 'cultivated' crossed out.
465. 'd' missing at the end.

October 14 Saturday, 1871

[Ink] Mrera. Sultan Mrera. 5h. 30 m. W. by N ½ North.

After a long march which sorely tried all the men we[466] emerged out of the forest & jungle, and arrived[467] at a ruined village where the clumpy jungles which we always saw in Ukwere on the Mrima, were seen here for the first time since leaving the coast.

In a narrow marshy[468] tract which we passed on the road we saw 4 elephants with enormous tusks. It was the first time I had ever seen wild elephants, and the first impression of them I shall never forget. I am induced to think that the elephant deserves the name of king of beasts. Their huge forms and the lordly way in which they stare at an intruder on their domain, and their whole appearance indicating conscious might, are good grounds on which to claim that title. They stopped to survey the caravan as it passed, about half a mile from them; and their curiosity satisfied they passed into the forest which bounds the marshy plain southward, as if caravans were every day things giving no trouble whatever to them, lifting their trunks high into the air. Close to them were giraffe & zebra.

Selim was attacked with severe acute dysentery which caused great alarm to us. He brought this attack of sickness from sheer wilfulness. He had been warned often & often that the way dunk[469] water, his own mbuga,[470] mine & two or three others would be emptied before arriving at a camp, of water none the least[471] in the world

October 15 Sunday, 1871

[Ink] Halt at Mrera.

Every body being well tired, Selim severely ill, a halt was ordered, which I was to improve by patching my clothes, & shoes, which the thorn species had almost destroyed. There were new cartridges to be made & filled up in place of those which had caused destruction to the game in the neighbourhood of Gombe Nullah.

3 doti were sent as presents to the moribund Mrera. His chief man received the gift with many praises of the Musungu's generosity and sent a return in Holcus Sorghum & beans & fowls which though not equal in price were nevertheless acceptable.

The people of this place[472] were great beggars after flint stones & powder & articles I could not part with. Had I a supply a dozen flintstone would have sufficed

---

466. 'arriv' crossed out.
467. 'upon' crossed out.
468. 'marshy' written above 'plain' crossed out.
469. 'dunk', ms., for 'drank'? 'he' missing.
470. *Mbuga* (a plain) is meaningless here. Stanley might have mistaken *mbuga* for *mabura*: gourds?
471. Word unclear.
472. 'place' written over 'people'.

to feed my caravan for 2 days. They are an idle set doing nothing but hunting & playing, dancing, beating the drum,[473] varying these occupations sometimes with fighting their neighbours. Seven skulls set on stakes placed near the principal gate of the boma.

 Mrera is well protected by a jungley hedge varying from one hundred to 30 feet in thickness. Against the attacks of naked Africans it is impregnable. But the position of the villagers would be bad indeed in case of an attack by men who knew how to fight, as it has only 2 outlets, these leading through a narrow lane between two hedges of jungle thorn, whiler[474] the

October 16 Monday, 1871

[Ink] Halt at Mrera.
water is more than half a mile away procured from a nullah.[475]
The mode of saluting a chief is by bending the back, and letting the arms drop down until the tips of the fingers touch the ground. The chief answers it by clapping his hands.

 Costume of women & mostly of[476] the men too poor to purchase cloth w[477] the necessaries for caravans is of the bark of trees well beaten & tanned. It has a leaden color & it soon wears out. Many[478] things are made of this same bark, round boxes called Kirindos, of all sizes varying from one holding but a quart to one able to hold 50 bushels, good rope and on the rivers Malagarazi, Muruya, Ruzizi & Ruffiji, canoes are made.

 Selim slightly improving, caravan marches to-morrow God willing. 2 kirangozis backed out of an Expedition[479] Engagement they had made to conduct my caravan to the Tanganika,[480] on the plea that my bales would be all eaten up & no provision left for their return.

 Wazavira from Simba brought me goats to sell. Uzavira is north by west from Mrera. Simba boasts of cows, goats & sheep[481] a fact which indicates population & fighting qualities. From before the boma of Simba, Mirambo retreated in haste to his own country last here, just after he had destroyed the villages of Akamba.[482]

---

473. 'beating the drum' added above the line.
474. ms., ending with 'r'.
475. This seems to be the end of the previous page.
476. 'of' added above the line.
477. 'with' under ink spot?
478. 'Many' preceded by 'a great' crossed out.
479. 'Expedition' added under the line.
480. Tanganika, 'i' written over 'y'.
481. 'which tells' crossed out.
482. About Simba, see Waters, "Social Organization and Social Status," 84, note 69.

October 17 Tuesday, 1871

[Pencil] Mtoni. W by N. 4h. 30 m. Mtoni in Kasera going South probably to the Rikwa. Sultan Simba son of Mkasiwa.

Along the march we caught glimpses travelling as we did along the spurs of one these ridgy waves, of magnificent & far reaching prospects. We crossed a running[483] stream of clear water the first we had seen since leaving the sea Coast – region, before the asscent of the ridge flowing N West. The country is cut up into parallel ridges, with deep[484] valleys[485] These valleys drain the ridges of water, and empty into the Tanganika, either by the Malagarazi & Rikwa or independently. As we crossed the ridge came to the sources of a small stream flowing southward into the valley.

Simba sent an embassy after me in this camp to scold me well for not travelling by his road and taking his villages on the way. Simba as usual received a present of a royal dabwani & kaniki.

October 18 Wednesday, 1871

[Ink] Misonghi. 4 h. 30 m. W.N.W.

Killed a deer or horned antelope, 2 Guinea fowl.

Many burnt up, and desolated tracts but lately cultivated, now given up to the elephant, rhinoceros & Buffalo whose tracks were numerous. Crossed several marshy ravines all of which drain to the Rungwa River. On the western side of a large ravine was the village of Usense. About a mile & a half northwest of this village was the deserted boma of Misonghi a village in Usavira. Numbers of guinea fowl, were seen of which[486] brace were shot as well as a horned antelope called Umbawala,[487] a short bushy tail, reddish brown & long hairs, a ridge of long hairs along the spine, short straight horns points very sharp.

[Pencil] Matonga fruit as large as an orange, outside it has the semblance of an orange, but not inside, flavor of stale cider.

---

483. 'running' added above the line.
484. 'hollows' crossed out.
485. Word unclear: intern… ?
486. 'a' crossed out.
487. *Mbawala (HIFL*, 366): bushbuck in Swahili.

October 19 Thursday

[Pencil] Mtoni. W. by N. 6 hours
[Ink] A long march through a forest where the sable antelope was seen for the first time. It stands about 4 ½ feet at the shoulder, is a strong compact animal with straight horns, belly dark brown, body black with long hair. Crossed two or three small streams, along the banks of which grew the enormous Mkuyu sycamore, some lofty tamarinds, and the Mbembu[488] tree. We halted at the base of a conical hill near a small stream of most clear water, buffalo plentiful.[489]

October 20 Friday

[Pencil] Mpokwa in Utanda 4 h. ¾ m.
[Ink] Leaving our camp we were in full view of what we so often desired – viz hills. Germany on a small scale. Conical hills rose all around us, and it gave me first rate opportunities to test my compass which I found to be perfectly correct. Bamboo grew on the hill slopes, feathery & graceful, the thickest the size of a man's wrist. After nearly a five[490] hours march we entered the deserted village of Mpokwa in Utanda, the inhabitants of which had been driven to flight by an advance of Simba Sultan of Kasera. Near the village grew a group of the borassu[491] flabelliformus. Every thing inside the boma indicated a hasty flight of the people who have gone to Usowwa.[492]
[Pencil] Numbers of birds catching fish which abound in the stream close by the boma. Mud fish about 60 were caught by the hand in a few minutes.

October 21 Saturday, 1871

[Ink] Camp on Mtoni. 3 hours. N.N.W.
Travelled up the marshy valley of Mpokwa, we came to the head of the stream where we camped. Antelope bark[493] like a dog, hides himself in a thick clump of grass, and when an intruder is near darts of with great speed keeping his nose to the ground. Plenty of honey near this river. This as well as others drains towards the Rungwa. An

---

488. 'Mbembu' written above 'Mpundu' crossed out. *Mbembu*, also spelled Mbemba, is a wood peach. About wild fruit-bearing trees, see *HIFL*, 526.
489. 'Matonga' in pencil, crossed out.
490. 'nearly' added above the line; 'five' written over 'four'?
491. For 'borassus' ['s' missing at the end of the line]: *Borassus flabellifer* L. should be the correct name.
492. Usowa (*HIFL*).
493. 's' missing.

African hunter armed with three heavy spears was seen by me while aiming[494] in his direction at an Umbawala, & doubtless suspecting that I was about to make a target of him, he set off also with the speed of an Umbawala.

October 22 Sunday, 1871

[Pencil] Mtambu
[Ink] Camp near River 4 h. 30 m. W. by N.

Saw for the first time the trees of which the Tanganyika mariners construc[t] their canoes.[495] They grow to the size & height of the loftiest pine trees, along the banks of the streams, and in the hollows of damp nullahs. All the streams & nullahs crossed on this day's march drained to the Malagarazi.

We camped this day on the banks of a river, the nearest approach to a river we have yet seen since leaving the vernal region on the sea-coast. As soon as we had unsaddled the donkeys, they made off for the river whose sweet & lucid water we had already tasted. While quenching their thirst a leopard sprang at the neck of one which happened to be a Myamwezi donkey the most intractable wilful & wild of its kind. The donkey uttered a terrible bray and was joined in chorus by the others which was so frightful a bray that the poor leopard must have thought he had attacked a small herd of lions and of course scampered away.

Shot a wild boar & a brace of ptarmigan with the Winchester Rifle. Lions roared the whole night close to the camp. There is a thick but narrow belt[496] of jungle lining both sides of this river which afford admirable dens for all sorts of wild beasts.

October 23 Monday, 1871

[Ink] Itaga in Rusawa. Sultan Imrera. N. N. W. 4h. ½

This district is thickly populated. People grow sweet potatoes, manioc, beans & matama. There is not one chicken in the village & the only goat that it[497] owend[498] we bought, a very lean & tough specimen. Mountains growing ever sublimer now surround the line of march. Sun getting hotter, & almost unbearable. Since leaving Mrera in Ukonongo we have been descending. Got a chill to-day from eating beans which previously had made me sick in the bowels.

---

494. 'at' crossed out.
495. Could be a 'Mvule', which Edward Coode Hore noted too: "Amongst the useful timber trees may be specially noticed the gigantic mvule, out of which the canoes are hewn." See Hore, *Missionary to Tanganyika, 1877–1888*, ed. James B. Wolf (London: Frank Cass, 1971), 93.
496. 'but narrow belt' added above the line.
497. 'it' written over 'was'.
498. 'owend', ms., for 'owned'.

October 24 Tuesday, 1871

[Ink] Halt to-day for rest

October 25 Wednesday, 1871

[Ink] Camp at base of Rusawa Mts. 2 ½ hours. N. N. East

We made a strike Easterly to-day in order to obtain a passage through the arc of mountains which environed us on the West & North. Crossed two or three small streams, along whose banks grew the wild date, Buffalo were numerous, but only one hartebeest & a guinea fowl were shot.

After resting yesterday the Wanguana did their utmost to prevent marching to day alleging as an excuse that no one knew the road, & that it would be better to stop one day more in order to have a talk with the people of Imrera's village, (but as I said, why did you not have a talk yesterday with them? If you do not know the road I will be your kirangozi.[499]

Towards night at this camp a Mshense shot a fat buffalo, and this turned out to be another cause of dissension. We were told by a Wakawendi Caravan that a wilderness of 2 days good marching had to be traversed before reaching a village. Immediately ensued a cry of No Posho, & as quickly[500] responded to by me Go & get it. Here is your cloth Go & buy. They were all too tired, they must have one day more to grind it in the village which lay to our right. But I was inexorable. All night long they were debating what to do, but I had forbidden all mention of a halt to Bombay & Mabruki upon pain of battle with me a la Heenan which[501] no Mgwana[502] ever relished.

October 26 Thursday, 1871

[Ink] Mtoni. N-N. East half way N.N.W., the other half N. 4 hours.

Early this morning I gave the order in as stern a tone[503] as possible to tie up & set out thus precluding any allusion to a halt. They were all in a fit mood to rebel & resort to extreme measures & the kirangozi was a fit man to lead them, but as no harsh word or offensive epithet challenged them the caravan set out without disturbance & by the time we had arrived at camp, they seemed to have forgotten the fat buffalo, & were in good humor.

---

499. Closing parenthesis missing.
500. 'as quickly' added above the line.
501. 'they' crossed out.
502. Singular of Wangwana.
503. 'a tone' added above the line.

Selim was flogged to day for eating the Mbembu fruit contrary to the orders & bringing on a second attack of dysentery.

A leopard was shot at, close to the[504] stream near which we camped.

A sugar loaf mountain was seen to the North West of the road. We ascended a lofty ridge – pretty animated – picturesque if you like is the character of the scenery of Kawendi nothing sublime. In the folds of this ridge we saw ruins of bomas.

October 27 Friday, 1871

[Ink] Camp on stream 5 hours. North half West

Found the khambi of Said bin Majid which we made use of. He had advanced thus far, but upon hearing unfavorable reports of the road had returned to Ujiji. We travelled close to a broad but[505] sluggish stream, the bed of which was choked up with gigantic grasses called Matete by the natives. The tracks of buffalo were numerous. Lions roared near the camp all night. On this stream were seen upwards of 50 large monkeys with beards.

October 28 Saturday, 1871

[Ink] Camp in Forest. 6 hours. North ½ East.

Just as we were leaving camp a herd of buffalo walked unconscious of the presence of man towards the stream near which we were camped. Only one however was killed the noise of the camp had already alarmed them, & they soon set off at a gallop towards the mountains which bounded the valley North East. One donkey died to-day. Bad water to-day. We walked over immense sheets of reddish rock having a metallic sound.

Famine in the camp. We live on mbembu & honey. There not being much grain at Itaga we had not sufficient & the road being unknown to us. According to the reports of the Itaga people we should have reached the Malagarazi to day, but we are two days off yet according to my map.

October 29 Sunday, 1871

[Ink] Camp in jungle. 5 h. 30 m. N. by E.

Descended 1000 feet down several terraces, through dismantled rocky gulleys, rocks all around us. Passed through miles upon miles of deserted land. At last descended

---

504. 'river' crossed out.
505. 'but' added above the line.

into a valley which would have been seductively pretty in Europe, but here was a hidden garden. Camped nea[506] a large rock, inscribed my name on a tree close to.

People very hungry & growling We have subsisted the last 2 days on mbemba & matamburu,[507] the last an acid fruit enclosed in a reddish pod. Not a grain of corn has been seen for 2 days & I have 45 mouths to feed. We are also unfortunate in game. The natives lied to us. Before retiring to sleep the Wanguana set up a loud prayer to Allah to give them food.

October 30 Monday, 1871

[Ink] Welled Nzogera. 2 ½ hours. N. by East.

Rhinoceros tracks abound, & the bois de vache of the buffalo travelling & desending the valley in which we camped last night, the humidity of the Malagarazi making itself felt in the air. Son of Nzogera posted on a lengthy triangul[ar] rock some 200 or 300 feet high, cunning dog, charged us 10 doti but contented himself with 7 ½ doti when we informed him that we would prefer paying it to his father, Nzogera, now at war with Locanda-Mira.[508] He is posted on an island.

We were all the afternoon diplomatizing with Nzogera's son.

People all happy at sight of food. 6 days posho & a goat & sheep were enough.

October 31 Tuesday, 1871

[Ink] Camp in jungle near village. 4 h. 15 m. N by East
[Pencil] Our road led E N.E for a considerable time after leaving the triangular post of Nzogera[509] in order to avoid a deep & impassable marsh that lay directly across our road to the Malagarazi. From the mountain the valley decended rapidly to this marsh, and it drains three extensive ranges. The crossing of the marsh caused terror to almost all my men for they had amongst their traditions a story of an Arab & his donkey, 35 slaves & 16 tusks of ivory being lost hereabouts in this marsh. It was a network of grass with a little decayed vegetation being mixed with it over which we walked. Underneath ran the stream. But this instable bridge moved for hundreds of yards on each side of the caravan like the swell of a sea after a storm. In the neighbourhood of the donkeys it waved in some places certainly a foot high. One donkey broke through

---

506. 'nea', ms., for near.
507. This is the name of the Sultan and his village visited by the Expedition on May 27 and 28, 1871. Is it a slip of the pen for 'mtamba' (*Ficus stuhlmannii*), a tree which produces a kind of fig, and is mentioned in HIFL, 522? 'Mbura' being a Kiswahili name for a tree also bearing edible fruits (*Par inari curatellifolia*), Stanley may have mixed up the two names (http://www.fao.org/forestry/25323-096344a3de335832e8f363c3ac5184a66.pdf).
508. Lokanda Mira (HIFL).
509. One word is unintelligible.

after a leap he has made, his feet broke holes through as if it had been thin ice, & with asinine stupidity doggedly lay until assisted by 10 men. The aggregate weight of the donkey & men caused a deep circular hollow in this bridge and I expected every minute to see the frail.

On reaching the other side we struck off North, found ourselves in a delightful country in every way suitable for agricultural settlements. Rocks rose here & there crowned with trees umbrageous under which nestled village after village. Sultan very greedy for Muhongo. Stopped on the road. Entering Luganda Nzogera's sons were out in full force for bakshish. 3 doti cheap. Wanguana feasting on flesh. Goats shukk.[510]

November 1 Wednesday, 1871

[Ink] Kiala, on the Malagarazi. N. W. 2 ¾ hours.
[Pencil] The Sultan last night relented & having received 3 doti permitted us to go – threatened to keep my kirangozi & stop the caravan. Striking N West and descending the slope of a mountain we soon saw the anxiously looked for Malagarazi a narrow & sluggish but deep stream running between mountains picturesque exceedingly, offering beutiful sites for settlements. The fish birds lined the trees on the banks. Villages thickly scattered about. Food abundant & cheap. Inhabitants more quiet & collected in their demeanor than the Wagogo though nothing abated in their pride & greed after Muhongo. Arriving at Kiala Eldest son of (Nzogera – now at war with Locanda Mira about the salt pans of Yambeho) waited an hour to exchange words. Made camp, 3 hours talking sufficed to elicit from Kiala the amount of his expectations 56 doti – in[511] 2 hours we reduced to 23. Sent a goat present – worth one shukka cordially thanked him for so munificently reciprocating the honga – 13 doti for Nzogera – 10 for Kiala – a faggot of Matete[512] stalks. Each bit of stalk represented a doti. Towards night while we were congratulating ourselves that the honga was settled came other words from Kiala, with 2 chiefs from the Capital, 2 doti more fine cloths for Kiala 2 doti for the King's Captains after paying which we should depart in peace. Until 10 P.M., poor Bombay & the kirangozi were negotiating arguing, quarreling until Bombay declared they would talk him mad if it lasted much longer. Their demands were settled.

---

510. End of the line unclear.
511. 'in' added above the line.
512. The word stands for reeds.

November 2 Thursday, 1871

[Pencil] Ihata, island in the Malargarazi.[513] 1 ½ hour. West. River makes a curve North from Kiala.[514]

Arrived before the island of Ihata about 5 P.M. when we at once proceeded to cross. The demand was first for 2 doti of cloth & 4 fundo of beads (samesame). 4 men were first permitted to cross with their loads, the 2 slave boatmen were ordered to halt on the other side, & another demand was made. The khete of Samesame were too short, 2 fundo more must be added before the crossing should proceed. These 2 fundo were given but not without considerable demurring on the part of Bombay & the kirangozi. Three times the canoes crossed backwards & forwards when there was another clamoring demand, 5 khete for the man who showed us the road, a kuto or shukka for the head man of the ferry, & a kuto or shukka for a babbling native the new covenanted brother of Jumah who did nothing but babble to no purpose but to increase the clamor. About sunset we endeavored to cross the donkeys. Simba went in first, bravely enough, and had arrived at the middle of the stream when he struggled, a crocodile was at his throat dragging him down. The struggles were terrific. Chompereh was dragging on the rope with all his might, but there must have arrived other crocodiles, for the poor animal suddenly sank like lead. The water at this place was about fifteen feet deep. We had seen the light brown heads[515] the glittering eyes and the ridgy trail of their bodies in the water, and I had shot one through the head with a 2 ounce ball. Left the other donkey on the other side in charge of Bombay. This morning about 9 A.M. the other donkey was crossed safely by the natives. They spat a chewed weed into the water which they said was medicine. Early in the morning & at night nothing can cross, as the crocodiles are in the water, but from 9 A.M. to 2 P.M. animals have been crossed in safety. Salt pans in the valley. Wash the salt in a trough. Thank God, it's finished. We propose to march in the after noon.

November 3 Friday, 1871

[Ink] Isinga. Sultan Katalambula.
Katalambula N.N.W. 1 ¼ hour.[516]

What talk, what excitement, what anxiety have we suffered since our arrival in Uvinza. Worse than Ugogo, and their greed is more esurient. The people are more

---

513. Here 'Malagarazi' is spelled 'Malargarazi'.
514. This sentence has been added between two lines.
515. 'and' crossed out.
516. In his fifth despatch (Bennett, *Stanley's Despatches*, 82–83), Stanley pretends to be quoting his November 3, 1871, Journal. In fact, his notes are not an exact copy of it, and he adds the news of Livingstone that a caravan of Waguhha gave him the next day.

noisy especially[517] those on the banks of the river. On crossing to the Northern side we seem to have arrived among new people. They appear more amiable, & more disposed to assist caravans than those on the Southern. Though their greed for cloth & beads is about equal. Before crossing the soldiers captured our native Kirangozi having recognized in him a spy in Locanda Mira's employ. The cry for rope to tie him was quickly responded to for every tree around them furnished them with enough bark to tie a[518] dozen spies. They took him to Kwi Kuru or the capital of Nzogera who is living on an island in the Malagarazi well guarded by crocodiles.

 We crossed the donkey with the aid of a Mganga, who spat chewed leaves of a tree which grows close to the river. He told us he could cross at any time after rubbing his body with these chewed leaves. He fills his mouth with this medicine into the water on each side as he swims, & the crocodiles will not attack him.

 We set out from the banks of the river with 2 new kirangozis furnished us by the old man (Usenge his name) of the ferry. Arriving at Isinga after traversing a saline plain which as we advanced into the interior grew wonderfully fertile, we were told by our native kirangozis that to morrow's march would have to be made with great caution as a band[519] the Warinza of Nzogera under Makumbi a great chief was returning from war – and it was[520] their custom to leave nothing behind them at such times. Intoxicated with victory they attacked villages, & caravans capturing live stock, slaves, and taking bales. The result of a month's campaign against Locanda Mira, were ten villages[521] captured with several men[522] killed[523] & a son of Locanda Mira was killed, while only 5 men of Nzogera were lost from thirst in crossing a saline desert. Over drinking.

November 4 Saturday, 1871

5 ½ x 2 ¼ =13 ¼[524]

Kawanga N.N.W. 5 ½ hours. (Uhha)

 Started early, with great caution & continued silence walked through the dwarf jungle now surrounded us, & which as we advanced grew shorter & shorter until by the time we had arrived at Kawanga,[525] villages were seen by the score on the plain. Sometimes one – sometimes a dozen, or a score of beehive huts formed of straw

---

 517. 'of' crossed out.
 518. 'hundre' crossed out.
 519. 'a band' added above the line.
 520. 'with' crossed out.
 521. 'being' crossed out.
 522. 'men' written above 'being' crossed out.
 523. '& a son of Locanda Mira was killed' added between two lines.
 524. The distance in miles.
 525. 'it had' crossed out.

formed a village – They were evidently living in perfect security for not one was surrounded with a boma a narrow dry[526] ditch runing North East & South West sufficed as a boundary line between Uhha & Uvinza. Their mode of life was the same, except the salutation. They folded each other hands, saying wake, wake, waky, waky, Huh, huh, like the Watusi. Dress Goat-skin, throw with a loop over one shoulder. Had solid brass collar and long coil[527] bracelets of wire over their wrists, but some like the Wanyamuezi wore ivory bracelets. The polished tusks of a boar seem to be a favorite ornament for the neck.

  Met a caravan of Waguhha bound to Unyanyembe with ivory & Ujiji they informed me that, the Musungu with a white beard, & wearing hat & shoes had returned from Maniema.[528]

[Pencil] Muhongo 12 doti

November 5 Sunday, 1871

[Pencil] Lukomo in Kimeni[529] – Mutware. Mionvu.
On the banks of the Pombwe runing S.W.
1 hour. N. N. W. Muhongo 75 doti

[Ink] The[530] talk about the muhongo last night lasted until 12 P.M. when I finally gave Bombay permission to settle it on the condition that I be allowed to pass to the Rusugi without paying more. At dawn this morning we started intending to make a good day's march of it and so get out of the country before we were utterly ruined. We were about crossing the stream Pombwe when we were halted by four messengers from the Mutware Mionvu, who asked us what we meant by passing through the country without paying the King's dues. He was informed that the Sultan had received his at the village of Kawaga. We were obliged to halt until the messenger sent had seen it.[531] Soon after his departure the Mutware himself came robed in new[532] crimson Joho, and a piece of American sheeting about his head and followed by a dozen spearmen, said "Yambo" cordially – then retired to consult by themselves. Result was after much useless talk on our part that we were compelled to go to the boma of Lukomo. Meanwhile as it was now noon the messenger was late coming we camped. Mionvu was under the shade making up listlessly a faggot of matete sticks, which we were to pay. We did pay 65[533] doti to the Sultan 6 doti to the Mutware, 5 doti to his sub.

  526. 'narrow dry' written above ['small'?] crossed out.
  527. 'coil' added above the line.
  528. In *HIFL*, this encounter takes place on November 3, 1871.
  529. Kimenyi (*HIFL*).
  530. 'The' in pencil.
  531. 'seen it' written above 'received his' crossed out.
  532. 'new' added above the line.
  533. '65' written over '64'.

And my God, what talk, what quarreling. About sunset it was settled, fore I perceive we are doomed to be ruined.

Water of this country as well as of Uvinza bad slightly saline. Malagarazi also.

November 6 Monday, 1871

[Ink] Kabirigi.[534] 4 hours. W.N.W. River Kanengi

At dawn we were on the road very silent & sad, not at all certain that we should ever reach Ujiji though we were so close to it & heard news of Livingstone.

We crossed the Pombwe this time[535] with a guide & crossed over 4 hours of country a mere plain slowly heaving higher towards the North, the depression through which the Malagarazi flowed was yet in sight. Villages of straw huts rose to view every where. Food was cheap, milk plentiful, butter good, goats, a shukka each. Crossing the Kanengi R. we came to a boma which we were told was our camp, we were in the country of the King's brother, & the King's brothers village was in sight of our boma. The announcement was anything but welcome, as soon after our arrival came a demand from the King's brother for 30 doti. We had been told by the Mutware that the honga of Kimeni was settled, and that we might travel to the Rusugi without paying more. This was the second time the lie was told and we are deceived.

In Kabirigi which is a large boma cont ing[536] two or three huts occupied by Watusi shepherds & their cattle we met 4 slaves of Thani bin Abdullah. These we enlisted by munificent gifts of cloth to talk for us & reduce the honga. Succeded to 26 doti. Much profond diplomacy on both sides. Tired of paying Muhonga which would absolutely deprive us of every yard of cloth, we contracted with these to guide us through the jungle to Ukaranga 12 doti, were paid for the services of two. They said as far as Ujiji we should have to pay no honga. There were 4 places more in Antari from which we were thus relieved & I was able to assist Livingstone.

November 7 Tuesday, 1871

[Ink] Lake. Musunia.[537] Rusugi R. 5[538] hours, Musunia Lake 4[539] hours. West ½ North.

Three hours before dawn we left Kabirigi very quietly without waking a single native. Strict silence had been ordered. We took for an hour a South West course then led straight west. By dawn we were in sight of the swift Rusugi, the banks

---

534. Kahirigi (*HIFL*).
535. 'under' crossed out.
536. 'cont ing', ms., for 'containing', at the end of the line.
537. Musunya (*HIFL*).
538. '5' written over '3'?
539. '4' written over '6'?

on both sides alive with buffalo, eland, antelope. It was very tempting but stayed our hands, crossed the Rusugi at a ford, and came across four natives carrying salt from Uvinza, who fled instantly. We halted until they were well out of sight then continued our course West. About an hour after leaving the river, we left the naked plain, and entered an extensive bamboo jungle. A long march brought us in sight of a small Lake wherein sported numbers of Kiboko[540]-Hippo-potamus. During the Masika season this Lake extends to about 3 miles in-length by 2 in bradth. We camped at Musuna[541] and were very silent.

2 ½ x 4 = 10[542]

November 8 Wednesday, 1871

[Ink] Sunuzzi River. Rugufu River 4 ½ hours. Sunuzzi River 3 hours W. N. W. Uhha. Antari.

Through bamboo jungle and over strips of naked plain we made our way for an hour came to another large pool, ducks snipe & wagtail.[543] Game abundant and remarkably tame. 3 ½ hours brought us to the broad & sluggish Rugufu – which I[544] would have taken for a long swamp – had I not been told it was the Rugufu. Halted here & cooked a breakfast, inside a small jungle. Heard the thunder of the Tanganika beating against Kabogo. Crossed extensive beds of primitive rock, & boulders thickly strewn about. Camped on the small Sunuzzi stream, & very very still though glad having run a gauntlet between several villages. Those under the rule of the Mutware on our left & those under the immediate rule of the King on our right.

November 9 Thursday, 1871

[Ink] 9 ½ x 2 ½[545]

Niamtaga Boma. Ukaranga 9 ½ hours. W by N ½ N.
on the Mtawe River

Two hours before dawn we left our camp, and struck off N by W lit by moon. Just at dawn met a small native caravan bound to Kimeni carrying salt. This caused

---

540. *Kiboko* is the Swahili word for hippos.
541. 'Musuna', ms., for Musunia or Musunya.
542. As before, Stanley estimates the distance by multiplying the length of the march by an average speed of 2½ miles per hour. In *HIFL* (398), Stanley placed here a long story of a woman that he whipped to make her stop screaming. Fiction or reality—or an attempt by him to add drama to a journey lacking trouble?
543. A passerine bird (genus *Motacilla*).
544. 'I' written over 'we'.
545. Usual for estimating the distance. See previous notes explaining these operations in the upper margin.

great consternation. We muzzled our milch goats, and slaughtered our chickens. We[546] were now travelling on the caravan road & in a few minutes the dawn permitted us to see villages all around us, which were at the base of the mountains range from which the Rusugi & other streams issue. In a great fright we plunged into the jungle again. We heard voices and prepared for a fight believing that the alarm was given & we were pursued. If we were we soon lost sight of the villages & the friendly jungle surrounded us on all sides. Passed several beautiful spots, and suny valleys containg[547] sweet water. In a short time we entered Ukaraga & were relieved of all trouble. Followed the great road boldly.

Arrived at the Mkuti river where two swift streams united & formed the Mkuti river, it empties itself into the Ruche River. The villages of the Wakaranga were all around us, but the people were sorely frightened at the sight of our flag, & many of them fled among whom was the Wami or king. Leaving these villages on the banks of the Mkuti, we entered a jungle & in an hour entered the Capital Niamtaga. The drums beat to arms every where & the jungle became alive with fugitives. We sent messengers ahead to inform the natives that we were not Ruga Ruga of Mirambo, or of those of Locanda Mira. King returned, visited me laughed together at the fright, exchanged presents & friendly words.

November 10 Friday, 1871

[The whole page crossed out with several perpendicular lines]
[Ink] Bandareen Ujiji 6 hours. West by S.

Left Niamtaga at dawn Wami at the gate to bid us good bye. Entered a bamboo jungle which after a slight ascent up the slope of a hill across two or three dry watercourses, beds of which showed traces of[548] furious torrents commenced our descent down to the valley of the Ruche which was separated by one low hilly prolongation hog-backed shape from the Bunder or port of Ujiji. After 4 ½ hours crossed the Ruche stream 15 yards broad 2 feet deep at the ford current four miles the hour, clear & sweet water as distinguished from all the streams & rivers running through Uhha & Uvinza. Having ascended the hog back hill commenced firing our guns. Mode of announcing new comers in Africa soon after the Wanguana residing in Ujiji came running up to ascertain the cause, much astonished to find it to be a caravan from Unyanyembe and led by a White man. Among those colored citizens of Ujiji thus eager were Chuma & two other men in the employ of Dr. Livingstone. Then Livingstone was in very deed in Ujiji. "Yes". Sure? Quite sure." Joy, heart beat fast, had

---

546. Stanley dramatized the situation in *HIFL* (402): "I ordered the goats to be slaughtered and left on the road…"
547. 'containg', ms., for 'containing'.
548. 'traces of' written above 'violent' crossed out.

to keep control over my emotions lest my face might betray them, or detract from the dignity of a White man appearing under such circumstances. But what would I not have given for a bit of friendly wilderness wherein I might vent my joy in some mad freaks, such as idiotically biting my hand, turning a summersault, slashing at trees, or something in order to purge these exciting feelings, before appearing in the presence of Livingstone. Soon after amid a large concourse of Arabs & blacks, I saw a pale looking White man, in a faded blue cap, with an arc beak, tarnished gold lace, red Joho jacket, sheeting shirt, tweed pants. As I saw him, I dismounted.

November 11 and 12, 1871[549]

[This page is missing. It seems to have been torn out. There is a loose page for October 24–25, which would have been attached to pages November 11 and 12.]

November 13 Monday, 1871

[Ink] Halt.

November 14 Tuesday, 1871

[Ink] Halt.

L. proposed to me to go with him & complete his work. It is an honor, but I must do my duty, which is to hurry to the coast & London & give the News to the "Herald"

November 15 Wednesday

[Ink] Halt

November 16 Thursday, 1871

[Ink] Halt[550]

[Pencil] Tanganika. Kigoma[551]

Started at dawn, found canoes too small for party, thinned it. Wajiji had loaded it with 10 bags of salt, discharged it started again. Canoes very cranky took down mast & sail. Steered, for Cape & Island of Bangwe, 2 hours. Snakes light brown

---

549. The account of the meeting is in Journal S.A. 11.
550. 'Halt' crossed out.
551. Under the lines 3 to 9, a sketch of Livingstone's head.

body, sunning on the shingle, bank of red-brown[552] soil mixed in with stones. Wind, East. The Eastern side deeply indented with bays, many affording excellent harbors, efficient protection from all winds. Arrived at Kigoma 10 A.M. western side of the harbor, opposite is Gunga harbor about a mile broad & long, but the bay is about 4 miles deep by about 2 ½ in breadth. 12 miles.

[Ink] On starting at dawn we find the wind blows from East, about ten A.M. it is North -12 to a little after sunset from South West.

Shot a dog faced monkey on Friday measure 4 ft 09 in[553] from tip of nose to tip of tail, face was 8 ½ inches long, body weighed about 100 pounds, teeth remarkably long canine 1 ½ inch long, had no mane or tuft at end of tail, but had long hair over his body.

Saw a large lizard (Monitor terrestris) 2 feet ½ long.

Chickens sold at Zassi at one khete each.

November 17 Friday, 1871

[Pencil] Halt.[554] [Ink] Niasanga. Tanganyika Lake. 12 miles
[Pencil] Determined after a decision of D[r] Livingstone to accompany him to Usige in order to find out exactly whether the river Rushizi flowed out or into the Tanganyika.

[Ink] Started at dawn. When about 4 miles from Kigoma, & half a mile from shore above which steep & lofty hills rose sounded & found 35 fathom. The color of the water was dark green. Saw a hippopotamus soon after starting within a sheltered nook. Our journey of this day ran by[555] most beautifully little nooks wherein fishermen had built their huts, and above which on the steep slopes their wives had contributed to the family by cultivating patches of land. Cassava, matama, & plaintains seemed to be the staple products. The canoes were drawn up on the strip of[556] pebbly beach under the shelter of the palm trees. Very picturesque indeed was the entire journey. It seemed to me[557] as if I were still journeying along the shores of Pontus, these rounded hills, these receding bays, and capes, & the noble array of tree clothed hills that rose steep & wooded above us.

Saw a gigantic lizard about 2 ½ feet long short legs about 3 inches high waddled as it ran. Close to the (about half a mile from the Kabongwe & a mile from[558]

---

552. 'red' added above the line.
553. 'ft and in.' written above '409'. Most probably a yellow baboon (*Papio cynocephalus*).
554. 'Halt' crossed out in ink.
555. 'by' added above the line.
556. 'strip of' added above the line.
557. 'to me' added above the line.
558. 'a mile from' added above the line.

the Cape Kazinga[559] halted[560] at the village of Niasanga. Struck our tent under a banyan tree. Doctor suffers considerably from diarrhoe[a] which seems to be of a chronic nature.

November 18 Saturday, 1871

[Ink] Zassi, Ujiji[561] Tanganyika 4 ½ hours.

Started at dawn, & continued our journey along the Eastern Shore which grew more romant[ic] & picturesque as we proceeded. The mountains towered above us to the height of about 2000 or 2500 feet above the Lake. The scenery rivals the best portions around Lake George or the Hudson. The cosy nooks at the head of the many small bays constitute most lovely features, filled in as they are with the ever beautiful palms, & umbrageous trees of the tropical Africa. These have all been taken possession of by fishermen whose conical huts of the beehive shape peep[562] from between the palms. The shores are thus extremely populous. Every terrace, small plateau, & level bit of ground are occupied. All these collections of huts have their canoes drawn up, their nets[563] hung up to dry.

One of the prettiest scenes of this nature we saw at a place called Mgongo a level amphi theatral[564] site through which ran a purling little stream, crowded with the dark green & graceful foliage of the palm & the light green plantain fronds. About a mile from shore sounded opposite Mgongo found 35 fathom. Coming abreast of Kirassa 2 miles further up, abreast of a lofty – conical hill which the Doctor thought was about 700 feet above the Lake, let go whole length of line 115 fathom found no bottom 1 ½ mile from shore. In drawing it up line parted, but this was the shortest of two lines we possessed.

November 19 Sunday, 1871

[Ink] Nyabigma, Urundi
Muzimu is an island peopled by Babwar.
Shot a monkey 5 feet long standing 3 feet high had an enormous head & teeth, canine inch & a half long.
The shores of the Tanganyika are surpassingly lovely.

---

559. Closing bracket missing.
560. 'under' crossed out.
561. 'Ujiji' written in a paler ink, same color and same hand as the next page.
562. 'in' crossed out.
563. 'drawn' crossed out.
564. One of Stanley's neologisms?

River Mabala passed to day is the boundary between Ujiji & Urundi. From Kisongo Cape to Kirassa Hills, slopes of mountains all wooded. Urundi is shorn of these but smooth topped & green.

Nyabigma is a sandy island. Here we prepared for a tuzzle against the Barundi of 2 stages ahead who were said to be hostile by distributing powder ball & flints.

Chickens abundant – a khete of same-same each. Soldiers fed on them.

Passed Kagunga a large village peopled by Barundi who ran away from their homes on Cape Kitunda. Cows and canoes in abundant[565] numbers.

Wajiji inhale the tobacco through the nose. Only occasionally is a pipe seen. A treatise could be written upon African tobacco smoking. As far as Unyanyembe.

November 20 Monday, 1871

[Ink] Mukungu. Urundi. 4 hours

Camped here on 5th day. At night were robbed of 1 bag of Flour 500 Cartridges of Double Barrel, Winchester & Starr Pistol Cartridges, 1 Sounding Line.

The fault was the excessive stupor of sleep into which the guardians of the boat Bombay & Susi had fallen.

November 21 Tuesday, 1871

[Ink] Mugeyo. Urundi

7 hours to Murembwe River

took lunch. 6 hours to a little above Damah River. 6 hours to Mugeyo. Total 19 hours at 2 ½ miles an hour. 47 ½ miles. arrived at Mugeyo about 3 A.M. of the 22nd.

November 22 Wednesday, 1871

[Ink] Magala, Urundi. 2 ½ hours

Arrived at Magala from Mugeyo. Soldiers very tired, made a halt here determined to rest. Mutware & people turned out to be very good. Got a sheep & milk from him, & we enjoyed it very much.

November 23 Thursday, 1871

[Ink] Kisuka Pt. Usige. 3 ½ hours.

A storm caught us but it was very fair wind and we drove before it a little in order to reach the safe anchorage which the port of the village hidden amongst dense reeds afforded.

---

565. 'abundant' written over 'abundance'.

November 24 Friday, 1871

[Ink] Mukanigi. Usige. 1 hour. N. by East.
Arrived past Mugera Delta to Mukanigi – Mokamba's[566] village. Put up in a little hut – very comfortable – but I had a terrible fever, here the result of exposure & sleeping amogst the dense reeds in the neighborhood of swamp where the luxurious matete grass and papyrus flourished.

November 25 Saturday, 1871

[Ink] Mukanigi. Usige.
 Sick of a fever & therefore a halt. The Doctor nurses me very well. Mokamba came to see us & after receiving his presents 10 doti, and 5 fundo cloth principally Kaniki sent us an ox, a sheep & a goat.

November 26 Sunday, 1871

[Ink] Mukanigi. Usige.
Sick of a fever & a halt until dusk. when we departed for Mugihawa[567] – Ruhinga's country who is the brother (eldest) of Mokamba. At 4 A.M. arrived across having pulled from 7 P.M. to 4 A.M. 9 hours at 2 ½ miles 22 ½ miles.

November 27 Monday, 1871

[Ink] Mugihawa. Uringa.[568]
Awaking found ourselves at the head of the Lake in the Delta of the Rusizi a broad & flat projection of land, through which the Rusizi with its waters augmented by the Ruanda entered the Tanganyika by 3 mouths
first 8 yds broad, very rapid & shallow
2nd 10[569] yds " , rapid but slower
3rd 6[570] yds " , deep but slow.

---

566. Mukamba (*HIFL*).
567. Mugihewa (*HIFL*).
568. Uringa =Ruwenga. "Ruwenga comprises the countries of Ruwenga and Mugihewa" (*HIFL*, 502).
569. '10' written over '8'.
570. '6' written over '5'.

November 28 Tuesday, 1871

[Ink] Mugihawa. Uringa

Exchanged presents with Ruhinga, sent off our canoe for Mukamba and eight soldiers with guns, having left two with him already for his protection.

Meet a most eccentric Mgwana one of the greatest of liars – most intriguing, yet most pious. It was elevating to hear his fervent Barikalla Inshallahs & Mashallahs upon the utterance of the least commonplace remark. He prevented us from getting any ivory from Ruhinga or Mokamba.

November 29 Wednesday

[Ink] Mugihawa. Uringa.

Went out to hunt, shot 2 fine geese, 1 ibis religiosa 1 duck & a crane.

November 30 Thursday, 1871

[Ink] Mugihawa. Uringa.

We delivered over the Muhongo to the good natured chief Ruhinga. The women have been celebrating Ruhinga's recovery from sickness, by besmearing their faces & heads with a pasty compound of dourra flour and arming themselves with their husbands & fathers' spears go about singing, and at certain intervals[571] relieve its monotony with dancing. For the first time since the day I arrived on the Tanganyika it rained to-day.

December 1 Friday, 1871

[Ink] Mugihawa. Uringa.

Ruhinga came to see us this morning and brought an immense two gallon gourd to drink coffee in. We had invited him last night to sit down & take a cup – & he had been pleased to defer the pleasure until this morning in order to give a whole day towards it. He had dressed himself with unusual care having a gay Manchester print folded about him like a toga.

December 2 Saturday, 1871

[Ink] Mugihawa. Uringa.

Our canoe went over to Mukanigi to day to fetch over Mukamba. His women & son have been very kind to us. Altogether we have had an ox, 3 sheep, fat browned tails,

---

571. 'have' crossed out.

and any number of pots of milk. They hollow these milk pots very well all through Africa. They hold from a quart to a gallon, & are beautifully white & clean. Though the churning gourd is by no means kept so clean.

December 3 Sunday, 1871

Mugihawa Uringa

To day we churned our milk presents & succeeded in making about 3 lbs of nice yellow fresh butter which was a great treat. We also made several pounds of cheese. The Doctor took a series of observations for Longitude. Chronometer did not go, but the D. fixed a rifle shell to the key and succeeded in making it go for an hour.

December 4 Monday, 1871

[Ink] **Mugihawa. Uringa**

Towards late in the afternoon the canoe & men sent after Mukamba returned bringing with them Mukamba & his force of 60 canoes. After landing his warriors surrounded him, and setting up a song while their arms encircled one another marched for Ruhinga's house. The women of Mugihawa came out to join in chorus, & dancing. Then followed Mukamba's wife & daughter very light complexioned, a sweet force of women came out to meet her dancing, like the companions of Miriam.

December 5 Tuesday, 1871

[Ink] **Mugihawa. Uringa**

Not feeling very well I left the Doctor to go alone to bid farewell to Mukamba & carry the parting present.

Went out in the morning to examine the bays, on Warumashania's[572] side.[573] were 3, Ruziz[574] 4, 2 more to us, 1 beyond us, 10 bays altogether.

December 6 Wednesday, 1871

[Pencil] **Mugihawa**[575]

Still here, but we purpose to go & sleep near the Lake to night so as to be off early to-morrow morning.

---

572. Warumashanya (*HIFL*).
573. One word under an ink spot there ?
574. Final "i" missing.
575. Mugihewa (*HIFL*).

D. took a series of observations to-day for longitude – & observations from Acanaur[576] last night for latitude 3. 19° – So.[577] mean latitude.

December 7 Thursday, 1871

[Ink] Kakumba,[578] near Chigongo River, & Cape.
[Pencil] From Mugihawa we went round South of the Katangara Islands and approached the highlands of Uashi near the boundary line between Mokamba's country & Uvira separated from each other by a wide ravine, in the bottom of which grew the tall beautiful & straight trees out of which the natives make their canoes. Their tall smooth grey trunks are topped with a round crown of deep green foliage. Passed Kanyamabengu river close to the market place of Kirabula – the extreme[579] point of Burton & Speke's Exploration of the Tanganyika. Half an hour south we halted at Kavimba[580] to cook breakfast. Here we met a party of plundered Wajiji who had been there punished for trying to evade the tribute to the Mutware.

[Ink] River Chigongo[581] at the point Kakumba small & rapid.
    Pt Kakumba nearly opposte Kisuka
S. by East from Kavimba.

December 8 Friday, 1871

[Ink] New York Herald Islets[582] 3° 41 South 5 hours.
After coffee before sunrise we quickly left our camp. Our fires had attracted the sharp eyed & suspicious fishermen of Kukamba, but the precautions we had taken proved an effectual safeguard against thieves. The Western shores are much bolder an outline than the Eastern & slightly loftier. There is a back ridge on this side as well as on the other which attains the average altitude of about 3 000 feet, and is the vanguard of the multitude of mountains which rise beyond. Within its folds however though the uniformity of the ridge itself is seldom broken rise hills isolated & of considerable magnitude precipitous & abrupt & sometimes of singular scenic beauty, but the majority of them have the rounded heaving top, or a tabular summit. The great ridge shoots out at intervals promontorial projection of sloping outline which on the map I have designated capes, or Pts. As soon as we rounded one of these lengthy capes up

---

576. 'Acanaur' *for* 'Achernar' *or* 'Achenar', the brightest star in the constellation Eridanus, best observed from the Southern hemisphere in November. Same mention in Journal S.A. 73.
577. '1' seems to be written over '4'. Stanley kept 3°.19 in *HIFL*, 506.
578. Kukumba (*HIFL*).
579. 'north' crossed out.
580. 'Kavimba' written in ink.
581. Kigongo (*HIFL*).
582. Name chosen by Livingstone, according to Stanley (*HIFL*, 510).

went our compasses to take bearings of distant points, & prominent objects. (See Note Book marked "Cash" outside)

December 9 Saturday, 1871

[Ink] Cape Luvumba. Basansi.[583]

At dawn set off. Once or twice we had been visited during the night, but the watchfulness of our people prevented any marauding. It seemed to me however that the people of the opposite shore who had visited us were prurient for the opportunity and our men seemed to be affected by it if we may judge from the hurry they were in to leave.

Coming to Cape Kabogi we left the Wavira & came to the Basansi we knew they were diffent[584] from the greeting "Maholo" which they gave us while the Wavira said "Wake". Arriving at Cape Luvumba, a sloping projection of the[585] mountain ridge which binds the Lake on the West, we shoved in, and made our camp. The natives who crowded about us were quiet & civil enough. They had bands of straw bound around their heads & their heads were shaved off after the eccentric manner of the Wajiji & Warundi. The women carried long staffs iron spiked at one end and carved at the other. These wore huge bunches of hair at the backs of their heads as if a chigon had been parted & a half adorned each back side of the head. There was but a sluggish disposition to trade amongst these people for the article they most needed was as might be expected among people travelling in canoes. This was meat.[586] Somewhat scarce. A few pink, blue & red beads, were taken in exchange for cassava which is here of the finest. Feeling somewhat drowsy I lay down for a nap & so did the Doctor. I had hardly been asleep half an hour when I was roused up by the boy Selim, with "Get up Master the soldiers are packing up & going to run away." The facts were indeed as Selim stated. The soldiers were packing up & going to run away.

December 10 Sunday, 1871

[Ink] Mukungu. Urundi.

From 4. 30 P.M. yesterday to 10 A.M. this morning at 2 ½ miles an hour 17 ½ hours = 43 miles.

---

583. In his book, Stanley kept the prefix Wa- when transcribing the name of this people as he did for any other, but he noted, "The Wasansi – or Basansi, as Dr Livingstone thinks they should be called…" (*HIFL*, 556). It shows the influence of Livingstone on Stanley's redaction of his journal.
584. 'diffent', ms., for 'different'.
585. 'the' added above the line.
586. This sentence was added between two lines, to be placed before 'somewhat scarce', according to Stanley's indication in the text. It would be more appropriate if placed after 'somewhat scarce'.

continued from 9th Dec. 1871

because soon after I had fallen asleep the son of the chief soon followed by his father & another chief of a village nearby had come into the camp excessively drunk, and excited, & had begun to spit at the soldiers & challenge them to fight, besides making indecent gestures, & once or twice endangered a man's life by slashing at him with a cane knife or billhook. The foolish young fellow was countenanced by the chiefs. They were followed by quite a crowd of people armed with spears, and hatchets, half of whom seemed to be of opinion that it were better not to trouble the Wanguana & the other half willing enough to engage in war. It was very foolish of the natives, for it needed only our word of command to scatter them right and left, but the Doctor and I were[587] of opinion that it were better to quiet the chiefs with presents rather than take offence at a drunken boy's extravagant freaks. So we set to listen patiently to what they had to say, which was as follows. The people of Basansi were subjects of Kisesa Sultan of Muzimu Island. Some two years ago during which there has been a cessation of trade between Kisesa's people & the Wujiji & Wanguana, Mombo the son of the Sultan had during a visit on

December 11 Monday 1871

[Ink] Zassi. River & Village 7 hours 21 miles.
From Cape Kitunda to South Pt of Muzimu Island a little South of W. S. W.
Kitunda to Zassi S. S East
"   " Kagunga S. E. ½ E.
South Point of Muzimu Island direct West of Zassi River & Village.

continued from page Dec 10th 1871

business to Ujiji been arrested & beaten from which soon after his return to Muzimu he died. (He has been caught peeping into the harem of an Arab as we subsequently learned). This was the cause of their hostility to us, & they saw no difference between us & Wanguana. Though the Doctor baring his arm earnestly protested against any such comparison. Musimu & Basansi are famed for the production of grain – dowora or matama.[588] When they traded with Ujiji Arabs could get from 30 to 50 bundles of[589] for 1 shukka of cloth. After a long tedious talk of the chief who during it cut himself across the knee deliberately asserted it to be the work of a Mguana he consented to receive 2 ½ doti & 5 fundo of beads as expiating for the deed of killing the son of the

587. 'evidently' crossed out.
588. 'Dowora' for 'dourra'. Stanley indicates an Arabic origin for this name of the holcus sorghum (*HIFL*, 526).
589. 'of' repeated twice.

Sultan Kisesa. But as we saw that he was inclined to rupture, we departed, the storm having abated & pulled across the Lake all night. We could have killed all.

December 12 Tuesday 1871

[Ink] To Niasanga. 3 hours – 7 ½ miles.
From Zassi to Niasanga, I felt very sick & the Doctor seeing my state obligingly turned the canoe in-shore at this place. It was the fever induced by a residence in the Delta of the Rusizi.

December 13 Wednesday, 1871

[Ink] Arrive at Ujiji at 1 P.M. 7 hours pulling from Niasanga at good 3 miles an hour.
Entered the port very quietly without any firing of guns, as we are short of powder and ball. As we landed we were met by our soldiers and the chief Arabs of Ujiji.
Mabruki had lots to tell of what had occurred during our absence. The faithful fellow had done excellently. Kalulu had scalded himself & got a frightful sore on his chest. Marora had been tied in chains for hitting my donkey with a stone or allowing him to be hit while he looked after them. Bill Alli had been making a row in the market place & destroying a poor woman's goods.
Most welcome was a letter from American Consul at Zanzibar waiting for me dated June 11th 1871.[590]

December 14 Thursday 1871

[Ink] Ujiji.
To day is resting day & visiting day. The Arabs call to congratulate Munia Kheri[591] & Mwhammed bin Sali, Munia Bwiri, and Mohammed bin Khari &c.
We asked Munia Kheri for his canoe to assist us in taking the goods down to Tongwe whence we propose to march for Unyanyembe by the Ugala road thus avoiding all Muhongo paying roads. The soldiers were also allotted their respective loads. We have got 40 men altogether, all armed & willing to carry goods, so that we shall have no trouble on that score.

---

590. See Appendix, S.A. 2654, Letter from Francis R. Webb to Stanley, Zanzibar, June 11, 1871.
591. Muniyi Kheri (S.A. 8); Moeni Kheri (*HIFL*, 565); Moenyeghere (*LJ* 2:154). A notable Arab of Ujiji who witnessed how Shereef sold off all Livingstone's goods.

December 15 Friday 1871

[Ink] Ujiji

I have commenced to work to get a saddle made for Livingstone's donkey, so that he can ride on his proposed march to Unyanyembe. We are also buying up the milch goats to be found in the market, to supply us with milk & meat on the road. Each goat yields a pint of milk. We have got five now.

December 16 Saturday 1871

[Ink] Ujiji.

At work on the Doctors[592] saddle to day. Very hard. Selim is helping me. The Doctor says he has finished all his despatches – all every one and copied them so as I am not going to ask him to stop until I finish writing. I expect we shall be off to Unyanyembe in a few days.

I made a second proposition to Livingstone to-day to write some letters to the New York Herald at £20 per letter of 8 pages of foolscap pretty close writing which will be equal to 400 lines of about 8 words each = 3200 words. He asked if I thought that America might be made to assist in suppressing the horrible slave trade of Africa. I said that whatever views he may have about the slave trade would be published, and read by the thousands of the Herald's readers & from thence would be copied & quoted into other journals, so that it must bear fruit one way or the other if he stuck to it, and did not give it up.

December 17 Sunday 1871

[Ink] Ujiji.

Had prayers to-day. The Doctor spoke to Habay (chief) yesterday about the Wajiji to pull boats back from Tongwe. So we propose soon to turn our faces towards Unyanyembe. I showed Rob Roy[593]'s introduction to Doctor to-day. He said he knew his mother & father very well – or his sister & father I forget which. He gave me a bit of history about East Indiaman Kent his father was Commander of ship.[594]

---

592. 'Doctors', ms., for 'Doctor's'.

593. See Appendix, S.A. 480, Letter of Introduction from John MacGregor to D. Livingstone, Suez, November 16, 1868. Stanley had received a letter of introduction to Livingstone from the famous canoeist and sportsman John MacGregor, nicknamed "Rob Roy," while he was on a prior *Herald* assignment to discover information on Livingstone's whereabouts. For further details of the meeting between Stanley and J. MacGregor, see S.A. 73, same date, note 53.

594. General Sir Duncan MacGregor, KCB, 1787–1881, father of John "Rob Roy" MacGregor. For further details of Duncan MacGregor and the *Kent*, see S.A. 73, note 54.

The Doctor's saddle being finished to day I put it on his donkey, and in order to quiet the ill-tempered brute – for the D. is not a rider – put a man on him to tame him a little. The man had several falls from which Livingstone augurs but doubtfully of his ability to ride him.

December 18 Monday 1871

[Ink] Ujiji.

Preparing for the road to Unyanyembe. Gave 4 days provisions to the people. Promise to go soon after Christmas. The D. says he has about finished his letters.

December 19 Tuesday 1871

[Ink] Ujiji

Sent 6 guns to be repaired to be resteeled.[595] Determine upon going to Ngondo, then strike off for Imrera in Rusawa.

December 20 Wednesday 1871

[Ink] Ujiji

Heavy rain & thunder, & storm on the Lake.
Was exceedingly sick last night had nettle rash, or acretaria.[596]

December 21 Thursday 1871

[Ink] Ujiji.

Busy writing all day.
Wajiji asked twelve doti for an ox or a slave. Took a pencil sketch of the Doctor while writing.[597]

December 22 Friday

[Ink] Ujiji.

Mukunguru – or -Homa -

---

595. Were repaired by Moeni Kheri's smithy (S.A. 11, same date).
596. Stanley ill-transcribed the word "urticaria" that he learned from Doctor Livingstone (see Journal S.A. 11, same date.)
597. This pencil sketch could be the one kept at the Peabody Essex Museum, reproduced in Bennett, *Stanley's Despatches*, 90. It is the source of the engraving for *HIFL*, facing 563.

December 23 Saturday 1871

[Ink] Ujiji.

    Mukunguru, or Homa.

December 24 Sunday

[Ink] Ujiji.

Mukunguru or Homa

December 25 Monday 1871

[Ink] Ujiji.

    Getting well again to day after a very severe attack. Tried to make something of a Christmas dinner – but the cook Ferazzi spoilt it – our custard was burnt, &c. Ferazzi with whom I had borne so long was dismissed for spoiling the dinner of all dinners.[598]

December 26 Tuesday 1871

[Ink] Ujiji.

    To morrow we shall leave. Everybody is ready, & every thing prepared. Why then should we stop?

December 27 Wednesday 1871

[Ink] Ukaranga.

    Bade farewell to Ujiji

December 28 Thursday

[Ink] Mouth of the Malagarazi.

December 29 Friday

[Ink] Kagongo.[599]

---

    598. Livingstone noted in his journal: "*26th December, 1871.* —Had but a sorry Christmas yesterday" (*LJ* 2:161).

    599. First spelled 'Kagogo', and corrected to 'Kagongo'.

December 30 Saturday 1871

[Ink] Kivoe

Account with the "New York Herald" taken from 1870		Dr.		
		£	s	d
1870	Already drawn since March 1st 1869	1050	0	0
Oct 7th	By draft on Dossabhoy Merwanjee & Co. Bombay	50	"	"
" 10	" " in favor of Capt T.G. Osborne, Str. "Comorin" Bombay	10	"	"
	Total Money received to Dec 31st 1870 £	1110	"	"

December 31 Sunday 1871

[Ink] Act. With the "New York Herald" taken from 1870   Cr

                                                                                                 £   s d

		£	s	d
Oct 1st	To money due me according to locked account book			
"	in my desk, to be found in large leather trunk	1411	2	6
"	care of Dossabhoy Merwanjee & Co, 7 Parsee Bazaar St Bombay India			
to 11th	Board for 2 weeks at Byculla Hotel	15	8	"
	Outfit for Africa			
	Treacher & Co's Bill for amunition	41	18	9
	I. W. Watson & Co. for blankets	8	18	"
	Macker Vining & Co for books upon Africa[600]	3	10	"
12th	Fare from Bombay to Mauritius per "Polly"	30	"	"
	Boats & Carriage to vessel	"	12	"
Nov 18	At Mauritius. Boat & Carriage to Hotel	"	8	"
19	To Mahebourg by rail	"	17	"
20	To Pamplemousses	"	3	"
21	3 days at Hotel de Masse	1	10	"
	Departure for Seychelle. Boat to Schr. "Romp"	"	8	"
	Fare to Mahe. Secheylle Islands per d[itt]o	10	"	"
Dec 9th to 13th	4 days board at Royal Hotel Mahé for self & 2 men	2	8	"
	14 Passage to Zanzibar for self, Interpreter & Superintendent of Negro porters, per Brigantine "Falcon" of Salem, Capt Josiah Richmond of New Bedford	30	"	"
	Repair & Purchase of hand Cart, Mahe	3	4	"
	To making of Ammunition Boxes $7	1	8	"

---

600. 'For amunition', 'for blankets', 'for books upon Africa' added with another ink.

Tools. Carpenters $6	1 4	"
Baggage & self from "Romp" ashore	" 12	
Oct 31st £33.6.8. Nov 31, £33.6.8. Dec 31, £33.6.8	100	"
Credit	£1663. 11. 3	
Debit	£1110. 0. 0	
Total due me	553 11. 3	

January
1871

	Dr
To draft drawn in favor of John Bertram of Salem	$3750
To 2nd draft drawn in favor of John Bertram of Salem	$3000
To 3rd draft drawn in favor of John Bertram of Salem	$1250
	$8000

January 1871

	Cr.		
	£	s	d
Jan 1st Amt brot forward from Dec 31st 1870)	553	11	3
	$2557	72	1/4
Expenses of Expedition	8000	00	
	10557	72	1/4
Salary	161	33	1/3
	10719	05	1/2
Money	8000	00	0
	2719.	5	1/2

February

2719	05	½	
161	33	⅓	5
$2880	39		

[Pencil] February

		Miles
1	Kikoka[601]	12
2	Rosaco	12 [written over 10]
3	Camp	8 ¼ [written over 10]
4	Kingaroo	5

601. From 1 Kikoka to 16 Camp, places and miles in pencil; from 17 Camp Makata to 19 Rudewa River, places and miles in ink. From 20 Camp to 28 Mpapaw, in pencil.

5	Imbiki	15	
6	Msuwa	10	
7	Camp	6	
8	Kisemo	5	
9	Moussoudi	11	
10	Camp	11	
11	Mikeseh	7 ½	
12	Ulagalla	7 ½	
13	Muhalleh	11 ¼	
14	Umgerengeri	7	119 ½
15	Simbo	5	4
16	Camp	10 ¼	124 ¼
		142 ¼	
17	Camp. Makata	6 ½	
		148 ¾	
18	Makata Valley	9	
19	Rudewa River	9 ¼	
20	Camp	1[?]	
21	Rehenneko	1[?]	
22	Camp	[?]	
23	Kiora	6	
24	Mukondokwa	10	
25	Madete	6	
26	Ugombo lake	6	
27	~~Mtoni~~ Mata mombo	11	
28	Mpapaw or Mbambwa	12 ¼	

March

[Pencil] 236 ¾; [Ink] 277 ½

29	Kisakweh[602]	4	
30	Choonio	5	
31	1st March Mar[en]ga Mkali	7 ½	
32	2nd " " "	15	
33	Umvoomi Small	10	
34	Umvoomi Great	10	
35	Matamburu	7 ½	

---

602. From 29 Kisakweh to 40 Mizanza in pencil; from 41 Mukonduku to the end, in ink.

36	Bihawana	5
37	Kididimo	5
38	Tirekeza	16
39	Pembera Pereh	4
40	Mizanza	12 Miles 337 ¾
[Ink] 41	Mukonduku	13 ½
42	Munieka	10
43	Mabunguru & Camp	20 [written over 16]
44	Unyambogi	5
45	Kiti	9
46	Msalalo	13
47	Weldo Ngaraiso	8 ¾
48	Kusouri	8 ¾
49	Nquala Mtoni	17 ½
50	Madedita	12 ½
51	Tura	7 ½
52	~~Tura~~ Ngwhalah Mtoni	17 ½
53	Rubuga. Wangwana Village	18 ¾
54	Kigwa	12 ½
55	~~Unyanyembe~~ Shisa	17 ½
56	[blank]	178 ½
		5

[On the right of this same page, an operation in pencil]

$$2880 \;\; 39$$
$$\underline{161 \;\; 33\,\tfrac{1}{3}}$$
$$3041 \;\; 72\,\tfrac{1}{3}$$
$$\underline{1453 \;\; 11}$$
$$4494 \;\; 83\,\tfrac{1}{3}$$
$$\underline{449 \;\; 48}$$
$$4944 \;\; 31\,\tfrac{1}{3}$$
$$\underline{968}$$
$$5912$$

[Another operation, in ink]

$$421\,\tfrac{3}{4}$$
$$\underline{103\,\tfrac{3}{4}}$$
$$525\,\tfrac{1}{4}$$
$$\underline{278\,\tfrac{1}{2}}$$
$$247$$

March
[numbers]

April
An operation
161 33 ⅓
___9___
$1453 11

[From May to November: pages missing]
[pencil] December

To Kawendi
1	Mkwe Kwe. com Ugonda
2	Kigandu
3	Ugoonda
4	Pakambabala Ugonda
5	Chonga
6	Mtoni
7	Wataka
8	Pakawano
9	Tolini
10	Sultan Nasangaro
11	Mtoni. Mtambwe
12	Usumbwri
13	Utanda
14	Pori
15	Sultan Pumburu
16	Katooma
17	Pori
18	Uyombeh
19	Uyombeh
20	Ugarawah
21	Mtoni
22	Usowa. Sultan Ponda

Get a man to show you the Usowa road but not take the Kataka road because the Wa…o are on it. When you get to Ukonon[go] must inquire from each village the name of the one ahead, the news & the direction to the Lake.

December
[Pencil] When we reach Usunga we are but four days from Kawendi when we see the Tanganyika Lake. Sultan Wgongehri.

Mkwekwe	3 ¾
Imesuka	5
Kangera	7 ½
Kigandu	7
Ugunda	17 ½
Benta	8 ¾
Kikuru	12 ¼
Ziwani	10
Maruara	16 ¼
Mtoni Gombe	10 ¾
Ziwani	13 ¼
Ukamba	3 ¼
Pori	13 ¼
Mwere[?]	7 ½
Utenda	19 ½
~~Ukum[?]~~ Mtoni	10
Mwara	13 ¼
Mrera [one word crossed out] –ny Ruwira	13 ¼
Utense [Mtoni added above the line] Kawendi	[?]
Mtoni	15
Mpokwa in Utanda	12
Usiemba	
Katooma	
Kazenga	
Mtoni	
Maponda	

[On the right side of this page, in the blank part after Mpokwa, in ink]

Mtoni	7 ½
Mtoni	11 ¼
Imrera	11 ¼

Camp	6 ¼
"	10
"	12 ½
"	15
"	13 ¾
N[zo]gera	6 ¼
[Total in pencil]	324 ½

[Pages inside the cover]

10 ¾
73 ¾
 3
13 ¾
 2 ½
10
22 ½
18 ¾
23 ¾
15
130 ¾
324 ½
52) 455 ¼ (
    525
    930 ¼

[Several calculations in pencil, and one in ink]

[Deciphered on a right side of a calculation:]

5 ½ miles per day from Bagomoyo
8 ¾   "   from Unyanyembe

Journal S.A. 11, Full Transcript
(10 November 1871–Unyanyembe, 8 May 1872)

[Page glued on the left side of the cover]
[Words in pencil at the top of the page]

"Africa!
"Would we were there – Under another heaven
In lands where neither love or memory
Can plant a selfish hope – in lands so far
I should not seem to see the outstretched arms
That seek me or hear the voice that calls.
I should feel the distance only and despair:
    So rest for ever from the thought of bliss,
    And wear my weight of life's great chain unstruggling".
    Georg Elliot[1]

shel.[?]

[Some pages torn off. First right page blank]

Nov 10th 1871. Bandareen (or Port of) Ujiji. (The diary entry of this date has already been published in How I found Livingstone)
    Copy that first then proceed to next Page.

Nov 11th 1871. Saturday. I woke up about dawn, with a delightful sense of pleasure, and fatigue of limbs. It was some moments before I could conquer a disposition to sleep. The faculties of the brain seemed to be in a state of pleasing confusion but gradually while yet drowsy, they arranged themselves in order, and suddenly with a quick start, came the consciousness that Livingstone had been found. I sprang up to a sitting posture, and took a quick survey of my lodgings. It was a large, and airy room, roofed with grass and palm brabs lying in rough ill arranged bundles over rafters cut

---

    1. 'Georg Elliot', ms. *Theophrastus Such, Jubal, and Other Poems and the Spanish Gypsy*, by George Eliot (Chicago: Belford, Clarke, 1839), 439. Stanley made two slight errors: "love or memory" instead of "love nor memory" and "or hear the voice" instead of "or to hear the voice."

from unbarked[2] forest saplings, & cross poles, which were lashed at the intersections with bark rope, & through the open squares of this crude roofing hung many pointed ends of spear grass. The walls were mere clay over wattle which here & there was visible, & gaped open in wide cracks. In one corner of the room were arranged my boxes tin & wood. The guns were huddled together & their respective amunition bags hung by straps from their nozzles. In another corner, and scattered[3] along the sides lay a strange assortment of a traveller's impedimenta, a broken wooden[4] box[5], or two, native made kirindos,[6] empty bale covers & sacking a heavy rifle, prismatic compass, sextant, bundle of coil rope, a bundle of Saturday Reviews, & a heap of 'Punches'.[7]

At the further end had been piles our expedition bales & boxes, which I recognised only two well. In the center between the piles of effects was the four poster of Arab make which I occupied and on which I had lain last night with a grateful heart.

A thick pile of palm leaves had been spread upon it for want of anything better & my bear skin thrown over the whole, had made it a place for a sound rest. By this time- I was quite awake, and strained my ears to catch the sound of Livingstone's voice if haply he was awake, as I remembered him to have said he was a poor sleeper & therefore an early riser, but I could only hear the dull boom of the Lake's surf, as it beat upon the shore.

Then I fell back upon the bed to indulge in the past time of those who enjoy that delicious early hour after hard work before whom there is a prospective holiday. My thoughts ran hurriedly, over many things, and all were[8] pleasant. How the men would rejoice that the march was over! Issat[9] as I do. Thank God no more marching for some time. Breakfast will be late. The cook will be too lazy to get ready the morning Coffee. He is fast asleep now & when he wakes he will cry Hamd il Allah! Yesterday's march ended the weary way. Wallahi! But we footed it yesterday & it is all over now! And the men, for reasons very like his will all cry out in the same way "the Thanks be to God". None of them can be so happy as I. Was there ever anything so lucky? To burst all of a sudden upon the very man we wished to SEE. Who would have thought it yesterday? Now here we are. This is his own house. There is his Compass hanging on the peg. There are English newspapers that he has read. How on Earth did he get them? I wonder how he has rested after yesterday's Event. That bag of letters must have kept him awake up to the small hours. If I had been him, I would have opened every one of them to get news of home.

2. 'unbarked' added above the line.
3. 'scattered' added above the line.
4. 'wooden' added above the line.
5. 'box[es]' crossed out.
6. 'made' added above the line.
7. From 'bundle of Saturday Reviews' to the end, added above the line.
8. 'were' added above the line.
9. Misspelling for 'I sat as I do'?

Well he is an extraordinary man! I wonder if he will be so kind today as he was yesterday. People say strange things of him. I heard that he was crabbed, and sour – & that he dislikes to see people poaching on his preserves. Well, thank God, I do not wish to do that. It will be enough to get some letter from him acknowledging the receipt of these bales, & goods. And then I'll foot it back to the sea again. I shall have to prepare to tell him why I came, and in order to do that I must glance over Anderson's letter of 1/68 which –by the bye- is the only written order I have got.[10] If it had not been for that letter I should not have been able to raise the money for this Expedition at Zanzibar. The old Consul was very suspicious of me until he saw that. If a business man was satisfied with its contents why surely Livingstone must be. But no one knows. He may be a very cranky fellow after all. If he gets into any tantrums off I go. I came to do him a service & whatever he wishes me to do he will find me willing, for I am not bound to run away with the news, as I should be in Europe."

Having dressed quietly, I hunted up all Anderson's & Levien's letters[11] & having furnished myself with the documents – I opened the door intending to see the Lake – but the Doctor was already up & on the verandah, meditating

"Halloa Doctor, you up already, I hope you have slept well." I cried

"Good morning Mr Stanley, I am glad to see you. I hope you rested well. I sat up late reading my letters. You have brought me a heap of good & bad news. But won't you sit down? He made a place for me by his side.

"Yes he continued "many of my friends are dead. It seems they die in Europe, as they do out here. My eldest boy has met with a sad accident – that is my boy Tom – my second son Oswell is at college studying medicine, and is doing well I am told. Agnes my eldest daughter has been enjoying herself in a yacht, with Sir Paraffin Young & his family. Sir Roderick (Murchison)[12] is also well & expresses a hope that, he will soon see me. You have brought me quite a budget.

The man was not an apparition, then, and yesterdays Events were not the result of a dream! I could not help commenting thus as I gazed upon him – for I had been perpetually haunted by the fears that the news of a white man coming to Ujiji,

---

10. It could be the letter that Anderson had enclosed within his mail: "I enclose you the letter that I told you I would send. If you should find Dr Livingstone you might read it to him if you think proper." See Appendix, S.A. 2589, Letter from Finley Anderson (*Herald*'s London Office) to Stanley, London, October 23, 1868.

11. Col. W. F. Anderson was a lifelong friend of J. Gordon Bennett. After the Civil War, he organized the *Herald* Bureau at Washington, and was then sent to the London *Herald* Agency, in 1866. Finley Anderson and Douglas A. Levien, who later replaced Anderson, were those *Herald* "folks" who handed over Gordon Bennett's orders and released mission funding. Their judgment seems to have been dreaded by the *Herald* correspondents, as Stanley notes: "I can finish my correspondence..., lest the "Herald "folks" deem me unworthy" [quotation marks as in original] (see Appendix, S.A. 5, August 2–3, 1870).

For letters from the *Herald* Office to Stanley, relative to this expedition, see Anderson's letters, S.A. 2586, 2588, 2589, and 2591; Levien's letter, S.A. 2626 (S.A. 2588, 2589, and 2626 are transcribed in the Appendix).

12. About Sir Roderick Murchison, see Robert A. Stafford, *Scientist of Empire: Sir Roderick Murchison, Scientific Exploration and Victorian Imperialism* (Cambridge: Cambridge University Press, 1989).

would cause him to hurry off – for so I had been told, by those who professed to know him.

The boys brought us our coffee, and Halimah brought a plateful of cornmeal dampers, and damp & soft enough they were I thought. I should have to teach the old woman to make them a little browner to take off the taste of mush, and having despatched our coffee, I said,

"Now Doctor you are probably wondering in your mind what mission has brought me to Ujiji? I said.

"It is true. I have been wondering a little. At first I thought you were an Emissary of the French Government, in the place of Lieutenant Le Saint[13] who is said to have died a few miles above Gondokoro. They told me you had boats, plenty of men & stores and I really believed you were some French officer until I saw the American flag & to tell you the truth I was rather glad it was so, because I could not have talked to him in French, and if he did not know English, we would have been a pretty pair of white men. I did not like to ask you yesterday, because it was none of my business."

"Well said I laughing "for your sake I am glad that I am an American, & not a Frenchman, & that we can understand each other perfectly without an interpreter. I see that the Arabs are wondering that you an Englishman, & I an American understand each other. We must take care not to tell them that the English & Americans have[14] fought,[15] against each other & that there are Alabama claims[16] left unsettled & that we have such people as Fenians[17] who hate you. But seriously Doctor – now don't be frightened when I tell you that I have come after you!

"After me" he asked in a tone of surprise

"Yes."

"How. I do not understand.

"Well. You have heard of the New York Herald"

"Oh – who has not heard of that despicable newspaper?"

"Sh-sh. I cried laughing. You will not call it despicable after you have heard what I have to say. You must know that the "New York Herald" you mean was formed by James Gordon Bennett Sr.[18] He is now an old man, and the conduct of the paper has

---

13. The French Lieutenant Le Saint died at Abou-Kouka (1868).
14. 'have' written above 'once' crossed out.
15. 'together' crossed out.
16. Alabama claims (1862–72): During the Civil War, the Confederacy used British-built ships (among them, the *Alabama*) as raiders. The toll on the U.S. merchant marine was heavy (more than 150 vessels were sunk), for which the United States demanded proportional compensation. The dispute between United States and Great Britain over payment was peacefully resolved in 1872 through arbitration (https://history.state.gov/milestones/1861-1865/alabama).
17. The Fenian Movement started in Ireland in 1850, with the hope of achieving Irish independence. It gained widespread support among the Irish Americans in the United States in 1858 during an Irish uprising against the British government.
18. Cf. D. C. Seitz, *The James Gordon Bennetts, Father and Son* (Indianapolis: Bobbs-Merrill, 1928; repr., New York: Beekman, 1973).

within the last three or four years been under James Gordon Bennett Jr. who without telling his father anything about it commissioned me to find you, to get whatever news of your discoveries you may like to give me, and to assist you if I can by every means in my power."

"Young M[r] Bennett told you to come after me to find me out – and help me! I see, it is no wonder then that you praised M[r] Bennett so much last night."

"I know him – I am proud to say – to be just what I said he was. He is a most generous enthusiastic & true man"

"Well, indeed! I am very much obliged to him, & it makes me proud to feel that you Americans think so much of me. You have come in the proper time too, for I was beginning to think that I should have to beg from the Arabs. But even they are in want of cloth, and[19] beads are now scarce in Ujiji. That fellow Shereef[20] – I told you of – has robbed me of everything. I wish that I could suitably express my thanks to M[r] Bennett, but if I am at all backward, or unable to do so, do not, I beg of you believe that I am ungrateful."

"Then as we understand one another, let me say that for my own part, I do not wish you to reveal[21] anything about your discoveries, that would in the least forestall what you would like to keep for yourself. A correspondent can do his duty without trenching[22] upon things in which he has no business. It will be quite enough so far as the "Herald" is concerned if you simply write a letter of thanks to M[r] Bennett, after I have turned over to you what I have brought & settled how you are to obtain the lot of Goods stored in Unyanyembe with M[r] Shaw. I am telling you this because I wish you to feel perfectly easy upon that score. The descriptions of Ujiji, native life, and what I have seen myself will give me ample matter, without robbing you of what you had better reserve for yourself.

I never knew a morning to pass so quickly. Just as my tongue revelled in speaking freely every though that came into my head after such a long silence, so I fancied Livingstone's must. It would be impossible to record the variety of topics touched upon. At one time I was deep & animated in descriptions of events[23] which I had witnessed during the Abyssinian Crussade – as I was pleased to call that campaign- Then he would take up scenes that he had witnessed on the Lualaba River, or during some tramp with one of his numerous Arab friends, in some unknown regions called

---

19. One illegible word crossed out.
20. Sherif Basheikh bin Ahmed sent news of Livingstone to Kirk (Letter to Consul Kirk, dated 20 Shaban 1287- November 15, 1870, a translated copy of which Kirk sent to Lord Granville on March 10, 1871; National Archives, Kew, FO no. 25, 84/1344; *PRGS* 15, no. 3 [1870–71]: 206). Though Sherif said he had sent off to Livingstone "all that he was in need of," some doubt remains, since Said bin Majid to Ludda Damji (n.d. letter, but in the same batch) indicates only the intention of doing so.
 The story of Sherif having sold off all Livingstone's goods in Ujiji is recalled in *LJ*, 2:155.
21. 'reveal' written over 'say'.
22. Trenching is used figuratively with the meaning of encroaching on.
23. 'in Abyssinia' crossed out.

Kamalondo, Bangweolo, Mweru – Nyangwe, &c. I am afraid I shall never understand what countries he refers to or distinguish one from the other, until he shows me some day on his map, which I am curious to see. At present these uncouth terms are jumbled in my head that I dare not write anything of them lest I make hideous mistakes. The interest I take in him personally is too overpowering. When he begins his narration of some incident in some place that I never heard of before, my mind wanders while my eyes rove over his face, & to[24] speculate upon every line, & facial movement, I am no short hand writer though I have a system of my own of abbreviating sentences which is intelligible to myself, & if I take too many notes, it occupies too much of the night to write them up. I suppose that by & bye all these things he tells me will arrange themselves in my mind in due order, but at present, I am bewildered.

About 11, we had breakfast. Ferajji & Halima did their work well. Masters & servants are in a state of[25] feverishly exultation.[26] The Doctor cries as he eats "Your coming has restored to me an appetite to which I have been a stranger for some time. Halima is a dear, good soul, and is one of the best of her kind, I think, but she makes odd blenders now & then. If I ask for tea she makes coffee, if I ask for coffee she almost invariably gives me tea. It is of no use to scold her, for when I look up at her conceited face, grinning & smiling, I lose courage.

I made a reference to the dampers, & he said that they had become[27] a necessity to him, as his teeth had been loosened by the Corn cobs of Manyema, wherever that is and the roasted corn of Lunda, and he had so few left now. Meat had been very scarce for months with him and to live at all, he had to feed on what he could get. Then he had to invent some form by which this corn could be made[28] digestible & so far he had found the corn flour converted into these[29] easily preferred & soft pancakes the best way. When he[30] could get sugar cane, he made a kind of molasses out of it, which enabled him to eat enough pancake so as to be "filling". Sometimes honey was useful as a substitute though the wild flowers on which the bees fed had frequently sickened him. Then again palm oil when fresh from the nut[31] which he could get in Manyema, did service as butter. Since he had come to Ujiji, he might have fared better for there was a well stocked market, but the depression from which he had suffered from the abominable conduct of the slaves to whom had been entrusted his goods at Zanzibar, had been such, that it seemed to him it had been scarcely worth while to struggle any more. "I had come to this place looking forward to my goods as a means of relieving

---

24. 'to' added above the line.
25. 'in a state of' added above the line.
26. 'exultation' written above 'pleased' crossed out.
27. 'had become' written above 'were' crossed out.
28. 'be made' written above 'be' crossed out.
29. 'these' written over 'this'.
30. 'he' written over 'I'.
31. 'when fresh from the nut' added above the line.

me from many troubles, making me independent of the Arabs, paying my servants, rewarding those who had been marked by Good Conduct – and having a good time after our long travels during which we would feed up a little & get strong for another bout. But[32] when we had landed & made inquiries – there was nothing left. The hogs had eaten up every thing. You will see them by & bye. They are still fat from the feasts they have had at my expense. Shereef who is the leader said that he looked into the Koran – and found that I was dead. He said he was sure it was true – for he had done it three times running. What did I do? What could I do? I could only dismiss him, and tell him never to come near me again. But he finds that as hard to follow, as it was to keep his hands from stealing my cloth. He comes round every day and touches his hand to his head & says "Spalkher[33] Bwana, (Good Morning, Master), but I wave my hand to him and sometimes say "Get away from me. I don't wish to see you!

"This is the eleventh day I believe, since I came here &[34] found I was ruined. I was obliged to go to my friend Mohammed bin Gharib,[35] & Muni Kheri & Said bin Majid[36] especially the first and tell them what had happened. They were very sympathetic and each of them lent[37] me some cloth of which I have a piece or two left. They sent me rice, & curry, & now & then a goat, but they could not go on for ever with this kindness. Each Arab you know has scores of dependants, and to feed them, they must have cloth & beads from the Coast. But the war with Mirambo has closed the road, and no caravans come in or go out. It has been attempted two or three times, but each time the slaves have come back, saying there was no road. You can now understand why your sudden coming was such a surprise to every body here – to me as well as the rest. No one would believe it. We all asked ourselves which way[38] you had come? How was it that[39] you had been able to come at all. Was the war ended? Or had you fought your way through Mirambo's ruga-ruga- or how?

"Truly the ways of God are wonderful. About this time yesterday I was sitting on this verandah – alone – thinking, and always thinking of the same thing. How would I ever let the people at[40] Zanzibar know I was here, and how I would in the meantime feed myself & my followers for it would take many months to go to the sea & back. I think that with economy we might have lived a few days longer upon the scanty bit of cloth I have left, & then I should either have to beg again, or begin selling my property. The rifle I have would prehaps bring most, then my dead chronometer, knives, &

---

32. 'But' written over 'when'.
33. Greeting in Arabic. See Norman R. Bennett, *Stanley's Despatches to the* New York Herald, *1871–1872, 1874–1877* (Boston: Boston University Press, 1970), 41.
34. 'here &' written above 'when I' crossed out.
35. Livingstone traveled with him in Manyema. See letters to Kirk mentioned in note 20.
36. 'Said bin Majid' added above the line.
37. 'lent' written over 'gave'.
38. 'had' crossed out.
39. 'that' added above the line.
40. 'at' written over 'of'.

knickknacks, but then you know that when[41] one begins to sell every thing in that way the end is not far. As for myself I loathed the very sight of food but I could not have lived long with that feeling. I think it required some such thing as has now happened – a shock like this[42] to give a sharp fillip to the system- to save me. Halima has good[43] cause to be amazed. I am amazed at myself.

We[44] lingered over the dejeuner. I could well believe what a[45] great change it seemed to him[46]. Even the articles & dishes, the Persian Carpet, the knives & forks – silver tea spoons – silver tea pot, bright & shining must have appeared unusual[47] to the old man who had been tended by one slave woman who had never seen the Coast, and who had been unable to find pleasure in any of her efforts. He himself directed my attention to these, & he[48] confessed that he thought[49] had he[50] only been permitted to see a breakfast laid out as it was by Ferajji & his willing helps, it alone[51] would have provoked appetite.

The Doctor's way of putting things has started me also into thinking that the way matters are arranged for us whether we wish them or not are very strange. Bennett gave me his order to find him in October 1869.[52] At that time he was enthusiastic about it. Yet brilliant as he thought the finding of him would be, he did not seem eager to order[53] me straight away into[54] into Africa, but thought it best to send me up the Nile, then up to the Crimea & round by the Caspian Sea & through Persia to the Eastern Sea, as though in[55] the interval it would be settled definitely that there was no need for me to undertake the Mission. Unless that was his reason, and he[56] innermostly[57] dreaded the expense of doing what he yet would like to do. I cannot understand it. However this hesitation on his part, has been the means of giving Livingstone

---

41. 'when' written above 'if' crossed out.
42. 'this' added above the line.
43. 'good' written above 'just' crossed out.
44. 'The breakfast' crossed out, preceding 'We'.
45. 'what a' written above 'the' crossed out.
46. 'it seemed to him' added above the line.
47. 'unusual' written above 'splendid' crossed out.
48. 'he' added above the line.
49. 'if he' crossed out.
50. 'he' above the line.
51. 'alone' above the line.
52. 1869 could be a mistake made by Stanley, since Anderson had sent a letter dated October 20, 1868, enjoining him to proceed to Suez or Zanzibar to meet Livingstone: "Having received the joyful news that Dr Livingstone is on his way home from Africa via Zanzibar, the New York Herald desires you to proceed to Suez, or if practical to Zanzibar, to meet him." (See Appendix, Letters from the *New York Herald* Staff in London to Stanley, S.A. 2588.) Or, did Stanley consider the commission Gordon Bennett Jr. gave him orally on October 28, 1869, in Paris as the true starting point of his mission?
53. 'order' written above 'send' crossed out.
54. 'in[to]' added above the line.
55. 'in' added above the line.
56. 'he' added above the line.
57. 'innermostly' neologism coined by Stanley.

time to finish his travels in[58] some far[59] country west of this lake. Then again as if that round-about course of mine was not sufficient circumstances comtinally accurred to thwart my eager desire to set off at once. There is no ship for Zanzibar to be found[60] at Bombay so I must after some three months try and obtain one at Mauritius. When I reach there, I am as badly off – and must go North again to[61] Seychelle's Islands. When I am almost despairing of finding a vessel there, in comes a Whaler the "Falcon" whose Captain must be pleaded with before he will consent to go cruising for whales towards Zanzibar. Finally though we have made no remarkable speed to Unyanyembe – a war happens to break out just at our arrival & the road to Ujiji is cut, & I am delayed three months more, in that country, and again I am on the verge of despair when the general fright at Mirambo enables me to enlist some more followers with whom after a prodigious curve round the disturbed country – I am permitted to drop upon Ujiji as it were from the clouds – at least to arrive within 400 yards of the town before a soul outside of our own party knows we are there – to discover that Livingstone had only reached Ujiji from the western country fourteen[62] days before. There is something curious about it. Had I not found Livingstone here, I might after a long stay here have either gone round the South end of the Lake, or gone to Manyema across the Lake to find probably[63] after reaching there that he had gone East by another road."

We have closed the day with prayers, & thanks and have had grace before & after food since we came here".

Nov 12th At 6 a.m. I was up & dressed, and soon after Livingstone came out of his room. Between our two rooms there runs a passage about 5 feet wide which admits entrance into a[64] court yard[65]. There Livingstone's servants are housed round the quadrangle – and Halima may be said to reign,[66] two milch goats & half a dozen fowls belonging to the Doctor to which are added our stock of goats & fowls form the other inhabitants of this yard. The house is about 45 feet long by about 27[67] feet wide. Two large rooms are in front separated by the passage. I occupy the one to the right.

---

58. 'Manyema' crossed out.
59. 'western' crossed out.
60. 'for Zanzibar to be found' added above the line.
61. 'Mauritius' crossed out.
62. 'fourteen' written above 'ten' crossed out.
63. 'that' crossed out.
64. 'a' written over 'the'.
65. 'the head of which is Halima' crossed out; 'which is looked after' written above 'the head of which' crossed out; 'by' written over 'is Halima' crossed out.
66. 'and Halima may be said to reign' added above the line. To be understood as: 'and [there] Halima may be said to reign'.
67. '27' written over '25'.

Livingstone retains those to the left of the passage. The verandah is[68] under[69] a five foot eave of the tall[70] roof. Its floor rises about 16 inches above the roadway & is made of hard tamped clay covered with mats and goat-skins[71]– which have been no doubt borrowed from his friend Mohammed bin Gharib from whom most of his comforts have come – it serves as an office, study, & reception room. Within the unwindowed rooms inside it would be too dark[72] and uninviting to read or write, so the best part of the day light from six to six Livingstone spends on the verandah, seated on a goatskin with his feet stretched[73] nearly across it & his back leaning on a goatskin tacked to the wall. Here is where he takes his meal exposed to view of every passer by, from here, he looks out on the market place every morning, here is[74] where he receives his[75] Arab visitors, where he reads prayers every morning & every evening, & here is the[76] place with which I shall always associate him.

After breakfast I[77] accompanied him to pay the return visit to his Arab friends, Mohammed bin Sali being the Governor,[78] and representative of the Zanzibar Sultan our first visit was due him. He is a grand & imposing looking personage with a full beard of silver grey & would be no discredit in any Eastern assemblage of elders. Livingstone has however two or three little things against him, the rights of which I do not quite understand. We next went to Said bin Magid who is the chief socially of the Arab colony. He is of the best family of Oman, and distantly related to His Highness of Zanzibar. His son Soud was my friend in the war with Mirambo, and he it was who headed the attacking party of 500 which entered that Chieftains stronghold, and which was immediately after assailed by the re-entering force of Mirambo's warriors & exterminated. According to Arab custom we had to take coffee here also, & were recieved most graciously. Then we went to Muini Kheris and lastly to Mohammed bin Gharib who has been such a friend to Livingstone. He is building a grand house – which is[79] a palatial affair compared to Livingstone's dwelling. The door is of teak[80] a magnificent piece of carving -lofty, broad & solid.[81] The verandah is quite 60 feet long by 15 feet wide & the columns supporting the projection of the roof. I hear it will cost quite a number of ivory tusks, before it is completed. As it is only in process

---

68. 'made out of' crossed out; 'covered by' written above 'made out of' crossed out.
69. 'under' added above the line.
70. 'sloping' crossed out.
71. 'goat-' added above the line.
72. '& gloomy' crossed out.
73. 'across' crossed out.
74. 'is' added above the line
75. 'guests' crossed out; 'here is where' crossed out.
76. 'the' written over 'where'.
77. 'I' written over 'he'.
78. 'under S' crossed out.
79. 'which is' added above the line.
80. 'is of teak' written above 'is' crossed out.
81. 'of teak' crossed out.

of erection Mohammed only took us to show what he believes will be some day his future residence. His present house is a modest structure, but cosy, and he played the host towards us in a manner quite worthy of the generous character Livingstone has been constantly giving him.[82]

Having performed our duties towards the principal residents, we walked to the Lake. It seemed to me as if I had come suddenly upon[83] the Ocean when I saw that grand expanse of water rolling in long lazy waves towards our feet. The surf that I had heard booming, and sighing, as it drawn backward baffled to the deep, was caused by a long stretch of shallow in front of the Bunder or port. Far away westward[84] Livingstone pointed the blue mountains of what he called Goma – and the part that he had crossed from the strange land of Manyema about which he talks so much lies towards the S. West but is of course invisible. Bangwe Island mentioned by Burton was also pointed out which I at first took for a headland to the right.

I asked Livingstone if he did not feel a desire to return home and take a rest after these continuous travels of five years. (He had left the Coast in 1866.)

Said he, I should like very much to go home once again, if I could only dare to[85] leave my work unfinished, but it is nearly completed. I have not the courge to forsake it."

"What work do you mean?"

"I came out with the intention of [86] exploring the watershed between the Zambezi & the Nile. After reaching Cazembe's I heard of any number of rivers all flowing into a Lake called Mweru, and I got Cazembe to assist me with guides, and I reached the Lake. At the North end the Luapula a large river flows northward, and I have been following that central line of drainage[87], which receives all the tributaries[88] from East & West, and as I have discovered that for 600 miles the course of that river is Northward I am convinced it joins ultimately Petherick's branch of the White Nile, or empties in Chowambé[89] the native name of Baker's Lake. Now before I ascertain whether this is true or not, why should I go home – now, to have to return to do what I can very well do now."

"But why did you come back then without doing what you say you must do."

"I was simply forced back by my own people. They mutinied against me – not by open force, but by assisting & urging every person who had the power to multiply obstacles to oppose me. If I[90] said, I should insist on advancing they threatened to

---

82. 'After partaking of another cup of coffee' crossed out.
83. 'up' added above the line.
84. 'we could' crossed out.
85. 'do so' crossed out.
86. 'finding' crossed out.
87. 'into' added above the line and crossed out
88. 'tributaries' written over 'rivers'.
89. [Sic], with "é".
90. 'insisted' crossed out.

raise a disturbance in the country & then to abandon me – by which of course I should be killed, and they would save themselves by flight. In every possible way they frustrated me. They intrigued with the Arabs not to lend me[91] canoes, the Arabs believing that I was not friendly to their methods of man stealing, gladly sided with them, and warned the Natives not to give me any assistance whatever. I was thus obliged to come back to Ujiji, to get my goods which I had heard had been brought here by a caravan and I thought that with those goods I could engage new men and strike away by a road that would take me clear of Arabs."

"Well Doctor – I dare say you will think me very simple – but I really have not the least idea of what you mean by this central line of drainage, and its junction with the Nile. I have no idea even of where Cazembe is, or Manyema, or Nyangwe, or any of these places" because on the maps which I have everything west of this Lake is a dead white. If you will let me have a glance at your map I shall be able to follow you intelligently, but just now I feel very dense & I can make nothing of it."

We got back to the house & Livingstone brought out his map, which is on a much larger scale than any I have – and long before the dusk made it difficult to see, I had grasped the position of places, so firmly & clearly that I can make at any time a rough copy to illustrate any geographical[92] intelligence I may receive from him.

(Note. About 300 miles of Lake Tanganika we must[93] a parallel course of a large[94] river. About the same distance abreast of[95] the S. W. extremity of Lake Tanganika we must draw the outline of a roundish Lake,[96] & call it Mweru. S. East of this say 200 miles or so draw another somewhat larger & call it L. Bangweolo, then unite these two Lakes by a curving river and from Mweru the Northernost Lake continue the river under the name of Luapula, to a point in that parallel river course which shall be[97] nearly abreast of the North End of Lake Tanganika, & call that point Nyangwe, the Capital, or principal residential place of the Arabs in the Country of Manyema. At any time henceforward Livingstone may mention Nyangwe I shall have a distinct understanding of it. I should say that a N West line from Ujiji about[98] as far Westerly of the Lake[99] as Unyanyembe is Easterly would about make it right.)

It[100] being Sunday we had service in the morning at 10 o'clock, and Livingstone expounded a chapter from the Bible to Susi, Chuma, Hamoiday & Gardner & Selim.

---

91. 'me' added above the line.
92. 'geographical' added above the line.
93. verb missing: probably 'follow'.
94. 'large' written over 'river'.
95. 'abreast of' written above 'from' crossed out.
96. 'S. East from' crossed out.
97. 'abreast' crossed out.
98. 'about' written above 'towards the' crossed out.
99. 'of the Lake' added above the line.
100. 'It' preceded by 'Nov 13th' crossed out.

After dinner he made a short prayer, and we soon after[101] retired each to our quarters to write. With[102] the Palm oil bought in the market, we have rigged out two lamps,[103] by the light of one of which I make my notes.

Nov 13th <u>Monday</u>. After our coffee, I took out my notebook & said, Now Doctor, after having seen your map last night I have a better[104] view of the regions you have been talking of[105] in my mind, and if you would not mind, I should like to take some notes for a resumé of your travels, but I must tell you frankly that I am very ignorant of everything concerning your[106] last journey. I do not even know the year you started. So if you begin from the beginning of your departure from England you will be educating me upon a subject upon which my mind at present is a blank.

"I left England in August[107] 1865, and went to Bombay which I reached in September,[108] and where through the kindness of Sir Bartle Frere,[109] & Dr Wilson, I was able to get a small force of Sepoys & Nassick school boys.[110] In January 1866[111] I reached Zanzibar, and two months later I sailed in the "Penguin" for Mikindany Bay with 12 Sepoys from Bombay, nine men from Johanna one of the Comorro Islands seven liberated slaves, and two Zambezi men. I also took with me as an experiment, 6 camels, 3 buffaloes, two mules & 3 donkeys. The Sepoys were to act as escort, & were armed with Enfield Rifles presented by the Bombay Govt. Our baggage consisted of 10 bales & 2 bags of beads,[112] some boxes containing[113] instruments, clothes, medicines & a few personal necessaries. We travelled up the left bank of the Rovuma River, mostly through jungle which gave us great trouble principally owing to the height of the camels, but the obstinate[114] laziness of the Sepoys & Johanna men was also a source of immense annoyance, and contributed as much as anything else to defeat any intention to push forward.

---

101. 'soon after' added above the line.
102. 'With' preceded by 'The Palm o' crossed out.
103. 'which' crossed out.
104. 'better' written over 'clear'.
105. 'of' written over 'off'.
106. 'your' written over 'this'.
107. 'August' added above the line.
108. 'and having seen my friends Sir Bartle Frere, and Dr Wilson got some Nassick boys' crossed out.
109. Sir Henry Bartle Frere (1815–1884) was Governor of the Bombay Presidency from 1862 to 1867. He encouraged British explorers to take African men from Indian orphanages for their expeditions. (See *Bombay Africans*, RGS, https://www.rgs.org/NR/rdonlyres/831B3822-2330-4773-8B53-A2E3328D2FBD/0/BombayAfricansPartTwo.pdf.) Stanley carried a letter to him from Livingstone (see Appendix, List of Letters Carried by Stanley from Dr. Livingstone, S.A. 4754).
110. The Nassick (Nasik) boys were children and youngsters liberated from Arab slaving boats by the Royal Navy, and taken to the first orphanage established for freed Africans in the town of Nasik.
111. '1866' added above the line.
112. 'We had other goods in the shape' crossed out.
113. 'containing' written above 'of' crossed out.
114. 'obstinate' added above the line.

The further we advanced, the more lazy they became instigated[115] in reality by their cowardly fears of the interior. As one way of stopping me from proceeding they ill treated[116] the[117] poor animals so cruelly[118] that in a short time they were all dead. When they saw that this did not succeed in inducing me to turn back they told lies about me to the natives, said that I practised witchcraft at children & did all sorts of horrible things which most of the ignorant people were only too willing to believe. On seeing this, I sent the Sepoys back to the Coast, – & having calculated the number of miles we[119] had travelled I rationed them for the number of days it would take them to reach the sea. They were a most worthless set of men & I should never recommend a traveller relying upon such a kind again. On the 18th July we came to a village in Uyeow,[120] after an[121] 8 days march to the[122] South of the Rovuma,[123] through an absolute wilderness.

Early in August we reached[124] Mponda's near Lake Nyassa. Two of the liberated slaves deserted. Here Wekotani insisted upon his discharge upon the plea that he had found his brother & that[125] his family was now living on the East side of the Lake. It was all false, and he tried to tempt Chuma to leave me also.

From Mponda's we came to the S. end of the Lake where we met a half caste Arab who reported that he had been plundered of all his property by the Mazitu. Chief of my Johanna men, though he knew the story to be a pure fabrication[126] affected to believe it & to be terribly frightened. I could not get him to follow my example & laugh at it but the day we[127] resumed our journey was the last we saw of Musa and the Johanna men. They ran away in a body. A day or two afterwards Simeon Price came to me with another tale of the Mazitu, but I ordered him not to mention the Mazitu any more to me. Had it not been for the Natives, I could not have continued my journey but fortunately I was well away from the districts haunted by slave traders, and as is always the case among unsophisticated Africans I found them hospitable & ready to help me. In December we entered a[128] country

---

115. 'instigated' written above 'caused' crossed out.
116. 'ill' written over 'moles[t]'.
117. 'the' written over 'our'.
118. 'cruelly' added above the line.
119. 'we' written over 'they'.
120. In *HIFL* (440), Stanley changed the name of the village "Uyeow" into "Wahiyou": "The Doctor and his little party arrived on the 18th July, 1866, at a village belonging to a chief of the Wahiyou." The prefix Wa- refers to the inhabitants of the area, while the prefix U- refers to their territory.
121. 'after an' added above the line.
122. 'march to the' written above 'march' crossed out.
123. 'which' crossed out.
124. 'reached' written over 'came to'.
125. 'that' added above the line.
126. 'to be a pure fabrication' written above 'was false' crossed out
127. 'moved on' crossed out.
128. 'a' written over 'the'.

devastated by the Mazitu and again we were distressed by[129] famine and had to live on the wild fruit which we found in the jungle. Several of my people deserted me, taking with them my personal kit. But still we pressed on, with our numbers getting smaller, & with the usual losses of property until we had travelled through Babisa, Bobemba, Barungu, Baulungu and a part of Lunda.

In this country lives the famous Cazenbe of whom you have heard me speak more than once. He is a most intelligent chief & wears a peculiar dress made of red cotton in the form of a kilt. He asked me what I had come for,[130] & I told him that I was looking for rivers & seas, & was surprised that I should leave my own country to look for such things. Then he asked me which way I proposed going. I answered that I thought of going to the South as I had heard of lakes in that direction. Cazembe said, Why do you wish to go that way. The water is here, & there is plenty of it in this neighborhood, & he gave orders that I should be permitted to go in any direction I chose, as I was the first Englishman he had seen.

Shortly after I[131] had entered Lunda, I[132] crossed the Chambezi R. which was quite an important river. On account of the name I at first believed that it was only another name or a native corruption of the Great Zambezi – & that it[133] had no connection with the Nile. An error[134] which cost me many months of travel.

From the begining of 1867, to the middle of March 1869, I was engaged in correcting this error into which I had fallen through the misrepresentations of Portuguese travellers. For the Portuguese invariably called the Chambezi our Zambezi. "In going from Nyassa to Cazembé"- they said you will cross our own Zambezi". But I soon discovered that they must be wrong & I had to retrace[135] my travels so often that the natives began to say[136] that I must be mad. But I have now established that the Chambzi which starts from about[137] S Lat. 11° is no other than the most Southerly feeder of the Nile which makes that famous river nearly 2000 miles longer than it was supposed to be.

To the N. East of Cazembé's I came to a Lake called Liemba, after the country round it. But tracing it northward I found it to be no other than the Lake we are on now – the Tanganika. The S. End is situate in about 8° 42' S. therefore this Lake is about 360 geographical miles in length. From the S. End of Tanganika I passed westerly & came to Lake Mweru, which is about 60 miles long. At the Southern end of this I found a large river entering it called the Luapula, & by ascending along its banks –

---

129. 'were distressed by' written above 'suffered from' crossed out.
130. 'from w' crossed out.
131. 'I' written over 'he'.
132. 'I' written over 'he'; 'had' crossed out.
133. 'that it' added above the line.
134. 'An error' added above the line.
135. 'retrace' written over 'retravel'.
136. 'say' written over 'hint'.
137. 'about' added above the line.

I discovered that it came from the large lake of Bangweolo. Through[138] all these travels I found that the Chambzi entered Lake Bangweolo & came out of it under the name of Luapula, & that the Luapula entered Mweru.

On returning to Cazembe's I met an old white bearded half caste named Mohammed bin Sali, who is now[139] Governor of Ujiji. He was detained by Cazembe because of certain circumstances which had made him suspected to be a slave trader. I used my influence and got him released. I had good reason to regret it afterwards, for while travelling to Ujiji, he ruined the fidelity of the few followers who still clung to me so that I was deserted at one time by all but two men Chumah & Susi.[140] He did it by selling the favours of his concubines to them. That alone will tell you what kind of wretch our old Governor is. The desertion of my men simply made me like a slave to every village chief I came across for the vile old man had a cunning way of scattering his remarks about me that made me deserve every one's contempt. In June 1869, I came to Ujiji & sent off some letters to the Coast. When that duty was done I intended to sail around this[141] Lake & examine it thoroughly but every Arab had combined to raise the price of canoes to such a rate that it became impossible, if I wished to settle the question of the Central line of drainage. So at the end of June I employed what goods remained to me in paying my way to Manyema, by which I discovered a Lacustrine river which connected the Luapula as it leaves Mweru, with the Lualaba which flows by Nyangwe. I went off with traders direct Westerly for Rua. After 15 days travel we came to Bambarré,[142] a sort of ivory depot on[143] the frontiers of Manyema. But for six months I was detained with bleeding ulcers in my feet at that place. On recovering I went in a Northerly direction, and struck the Lualaba, flowing river. It was from one to 3 miles wide according to the season. After making great curving bends this river enters Lake Kamalondo. In memory of the kindness of Webb of Newstead Abbey I called it Webb's Lualaba.[144] Webb was my companion in S. Africa. Away to the S. West is another large lake which sends out its waters to form the Lumani, a feeder of the Lualaba. I called that Lake the "Lincoln" in memory of the great American Emancipator[145] who freed four millions of slaves.

---

138. 'Through' added above the line.
139. 'who is now' written above 'the' crossed out.
140. From here, text written in black ink.
141. 'this' added above the line.
142. From time to time, Stanley spelled Bambarré with an accent.
143. 'on' written over 'in'.
144. As several rivers bore the same name of 'Lualaba', the Doctor gave this one "the name of 'Webb's River,' after Mr. Webb..., one of his oldest and most consistent friends" (*HIFL*, 451). On Webb of Newstead Abbey, see S.A. 8, "Byron's Home."
145. Livingstone reasserted his admiration for President Lincoln in several letters: "[I named] Lake Lincoln as my tribute of love to the great and good man America enjoyed for some time and then lost." See *Livingstone's Africa: Perilous Adventures and Extensive Discoveries in the Interior of Africa, from the Personal Narrative of D. Livingstone ... together with the ... Results of the Herald-Stanley Expedition* (Philadelphia: Hubbard Bros., 1872), 523, letter to James Gordon Bennett Jr, telegraphed from London, July 26, 1872.

There is another river to the North of Kalamondo called the Lufira, – but I heard of so many that I left them all out from my map[146] except the most important. I followed the Lualaba to 4° S. & that is the furthermost point I reached. Every one maintained that it still continues flowing northward as far as they knew. Now don't you think that is worth following up. If I went home now I could never feel easy in my mind about the destination of the river. I fully believe that it is the Nile, but it may not be that river. It may be the Congo, or the Niger. If it were either of these two, I should not feel so interested about it. Who would care[147] to die for anything less than the Grand Old Nile.[148]

You can imagine how my mind has dwelt upon this question. I have revolved it over & over, but for every thing that inclines me to the suspicion that it may be some other river I have a host of reasons for sticking to the belief that it is the Nile. It is strange also how facts told by Natives crop up to remind me of what Herodotus says.[149]
Not far from Chebungo Lake to which I have given the name of Lincoln there is a mound or small[150] hill which gives birth to two[151] rivers, and in view of it is another hill where two other rivers rise. It reminds me of Crophi & Mophi near which Herodotus said rose four rivers – two went to Ethiopia & two flowed towards Egypt". When you get home you had better look up Herodotus & pen what he says about it.[152] I have been more than once within a short distance from those singular mounds but surrounded as I am by slave traders I cannot always go where I wish. One of the fountains is said to be so large that a man standing on one side, cannot be seen from the other, which gives it a decent size. This is an important matter which I have not the heart to leave. Then there is Webb's Lualaba. I shall have to connect it with the Nile. There is a big gap between S. Lat 4°, and Baker's Lake or Petherick's Nile. You see there Natives stick in their little districts, & never know what lies in the next. 30 miles from the Lualaba I met natives who had never seen the Great river. It is most tantalizing to feel that you are probably within a few days march of the very thing that you are in search, the one link in the chain of Evidence as it were, & yet not until you are well away from it, not to have known that it had been so accessible.

---

146. 'from my map' added above the line.

147. 'care' written over 'die'.

148. Livingstone referred to the Nile the same way in a letter to Lord Clarendon (Ujiji, November 1, 1871), *Livingstone's Africa*, 550.

149. Livingstone seemed haunted by descriptions Herodotus narrated in his *Histories*. In spite of his doubts that he "might be exploring the Congo instead of the Nile," the doctor found many similarities between the watershed of Central Africa and "the description given of…the fountains of the Nile by the Secretary of Minerva, in the city of Sais, in Egypt, to the father of all travellers, Herodotus" (*Livingstone's Africa*, 548; letter to Earl Granville, Ujiji, December 18, 1871, ibid., 570; letter to James Gordon Bennett, July 26, 1872, ibid., 525).

150. 'small' added above the line.

151. 'two' written over 'four'.

152. Apparently Stanley followed Livingstone's advice and inserted in his book three pages of Henry Cary's translation from Herodotus, "for the information of such readers as may not have the original at hand" (*HIFL*, 455–59).

Then the state of terror into which the tribes of Manyema have been driven by the noisy boom of the slave traders muskets[153] has so unsettled the nerve of the natives that they mistake their friends for their foes. My life has been frequently attempted by them. In that tin box I have preserved some spears that narrowly missed me. The fire rushing out from the guns has made the ignorant native believe that the Arabs have made use of lightening, and that is what most fills them with fear. Otherwise I think the Natives, who are not at all deficient in courage would make short work of them.

I have never seen a country I like so much as Manyema. It is a veritable Eden. The women are pretty, and have such ways which are very pleasant.[154] Markets are regularly held every other day where you would be amazed at the products of the land.

Then the Doctor went into descriptions of habits & manners of the Natives & every now & then he launched out into denunciations of the slave traders especially of one called Tagomoyo[155] who is a terrible villain according to the way that he perpetrated an awful massacre of unoffending peoples at a big market.[156] But he tells me that he will write a letter to the "New York Herald", and give a written account of some of his Experiences which will even be better than what he tells me viva voce.

What date was it you arrived in Ujiji this last time, Doctor?

Well I must have[157] arrived here according[158] the new calculations on the 21st October.[159] I[160] have been far ahead of my reckoning, which is[161] & probably due to my

---

153. 'make' crossed out.
154. Stanley pointed out in his book how "the Doctor said repeatedly the women of Manyema were remarkably pretty creatures" (*HIFL*, 464).
155. Spelled 'Tagamoyo' in *HIFL*, 463.
156. This refers to the massacre at Nyangwe, which Livingstone described to Stanley (*HIFL*, 463). A firsthand narrative of it is in Livingstone's letter sent to Earl Granville (Ujiji, November 14, 1871), *Livingstone's Africa*, 564–65.
157. 'must have' added above the line.
158. 'to my' crossed out; 'the new' added in the margin before 'calculations'. The "new" calculations imply that both travelers were trying to readjust to the right chronology, and Livingstone had agreed on the 21st as his arrival date at Ujiji. However, Stanley stands by October 16th (*HIFL*, 465).
159. '21' written over '23'[?]. From here three lines of the manuscript are littered with numerous corrections, alterations of dates, and additions: '21st' [written over 23] October' has been written above '22nd November', which was crossed out, the number '22nd' having been written over '10', and 'November' over 'October'. The two following lines show various attempts of corrections:
—but if I am [number crossed out] [another number crossed out] [word indecipherable crossed out] days out. . . ['out' crossed out, and replaced by 'ahead as you say' written above 'out'];
— it must have been the 14th, [16th having been first written over '20', and '14th over 16th];
—Finally these lines from 'but if I am' to 'must have been the 14th' were crossed out, and only the first date of 21st remained valid.
These many changes of dates may indicate that both travelers could not make the figures tally. Stanley took refuge behind the fevers that plagued both travelers to explain the discrepancies.
Scholars are still debating the exact dates of Livingstone's arrival at Ujiji and his meeting with Stanley. Cf. François Bontinck, "La date de la rencontre Stanley-Livingstone," *Africa: Rivista trimestrale di studi e documentazione dell'Istituto italiano per l'Africa e l'Oriente* 34, no. 3 (September 1979), http://www.jstor.org/stable/40759179, and the more recent survey of this question, "The Date of the Livingstone-Stanley Meeting," by Justin Livingstone and Adrian S. Wisnicki, http://livingstone.library.ucla.edu/1871diary/meeting1.htm. Unfortunately, these alterations do not solve the problem.
160. 'must' crossed out.
161. 'which is' added above the line.

illness[162] at Bambarré. Of course had I suspected I was so wrong a glance at the Nautical Almanac would have discovered the Error. But I am glad to have had my attention called to it, and as I hope[163] to go back the way I came, it will not matter much.

"I tried to cheer myself all the way from Nyangwé that the great object of my heart was only postponed. The 300 miles or so between this place and the Lualaba seemed nothing when the way was lightened by the thoughts of the abundance of stores waiting me. "Never mind" said I to myself. "It is only a few months, & then I shall be able to say "finished". I came to Ujiji a mere knuckle of bones", but soon after my arrival Susi & Chuma were seen crying and I asked them what was the matter.

Said they "All our things are sold Bwana. Shereef has parted with everything for ivory!" I was a beggar there was nothing left neither cloth nor beads.

Late in the evening Sherif came to see me & saluted & offered his hand, but I could not touch the hand of a thief.[164] When I asked him why he robbed me, he said he had searched the Koran & the Koran had told him I was dead. I cannot imagine why Kirk who was once of my opinion about the employment of slaves should have trusted my all into their keeping, and I have so often implored him[165] to send only freemen. If he had only taken[166] a little trouble[167] he might have found honest freemen, but he must have sent to Ludha Damji the Banyan for men & of course he sent what men he chose, hiring them I suppose from some of the Arabs in his debt. I am almost tempted to laugh at the plight in which I was only a few days ago & in which I should be stil but for you. Really you have been a good Samaritan to me & I do not know how to thank Mr Bennett for his munificent help. It will all come out right please God, and that is our comfort.

Nov 14th Tuesday. Halt at Ujiji.

The mornings in Ujiji are divine, and I never feel so bright and clear headed as after the morning coffee. Livingstone seems to me much more hopeful this morning than he was yesterday and in a short time he made me conscious of it by proposing to me to accompany him into Manyema and help him to finish his discoveries. Had he knocked me down he could not have more astonished me, and I did not know what to say, but feared giving him a downright answer lest he might suspect that I had a personal objection to him. I do not think I was made for an African Explorer for I detest the land most heartily, & I doubt whether he could have a worse companion. I seldom am well, except for a day or so when sleeping in quinine. To be constantly

---

162. 'have been far ahead … to my illness' written above 'lost most of those dates while' crossed out.
163. 'hope' written above 'intend' crossed out.
164. See notebook S.A. 8, pp. 72 and 75.
165. 'not' crossed out.
166. 'If he had only taken' added above the line.
167. 'on his part' crossed out.

obliged to dose oneself with aperient[168] medicines, and on top of these take from six to 20 grains of Quinine is not very alluring. Then the anxieties of the life are very wearing on the nerves. The blacks give an immense amount of trouble – they are too ungrateful to suit my fancy. I thought I liked it when we started. There was so much novelty in it, and I had a romantic[169] that among some of them I should find some sterling examples of native faithfulness & devotion, that a steady course of kindness would win a few over to my side which should make me feel strong in moral courage to resist the depressing feeling that sometimes came over me. Then again I serve a hard taskmaster. I should say Bennett would never forgive me for running away from my duty to him. From what I know of him he would even begrudge the few days I must naturally stay here, & would say "Your duty was to ask questions & note answers, obtain a formal acknowledgement that you had seen him, & hurry back to the Coast with the news." So thinking these thoughts I answered Livingstone, that I was afraid I could not see my way to accompany him, as I was in the service of a newspaper which of course would expect the most implicit obedience. His face was shaded for a brief time, & he said, "I see how it is. "You would come if you thought you would be permitted. Well there is nothing like sticking to duty, & I will not be the one to tempt you, but I hope that before you leave me you will be able to look kinder on Africa. It is a great pity that there are so few who come to Africa that can divest themselves from their personal feelings, and look at the land apart from themselves. Now just look around the shores of this Lake and tell me honestly if you saw in any country any thing to excel it. Take the grand uplift of the mountains, the rich vegetation in the valleys, the spaciousness of the Lakes – the warmth of the sun – the bursting greenness all around us. Look at the Natives. Where would you find so many finely formed bodies, such physical strength, such mild manners. I wonder that people are so long in finding these things out for themselves."

"Well Doctor" said I smiling at his unusual grand way of talking "I have been something of a traveller myself. I have been in nearly every state in America, I have been much in England, I have been in France, Spain, Italy, Egypt, Greece, Crete, Asia Minor, Abyssina, the Caucasus, Persia, Mauritius, Seychelle, & I have reached Tanganika. Though I admit that all this is fair to look on, it would be hard to say that I have seen nothing superior to it. I think that so far as scenery Africa will do well enough but I can never dissociate it from the cursed fever which clings to me continually – and whether the cause is in me myself, or in the land – I fancy something of a sadness in what I see.

"I know what you mean" said he. That is bile, nothing more than the effect of bile in your own system. So long as you look at Africa with eyes full of yellow bile, you can

---

168. Aperient medicine: laxative. Constipation is a side effect of quinine.
169. Word missing.

not help but feel that. Well, I get bilious too sometimes, but I have long ago got beyond fancying that every one was hideous, because my inside was wrong, and when I come out of my house in the morning, and look abroad I feel sometimes overpowered with feelings of gratitude that the Earth is so fair and the air is so soft and balmy. The waving of the palms when the branches[170] rustle one against the other sends something like a thrill through me, and if I felt at all dispirited within the house, I soon am different when I see & hear all that I see without. Take my word for it – before you go home you will be able to see things differently."

"There is no knowing what I may feel, when I am in health, said I, but if I am sick I am sick & can not forget it. If I am well, I know nobody so well able to find delight or be ready to enjoy himself. But Doctor to turn to another subject, I understand that you have not explored this Lake, that you tried to get canoes, but you did not have[171] means enough to pay the Arab demand?"

"No, I have not explored the Lake. As I said I intended to with a view of ascertaining which way the surplus waters went, but the Arabs chucked that intention by asking so much for canoe hire that I could not afford it – & then again the importance of this Lake was nil against that of the Central line of drainage of a Continent."

"You have seen the S. end?"

"That is what the Natives call Liemba which is another name for the Tanganyika."

"I read Burton's account of the Lake Regions & it appears that he and Speke did not reach the North end quite. Which way do you think the Lake discharges its super-[172] abundance of water?"

"I am of the opinion that the waters go northward to the Nile. While standing on the beach – the water plants, & vegetable debris – are always noted to be drifting to the North. There are several Arabs here who have reached the North End, and they say that the mountains[173] on both sides of the Lake come together there, & that right in the middle there is a gap through which the river from the Lake flows northward."

"The last note that I recollect to have seen in a newspaper referring to the Tanganika was that Sir Roderick Murchison was sure that whatever doubt was entertained with regard to the outlet of the Tanganyika would soon be dispelled by the researches of Dr Livingstone. I think he will be dreadfully disappointed to learn that it is still a mystery."

"Well, you know I have sometimes felt that too, but then what can a poor fellow like me do. It is only want of means that has prevented me from settling it long ago."

"I dare say you will think me very presumptious, but I should like to make a proposition. You have been good enough to ask me to accompany you on your travels

---

170. 'the' written over 'they'; 'branches' added above the line.
171. 'the' crossed out.
172. 'super' added above the line.
173. Word indecipherable, crossed out.

to the West, & I have been obliged to decline for the reasons stated, but a month or so would not much matter especially when one is rewarded by being able to give an answer to such a question as this. What would you say to as hiring a big canoe from Said bin Majid or[174] Muini Kheri & filling it with provisions & goods and sailing straight to the N. End of the Lake, and settle that question once & for all."

"I should be very willing indeed, for[175] I should look upon such a trip as a holiday."

"Well we have plenty of means to pay any price for a canoe & have abundance to spare. We have good men, better never came from Zanzibar. Now if you ask Said bin Majid[176] to let you have a[177] proper sized canoe, the thing is as good as done."

"Capital. Nothing could be better."

It will be[178] so easy you know Doctor, compared to what Burton & Speke had to endure. They had to beg Kannena for canoe, & men, and were entirely at the mercy of a native chief & could do nothing without an awful amount of worry & vexation. Burton's[179] account of the trip really made me wish that I could have Kannena in my caravan for a month – just to give him another view of a white man, & reduce[180] that big head of his. I wonder if that fellow is alive to day. Just fancy after getting within view of the head of the lake to be turned back! They were like slaves!

The upshot of this long conversation was that Livingstone after pondering awhile suggested that we should go together to Said bin Majid[181] which we did. Said bin Majid[182] saw no difficulty at all in allowing us to have a canoe, and I thought his manner exceedingly gracious, partaking of that Grand Seigneur way that attracted me so much in Khamis bin Abdullah at Unyanyembe.[183] He said it would carry 25 men and hundred frasilah (3500 lbs) of ivory, from which we thought it would be very suitable for our purpose.

While returning to our house Livingstone said that his reception by the Arab had made him feel several inches taller. It was quite unexpected. Said had always been kind, but he had been made to feel this time that he was of importance. "Ah well, said he, had you not come & had I come to beg, I should have had a different reception. Then even if he had[184] given me[185] what I asked, I should have been made to feel that it was out of pity – but now you see I receive as if it were my due. That's just the difference."

---

174. 'Said bin Majid or' added above the line.
175. 'for' added above the line.
176. 'Said bin Majid' written above 'Muini Kheri' crossed out.
177. 'a' written over 'the'.
178. 'will' written over 'is'; 'be' added above the line.
179. 'Burton's' written above 'His' crossed out.
180. 'reduce' written over word indecipherable.
181. 'Said bin Majid' written above 'Muini Kheri' crossed out.
182. 'Said bin Majid' preceded by 'Muini Kheri' crossed out.
183. Khamis bin Abdullah, an influential sheikh of Unanyembe, was killed in Mirambo's attack on Tabora, August 22, 1871 (S.A. 7).
184. 'he had' written over 'it was'.
185. 'me' written over 'to'.

Nov 15th Wednesday. It is decided we shall set of tomorrow and we have each of us been busy. Livingstone wrote letters[186] and I prepared for the trip by buying provisions, salt for barter special beads for the Warundi, selecting the cloths most suitable, making samples of cloth presents, packing baggage ammunition for sport & defence, & picking out the crack oarsmen, repairing oars & canoe. The vessel must have been when cut down a splendid tree. It has been hollowed out, and built upon. It will not be fast, but is capacious and having rigged an awning over the after part – and a platform 2 feet above the keel we ought to be comfortable unless the Lake is very stormy. I am too tired with my work to write.

Nov 16th Thursday. From Ujiji to Kigoma, which Livingstone insists on spelling Chigoma.

Started at dawn after an early dish of coffee. Before we had proceeded very far, I experienced an uneasy feeling. One who has been much at sea & knows by instinct almost when the vessel under his feet has been overloaded will understand it. The roll was sickening & lifeless, so after consulting with the Doctor turned in shore, dismissed 9 men & discharged a good deal of the salt. Started again she was still cranky & found the mast & sail made her dangerous. She then rode better & with delicate treatment found she would do. We headed for Bangwe island, and after 4 hours landed at Kigoma.[187]

Nov 17th To Niasanga 12 miles. Started at dawn. About 4 miles from Kigoma sounded & obtained 35 fathom. The water was dark green. The lake was lovely & the[188] shores reminded me of the Turkish shores of the Black Sea. And seemed deliciously happy in their warm bath of sunshine.[189] As the Doctor suffers[190] from intestinal ailment we are obliged to take it much easier than we would have done otherwise. His manner suits my nature better than that[191] of any man I can remember of late years. Perhaps I should best describe it as benevolently[192] paternal. It[193] is almost tender, though I don't know much about tenderness but it steals an influence on me without any effort on his part. He does not soften his voice,[194] draw back his lips in an affected smile, mince his words,[195] or courtsey to my wish, or will – but is sincerely natural and converses with me as if I were of his own age, or of equal experience. The consequence is that I

---

186. 'wrote letters' written above 'began to' crossed out.
187. 'On the way shot a dog-faced monkey' crossed out.
188. 'Eastern' crossed out.
189. This sentence was added between two lines.
190. 'suffers' written over 'suffered'.
191. 'that' written over 'of any'.
192. 'benevolently' written above 'truly' crossed out.
193. 'It' preceded by word undecipherable.
194. 'or' crossed out before 'draw'; idem before 'mince'.
195. 'mince his words' added above the line.

have come[196] to entertain an immense respect for myself, and begin to think myself somebody though I never suspected it before. If it were other than perfectly natural with him my conceit tells me I should discover it. It was all right to be acknowledged as some one by my own paid followers but when a man old enough to be my brother manages to[197] convey it to me in every action I get as proud as can be, as though I had some great honour thrust on me. I therefore think nothing too good for him – and pester the cook more than enough about getting the food done up properly. In the boat while on the Lake I have been struck by his broad views in regard to this Continent. He is so serious & genuine in his interest in its redemption from the slave-trading blight that I fancy there is something seer-like in him. I am not able to sympathise with every thing he says because underlying the beauty of the land I always feel that the fever is not far off – but if it were not for that – I think his influence & example of sweet patience, and grand hope that everything will come out all right at last would have effect on me. However I honour him all the same, & think it a thousand pities that such doings as he daily talks about as having occurred before his eyes in Manyema should be possible.

Nov 18. Zassi Village. District of Ujiji reached after 4 ½ hours rowing. Started at dawn & journeyed along the Eastern shore which grows more picturesque as we proceed northward. The tops of the mountains are from 2000 to 2500 feet above the Lake. The cool[198] nooks are enchanting & the bays are lined with umbrageous tropical trees. The beehive huts of the fishermen peep out from under deep shadow of the leafage. The shores are extremely populous & every terrace and bit of plateau are crowned with dwellings. Pulled out 1 ½ mile and at 115 fathom found no bottom. In pulling line up it parted.

Nov 19th Nyabigma Island. Off Urundi Country. The river Mshala is the boundary between Ujiji & Urundi. Traded freely for fowls. We prepared here for a tuzzle with the Warundi of whom we hear bad accounts.

Nov 20th Camped at Mukungu Urundi after a row of 4 hours. Our first night in the Urundi Country very inauspicious. We lost I bag of Flour, 500 Cartridges & the remnant of the sounding line. This was due to the excessive stupor of sleep into which the guardians of the boat Bombay & Susi had fallen.

Nov 21st Slept at Mugeyo after 7 hours pulling to Murembwe River, 6 hours to Dama R. and 6 hours thence to Mugeyo during which exertion we must have gone 47 miles.

---

196. 'come' written above 'got' crossed out.
197. 'to' written over 'it'.
198. 'cool' written over 'cozy'.

We reached Mugeyo at 3 A.M. of the 22nd. The reason of this uncommon journey was the undoubted hostility of the Natives. The further we went the more decided were the evidences of unfriendliness. Our Wajiji guides continually harped on the attitudes exhibited, and as we were a small party & the Doctor was as it were in our care I weighed carefully every action. We were inclined to stop for the Doctor's sake at Bikari, but the insolent calls shouted out to us, caused us to sheer out again. Friends do not use those gestures & tones we said & continued on. Wherupon they flung stones at us. If Livingstone had not been in the boat, I would certainly have tried to teach them a lesson – for I have already begun to learn that the weaker we are, the more natives of this temper encroach upon forbearance. Coming to Morembe Pt[199] we halted to prepare lunch. While we were fortifying ourselves with this repast the Doctor said that from his experiences elsewhere the Arabs slave traders must have been here & angered these people by their conduct. His[200] explanations were so wise, that I was glad we had not been driven to retaliate.

Having finished lunch we steered for distant Sentakeyi Cape which we hoped to make before dark. But the night came & we were still at the oars & the boatmen fully understood that this was none of our choice. About 8 P.M. we pulled in shore at what we thought was a deserted spot. Keeping as quiet as possible we began to prepare dinner with a view to be off before dawn, but while thus occupied the look outs hailed some natives who were stealing cautiously towards us. They answered the hail with the Barundi greeting Waké. We explained to them who we were & said we should be glad to trade with them in the morning. They seemed quiet enough but I observed their roving eyes, & having had reason to be suspicious, I doubted them. They went away & another party came & did likewise & these also departed with an overacted pleasure. A third & fourth party came & went, too boisterous altogether for friendship. Our supper meantime had been by then nearly[201] despatched & we were debating whether we would risk staying, when something decided us for resuming our journey by night. Our men were only too pleased for they were wide awake with uneasiness, we soon loaded quietly and after the Doctor had taken his seat, & every oar ready to back water, I lifted the prow & shot the canoe[202] into the water, springing in as she glided off. Not a moment too soon, for as our eyes searched the shore in the moonlight, we saw that our[203] comfortable nest[204] under a shelf of land was surrounded by dark forms. They hailed us, but we did not respond. "Neatly done" cried

---
199. Murembwe Point (*HIFL*, 490).
200. 'His' preceded by 'from' crossed out.
201. 'nearly' added above the line.
202. 'the canoe' written above 'her' crossed out.
203. 'our' written above 'we had been in a' crossed out
204. 'and that' crossed out.

Livingstone as I showed him how from all sides – but the Lake – the natives were converging upon our camp.[205]

"Do let me fly a couple of shots on the rascals!" I said. "What is the use? Let them be. We are safe, let us bless God for that." He said putting his hand gently on mine[206] and I put down the gun thinking what a pity it was that I should not send them home to meditate, and learn, that some people had their wits about as well as they.

While we dozed under our awning the stout rowers labored[207] until 3 in the morning when the Wajiji said that we were well away beyond the dangerous port of Urundi. We pulled it towards the beach of Mugeyo & camped unmolested.

Nov 22nd At dawn we set to again for 2 ½ hours and reached friendly Magala. As the people were naturally very tired & we felt stiff from the hard seat[208] under the awning & the Natives were civil we rested. We exchanged presents – and had every reason to[209] be pleased with our reception by the Mutware and his subjects. The boatmen were also[210] well-fed on meat, & four days rations[211] which they well deserved.

Nov 23rd We reached Kisuka P^t in Usige after 3 ½ hours rowing. A storm overtook us while we were under weigh between two capes or headlands, but as it was fair it drove us at a rattling pace, until we came to the safe port of Kisuka & beached our boat close to a village half buried by tall reeds.

Nov 24th One hour took us to Mukanigi on a N by East course. This is the Great Mukamba's village. We were housed in a small but comfortable hut, but it was not long before a violent fever prostrated me, and I became indifferent to every thing. Indeed it was time, for since leaving Unyanyembe I had escaped, but lake, swamps & river Deltas & reed beds are not healthy to me. So I saw everything as through a dream, for the fever had come upon me with full force. I had an idea that Livingstone was nursing me, & sometimes feeling my hand, and that Mukamba appeared to shake hands, but it was all so vague & unreal that I think I must have been a good deal delirious.

---

205. This incident is described with minor changes in field notebook S.A. 8.
206. 'He said… on mine' added above the line.
207. 'all night' crossed out.
208. 's' of seats crossed out.
209. 'rejoice' crossed out.
210. 'also' added above the line.
211. 'of beads' crossed out.

Nov. 25[212] Saturday. Continue prostrated – but sensible. We halt. A Mgwana from Zanzibar says that he knows the Rusizi well & that it flows out of the Lake.[213] I thought the news too good to be true", for it would be a grand discovery. Livingstone however more than half believed it & he cited stories of the father of Rumanika having had the idea of excavating the bed of the Kitangule River in order that his canoes might pass on to Ujiji! I hope it will prove true, but in a day or two we shall see for ourselves.

Nov 26. Sunday. Fever still on me but at dusk we departed for Mugihawa. Susi got drank last night & crept into Livingstone's bed, and I was wakened by hearing him slap the hard sleeping Susi.[214] At 4. A.M. we reached Ruhinga's territory having gone 22 ½ miles

Nov 27th Monday. On awaking this morning found ourselves at the Northern head of Lake Tanganika, in the Delta of the Rusizi with rank matete & papyrus all round us. Ruhinga[215] received us most[216] courteously & gave us a great deal of information respecting the Rusizi which was the object of our voyage and its many affluents. He said it rose in Kivoe Lake, lagoon or marsh which must be about 18 miles by about 8, and is surrounded by montains. On leaving the lake it begins to recieve many little streams (he named them all). After a while it connects with the Ruanda R. and flows into the Lake.

Nov 28th Tuesday. We mustered ten paddlers & set out to explore the Rusizi. There was not a doubt of it the Rusizi came into the Lake by three mouths the left 8yds[217] broad very rapid & shallow[218] the central one 10yds rapid but slower[219] the right or Eastern most 6yds[220] wide, deep but slow. We ascended high enough up each mouth to ascertain the character of each stream. As regards this river then the question is settled forever but the Doctor is strongly of the opinion that there must be an outlet somewhere. We are also both firmly convinced that Baker has overdrawn the Albert Lake & that much of it must be cut off to allow of Kivoe Lake & the length of this river, which comes from Northward &[221] from our knowledge of African Rivers[222] should have its source at least[223]

---

212. '5' written over '6'.
213. Field notebook S.A. 8 and *HIFL*, 495 and 497. Same story in *LJ*, 158, but on November 24, 1871.
214. A slightly different rendering of the story is in field notebook S.A. 9 and *HIFL*, 498–99.
215. Ruhinga was Mukamba's elder brother (*HIFL*, 500), and his superior.
216. 'most' written over 'very'.
217. '8' written over '10'.
218. 'very rapid and shallow' added above the line.
219. 'rapid but slower' added above the line.
220. '6' written over '5'.
221. 'comes from Northward and' added above the line.
222. 'we think' crossed out.
223. 'at least' written above 'say' crossed out.

in 2°. 19[224] or a degree further North than the head of the Lake, and probably still further. By star observation the Doctor made Ruhinga's village to be on 3°.19

Nov 29[225] Wednesday. I went out to hunt leaving Livingstone to write his letters & make copies of the most important. I shot some fine geese, an ibis, a duck & a crane, all of which are eatable.

In the evening after dinner we sat under the eaves of our beehive shaped hut, and as it was a beautiful moonlight & we could do nothing else, Livingstone who was in a good vein told me for the first time the extraordinary story of the death of Speke[226] the Companion of Burton during the journey to this Lake some 14 years ago. I knew Speke was dead, but[227] nothing of the circumstances. He said, among other things "Of the two, Speke was by far the best as a traveller. He was one of those frank, soldierly fellows who go to India, and love shooting upon every occasion. He was rather fond of natural history, could use his sextant & so on,[228]

He had a keen eye for country, and was much better fitted for African travel than Burton in every way. Burton was a clever fellow – much cleverer in a literary sense[229] than Speke. He knew languages, he had a gift that way – could write well. I have read his book, but though I don't like him I must say it is well written. It is spoiled I think by his intense spite against the people – against Speke – against everybody but himself. He must be a quarrelsome fellow. But the big quarrel between the two[230] was about that[231] Victoria Nyanza. You who have read the "Lake Regions" can understand the matter as well as myself. When they returned from this Lake to Unyanyembe, Burton sat down in the bazah of his house to enjoy his rest. He loved to chat with the Arabs, and affected to be while with them a Hajji, one who had been to Mecca, which is of course a great thing with Mussulmen. While he rested in this way Speke was flying about[232] the country shooting. He came across some men who told him that a little distance to the North there was a bigger lake to be seen there than even Tanganika. Speke reported it to Burton who was not much impressed with it seemingly. Finding that Burton did not[233] care for it as it had struck him[234] asked[235] for permission to go & have a look at it. He went & in a short time returned saying that he had

---

224. '9' written over 'o'.
225. From November 29, change of ink.
226. 'who was' crossed out.
227. 'I knew' crossed out.
228. 'and' crossed out.
229. 'in a literary sense' added above the line.
230. 'two' added above the line; 'the' written over them.
231. 'that' written over 'the'.
232. 'about' written over 'through'.
233. 'seem to' crossed out.
234. 'as it had struck him' added above the line.
235. 'him' crossed out.

found the source of the Nile. Burton was taken much aback by this, and then tried to laugh the idea down. He ridiculed it, and poor Speke too. He said that he had made all sorts of inquiries among the Arabs & that they all said it was only a marsh – a puddle & so on. But Speke perested in his idea, and was offended at Burton's manner who was a man who never minced his words. It seems that they were not on speaking terms from that day to the Coast. After reaching the Coast Burton took into his head that he must do some more exploring on the Coast & I believe he visited several places, but Speke was glad to be rid of Burton & insisted on going home, – for everything seemed tame to him compared to what he had already seen. Before they parted they made some agreement together. Speke[236] undertook not to read any paper before the Geographical Society until Burton had come home. But when the Geographers got hold of Speke it was all up with him. Sir Roderick was one of the worst men to be met when there was anything about Geography to be talked and Speke was coaxed by the dear old fellow in his usual familiar & friendly manner & Speke yielded, and read a paper about his discovery of the Source of the Nile. The paper made a great sensation at home and Sir Roderick taking his cue from the general interest tapped Speke on the shoulder and said, Ha, My dear Speke I see we must send you out again to settle that question for you have won the blue ribbon. It was impossible to resist him and Speke[237] came out once again with a Captain Grant this time. To cut a long story short, Speke & Grant came to Unyanyembe & went to Uganda and not far from that country saw the river tumbling down the Ripon Falls as it left the Lake. They then[238] followed that river down until it came into Egupt. It was the Nile of course. Burton did not give in however. He hammered away at poor Speke, and with his friends made things very hot for him. At last it was decided that they both should meet before the British Association at Bath, & have it out. In expectation of a grand field day between the two travellers – all the world – that is all those who knew anything in Geography had met, & we expected to hear grand passages between them. I went there too for I was to read a paper before the Geographical Section.[239] My sympathies to tell you the truth were entirely with Speke – for after all – however Burton, clever as he was could make Speke ridiculous. Speke had done the trick. It was an exciting time. Burton had done his best for the debate, and the man can talk. The place was crowded & Burton being the senior was allowed to speak first. As he went on, and got warmer my informant told me that he[240] cast a look at Speke & saw that he was getting more & more uneasy – and that[241] at last he got up and said "By George

---

236. 'was' crossed out.
237. 'out' crossed out; 'came' written over 'went'.
238. 'then' added above the line.
239. This sentence was added between two lines, above 'I happened to be there, and' crossed out.
240. 'my informant told me that he' added above the line; 'I' crossed out.
241. 'that' added above the line.

or something of the kind, I cannot stand this", and walked out to amuse himself shooting birds,[242] while Burton continued his speech, smiling with a kind of triumph as was[243] thought. Well not long afterwards while the section was[244] still setting,[245] the news reached[246] that Speke had shot himself."

"What committed suicide."

"No it seems not, for of course there was an inquest, & it came out that he had borrowed a gun & gone to do some[247] shooting,[248] & that in jumping over a hedge,[249] or forcing his way[250] through it the trigger of the gun was caught by a bush[251] & the contents were lodged in his side causing death immediately afterwards. Burton tried to spread the report that Speke had committed suicide to avoid having to answer what he thought was unanswerable, but there is no doubt that it was a pure accident. However as Speke was such a noted sportsman, Burton's story was believed by many, though in my opinion it is just what might happen to a carless sportsman – whereas a novice would have been more careful." I suppose his mind was full of Burton's speech at the time & did not think of his gun.[252]

"What a sad story, I said. But I cannt imagine why a man like Speke – knowing that he had done what the other would not, or had not done should have been afraid to face the best orator that ever lived. It seems to me that had I been in his place I would have sat that paper quietly out, and after Burton had concluded, I would have walked to the platform & said Ladies & Gentlemen I have not the gifts of speech of Captain Burton, and cannot hope that I shall succeed in saying what is in my mind. I beg to say however that I first saw the Lake while Captain preferred to stay in Unyanyembe & that the second time I travelled with Captain Grant & saw the Lake again,[253] & having seen its southern & northern ends & the river coming out of it, I followed that river to Egypt. That is all I have to say Good Morning."

Livingstone laughed and remarked "Yes, I quite agree with you – and English people are not fools but are in the main generous[254] & however they might admire[255] Burton's grand way of putting things – every sensible person would have sided with

---

242. 'to amuse himself at shooting birds' added above the line.
243. 'was' written over 'I'.
244. 'the section was' written above 'we were' crossed out.
245. 'setting' written above 'in the hall' crossed out.
246. 'reached' written over 'came'.
247. 'do some' added above the line.
248. 'shooting' written over 'shoot birds'.
249. 'the trigg' crossed out.
250. 'forcing his way' written above 'going' crossed out.
251. 'by a bush' added above the line.
252. 'I suppose his mind was full of Burton's speech at the time & did not think of his gun'. This sentence was added between two lines, and quotation marks are missing.
253. 'again' written above 'a second time' crossed out.
254. 'but are in the main generous' added above the line.
255. 'admire' written above 'have' crossed out.

Speke – because no amount of talkee-talkee could disprove the great fact. But Speke poor fellow was so nervous, that he could not speak.[256] It was said that[257] he could scarcely get one sentence smooth and straight out. I am a poor speaker myself & could sympathise him. To get up & face an audience is not easy. While we are sitting down, we are full of matter, but when we stand we are dumb, the words will not come out. I suppose after plenty of practice we should improve. Your time will come, and you will see for yourself whether it is easy or not."

Nov 30th Thursday. We delivered over the Muhongo (tribute) to the good natured chief Ruhinga. Livingstone undertook to see to this business, as he is more used to native ways. The women have been celebrating the chief's recovery from sickness, & have besmeared their faces & heads with a pasty composition of dourra flour & oil, & arming themselves with their husbands & father's spears go about chanting & at certain intervals relieve the montony with a dance. For the first time since I arrived on this Lake it rained to-day.

Dec 1st Ruhinga came to see us this morning bringing an immense two gallon gourd to drink[258] coffee out of. We had invited him last night to sit down & take a cup of coffee, much sweetened but he had deferred that pleasure until he could bring his own drinking vessel. He[259] seems to have thought that he should give a whole day to it & had dressed himself with unusual care with a gay Manchester print folded around him like a toga. We explained to him the use of coffee, & after a long chat about the Geography of this region he retired.

Dec 2nd Our canoe went over to Mukanigi to day to fetch Mukamba. His women & son have been very kind to us. Altogether we[260] received an ox, 3 sheep with broad fat tails, and any number of pots of milk, eggs, honey[261] & a quantity of flour. The wooden milk pots in which they bring the milk to us are beautifully carved & exquisitely clean, but their churning gourds I doubt are ever[262] washed.
    This evening while we were under the eave of our hut & indulging in gossip about various things, a sound escaping[263] from the interior of our hut attracted me, & peeping in through a crack saw Selim on his knees with his head well back & mouth

---

256. 'I heard him more than once try hard, but it was of no use' crossed out.
257. 'It was said that' added above the line.
258. 'our' crossed out.
259. 'He' preceded by 'and' crossed out.
260. 'have' added above the line.
261. 'honey' added above the line.
262. 'ever' written over 'never'.
263. 'escaping' written over 'escaped'.

open under our honey bag, which was dripping clear honey into a basin set underneath. I nudged Livingstone & whispered[264] to him to look in. He turned away with a disgusted face, & said, "There, we[265] have a proof of the way servants behave when their masters are absent. I should never have believed had I not seen it that Selim would have behaved in that way. Clearly the Christian Religion has had not much real effect on him."

Dec 3rd Sunday. Had prayers & service after a brief fashion.

At night the Doctor took a series of observations for longitude. As his chronometer had stopped & would not go, he tied an empty rifle shell to the key & succeeded in[266] measuring the time between the Lunar sights.

After this we had a warm political argument about the merits of Disraeli & Gladstone. The Doctor seems to have got all his ideas from the Saturday Review & is strong for Disraeli, while I am as ardent on the other side. He was pushing me rather hard, when the fever obliged me to cry out. It is of no use Doctor, I must be off to bed, my head aches tremendously. In an instant his tone changed, and had he been my own father, he could not have been kinder. He wrapped me in rugs, brought hot bottles to my feet, and after thanking him I was soon steaming & perspiring under my load of clothes. He himself has not been over bright the last two days but it does not appear to make any difference in his manner.

Dec 4th Monday. Late in the afternoon our canoe & men returned bringing Mukamba & his force of 60 canoes. After landing his warriors surrounded him & setting up a song while with[267] their arms then encircled one another they marched towards his brother Ruhinga's house. The women of Mugihawa came out to meet him footing it bravely & singing. Behind Mukamba came his wife & daughter both very light complexioned & these were received by another party of women who danced as they drew near to them very much like the companions of Myriam, as recorded in Scripture.

Dec 5th Not feeling very well I left the Doctor to go alone to bid farewell to Mukamba & carry the parting present.

In the afternoon feeling better we went out to examine the bays on the Eastern side of the Rusizi of which there are three – Altogether 10 in the shore at the N. End of the Lake.

---

264. 'whispered' written over word indecipherable.
265. 'we' written over 'he'.
266. 'taking the' crossed out.
267. 'with' written over 'their'.

Dec 6th Still at Mugihawa, but we purpose to go & sleep nearer the Lake tonight so as to be off early in the morning

Doctor took a set of observations last night again for longitude, & another set for Latitude.

Dec 7th Thursday. Reached Kakumba near Chigongo R. & Cape of that name. From Mugihawa we went S of the Katangara Islands & approached the highlands of Uashi near the boundary line between Mukamba's country & Uvira. Passing Kanyama & the market place of Kirabula – the furthest point N. reached by Burton & Speke in 1858, half an hour later we halted at Kavimba to cook breakfast. Here we met a party of plundered Wajiji who had been thus heavily punished for trying to evade the tribute to the Mutware or chief.

Dec 8. Friday. Arrive & camp at New York Herald islets 3.41. S. after 5 hours. We had taken precautions against thieves last night, so missed nothing. The Western shores of the Lake about here are much loftier & bolder than the Eastern – and many parts show singular scenic beauty. Ridges drop down in bold spurs towards the lake & form so many points at sight of which our compasses go up to take bearings of the prominent objects revealed.

When not thus occupied Livingstone kept me pretty busy with adds and end of stories about his[268] journey to Manyema. He said that he would have settled the Nile problem long ago had he a sufficient force, or anything like the number I have at Ujiji, but his time was frittered away in quieting the cowardly fears of his few men, & though after much persuasion he manages to get from a village he is obliged to be perpetually alert, because on the first alarm they would fly & leave him to his fate.

Muini Dugumbi the greatest Arab at Nyangwe told Livingstone one day that his own people were his worst enemies. He had thought of descending the Lualaba in a canoe, but when he tried to obtain one his men spread a report that he wanted it to kill Manyema, and as they had never seen white men before they could not help believing it. He was in the sphere of bloodshed & strife and the Arab slave traders gladly conspired with his men to baulk every intention.

He told me also a story of how he went to a meeting in Glasgow where he met an enthusiastic admirer who turned out to [be] a Mason,[269] & a very warm Mason too. "Said he to me "I will make you a Freemason if you like free of charge. Come now it will do you a vast deal of good. "But", I answered "it is a secret thing this Masonry. I do not know anything about it, besides so far I have managed to do very well without

---

268. 'last trip to' crossed out.
269. 'be' missing in the text.

it. Why should I become a Freemason now?" Ah", he said it wont cost you anything not a single farthing. I will get you in free of charge."

"Yes, so I understand, I said, but your Society is a secret one & I am opposed to do[270] anything without knowing first all I am expected to do."

"But "Man alive, he continued it will do you a world of good in Africa, where you are going."

"I cannot see how, said I. I never came across a Free Mason in Africa, nor heard of any place where if I had filled the office in your Society, the fact would do me any good." But he was not convinced & I suppose he still thinks me as stupid as at the moment I was obliged to escape him to turn my back to him."

This[271] evening while snugging[272] before the fire on this[273] largest of these islets he told me of an[274] experience he had with a secretary of a Young Men's Christian Association who called on him with a view to engage him to lecture on Africa.

The lecture was to be at Exeter Hall and the young man offered him £20 for it. "I am sorry to say that it is not quite convenient for me to lecture just now, as I am very much occupied, I said.

"Ah but £20 you know is to be given to you. You really must, "for £20."

"Ah but I really can't", I answered.

"Ah, but please remember we are to pay you £20."

Why he did not seem capable of understanding how a man could refuse £20, and that by obstinately dangling his £20 before me, he could beat down what he took to be my obstinacy, & at last I had to get up, and literally open the door for him to get him to leave. I bade him a very polite good morning."

At Bemba as we came to these islets we took a lot of pipe clay on board to satisfy our Wajiji guides who mentioned the custom to us, & who believed that it would give us a safe passage across the Lake.

These islets have been so named because it is not likely we shall make any more discoveries and as it is through the bounty of the "Herald" & the native name of Kavuruwé[275] is as unspellable as it is gross the Doctor shook me solemnly by the hand as we agreed they should be called by the name of Bennett's paper.

Dec 9th Saturday. Reached Cape Luvumba. Basansi.

---

270. 'do' written over 'join'.
271. 'This' written over 'the' and preceded by 'In' crossed out.
272. 'snug' corrected into 'snugging', for 'snuggling'.
273. 'this' appears needless. Stanley had probably written 'on the largest of these islets', then added 'one of the' above the line but crossed out 'one of', and may have left 'this' by error.
274. 'an' written over 'his'.
275. 'Kavuruwé' written in big letters.

We came[276] into[277] a cove behind the Cape and made our little camp. The aborigines who came to see us upon landing seemed civil enough. They wore bands of grass round their heads & they wore[278] their hair shaved in eccentric fashion which tufts either singly or[279] scattered about their bare skulls like an archipelago of islets in a sable sea. The women carried lengthy staffs spiked at one end & carved at the other, & wore their hair in heavy chignons. There was not much desire to trade on their part as we did not possess the peculiar kind of beads they fancied. Being somewhat drowsy after breakfast I lay down for a nap & the last thing I was aware of was the Doctor preparing to follow my example but I could not have been asleep long before I was roused by Selim who cried Wake up quick our men are packing & are going to run away. I hastily getting out of bed, I found the facts to[280] be as stated. It seems that shortly after I had retired the chief's son followed by his father & another chief had entered the camp extremely drunk & noisy, and had amused himself by spitting at the boatmen, & making indecent gestures, and then growing bolder by impunity had viciously slashed at one of them with a billhook. The older chiefs stood by laughing at his antics, while their followers were divided in opinion a half of them appeared to favour indulging the young man but the other half seemed to think that it would be well to drop that kind of[281] horse play which might prove serious. The Doctor had crept away to take observations & no one knew which way he had gone. I sent two or three runners to hurry him to camp while I sat down & tried to be[282] interested in what the drunken youth was bellowing as he pranced about. As my anxiety for the Doctor was increasing I saw him leisurely advancing from somewhere in land, & standing sometimes as though he were trying to make out what was going on.

When he arrives, I gladly turned the affair into his hands for the naked brute who bellowed himself hoarse & behaved so fantastically might if he had come too near me[283] in his wild motions have got hurt. Our boatmen were of one mind in thinking that we were not far from trouble for most of them were crouching behind our canoe.

In a short time the Doctor understood that these people wished us to leave their country as they were hostile to the Arabs ever since a[284] chief's son had been beaten to death by a Baluch,[285] because he had peeped into his harem. Then the Doctor bared[286]

276. 'came' written above 'shored' crossed out.
277. 'and' written over an indecipherable word crossed out.
278. 'wore' written over 'had'.
279. 'either singly or' added above the line.
280. 'to' written over 'as'.
281. irritati[ng]: this word is unfinished and crossed out.
282. 'be' added above the line.
283. 'me' added above the line.
284. 'native' crossed out.
285. Baluchi communities derived from Iran settled in East Africa (Kenya and Tanzania) as early as the 1820s. Squadrons of them were dispatched from Zanzibar into the interior to such places as Tabora and Kigoma. See Abdulaziz Y. Lodhi, "The Iranian Presence in East Africa," in *Haft kongeree wa haft murraka*, ed. M. A. Khajeh Najafi and M. Assemi (Uppsala, 2007), 267–74.
286. 'his arm, which' crossed out.

an arm, whose whiteness even I wondered at, & asked if they had known any man of that colour to hurt them. They all crowded around it & indeed it was worth looking at. Then he told them that there was more difference between white men, and Arabs, than there was between the Arabs & Basansi etc. etc., which had a great effect, for after a little more persuasion the drunken young rowdy collapsed, for a time. But[287] suddenly the boy's father got up & he went through a pantomime of frenzy & I saw him cut himself on the leg with his spear, after which he cried out that our black boatmen had wounded him.

At this one half of the mob fled, but an old woman – who carried a long staff commenced to abuse the chief & accused him[288] of a desire to make a row in which many people would be killed, and her companions chimed in with such lungs that the old man was so sobered that he finally condescended to receive a present of cloth & hold his tongue.

Well, this is[289] the third time the Doctor has stepped in, and saved us from extremities. All this scene has been a trick of course to get cloth, which they might have had for the asking as a right, for had we not landed on their own soil? Were we not cutting their wood? Were we not rich & they poor? They had plenty of good reasons to demand[290] cloth, but they had no right at all to come & flourish weapons in our faces under the pretext of being drunk.

The motive for all this hysteric by-play was so obvious that I was thoroughly disgusted – though it rather increased my admiration for the Doctor who at his age & with all his vast experience could keep his patience & be so simple in heart that he never cared to ask the why of anything. I begged the Doctor to take his seat in the canoe, becausse – they have succeeded so easily in getting cloth, they may try something else, & our men are such that I believe they would push off & leave us, if any disturbance ruses in the night.

Only this scene would have induced us to prefer to begin[291] crossing the Lake at half past 4. Fortunately the elements were tranquil.

We continued the argument on board – and as the boatmen were subdued being a little ashamed I have no doubt – we had the evening to ourselves, and interesting it was. We talked of so many things that I[292] have not the[293] time to record what he said, but I am more than ever convinced that the people at[294] Zanzibar who pretended to know Livingstone & told me such extraordinary stories about him must have been

---

287. 'But' added above the line.
288. 'him' written over 'of'.
289. 'is' written over 'was'.
290. 'demand' written over 'get'.
291. 'to begin' added above the line.
292. 'cannot' crossed out.
293. 'not the' added above the line.
294. 'at' written over 'of'.

dreaming.[295] He no more resembles their Livingstone, than I do. My impression is that he would rather be killed himself than be compelled to kill another even if he is a black man. At the same time on[296] three or four occasions[297] I think he has allowed himself to tell me incidents wherein he showed himself capable of a[298] flaming anger. "I came near shooting him" is an expression, "I have observed to escape him,[299] and the provocation was doubtless strong, but he has never done so, and if it came to the pinch my belief is, he would resign himself to the other alternative rather than do it. I admire this as I say but I am afraid that I could not yield my life to every Tom, Dick, & Harry who chose to demand it. The waste of good material for bad, would strike me as wrong.[300]

If that[301] drunken young fellow had slashed me across the throat with his billhook, or the cunning old chief instead of cutting himself had prodded me with his spear point,[302] I think the world would lose more in my death, than the whole of their tribe could possibly benefit it, but what[303] would it be to me? I wish to harm no one quite as little[304] as the Doctor, the wish to do them some good is just as spontaneous in me as it is in him, but where we differ is, that whereas every instinct is prompt in me to resent evil, or a deadly menace – he[305] appears indifferent, almost to carelessness. Perhaps the 30 years difference in age has something to do with it, and[306] while my blood is as mercury,[307] his never rises above[308] normal temperature – and I pray that it will always keep so.

Dec 10th Sunday. Thank Heaven we are across the Lake and are on the Eastern shore. We reached Mukungu after 17 ½ hours rowing and I take it that we have come 43 m.

Dec 11th Monday. Zassi once more after another 7 hours. The men do not require any urging. The fish of Ujiji invites them.

---

295. While changing 'people of' into 'people at Zanzibar', Stanley could have meant to limit to fewer people this rumor about Livingstone's character, without naming Dr. Kirk. However, he took the opportunity to underline how Kirk misled him, by giving "a very bad impression of Livingstone," on January 17, 1871 (S.A. 7).
296. 'on' added above the line.
297. 'occasions' written above 'times' crossed out.
298. 'a' added above the line.
299. No quotation mark here.
300. 'Supposing that' crossed out.
301. 'If that' added in the margin.
302. 'would' crossed out.
303. 'it' crossed out.
304. 'little' written above 'far' crossed out.
305. 'assumes' crossed out.
306. 'and' written over 'but'.
307. 'his I have not been cons' crossed out.
308. 'never rises above' written above 'is steadily at' crossed out.

Dec 12th To[309] Niasanga 3 hours. I feel too sick to proceed. Fever is in my veins, & the Doctor ordered a halt.

December 13th Wednesday. Arrived at Ujiji at 1 P.M. 7 hours, at a good three miles an hour. We entered the port very quietly without any firing of guns as we are short of powder. As we landed we[310] were met by our men and the[311] principal[312] Arabs.[313] Mabruki Speke had lots of news to tell us regarding every thing that had happened during our absence. The faithful fellow had done excellently. Kalulu had scalded himself. Marova had been put in chains by Mabruki for wounding one of the asses in the head with a stone. Bill alli had made a row on the market place, and Mabruki had laid the stick freely on his shoulders. Most welcome of all was a letter from Zanzibar dated June 11th containing telegrams from Paris[314] to Aden up to April 22nd. Poor Livingstone when he saw my delight said[315] "And I have none. What a pleasant thing it is to have a real good friend.

December 14th Thursday. To day is a resting & visiting day. The Arabs are punctilious in observing social forms. We had to sit on the barza (verandah) for a greater part of the morning while they called to pay their respects one[316] after another until it grew somewhat tedious. After they went home one sent a dishful of cookies, another a huge tray full of pilaf & a bowl of ghee flavoured with garlic, another rice, another Coffee & so on.

In the afternoon Livingstone and I had a long discussion about future movements. We have touched these points several times while on the Lake, and I had an idea what[317] he would eventually determine to do, but there has been no definite settlement, as it was unnecessary. Now however as I must shortly be moving I broached the subject as to his future.

"Well, said he[318] the[319] things which you have[320] suggested have been frequently discussed between us.

"Go home I cannot until I have finished what Sir Roderick gave me to do. I would scarely dare to show my face, and to explain to people who have no idea of my difficulties would be impossible.

---

309. 'To' added above the line.
310. 'we' written over 'were'.
311. 'the' written over 'our'.
312. 'principal' added above the line.
313. 'friends' crossed out.
314. 'up' crossed out.
315. 'said' written over 'cri[ed]'.
316. 'one' written over 'once'.
317. 'what' written over 'which'.
318. 'of' crossed out.
319. 'three' crossed out.
320. 'have' added above the line.

To go, and join Sir Samuel Baker would be to poach on his province – and I think my district more interesting & far more important.

To go to Unyanyembe with you – and then make for Uganda & Unyoro would be to travel over beaten ground, is to go[321] where at my time of life I have no hurries.

To accompany you to Unyanyembe & receive[322] such goods as you have in store then enlist new men & go back either to Manyuema,[323] or Rua, is the best with modifications.

I decide then on accompanying you to Unyanyembe accept such goods as you will be pleased to give me & wait there until you can send me proper men from Zanzibar such as you have here, and while you are there buy such things for me as I shall mention, for they might as well have little of something to carry as come empty handed, and one can scarcely have too much of necessaries in a land like this. If of course these men which you have were willing to go with me from Unyanyembe I would not require anything from Zanzibar, but as they are unwilling, it would be best to equip a proper force pledged to my service, and once let me have that I shall have no fear of not being able to discover the solution to my great problem.

This was the decision uttered in the tone of a man who has made up his mind unalterably.

In the afternoon about four o'clock we went together to Muini Kheri to negotiate for the loan of his huge canoe -the biggest at Ujiji- in which we could load our goods – and sail South to a point abreast of Imrera's in Ukonongo, which would shorten our journey to Unyanyembe[324] considerably, & will obviate any hongo paying to the rascally chiefs in Uvinza & Uhha. The Muini closed with us so that matter is settled. To morrow I shall begin apportioning loads, and try to make a saddle for Livingstone who will perhaps be compelled to ride – as some of the marches will be rather long for him.

Dec 15th Friday. I spread out my map before Livingstone today, and showed to him our intended[325] course. I pointed out how when coming from Unyanyembe we struck[326] southerly, then westerly towards the Lake – and how when about nine days journeying from it, we turned N & travelled parallel to the Tanganyika,[327] in order to avoid Mirambo & his bandits, but that when we approached the Malagarazi we had been daily mulcted of cloth & beads to such a degree, that we lost many bales. By sailing

---

321. 'to go' added above the line.
322. 'all your' crossed out.
323. Manyuema is the spelling Stanley adopted in *HIFL* based upon what Livingstone told him about its pronunciation in local languages (*HIFL*, 450).
324. 'to Unyanyembe' written above 'there' crossed out.
325. 'intended' written over 'new'.
326. 'to' crossed out.
327. This is one example of the few spellings of Tanganyika with 'y' in Stanley's journals.

along the eastern shore of the Tanganika as far as Tongwé,[328] & cutting across country to the point where we turned northerly we should escape being obliged to pay a single doti, and the tedious annoyance of daily chaffer, with natives who were masters in the art of bargaining & were quite ready if an excuse was offered of taking our goods by force. This plan Livingstone thought was excellent. It has therefore been adopted.

I began to work on Livingstone's saddle & set our trailors with palm and needle on the canvass. I bought several milch goats in the market to supply us with milk on the road, so that when the milk fails we can have meat. We have already got five & each goat yields a pint. Got out the bales made lists of them – and apportioned them to[329] their carriers. We have 40 carriers, and all are armed & willing, and while returning we need have no fear of trouble or mutiny.

December 16th Saturday. At work on the Doctor' saddle. Selim is my assistant. Livingstone writes in his big journal a Perpetual Lett's Diary which has a lock & key. He says he has finished all his despatches all, &[330] every one & also copied them, so as I am not going to detain him while I write my letters to the "Herald" I expect we shall be on our way to Unyanyembe very soon.

I proposed to Livingstone today to write a few letters to the "Herald" himself at £20 per letter of 8 pages of foolscap which will be equal to about 3200 words. He asked me if I thought America might be induced to assist England in suppressing the horrible slave trade in[331] Africa. I replied that whatever views he might have about the slave-trade would be published and read[332] by countless thousands of people so that eventually the outcome would be an immense & widespread[333] public sympathy sure to produce some kind of action, that the "Herald" meant nothing but the agency whereby hundreds of other joural[334] would be influenced to join in his propaganda. He says he will think of my proposal. When he talks like that it means that he is favorable to it, and will meditate upon how to do it.

Dec 17th Sunday. Ujiji. Had prayers today longer than other days. After reading a chapter he translated it into Swahili, and expounded it to his men. Some of my people also sat & listened, so that we had a respectable attendance.

Yesterday Livingstone spoke to Habay the native chief of Ujiji about boatmen to bring our boat back from Tongwé.

---

328. 'we sho' [word unfinished] crossed out.
329. 'them to' written over 'the car' [word unfinished].
330. 'and' added above the line.
331. 'in' written over 'of'.
332. Stanley first wrote 'ready' but corrected his mistake.
333. '& widespread' added above the line.
334. 'joural', ms.

Today I showed Rob Roy's letter of[335] introduction of me to him in 1868, when he was supposed to be approaching the Coast.[336] He said he knew his mother & father very well, or his sister & father. I forget which. He gave me a bit of the history about the East Indiaman the Kent,[337] of which Rob Roy's father was commander.[338]

The Doctor's padded saddle was finished last night. I tried it on to-day & asked a Zanzibari to ride the donkey – but the poor fellow though he bravely repeated his attempts several times was disastrously thrown from which the Doctor argues but doutfully of his ability to ride him.

Dec 18. Monday we are still preparing for the road, but I do not suppose that we shall be able to depart before Christmas.

Dec 19th Tuesday. I sent 6 guns to be repaired at Muini Kheri's smithy, today. The Doctor has now commenced to write his private letters.

He told me to-day that he first heard of Lake Bangweolo as Lake Bemba in 1863 & was then within 10 days journey of it but as he had been enjoined by Earl Russell to return before the fall of the Shiré, he had to abandon the region.

Also that had the Mazitu not devastated the land, he had intended to follow the Rovuma River to its Source – but every article in the shape of provisions had been clean swept by those vengeful fellows. That he was deterred from going to the head (N) of[339] Lake Nyassa by the reputed ferocity of the tribes, and as his men especially the Johannese were continually straining their ears after these foolish reports. That then he intended to cross Lake Nyassa at the middle but no dhows were procurable, he was therefore compelled to travel[340] round about the S. End of the Lake.

He said the Zambezi Expedition had not been written at all as it ought to have been written. Several things must take place before it can be done properly. Several personagges who shall be nameless must die before the truth can be published. He doubted that it would do any good to tell the truth, & it certainly would not redound to his benefit – because it was too late. Then again the true[341] history of the Missionary Effort on the Zambezi has been kept dark for various reasons. Six people volunteered

---

335. 'letter of' added above the line.
336. About the letter of recommendation from John MacGregor ("Rob Roy"), see Journal S.A. 73, same date, note 53. For the letter, see Appendix, Letter of Introduction from John MacGregor to David Livingstone, Suez, November 16, 1868, S.A. 480.
337. East Indiamen were sailing ships carrying passengers and goods for the East India Company. The Kent ran twice from England to Bombay and China before being destroyed by a fire on her third trip, in 1825.
338. About John MacGregor's father, Sir Duncan MacGregor, see Journal S.A. 73, same date, note 54, and Journal S.A. 7, same date.
339. 'the' crossed out.
340. 'travel' written over 'go'.
341. 'true' added above the line.

at first who were really capable men – but when it was time to depart they withdrew, then another party of six was taken & these gentlemen[342] were extremely new to Missionary work. When they reached the Zambezi they made their Camp at the end of a 200 mile swamp. I persuaded them to ascend the Morambala mountain where they might breathe fresh open air; but after trying it awhile[343] they soon returned[344] – afraid – as they said – of the Wahiyou.

Bishop Mackenzie[345] enjoined on them not to try to teach until they were familiar with the language of the natives but he did not tell them that they should abstain from visiting them and acquainting themselves with their natures. On the pretence however that they continously engaged in learning the language they refrained from putting their dainty hands to anything other than pinning beetles & butterflies. The men of the Zambezi Expedition used to chaff them often upon these[346] noble pursuits, and used to say that they had a good mind to become Missionaries also. Talking about unhealthiness of the climate, what could they expect where they had[347] established themselves. When they came to visit him at his place 7 miles above, they invariably went away declaring that they were greatly benefited by the change. The bishop was a real, noble fellow, worked with his own hands like a common mechanic, he built the houses for his assistants – because as he said – he could not find it in his heart to ask his gentlemen to work. It astonished the natives to see the "big father" work on the roof of a house for one of his young men while he & his companions[348] sat in the shade encouraging the good bishop with their kind comments on his industry & cleverness. The Natives could[349] mimic them perfectly, and hold their heads on one side & cock one eye & cry Hah goot! And they would imitate them sitting on the ground writing their journals, while their Father was toiling in the sun. Failure marked that mission from the beginning. I never saw people with less of the common sense that was wanted.

When Bishop Tozer came he said it was an astounding fact that the missionaries had as yet taught the natives absolutely nothing. In their defense they said – forgetting I suppose what they told me – that I had deserted the Makolola, & the Makolola[350] had nullified their teaching. I assure you that if it had not been for Sir Roderick's adwice – whose worldly wisdom was something on which one could rely. I should

---

342. 'knew' crossed out.
343. 'awhile' added above the line.
344. 'returned' written above 'fled' crossed out.
345. For Bishop Mackenzie, see Henry Rowley, *The Story of the Universities' Mission to Central Africa, from Its Commencement, under Bishop Mackenzie, to Its Withdrawal from the Zambezi* (London: Saunders, Otley, 1866).
346. 'these' written over 'their'.
347. 'had' added in the margin.
348. 'he and his companions' written above 'they' crossed out.
349. 'could' written over 'would'.
350. Makolola, ms. Stanley opted for the spelling Makololo in *HIFL*, 542.

have written very strongly upon several points especially what a[351] well known Coburg[352] had to do with maintaining the Portuguese Slave Trade. It is a long story but I think if I outlive some people it will surprise people to find wheels within wheels even[353] in African[354] affairs. It is gall to my soul to think of it. But for this curiously complicated system of politics, we should be able to stamp out the Portuguese slave trade in a very short time. Another thing[355] which grieves me has been the loss of life & bad success attending the Zambezi Mission which I am confident could have been avoided.[356]

(Note. I regard these matters as in the light of confidences more for my own instruction & entertainment & relief it gives him to talk of them, than for publication. I observe that he fears for my indiscretion,[357] by the hints which are dropped, the pauses he makes, & so on, but as he suggests half-confessedly that their revelation would not avail anything – I shall not meddle except in what I think will do him good.)

I suspect that thoughts of these matters occupy much of his silence. He is terribly in earnest about this slave trade, there is no doubt. I sometimes see him with uplifted finger & fixed gaze & moving lips as if he were in the act of addressing an audience. The first time I saw him do this, I asked him to whom he was talking upon which he drew back, & said he probably was thinking his thoughts aloud, but I was to take no notice of that.

Dec 20th Wednesday.[358] Ujiji. Heavy rain & thunder & a grand storm on the Lake. We had some fat fish from the Lake yesterday which last night, after I had retired gave me a very prickly & nauseous feeling. The Doctor called it Urticaria.[359]

He told me to-day that Hayward, Q.C.[360] brought a message from Lord Palmeston to him wishing to know what distinction could be conferred on him. He damned that he did not want anything for himself but for Africa and if Lord Palmerston would only remember that the crying need was for a free entry by the Zambezi and Shiré into Africa – & could obtain that – by a treaty with Portugal all that he hoped for

---

351. 'a' written over 'the'.
352. 'well known' added above the line. Prince Ferdinand of Saxe-Coburg and Gotha (1816–1885) was the husband of Queen Dona Maria II of Portugal, and the first cousin of Queen Victoria and Prince Albert.
353. 'even' added in the margin.
354. 'African' added above the line.
355. 't[hing]' written over 'g'. Stanley probably considered writing 'grief'.
356. Stanley records numerous "grudges" from Livingstone against Portuguese and the Portuguese government for its support of the slave trade. See the Portuguese reply to Livingstone in José Maria Almeida e Araújo de Portugal Correia de Lacerda, *Portuguese African Territories: Reply to Dr. Livingstone's Accusations and Misrepresentations* (London: Edward Stanford, 1865).
357. 'in-' added above the line before 'discretion'.
358. '20' written over '19', and 'Wednesday' over 'Tuesday'.
359. 'Urticaria, or nettle rash' is a skin rash that may have been caused by the ingestion of this fat fish. In *HIFL*, 564, Stanley does not mention this fish dish but he reports it was his third attack with urticaria, in which he recognized "the forerunner of a remittent fever."
360. Abraham Hayward, Q[ueen's] C[ounsel], 1801–1884.

Africa & all that it needed would follow. Now, sometimes I think I made a great mistake & ought to have taken the opportunity to have done something for my children.[361]

Also that it was wholly due to Sir Roderick that he had come to Africa on this last Exploration. He was writing his book on the Zambezi when Sir Roderick sounded him upon devoting himself to Exploring the watershed between the Zambezi, and the waters flowing North, and[362] suggested his[363] going[364] a second time across Africa to the W. Coast or making his[365] way to the White Nile, winning a name superior to all. "That was Sir Roderick's way you know. I recommended him to apply to Kirk as he was the best I[366] knew of – for I was so engaged on my book upon[367] the Zambezi Expedition[368] that I could do nothing else. By & bye Sir Roderick sounded[369] Kirk & found[370] him strongly averse to the idea as there was no permanency to it, and he was a poor man. Then I recommended him to Sir Roderick for an appointment, and finally I persuaded Sir Bartle Frere to appoint him to Zazibar as it is a dependency of Bombay. He is there now. I think he might pay more attention to his friend than he has done for the sake[371] of common gratitude.

Dec 21st Thursday. Ujiji. Have done a considerable amount of writing to-day trying to reduce into shape what I have gleaned from Livingstone. As he was busy writing in his big journal I attempted a sketch of him in pencil. While doing so the manner of catching his journal when he changed the position of his legs attracted my attention, made me think his left arm was half paralysed. I asked him if anything was the matter with it. He said, "Did you never hear the story of how I was attacked by a lion!" I think I have I answered but it has been so long ago that I do not remember a single detail of it.

"Well feel my arm" he said "first & then I will tell you about it."

I did as requested and distinctly felt that the[372] left arm half way between elbow & shoulder[373] was quite broken but joined as though the inner rim of the lower piece had become attached to the outer rim of the upper, – so that it resembled an overlap of the lower half of the upper arm, over the upper half. He stretched his two arms out & I saw that his left arm was considerably shorter than the right. The reason of a peculiar disproportion somewhere, or a peculiar pose of the shoulders then dawned

---

361. This sentence was added on the line above the following paragraph.
362. 'talked' crossed out.
363. 'his' written over 'my'.
364. 'out' crossed out.
365. 'his' written over 'my'.
366. 'I' written over 'he'.
367. 'upon' added above the line. All corrections of this paragraph in black ink.
368. 'Expedition' added above the line.
369. 'sounded' written over 'sounds'.
370. 'found' written over 'finds'.
371. 'for the sake' written above 'even out' crossed out.
372. 'upper' crossed out.
373. 'half way between elbow & shoulder' added above the line.

on me I knew there was something the matter somewhere, but I was too shy to stare at a man so much my superior in age & who whatever[374] his present condition was one for whom I had something of a reverent regard.

"Well, he said, I don't like to speak about it much because it is so easy to imagine a man telling of such adventures, & boasting of it & I have been so often asked about it that I became[375] rather sick of the subject. It took place in the Country of the Mabotse, or Mabatsa, nearly 30 years ago. The lions were very numerous & some of them had become very bold. One day it was told to me that nine sheep had been killed by a lion not far from my house in the day time. There was a great excitement among the natives & I became as interested as any one in the story, and I walked towards the spot. The lion was still there, & wishing to see the fun. I shouted to the people to go & hem him in. Some appeared very willing to go to any lengths others held back & the lion at last got away, as[376] I thought for good, and so turned homeward, passing by some of the people who were still talking of the affair. But I had not gone many paces beyond them when he sprang out of the bushes upon me knocking me down, & with one crunch he broke my arm – and I expected it was all up with me, I lay still, under him when one of my men crept up –very bravely & planted a shot in him which dropped him[377] dead, and I was dragged away feeling somewhat dazed but[378] less[379] pain than I would have expected."

"That was a narrow escape" I said, what were your feelings while expecting his last snap?"

"To tell you the truth, I cannot say I felt anything very much, except that I was in a position wherein it was useless to struggle. I did not think of my last end or anything like that, but if I can say I thought of anything it was of the exceeding masterfulness of the beast, & his immense strength & that it would be all[380] up with me in a short time. There was no fear, but an unusual calmness,[381] & the mind seemed to work as before, but I did not care, or could' nt speak my thoughts"

One of his fore[382] paws was on my body & the other on the ground and he was looking up away from me."

"What do you think made him pause when you lay under him?"

"Oh, I suppose the noise of the people around him, and having his attention attracted by my man creeping up to him, but there you have got the story & you need

---

374. 'who whatever' all attached.
375. 'became' written above 'am' crossed out.
376. 'as' written over 'and'.
377. 'him' written over 'away'.
378. 'very' crossed out.
379. 'less' written over 'little'.
380. 'all' added above the line.
381. 'Why' written over 'though' and crossed out.
382. 'fore' added above the line.

not put that in your letter to the "Herald". I have always thought of it as a story to tell my grand children when I am quite toothless & old & past work."

"Have you had many such escapes Doctor?

No I can't say I have but I have seen some curious things.

"I winna blow about mysel'

As ill I like my fault to tell"[383]

A far more serious accident happened one time to a companion of mine named Murray,[384] a Scotch traveller near the Zouga R. He went out shooting ducks one day, and you know how some of these African rivers when sluggish spread out very wide especially where th[e] country is flat, & the body of the stream is far away from the dry shore. Well the Zouga was something like that and Murray saw a bird among the floating lotus[385] leaves & shot it. There was no way to get at it except by wading & he went in, but as he drew near the water deepened to his waist, and he turned back to[386] the shore. He had almost got on shore, when he was whisked from his feet & began to be dragged towards[387] the river. He was in the maw of a crocodile which has fastend its teeth in the[388] calf of one[389] of his legs. Murray saw his danger & threw out his arms[390] to catch at any thing within reach, & in so doing he caught a young tree to which he held fast with all his strength. He roared out for help & by good luck some of our men heard his cries, and ran to his assistance, but in the meantime the crocodile was tugging at his leg & the wounds made by them were opening out & spurting blood. Fortunately the men arrived just[391] in time before he gave out, and fired at the brute who finally let go & disappeared in the water. Now I consider that a much more desperate position that I was in. Poor Murray was in a bad way for a long time. We did the best we could for him, but he had had enough of Africa. The wounds quite crippled him & the last time I saw him which was years after that terrible accident, they[392] were occasionally running sores in the place rent by the sharp teeth.

"Talking of crocodiles reminds me of the tuzzle we had with one, who caught my poor donkey "Simba" the finest of his kind I ever saw. We were on the Malagarazi &

---

383. From "Epistle to J. Lapraik," by the Scottish poet Robert Burns (1759–1796), *The Works of Robert Burns*, vol. 1 (Glasgow: A. Fullarton, 1834), 165. This verse was added between the two lines, with a different ink and pen.

384. Mungo Murray, of Lintrose, and William Cotton Oswell accompanied D. Livingstone to River Zouga and Lake Ngami. See William E. Oswell, *William Cotton Oswell, Hunter and Explorer*, 2 vols. (New York: Doubleday Page, 1900), chap. 7, "3rd Expedition with Livingstone and Murray…Discovery of River Zouga and Lake Ngami, 1848–1849," 172.

385. 'lotus' added above the line.

386. 'to' written over 'near'.

387. 'towards' written above 'into' crossed out.

388. 'thigh' crossed out.

389. 'one' written over 'his'.

390. 'out' added above the line after 'threw', and crossed out after 'arms'.

391. 'just' added above the line.

392. 'they' written over 'there'.

crossing, one held the donkey's head, and the others were paddling across as hard as they could. On the bank my men & I were shouting Pull boys – pull – encouraging them by voice & gesture for the river was full of the vicious[393] brutes. In mid-river the donkey tried to leap up into the canoe with a sudden spring. We thought at first he did not like the river & would prefer being in in[394] the canoe, but we soon realised as he made a second & third effort that a crocodile & perhaps more than one had fastened on him. Then the excitement became tremendous. The men shouted from both sides, the ropes was held still firmer, the men franctically paddled, but you could tell by the stiff[395] way that the canoe moved, that something more than the donkey held it – and presently the rope parted and the donkey disappeared.[396] Ah – the rage we were all in was something to be seen. I snatched my riffle & potted away for over an hour at the cruel, deadly eyed creatures, which came up to the surface every now & then to breathe. Ever since at every opportunity I have lost no chance to pour lead into them. I do not think I hate anything as I do a crocodile."

"Yes, they are very cruel creatures & number of times they have caused me great grief, said Livingstone. I remember once on the Zambezi Expedition, when I was at some distance from the river I had to send a note back to the camp – to catch the mail by one of the men. He took it & folded it in his loin cloth for safety. On the way however there was a deep river which he had to cross, & being obliged to swim it, he stripped his loin cloth &[397] wrapped the cloth with the letter in it round his head leaving his belt & knife, around his waist. He plunged & had[398] got half way across when he felt himself seized by a leg by a crocodile. He was dragged under water, and not losing his wits, he doubled and felt for one[399] the crocodile's eyes which he tried[400] to gouge out with his thumb. The pain was more than the crocodile could endure, & he let the man go, which the man no sooner felt than he rose to the surface, & swam as he does when he knows he swims for his life. He had almost got hold of the grass on the[401] bank of the river when he was seized again & taken below. The man a second time used his thumbs to such a purpose that the crocodile gave it up as a bad job and let him loose again, and you can imagine how the man sprang out of the river, & rushed away from it."

"By George, that was a plucky fellow", I said enthusiastically."

---

393. 'vicious' written above 'nasty' crossed out.
394. 'in' written twice.
395. 'stiff' written over 'way'.
396. See Journal S.A. 7, November 2, 1871.
397. '&' preceded by 'having his' crossed out.
398. 'had' added above the line.
399. 'one' added above the line; 'of' missing.
400. 'tried' written over 'gouged'.
401. 'grass of the' added above the line.

"Yes he was uncommonly brave. Some of these blacks are extraordinarily so, and fortunately this fellow was a good swimmer."

"I suppose you were very proud of that man after such a feat."

"Yes, he was made much of, & several of rewarded him handsomely" – but I must go on with my work or else, I shall not be ready with my letters when you go."

I proceeded with my sketch, and while touching up his face, I noticed that his face was smoother, & less wrinkled than according[402] to my first impressions. He seemed much younger & far more vigorous than[403] at my entry into Ujiji. His hair was almost brown fine & well brushed with a distinct parting on the side[404] though the grey was marked in the side whiskers & moustache. His chin was clean shaven every day & altogether there were signs of punctilious habits about his personal appearance. He had doffed the faded[405] scarlet jacket of coarse red blanketing[406] which he wore when I first saw him and was now clad in a suit of dark Norfolk gray tweeds which I had ordered when at[407] Bombay, though before they would fit him the legs of the trousers[408] & the arms of the jacket had to be lengthened a couple of inches, & a seam opened at the back of the jacket. I should say he must be about 5 feet 9 or 9 ½ in height & an altogether larger man in the chest than I am. His old blue cloth Cap he has promised to me as a souvenir. It has a band of gold lace set on a lower & broader[409] band of Turkey red cotton, which probably has been sewn on as a protection to[410] the temples. The vizor is of[411] black leather & rounded, & the glazing is most crinkly as if had been subjected to a roasting heat.[412] His new cap is in the hands of Hamadi one of my men who is[413] an expert with the needle, and the same arrangement is carried on with it.

December 22nd Friday. Ujiji, am down with the Mukunguru the local fever.

Dec. 23rd Saturday. Still on my back in bed. Livingstone whom I initial as L. in my diary, calls to see me now & then. What a hardy, old veteran he is. I get three fevers to his one.

---

402. 'according' written over 'it'.
403. 'than' written over 'that'.
404. 'fine & well brushed… on the side' added above the line.
405. 'faded' added above the line.
406. See Journal S.A. 7, November 10, 1871.
407. 'when at' written above 'in' crossed out.
408. 'had to be lengthened a couple of inches' crossed out.
409. 'lower & broader' written above 'scarlet' crossed out.
410. 'to' written over 'round'.
411. 'of' added above the line.
412. Livingstone wore the consular cap because he had been appointed HBM Consul at Quelimane (Mozambique) for the East Coast of Africa.
413. 'one of my men who is' added above the line.

Dec. 24th Sunday. I heard Livingstone's voice at prayers at 7 o'clock from my bed. This is a severe bout, bilious & very seedy.

Dec 25th Monday – Christmas. The fever went away yesterday afternoon just in time for Christmas pudding. Am getting well again but my ears are ringing with quinne. I pottered about at an early hour & had a friendly chat with Ferajji.[414] I told him this was the day of days for white men & that he must cook something extra good. He mentioned a number of dishes as though he were in a galley on a well provided ship, soup, steer, roast duck, greens, sweet potatoes, basted mutton & chicken for the Doctor, slap jacks & honey, and a Custard. I prepared the Custard but the villain burnt it. The love for gossip which these fellows have ruins every delicate preparation. I believe he is courting Halima – though Hamoidah's lawfully married wife. At any rate they were so absorbed with one another, that Ferajji kept[415] heaping[416] on the red embers[417] on the skillet, that the Custard had become so[418] scorched[419] throughout[420] was bitter. I was not strong enough to thrash him so soon after the fever, but I reduced him to take[421] a spell among the carriers where he will feel the difference though he is as strong as a horse.[422] I heard him as he went away exchange his opinion with another as to how very "kali" or hot I was, compared with the Fartib, or "gentle" manner of the big Master (Livingstone).[423]

Dec. 26th Tuesday. To morrow we hope to be able to leave Ujiji – as everything is now ready for the homeward journey. Why should we stop longer? Yet, I could well afford to linger. I have become attached to the life in Ujiji, & most of the hours spent here have been indescibably happy, despite the local fever. The inevitableness of it makes me quite melancholy, though I bare no reason to like the place except for the sentiment which must always cling to it in my mind. To be accurate I ought to say that something too belongs to the palms & the steady murmur of the Lake[424] sounding

---

414. Ferajji (or Ferrajji) was the cook of the expedition and as such he carried kitchen utensils during the journey (cf. the details of the carriers' loads in Field Notebook S.A. 9). When back at Zanzibar, he re-enlisted in the caravan for Livingstone (cf. Appendix, Contracts of African Soldiers, May 21, 1872, S.A. 4749). For Ferajji's biography, see François Bontinck, "Voyageurs africains en Afrique centrale, VII. Ferrajji le cuisinier," *Zaïre-Afrique*, no. 128 (1978).
415. 'kept' added above the line.
416. 'heaping' written over 'heaped on'.
417. 'until the' crossed out.
418. 'so' added above the line.
419. 'scorched' preceded by 'burnt' crossed out.
420. 'that it' crossed out.
421. 'to take' added above the line.
422. Stanley found it hard to forgive Ferajji for spoiling this Christmas dinner as it is also mentioned in Journal S.A. 7 (December 25, 1871) and again in Field Notebook S.A. 9 (February 10, 1872). Even Livingstone noted this "sorry Christmas" in his journal (*LJ*, December 26, 1871).
423. This sentence is added between two lines.
424. 'of the Lake' added above the line.

solemn on the shore. The nerves feel the influence & I am in no way[425] insusceptible to these things.

Dec 27th Wednesday. Ujiji has been left behind perhaps for the last time and we are on the South side of the Liuche[426] or Riuché R in Ukaranga Bay.
The canoes, Said bin Majid's & Moeni Kheri's were at the beach in good time, & the rowers in their places. Over[427] the Doctor's canoe, the English flag has been raised, & over the one I was to command was the American. It made a pretty sight. Quite a gathering had assembled to see us depart, Arab traders, Zanzibaris, & Natives. The hateful hour of farewell came & we pushed off, with many a kindly wish ringing in our ears. The land party filed away along the shore under Asmani & Bombay, and we were to meet at the Liuche R. to ferry them across. Our canoes held on side by side. The Doctor admired the appearance of my canoe, & I paid him a similar compliment. Never at a loss to utter his humour he affected to be jealous of the prodigious height of my flagstaff he remaked he would have to cut down the tallest palm tree, as he did not like seeing the English flag at a lower altitude than that of the United States.

The boatmen were lighthearted at least such as were not Wajiji & roared out a steering song with a chorus of "Kinan de ré ré Kitunga,"[428] and as the thought glanced across their minds that we were able[429] to slip by the Wahha & Wavinza by our intended route, they improvised a song about it to one of their well known tunes.[430] They are ably bardic sometimes & full of quaint humor when they are not sullen. The fellows on shore hearing our sailor's chorus joined in & as they[431] carried nothing but their own kits they were seen to race trying to reach the Liuche ahead of us. The little goat herds driving our flock at full speed after the caravan amused us. About 10 o'clock we came to Kirindo's a native chief who had a special affection for Livingstone but detested the Arabs.

The Liuche is wide at the mouth & issues into the Lake through wide growths of the scraggy pith tree,[432] & forms a bay which is called Ukaranga, from a village on the South side. Long before dark we had crossed the land party, donkeys & goats over the S. side. The crossing had not occupied more than four hours.

---

425. 'in no way' written above 'not the most' crossed out.
426. Stanley ultimately opted for Livingstone's spelling Liuche and not Riuche, which he used in his field notebook S.A. 9. Similar differences are shown in Stanley's and Livingstone's transcriptions of other native names, such as Stanley's use of Rusizi and Livingstone's, Lusizé (*LJ*).
427. 'Over' written above 'on' crossed out.
428. Kinan de ré ré kitunga: "the exhilarating song of the Zanzibar boatmen" (*HIFL*, 568) but in notebook S.A. 9, Stanley says it is "one of the chorus used by boatmen of the Lake [Tanganyika]".
429. 'able' written over 'possibly'.
430. Stanley elaborates on the notes taken in his field notebook S.A. 9. He gives a translation of this song in *HIFL*, 568.
431. 'were' crossed out.
432. Pith tree, light and thin tree, also known as ambatch (*Aeschynomene elaphroxylon*).

Dec 28th Wednesday. Our course was southerly along the Eastern shore, the land party filing in a parallel course as well as they were able, by a path which dipped close down to the water & then curved well in land. The shore was[433] beautifully green – from the effects of the rains – the season here corresponds to our Spring. Stopped at a camp which Mohammed bin Gharib had established for his workmen who were preparing timber for his new house, as well as for that for[434] his friend Mohammed bin Sali the white bearded Governor. Bin Gharib evidently has a fancy for architectural works. We drank a cup of coffee & ate some sweetened vermicelli with him. I am told we shall stop at Karah tomorrow. We reached the mouth of the Malagarazi at 2 P.M. We then hoisted a flag on a tall punting pole to attract the attention of the land party which happily arrived at 5 o'clock. In the soft chalk-like stone (of[435] which most the cliffs & buffs seemed to consist the surf has worn fantastic holes & chiseled[436] strange forms resembling arm-chairs & couches, in another place[437] tunnels like that we read of in Melvilles "Omoo".[438]

Dec 29th Thursday. Crossed the Expedition across the mouth of the Malagarazi. I measured Moeni Kheri's canoe today & found her to be 45 feet long 5 beat beam & 6 feet deep, while Said bin Magid's was only 33 feet by 4. Tired & turned in early.

Dec 30th Friday. Started this morning from Cape Kagongo then rounding Mviga, we came in view of P^t Kivoe, & reached the Rugufu at 9. A.M. in which river I shot a crocodile. Crossed the caravan over to the S. side.

Dec 31st Saturday. Sent out a canoe at an early hour to procure food, and obtained 4 days rations for all hands 48 people. Plaed all the children & weakly goats in the canoes & lightened the people of some of their luggage and pushed off on[439] our Southerly voyage. Steering straight for Mizohazy behind which owing to a foul wind & a chopping sea we camped for the night. Our people did not arrive – they probably marched on ahead.

Jan 1st 1872. Sunday. Started at our usual hour, wind & Lake calm, & passed the dreaded Kabogo, on whose heights & slopes are some splendid Mvule trees. At lunch time we put in at Sigunga, which was in a cozy nook. An afternoon's spurt brought us

---

433. 'was' written over 'were'; Stanley also barred the 's' of 'shore'.
434. 'that for' added above the line.
435. 'of' written over 'it'.
436. 'arm chair looking' crossed out.
437. 'place' added above the line.
438. 'Melvilles', for Melville's, added above the line. Herman Melville, *Omoo: A Narrative of Adventures in the South Seas*. Also mentioned in Field Notebook S.A. 9, same date.
439. 'on' added above the line.

after three hours pulling to Uwelasia River, where we amused ourselves by[440] shooting the crocodiles & hippos, and we hoped the sound of our guns might be responded to by the absent caravan.

Jan 2nd Monday. Rowed beyond[441] Herembe P^t & then[442] entered the bay of Tongwé. We passed the villages of[443] Urimba[444] to a suitable[445] camping place at the extreme S. East corner of the bay, a mile & a half due W of Kakungu Peak.

By observation the Doctor found that we had reached S. lat 5° 54' about a degree South of Ujiji. Shot a fine spur winged goose soon after landing. Then as our Camp commanded an extensive view of the mountains slopes as far as Kabogo P^t we hoisted an[446] immense flag on the top of the highest tree[447] to catch the eyes of our absentees.

January 3rd Tuesday. Had some modest[448] sport among some[449] zebras, & secured a[450] quantity of meat, which will be useful.

Livingstone this afternoon got upon his favorite topics the Zambezi Mission, the Portuguese and Arab slave trade, and these subjects invariably bring him to relate incidents about what he has witnessed of African nature & aptitudes. I conclude from the importance he attaches to these that he is more[451] interested in Ethnology than in topographical Geography. Though the Nile problem & the central line of drainage are frequently on his lips they are secondary to the humanities observed on his wanderings which whether at the morning coffee, tiffin, or dinner occupies him in the intervals of mastication. The Manyema women must have attracted him by their prettiness from which I gather that they must be superior to the average female native. He speaks of their large eyes, their intelligent looks, and pretty expressive arch ways. Then he refers to the customs at Cazembe's Court, & the kindness received from the women there. In a little while I am listening to the atrocities of Tagamoyo the half-caste Arab, who surrounded a Manyema market, & with his long shirted followers fired most murderous volleys on the natives as they were innocently chaffening[452] about their wares. There then is real passion in his language & I fancy from the angry glitter in his eyes – that were it in his power – Tagamoyo & his gang should have a

---

440. 'pott' crossed out.
441. 'beyond' written above 'past' crossed out.
442. 'then' added above the line.
443. 'the villages of' added above the line.
444. 'and found' crossed out.
445. 'suitable' written above 'proper' crossed out.
446. 'an' written over 'two'; 's' of 'flags' crossed out.
447. 'on the top of the highest tree' added above the line; 'to which should' crossed out.
448. 'modest' written above 'excellent' crossed out.
449. 'some' written above 'a herd of' crossed out.
450. 'large' crossed out.
451. 'of an' crossed out.
452. One of Stanley's neologisms made up from 'to chaff'.

quick taste of the terror he has inspired among the simple peoples of Manyema. He is truly pathetic when he describes the poor enchained slaves, & the unhappy beings whose necks he has seen galled by the tree-forks lumbering & tottering along the paths watched by the steady cruel eyes of their drivers, etc. etc. The topics change so abruptly, that I find it almost impossible to remember a little of them & they refer to things about which I know so little that it will be hard to make a summary of what I am told at each meal. One cannot always have his notebook handy, for we drop upon a subject so suddenly & I often in my interest forget what I ought to do. I must trust largely to[453] the fact that I am becoming steeped in Livingstonian ideas, upon everything that is African, from pity for the big stomached picaninny clinging to the waist strings of its mother to the Missionary Bishop & the Great Explorers, Burton – Speke & Baker.

He is a strong man, in every way with an individual tenacity of character. His memory is retentive. How he can remember Whittier's poems, couplets out of which I hear frequently as well as from Longfellow. I[454] cannot make out. I do not think he has any of these books with him. But he recites them as though he had read them yesterday. The only books I have seen with him are the Bible – Prayer book – Hymn book, Smith's Dictionary of the Bible, an Epitomé & nautical Almanacs, and I gave him one of Hugh Miller's books on Geology.[455] At Ujiji there were Saturday Reviews, Spectators, & Punches, and it is possible he may have seen reviews of the poems there, if not – his memory is astonishing. On other subjects his allusions, to events, & scenes, of African Life,[456] names of persons whom he met years ago, anecdotes and incidents connected with them, have attracted my notice, whereas I would be very hard set if I were expected to entertain another with what had happened at meetings, or in society.

Our men have not come in to-day, and I feel the symptoms of a fever hanging about me.

January 4th 1872 Thursday. Hunted again but was unsuccessful the game seems to have fled – though I came close upon a hartebeest. In the afternoon the fever which threatened me, has floored me.

Jan 5th Friday. Sick of the Homa. Shore party arrived all safe. I heard something of the Lindi flowing from East to the Luaaba,[457] but from what part East I do not know.

Mabruki Speke has had his beard shaved off, and it has been great fun to all hands, for he was so proud of it. His long face bereft of its usual appendage appears quite

---

453. 'being steep' crossed out.
454. 'I' written over 'He'.
455. Hugh Miller (1802–1856), a Scottish geologist and writer.
456. 'African Life' written over undecipherable words.
457. Lualaba (*HIFL*).

feminine now.[458] If he only put on an old lady's cap I would recognize his likeness to some one I have met elsewhere. Burton called him the "Bull-headed".[459] What a strange perverse way Burton had of looking at people! Rivers Loajeri & Mogambazi

Jan 6th 1872. Saturday. Recovering from the fever.

Livingstone tells me he has been only twice at a theater in his life, and would not give a sixpence to see the best play ever acted.[460]

He says that the native tales regarding Kabogo deserve our attention now – as it is just possible that the hollow cavernous sounds heard & reported by many may indicate some remarkable freak of nature.

He reverted again to the Zambezi Mission during which he expressed a strong contempt for the weak dawdling creatures who called themselves Missionaries, and who when confronted with their fields (Note. Repeat the invitation which he & the Captain of the Man of War – (Bedingfield[461]?) received from Bishop Mackenzie to breakfast) resorted to so many subterfuges to escape the necessity of going there.

Tozer, Bishop of Central Africa[462] as he is called has not yet ventured upon his diocese, Central Africa indeed!

He tells me has been a little into the Balegga Country, which he supposes to be identical with the Balegga mentioned by Baker as being West of the Nyanza (Albert)

The coffee in Manyema is very bitter to the taste as the natives burn husks & all.

A great many travellers attempted to reach Lake Ngami & failed among whom, were Smith,[463] Alexander,[464] Galton.[465] The last who is Francis Galton gave it up, about half way on his journey to the West Coast. You should read what Andersson[466] his

---

458. The same anecdote under the same date appears in Field Notebook S.A. 9.

459. Stanley mentions the nickname "Ras-bukra" Burton gave to Mabruki in *HIFL*, 347.

460. Same entry, except the end of the sentence "to see what people call the best," in S.A. 9, same date.

461. Captain Norman B. Bedingfield, RN, FRGS, then a lieutenant, had met Dr. Livingstone in Loanda in 1854. Chosen by Livingstone as the second for the Zambezi Expedition (*PRGS*, January 11, 1858, p. 82), he quarreled with everyone and finally resigned (September 28, 1858, letter from D.L. to Braithwaite, https://www.livingstoneonline.org/in-his-own-words/catalogue?query=liv_001365&view_pid=liv%3A001365). He resumed his career as Commander of the *Prometheus* in 1860. After several commands, he retired in 1877 (http://www.pdavis.nl/ShowShip.php?id=185). Cf. Michael Appleton, *Time Is for Slaves: Yorkshiremen in Nineteenth Century Matabeleland* (Bloomington, IN: AuthorHouse, 2008), 167.

462. See the diatribe against 'our Central Africa bishop' in D. Livingstone's letter to J. Gordon Bennett, April 9, 1872, S.A. 481.

463. This is likely John Smith Moffat (1835–1918), British missionary, and D. Livingstone's brother-in-law.

464. Sir James Edward Alexander (1803–1885), Scottish officer and explorer, FRSE, FRGS.

465. Sir Francis Galton (1822–1911), explorer, geographer, and prolific writer. From 1865, his interest switched to heredity and he became a leading eugenicist and proponent of the "new science of race." On Galton's African Expedition, see Maria Berclouw, "The Travels of Francis Galton" (Masters advanced seminar and shorter thesis, University of Melbourne, 2010), http://dtl.unimelb.edu.au//exlibris/dtl/d3_1/apache_media/L2V4bGlicmlzL2RobC9kM18xL2FwYWNoZV9tZWRpYS8yNTQ0OTk=.pdf.

466. Charles J. Andersson (1827–1867), hunter, explorer and naturalist, joined Galton's Expedition to Southern Africa in 1851. He would go on to document the location of Lake Ngami. See Charles J. Andersson, "Explorations in South Africa, with Route from Walfisch Bay to Lake Ngami, and Ascent of the Tiogé River," *Journal of the Royal Geographical Society of London* 25 (1855): 79–107, http://www.jstor.org

companion said of him in his book. Yet when he reached home the Royal Geographical Society presented him with their Gold Medal for his failure to reach it. Just like some people's marvellous luck you know. I am told he has twice written about the Art of Travel.[467] I think it strange that such an accomplished Master of the Art, did not succeed in reaching the Lake.

I did not want any credit personally for the share I had in the discovery for I did my best to palm the honour of it upon my friends Oswell and Murray. They were however so good natured as to insist that the honour of the find should be mine. It was so like them.

I was very fortunate in meeting so many good people who became attached to me through years, & whom I always love to think of – among the fine, spirited manly English gentlemen who came to South Africa to hunt. That was how I became acquainted with Col Steele of the Guards,[468] a soldierly, chivalrous man, a perfect gentleman[469] whom it was an honour to meet. Then there was Mr Webb – Cap Webb of Newstead Abbey with whom I stayed while writing my first book. He & Mrs Webb are among the best friends I know. They seemed never to tire of looking after me. In every thing they did, they were real & genuine.

Frank Vardon[470] was also a very good fellow, full of fun & spirits. I also met Gordon Cumming the Lion hunter who[471] I dare say you know has written a book about his exploits.[472] I think though he has made a little too much of the lion, for taking the lion – altogether he is rather a currish character considering how we have been in the habit of magnifying him from infancy. A near acquaintance has deprived him of his nobleness. In Majesty he still holds his own from his big mane & fierce eyes, but he seldom acts like a King. Cumming I think has here & there embellished much, but then every one has his own way of telling a story. It would be wrong to regard[473] his exaggerations – as lies, but – well, it is not the style I should adopt of telling of my adventures.[474]

/stable/1798105?seq=31. Stanley may have recalled Livingstone's poor opinion of Galton, resulting from their heated exchanges upon his return to England in 1872.

467. Francis Galton, *The Art of Travel; or Shifts and Contrivances Available in Wild Countries*, 1st ed. (London, J. Murray, 1855).

468. 'of the Guards' added above the line.

469. One word undecipherable added above the line after 'gentleman'. Could be in fact ?

470. Major Frank Vardon, Colonel Steele, Murray, Oswell, and Webb were Livingstone's close friends during his first years in South Africa.

471. 'who' written over 'whom'.

472. Roualeyn George Gordon-Cumming (1820–1866), Scottish traveler and sportsman. He is the author of *Five Years of a Hunter: Life in the Far Interior of South Africa* (London, 1850), http://archive.org/stream/fiveyearsahunteoocumgoog#page/n14/mode/2up/search/livingstone. His collection of hunting trophies was first exhibited in 1851 at the Great Exhibition in London.

473. 'to regard' added above the line.

474. 'of telling of my adventures' added between two lines.

Jan 7. 1872. Sunday. Struck Camp, and marched East through the delta of the Loajeri 1½ hour. We then mounted a knoll, then a terrace, then a hill & lastly a mountain where we halted to encamp.

I observed the Doctor who was ahead of me silently pointing to some object. On coming up to him I saw across a ravine a cow buffalo scrambling upward. He lent me his 10 bore rifle, & trembling as I was from a full dose of quinine, I planted my shot fairly a third shot finished her, to the gratification of every-body. We had the tongue & some choice pieces to salt for the road.

Immediately after the depression produced by the approach of fever, and the sickness caused by it there is a lively reaction created by the enormous doses of quinine I take, and when the system has been thus relieved & the excitement occasioned by the medicine has somewhat subsided I always feel energised as it were, and more capable of entering into the enjoyments of travel. This afternoon was one of these periods when I felt as if recharged with vitality and as we had plenty of food in the camp meat & grain I was uncommonly gay – and Livingstone was somewhat exhilarated by the beauty of the Camp's situation – and probably infected by my high spirits. We had a long talk outside[475] of our little tent about a number of things connected with his earlier years.

He told me that a great friend of his while studying medicine at Glasgow – I think he said, was one James Young an Assistant Professor who afterwards became a chemist, and made a notable discovery in Petroleum – inventing paraffin for which Livingstone dubbed him Sir Paraffin Young, – that another great friend for whom he had a warm admiration was Lyon Playfair.[476]

His attention to Africa was first brought about during his medical studies when he made an application to the London Missionary Society to be sent as a Medical Missionary to China, or some distant Eastern land. But on account of the Opium War the Directors did not think that they would send any one to China but they asked him to call on them when after examining & hence they concluded that he was best fitted for South Africa. At that time[477] Dr Moffatt who afterwards became his father in Law was creating a lively interest by his narrative lectures on Missionary Life.

I went to see him, and we became as[478] intimate as the disparity of our ages would allow and he it was who confirmed me in my belief that I had best accept Africa as my field, though I had a real hankering for the East.

---

475. 'out' written over 'in'.
476. Lyon Playfair (1818–1898), first Lord Playfair of St. Andrews, Scottish scientist and politician. His friendship with David Livingstone and James Young is recalled in Wemyss Reid, *Memoirs and Correspondence of Lyon Playfair* (London: Cassell, 1900), 36–37.
477. 'the f[ather in law]' crossed out. Instead Stanley wrote the name of Dr. Moffat, but spelled it wrongly!
478. 'as' added above the line.

On going to London to finish my medical studies I made the acquaintance of Richard Owen who has since become distinguished for his science[479] in Anatomy.

I landed in Africa in 1840 at Algoa Bay, and waggoned into the interior some 700 miles to a place called Kuruman which was Moffatt's Station. After a few years I went to Mobotza where I practised medicine, conducted missionary duties, and built a Mission.

"Yes. I have built more than one Mission station, and was in those handy with tools of all kinds. I do not occupy myself so much as I used to do with tools but I have built houses of stone, clay[480] – and wood – which occupied months in construction. I have done almost everything in the way of ordinary trades, patched my own shoes, mended gun-locks, planted & sown. Misfortunes sometimes in the rough country we had to travel in happened to my wagon, perhaps an axle broke down, or a felloe[481] was smashed, the canvass wanted sewing. Who was there to do it but I myself. I once made a wheel[482] which did not wobble as it would have done had I been a bungler.

"Surprising as it may appear Doctor I never thought of you as ever having been qualified that way. I don't know why. Made wagon wheels which did not wobble! Well! I must say you are a much superior man than I thought you."

"Ho,[483] I should have been very unfit for my position if I could not have turned my hand to supply my wants. Our gardens were really worth looking at, & supplied our table at Kolobeng so well that we seldom had to buy anything but tea & coffee & articles of that kind. There I was mason, carpenter, gardener, farmer, Doctor, preacher, schoolmaster[484] and administrator. What with one thing or another I seldom stopped work from the time I rose from bed till I[485] was so overpowered with fatigue that on entering the house, I was not fit for anything but sleep. That is the place where my children were born, and after years of work I was obliged to leave it.

"Why – was it unhealthy?"

"No – on the contrary it is one of the healthiest spots in the world, but the Boers thought fit to visit my house when I was away on my duties – & destroyed my furniture, and all my books – scattering them promiscuously in fragments all about, and gave me notice to quit.[486] You see – they had an idea we Missionaries were a stumbling block to their proceedings with the Natives. We were a curse to the country according

---

479. 's' of sciences crossed out.
480. 'clay' written over 'mud'.
481. 'felloe' written over 'fellow'. A felly or felloe is a part of the rime of a wooden wheel into which the spokes are fitted. Kelsey B. Harder, "A Vocabulary of Wagon Parts," *Tennessee Folklore Society Bulletin* 28 (1962): 12–20.
482. 'and' crossed out.
483. 'Ho' preceded by 'Why' crossed out.
484. 'schoolmaster' added above the line.
485. 'I' written over 'it'.
486. Ransack by the Boers, 1852. Letter from Livingstone to his wife: "The Boers gutted our house; they brought four wagons down, and took away sofa, table, bed, ... your desk,... tore out the leaves of all the books and scattered them in front of the house, smashed the medicine bottles, windows, even door." Cited by Thomas Hugues, *The Life of David Livingstone* (New York: A.L. Burt, 1902), 43.

to them, in other words we were teaching the Natives so fast that they thought so much education among the Natives would cause them one day to rise against them & drive them out.

Well, I[487] suppose[488] it was the will of God. If it had not been for the Boers treatment of my belongings & their savage conduct towards my pupils & their threats that on their next visit[489] they would[490] make a clean sweep of all missionary work, I should not have been so anxious to move northward. I had always thought however that a Missionary should go out boldly among the heathen, & in my opinion there were too many of us crowded in a small corner of S. Africa when all the continent required our services. The rough visit of the Boers decided me, to go forward and search for sites far removed from Boer visits, which would yet be healthy enough for white men to live. One thing then[491] led to another. We came to the malarious country – & when I saw the Zouga & Lake Ngami I really thought that I had found a paradise at last, but my children sickened, one died & then my wife began to be afflicted, and I yielding[492] to my fears I drove back with them again to the Cape & sent my family to England. Then[493] freed from anxiety for their sakes, I resumed the search, & travelled North again. Here & there I came across lovely places with grass, trees & plenty of sweet water – the want of[494] which was always a great drawback at Kolobeng – but the fever in a short time made its appearance, & I moved off again to another place, & finally I pushed so far, that I reached the West Coast at Loanda in 1854.

Jan 8. Monday. 1872. Arrived at a small stream after 3 hours march. E by S from Kakungu Mᵗ. The guide was bewildered, so after consulting with Livingstone, I led the column, from the swollen Loajeri. He was about to lead us into a labyrinth of gullies, & towards a roaring cataract which even had we succeeded in crossing would have been most fatiguing without having made any progress. The game appears to be abundant. The country is grand, our Camp lies between the peaks of Kakungu & Kivanga.

In the afternoon Livingstone talked of his son Robert Moffat[495] Livingstone. He would like to have him traced as he is reported to have died in a hospital Newbern, North Carolina but I am to ask Miss Agnes if she has discovered anything new. He fell before Richmond on the Union side. If it is possible to have his grave discovered he

---

487. 'I' written over 'in'.
488. 'that' crossed out.
489. 'on their next visit' added above the line.
490. 'they would' written above 'they would the next time' crossed out.
491. 'then' written over 'led'.
492. 'yielding' written over 'yielded'.
493. 'I resolved to' crossed out.
494. 'the want of' added above the line.
495. Livingstone's eldest son was named after Dr. Moffat, his maternal grandfather. In *HIFL* (601) Stanley included this conversation about Robert's enlistment in the Union army and subsequent death on February 2. Further information related to his son's death is provided in S.A. 9, p. 320, note 159.

would like a stone inscribed "Here lies Robert Moffatt Livingstone (who enlisted in[496] New Hampshire Volunteers under the name of Rupert Vincent.) Eldest son of Dr David Livingstone the African Traveller, one of the brave men who fell before Richmond in behalf of the Union.

He has told me of the love the natives entertained for the boy by one of the Zambezi tribes, and how Mrs Livingstone was known to them by the name of Ma-Robert,[497] in such a manner that I have concieved quite a liking for the romantic high spirited youth, & will gladly see what I can do towards discovering his remains.

Mrs Livingstone died on the Zambezi just after she had landed – or rather as she was ascending the river to join him.[498] The place of her death is Shupanga. She seems to have been stopped longer than was necessary at the mouth of the river. His steamer the "Pioneer" had gone[499] down the river to meet the "man of war" but[500] was stranded on a sand bank for a long time. There were some other ladies came out with Mrs Livingstone, Missionaries' wives, & sections of the new steamer for the Zambezi. The "Pioneer" was too deeply laden with her cargo,[501] & she found great owing to[502] the sand banks. The naval[503] Captain[504] undertook to take the ladies[505] up river but they arrived only to meet the dead bodies of their relatives.[506] Finally reaching Shupanga Mrs Livingstone became ill with the fever. "Kirk was with me and we both attended her, but it was of no use, as we could not rouse her. I have often thought since that if we had given her a hot bath with some muriatic acid (?) in it we should have been able to overcome the coma in which she had fallen. But everything was done that we knew, and she sank. For some time I thought that I should never get over it. Aye[507] – She was a grand woman – very quiet – but with a great heart."

This has been a doleful day, with memories of his son & wife, told in snatches. The pathos of his voice sent quite a thrill through me. The death of his wife was so affecting that I thought saw the river – the deep green shade on the bank – the husband &

---

496. 'in the N' crossed out.
497. 'that the' crossed out.
498. Mary Livingstone died on April 27, 1863.
499. 'gone' written over 'come'.
500. 'not finding her' crossed out.
501. The "Pioneer" was overladen with the sections of the "Lady Nyassa" that the "Gorgon" had conveyed from England and transshipped on the "Pioneer." Cf. infra 108, and W. G. Blaikie, *The Personal Life of David Livingstone* (London: John Murray, 1913; 1st ed. 1880), 247.
502. 'owing to' added in the margin above 'into'; 'in[to]' crossed out.
503. 'naval' added above the line.
504. 'of the' crossed out; 'went' crossed out.
505. The ladies were Miss Mackenzie, Mrs. Burrup, and Mrs. Livingstone. By the time they arrived, Bishop Mackenzie and Mr. Burrup had died. Blaikie, *Personal Life*, 248, and J. E. R. Emtage, "The First Mission Settlement in Nyasaland," *Society of Malawi Journal* 8, no. 1 (January 1955): 16–24.
506. On the detailed ordeal of the journey ascending the river, see Rowley, *Story of the Universities' Mission*, 326–28.
507. 'Aye' added above the line.

friend striving anxiously and unweariedly to save, and bending over[508] the brave woman who had insisted on leaving Scotland to join her husband in Africa.[509]

After a little time I asked him if they had tried injection – as I had read in a medical book that injecting quinine had succeeded where the stomach was unable to retain it. "No, he answered, but Kirk was about as clever in cases of fever as any man & did the best he could. I was myself there, and I was a Doctor myself. No, if I could only have wakened her into consciousness, I should[510] have had[511] some hope of saving her, but the attack was so severe that it quite overpowered her. She rejected every kind of medicine, & soon became delirious, then fell into a heavy[512] stupor out of which we could not wake[513] her.[514]

January 9th 1/72. Tuesday. March E ½ N. 3 ½ hours. The land is rising steadily, and I feel quite recovered. Wounded a buffalo cow but she escaped. Had a view of zebra. Have[515] not come across a single native, or sign of a village, since leaving the Lake. It has been raining all day. Miserable weather. Our marches are[516] short.

After lunch Livingstone pointed out the ginger plan, indigo, sarsaparilla plant,[517] and the Borassus palm. We saw to-day a tree bearing fruit of the size of a 200 pounder cannon ball.[518]

He turns out to have a most familiar knowledge of African vegetation from which I get the benefit. He seems to be also quite a naturalist. I have had[519] quite a lecture on tsetse, beetles, insect pests as well as butterflies. Had I left Ujiji without tramping with him overland I should have had[520] but a poor opinion of his universality of information.

The[521] story of his[522] Zambezi experiences which he related yesterday cleaved to my mind, & I[523] thought of them while travelling this morning, and made me quite melancholy. I remarked to him that he must have had a trying time on his second Expedition.

---

508. 'to save, and bending over' added above the line.
509. After full stop, 'and hanging over her' crossed out.
510. 'had' added above the line and crossed out.
511. 'had' added above the line.
512. 'heavy' added above the line.
513. 'wake' written over an indecipherable word.
514. 'round' crossed out.
515. 'Have' written over word undecipherable.
516. 'therefore' crossed out.
517. Sarsaparilla was quite well known in nineteenth-century United States for its supposed medicinal properties.
518. The size of the fruit became 'a 600-pounder-cannon-ball' in HIFL, 579.
519. 'had' added above the line.
520. 'a' crossed out; 'but' added in the margin.
521. 'The' written over 'His'.
522. 'his' added above the line.
523. 'I' added above the line.

"Yes, he said, the story of it was never written, as I felt it ought to have been. In fact many parts of it (or much of it) was written by my brother Charles. I made a resolution then that if I ever went into Africa a third time, I would never entangle myself with other people. The more you do for them, the more ungrateful they are. I cannot get rid of the unpleasant thoughts relating to that Expedition. As it was through my addresses & appeals that the Missionaries were sent out I was in honour bound to assist, & advise them.

They had a Bishop of their own, & of course I could not interfere so much as I should have done had he not been there, but the Bishop though a very worthy and excellent man,[524] a hard worker, with nothing of the "kid glove"[525] about him had a will & mind of his own, and was in an altogether independent position from us of the Zambezi Expedition.[526] Where it suited him, he of course followed my suggestions, – otherwise, he would not. I had therefore to be an onlooker of many acts I condemned. Up to the time of the arrival of the mission affairs had got on very well with us, and we had been about two years in Africa[527] before the Bishop & the University-people came out.[528] – And then came ill-luck. The slavers[529] carried their trade with more energy & boldness than they had done before. The Bishop was invited to settle at a place, and while he was going with me to see the chief, we were attacked. Then the Missionaries began to meddle with native affairs, far more than I liked, & entirely against my advice. They were new to the country, and had enormous confidence in themselves. But the worst of it was when they found that the people at home did not approve[530] these militant proceedings, the Missionaries, and imputed the blame to me, and said that the troubles were caused by my acts, especially a Mr Rowley – and the newspapers took it up & repeated his charges, and so we began to be decried right, and left. In a few months the Expedition was recalled by Government & the Missionaries were removed by Bishop Tozer.[531] The truth is[532] we owed our misfortunes to the Portu-

---

524. 'man' added above the line.
525. Stanley uses this expression again when describing the ideal missionary (*HIFL*, 235): "He must be no kid-glove, effeminate man, no journal writer, no disputatious polemic … a man of the David Livingstone, or of the Robert Moffat stamp."
526. During his visit to England in 1857, Livingstone had proposed that the Church of England, represented by its two oldest Universities, plant a mission in Central Africa. An association, the Oxford and Cambridge Mission to Central Africa, was formed (1859), and in 1860 it became the Oxford, Cambridge, Dublin and Durham Mission to Central Africa under Bishop Charles F. Mackenzie. About missionaries and Livingstone's relationships, see A. E. M. Anderson-Morshead, *The History of the Universities' Mission to Central Africa*, London, Office of the Universities Mission to Central Africa, 1897, p. 1-43.
527. 'in Africa' added above the line.
528. See H. Rowley, *Story of the Universities' Mission*. Rev. Rowley is quite critical of Livingstone's management.
529. 'were' crossed out; 'carried' written over 'carrying'.
530. 'approve' written above 'like' crossed out.
531. 'by Bishop Tozer' added above the line. Bishop Tozer was Bishop Mackenzie's successor. Facing a heavy death toll among missionaries and hardship for settling in the interior of Africa, he decided to withdraw, and established the mission in Zanzibar. Livingstone criticized that move. See Letter from D. Livingstone to J. Gordon Bennett, April 9, 1872, S.A. 481.
532. 'that' crossed out.

guese government who represented at home that we had only rediscovered what was very well known to Portuguese travellers & that we had designs on their country. Their representatives were seconded[533] by a Prince allied to the Royal Family of Portugal[534] and our Ministers withdrew[535] their support.[536]

I had also great trouble with the steamers sent out to me. The "Ma-Robert" our first vessel was so slow that she could scarcely breast the current. We called her the "Asthmatic". The second vessel the "Pioneer" was to deep, & drew to much water. Then I purchased one out of my own money, the "Lady Nyassa. My wife came on board the vessel which brought the new boat[537] out to us in sections. The "Lady Nyassa"[538] cost me £6000, just double the estimate. We were carrying her overland to lauch her on Lake Nyassa when our[539] recall came." I was blamed for the disasters that happened to the Mission – as well as for its removal by Mackenzie's successor, I was blamed by the Portuguese for taking discoveries which they never made[540] – and I was blamed by the Press for every error connected with everything on the Zambezi.

I sailed with[541] the Lady Nyassa[542] from Mozambique & Zanzibar for[543] Bombay with twelve hands in 25 days[544] & when I entered the harbour she was so small – a mere river steamer – that the harbour master did not appear to[545] think her worthy of notice, as it was some time before he[546] knew of our arrival.[547]

"Ah, yes. I had a black time of it the last two years on the Zambezi, and all the world in Africa or out of it were against me. It is hard to lose one's best[548] companion[549] the mother of one's children,[550] to see one friend after another carried away by death, to be smitten unkindly[551] by those who are left, to be accused of doing what was wholly against one's nature, to find every step, no matter how righteous you know your acts to be, followed by slander & calumny and every endeavour blighted by malice, and uncharitableness. But the Lord gave & the Lord has taken away. It will all come out right at last, not in my time perhaps, but it must come eventually, and there will be no arresting it.

533. 'were seconded' written above 'was supported' crossed out.
534. He is clearly referred to by his name "a well known Coburg" in this notebook, p. 71.
535. 'from' crossed out.
536. 'support' written above 'effort' crossed out.
537. 'the new boat' written above 'her' crossed out.
538. The 'Lady Nyassa' written above 'she' crossed out.
539. 'our' written over 'the'.
540. See Lacerda, *Reply to Dr. Livingstone*.
541. 'with' added above the line.
542. 'for' crossed out.
543. 'from Mozambique and Zanzibar for' added above the line.
544. 'twelve hands in 25 days' added above the line.
545. 'appear to' added above the line.
546. 'it was some time before he' added above the line.
547. 'until I went up to him and reported her' crossed out.
548. 'best' written over 'dear'.
549. 'co[mpanion]' written over 'wo[man?]'.
550. 'the mother of one's children' added above the line.
551. 'unkindly' added above the line, and crossed out after 'who are left'.

Jan 10th 1872. Wednesday. March to camp near River 3 ½ hours, through a beautiful park land. I led the way straigh across country which had not the least sign of a path.

Jan 11th 1872. Thursday. Two hours march brought us to a rivulet[552] whose smooth slippery bed rock showed the powerful wearing action of water. Mushrooms in abundance & very large. Our course then lay along the base of a hill range runing due East & West, on our right. At the third hour & a half we halted for lunch then proceeded for two hours more to a river. The Doctor was much fatigued when we reached camp, and said that he had once a suspicion that he was being "Rowleyfied".

Jan 12th 1/72 March for 3 hours to camp on stream flowing from S. E. We thought we saw[553] the great "Magdala" Hill[554] that I remember to have seen two days after leaving Imrera when proceeding to Ujiji last October. Saw an elephant, and while I was admiring him a wasp stung me on the neck. Men begin to feel anxious about food. They hunt for mushrooms, and a large flat thick root which has a turnipy flavour. Mbembu & Matambu fruit not in season.[555] This is the 6th day since leaving Urimba & the country is utterly uninhabited.[556] The men complained to Livingstone of their hunger but he turned & chaffed them so cleverly that they were silenced.[557]

Jan 13th Saturday. Camped[558] by a stream[559] with a broad belt of fine timber[560] on each side. Men pick mushrooms. A herd of 12 elephants passed by us not far from Camp. Our hunters followed them but were unsuccessful in getting meat.
    This brought out stories about shooting elephants from Livingstone, wherein Gordon Cumming Murray, Oswell, Pringle & Vardon figured – but I am too tired to write them.[561]

Jan 14th Sunday Marched 5 hours S. East. After the fourth hour lunched looking down upon a grand feature of Kawendi scenery. Saw a colony of large reddish monkeys of the howling Class. I think the rainy season is on us for it rains every day about[562] the same hour. Saw a herd of animals I took to be gnus

---

    552. 'with slippery rocks in its bed' crossed out.
    553. 'We thought we saw' added above the line.
    554. 'is in sight' crossed out.
    555. About trees, see *HIFL*, 522–26. The Mbembu is the wood-peach. The Matambu (Matamburu in S.A. 9) could be the Mtamba, which produces a kind of fig (*HIFL*, 522).
    556. 'Expect and hope to reach Imrera to morrow' is crossed out, but mentioned in S.A. 9.
    557. This last comment is not mentioned in S.A. 9.
    558. 'Camped' preceded by 'Reached Imrera' crossed out.
    559. 'belted on' crossed out.
    560. 'Fine' added above the line before timber. In S.A. 9, Stanley specifies "a broad belt of timber of which canoes are made," which refers to the mvule tree (*HIFL*, 524).
    561. No mention of hunting stories under this date in S.A. 9.
    562. 'at' changed into 'about'.

January 15th Monday, 1872. Went up a long valley &[563] past a deserted village which had been palisaded, ascended a ridge up to the summit. Four lions roared in concert not far from us. Proceeding S. E. about 2 miles came upon a herd of hartebeest & zebra fired & missed being too anxious for meat for our desperately hungry men. Came to a stream flowing S. W. Sighted a wild sow with a little & a boar. Camped near a stream on the trees of which a species of wild plum. The African wilderness is kind – one day we find fungi, on another wild fruit, on[564] a third we find meat. If the people were only prudent with what they obtain they would relieve us from much anxiety.

January 16th Tuesday. Arrived at Imrera – the long sought for village (21 days from Ujiji) to the wonderment of the caravan who cannot imagine why the little[565] compass should be a better guide than the old veterans of travel among them. We are all fatigued, & hungry.

January 17th Wednesday. Halt. Plenty of food in Camp. Men munching contentedly & continuously maize, millet, beans & early sweet potatoes. What a change has come over the country. Last October the country was in its golden Autumn coloring it is now one vivid green from the rains.
The Doctor's feet are very sore from the late marches & he has[566] cut & slashed his boots[567] ruthlessly. Though he[568] might well ride on his donkey he will not. I ride about one half the march so that when I reach camp I feel able to do as much more after[569] a little rest & feed. I look upon the march as a kind of task work which must be done as quickly as possible for the sake of the carriers and though it is delightful to walk in the cool of the morning, it becomes distressing in[570] the[571] hot sunshine three hours afterwards. Then it is that the donkey's back is a relief, & I save my strength for the afternoon hunt which occupies from one to sometimes three hours, – and my diary which often takes quite an hour in writing up. To see the old man tramping it on foot, like a hero makes me feel a little ashamed – and sometimes an unworthy thought comes into my head that he does it to vex me. He must be a rider – having been in South Africa, – but it is an odd taste to prefer walking to riding. However if he won't, he won't & there's an end on it

---

563. '&' added above the line.
564. 'on' added above the line.
565. 'little' written over 'com[pass]'.
566. 'has' added above the line, in black ink.
567. 'his boots' written above 'them remorselessly' crossed out.
568. 'owns a donkey' crossed out. From 'Though he owns a donkey' to 'which must be done as', text in black ink.
569. 'lunch' crossed out.
570. 'in' written above 'when' crossed out.
571. 'sun' crossed out.

January 18th Thursday. 4 hours march S. S. E to Miunyo Mansu. R. flowing N. to Malagarazi – narrow – but deep being in flood. The Kirangozi lost the road again twice. I put him right, and gained additional honour as a guide. The[572] feet of both the Doctor & myself are sore from the wet, & cut great slivers out of our boots round the chafed[573] spots.

Wild grapes are abundant, & of various species. Our singwe (oval[574] wild plum) jam having been exhausted we have taken to stewing the grapes in honey. Were we a fortnight or a month later we should have ripe grapes.

January 19th Friday March 5 hours S. S. E to Mpokwa in Utanda. The Doctor stopped a few minutes on the road to show me the gum copal tree, & to talk about the fossil Gum which is sometimes found in places where the tree has long ago disappeared. He also showed me the Chili, and the Sarsaparilla plants.

We made ourselves comfortable in the deserted village – two huts having been swept clean for our use.

Soon after tiffin our men sighted herds of game in the neighborhood & I rushed off with Billalli for a gunbearer carrying the Doctor's Reilly Rifle No 10. Shot two zebra, & obtained 719 lbs of meat which allowed 16 lbs to each person. I weighed them & the Doctor marked the figures in my notebook.[575] Every one of course was hugely delighted. The Doctor applauded me much. Bombay said he had dreamed a dream wherein I had shot animals right & left.

January 20th Saturday. Halt to day to eat meat. On going out to hunt I saw eleven giraffes. After crossing the Mpokwa river I got within 150 yards of one. I wounded one, but he got away.

In the afternoon I went East of Mpokwa & came across six giraffes. I wounded one, but it escaped. What remarkable creatures they are! How beautiful their eyes! I could have sworn from their manner of sidling off that both shots had succeeded, but they disappeared like clippers, about to tack.

The Doctor knows the art of consolation very well. He said that my non-success was due to using leaden balls which were too soft to penetrate their thick hides, and advised me to melt my zinc canteens to harden the lead with.
It is not the first time that this quality in the Doctor makes me think him an admirable travelling companion – nobody knows so well how to console one for bad luck, or how to elevate one when in low spirits. If I killed a zebra, did not Oswell & himself

---

572. 'The' written over 'our'.
573. 'chafed' written over 'bruise'.
574. 'oval' added above the line.
575. See S.A. 9.

decide long ago that zebra meat was the best in Africa. If I shot[576] a buffalo cow she is sure to be the best of her kind, & even the horns are worth carrying home. If I am unsuccessful, the game must be wild, or frightened & it is poor sport to stalk animals when alarmed. Indeed his considerateness makes him loveable, I am proud when he applauds, and consoled when I fail.

Ibrahim whose Kibuyu (gourd) when broken the other day made him exclaim – My Kibuyu is dead, bought a slave in Ujiji, who was called Ulimengo or the "world". The "world" has absconded with his owner's Kit – clothes & salt, and Ibrahim has been lamenting it in such a way that the people laugh at him I asked him "Why he bought such a slave, & why he did not feed him when he had him? He turned round sharply & asked "Was he not my own? Did I not buy with my very own cloth? If the cloth was mine, could I not buy what I liked? Why will you talk so?" But Ulimengo came back this evening & the one eyed[577] old fellow is glad & came to me & said "So, the "world" had returned Sure! My salt & clothes too! Sure! Then I advised him to be careful & feed him, as slaves want food as much as their masters.

The Doctor sat up from 10 – to midnight taking observations from Canopus[578] & I find we are in S. Lat 6°. 18'. 40". By dead reckoning I was 6°-15 just 3 miles wrong.

January 21st Halt. The Doctor's feet are too much inflamed for travel & my heels are raw.

Having melted[579] my zinc canteens, I hardened some bullets & set off West of Mpokwa to hunt, and in a short time I saw a group of giraffes nibbling at tree branches. After a laborious[580] stalk I came within 175 yards & then rested to get my breath & pulse steady & to cool for I was bathed in perspiration. Then cooled down a little, I aimed. I then[581] put the rifle down, arranged sights, passed my hand over the barrel, played with it until quite calm. I aimed once more & fired. For a short time I feared I had again missed him but after hobbling 200 yds away, he drew his ears back & stood. A second shot laid the giraffe dead.

"Allaho Akhbar" cried Khamis this is meat master!

What a splendid animal a giraffe is! I felt such a pity for it now that I would willingly have given it the life I had taken had it been in my power.

The dead giraffe measured 16 feet 9 inches from right forehoof to the top of his head & was one of the largest of his kind. He was spotted all over with large black, nearly round patches

---

576. 'shoot' changed into 'shot'.
577. 'one eyed' added above the line.
578. Canopus: the second brightest star of the southern hemisphere.
579. 'melted' written above 'cut' crossed out.
580. 'a' added above the line before 'laborious'; 'laboriously' changed into 'laborious'.
581. 'I' preceded by 'again' crossed out; 'then' added above the line.

Men came to cut it up, but Khamis for fear of lions crept up to a tree. The meat was hung in the scales & weighed

1 hind leg,	134 lbs
1 " "	136 "
1 fore "	160 "
1 " "	160 "
Ribs	158 "
Neck	74 "
Rump	87 "
Breast	46 "
Liver	20 "
Lungs	12 "
Heart	6 "
	993 lbs
Skin & head	181 "

Bombay's dream was fulfilled. The people who[582] had been crying for giraffe meat were pacified, Young Kalulu my infant cannibal, and Billalli another young toto[583] fond of meat had been hoping & wishing the "little master" as I was told to distinguish me from the "Great Master" would procure meat. Bombay had by his dream been persuaded that if I took a Zanzibari, I would succeed, & according to him I owe my success to that fact.

The village of Mpokwa is the most comfortable camp we have had since leaving Ujiji. Castor oil plants flourish between the huts. There is always plenty of game & fish to be found here. It is also[584] at the junction of several roads, to Ufipa, to Msowwa, to Ukawendi & to Maungu.

January 22nd Fever
    23rd "
    24th "
    25 "

26th Friday. March to Camp on Mtoni (river) Rain incessantly. The land is pretty. But I am still too shaky for anything much.

Livingstone's prescription for a fever is

3 grains Resin of Jalap
2 " " " which must be got pure at Apothecaries Hall, with just enough Tincture of Cardamoms to make into a pill to prevent irritation of Stomach,

---

582. 'who' added above the line.
583. 'Toto' refers to young ones, but the correct rendering is in Kiswahili is mtoto (sing.) and watoto (pl.).
584. 'also' added above the line.

an hour or so later take a cup of pure coffee unsugared & without milk.[585] 3 grains of Rhubarb may be added with benefit. He thinks also that quinine ought to be taken at the same time, but my opinion is different from this.

January 27th Saturday. A long march to the Misonghi Stockade[586] 6 hours. Or 10 ½ hours from Mpokwa. We were attacked by wild bees about halfway. Every body ran on wildly and I could not help laughing at the antics, the cries & struggles though I was stung several times in the face & hands. The Doctor was behind me & in view. His poor donkey got stung unmercifully about the head, and raced, blindly on, running his head into a thick bush. Then kicking himself free he galloped again, and the last I saw of him as my donkey plunged recklessly on was the Doctor sprawling on the ground & struggling with the bees.

It was suave qui peut.[587] I let mine go-, as he was in torments,[588] screams, & tremendous excitement all along the line & the vicious bees stinging with all their energy as fast as we went. Selim who is always peculiarly unfortunate with insects red & black ants was of course a special object of malice to the bees & was dreadfully stung in every exposed part – but my poor donkey was in the worst condition, his nose is so swollen that it resembles that of a giant moose, or the curved snout of a gnu.

The Camp was uncommonly distant – but finally we reached it, thirsty, and hungry. After setting up the tent & refreshing myself with a cup of tea, I began to think of Livingstone. Aware of his misadventure with the donkey & sure that he would not venture on his back again, I became uneasy. The men were dropping in to Camp at long intervals & one of them told me that the Doctor was very tired. I bestirred the guides & the best men to[589] prepare a hammock & sent them off with promise of reward. After two hours they returned they returned[590] saying that they had[591] found the Doctor resting under a tree. They offered to carry him but he said "Get away with you – do you think I am a woman?"[592] quite sharp. I then began to suspect that the Doctor must be in a bad temper – what with the bees, the fall from the donkey, the long march & the wretched boots so posted a couple of men along the road at a good distance from the camp to give me warning of his coming. Meantime I

---

585. In Field Notebook S.A. 9, Stanley gave the following prescription: 3 grains resin of Jalap, 2 grains of calomel. The rest of the prescription is identical. Stanley must have made a mistake here when repeating Resin of Jalap instead of writing calomel.

586. 'Stockade' added above the line.

587. "Sauve qui peut" is a French expression for "Run for your life." Stanley incorrectly wrote 'suave' instead of 'sauve'.

588. 'as he was in torments' added above the line.

589. 'get rea[?]' crossed out.

590. 'they returned' repeated.

591. 'had' added above the line.

592. "I have done it all on foot…. I could never bear the scorn the Portuguese endure in being carried when quite well." Letter from Livingstone to R. Murchison, March 13, 1872, *PRGS* 16, no. 5 (1871–72): 435.

bribed Ferajji to get ready a hot & bounteous meal of Tea, basted balls, mush & goat[593] milk, & lots of dampers ready. The bed was made quite comfortable & cheery, and slippers[594] laid ready, & Billalli was instructed to stand by to take off the Doctor's boots. The people struggled in very slowly, and long after sunset, the messengers came and announced the Doctor to[595] be coming. The table was quickly set, & the smoking dishes were laid.[596] I went and hid myself in the shadow of a hut. & saw that he was tired and grave.[597] From my place of observation, I saw Billalli bending down as the Doctor seated himself on the head,[598] & threw off his cap, the steam from the smoking dishes curling about his face, then after wiping his face & set to, I waited until quite ten minutes watching the effects of these preparations. I then sauntered up, and gave him "Good evening". The Doctor was very grim at first, but he soon relaxed, & said "Well I had thought you were going on to Unyanyembe without stopping. It is rather a long march is it not? I excused myself as best I could. The people knowing the road & that they were going to Unyanyembe & having made up their minds to reach Misonghi could not be stopped, &c &c. Before long the Doctor was in his usual sweet temper & we laughed over our misadventures. But a good hot meal is a great restorer of the spirits!

January 28th Sunday. Marched 2 ½ hours E ½ N. Crossed 3 streams inclusive of Usense & camped on E. bank of 3rd River. Rain again & much discomfort from the wet.

January 29 Monday. Arrived at Mrera of[599] Ukonongo, having travelled by a shorter route & a better one[600] than that[601] taken when going West towards Ujiji.

January 30th Tuesday. A halt, for caravan people to grind corn & prepare rations for the long wilderness in front of us. Rain & Rain ever since leaving Urimba on the Tanganika. We are contending for comfort, to-day the Doctor & I, which is so difficult to obtain in this weather.

January 31st Arrived at Kamirambo's, Mwaru. Met a caravan under a slave belonging to[602] Said bin Habeeb, who paid us a visit.

---

593. 'goat' added above the line.
594. 'stood' crossed out.
595. 'to' written over 'com'.
596. This sentence was inserted between two lines.
597. 'grave' written over 'subdued'.
598. Evident slip of the pen for 'bed'.
599. 'of' added above the line.
600. 'and a better one' added above the line.
601. 'that' written over 'the one.'
602. 'belonging to' written above 'of' crossed out.

We asked him the news about Mirambo, Unyanyembe. He told us that his master had taken Kirira, that Said bin Majid (of Ujiji) had killed Moto, that Simba of Kasera was fighting for Mkasiwa of Unyaynyembe that the chief of Ugunda had sent 500 men to fight Mirambo, and that Mirambo was[603] so closely pressed that he would die of hunger in a month.

We[604] next asked him where he was going? In answer he said that as I had been able to reach Ujiji by this new road that his master had thought he had better try also, & that many Arabs intended to follow him. He had heard that I was dead, killed by the Wazavira – but affected to be astonished when he was told by the white man who had opened the road was myself.

I then asked about Shaw, whom I had left at Kwihara Unyanyembe[605] in Said bin Salim's house & was shocked to hear that he was dead, from a fever.

I looked at the Doctor, & he said, "I told you so for when you described him to me as a drunkard, I knew he could not live. Men who have been habitual drunkards cannot live in this country any more than those who are slaves to other vices. I attribute most of the deaths on the Zambezi to much the same causes."

"Ah Doctor there are two of us gone. I shall be the third, if this fever lasts much longer."

"Oh no, not at all. If you were going to die from fever, you would have died at Ujiji from that severe remittent. Don't think of it. Your fever is only due to exposure to wet. I never travel during the rainy season. This time I have done so because I was anxious & did not wish to detain you."

"Well, there is nothing like a good friend at one's back in this country, to keep one's spirits up. Poor Shaw! He was a bad man, but I am sorry – very sorry for him. How many times I tried to cheer him up! But there was no life in him. Among the last words I said to him before parting were: Remember, if you return to Unyanyembe you will die."

We also heard that several packets of letters, newspapers, & boxes, had arrived from me for Zanzibar,[606] & that Selim bin Hasheed had also come. The Doctor also reminded me – goodnaturedly that he had a stock of jellies & crackers, soups, fish & potted ham & cheese waiting him at Unyanyembe & that he would be able to share with me, as I had shared with him.

Today as we passed through a quiet bit of forest, he pointed his stick at a deep[607] shady place & said, That is the kind of place I should like to be buried in. In England

---

603. 'was' written over 'would'.
604. 'We' written over 'where'.
605. 'Unyanyembe' added above the line.
606. instead of 'for me from Zanzibar'.
607. 'deep' added above the line.

there is no elbow room. I should feel suffocated. I have[608] often & often looked at such spots with just such thoughts – ever since my poor dear Mary was laid at Shipanga (?)

Feb 1st Thursday. Through forest E by N 4 ¼ hours.

Among the blessings of this life I count wheaten bread & good fresh butter. Molasses, Hams, bacon, caviar &c such things are beyond our reach. While suffering from fever I find myself[609] wondering that people should ever be ill who can have access to such luxuries as are denied to me. I fear I shall surprise people when I renew my acquaintance with wheaten bread & fresh butter.

We have salted giraffe meat, & pickled zebra tongues, porridge, sweet potatoes, tea, coffee, and dampers, but we have fed on these things so often that I begin to loathe them. The Doctor shows me a good example however by his persevering attention to the demands of the stomach. He has a thorough[610] knowledge of all[611] that is African. The trees are familiar to him also their fruits, and their virtues. When[612] we come across any rocks, I get a lecture from him about their composition. He is[613] interested in anthropology and whether on the road or in the camp he imparts to me his wise reflections. In Camp craft he is an adept. His bed is rather luxurious considering its materials. His servants Susi & Hamoidah take special charge of constructing it afresh at each camp – two thick logs[614] 3 feet apart & parallel to each other with cross sticks just strong enough to support his weight lashed to the logs with bark rope. On top of these a thick layer of dry[615] grass – and with a waterproof thrown over – furnishes him with a bed that is soft, dry & at the[616] agreeable height of a drawing room lounge from the ground. It[617] is not only his bed, but his sofa & chair. A couple of tin boxes in front of him, become his writing, study & dining table. He & his goods occupy one half of the tent, my cot & boxes are on the opposite side. An[618] unoccupied space the width of the tent door[619] running from end to end serves as a passage & boundary between us.

The Doctor's donkey died yesterday from the effects of bee stings probably. Our goats are still thriving & give us a fair supply of milk morning & evening certainly more than enough for our tea of which we are almost inordinate consumers. Both[620]

---

608. 'I have' written above 'He had' crossed out.
609. 'find myself' written above 'sometimes' crossed out.
610. 'thorough' written above 'good' crossed out.
611. 'all' written above 'everything' crossed out.
612. 'When' preceded by 'A rock met' crossed out.
613. One word above the line, unclear.
614. 'laid parallel' crossed out.
615. 'dry' added above the line.
616. 'the' written over 'that' above 'an' crossed out.
617. 'It' written over 'this'.
618. 'An' preceded by 'A passage of three' crossed out.
619. 'the width of the tent door' written above 'of 3 feet wide' crossed out.
620. 'Both' written over 'each' preceded by 'We' crossed out.

of us absorb from five to seven cups at each meal – sometimes even more. Once Livingstone drank thirteen cups, and I took eleven which was due to[621] a long march, and an almost[622] rabid thirst.

The five parrots brought from Manyema by Livingstone's servants have had an easy time of it. They have been carried & well fed, & consequently we know when all the Doctor's people have reached Camp by the screeching & whistling greetings they[623] give to their compatriots.

Cut our initials on a tree at this camp L & S Feb 1. 72

Feb 2nd Friday March through forest 5 hours to Ukamba
Livingstone was in excellent humor for narration[624] in the afternoon, but it was principally on the subject of his grudges against the Portuguese for their machinations on the Zambezi, and at home, & their support of the slave trade.[625] He referred to the Señhores with grand names who was reported to have crossed Africa being no other than half-caste slave-traders of Portuguese paternity & negroid maternity, but Lacerda[626] was different being a Portuguese gentleman of great intelligence Being on[627] Zambezi topics[628] I had some further details respecting the deaths of Mackenzie Burrup & Thornton[629] – of the goodness of a Mr Waller[630] who acted as Secretary to the Mission – then he told me of Morambala Mountain, of the certainty that he had of the habitability of the Zomba plateau – of the Elephant Marsh – of his discovery of the Shirwa, & Nyassa Lakes. Then he ranged back to Shupanga, the place of Mrs Livingstone's burial, and said that as he once passed that place he had looked at it with more than ordinary interest little thinking that his memory would ever have cause to[631]

---

621. 'which was due to' added above 'but' crossed out; 'a' written over 'the'.
622. 'an almost' written above 'a quenchless' crossed out.
623. 'they' written over 'these'; 'parrots' crossed out.
624. 'for narration' written over 'in gossip'.
625. See note 356 to the entry for December 19.
626. Livingstone probably alluded to Dr. Francisco José Maria de Lacerda e Almeida (b. Sao Paulo, 1750, d. Zambia, 1798), mathematician and astronomer, explored a large part of Brazil in the 1780s and afterward undertook travels in South Africa. He attempted a coast-to-coast journey from Angola to Mozambique and died at the court of King Cazembe in 1798, before completing the journey. The RGS published his diary, *The Lands of Cazembe: Lacerda's Journey to Cazembe in 1798*, translated and annotated by Captain R. F. Burton (London: J. Murray, 1873), https://archive.org/details/landsofcazembelaooroya.
627. 'the' crossed out.
628. 'topics' added above the line.
629. Geologist Richard Thornton (1838–1863) was hired to serve with Livingstone's Zambesi Expedition.
630. Rev. Horace Waller (1833–1896) edited and published the last journals of Dr. Livingstone, though he was not the first choice of Livingstone's daughter. See letter from Agnes Livingstone-Bruce to Stanley, January 31, 1878, S.A. 518: "[The book] has been a grand failure, but this must be "entre nous". Poor Tom [Livingstone] felt unequal to the task of editing it, and Mr Murray proposed Mr Waller should help him, and their joint names would appear. I did not approve of Mr Waller doing it, and we thought of asking you, but when Mr Murray went to do so we got the news that you were leaving in a day or two for Africa. It ended in Waller undertaking it, and by some means or other he kept Tom's name out, and took all the glory of editing the book! It was a cruel thing, and the book has not sold."
631. 'remember it' crossed out.

retain an indelible impression of it. He repeated to me the story of his son who enlisted in the Union Army & he hoped we should be able to ascertain where he was buried. I might have made quite long entries of his conversation this evening but, I fear that I am in for another dose of the fever.

Feb 3rd Saturday. Halt. Fever.

Feb 4th Sunday. March 3 hours. I was carried

Feb 5th Monday. March. Carried in a cot.

Feb th Tuesday. March. Carried for 2 hours. Reached a spot three miles beyond Ukamba.

Feb 7th Wednesday. Arrived at the Gombé. Sent Chowpereh and another man to Unyanyembe to bring our letters and medicines. Am a little better. After breakfast I went out to hunt. While wondering at so many game tracks along the Gombé, I heard Khamisi cry out "Simba!" a lion, and I caught sight of his head. Before however I could get behind a tree to steady my hand which trembled with quine – the animal bounded away.

Feb 8th Thursday. Halt.[632] In the morning[633] I went out again to hunt after despatching two men to Ma-manyara with presents, and I had not gone far from camp before we were stopped by hearing close to us on the other side of a clump of bush a triplet of lions roaring together. While trying to pierce the bush screen I happened to look around, and saw within easy rifle shot a fine hartebeest cowering behind a tree & trembling. I fired into it, but when it recovered itself it dashed away – and as the lions had ceased their roaring, I crept around to have a view of them, but they also had disappeared.

    In the afternoon we made a 4 hours[634] march for Manyara, by[635] whom we were hospitably received at the gate of the village

Feb 10th Friday March to the Ziwani or the Pool Camp under a splendid[636] Sycamore, arriving about 2 P.M. having breakfasted on the road.

---

632. 'Halt' written over 'I went'.
633. 'In the morning' added above the line.
634. '4 hours' added above the line.
635. 'by' written over 'who'.
636. 'Mkuyu' crossed out.

The Doctor read out his list of stores that ought to be in Unyanyembe for him – and said that we should make amends for our spoiled Christmas dinner when we reached them.

Feb 11th Saturday. Arrived at Kwikuru a palisaded village. Several Arab caravans are met each day. The news that I have reached Ujiji safely despite Mirambo has had the effect of inducing them to[637] hazard their lives outside their strong tembes.

I find that they have been nicely calculating how many months ago it is since I left. We hear favourable accounts of the progress made by the Arab heroes in the war with Mirambo. The fiery old Chief Said bin Majid[638] angered for the loss of his son Soud at Wilyankuru seems to have been distinguishing himself, and has attacked Usagozi & the other villages under Simba the son of Moto with considerable success.

Livingstone came across a review of his book the "Zambezi & his tributaries" & handed it to me saying, "Read that. There is a cordial now for a man so badgered as I have been."

I read it & thought it very favorable and asked, "But were you harshly reviewed, Doctor?"

"Yes, by nearly every writer.[639] My critics seemed to have made up their minds that the Missionaries were right, and I was wrong. It was a kind of damning with faint praise, you know. They were kind enough on matters that I did not care about, for I never pretended to be a fine writer – and if they had said the book from[640] a literary[641] point of view was a disappointment and that kind of thing they would not have been far wrong but when they charged me going against life long principles & the rules of Common Sense they touched me to the raw[642] – as though they knew instinctively how to make me[643] smart, & feel small. Well- well- one learns something every day but I never thought that after being 23 years among Africans, I ought to have gone to those young Missionaries fresh from College to be taught how to treat natives, or how a mission ought to be conducted."

"What you tell me surprises me a great deal – for since 1868 when I was sent to Aden to await your coming – I have read considerable about you – but I do not remember to have seen anything in any Newspaper or Magazine that was in the least derogatory. It may be that if I had I should not have remembered it – and probably that is the opinion of the world at large. Just think of the sentiments which I uttered

---

637. 'attempt' crossed out.
638. Change of ink.
639. 'writer' written over 'author'.
640. 'from' added above the line.
641. 'literary' preceded by 'literary compos' crossed out.
642. 'raw' written over 'quick'.
643. 'feel small' crossed out.

about Speke & Burton. Speke was the traveller, the explorer the man who discovered – therefore[644] who cared what Burton had to say, however ably he said it against Speke. One was a genius as a geographer the other was clever as a writer, but the writer bears no comparison in my mind with the Man of Action & the Discoverer. I have read Burton's Lake Regions thoroughly, but withal that Speke has my sympathy I have not met either of them. I do not know anything about them except what I have gleaned from[645] Burton in his book & from your lips. Yet I side with Speke wholly in the dispute. Now try & judge of the world in regard to yourself, from my sentiments about Speke. There is Bennett for instance who may be taken as a fair example of the world. He[646] is a newspaper man all over, lives on Newspapers why should he have sent me after you, if he had not gaged the world's opinion & divined that underneath all that blind criticism, there was the greatest possible admiration for you.

I am a newspaper man myself, and know how these criticisms are written. Many of them have only a desire to be considered smart writers, & really manage to string their remarks together with due grammatical correction fluency & an appearance of wisdom, but if you saw them & heard them speak – & understood their motives I doubt whether you would respect them. At the American consulate at[647] Zanzibar I came across a number of bound volumes of the "Saturday Review" & examing the index I found a number of references to America & read several – but a child might have been able to pick out in every article any number of mistakes. These are not the kind of people, Doctor to which the world listens."

"You are my kind I am sure, but I am thinking that you have also a pretty way of saying pleasant things, to one who is low spirited. I return you the compliments you paid me the other day."

Feb 12th Monday. A Halt. People grinding corn for the last stretch to Unyanyembé.

Had a talk today with Livingstone about the floating island of Tanganyika which was reported to us by the Zanzibaris as moving from place to place in a most mysterious manner.

He said he had heard of it also and he was reminded of what Herodotus described in one of his books of a similar island in an Egyptian Lake which remained undiscovered for a long time until one day a King hotly pursued by his enemies sprang into the water, and when he rose to the surface he found himself all of a sudden[648] on[649] the shore of the fabled island where it was said he passed a pleasant

---

644. 'therefore' added above the line.
645. 'I have gleaned' added above the line.
646. 'He' preceded by 'He sent me after you' crossed out.
647. 'at' written over 'I came'.
648. 'in the midst' crossed out.
649. 'on' written over 'of'.

time. He thought probably that the tradition has been handed down – and as people invariably in the course of repeated telling exaggerate or distort the original story – the story of the floating island must have had some connection with the old Egyptian fable.

This reference to the Nile Land started him on his pet hobby the Nile problem. He asked me "Have you never when a boy tried to race with your own shadow?"

"Ah yes often – & found that it always went as fast as I did myself."

"Well now, I am very much in that predicament with this Nile question. Whether I go to Bangweolo, Nyangwé, Cazembé or Ujiji or even here something happens always to corroborate my own opinions that these waters that we have been passing lately, or the Chambezi & its affluents, or that immense river the Lualaba have a connection with the Nile. Even that story of the fabled island of the Tanganyika – the steady Northward flow of the great river – the Mound from[650] which those four rivers spring – Two to the South & two the North – all tend to confirm me that it is the Nile & no other. Really if it were not I would not risk being made black man's meat but would go home with you now.

I wonder whether I shall be able to satisfy my old friend Sir Roderick that I am doing what I ought to do. If he were here I think he would understand better. He has a fair & discriminating mind, and would know how desperate my position has been. I look at it this way. I am in the midst of an intense darkness – and I hold up a little farthing rushlight[651] to see what I am about. About my feet I can see very well, & see which way the streams flow. I can see the rocks on banks & the vegetation, but while I hold my little light up I hear the sound of waterfalls and roar of cataracts in the distance, and my rush light goes out, & I have to go on, & on groping my way feebly to guide my steps to the distance where my queries will be answered."

I wish that I were in the vein of writing – as he is of speech this evening; but my fever is on me again & I think that I shall go mad with these continual attacks.

Feb 13th Tuesday. March from Kwikuru. Am carried again as I cannot even ride my donkey.

I am in such a state to-night that I can neither lie down, or sit quietly in one position long. Livingstone is calmly asleep – I am nervous and my head is very strange. I[652] have the most fearful dreams every night – & I am afraid to shut[653] my eyes lest I shall[654] see the horrid things that haunt me. I will go walk – walk walk[655] in the forest to get rid of them.

---

650. 'from' added above the line.
651. 'ushlight', ms. A candlelight with a wick made of rush.
652. 'must go' crossed out.
653. 'even' crossed out.
654. 'shall' added above the line.
655. 'walk' written three times.

Feb 14th March to Ugunda through flat, open forest. Last night I travelled round & round the Camp – and among the Camp-fires. Stopping a little at one & then at the other & then resuming my midnight walk. It must have been two o'clock this morning before I lay down. I think it must be the quinine which I have taken in unusual doses that[656] that created this extraordinary state of nervousness – singing in the head, twitching & uneasiness of the head. After a hard wrestling with myself, I fell asleep & woke up relieved.

Soon after we reached this large palisaded[657] village & had made ourselves comfortable in our new quarters in came Ferajji & Chowpereh with our messengers from Zanzibar.

They brought no less than seven packets of letters, which had been collecting at Unyanyembe during my[658] absence. They confirmed the news of Shaw's death but they stated that one[659] of the men in his tembe had reported that while in a raging fever he had cut himself open with a jack knife – but the other man with him said it was a[660] lie.

I had one packet from Dr Kirk which contained two or three letters for Livingstone to whom they were transferred with my congratulation that he was not forgotten by his friend. In the same packet was one to myself from Dr Kirk requesting me to take charge of Livingstone's goods & do the best I could to forward them on to him. This was dated 25th Sep. 1871 five days after I had set out from Unyanyembe for Ujiji.

"Well Doctor, said I to Livingstone "the English Consul requests me to do all I can to push forward your goods to you.[661] I am sorry that I did not get the authority sooner for I should have attempted it, but it does not matter as you have been pushed towards your goods. The mountain has not been able to advance towards Mohamed, but Mohammed has been compelled to advance towards the mountain.

But Livingstone was too deeply engrossed in his letters from home which proved to be a year old.

On opening my letters, the first that came to hand gave me a shock that in my weak nervous state, seemed to strike me to the heart, and caused me an attack of vertigo.

The paragraph that was the occasion of this was in a letter from Francis R. Webb, American Consul at Zanzibar, & ran as follows,

"I am distressed not only in my private capacity as a gentleman, and business man but also as a Consular Official to hear from my correspondents in New York that

---

656. 'that' written above 'which has' crossed out.
657. 'palisaded' added above the line.
658. 'my' written over 'our'.
659. 'one' written over 'some'.
660. 'a' added above the line.
661. See Appendix, Letters from John Kirk, British Consul in Zanzibar, to Stanley, Zanzibar, September 25, 1871, S.A. 2656.

your draft for $3750, which was the first sent has been protested, and that Mr James Gordon Bennett disclaims all responsibility in connection with it. As I was the cause of your being able to obtain funds, and guaranteed to Tarya Topan the Hindi Merchant who advanced the money that the money would be forthcoming[662] you will understand that Tarya Topan will look to me to be refunded, and as there are other drafts of yours on the way, the amount will ruin me, unless you can certify me that you will be able with private means to meet all these obligations. I departed from strict business principles for your sake, and because I believed that the private letters you carried from the Agent of the "New York Herald" would ensure against any[663] loss, but as Mr Bennett has peremptorily declined to pay I must look to you for repayment and I hope you will send a courrier to inform me how you propose to do so at your earliest opportunity."[664]

Here was a blow! After a while an official looking letter from New York attracted my attention and I opened that. It contained the legal protest & was as follows:

New York Mch 29, 1871

"Please to take notice, that a draft drawn by you on James Gordon Bennett Esq Jr. at Zanzibar Jan 17, 1871 3ds/s for 3,750 Gold Dollars is <u>Protested</u> for non=acceptance & that the holders look to you for payment thereof.[665]

Your obedt. Servant

J. F. Lockwood

Notary public

214 B.dy New York

To Henry M. Stanley Esq

There was not a doubt of it! Bennett was about to treat me as I had heard he had treated others of his unfortunate correspondents. For a minute I looked at Livingstone, and held the letter & the protest suspended in my hand ready to denounce in the fiercest terms the man who had sent me into Africa & treated me so disgracefully. Visions of the thousands of dollars I should have to pay out of the salary of £400 a year which I had received since 1868 floated before my excited brain – and a stern angry Consul at Zanzibar awaiting me there on the beach, to tell me in no choice language what he thought of me & so on. But the quiet pleasure on Livingstone's face

---

662. 'that the money would be forthcoming' added above the line.

663. 'any' written over 'my'.

664. There is no such letter in the Stanley Archives kept at the RMCA. However, there is another letter from Francis R. Webb, informing Stanley that he had indirectly received news from the United States that the draft was protested, and from London that the proceeds were received in Salem (Appendix, S.A. 2655). This letter is dated July 16, and most probably did not reach Stanley before his departure to Ujiji, but it should have been awaiting him at Unyanyembe. However, Stanley did not mention this letter in his journal.

665. S.A. 4751.

as he read his children's letters, & his[666] utter unconsciousness of the misfortune that had overtaken me restrained me. Then laying the letters down, I rummaged among my papers[667] that[668] I might refreshen my mind with[669] those missives[670] from the "Herald" Agent which I as well as the Consul had taken to be evidence that Mr Bennett had despatched me into Africa. The first was dated 14 Cambridge Sq. Hyde Park London Nov 29, 1869, & said,

"My dear Stanley

I enclose you a letter of credit for £600, and I send with it my best wishes for your signal success in your great undertaking. I have no doubt you will carry it through in perfect style. The latest news from Livingstone seems to render it certain that he is alive, and that after all is the most important feature of your commission. I talked the matter over with Mr Bennett, and his idea is decidedly Napoleonic. In the expectation of hearing great things from you I wish you all health & comfort on your extended pilgrimage.

By the way I hear indirectly that the Canal will be a failure after all. If this is so, do not conceal the fact. It is none of our profit or glory, &c &c &c.

You may fully rely on my sending you supplies of money & I make the present letter £100, more than you asked for, because I am sure you will be careful as you always have been in regard to Expenditure[671]

Very truly your friend
Douglass A Levien

"They objected to make the letter of credit run over 12 months but wherever you may[672] be at the end of a year, you will no doubt have used up the amount."

2nd letter from the same address 31, January 1870

"My dear Stanley

I have a sort of presentiment that there will be a break up after all between the Khedive & the Sultan. If it does come, I hope to gracious[673] it may be before you leave that part of the world (Egypt) as I should like to have you there. Of course you will not forget that you are to see it through before any thing else if there should really be a row, &c &c.

---

666. 'his' written over 'the'.
667. 'papers' written over 'letters'.
668. 'that' written over 'for'.
669. 'refreshen my mind with' written above 'reread' crossed out.
670. 'missives' written over 'documents'.
671. 'Expenditure' written over 'your'.
672. 'may' written over 'are'.
673. For 'good gracious'.

If you do not find your money likely to hold out, you can let me know in time where to send you another credit before you get out of reach of letters & I will do so.

Very truly yours

Douglass A Levien

Henry M Stanley Esq

The[674] reperusal restored me to calmness for it appeared to me that though[675] they were not in official form, they corroborated my story, and would prove that I had not been romancing. True M[r] Bennett could swear that[676] the verbal account of my commission that I had given was an exaggeration or something else, but what else[677] could M[r] Levien have referred to as "Great undertaking, "Napoleonic idea"[678] and the fact of Livingstone being alive, as[679] "the most important feature of my commission". I had a weak case perhaps in a court of Law which could distort any thing – but not in equity. It is no matter however – I must pay the bills myself.

I had no stomach for the other letters after this shock – and lay down silent revolving the extraordinary disclosures of these letters. After resting I took up a third letter which was in a strange handwriting from Zanzibar. I looked at the signature. It was signed John F. Webb, whom I did not know. I began to read it languidly – but before I read many lines, I was staring at them[680] with a fixed gaze, & wondering if I read aright. In my present state of weakness, the news was almost too much. It was dated Dec 23, 1871 and contained[681]

"H. M Stanley Esq

My dear Sir

I avail myself of an opportunity today by the return to Unyanyembe by the return of one "Zede", a slave of Said bin Salim to forward to you a small package of the latest despatches we have received from Aden, and to wish you God Speed in your undertaking.[682]

Capt Webb and family left here (Zanzibar) Nov 13th in the Barque "Glide" for home. He left with me a copy of a letter he had received from London dated Sept 25th 1871 which is as follows: "M[r] Webb &c &c. I write this to inform you that a change has been made in the N. Y. Herald Office Agency here & that I am in charge while M[r]

---

674. 'The' written over 'they'.
675. 'though' written over 'they'.
676. 'they' crossed out.
677. 'else' added above the line.
678. S.A. 2626, Letter from Levien to Stanley, November 29, 1869.
679. 'as' added above the line.
680. 'the' changed into 'them'; 'lines' crossed out.
681. The letter Stanley quoted here is incomplete. See the original letter in Appendix, Letters from John Webb, American Consul in Zanzibar, to Stanley, December 23, 1871, S.A. 2658.
682. The following sentence 'I am requested to inform you that a change has been made in the "N. Y. Herald"' was crossed out.

Levien the former Agent has gone home. This you will understand may be of special interest in view of matters relating to the Expedition of Mr Stanley. Will you kindly make note of the fact, that I am ready to cash here at any moment any draft that you or others at Zanzibar may cash for Mr Stanley or to order by telegraph that the same be paid at Bombay or Alexandria. Will you be so good as to acknowledge receipt of this & let me know if there is any way in which I can facilitate the operations of Mr Stanley &c &c

Geo Hosmer"

&c &c &c I remain yours truly
Jon F Webb

It required some time for me to recover my[683] equanimity and to engage in conversation with the Doctor without letting him perceive through what a furnace of emotions, I had passed. We sat until late in the evening talking about the Franco-German War which was now terminated long after the stars had appeared in the milky way above. I never thought that I had such a good memory, or could be so fluent, about a hundred events that had been consigned to oblivion – as things of no further concern. I was the principal talker this evening & I go to bed a different man from what I was this morning.

Good bye Levien, & long live Hosmer.

February 15th Thursday. A march, through open Forest, for Unyanyembe.

We are both in better spirits to-day owning to the fact that we are inspirited by our approach to Unyanyembe.

The two messengers from Zanzibar tell us that Hamdallah a[684] "bounty-jumper" who made his escape soon after leaving the sea as been arrested & is a close prisoner.

The Doctor told a story about Speke & the Duchess of Sutherland today. He said that the Duchess before whom Speke was brought at a ball or something of that kind began to cross[685] examine him rather closely about various African matters and was especially anxious to know from him whether when he said that the Native women were naked he meant the term in its literal sense.

"Yes certainly" said Speke.

"Oh, but surely they wore something the Duchess insisted.

"No not a thing", said Speke bluntly except a string or so down here, and suited the action to the word in a manner that caused several ladies to cry, "Oh! Captain Speke! And the Duchess to hide her face with a fan, which the gallant traveller no

---

683. 'my' added above the line.
684. 'deserter' crossed out.
685. 'cross' written over 'address'?

sooner saw than he beat a hasty retreat thinking he had done for himself that time & no mistake."

"I[686] do not see that it was poor Speke's fault" I said.

"No, of course not", replied[687] Livingstone. The Ladies will sometimes you know, insist to know about things they ought not to know – & Speke was caught unprepared that time."

He also told me that when he first obtained the privilege of sleeping on a four post bed stead, he cannot contain[688] himself to one position in it but must try the luxury of rolling in it like a buffalo in his wallow, & then stretching himself diagonally, transeversely obliquely & every other way & sometimes[689] with his feet where his head ought to be, or hanging over the sides.[690]

Looking at him to day closely, I think his face appears remarkably youngish. The furrows noticed at first are now mere slight puckers about the eyes, & the skin is much smoother and settled. He is stouter also – having filled out considerably. His sight is as good as[691] mine, at long range, & though his writing is unusually large, he reads printed books without trouble.

February 16th Friday. Arrived at Kigandu. Continue to be much absorbed in the news from Europe, brought from Aden in telegrams, and in the New York Herald's & Punches, & the condition of things around Paris, greatly exercised us, so much so indeed that we recklessly kicked the journals under the beds, though "Punch" made us laugh.[692]

Feb 17th Saturday. March to Inesuka which has a new palisade. To morrow please God we shall be in Unyanyembe.

Feb 18th Sunday. Unyanyembe.[693] On the 53rd day[694] from Ujiji. We entered in fine style. The flags were flying and the men shot tremendous discharges of gunpowder.
It is the custom, for as they say "a great man does not enter a town like a sneak", numbers of Arabs came to meet us & give a cordial welcome. Among[695] them was[696] Sheikh

---

686. preceded by 'Spe[ke]' crossed out.
687. 'replied' written over 'said'.
688. 'contain' written over 'confine'.
689. '& sometimes' added above the line.
690. This is also noted in the inside cover of Field Notebook S.A. 8.
691. 'that of' written above 'any of an'? 'ou[r]'?, all crossed out.
692. An example of Stanley's erratic punctuation.
693. Written in big letters.
694. '53rd' written over '54th'.
695. preceded by 'Said' crossed out.
696. 'Said bin Salim the Governor' crossed out.

bin Nasib the philosopher, and Thani bin Abdallah a notable gailliard,[697] among many other Notables. Since I had departed from Unyanyembe 131 days had elapsed, & we had journeyed meanwhile 1200 miles – &[698] I felt very proud when I entered my old house arm in arm with Livingstone & said "Doctor, we are at last At Home.[699]"!

We[700] did little else in the afternoon[701] than eat the cookies, pilaf, & curried[702] rice that came pouring in from our Arab friends, as[703] our bodies after the journey well deserved some pampering.

Finished the day with prayers & one of thanksgiving from the Doctor.

Feb 19th Monday. We began our new life in Unyanyembe after the morning coffee with a little service, at which many of our men attended. I then[704] took the Doctor round the store rooms of the big tembé of the Governor which was like a palace compared to the hut at Ujiji. In the storerooms there were 74 loads of miscellanea, the most[705] of which were to be turned over to the Doctor, for I needed only sufficient to take me to the Coast.

We rousted out the Doctor's property for the sake of those jams & jellies, potted hams & biscuits of which he had spoken. The first box when opened contained 3 tins of biscuits, 6 small[706] tins of potted ham, – 5 stone[707] pots of jam, one of which was uncovered[708] & was empty, each[709] the others had a little over a tea spoonful! Besides those[710] there were 3 bots of[711] curry. The second box and out tumbled a fat dumpy Dutch cheese, but it was a hollow cheese – the inside was eaten clean by rats, or two legged thieves I cannot say. The third-box had two loaves of white sugar, the fourth, had candles, the fifth table[712] salt in bottles, sauces,[713] essence of anchovies, pepper & mustard. In[714] the sixth box[715] were some clothes

---

697. Probably for the French "gaillard", as in S.A. 9, February 12–15, 1872.
698. '&' written in black ink over 'but'.
699. 'At Home' with capital letters.
700. Text in black ink from here.
701. 'in the afternoon' added above the line.
702. 'curried' added above the line.
703. 'as' written over 'and'.
704. 'then' added above the line.
705. 'valuable' crossed out.
706. 'small' added above the line.
707. 'stone' added above the line.
708. 'uncovered' written above 'opened' crossed out.
709. 'each' added above the line.
710. 'Besides those' written above 'there' crossed out.
711. 'bots' for 'bottles' added above the line.
712. 'table' added above the line.
713. Preceded by 'Harvey' crossed out. "Harvey" sauce has been kept in *HIFL*, 609. Stanley is even more specific, adding Worcester and Reading sauces. But he is also quite critical about the whole content of this fifth box: "What food were these for the revivifying of a moribund such I was!"
714. 'In' added above the line.
715. 'con' crossed out.

four flannel shirts, two pairs of stout[716] russett leather boots stockings & shoe strings the last of[717] which delighted the Doctor so much that he exclaimed after he put on a pair now Richard is himself again",[718] and stamped bravely on the floor."[719]

"That man who gave you those is a friend indeed"

"Yes that is my friend Waller."

We opened 5 other boxes which contaned potted meat & soups, but the twelfth supposed[720] to contain one dozen bottles of medicinal brandy, was not to be found. We cross-examined Asmani the head man of[721] Livingstone's caravan & discovered that not only was the brandy missing but also 2 bales & four bags of beads. We were both grievously disappointed I especially – for during my late fevers these luxuries at Unyanyembe had floated before[722] my crazed mind. There was only one tin of biscuits, and as for the soups we did not care for them in a land of cattle & sheep.[723]

We then overhauled my stores & found some fine old brandy & a large bottle of Champagne still left – though it was clear that some of the articles had been rifled.

Some one suggested that Asmani who had been in charge must have been the thief, & Susi & Chuma were empowered to seach[724] his effects which[725] resulted in 8 or 10 colored cloths with the mark of my own agent on them. Other[726] charges were brought forward by the watchmen against Asmani which on Livingstone finding them proven caused him to[727] dismiss Asmani[728] as another of the "moral idiots".[729]

Unyanyembe however being a great Arab rendezvous & rich in herds, sheep, goats, & poultry, eggs & milk besides millet, rice, & maize we did not feel the loss of the stores very much. We had abundance of material to buy any thing we chose & we all resolved to have our Christmas dinner as soon as we can obtain the articles needed. In the meantime we feasted on the cooked viands sent to us from Tabora with the Arab Compliments, & congratulations, though many of the principal men are absent in the field against Mirambo.

---

716. 'stout' added above the line.
717. 'the last of' added above the line.
718. A famous (but interpolated) line from Shakespeare's *Richard III*.
719. 'floor' written over 'gro[und]'.
720. 'supposed' written over 'whi[ch]'.
721. 'the head man of' added above the line.
722. 'me in' crossed out.
723. Most of this account was kept word for word in the description of the opening of Livingstone's boxes (*HIFL*, 609–10). Slight additions and changes provided an opportunity for designating Kirk to be responsible for the poor choice of Asmani as the headman in charge of Livingstone's goods and, indirectly, for the content of the boxes: "who cares for curry?" (*HIFL*, 609), "who cares for meat soup in Africa?," "chicken and game soups! – what a nonsense!" (*HIFL*, 610).
724. 'seach', ms.
725. 'which' written over 'with'?.
726. 'Other' added above the line.
727. 'be' crossed out; 'dismissed' corrected to 'dismiss'.
728. 'As' of 'Asmani' written over 'the'.
729. Here Stanley must be quoting Livingstone, who applied the same term to Shereef (*LJ*, 2:155).

Feb 20th Tuesday. Cooked our Christmas dinner to day, & being in good health, I personally[730] superintended it. We had roast beef, soup, rice, sweet potatoes, boild fowl, curried stew, rice pudding rich with milk & eggs, & papaws for dessert, and Champagne. There was no fault with anything. The wine was certainly a blessing and it rendered us very talkative.

Livingstone said after dinner that he did[731] not believed in hurrying on while travelling, because the poor carrier suffers too much. Five miles a day he thought quite sufficient. If he comes to a locality worth exploring he likes to do it thoroughly lest he should never have the chance again. Hunger combined with weariness kills in a short time. To[732] rush through a country can only give one a superficial knowledge – therefore take it easy & in the end you will find it more advantageous.

Though elderly in years – I am told he is[733] drawing near 60 – does not appear so in body – & in heart & mind is still younger. It was[734] the first appearance at Ujiji that gave[735] me the impression that he was old. I was then somewhat shocked by the ravages in his face & bowed bearing, but he is now not the same man at all. When I turn my face away from him I[736] fancy myself talking to a man full of vigour. The loose front[737] teeth which play while he talks add to the appearance of age a great deal. He uses humorous Scotticisms frequently – but I cannot remember them. He is full of sly jokes. When he begins one of his[738] funny stories, I see how it is going to end by the gleam in his dark hazel eyes, & the puckers gathering about the eyes, & the uplifted forefinger.* They all seem to say, Now look out there is a joke coming."

He retains habits of carefulness, & order. His tin boxes are in a better condition than my own though this is his seventh year of travel & I am[739] only 11 months from the Coast. The black Japan on his[740] tin boxes[741] is scarcely[742] rubbed off, while my[743] tin is almost naked of the varnish. His compasses & sextant are in first rate order, his journals are comparatively clean, & almost blotless, as if a copyist had been lately writing it up.[744]

---

730. 'personally' added above the line.
731. 'did' written over 'does'.
732. 'To' preceded by 'and' crossed out.
733. 'is' added above the line.
734. 'was' written over 'is'.
735. 'has' crossed out; 'gave' written over 'given'.
736. 'can' crossed out.
737. 'front' added above the line.
738. 'his' added above the line.
739. 'I am' written over 'is any'?
740. 'his' written above '(the)' crossed out.
741. 'boxes' added above the line.
 Black Japan was a coating varnish made of a solution of bitumen, turpentine, and linseed oil for protecting the metal.
742. 'scarcly' ill-corrected by Stanley.
743. 'my' written over 'mine'.
744. This is quite contrary to what Stanley had noted about Livingstone's journals, after his meeting with Dr. Kirk at Zanzibar, on January 17, 1871, Journal S.A. 7.

He told me also of his children. Agnes his eldest child[745] is quite a young lady now.

*Livingstone when about to begin his narration was always in the habit of holding out a crooked forefinger. Gibbon the historian used to hold his forefinger straight on similar occasions.[746]

Tom his oldest son is in the employ of a Mercantile firm – Oswell – who was[747] named after his dear friend the South African[748] hunter[749] is studying medicine & Anna Mary is still[750] a school girl.[751] Robert Moffat died in the company of brave men & sleeps with them.

[change of ink]

Feb 20th Tuesday. Went to Tabora to pay our respects. Visited Sultan bin Ali who held the rank in Syed Barghash's army equivalent to a colonel at $1,200 a year. He is an old Tory who persisted in believing that his old Muscat flint-lock is superior to the Winchester Repeating Rifle until I fired 14 shots at a target from it. He gave us some wheaten bread, cakes fried in ghee & a bountiful supply of lemonade. He also presented an ox to our men.

Then we visited Massoudi another old Arab who has anchored here & will probably never leave.

We saw in the Arab houses papaws, bananas, mangoes, lemons, citrons & a few grapes in the gardens. They also had onions, rice, millet, maize, beans, field peas, peanuts, sweet potatoes, cucumbers, milk, eaggs[752] butter. They seem to live luxuriously.

Got home again in good time, then measured the cloth in the store room before preparing a few[753] bales for the Coast, & discovered that over 700 yards have been abstracted by some one during my absence. The red sami-sami beads have also been used with a heavy hand quite 70lbs gone. Such a quantity means nearly two months rations for a respectable Caravan in Unyanyembe.

Now that we have candles & have an immense amount of work to do in writing up notes & letters, the evening are very pleasant. Every spare moment during the day Livingstone spends on the verandah copying from his little notebooks into his journal,

---

745. 'child' added above the line.
746. This note and its asterisk were added in another ink.
747. 'who' was added above the line.
748. 'South African' added above the line.
749. 'Oswell, who' crossed out. Oswell joined the "Rescue Expedition" organized by the RGS that Stanley would meet when arriving at Zanzibar in May.
750. 'is still' added above the line.
751. See S.A. 488, 490, 491, 492, 493, Letters to Stanley from Thomas Steele, William Oswell, Anna Mary, and Agnes Livingstone.
752. 'eaggs', ms.
753. 'a' added at the beginning of the line; 'few' written over 'our'.

but after the dinner chat is over, he finds it necessary to make use of candle light. He told me of his row with a Naval Captain which he had on board the Pioneer (?) I think. It started because Livingstone according to him was descrating the Sabbath! "What a foul of a man he was to think that doing necessary work was desecration. He was my navigator, or Sailing Master, and he had the impudence to come to me and protest against my ordering the men to clean up. The Sabbath he seemed to forget was made for man – and not man for the Sabbath. Besides the ostentatious manner of it was most objectionable just what you would expect from a man bred up in the forms of a Pharisee. I had to get rid of him – for that, and other things. He had got to believe himself indispensable. So I became the skipper myself.[754] We were as the saying is too incompatible to get along smoothly. Among the Commoner men we had some rare good chaps."

When people heard that I was going to return to Africa on this last journey I had any number of applications – but as you can imagine after my Zambezi experiences I would have none. Squabbles are not pleasant.[755] Even little boys of 11 & 12 wanted to go out with me. There was one little fellow who scarcely reached my waist who begged hard, & cried when I told him it was impossible. I gave him a box of candy, I had bought for my child Anna Mary, and I took him out by the hand, and he went away smiling.

A[756] reference to the Arabs we have seen made him say: "When the native is not contaminated by contact with the Arabs[757] one[758] is wrong to call these[759] half Castes by that term – though some of the pure breed are just as bad. I use it because it is comprehensive and short, & as handy as the word Englishman which we use for an inhabitant of the British Isles. – The native is more amenable. There is a little commotion at first, but they soon settle down, and one is as safe in their villages as elsewhere."

"What about those Manyema who tried to spear you, and the Warundi on Lake Tanganyika I asked."

Well, I think I have told you about that hellish creature Tagamoyo having murdered wholesale in the market place? Do you think that what took place would not be rumored widely among the Manyema? The Arabs were in Manyema a couple of years before I reached that country. And the Warundi must have been often vexed by them – for the Arabs have been on the Lake as much as thirty years ago – perhaps more.

---

754. From 'He had got to believe…' to 'the skipper myself' added above the line.
755. 'Squabbles are not pleasant' added above the line.
756. 'A' preceded by 'Referring' crossed out.
757. 'Arabs' written above 'half–castes from the Coast' crossed out.
758. 'one' written over word undecipherable.
759. 'fellows' crossed out.

No. I maintain that the Manyema who tried to spear me took me for another specimen of those who were hunting them down. They did not know poor things, that I was their best friend. There is a verse in Coleridge somewhere about the angel loving the bird that loved the man that shot him with his bow. I love the Manyema too – and when I was at Ujiji I wrote a letter for Mʳ Bennett of the New York Herald" which I think will prove it, for why do I write at all but in the hope that somehow this system of unmitigated ruffianism – which was born of hell will be stopped.[760] You told me yourself that if I wrote to the "Herald" other papers will publish[761] my letter – and in that way my words will[762] touch the hearts of some who will stir – and not rest until the system is put down with the strong hand.[763] May God Speed that day – I cry with all my heart.

I will write other letters to the "Herald" and try to make people at home realise the horror & grief I have felt in the sights I have seen. Long before I reached Nyassa, & from Nyassa to Manyema what have I seen – but the provision of horrors that these villains had provided for my eyes. I quite understand why my friends have believed me dead. I have sent letters enough at every opportunity – but they have been destroyed by these rascals for fear, that they contained my revelations of their atrocities. Consequently you have gone on either believing that I was dead & buried, or that I have become so morose & sour that I never wish to see my family again. I have not been ignorant that while my wife remained home[764] at my bidding to look after our children, she was said to have made my life so uncomfortable that I could not live with her, and a more gentle companion never lived. The one story is just like the other, both are the fictions of long tongued gossips.

Feb 21ˢᵗ Wednesday. The rain continues pouring all day, but we have both so much to do that we do not mind it, and I rather enjoy the whisk of the driving, & the heavy patter of the falling drops. We are well furnished with all that contributes to comfort. I have been busy enlisting new men, & settling[765] with those who went to Ujiji with me.

After dinner, the subject of his connection with the Geographical Society was broached. He said,

---

760. The Stanley Archives (KBF/RMCA) keep two incomplete long letters from Livingstone to Gordon Bennett about the slave trade (S.A. 481, 8 pp. and 7 pp.).
761. 'it' crossed out.
762. 'reach' crossed out.
763. See Stanley's proposition to Livingstone to write letters to be published in the *New York Herald*, S.A. 7, December 16, 1871.
764. 'home' added above the line.
765. 'sett[ling]' written over 'pay'.

"The Society only gave[766] £500 towards this journey of mine – yet they expected that I would them[767] the fullest reports of all my discoveries.[768] It is odd how a big Society composed of learned & rich men, should[769] collectively have so little sense as to expect that I was bound to think only of them, and not of my family. Was I bound to serve them with[770] my body & soul for £500? Kirk's answer to Sir Roderick ought to have made them ashamed to ask me to do what no one else was prepared to do. Before any correspondence was begun upon the subject of my coming I remember Sir Roderick putting his hand on my shoulder and saying coaxingly "Well Livingstone my dear fellow, we must get you to go & settle that watershed. Nobody else can do it but you" When I got my book off my hands and the subject was renewed by Sir Roderick, I told him plainly that I was quite prepared to go but not as an[771] explorer only.[772] I had other views which were to open up Africa, expose the slave trade, and explain to the natives wherever I went about our Redeemer & our religion. I was not unwilling to do Geographical work as I went along but I did not wish to abandon altogether[773] my own particular work, wherein I felt I could do most good.

I therefore welcomed the Geographical fund as an aid to the great[774] humanitarian object to[775] which my own inclination was driving me. Of course for either Geography, or humanity, or Christianity the sum was a mere sop[776] by itself,[777] it would just enable me to pay my fare to[778] Zanzibar & back[779] with a tropical kit. Government granted a similar sum, and when I reached Bombay, my friend Dr Wilson[780] appealed for subscriptions -which brought in between £900 & £1000. Then I sold the Lady Nyassa for £2,300. I took £300 for Expedition & invested £2000 in[781] bank

---

766. 'me' crossed out.
767. Verb missing.
768. On the detailed funding of this journey, and the role of Sir Roderick Murchison, see R. C. Bridges, "The Sponsorship and Financing of Livingstone's Last Journey," *African Historical Studies* 1, no. 1 (1968): 79–104.
769. 'when' crossed out.
770. 'all' crossed out.
771. 'a' changed into 'an'; 'mere' crossed out.
772. 'only' added above the line.
773. 'abandon altogether' written above 'drop' crossed out.
774. 'great' added above the line.
775. 'to' added above the line.
776. 'for' crossed out.
777. 'it was useless' crossed out.
778. 'it would just enable me to pay my fare to' written above 'not have done much more than to take me to' crossed out.
779. 'and back' added above the line.
780. John Wilson (1804–1875), Scottish missionary and head of the Free Church of Scotland Mission School in Bombay. Cf. George Smith, *The Life of John Wilson, D.D. F.R.S. for Fifty Years Philanthropist and Scholar in the East* (London: J. Murray, 1878).
781. 'Agra' crossed out. In 1866 a financial crisis drove a series of banks to failure, among them the highly regarded Agra & Masterman's Bank. It was established at Edinburgh, London, Paris, and many cities in India, which explains Livingstone's choice for his place of investment. At the time, Stanley was engaged in an adventure in Turkey and he may have ignored the fate of the bank. However, it is not clear that this investment had been lost in the bankruptcy, since Livingstone tells Kirk that he

which[782] bankrupt soon after.[783] As another kind of[784] aid I accepted the merely honorary office of H. B. M. Consul for Africa,[785] without pay. It would give me the name of "Balyuz" which the Arabs bestow on[786] a Consul[787] or an Ambassador indiscriminately a title that would command respect, and explain my business in Africa to every fellow curious to know what engaged me in the wilds & led me to wander from home.

In other respects besides expecting to reap all the benefit from my labours the Society has not treated me well. I had a bone to pick with it before leaving England. From the Zambezi I had sent a sketch map to the Society and a member had made free use of it. When I[788] returned I[789] wished to have a correct map made after the corrected observations – verified by Sir Thomas Maclen[790] the Cape astronomer, but this gentleman turned round to me & said he should charge me £200 for the trouble of making a new one. Now the Society, mind you is a rich & influential body, & consists of such men as Sir Roderick Murchison, Bates of the Amazon, Webb of Newstead Abbey, and scores of other friends, and when I complain of the Society, I only wish to complain of those Fellows on the Council who appear to forget what is due to the poor traveller – and remember only what is due to the Royal Geographical Society. As in every great body, there are some terrible faddists in it – of the Cooley[791] type – there I am afraid there is far too much cliqueism.

One time also I saw a grand map of Africa[792] in[793] the Society's rooms – and most of the information was derived from me – yet it bore another man's name. Now fair play is a jewel but I doubt whether there is much fair play in tacking somebody else's name to my discoveries. If some of them only came to Africa they would know what it costs to get a little accurate information about a river, or a mountain, & how many months of labour & suffering are[794] involved in travelling round a Lake.

---

had given Stanley a draft of £1000 on Bombay to pay for his expenses if needed (cf. letter published in *HIFL*, 707).

782. 'Went'? written over word undecipherable.

783. From 'Then I sold the Lady Nyassa …' to '… bankrupt soon after' written above 'Altogether I got about £2,300' crossed out.

784. 'kind of' added above the line.

785. 'the' crossed out.

786. 'bestow on' written above 'give' crossed out.

787. '& which means' crossed out; 'or' added above the line.

788. 'I' written over 'he'.

789. 'I' written over 'he'.

790. Sir Thomas Maclear (1794–1879) was the director of the Cape Observatory from 1834 to 1870. Besides having proved the Earth is round, he started to prepare a catalogue of Southern hemisphere stars. See "Astronomical Society of Southern Africa," http://old.assa.saao.ac.za/html/his-astr-maclear_t.html.

791. W. D. Cooley (b. 1795?–d. 1883), author of *Inner Africa Laid Open, […]* (London, 1852). (See complete title in Bibliography.) About Cooley, cf. R. C. Bridges, "W. D. Cooley, the RGS and African Geography in the Nineteenth Century," *Geographical Journal* 142, no. 1 (March 1976): 27–47, and no. 2 (July 1976): 274–86, http://www.jstor.org/stable/1796601.

792. 'of Africa' added above the line.

793. 'in' written over 'on'.

794. 'are' written over 'is'.

Then again when I do send a letter home, the Council has a curious way of excising some of my views, and thrusting their own in – as if they knew better than I what I have seen. Where is the harm of letting my own letters stand just as I write them? I do not see that the Society's fame depends upon revising my letters however wrong-headed I personally[795] may be. My name is at the foot of the letter and makes me alone responsible for what I write. I call this[796] unnecessary Doctoring and I am old enough not to like it. In my private correspondence I have often called their attention to this, but they keep on doing it[797] all the same.

Feb 22nd Thursday. Had prayers this morning at which there were fourteen people present. He read the 2nd & 3rd Psalms, and I thought the tone singularly appropriate especially the verse, "Ask of me, and I will give the heathen for thine inheritance, and the uttermost parts of the Earth for a possession." He expounded some of these verses as he came to each, and he interpolated personal references to his many periods[798] of suffering & illness, and asked "Has not something higher than man sustained me?" and when he came to the verse "I will not be afraid of ten thousands of people that have set themselves against me[799] round about."[800] He reminded them of the Mazitu,[801] the natives of Cazembe, & the Manyema.

Soon after an Arab fresh[802] from the Coast brought another packet of letters for Livingstone.

Several Wanyamwezi desirous of going to the Coast have made applications for loads to carry. I engaged them.

Feb 23rd Friday. Livingstone having heard that some goods of his were in charge of Said bin Salim the Governor he sent some men to bring them to our house. The Governor says he is ill as a reason for not paying his compliments to the Balyuz. As Livingstone stated that he had sent two letters to the Coast in charge of the Governor, I reminded him to ask if they have been received. The Governor replied they had. &[803] as for the goods, he hoped the Doctor would not be very angry at their condition as the white ants were very destructive in Unyanyembe.

The stores were in an extremely sorry state. The expenses had been prepaid for their transport from the Coast to Ujiji but had been detained by the Governor since

---

795. 'personally' added above the line.
796. 'Doctoring' crossed out.
797. 'doing it' added above the line.
798. 'periods' written over word undecipherable.
799. 'against me' added above the line.
800. 'against me' crossed out.
801. 'and' crossed out.
802. 'fresh' written over word undecipherable.
803. '&' preceded by 'The goods came' crossed out.

1867. The white ants had made havoc with the box in which two guns had been packed, & had eaten the gunstocks. The barrels were corroded & the locks quite destroyed. The case containing 12 botts[804] of brandy had also been consumed, & strange to say the brandy had been drunk, and in place of the corks, corn-cobs had been substituted & driven into the bottom of the[805] bottles. Medicines had also vanished and the zinc casing & pots in which they had been packed[806] were corroded. Two bottles of brandy & 1 zinc pot and a cheese[807] alone remained out of the goods in Said bin Salim's charge.

Feb 24 Saturday. After prayers, Livingstone resumed his letter writing. He says he is writing to Lord Granville about the slave trade.[808] I continued packing.

I learn that Sir Samuel Baker received a baronetcy for his discovery of the Albert Nyanza – and that another traveller has had the good fortune of securing a charming lady with £7,000 a year for a wife, which impelled me to think that if desert was thus liberally rewarded what fair proportion of honour, and fortune should be given to this simple & single minded man, who not satisfied with discovering the Zambezi, and the Lualaba, and Lakes Nyassa, Shirwa, Bangweolo, Mweru –[809], and who has now been 31 years in Africa, during which he has torn off the mysterious mask that shrouded the heart of the Continent. He is about to set off again with the purpose to finish the revelations of the Central line of drainage which fills his thoughts & so fascinates him. He is talking about the Nile of Joseph, & Moses[810] & the Pharoahs, & its connection with Herodotus & so on but at his age drawing near his 60th year – it appearss to me to be a big task – from the cannibals on its banks, & the multitude of rivers which he had mentioned. Ali bin Sultan the other day when visited him though he must be certainly[811] over 65, talks as if he knew from Father Time how many years he was yet to live & was quite contented with the promise. So I think Livingstone takes life in the same cool & assured manner as if it had been whispered into his ears[812] – the assurance of enjoying[813] a few more decades. Strange people these. I wish I could have the same comfortable feeling about[814] longevity, but my shrunken muscles & whimpering stomach urge me to leave the black man's land before another bout of fever lays me low under the sable soil of this malarious clime.

---

804. 'containing 12 bott[le]s' added above the line.
805. 'bottom of the' added above the line.
806. 'had been destroyed by corros' crossed out.
807. 'and a cheese' added above the line.
808. 'I went on' crossed out.
809. 'proposes to finish with this central line of Nile waters of which I have heard so much about' crossed out.
810. 'its' crossed out.
811. 'certainly' added above the line; 'certai' crossed out after '65'.
812. 'ears' written over 'years'.
813. 'enjoying' added above the line.
814. 'about' added above the line; 'that' crossed out.

Feb 25th Sunday After prayers & breakfast we[815] took a walk around Kwihara, & paid visits to Sheikh bin Nasib, and Muini Mokaya an old friend of Livingstone. We admired the tembes, and gardens. I showed Livingstone how I had prepared a warm reception for Mirambo & his desperate followers during their invasion and told him how by the death of Khamis bin Abdallah on that day he had missed seeing a princely & noble hearted & noble mannered Arab.

The Arabs are still fighting or rather indulging in the usual tactics of inactive generals. They hope to starve Mirambo to capitulation and make requisitions on those of their friends who have chosen to remain in Unyanyembe.

Some women of a highly amiable tribe called the Watusi visited us today, and both Livingstone & myself remarked their pleasing & regular features. I asked Livingstone if the Manyema women were at all equal or superior in their attractions to these. His answer was rather ambiguous. In some senses, they were, in others they were not. The Manyema were fleshier, not so thin or graceful, or so refined in feature but they had larger eyes, and more pleasant in expression &c, &c.

Feb 26th Monday. At the village of Kwikuru near Ugunda. I was lying inert in my bed, and a fly – a black, ugly, importunate fly settled on my leg under my pyjamas – & irritated by its pertinacity, I crushed it. I find that a pimple near the fly bite[816] has now grown to the dimensions of a goodly sized boil which pains[817] me exceedingly. It woke me up last night from a delightful dream, & the pain was as if a pin was being driven to the bone. I consulted the Doctor this morning & he said it reminded him of one of his own experiences, & that the fly must have deposited an egg, which had become a worm. He examined it, and pressed upon it, and there was ejected a similar creature to what he had described. The pain ceased almost immediately & I am assured that the inflannation will have disappeared in a couple of days – as he has suffered from twenty one of these worms.

Feb 27th Tuesday. Still engaged in packing goods and caravan arrangements. The Men received their Christmas feast for which we had been making preparations. Every copper pot held rice, & the native pots fowls, an ox was killed & roasted, and a grand attempt was made at a rice pudding with several dozen eggs.[818] Livingstone[819] was called towards evening[820] by a message from Muini Mokaya – to go & visit him as he was ill. He

---

815. 'have' crossed out; 'took' written over 'tak'.
816. 'near the fly bite' added above the line.
817. 'pains' written over 'pained'.
818. From 'The Men received their Christmas feast …' to 'with several dozen eggs', these sentences are written above 'Visited Tabora again and returned at 4 o'clock, having been lavishly entertained by the Arabs' crossed out.
819. 'Livingstone' preceded by 'On returning to our house' crossed out.
820. 'towards evening' added above the line.

came back and obtained a blisterring fluid. I am told that the Arab not only suffers from an abscess of the liver – but has also heart disease & that his case is hopeless.

Feb 28th Wednesday. [Change to black ink] We have had no rain for some time nearly a week, which enables us to spread out the bales and cord & sew up, for the march. Among the goods to be turned over to Livingstone are 2788 yds Cloth, 992 lbs Beads, 350 lbs Wire, 1 Canvass Tent, air bed, canvass Boat bag of tools, 3[821] breech loaders & revolver – ammunition to suit, medicine Chest, Cooking Utensils, books, sextant, &c &c &c. These will make about[822] 40 loads. The amount of cloth alone will purchase rations enough for a small caravan for 4 years, but he will have many more demands than rations & 16 sacks of beads & wire will enable him to ration his men & reserve the cloth for presents to chiefs, or hire or purchase of canoes for exploration.

Before I leave we must put our heads together to make a list of[823] what to send to him from Zanzibar by the men he wants. He has long ago come to my way of thinking that these small expeditions are ruinous to the health of a white leader. All his travels that he has accomplished[824] between 1866 – and now, nearly six years might have been performed within 30 months comfortably, but the smallness of his caravan has caused him to be detained by every chief who thought he was stronger than Livingstone until the novelty of having white man in his village wore away, & the old man became too obstinate to hold back without violence.

Then long periods of illness -3 months & 6 months at a time, – which might have been curable by medicine – were also the results of the fewness of his followers – as well as the marching & countermarching for more supplies, & the necessity he has been under of sticking to the Arabs for protection as with Mohommed bin Gharib in Marungu, &c &c. Had he but 40 men with him he would long ago have finished the task he has set himself to do. Now he is already so advanced in years that he cannot afford to lose so much precious time in an obscure village and is resolved to follow my advice, and take such a force of good choice fellows as will make him independent of the caprices of savages & the dawdling habits of Arabs.

1st March Thursday. I mustered about thirty men this morning, and we have been occupied[825] the whole day in[826] raising a cairn of stones over the grave of John W. Shaw, who died in October last while I was on the way to Ujiji. I heard no more of the rumour of his having committed suicide while in delirium.

---

821. '3' written over '4'.
822. 'about' added above the line.
823. 'to make a list of' added above the line.
824. 'accomplished' written above 'done' crossed out.
825. 'occupied' added above the line.
826. 'in' added above the line.

2nd March. Friday. We have drawn up a list of the little extras Livingstone[827] will expect by his men from Zanzibar

A few tins of Flour
"   Crackers or biscuits
"   preserved fruits
"   sardines
"   salmon
Tea about 10 lbs of Hyson[828]
Sewing thread & needles
Official Envelopes
Nautical almanacs for 1872 & 1873
A blank Journal
A Chronometer stopped
A chain for refractory people.[829]

I am to enlist 50 Zanzibaris – who shall be freemen & not slaves. They are to be armed with a gun and hatchet each man. He will want for these 2000 bullets, 1000 flint stones, & 10 kegs of gunpowder. They will have to sign contracts to follow Livingstone in whichever direction he chooses to travel. On leaving him I am to strive to reach the Sea as soon as possible so that he will not be detained here too long in waiting. He says he will be counting every day, while I am gone.

I am eager to start even now but the Doctor is still busy writing letters which will take him a few more days. He has again proposed that I shall accompany him – but that is impossible then he has urged me to stay until the rains are well over, and the country dry[830] enough for safe travel – but that will not mend matters. I shall to leave some day[831] and the sooner the better for him, for me, for all of us. I should like to stay with him longer – if the march of time could be arrested – and the hours could be so prolonged that they would not multiply into days. I have done my duty strictly by him, and now another duty siezes upon me to sever us.

March 3rd Saturday. Livingstone reverted again to his grudges against the missionaries on the Zambezi – and some of his Officers (Naval) on the Expedition.

---

827. 'Livingstone' written above 'he' crossed out.
828. Chinese green tea.
829. The fact that Livingstone might have chained his porters and servants in the manner used by slave-traders raised an issue in Great Britain, among RGS members in particular. See letter from Agnes Livingstone to Stanley, August 12, 1874, S.A. 516.
830. 'eno[ugh] for travel' crossed out.
831. Change of ink.

I have had some intrusive suspicious thoughts that he was not of such an angelic temper as I believed him to be during my first month with him – but for the last month I have been driving them steadily from my mind, or perhaps to be fair – he by his conversations, by his prayers, his actions, and more careful weighing and a wider knowledge[832] of all circumstances, assist me to[833] extinguish[834] them. Livingstone with all his frankness does not unfold himself at once, and what he leaves untold may be just as vital to a righteous understanding of these disputes as what he has said. Some reparation I owe him for having been on the verge of prejudice before I ever[835] saw him. I expected & was prepared to meet a crusty misanthrope, and I was on my guard that the first offence should not[836] come[837] from me – but I met a sweet opposite – and by leaps & bounds my admiration grew in consequence. When however he reiterated his complaints against this man and the other – I felt the faintest fear that his strong nature was opposed to forgiveness & that he was not so perfect as at[838] the first blush of friendship I thought him. I grew shy of the recurrent theme lest I should find my fear confirmed. Had I left him at Ujiji[839] I should have lost the chance[840] of viewing him on the march. – and obtaining that more detailed knowledge I have – by which I am able to put myself into his place & feeling something of his feelings understanding the position better.

It was bad enough to have to rebuke an officer[841] for his[842] ostentatious reprimand of one who all his life had professed himself to be a religious man to have to dismiss him, it[843] was an ungrateful task to reproach the Missionaries for their over zeal against the slave-traders – though he quite shared their hatred of the trade & all connected with it – but to be charged as he was with having been the cause of their[844] militant behavior – to be blamed for their neglect of their special duties, & for their follies by the very men[845] whom he had assisted, & advised was too much.[846]

But in thinking that it was rather a weakness to dwell on these bitter memories, I forgot that he was speaking to me, who had reminded him of his experiences, & who pestered him with questions about this year, and another – upon this topic & that,

---

832. 'and a wider knowledge' added above the line, in black ink.
833. 'assist me to' written above 'they are being' crossed out.
834. 'extinguished' changed into 'extinguish'.
835. 'ever' added above the line.
836. 'should not' added above the line.
837. 'came' corrected into 'come'; 'not' crossed out.
838. 'at' written over 'on'.
839. 'it is probable' crossed out.
840. 'chance' written over 'benefit'.
841. Plural of 'officer' crossed out.
842. 'his' written over 'their'.
843. 'it' written over 'to'.
844. 'becoming' crossed out.
845. 'for' crossed out.
846. 'for any kind of mortal to bear' crossed out.

and I thought that it was not fair to retaliate with inward accusations that he was making too much of these things when it was my own fault. Then I thought of his loneliness, & that to speak of African Geography to a man who was himself in Africa was not only not entertaining – but unnecessary & that to refuse to speak of personal events would from the nature of a man be imputed him as reserve & perhaps something worse. These things I revolved, caused by observations on his daily method of life, his pious habits,[847] in the boat, the tent & the house.

At Kwikuru just before the day we got our letters from Europe I went to the Cook Ulimengo who was acting in Ferajji's place – and being half mad with the huge doses of quime I had taken & distressingly weak I sharply scolded him for not cleaning his coffee pots, & said that I tasted the verdigris in every article of food, and I violently asked if he meant to poison us, I showed the kettles & the pots, and the loathsome green on the rims. He turned to me with astounding insolence, and sneeringly asked if I was any better than the big Master – & said[848] that what was good for him was good for me – the little Master.

I clouted him at once not only for his insolent question, but because I recognized a disposition to fight. Ulimengo stood up – and lay[849] hold of me. On freeing myself I searched for a club, or[850] some handy instrument – but at this juncture Livingstone came out of the tent and cried out to Ulimengo. "Poli-Poli-hapo" Gently there! What is the matter Mr Stanley? Almost breathless between passion & quime I spluttered out my explanations. Then lifting his right hand with the curved forefinger, he said, I will settle this: I stood quieted, but what with unsatisfied rage, and shameful weakness the tears rolled down as copiously as when a child.

I heard him say, "Now Ulimengo, you are a big fool, a big thick headed fellow. I believe you are a very wicked man. Your head is full of lying ideas. Understand me now, and open your ears. I am a Mgeni (guest) and only a Mgeni – and have nothing to do with this caravan. Everything in the camp is my friend's. The food I eat, the clothes on my back, the shirt I wear, all are his. All the bales and beads are his. What you put in that belly of yours comes from him – not from me. He pays your wages. The tent & the bed clothes belong to him. He came only to help me, as you would help your brother or your father. I am only the big Master because I am older, but when we march or stop must be as he likes not me. Try & get all that into that thick[851] skull of yours Ulimengo. Don't you see that he is very ill? You rascal. Now go and ask his pardon. Go on." And Ulimengo said he was very sorry & wanted to kiss my feet. – but I would not let him."

847. 'habits' written over 'duties'.
848. 'said' added above the line.
849. 'lay' written over 'took'.
850. 'or' written over 'and'.
851. 'tkick' for 'thick' written over 'sk[ull]'.

Then Livingstone took me by the arm to the tent, saying, "Come now you must not mind him. He is only a half-savage & does not know any better. He is probably a Banyan slave. Why should you care what he says? They are all alike, unfeeling and hard."

Little by little I softened down – and before night I had shaken hands with Ulimengo. It is the memory of several small events – which though not worth recounting singly – muster in evidence and strike the lasting[852] impression.

"You bad fellow – you very wicked fellow – you blockhead – you fool of a man" were[853] the strongest terms he employed where others would have clubbed or clouted, or banned & blasted. His manner was that of a cool – wise old man, who felt offended & looked grave.

March 4th Sunday. Service at 9 A.M.[854] Referring to his address to his men after the Sunday service was over he asked me what conclusions I had come in regard to the African's power of receiving the Gospel.

"Well, really to tell you the truth – I have not thought much of it. The Africans appear to me very dense, and I suppose it will take some time before any head way will be made. It is a slow affair I think altogether. You do not seem to me to go about it in the right way. I do not mean you personally but Missionaries. I[855] cannot see how one or two men can hope to make an impression on the minds of so many millions when all around them is the whole world continuing[856] in its own[857] humdrum fashion absorbed in its[858] avocations, and utterly regardless of the tiny village, or obscure district where the Missionaries[859] preach the Gospel."

"How would you go about it? he asked.

"I would certainly have more than one or two missionaries. I would have a thousand, scattered not all over the continent – but among some great tribe, or cluster of tribes, organized systematically – one or two for each village, so that though the outskirts of the tribe, or area where the Gospel was at work might be disturbed somewhat by the Evil example of those outside all within the area might be safely, and uninterruptedly progressing.[860] Then with the pupils who[861] would be turned out from each village there would be new forces to start elsewhere outside[862] the area."

---

852. 'lasting' written above 'strong' crossed out.
853. 'were' written over 'was'.
854. 'at 9 a.m.' added above the line.
855. 'I' preceded by a hyphen crossed out.
856. 'continuing' written in black ink above 'going on' crossed out.
857. 'own' added in black ink above the line.
858. 'its' written over 'their'.
859. 'are located to' crossed out.
860. 'progressing' written over 'pursuing'.
861. 'who' written in black ink over 'which'.
862. 'outside' written in black ink over 'without'; 'and attack' crossed out.

"In a way that is just my opinion, but some one must begin the work. Christ was the beginner of the Christianity that is now spread over a large part of the world. – then came the twelve Apostles, & then the disciples. I feel sometimes as if I was the beginner for attacking Central Africa, and that others will shortly come, and after those there will come the thousand[863] workers that you speak of.[864] It is very dark and dreary – but the promise is "Commit thy way to the Lord, trust in Him,[865] and He shall bring it to pass." I may fall by the way being unworthy to see the dawning. I thought I had seen it when the Zambezi Mission came out, but the darkness has settled again darker than ever. It will come though, it must come, and I do not despair of the day one bit.[866] The Earth – that is the whole Earth shall be filled with the knowledge of the Lord – as the waters cover the Sea.

Loneliness is a terrible thing – especially when[867] I think of my children. I have lost a great deal of happiness I know by these wanderings. It is as if I had been born to exile, but it is God's doing and he will do what seemeth good in his own eyes. But when my children & home are not in my mind – I feel as though appointed to this work & no other. I am away from the perpetual hurry of civilization – and I think I see far & clear[868] into what is to come. And then I seem to understand why I was led away here & there, and crossed and baffled, over and over, to wear out my years, & strength. Why was it but to be a witness of the full horror of this slave trade which in the language of Burns is sending these pitiless half-castes:

Like bloodhounds from the slip

With woe and murder o'er the land."[869]

My business is to publish what I see to rouse up those who have the power to stop it once & for all. That is the beginning – but in[870] the end they will also send proper teachers of the Gospel, some here, & some there, and what you think ought to be done will be done in the Lord's good time.

"See yonder poor o'er laboured wight[871]

So abject, mean & vile

Who begs a brother of the Earth

To give him leave to toil."[872]

---

863. 'the thousand' written in black ink above 'an army of' crossed out.
864. 'that you speak of' added in black ink under the line.
865. 'H[im]' written over 'h[im]'.
866. From here, text in black ink.
867. 'when' was crossed out and rewritten above.
868. 'and clear' added above the line.
869. From "A Winter Night," by Robert Burns:
   "See stern Oppression's iron grip,
   Or mad Ambition's gory hand,
   Sending, like blood-hounds from the slip,
   Woe, Want, and Murder o'er a land!"
870. 'in' written over 'the'.
871. wight: archaism for human being or living creature.
872. From "Man Was Made to Mourn," by Robert Burns.

I have often quoted those lines of Burns to myself[873] on my travels in Manyema when I saw the trembling natives just on the run when they suspected that we were Arabs about to take them from their homes & compel them to carry their stolen ivory. Ah – well – there is a good God above who takes note of these things & will at the proper moment see that[874] justice will be measured out, to these monsters.

March 5th Monday. Muini Mokaya is worse. I am told that he was the first Arab who reached Manyema, which was[875] eleven[876] years ago. He probably absolves him from the iniquities which drives Livingstone almost into a passion when the subject of the atrocities[877] crops up in conversation. He always talks of him with affection, and respect. He sent him some more medicine, but he believes his case to be[878] hopeless.

Livingstone told me that his weakest point is his susceptibility to dysenteric attacks, ever since his journey to St Paul de Loanda in 1856.[879] Any wetting, afflicting agitation, disturbing scene worry, anger, or anything of that kind revives the malady, which requires weeks to recover from the attack & regain lost strength. "But I suppose" said he "I ought to be grateful that I suffer from dysentery instead of fever – for nine times out of ten it is a safety valve perhaps to what might end in worse if anything can be worse than this constant internal[880] hemorrhage."

March 6th Tuesday. Muni Mokaya the path-finder to Manyema died to-day, and Livingstone showed genuine & unaffected sorrow.

I emptied my private boxes, and most of the morning was passed in pressing upon Livingstone odds & ends of things which may come useful to him & which I can do without between here & the Coast.

I explained to him how the small boat would save him many a mile of water – especially in swamps like the inundated Makata valley which is always subject to overflow in rains. It draws only four inches, and often there is[881] quite as much water as that in these[882] native troughy[883] roads. But I suspect that he will not[884] use it so often as I think he ought from a certain kind of indifference which I see in him in

---

873. 'to myself' added above the line.
874. 'that' written over 'jus[tice]'.
875. 'which' was added above the line.
876. 'ele[ven]' written over 'ei[ght?]'.
877. 'of the atrocities' added above the line.
878. 'to be' added above the line.
879. Livingstone reached St. Paul de Loanda on May 31, 1854, and remained until September. From there he retraced his path back to Linyanti. Then he undertook to open a new route to the East Coast and reached Quilimane on May 26, 1856. The closeness of the dates in May could be the origin of the confusion in the years.
880. 'internal' added above the line.
881. 'enough' crossed out.
882. 'e' written over 'o'.
883. Troughy is one of Stanley's neologisms, from trough, a descriptive image for a sunken road.
884. 'not' added above the line.

small matters. His age prevents him from taking that lively interest which a younger man for the mere love of stirring would, and which to him will be only a bother. I[885] must send him also a good donkey & saddle from Zanzibar. I cannot understand his love of tiring himself by walking, when his business in this country is not for his personal pleasure but for doing a special work, and the more he saves his strength, the more certain he will be able to accomplish it. It must be a kind of vanity from which I should like to see him free for his own sake.

March 7th Wednesday. In a week more I shall be off – and the hours seem to be flying when I shall see Livingstone no more – unless he finishes his task.

We had a basket of pomegranates from Sheikh bin Nassib to-day. This fruit looks beautiful but there is nothing within except a tartish acid, in an abundance of pellets.

March 8th Thursday. Livingstone races over sheets of blue foolscap as his time is getting more & more limited, & appears to be very earnest upon something.

We had a little talk after dinner about the Royal Geographical Society's dinners & the rich viands that then appear on the table's. He remembers the juicy marrow bones served on toast and laughed as he spoke of the yellowy[886] marrow streaming from them. This led him into a digression on the excellent living he had at Newstead Abbey, & of the Devonshire cream he used to get at the Webbs – & how Mrs Webb even mindful of his partialities insisted on serving most mornings fresh pots of this. As I have never tasted it, I do not know what it is like, except that it must be something[887] very good.

"You will[888] think of me when you taste those marrow bones at the Geographical & the Devonshire Cream in London." I will be then feeding on corn cobs, & husks, & horse beans when you will be luxuriating."

"But I do not know anybody in London" I said.

"Oh Sir Roderick will be sure to find you out & fasten on you, & get you to read a paper on Tanganika I have left all that to you – so you will have something fresh to say – because the Rusizi is a real discovery – and it settles an important point".

March 9th Friday. We obtain milk every morning from our friends the Watusi – and sometimes from[889] the Arabs who keep cows. The milk vessels are extremly neat & made of very light wood as well as though they were turned by the lathe.

---

885. 'I' preceded by 'He' crossed out.
886. 'yellowy' added above the line.
887. 'something' added above the line.
888. 'will' written over 'think'.
889. 'from' added above the line.

Articles[890] of food are very dear just at present. 1 necklace of sami-sami beads can only purchase 1 egg whereas formerly we could obtain 4. I suppose this is due to the war. I often twit Sheikh bin Nassib for his prophecies that the war would soon be over, & his advice that I should wait for the termination before going to seek Livingstone. The old four pounder carronade in front of his barzahr still stares out with its round eye on vacancy – and he will have to wait a long time before he celebrates with it the return of peace. But no Arab appears to understand the value of time, and the best of them would make but a poor Newspaper Correspondent.

Mach[891] 10th Saturday.

We packed up today for Capt W. F. Webb of Newstead Abbey one box containing 1 Spear from Manyuema[892] with ball at pond. 2 Heavy Manyuema Spears for elephant killing, 3 assegais from Unyamwezi.

For Livingstone's children – there were put up 1 Large Manyema Spear. 1 Casting spear – 1 Spear with ball at end. 3 Wanyamuezi Assegais & one broken spear which has to be kept for its association for the Doctor.

Livingstone drew a draft[893] to-day on Messrs Ritchie, Stewart & Co of Bombay for £500.[894] If Dr Kirk holds[895] any money[896] for his benefit,[897] then I am to make use of what is needed for the Equipment & Enlistment of his caravan of 50 men, and tear up the draft – if he has none I cash it & devote the money to his purposes.

March 11th Sunday. This is to be the[898] last Sabbath with Livingstone! The service was slightly longer than usual and there was a prayer for our[899] safe arrival at the Coast. He read the 35th Psalm and in prayer he referred to me as "one who had behaved himself to him[900] as though he had been his[901] friend & brother" and he[902] asked blessing on those who favoured his righteous cause". – the cause of the poor slave.

After breakfast he told me that[903] as soon as he gets away from Unyanyembe he intends proceeding to Ufipa, & cross Rungwa R. strike Southerly and rounding the S.

---

890. 'Articles' preceded by 'Other' crossed out.
891. 'Mach', ms.
892. Manyema is the more proper spelling.
893. 'draft' written over 'cheque'.
894. *LJ*, 2:173, same date: "Gave Mr Stanley a cheque for 5000 rupees on Stewart & Co., Bombay. This £500 is to be drawn if Dr Kirk has expended the rest of the £1000."
895. 'holds' written above 'possesses' crossed out.
896. 'belonging to, or given' crossed out.
897. 'by some person' crossed out.
898. 'the' added above the line.
899. 'our' added above the line.
900. 'him' written above 'me' crossed out. 'Me' had already been written over 'him'.
901. 'his' written over 'my'.
902. 'he' added above the line.
903. 'he' crossed out.

head of Tanganyika Lake 8°. 42' S. Lat. take a South westerly course for Chicumbi's on the Luapula. Then crossing the Luapula proceed direct West to the Copper Mines of Katanga, thence to a point eight days march to the South to discover those mysterious & sacred fountains (of the Nile) which have been reported as existing in that locality. He then hopes to return by Katanga, and be able to make his way to the underground dwellings said to be in Rua, which are remarkable for certain inscriptions, or drawings on the rocky walls which are about 10 days journey to the N. East of Katanga. After satisfying his curiosity about these he will go in quest of Lake Kamolondo & thence by the river Lufira to the Lake which he has called Lincoln. From this lake he will retrace his steps to the Lualaba R. & follow that river to the fourth Lake of which he has heard & which he thinks will prove to be the last link connecting the great Lualaba to the White Nile. All these journeys he hopes will not occupy him more than a year & a half from the time he leaves Unyanyembe.

I roughly traced this proposed series of travels on my old[904] Stanford's map which is blank west of Tanganyika, and on[905] comparing their length with his travels elsewhere, I do not think that they can be performed by him under two years. & then if he lives we may begin to expect him back with volumes about the wide virgin land he will have explored.

He will not travel during the rainy season, as it will be too terrible an exposure. He has already tried it often enough and each time he has had to endure severe suffering through his old[906] bowel complaint.

He does not need rest & has not felt it at any time. His crying need was supplies, and free men. Once having made himself independent he will waste no more time – as he has none to lose, if he would see his home again.

March 12th Monday. The Arabs have sent me 45 letters to carry to the Coast. I am turned courier in my later days. The reason is that no caravans leave Unyanyembe, or are permitted to, indeed because of the war with Mirambo, which will probably last 9 months yet.

In the evening the natives gathered together to celebrate our departure with a dance. Many[907] of them belong to the Caravan of Singiri – one of Mtesa's chiefs. My men joined in, and inspired by the stirring music I also joined. Bombay wore[908] my water bucket on his head, Chowpereh carried & flourished an axe, Baraka had donned my bearskin, Mabruki the "bull headed" stepped up and down as solemn as an

---

904. 'old' added above the line.
905. 'on' added above the line.
906. 'old' written over 'anc[?]'.
907. 'Many' written over 'they'.
908. 'wore' written over 'had [?]'.

elephant, Ulimengo had a gun and never looked so ferocious[909] – one would think that he thought himself a match against a hundred thousand, Khamisi, and Kamna posted themselves back to back, and kicked ambitiously at the stars, Asmani held a gun with which he now & then dealt wild blows at imaginary enemies. When that dance was over another was begun, where the leader fell on his knees, and dipped his head into a hole two or three times & the singers in full chorus imitating his motions sang a slow & mournful refrain, about the white man going home – Oh, oh, oh Going home – oh – oh."[910]

Livingstone continued writing far into the night.

March 13th Tuesday. This is[911] the last day[912] of my stay with dear, old Livingstone, and the last night we shall be together is present, and I cannot evade the morrow. I feel as though I should like to rebel against the neccessity of departure. The minutes beat fast, and grow into hours. Our door is tonight closed – and we both think our own thoughts. What his are I know not. Mine are sad. My days seem to have been spent far too happily – for now that the last day is almost gone – I bitterly regret the approach of the parting hour. I now forget the successive fevers, and their agonies, and the semi-madness to which they often plunged me. The regret I feel now is greater than any pains I have endured. But[913] I cannot resist the sure advance of time which is flying to-night far too fast. What must be, must be. I have parted often with friends before – and remember how I lingered, & wished to put it off – but the inevitable was not to be prevented. Fate came and at the appointed[914] hour stood between us. To night I feel the same aching pain, but in a greater degree – and the Farewell – I fear – may be forever. "For ever? And For Ever echo the reverberations of a woful whisper.

I have received the thanks that he has repressed all these months in secresy of his heart uttered with no mincing phrases but poured out as it were at the last moment until I was so affected that I sobbed as one[915] only can in uncommon grief. The hour of night[916] & the crisis – and oh – as some dreadful doubts suggested, the[917] eternal parting – his sudden outburst of gratitude with that kind of praise that steals into one & touches the softer parts of the ever-veiled nature – all had their influence. & For a

---

909. 'ferocious' written over 'fierce'.
910. The full song appears in S.A. 10 under the same date, and figures in *HIFL*, 621–22.
911. 'This is' written above 'this is' crossed out.
912. 'day' written over 'night'.
913. 'But' added above the line.
914. 'appointed' added above the line.
915. 'one' written over 'if'.
916. 'of night' added above the line.
917. 'the' written over 'an'.

time I was as[918] sensitive child of eight or so, and yielded to such bursts of tears that only such a scene as this could have forced.

I think it only needed this softening to secure[919] me as[920] his obedient, and devoted servitor[921] in the future should there ever be[922] an occasion where I could prove my zeal.

We have folded up the great journal in several wrappages, of cloth, and over all a waterproof canvass cover strongly sewn. It contains the accounts of his travels, notes, letters between 1866 and March 1872. It was sealed with five different[923] seals – and the coins which stamped them were turned over to him, and the words "Positively not to be opened" in German text & round hand were written in bold letters on the cover & signed by him.[924] I have taken notes of his instructions regarding the distribution of certain curiosities, to Mr Webb, Mr James Young, Scotland, Chronometers & Watch to Capt Richards Admiralty, to get Champagne, India rubber coat, 2 pair trouzers, looking glass, dishes, Boat colors &c,[925] & his last wish about his dear old friend Sir Roderick – about whom he has been anxious ever since we received news about his affliction at Ugunda.[926] I am[927] to be sure to send him news from Aden, & I have promised that he shall receive it in a shorter time than anything was ever received before in Central Africa.

He has given me also an order which is as follows. It is dated to-morrow.

"Unyanyembe, 14th March 1872,

I have been subjected to so much loss by the employment of slaves in caravans sent to me by H. M. Consul, that, if Mr Stanley meets another party of the sort, I beg of him to turn them back, but use his discretion in the whole matter.

David Livingstone."[928]

He then repeated his intentions after the arrival of his Caravan, said that he hoped I would not forget to explain them, & all the reasons why he has been so long delayed.

"To-morrow night at[929] this time you will be alone Doctor."

---

918. 'child' crossed out.
919. 'secure' written over 'make'.
920. 'as' added above the line
921. 'should anything' crossed out.
922. 'should there ever be' written above 'make' crossed out.
923. 'different' added above the line. *LJ*, 2:173: "The impressions on them are those of an American gold coin, anna, and half anna, and cake of paint with royal arms." The anna is an Indian currency unit.
924. H. M. Stanley handed D. Livingstone's Journal to Tom S. Livingstone on August 2, 1872. See Tom S. Livingstone's statement, S.A. 4753.
925. From 'to Mr Webb' to 'Boat colors &c.' added above the line.
926. For the list of letters handed by D. Livingstone to H. M. Stanley, to be carried back, see Appendix, S.A. 4754.
927. 'am' written over 'must'.
928. See Appendix, Letters from Dr. Livingstone to Stanley, Unyanyembe, March 14, 1872, S.A. 477.
929. 'at' written over 'you'.

"Yes this house will look as though a death had taken place. Had you not better stop until after the rains which are now near, are over?"

"I would to God, I could my dear Doctor, but every day I stop here, now that there is no necessity for me to stay longer, keeps you from your work & home."

"I know; but consider your health – you are not fit to travel. What is it? Only a few weeks longer. You will travel to the Coast just as quickly when the rains are over as you will by going now. The plains will be inundated between here, and the Coast."

"You think so, but I will reach the Coast in forty days: if not in forty, I will in fifty – certain. The thought that I am doing you an important service will spur me on."

At last near midnight we retired.

March 14th Wednesday.

At dawn we were up, the bales &baggage were taken outside of the tembe & the carriers prepared for the first mach towards home.

We had a sad breakfast together. I could not eat, my[930] heart was too full, neither did the Doctor seem to have any appetite. We found something to do which detained us beyond the intended hour of departure. At 8° clock I was not gone & I had[931] thought to be off at 5 A.M."

"Doctor" said I, "I had better leave two men with you, who will stop here to-day & tomorrow. It may be you will have forgotten something at the last moment. I will halt a day at Tura for your last word & your last wish & now we must part – there is no help for it. Good bye."

"Oh I am coming with you a little way. I must see you fairly off on the road"

"Thank you. Now my men Home! Kirangozi, lift the flag and <u>March!</u>"

The house looked very desolate. – it faded from my view. Old times & old memories thronged thickly to the mind. The old hills round about that I once thought so tanne & uninteresting, were at this time invested with new interest. On the barzah of that home I had often sat dreaming & hoping & sighing. On yonder col I stood watching the battle & the burning of Tabora. Under that roof, I had often sickened & been delirious. Under that banian tree & the cairn near it lay my comrade Shaw. I would have given much to have had him at my side now. From the house I had started on my journey to Ujiji, to it I returned as to a friend with a newer & dear Companion and now I leave all. Already it appears to be like a dream.

We walked side by side. The[932] men lifted their voices in a song – for they were glad. I took long looks at Livingstone to impress his features thoroughly on the memory.

---

930. 'feelings' crossed out.
931. 'intended' crossed out.
932. 'The' written over 'for at'.

"The thing is Doctor – so far as I can understand it – you do not intend to return home until you have satisfied yourself about the Sources of the Nile. When you have done that you will come home & satisfy others. Is it not so?"

"That is it Exactly. When your men come back, I shall immediately start for Ufipa – and go on to the S. end of the Tanganyika. Thence a South-East course will take me to Chicumbi's on the Luapula. From[933] the other side of the Luapula I shall go West to Katanga. 8 days South of Katanga are the fountains. When they are found I shall return & seek the underground houses of Rua. From those Caverns, 10 days North Easterly will take me to Kamalondo. I shall travel from the Lake in your boat up[934] the Lufira to Lake Lincoln. Then descending I can go North by the Lualaba to the fourth Lake which I think will settle the problem & I shall probably find that it is either Chowambe (Baker's Lake) or Piaggia's Lake". In a year & a half at the farthest I shall have done.

"Supposing we say two years. And[935] I had better hire these new men for that period – the day of Engagement to begin from the date of their arrival in[936] Unyanyembe.

"Yes that will do excellently well""

"Now, my dear Doctor, the best friends must part. You have come far enough, let me beg of you to turn back".

"Well I will repeat to you what I said last night. You have done what few men could do . – far better than some great travellers I know. And I am very grateful for what you have done for me. God guide you safe home, and bless you my friend."

"And may God bring you safe back to us all my dear friend. Farewell!"

"Farewell."

We wrung each other's hands & I tore myself before I unmanned myself again before others, but Susi, & Chumah & Hamoydah – the Doctor's faithful fellows – then came to shake & kiss my hands, before I could turn away.

"Good bye Doctor, dear friend! Good bye!"

"March! Why do you stop? Go on! Are you not going home? The men struck out, and we were soon swinging along at 3 miles an hour.

[Change of ink] We came to a ridge, and I looked back & watched his grey figure fading dimmer in the distance for a presentiment, or a suggestion stole in – to my mind that I was looking for the last time at him. I gulped down my great grief, and turned away to follow the receding Caravan.[937]

---

933. 'From the other side' preceded by '8 day So' crossed out.
934. 'up' written over 'to'.
935. 'And' preceded by 'There' crossed out.
936. 'the date of their arrival in' added above the line.
937. The rest of the page and the next page barred with a vertical line in the middle.

Bombay[938] as usual acted like a donkey, today. He is never ready, and all through the day he committed blunders enough to deserve the character[939] Major Grant gave of him that "he was a first rate fellow for humbugging the natives". The men marched like raw recruits though they have been to Ujiji & back. Selim also has forgotten a few things.

I have 45 letters in the Arab mail bag for Zanzibar and from Livingstone there are six for Bombay,[940] 1 for Zanzibar, twenty for England,[941] & two for the New York Herald.[942]

March 20th Tuesday. We arrived at day at Eastern Tura. Soon[943] after a gun was fired and in came Livingstone's messengers, Susi, & Hamoidah & my[944] two men with a big letter for Sir Thomas Maclear Observatory, Cape of Good Hope & one for myself which was as follows: -

Kwihara March 15th 1872

"Dear Stanley

If you can telegraph, on your arrival in London be particular, please to say how Sir Roderick is. You put the matter exactly[945] yesterday when you said that I was not satisfied about the sources, but as soon as I shall be satisfied, I shall return & give satisfactory reasons fit for other people." This is just as it stands.

"I wish I could give you a better word than the Scotch one to put a stout heart to a stey braé (a steep ascent) for you will do that, and I am thankful that before going away, the fever had changed into the intermittent, or safe form. I would not have let you go, but with great concern had you still been troubled with the continued type. I feel comfortable in commending you to the Guardianship of the Good Lord & Father of all.

I am gratefully yours

David Livingstone."

"I have worked as hard as I could copying observations in one line of march from Kabuire, back again to Cazembe, and on to Lake Bangweolo, & am quite tired out. My large figures fill six sheets of foolscap, & many a day will elapse ere I take to copying

---

938. On the first line above this paragraph, 'March 17th Saturday' crossed out.

939. 'the character' added above the line.

940. One of them must have been addressed to the governor of Bombay, Sir W.R.S.V. Fitzgerald (see RGS-IBG Collections, DL/4/10/3, true copy, 12 pp.) who had replaced Sir Bartle Frere as governor in 1867.

941. 'England' written over 'London'. ('London' in Field Notebook S.A. 10, March 15, 1872.)

See Appendix, "Letters carried by me from Dr Livingstone from Unyanyembe & delivered to Lord Lyons, August 1872," S.A. 4754. The list of addressees has 19 names. Since Livingstone had written to each of his children, and William Oswell is not mentioned in the list of addressees, Stanley may have handed him a letter at Zanzibar (see this journal, May 7, 1872).

942. The whole paragraph that follows has been crossed out: "I have felt very lonely all the day. Pity that partings should be necessary. I never thought while a victim to African fever that I should even grieve to ['grieve to' added above the line] leave this country ['with such grief' crossed out]".

943. 'Soon' preceded by 'When' crossed out. Change of ink to correct the capital letter S.

944. 'my' written over 'tw...'

945. 'exactly' added above the line.

again. I did my duty when ill at Ujiji in 1869, and am not to blame, though they grope a little in the dark at home. Some Arab letters have come, and I forward them to you. D. L."

March 16, 1872.

P. S. – I have written a note this morning to Mr Murray, 50 Albemarle St the publisher to help you if necessary, in sending the Journal by book post, or otherwise to Agnes. If you call on him you will find him a frank gentleman. A pleasant journey to you.

David Livingstone
To Henry M. Stanley Esq
Wherever he may be found."

By return of the couriers I[946] sent an[947] answer of which the following is a rough copy.

Tura Unyanwezi
March 20th 1872.

My dear Doctor

I feel I have parted from you too soon, for I am very depressed. The time I have spent with you I have mostly spent in work for you & for myself. & you have been so engaged in writing your journal & letters that much as we have been together it seems insufficient and I regret that I have had so little of you.

In writing to you it is a comfort that I am[948] writing to one who embodies warm, good fellowship & every thing that is noble & right. You are no longer an abstraction to me such as you formerly were. I can image you for all future time with fidelity, and though you are absent it will be as though I were addressing a very palpable personage. It has been a severe wrench to me to leave you. And[949] I feel an aching void. Why should people be subjected to these partings & the pangs that follow them? It is a consolation however that though parted – I am in the act of doing you a service so that we are not quite separated. You will be thinking of me daily until your caravan reaches[950] you – and I must bear you[951] constantly in mind until my[952] promise has been fulfilled. And this Dear Doctor believe me is consoling. Had I a series of services to perform for you it would be still better.

I had to turn away from you rather abruptly for it is doubtful whether the Arabs would have understood my feelings, but I am sure you did, and by the faithful

---

946. 'I' written over 'the'.
947. 'an' written over 'the fo…'
948. 'not' crossed out.
949. 'And' written over 'for' with another ink.
950. 'reaches' written over 'arrive'.
951. 'bear you' added above the line.
952. 'my' written over 'your'.

attention with[953] which[954] your wishes shall be observed I will prove their sincerity. Do not attribute these professions to interested motives but accept them in the spirit in which they are made in that true[955] Livingstonian spirit which I have learned[956] to honour.

The road is good so far and the Wangwana (Zanzibaris) now travel with a will. The bag of shot has been received but I return it to you as you will need it more than I do. You did not tell me where to address your letters but I will send them care of your neighbour Sheikh bin Nasib who is more honest than the Governor. Praying that you will be wholly successful in your great journey & that you will return to England safely I remain[957]

Yours ever faithfully,
Henry M Stanley
Dr David Livingstone
&c &c &c &[958]

May 2nd 1872. Rosako. One of my letters from Zanzibar just arrived[959] states that there is an Expedition at Bagamoyo called the Livingstone Search[960] Relief Expedition.[961] What will the leaders do now? Livingstone is found & relieved already & says that he requires nothing more. It is a misfortune that they did not start earlier – then they might with propriety proceed & be welcomed.

May 6th. At sunset we reached Bagamoyo on the Sea. "The White man has come to town" were the words we heard as we entered it.[962] As we reached the middle of the town I saw standing on the steps of a large white house a White Man in flannels & helmet,[963] young, & reddish whiskered with a bright humorous face. He advanced towards me & we shook hands heartily.

---

953. 'with' added above the line.
954. 'which' written over 'I will'.
955. 'true' added above the line.
956. 'learned' changed into 'learnt'.
957. From 'Praying that you will' to 'I remain' added above the line, with another ink. There is no mention of this letter in *HIFL*.
958. For Stanley's return to the coast from March 13 to April 30, see Field Notebook S.A. 10.
959. 'just arrived' added above the line.
960. 'Search' added above the line.
961. Stanley had dispatched three messengers ahead who discreetly met with the American Consul J. F. Webb, bringing him news from Zanzibar. See Appendix, Letters from John Webb, American Consul in Zanzibar, to Stanley, April 30, 1872, S.A. 2659.
962. 'it' written over 'the'; 'town' crossed out.
963. 'A' crossed out.

He invited me in & asked what I would take to drink, beer, stout, brandy? and then he impetuously congratulated me. "Lets have some beer boy, quick or I will knock seven d... out of you – he said in a lively tone.

He soon informed me[964] in his vivacious way who he was, what he came for, what were his hopes, his ideas & feelings in a delightfully frank way. He was Lieut Henn R. N. Chief of the Expedition for the Search & Relief of Livingstone which had been sent out by the Royal Geog- Society.[965] The former chief Lieut Dawson R. N. had immediately resigned after hearing from my messengers that Livingstone had been found, and was so advised by Dr Kirk. There was a Mr Chas New – a missionary from Mombasa lately been attached but he had also resigned.[966] At present the only European members of the Expedition were himself & Oswald Livingstone the second son of the Doctor.

"Is Mr Oswald Livingstone here?" I asked with considerable surprise.

"Yes he will be here directly

"And what will you do now?

"Oh, I don't think it worth my while to go[967] now.[968] You have taken the wind out of our sails completely. If you have relieved him I don't see the use of my going. Do you?

"Well it depends. You know your own orders best. If you have come only to find & relieve him, I can tell you truly he is already found & relieved & that he wants nothing more than a few canned meats & some other little things which I dare say you have not got. I have his list in his own handwriting with me. But his son must go anyhow & I can get men easily for him."

Well if he is relieved it is of no use my going.

Mr Henn said that he should like sport – to have a shot at an African Elephant, for that was really what he had come for, & he did n't care &c. &c. &c.

Henn's manner simply roused me & I said and he does n't want you. And[969] any more things than he has got already would be an incumbrance without men.

---

964. 'me' written over 'in'.

965. Lieutenant William Henn (1847–1894) belonged to the British social elite. After having retired from the Royal Navy, he and his wife led a leisurely life, cruising with their own yacht. In his official report, dated May 10, 1872 (*PRGS* 16, no. 5 [1871–72]: 424), Henn situates the arrival of Stanley on the evening of the 7th.

966. Rev. Charles New, of the Methodist Free Church, was on his way to England from Mombasa when he met the party of the RGS Expedition. Kirk persuaded him to join the Livingstone Search Expedition, as an interpreter (Agreement between Cs. New and L. S. Dawson, March 25, 1872, ibid., 428). According to it, New agreed to take command of the Expedition in case of Dawson's & Henn's incapacity. After Dawson's resignation, "complications and misunderstandings" arose with Henn, as New said in his book's last chapter (Charles New, *Life, Wanderings, and Labours in Eastern Africa* [London: Hodder & Stoughton, 1873], 509–22). New informed Kirk on May 3 (his letter, ibid., 428) and retired on May 4 (letter to Henn, ibid., 423).

967. 'go' written over 'do'.

968. 'anything, now' crossed out.

969. 'And' written over 'any'.

He said with a light laugh – "we have the store room full of cloth & beads. We have over 192 loads of stores." &c &c.

A young man now walked in, tall, slight, & gentlemanly – he was introduced as Mr Oswald Livingstone.

"I was telling Mr Henn that whether he goes or not, you must go to your father Mr Livingstone.

"Oh I mean to go

"Yes that's right. I will furnish you with such men & stores as your father needs, & the men will take you to Unyanyembe without any difficulty. They know the road well & that is an advantage. The great thing required is speed. Your father will be waiting for the things."

"I will march them fast enough if that is all".

"They will be going up light, & can easily make long marches."

It was settled. Henn made up his mind that as the Doctor was relieved he was not wanted, but before resigning would consult with Dr Kirk.

At 2 A.M. I retired to sleep on a comfortable bed, and as I threw myself on it, I[970] murmured "Thank God my marching is ended".

May 7th Zanzibar. Reached the island in a dhow at 5 P.M. On reaching the shore the men scattered to their homes and I proceeded to the American Consulate & was received very cordially by Mr John F. Webb – the present Consul. Later in the evening Mr Charles New the missionary called. He is rather[971] a weakly looking man of a[972] nervous temperament & active habits.[973] After dinner Mr Dawson called. He is[974] of splendid physique & particularly[975] handsome. He congratulated me & stated that he envied me my success,[976] "I had taken the wind out of his sails" & so on. He told me how as soon as he had heard the news he had crossed over & resigned after a talk with Dr Kirk. He agreed[977] that perhaps he had been hasty but after Livingstone & I had found the Rusisi to be[978] flowing into the Lake & as[979] I had obtained[980] the Doctor's letters & despatches, he thought[981] there was nothing left for him to do." He said his orders had been to seek, find & relieve Livingstone, and afterwards[982] to direct

---

970. 'said' crossed out.
971. 'He is rather' added above the line.
972. 'of a' written above 'but still' crossed out.
973. 'temperament and active habits' written above 'active' crossed out.
974. 'He is' written above 'a young man' crossed out.
975. 'particularly' written over 'extremely'?
976. 'though' crossed out.
977. 'agreed' written over 'said'.
978. 'to be' added above the line.
979. 'as' written over 'that'.
980. 'obtained' added above the line.
981. 'he thought' added above the line.
982. 'afterwards' written above 'I was then' crossed out.

his attention to exploration but as in[983] the primary object he had been forestalled, and the Admiralty had only granted him leave for the Search he felt it his duty to return home.

Dawson also said[984] that my Expedition was regarded with great jealousy by the Geographers, and that it was hoped I would fail.

Mr Webb sent over one of his boys[985] to the English Consulate with Livingstone's[986] letters to Dr Kirk & Mr Oswald Livingstone. Capt Fraser called[987] and when he saw me he said I was not the person who went into the interior last year. He solemnly shook his head, and said – It appeared "like another Tichborne affair".[988] Dr James Christie & two or three German residents called & spoke kindly of my success.

May 8th 1872. Discharged my men and at the same time reengaged 20 of them to return to Livingstone. Stupid Bombay though he had more than once expressed his scorn of dirty money was glad to take a present of $50 besides his pay – and every deserving man received from $20 to $50 reward.

When by the morning light I viewed myself in one of Mr Webb's tall mirrors – I was shocked by my emaciated & aged appearance, and discovered that my hair had much grey in it. The little circular mirror of the camp had not revealed the havoc which the wearing life of Africa had caused.

Lieut Henn came over from Dr Kirk's house & asked to see Livingstone's order – which was to the effect that as he had been subjected to so much loss of time & money by the employment of slaves in the Caravans sent by the Consul he desired me to turn them back, if they appeared to me to be such.[989]

"This does not refer to our Expedition at all" he said. I therefore explained that I had nothing to do with his Expedition, & that if he thought he ought to proceed into the interior – I should advise him to do so by all means – at least not to part with the goods if he had any doubt in the matter until he heard from the Geographical Society as they might have other views besides relief. But he quickly rejoined that he intended to resign, and turn over all[990] the effects to young Livingstone.

---

983. 'in' added above the line.
984. 'Dawson also said' written above 'I was also told' crossed out.
985. 'with Livings[tone]' crossed out.
986. 'Livingstone's' added above the line.
987. 'ca[lled]' written over 'al[so]'.
988. The issue of the Tichborne trial was to define whether the claimant was or was not Roger Tichborne, heir of Sir James Tichborne. *The Tablet*, January 27, 1872, Memoranda, 113–16, http://archive.thetablet.co.uk/article/27th-january-1872/21/memoranda.
989. See Appendix, Letters from Dr. Livingstone to Stanley, Unyanyembe, March 14, 1872, S.A. 477.
990. 'all' written over 'the'.

He returned to the British Consulate and wrote[991] his formal resignation & young Livingstone is now in sole charge, & he[992] has concluded that it will be best to sell most of the stores retaining such as may be useful to his father.

When Dr Kirk called to see me[993] I suggested[994] to him[995] that it would be to store the goods as the Society might wish to do something in the way of Exploration.

"No, said Dr Kirk, "these goods belong to Dr Livingstone & as he does not need them they can be converted into money for him without much loss."

I do not agree with Dr Kirk at all, and I am surprised that these young men should throw up their commissions so readily. I feel sure that he is at the bottom of all these changes though the motive is difficult to understand. Lieut[996] Dawson evidently acted on his advice, Henn must have done so.[997] They are evidently piqued at my success, but why Kirk should strengthen this pique – instead of encouraging them to proceed up country is hard to discover unless he suspects that there is some weakness in the organization of the Expedition.[998] I[999] am inclined to think that.[1000] Or he probably has contrived[1001] to insinuate some such notions into their minds, as he did into mine last year.[1002] But young Livingstone will manage well enough with a good & experienced Arab as head of his caravan.[1003]

---

991. 'wrote' written over word indecipherable.
992. '& he' written over 'who'.
993. 'When Dr Kirk called to see me' added above the line.
994. 'suggested' written over 'advised'. Stanley kept 'advised' in his book (*HIFL*, 664). When reporting his conversation with Dr. Kirk, Stanley mentions "it would be best to store them." The word 'best' is missing here.
995. 'him' written over 'Dr Kirk'.
996. 'Lieut' added in the margin in black ink.
997. 'but why he should second' crossed out.
998. From 'unless he suspects' to 'the Expedition' added above the line.
999. 'I' preceded by 'He probably' crossed out.
1000. 'he has contrived' crossed out. This sentence was left in abeyance.
1001. 'Or he probably has contrived' added above the line with black ink.
1002. 'into mine' written in black ink, above 'with me' crossed out; 'last year' written above 'before' crossed out.
1003. End of the Journal. Several pages torn out at the end. For the caravan to Livingstone preparations and Stanley's last days at Zanzibar, see S.A. 12.

Field Notebook S.A. 8, Full Transcript

[Notebook still in its wrapping]
[Inside page cover: Almanack 1868, pasted]

[Pencil] Places to pay Muhongo
[Calculation scattered on the page]
[Ink] Henry M Stanley Correspondent New York Herald

[A large "$" in the middle of the page]
[Pencil] Elephant oil from Mohuma Sultan near Sagara for horses to be rubbed all over against attacks of horse flies
days grass [f]rom Shaw to Ugogi [?]
Grass to [?] Ugogi[?]
Mkue. Mtonee
Grass arriving at Ugogo
[Same page but upside down]

M Kaniki[1]	11.00
Merikani[2]	257.50
6. Samesame[3] 12	1.50
Lunghio "	1.50
Lakkior[4]	2.00
	273.50
	91.12 ½
	364.62 ½

[Some other figures scattered on the page]

[Left corner: 8]
[Pencil] 2 khete of beads to be given to each Pagazi every day after crossing the river
3 khete to each soldier

---

    1. Kaniki: cloth. On cloth, see *HIFL*, 23.
    2. Merikani: white beads. On beads, see *HIFL*, 24–25.
    3. Samesame [sami-sami]: red beads. Ibid.
    4. Lakkior [Lakhio]: beads. Ibid.

Given one doti to Bomb[ay] & send him to buy grasses
One goat every day to soldiers & pagazis.
Sunday 19th Zanzibar[5]

[Upside down] 5/ 17 bales

[Pencil] Trees
[Ink] Mparamusi - like the plane or chenar[6]
Mbuyu[7] – baobab or calabash
Mvumo[8] - . . . tree
Ukhunbu
Nyara[9]
Mtobwe[10] – Stick trees [above, pencil] Kingaroo
Mbungo[11]-bungo – Ungerengeri R. [under, pencil] River; [above, pencil] Nux vomic[a]

[Pencil] The Northern road for caravan was only opened last year.[12]

[Ink over pencil] Mtobwe - the stick tree grows extensively in Mtambo in Uruguru. It is cut up & carried to Zanzibar and used by the dusky fops as walking canes.
Uruguru commences directly South of Simbawenni and stretches across the Mgeta to Mvuha South of it
South East of it is Ukwenhe & South East of Ukwenhe is Kirangawana.
Donkey's ears bleed freely from the rupture of Epicene ticks.

Red ants at Kisemo invade our tent & cause an uproar from Selim & Omar.

[Pencil] his master's door is made the first [within?], and which Selim <...> to relieve him. He with a blissful innocence declares "Ah master there is something the matter with me. Next I am conscious of the sound of the piteous words of
[Ink over pencil] In passing through the forest I constantly felt some insect clinging to my neck either a tick – a tsetse a white, red or black ant or a gadfly a chufwa, a yellow worm or a tenacious wood tick.
Crickets preserve their noisy status the day & night without rest.

---

    5. Sunday 19th could be February, March, or November 1871. Since Stanley was not in Zanzibar in November, it must be either February or March.
      6. Mparamusi, unidentified.
      7. Mbuyu: Kiswahili name for the baobab tree (*Adansonia digitata*), used for food, fodder, ropes.
      8. Mvumo: vernacular name of several kinds of *Ficus*.
      9. Ukhumbu, Nyara: unidentified. Stanley first wrote an equivalent in pencil, then erased it.
      10. Mtobwe: vernacular name (Shambaa) for the *Mimusops*, used for medicines and firewood.
      11. Mbungo: Kiswahili name for the *Saba comorensis*, used for medicines and edible fruits. Mbungo is also the tsetse fly (S.A. 10).
      12. Text in pencil was obviously written before the names of trees in ink.

[Pencil] Course to Ulagalla
West ½ N. mountains stretching on each side parallel with the road.
Distance 7 ½ miles

[Pencil] The Wamrima Clans.
It were a difficult task to distinguish nice ethnological differences between the Wamrima & the more Occidental Washense. I[13] have seen customs at Bagomoyo similar to the one in Abyssinia. And as far as Usegura there is no essential difference. Strange as it may appear the moral character of the East African barbarian,[14] compares favorably with that of the Arab of Zanzibar, the Persian vendor of silks in the bazaar of Ispahan, with the Coptic Christian resident in Cairo the Turkish diamond merchant of Stamboul, and alas that I should say it, with the sailors boarding house keepers of New York, & Boston. I have studied the character of all these, & truth conpels me to state that I see no difference between them. The East African barbarian checked by no fear of sweeping[15] justice, by no code of laws, knowing no God, ignorant of the idea of virtue, or morality will yet meet you with deadly weapons in his hands & ask you to trade. He perceives his shukka getting threadbare & old & if he sees a caravan halt in, or near his village he does not say to[16] himself "Lo! here is a chance to obtain plunder. My loin cloth is all but worthless I will go &[17] steal a new one." but, "Here comes a caravan. Let me see. I want a shukka. What have I to exchange, I have some tobacco, a few eggs & chickens, a few measures of rice or Matama. I'll go & see what they want." Let us follow this black pagan into the camp. He does not stalk amongst the strangers with any haughty demeanour, or defiant face nor does he regard them with suspicion – but he enters the boma to seek the master's tent or hut whom he salutes with "Yambo, Bana", Sana? (How are you Master? Well[18] and he lays his stock in trade before the stranger with an enquiring face. If the master of the caravan is in need of food or[19] trifling luxuries he opens trade by enquiring "khete ngapi" "How many Khete or necklaces" or shukka ngapi" "How many cloths". Do not wonder at his[20] exorbitant demand. It is common to all natives & lands. Do not wonder that he tells lies. Such is the practice of all tradesmen, sellers, buyers, merchants, farmers & especially peddlers throughout the world. But express open eyed wonder that this untaught black pagan stoops to buy when he could waylay & kill a stray pagazi & the master of the caravan himself if he chose.

Have you my friend, you who hate all ebony skins & long heels [?] &[21] dress-less pagans. You who choose to differ with me ever had occasion to deal with a Zanzibar Arab, or an

13. 'I' preceded by 'customs' crossed out.
14. 'who' crossed out.
15. 'fear of sweeping' added above the line.
16. 'say to' written above 'converse, with' crossed out.
17. 'go &' added above the line.
18. No closing parenthesis.
19. 'the' crossed out.
20. 'pertinacity' crossed out.
21. 'undressed' crossed out.

Indian-banyan, or a consum[ate?] rascal such as the Ispaham Merchant or the Copt of Cairo, or the Turkish vendor in a Stamboul bazaar, the Greek or Armenian loafer or have you ever had dealings with a Chatham Street Jew, or were you ever shanghaied by a keeper of a sailor's boarding house in New York & Boston. If so did you number the untruths told you, or measured the villainy of which you were the victim. No! then forbear to be judge.

It is true that you have to keep your weapons at all times ready – for that is no more than common prudence, because the policeman, the dread representative of the law is not found in these lands, nor does the Cadi or recorder hold court. But wise words are these. Keep your[22] powder dry, and pay your tribute. The man who[23] molests your caravan is a robber whom you are licensed to shoot.

[Ink over pencil] Nyomba tapped like Maple trees or Pine.
Ambito very shapely tree.
Large spiky leaves probably sycomore
Ugongo
Njaza

[Pencil] **Stations from Rudewa**
1 Renneko
2 Maweni
3 Mukondokwa
4 Kadetamare
5 Masua Usagara
6 Madete
7 Ugombo (Lake)
8 Matamombo
9 On the road
10 Umpopaw[24]
11 Choonio[25]
12 Wakaniamara
13 Kisokwe
14 On the road
15 Umvoomi[26] Ugogo
16 [blank]

---

22. 'arm' crossed out.
23. 'then' added above the line.
24. Mpwapwa (*HIFL*).
25. Chunyo (*HIFL*).
26. Mvumi (*HIFL*).

[Pencil]1 Quitamani
2 Mwrinyo
3 Madete
4 Ugambo[27]
5 Mtoni
6 Umpawpaw
7 Polini[28]
8 Umvoom[i]

[Ink over pencil] I never found the Arab or Mswahili yet who could give me the correct list of ten station[29] ahead. For example (Here give the list of the Kirangozi from Rehenehko to Mvumi and the list from Mwmi to Unyenyembe)
Sheikh Thani informed me[30] that Wanyamuezi had to be closely watched when hired to string beads, that immediately the owner of the servants eyes were turned away that they swallowed them[31] and recovered them after evacuation a similar trick to the slave diamond diggers of Brazil.

[Ink over pencil] We had a great deal of trouble with the first Mgogo Sultan that of Mvumi: I augured ill of our transit through Ugogo but as it turned out none were so bad as this.[32]
[Pencil] Pole 6 feet 7 inches
[2 sketches of a tent after the previous sentence] 6 feet

[Several calculations probably for the measurements of the tents scattered on the page]
[Pencil]9 feet long   52 inches high
9 feet 3 inches
11 feet long

	yrds	ft	inches
sides	14	1	4
top	18	1	6
	14		
yds	46	2	10

---

27. Lake Ugombo.
28. For porini, a camp in the bush.
29. 'station' in ink written over 'stations' in pencil.
30. 'Upon' in pencil, crossed out. Words in pencil from a previous text are still visible in between words in ink.
31. 'like' in pencil, crossed out.
32. This paragraph is written in pencil over calculations for a tent.

6 feet wide
　36
　35 lbs
　 12
　47

[Numbers scattered over the page]

[Pencil]

　　Pagazis wanted
　　2 for tent
　　1 for kettles & pans
　　2 for Boxes
　　1 for Clothes & Bed
　　1 for Spencer Cartridges
　　1 Pistol Cartridges & Shot
9. 1 Winchester Rifle
10. 1 Box Bullets
11. 1 Load of Powder
12. 1 Tin Box Cartridges
　　6 cloth
　　4 Wire
　　6 beads

[Pencil]

7 feet slope long side
5 feet slope short side
8 feet long, one side
11 feet long, long side
2 yd. pieces or 6 feet

[several calculations]
6x12=72
8 feet
96:22
4 cloth 8 inches
30 feet ends ⎫
48 feet sides ⎭ Roof
45 feet side walls

27 feet end walls
150:3 =50 yds

96 inches
4 cloth. 8 inches
5
20
25 feet ends ends ⎫
42 feet sides   ⎬ Roof
42 - 6 in
25 - 6   132 in – 6 cloth
135 : 3 = 45 yds
[and more calculations…]

[Pencil]

6 ½ feet long slope { Roof
4 ½ feet short slope {
7 feet short end
10 feet long end

30. 0 feet short end }
30.0   "   "   "   }Roof
70.0   }
130.0 : 3 = 43
[The previous page and this one are covered with calculations, most probably for the tents]

[Ink over pencil, but most of the punctuation left in pencil]

Tanganyika[33]
4 miles from Kigoma about half a mile from shore where steep hills rose to about 200 feet above the water the lead had 35 fathom – 210 feet water color dark green
Island Muzimu South pt bore N. W. from Kigoma North pt.
N. by West[34]
The shores of the Lake open out & in; recede into comfortabe bays protected by rounded hills or extend out into promontories or capes.

---

33. Travel to the north of the lake started on November 16, 1871 (Journal S.A. 7). Livingstone gave the same date (*LJ*, 2:157).

34. 'Pt' in ink is written over 'point' in pencil; 'N. by W.' in ink, over 'North by West' in pencil. The account of Stanley's and Livingstone's journey to the mouth of the Rusizi was first written in pencil. Then Stanley went back over his pencil notes with black ink. It is hurried writing, with missing letters especially at the ends of words, or when there are double letters. Some words are even half in pencil and half in ink.

When sighting fishermen boats the Wanguan[35] gave way with right good will. The fishermen seeing their efforts then make & stak[36] naked & standing up afford us a perfect view of their muscular bodies.

[Ink over pencil] [Map of the North East coast of Tanganyika, both in ink and in pencil. Distance given in hours of navigation. Measures of depth]

[Ink over pencil] Muzimu is an island. Babwiri
Shot a monkey 5 feet long standing 3 feet high had an enormous dog head and canine teeth 1 ½ inch long[37]

[Pencil] ~~Barundi~~
[Ink over pencil] a great many palm trees are found at the base of the enormous folds of mountains rising immediately above the Lake above Niasanga our second camp. The shore[38] of the Tanganyika are surpassingly lovely in some places from Ujiji to Urundi the best portion, mountans[39] round Lake George, beat scenery along the Hudson.
Mgongo remarkably pretty villages cresting each knoll. Palm trees & banyans affording exquisite shade. Valley very [?] Mgongo stream, a pretty little rivulet: lik[40] an amphitheatre. Among the prettiest.
Sounded at a point 1 ½ mile[41] Kirassa a conical line,[42] 115 fathom no bottom. Lost line Appear like a crater
Muzmù island West[43] from Zassi.
Zassi third day 4 ½ hour to day
Wagigi inhale the tobacco through the nose. Only occasionally is a pipe seen. A treatise could be written upon African tobacco smoking. As far as Unyanyembe the people use a pipe similar to the Cheyenne Pipe. In Ukonogo they use a pipe which may be said to resemble the funnl[44] of a miniature steamer. In Uvinza we begin to see people holding their fingers to their noses as if it wer[45] an abomination to be near us. The cause of this we find to be that they have put tobacco in their nostrils. Ujiji Uhha.

---

35. Wanguana. The correct spelling should be Wangwana.
36. stark.
37. Most likely a yellow baboon (*Papio cynocephalus*?).
38. 'shore' written in ink over 'shores' in pencil.
39. 'mountans' written in ink over 'Mountains' in pencil.
40. 'lik' written in ink over 'like' in pencil.
41. 'mile' written in ink over 'from' in pencil.
42. 'hil' written in ink over 'hill' in pencil.
43. 'Muzmù island' written in ink over 'Muzimu' in pencil; 'West' written in ink over' West N[?] West' in pencil.
44. 'funnl' written in ink over 'funnel' in pencil.
45. 'wer' written in ink over 'were' in pencil.

Kagunga a large village, several cows & canoes, has a mutuare who ran away from Kitunda.

R.[46] Mshala form the boundary between Ujiji & Urundi. It is also the terminatation[47] of the great deep bay which commences at Kazinga and ends at Kitunda in Urundi.

Kitunda Cape, N. W. by West from Namisinga River

[Ink over pencil] 4th day

Nyabigma, a sandy island 4th day on Sunday 19th we prepared for a tuzzle against the Barundi of 2 stages ahead by distributing powder lead & flints. Chickens abundant Soldiers fed on them.

5th day. Monday

Uninteresting. Low Cape prolonged of. Kitunda formed by the numerous streams which descend from the mountains[48] which at a distance of 8 or 10 miles[49] form such an imposing picture.

Frequently we passed travelling parties in canoes loaded with salt, dried fish goats & sheep holding ma[r]ket on their own account on the banks

Or groups of fishermen canoes.[50] Sitting quietly plying the fish line rod & hook. Small circular nets, hand nets, casting nets and the drag net.

Cape Kitundu ends with a small rocky knoll from which extend into the interior for 5 or 6 miles[51] a low rocky platform covered over with a reddish soil well cultivate[d]. It is a low ridge separated[52] the Luaba from Namsinga & Kasokwe[53] – Schist – conglomerate sandstone.

Caves sometimes are seen.

Birds, kites, fish hawks in a quiet bend, sitting on a tree or rock brooding over the scene. Whitish black on wings, white heads & throats

Gulls.[54] Geese with spur on wings.

Cranes, ibis, darters with their snake like heads.

White paddy birds, weaver birds suspending their nests to a branch hanging[55] over the Lake. Kingfishes

[Pencil] Kingfishes

[Ink over pencil] Canoes are 30 doti, 10 bundles of salt, 10 goats, 10 pots of palm butter.

---

46. 'R.' written in ink over 'river' in pencil.
47. For 'termination'.
48. 'montans' in ink written over 'mountains' in pencil, as note 39.
49. '8 or 10 miles form' written in ink over 'ten or 12 miles formed' in pencil.
50. 'canoes' written in ink over 'K[…] canoes' in pencil.
51. 'for 5 or 6 miles' added above the line.
52. 'separated' written in ink over 'separating' in pencil.
53. Text in pencil under text in ink is unintelligible.
54. 'Gulls' in ink over 'sea gulls' in pencil.
55. 'haging' written in ink over 'hanging' in pencil.

Except in the neighborhood I do not think many crocodiles are ever found. I have seen as many eight children at least 30 yards from the beach swimming while their parents looked on approvingly from under the shade of a tree.

[Ink] Largest canoes comm[an]d as high as 80 doti, but it is customary to take a selection of such things as are cheap at Ajiji,[56] and sell largely with a profit at Goma, where they are made

Remember L.'s description of how they are made

[Page widthwise]

[Sketch] View south of Cape Kazinga
[Top of the sketch] Tree covered
[Bottom] Grass [?] village. Palms. Tall weeds

[Sketch] Close to Zassi
[Legend] trees. Precipitous. Trees. Clothed with brush.
Bald but green grass

[Double page widthwise]

Outline of Island Muzimu from Cape Kitunda distant over 30 miles.
[Legend: left page] Mainland Ukaramba. Dim and indistinct. [Legend: right page] Mainland. Dim and indistinct

[Ink over pencil]

Customs of Barundi[57]

No more customs have I observed any where in regard of the dress of the hair than in Urudi, diagonal horizontal comb ridges, knots, strips, tufts, curlets temple, forhead curl or front band, sometimes only lines cross lines straight wavy tatooed round the[58] navel like a wheel around the bosom on the arms in wavy lines runing from shoulder to wrist while round the wrist runs a tattooed bracelet. Diagonal lines from right shoulder to left hip & from left shoulder to right hip over the stomach runs a most intricate system of lines both wavy & horizontal though often are seen small wheels & blotch work.

Wear[59] ivory tusks thinned and filed around the necks, hippopotamus tusks, boar tusks while down the back of the neck are hung three or four orannental pieces of ivory. Samesame beads white called merikani, long narrow miniature bells of native iron twisted iron wire & charms, besides a white stone, or a shell as an amulet around the neck.

---

56. 'Ajiji' for 'Ujiji'.
57. Most of the following observations are taken up in *HIFL*, 553–55.
58. 'wheel' in pencil and crossed out.
59. Small sketch of this ivory ornament.

Around the wrist are samesame khetes or blue mutomdu[60] which is a favor[i]te around the waist. From the left shoulder is strapped the syme or native dagger about 18 inches in length.

Their clothing consists of a tanned goat, calf or sheep skin dyed with the red ochre and painted with black lines, spots & circles after the manner of our Indians.

Like the Wagogo they are fond of ochre on their bodies perhaps to a greater extent, besides rubbing their bodies with ochre soil, so as to considerably lighten their original color. They daub their faces, heads, eyelids & eyebrows a deep red with it.

Carry heavy spears for close fight, & light weapons for hurling. Arrows are short compared to those generally seen but like all the tribes bordering[61] the Tanganyika, the feathers of their arrows are beautifully arranged.

Their women tie down the long purse like bosom upon their breasts. Carry for defense & for habit long sticks. Women and male dandies sometimes carry a wealth of beads either round their necks or waists. And several circlets of twisted iron wire or brass wire coils until their legs seem to be attacked with Elephi[62]– the effect is as that of one afficted with Elephantiasis.

Middle tooth of top row extracted, rest filed.

Both Wajiji and Warundi weave excellent thick[63] cloths of cotton, striped[64] tastefully yet they will readily part with a native-made for one of the flimsiest American sheeting, which for purpose of wear & durability the home made is infinitely superior.[65] It is possible[66] that they prefer the American because it is lighter.

The operation of tattooing must be very sore if one may judge from the immense blisters raised after the puncture

In ornament nothing limits their vanity except poverty. Those who can afford it[67] wear as many as 3 or 4[68] fundo of samesame merikani sofi or pipe stem bead kadunduguru & the Pink bead.

[Ink] Stopped at Mukungu on night of 5th day

6th day Tuesday. Upon starting from our camp at Mukungu and wishing to be prepared against contingencies which the well known hostility of Warudi[69] to strangers I

---

60. Mutunda (*HIFL*, 473)
61. 'bor' written in ink, 'd' in pencil, 'ering' in ink.
62. 'Elephi' for 'Elephantiasis'.
63. 'thick' added above the line.
64. 'strped' written in ink over 'striped' in pencil.
65. 'but' crossed out.
66. Between the two lines rewritten in ink, this line in pencil "climate of Tanganyika except" is visible but crossed out.
67. 'who can afford it' added above the line, 'i' in pencil, 't' in ink.
68. '4' left in pencil.
69. Warundi.

ordered Bombay who was storing the baggage to leave the box containing the pin cartridges for smooth bore for rim & central fire. This order about to be executed revealed to us that we had been visited by a party who were travelling during the night & had been robbed of the box containing them & further search we found that the Doctor's box of sugar had also gone. Bombay & the Doctor's invaluable adjunct Susi had slept so soundly from the effects of palm toddy that it was only the natural cowardice of the native breast that had prevented from decamping with the boat & property altogether. They seem however to have satisfied themselves with these two boxes & I can imagine the joyful suspense which the Doctor's sugar must have brought forth & the wonder excited as the strange cartridges were revealed to them.

[Pencil] Last night
[Ink] Map of the N E coast of Tanganyika with rivers
[Distances and some remarks on vegetation in pencil]

[Ink over pencil and pencil]
Last night we paid Muhongo to the extent of 2 ½ doti. The Doctor taught me a lesson of diplomacy. Mateko wanted to take muhongo & give nothing in return[70] & gave us an excuse our departure on the morrow. When we should return we might get something then the Doctor said "as you mean to give us something when we come back, suppose we give you the cloth when we come back." We then said perceiving them quite taken aback "We are hungry we have not eaten much today bring us a sheep only, and make us glad, only one little sheep." Then the old man brought a lamb & a pot of plaintain wine. 2 doti & a fundo.

[Pencil] Southern end of Muzimu from Mwrembere R. S. W. by S.
North West

[Ink over pencil] At villages of Bikari low point commences at Kisunwe Pt[71] & terminates at Murembwe R. we were stoned, scoffed, and threatened with the dire vengeance of the great Wami.

As these demonstrations of hostility were very unwelcome we kept at the distance of half a mile or a mile from the[72] shore but at almost every village we were invited to come closer in anything but a syren voice. We landed on a low spit towards noon protected by a breadth of swamp & depth of thorny jungle & spiky cane from which the boldest might well shrink especially if he called to mind that behind this swamp world be the guns of those they had so rudely challenged.

---

70. 'but the Doctor' in pencil and crossed out.
71. 'Pt' in ink over 'Point' in pencil.
72. 'coast' in pencil and crossed out.

Our coffee was cooked & drank in peace the Doctor spicing the humble meal with a few details of his experiences amongst people of[73] similar dispositions.

Our men were by this time thoroughly alive to the dangerous positions in which we might find ourselves should we relax our energies or vigilance and were therefore most willing to proceed & pulled until an hour[74] or two after dark. We then drew in & landed on a clean shelf of sand about 15 feet broad by 30 long. Behind us rose a clay bank to the height of ten or twelve feet which formed an arc. Within this arc we thought we might be able to pass a few hours undisturbed. Our kettle was boiling on the fire for tea, & the men had built a little fire for themselves & had filled their black earthen pot with water for porridge when our look outs perceived

[Sketches of natives rowing]

darks[75] forms creeping towards us. But on being hailed they came & saluted us with the native "Wake, Wake." They exchanged a few words more & were glad to hear we intended to stop until morning. Upon leaving they promised to bring food in the morning & make friendship. While drinking tea other suspicious forms were seen standing a distance of 25 yards evidently watching us, & from another direction came another set of men to[76] exchange the same salutations, & profess the same readiness to make friends as the first party had done. Soon after this party had left, a third party came & went and shortly after were replaced by a fourth. Our indefensible position, the knowledge that the Barundi were hostile towards us, the suspicious conduct of these several parties had soon impressed upon us an idea, that a misfortune worse than that of the previous night would occur, should we halt much longer at such a time & in such a spot and it was almost in the same breadth that the Doctor & I exchanged our ideas. So after the fourth party had gone our[77] things were replaced in the boat & it shoved off into the water, & the Wangwana hurried in, but not a momt[78] too soon. As the canoe was gliding from darkness of the ultra night that we were in I called the Doctor's attention to several forms hurriedly scrambling towards over the rocks which lined the beach to our right while at the same time natives[79] were seen to our left, and directly we heard a voice hailing us from the bank overhanging the sandy

---

73. 'people of' added above the line.
74. 'an hour' written in pencil.
75. A slip of the pen.
76. 'wake' in pencil and crossed out.
77. 'Wangwana' in pencil and crossed out.
78. 'momt' in ink, over 'moment' in pencil.
79. 'natives' in ink above 'they' in pencil, crossed out.

shelf where we had lately been cooking our suppers. "Neatly done" said the Doctor, as we were shooting through the water leaving the discomfited natives far[80] behind, with which I heartily agreed, for knowing the true natures of our perils. I should have expected nothing less than a frightful confusion & perhaps a capsize as our cranky canoe was one well adapted for such a catastrophe.

This took place close to Cape Sentakeyi.[81]

Slept after pulling six hours more at a small fishing village called Mugeyo and about dawn continued our journey unmolested

Seven[th] day

About 8 A.M. arrived at Cape Magala.

West side about 10 miles off extremely lofty mountains 6 to 7000 feet, we hear Mukamba is fighting a chief near whose country we must pass

[a calculation] 18x 2 ½…

[Ink over pencil]

Still those Warundi at whose villages you effect a landing that boisterous impudence which characterizes the Wagogo[82] has the effect of making one defiant despite virtuous & strenuous exertions to be the contrary treat one far more amiably & leave a more agreeable impression than the Wagogo

Sultan Mwezi of Urundi & Usige lives at Murukoko North East of Magala close to Karagwah, between 3 & 4 months' journey.

Mutware of Magala visited us and proved a most agreeable boy, gave us a fine sheep & milk for a present, for 2 doti &[83] a fundo of samesame.

Eigh[th] Day

Arrived at Cape Kisuka. Western end of Ramata Hills. bears N by E ¼ East from Kisuka.[84]

Highest peaks of Luhunga,[85] Uvira rise N by North from Kisuka 600 to 7000 feet.[86]

Storm rose in a few mintes[87] and the fearful yawing of our canoe into the depths of the waves warned us to desist from proceeding.

---

80. 'far' added above the line.
81. Cape unidentified in modern maps.
82. 'characterizes the Wagogo' added above the line.
83. This sentence was written over and in between the following lines in pencil: 'thought of visiting us in person but the delights of pombe prevailed and he could not come. Hongo, 2 doti and a fundo of [next page] samesame'.
84. This sentence was written in ink over the following in pencil: 'Arrived at Cape Kisuka Pt. End of range running across Northern End of Lake bears, N by E ¼ East from Kisuka Pt'.
85. Luhanga (*HIFL*, 493). The altitude given in *HIFL* was divided by two.
86. This sentence was written in ink over the following in pencil: 'Highest peaks of Uvira, named Sumburizi rise N by North from Kisuka 6000 to 7000 feet'.
87. In ink over 'minutes' in pencil.

Usige commences at between Mugera[88] R. & Kisuka Pt ruled over by Mukamba under Mwezi Sultan of Urundi.

[Sketches of warriors and spears, one man in full garb, sword, feathers]
Some have shave heads.
Some laughing
10 or 12 people
Doctor L. writing
Heads of people looking separate ways boys and girls sitting down
Levee at Magala Urundi[89]
[Mentions of ivory and cloth on the sketches of people]

[Sketch of a part of a canoe with portrait of] Khamis negro of 20
[At the bottom of the page, sketch] On the sand Selim an Arab boy
[Legend] sand, water, distant view of mountains.
[Ink over pencil]

Wagtails numerous & tamed at one place they flew to meet us, & a couple of them landed on our awning within easy reach of our hands. The natives regard them highly & resent any harm done unto them as much as if done to one of their own people.
A Mgwana living at Mukamba came to see us said that Ruzizi flowed out of the Lake and in the interior was joined by the Ruanda or Luanda River, went to Suma's[90] at Karagwah.
Kirubula[91] market where Burton & Speke went to Uvira
Sultan Mruta[92] lives near Sumburizi Peaks
Nin[th] day
End of rounded hill on left & in front North ½ West opening North ½ West.
[Pencil] End of range across head of Lake from Right North
[Ink over pencil] Mugera River quite a stream
Cape very fertile abounding in Palms and Plaintains. Stream flows North to the Lake. In[93] the bend behind the point formed by the Delta of the Mugere we steered for a[94] collection of villages visible on the bank. Landing the Natives crowded to meet us & greet us with one universal stare: we were told our khambi would be on the bank. A

---

88. Mugere (*HIFL*, 496).
89. These various sketches were used as the basis for the engraving "Our levée at Magala, Urundi" (*HIFL*, facing 494).
90. 'Suma' in ink over 'Suna' in pencil. Suna is King Mtesa (*HIFL*, 495).
91. Kirabula (*HIFL*, 507).
92. 'Mruta' in ink written over 'Mrutha' in pencil.
93. 'In' preceded by 'about' in pencil, and crossed out.
94. 'large' in pencil, and crossed out.

small hut was shared between us. But soon after entering I was attacked with a severe fever. I had suffered several fevers between Bagomoyo & Ujiji, without anything to relieve me of the tedious racking headache, and pains, or any kind friend illumining the dark & gloomy prospect which[95] must necessarily surround the bedside of the sick & solitary traveller.[96] But though this fever was more severe than usual having enjoyed[97] immunity from it for 3 months I was not very sorry when I became the recipient of the very tender & fatherly kindness of the good man having enjoyed[98] whose companion I had become.

[Sketches of map: deltas of the Mugere, and the Rusizi R.]

The chief Mukamba came to see us, a[99] man[100] about 40[101] years old had on his head an ornament (see Dictionary of Antiquities)[102]
[Sketches of ornaments: bracelets, necklace, armlet, headdress . . .]

[Pencil]

Upon asking Mukamba through the medium of that over cheerful Mgwana whose Barikallahs & Inshallahs were still fresh in our ears, we were told that the Ruzizi flowed into the Lake that it was joined by the Luanda or Ruanda River at a distance of 2 days by water or 1 day by land.
Thus our hopes which had been somewhat excited by the positive & oft repeated assurances that the river flowed out, away towards Suna of Karggwah collapsed as speedily as they were roused.
Mukamba appeared very amiable & well disposed. Sent 1 bullock & a sheep[103] for the Doctor[104] & myself, & a goat for the boy Selim and a pot of pombe.
A war was[105] being waged between Warumashania[106] & Mukamba & our advent into his country he[107] regarded with favor at such a time hoping no doubt that we would aid him directly or indirectly.
W. not of the same blood.

---

95. [word?] 'of' in pencil, and crossed out.
96. 'tr' in ink, 'a' in pencil, 'veller' in ink.
97. 'an' in pencil, and crossed out.
98. Change of writing. Those words are not connected with the previous page.
99. 'young' in pencil, crossed out.
100. 'man' written in ink over 'chief' in pencil.
101. '40' written in ink over '35' in pencil.
102. 'Dictionary of Antiquities' written in pencil.
103. '& a sheep' added above the line.
104. 'a sheep for my' crossed out.
105. 'raging' crossed out.
106. Warumashanya (*HIFL*).
107. 'appeared' crossed out.

10th day

Paid Muhongo to day 9 doti & 9 fundo. Samesame Lungio, Muzuri N'zige, hkfs[108] very much prized brass wire & heavy brass bracelets.

Mukamba introduced his son & a friend to the Doctor of course to get a few more but the Doctor with a good-natured laugh utterly scouted all ideas of relationship with[109]

Ask the Doctor about Speke's Copper mines of Ruanda

11th day

Tuesday

Copper mines Katanga worked for ages, in Manyema.

Doctor still sanguin[e] that the Tanganyika flows out somewhere even after scouring the head of the Lake.

About dusk the chief Mukamba came to see us before our departure. He evidently wanted us to do him a favor, by hurrying away before Warumashania of Ramata, so that we could[110] return the canoe to fetch him from his country before his enemy could gather his people to attack him. The cause of the war seems to have been the seizing of ten canoes[111]

[Upside down]

Naviungo Sultan of Mutumbi. Gitara Sultan formerly of the country called Itara

---

Quangeregere head of the Ruzizi near to Unyambungu

rises in Kivo, Unsubura Chief – 1

On one side is Mutimbi on the other is Ruanda near Urundi, which may be the most North Western portion of Ruanda

Mugera[112]	Mokam[113] Tanganika
Mpanda	Ta….. Warumashana
Karindwa	"
Mugera wa Kanigi	" Waru
Mugera Kagunissi	Riv[114]
" Kaburan	"
" Mohira	"

---

108. Abbreviation for 'handkerchiefs'.
109. Notes on Stanley and Livingstone's trip on Lake Tanganyika are split into two parts. For better intelligibility, they are published without interruption.
110. 'we could' added above the line.
111. For the end of the sentence and the continuation of the story, see two pages further on in this notebook (S.A. 8), "in which were 10 fishermen…"
112. Mugere (*HIFL*, 501).
113. For 'Mukamba'.
114. River. This is the list of the tributaries of the Rusizi.

"	Nyamagana..............................	"
"	Nyakagunda	"
"	Ruviro	"
"	Rofubu	"
"	Kavimvira	"
"	Myove	"
"	Ruhuha	"
"	Mukindu	"
"	Sange	"
"	Ruvirizi	"
"	Kiriba	"

in which were ten fishermen by a flotilla of 60 canoes containing nearly 200 men. This flotilla had advanced under cover of the low ground formed by River deposits at the head of the Lake as far as an island situated about a mile from the Rusizi and[115] the eastern side of the island had remained[116] secretiv[e][117] until the fishermen had come out at early dawn to follow their usual avocations, when they were suddenly surrounded & slaughtered.

As a kind of protection to him, and no less as I supposed as a guarantee that we would keep our word we were asked to leave 2 soldiers with their guns. Mukiamba having been kind to us we had no hesitation in granting his request, though he had put too many requests. The Doctor was exactly the man with the proper way of checking him. Starting about 7 P.M. we steered W. by N ½ North until[118] we drew near the land, Sumburizi Peak and Mruta's country being a little to our left. We then steered,[119] following the Western shore of the Lake until

[Pencil]

12th day [page blank]

[On the double page, sketch of a map with names and orientation]
3 islands Katangara; Mugehera; Mugihawa of Ruhinga; Kagando; Murambira North East; landing.[120]
[A line on the left part with indication of direction] S by West.

---

115. 'and' is repeated.
116. 'remained' added above the line.
117. Unintelligible word crossed out.
118. 'until' written over 'and'.
119. 'steered' followed by a blank or a word erased.
120. Sketch of the northern part of the lake. See the following page.

13th day
Left about 8 A.M. took boat, pulled to a first bay swarmed with crocodiles. Very shallow water canoe drawing but a foot of water, aground several times. Went round the small island at the foot of the Bay then came to a second bay at the point of which distant a mile lay the larger island told by some fishermen that the mouth of the Rusizi was in the third bay. 3rd Bay very large widest past 3 miles that is from point to point, depth as far as can be seen 2 miles, at the extremity of the Bay it narrows to about ½ a mile, sluggish current visible even on entering the bay, surrounded seemingly by sedgy reeds,[121] sounded 1 fathom at the mouth of the river. The[122] mouth river North by East from the point[123] turns N-E. in a narrow rapid 10 yds broad, expands, become[s] less rapid, oozes out between myriads of reed & sedge clumps – had quite a flotilla of canoes to accompany us, went in about half a mile. It shallowed to four and then 3, as it broadened. Coming out we visited that on the right, 10 feet deep, narrower and not so rapid.

Reeds marked distinctly above 3 feet from the water with the high water mark

a line draws from SW by S to North represents the[124]

14th day
[Sketch of a map of the mouth of Rusizi R.]

Small lake of Kivo about 15[125] miles in length by about 8 in breadth
Kwansibura chief of Kivo

Kivo seems to be the source of the Rusizi. A mountain rises between them. On one side is Kivo, from the other side springs the Rusizi River.
These are the words of Ruhingo, chief of Gihawa.

[Sketch of map of North of the Tanganyika Lake]
[Clockwise from left, one can read] Uvira, Mugehawa,[126] Uringa, Washi, Sultan Unonoro,[127] Chamate, Usige, Ramata, Uzumbara,[128] Mukanyigi.[129]
[At the bottom of the page] Rutwe Sultan of Uzige

---

121. 'no river to be seen' crossed out.
122. 'direct' crossed out.
123. 'went' crossed out.
124. Sentence incomplete.
125. '15' written over '25'.
126. Mugihewa (*HIFL*, 500).
127. 'Washi, Sultan Unonoro' encircled.
128. Usumbura (*HIFL*, 501).
129. Mukanigi (*HIFL*, 501).

North of the Tanganyika is Ruanda.
Usumbara & Mukanigi are in Usige.
Mugehawa & Ruwenga are in Uringa
All are in Urundi

[Page widthwise]

"Sketch of Point of Lake"
[Calculations on the right part of the page]

[Pencil]

Dr Livingstone
What date is it (then the 11th) the 23rd Nov. I believe
Sonded L. Tanganika 300 fathom close to Gomba, on the West opposite Ujiji, 1800 feet. Line broke.
Supposing that all[130] West of[131] the Hudson & Albany was all a blank unknown to us. Crowd that with immense Lakes & noble Rivers, remarkable Mountains &c., & you will have some idea of what Livingstone has now done for African geography.
If Baker deserved a baronetsy for naming the N'Zige, or Unyoro Lake the Albert what does Livingstone deserve for discovering half a continent.

Lake Camolondu – Central Lake – Rivers Lafui, & Lomami coming into the Lualaba, thought at first it was the Congo, but as it still continues to flow North he has come to the conclusion that it is the Nile.

 Thinks that if it does not flow into the Pethericks branch the Lualaba must enter the Albert NYanza in or about the middle of the western shore.

 Ptolemy seems to be correct. The fountains spoken of to Herodotus, he has heard[132] from the natives repeatedly, Two of which are the sources of the great Zambezi, & two of the Lualaba – This task to find them Doctor has undertaken he has been several times within a hundred & 200 miles of them, but always something turned up to prevent him. They rise on either side of a mound (Earthen) which has no stones in it – (some have called it an anthill (Natives). These fountains seem to be very peculiar besides being remarkable. One of them is said to be so large that a man can not be seen on the other side.

 He suffers considerably from bowel illness, discharges blood frequently.[133] - Mind preys on body – inflammation of eyes. But all this has resulted from being compelled to turn back by cowardice abject of his fellows.

---

130. 'behind' crossed out.
131. 'Rochester' crossed out.
132. 'abou[t]' crossed out.
133. Livingstone suffered from severe bleeding hemorrhoids. See G. Shepperson, "David Livingstone 1813–1873," *British Medical Journal* 2, no. 5860 (April 28, 1973): 232–34, http://www.jstor.org/stable/25425436.

The sources of the Nile have not been discovered, so long as these remarkable fountains have not been seen & their position taken. He does not think them South of some of the feeders of the Bangweolo, for instance the Chambezi.[134]

The[135] real name of the river Kwviru [?] as the Zambezi – is the Dombazi, Zambezi is a mere Portuguese corruption from the latter name, so that when the Portuguese came to Cazembe the[136] immediately set down the river Chambezi which they had to cross as "our own Zambezi". Livingstone followed them but as he has been nearly two years correcting it, he has discovered that the Chambezi is one of the many feeders of the Bangweolo, & continuing North becomes known as the Lualaba.

He was so long engaged in correcting this corruption of the Portuguese travelled backwards & forwards, to & fro like an uneasy spirit that the natives began to say, "He wants only water. His safari[137] is to find water. He was afraid that the natives would think he had hydro[138] on the brain!"

But it is certain that he has got the Sources of the Nile on the brain, nor will he give up until he has found them, so that none may come here after & say, "Oh I have found the Sources & none other. He is now in a virgin country, a country that no Frenchman or German or Italian or Portuguese can say, "I have been there."

Lualaba a great river. Sonding going across - 9 feet close to the bank - 15 feet in the middle, 9 feet on the other bank. One & one & a half to three miles broad. Between 1 ½ & 2 miles an hour current.

Altitude of Lualaba where he loses sight of it- is about 2000 feet high.

River L. can not be waded any part of the year by natives. Crocodiles & hippo plenty fish abundant.

15 varieties of fish in the market.

Oysters, within.

Women expert divers for them. Pearls said to be in them but Livingstone doubts it, though the Congo contains some.

Livingstone is poor, sold his steamer, got £2,300. Employed £300 on his own account left 2000 in bank, for his daughters, bank broke, prospects of the daughters but poor now.[139] If England's gratitu[de] manifests itself in bestowing titles, let her follow America's example & bestow something solid on this hardworking man.

---

134. 'There are' crossed out.
135. This paragraph is preceded by 'There are' crossed out.
136. Word incomplete, for 'they'.
137. Swahili word from the Arabic meaning 'journey'.
138. Blank space after this word.
139. See Journal S.A. 11, February 21, 187..

L. left Zanzibar in March, left Mikindyni[140] bay, 7th Ap. 1866 with 12 Sepoys, 9 Johanna men, 7[141] Captive slaves 2 Zambezi Men, 6 Camels, 3 Buffaloes, 2 mules, 3 donkeys. Sepoys to act as guards 12 Bales of cloth, 2 Bgs Beads & few[142] Boxes of instruments & personal necessaries Chronometers, Barometers, Thermometers, Air Thermometers, Sextant & Artificial horizon.

Went up the left bank of the Rovuma River & arrived at the Chief of the Wahiyou 18th July 1866. Animals all killed by the cruelty of the Sepoys, in order to defeat Livingstone's march to the interior to which early after the departure from the Coast they showed decided hostility. Had to cut his way for miles through dense jungles with axes assisted often by the natives. Seeing their unwillingness to accompany him L. decided to discharge them & accordingly sent them back after furnishing them with the means. They were such a disreputable set that the people through whose countries they passed set them down as his slaves.

Leaving the Chief of the Wahiyou he sent[143] off for the Nyassa, from the Rowuma River.[144] This chief dwelt 8 days march through an uninhabited wilderness, on a high ridge overlooking the watershed of the Nyassa.

Arrived at the Nyassa early part of August Two of the liberated captives deserted him on the road. Near the Nyassa Wakotani a protégé, was permitted to go to his own people, simply at his own request nothing the matter with him. He saw his brother or one he said was his brother. L. gave him permission after he had elicited from him the information that his family was on the east side of the heel of the Nyassa. L. gave him some writing paper, as he could write a letter, to write to Mr Waller or himself & strictly enjoined on him, not to join the slave raids of his countrymen.

L. took him to the chief Mponda & asked him to take care of Wakotani, until as it was stated his big brother should come for him. Mponda promised. He found out then that Wakotani had been telling lies for he had said that Mponda's chief wife was his sister. Mponda knew nothing about him & he asked him how he had come to be with the Wasugu.[145] Wakotani said that he had been captured by the Portuguese & that they had liberated him. He said that he had been sold by his people during a famine, when the Doctor asked him if he was not afraid to be resold. He tried to induce Chuma to go with him, in order as the Doctor thinks to make Chumah his slave.

---

140. Minkindiny (*HIFL*, 438).
141. '7' written over '9'.
142. 'few' added above the line.
143. 'set', ms.
144. 'leaving the Rowma' crossed out. Here is an arrow to indicate that "from the Rowuma River," which is at the end of the next paragraph, must be read here.
145. For 'Wasungu' plural of 'Msungu': the white man.

He had told Chuma that his big brother had 14 slaves, & he would get a wife & plenty of pombe as soon as he reached [h]is family. Chuma was of the same tribe. This story was false. Doctor gave him some cloth & beads as a parting present.

Leaving the Nyassa deprived of most of his men L. struck off for the highlands west of the Lake and arrived in a country where there never was a slave trading party, & the Doctor got along very well.

"When we came to the heel of Nyassa (Wakotani had not left them) at a village of a Babisa chief who required medicine for a skin disease. Stopped 2 days to treat him. While staying here a half Caste Arab arrive[d] from the Western shore who told Musa that he had been plundered by a band of Mazitu, at a place which Mussa & the Doctor knew was 150 miles Nor Nor West of the village, 20 days march – because he had been with the Doctor during the Zambezi Expedition, much beyond it. Musa upon imparting the news to the Doctor, was asked if he believed that man. "Yes said he "he tell true true. I ask him good & he tell true, true."

D – I don't believe him for the Mazitu if they had plundered him would have killed him. Now this chief is a sensible man let us go ask him, as he must know all about it.

D – asked chief about Arab statement who said he believed he was telling lies. He had heard nothing about it.

Musa said, "No, no, no, Doctor. No, no, no, I no want go to Mazutu I no want Mazitu to kill me. I want see my father, my mother, my child in Johanna. I no want Mazitu kill me. Ipsissima verba.[146]

D. said I don't want Mazitu to kill me either but as you are afraid of them I will go straight West until we are far past the beat of the Mazitu.

He said If we had 200 Arab guns, I would go – but they will come by night & kill us all.

D. said but I will not go near them, I will go west.

As soon as he turned his face West, he & the other Johanna men ran away.

D. felt inclined to shoot him & another ringleader, but is glad he did not soil his hands with their dirty blood.

A day or two afterwards another Simon Price by name came to the Doctor with the same tale, but the Doctor was necessitated by the scant number of his men, was compelled to be careful.

Had the natives not assisted him, he must have despared of succeding but fortunately they conveyed his goods for a very small portion of cloth & in other ways manifested kindly feelings towards the White Man. Chuma, Mabruk, Garner,

---

146. Latin for 'His very words'.

James, Simon Price & Abraham, the rest of the liberate captives did very well for a long time.

Went to the Highlands left Nyassa on the 8th October. Leaving the Highlands they came to a country where the Mazitu had swept everything Consequently they suffered famine. Passing through the Babisa, Babembe & Barungu & Baulungu[147] countries he came to Lake Liemba which L. found out afterwards was the Southern[148] point of the Lake Tanganyika.

In the Baulungu country he was detained 3 months on account of a war, between that chief & the Arabs. When the Doctor had to make peace.

From Lake Liemba to L. Moero, a long distance. Thence to Cazembe (see notes already taken) many times detained. Many times sick, traping round & round in search of waters. His people mutinied – Arabs conspired against him, tempted his people to desert him. He had ulcers on his feet from which as soon as he set them on the ground was a discharge of bloody icor[149]– detained 6 months by this in Maniema.

First came to Ujiji the middle of March 1869. Came from Marugu up the Tanganyika in a Dhow, stopped until the end of June to recruit whence you set out for his last & greatest discoveries the region of Manyuema, the wonder-problem of the Nile valley was being slowly but surely revealed until he was turned back from its completion by the arrant cowardice of his followers.

He had intended to have sailed round the Tanganyika, but the natives & Arabs were so bent in fleecing him that had he done so his goods would not have enabled to travel to Manyuema.

The central line of drainage he though was of more importance than the Tanganyika.

He had observed that there was a current in the Tanganyika stadily set towards the North 9 months through the year.

Lake Bangwelo, Moero Kamolondo – Lualaba

Took him 4 months to travel 400 or 500 miles – Manyuema is a big country, people do not know thirty miles off from the river Lualaba.

4 trips through it trying to get down the Lualaba.

D. calls Wakotani Wikotani.

Found Mohammed bin Sali, an Arab at Cezembe, influenced Cezembe[150] to release him.[151] Yet this Mohammed bin Sali moral ingrate induced his people to

---

147. 'Baulungugu' added above the line. Then Stanley corrected this name, adding "u" before "l", and crossing out the last syllable. Spelled Ba-ulungu in *HIFL*, 444.
148. Word crossed out.
149. 'icor': most likely ichor, an antiquated term for a watery or bloody discharge.
150. Cazembe (*HIFL*).
151. him=Wakotani.

desert. Sold the favors of his female slaves, to them. Had considerabe[152] with his people since Sali was of his party.

He is now the big man of Ujiji & here I was introduced a cunning fellow pretending to be very frank & friendly – but a bad old man.
L. found when he had returned to Ujiji that he was destitute.

4 children.[153]

Agnes[154] is an accomplished young lady. Tom oldest boy is the employ of the Mercantile line,[155] Oswell named after the hunter of South Africa one of his dearest old friends,[156] is studying medicine.[157] Anna Mary is a school girl.[158] Robert Moffat L. died before Richmond fighting in the cause of Emancipation – a case that L. himself has fought life long.[159] What an ardent admirer of Abe Lincoln is he? He has immortalzed the mourned President by calling a large Lake after him. His son Robert as his officer wrote was much of the same nature as his father – brave – ardent and always cheerful. "He died in the company of brave men, and sleeps with them."

[From this line to the end of the page, struck out across the page]

Livingstone is a most careful man, his boxes appear like new, his compasses & instruments are in first rate order. His journals are clean & orderly kept – blotless as if a copyist had been lately transcribing them.

[This page too struck out across]

Livingstone though old in age does not appear so old in body & is quit[e] young in heart & mind. It is only at the first look of him that I felt shocked but when he began to talk I quite lost sight of his age. If I turned my face away & listen I imagined myself in the company of a sociable young man.

[The following paragraph is crossed out with one vertical line.]

---

152. Word missing.
153. Six children were born to Mary Moffat Livingstone. One died in infancy.
154. Agnes Livingstone (1847–1912) married Alexander Bruce (1875). Her father singled her out as the addressee of the diary Stanley brought back. See her letters to Stanley upon his return from Africa, S.A. 492, 493, 494.
155. Thomas Steele Livingstone (1849–1876). See Letter from Thomas S. Livingstone to Henry M. Stanley, S.A. 490.
156. William Cotton Oswell (1818–1893) traveled with D. Livingstone in 1848–49 and 1851–52. See Oswell, *William Cotton Oswell, Hunter and Explorer*, 2 vols., Cambridge Library Collection—African Studies (New York: Cambridge University Press, 2011).
157. William Oswell Livingstone (1851–1889) married Kate J. Anderson. See letters from William O. Livingstone and his widow to Stanley, S.A. 488 and 489.
158. Anna Mary Livingstone (1858–1938), spouse Wilson. See letter from Anna Mary to Stanley, S.A. 491.
159. Robert Moffat Livingstone (1846–1864), known as "Private Rupert Vincent." Although only seventeen, he joined the Union Army, 3rd New Hampshire Regiment, 10th Army Corps, in 1863. The place of his death is not certain. About his son, Livingstone said he fell before Richmond and was reported to have died in a hospital in Newbern, North Carolina (S.A. 11, January 8, 1872).

L. does not believe in hurrying on while travelling, that is weary but in taking it easy. If he comes to a place worth seeing he likes to see it thoroughly. Hurrying on wearies & finally kills, & is superficial.

Tagomoyo a half caste Arab, second in importance to Dugumbe, massacred the inhabitants of a populous[160] district on the Lualaba. Livingstone was a spectator, & can not describe his loathing of the horrible deed.

Liv. made 4 or 5 trips through the country.

Webb's River called after the wealthy proprietor of Newstead Abbey.[161] Byron's home.

Leaves Moero to Kamalondo[162]

Webb is 6 feet high, stout, double chinned, large bearded: worth £ 25 000 per year.

When L. returned to Ujiji that evening his faithful Chuma & Susi returned to L. crying bitterly: "All our things are sold. Shereef has sold everything. Later Shereef returned & saw the Doctor at Muniyi-Kheri and offered his hand to shake L. refused saying he would not shake hands with a thief. L. was in great misery being thus destitute & must have felt as miserable as the poor man who in the London streets knows not where or how to get the next meal.[163]

The Doctor upon hearing that a Muzungu was lost in conjecture as to who it could be. He thought that it might be a Frenchman having heard of Lieut Le Saint's effort to reach the Albert & of his subsequent death & that this one might be sent by French Govt. to go down the Nile.

Tanganyika stretches down to 9° South. Two or three rivers inflow but Marugu is the largest.

The Wanguana are fearfully timid and such irresolute brave-hearted people that one could not trust himself in war with a thousand of them as witness Zimbizo and the shameful retreat to Unyanyembe.

The Wavinza & Wagogo need a good whipping to bring them to their senses, and a strong-minded prince of Zanzibar seeing that the principal part of his revenue is derived from ivory & slaves imported from the interior would do well to send a thousand Baloch & Haramaut[164] Arabs & Persians under a good officer if not to clear

---

160. 'populous' added above the line.
161. Newstead Abbey was a twelfth-century Augustinian priory, granted to the Byrons by King Henry ?, and converted into a family residence. It remained in the family until the poet Lord Byron sold it. William Frederick Webb (1829–1899) was a very wealthy landowner. He bought Newstead Abbey in 1861 and added his mark by remodeling and decorating it with his game trophies and African artifacts. D. Livingstone when parting from Stanley gave him a bale of spears to be delivered to Webb (see Field Notebook S.A. 9).
162. Kamolondo (*HIFL*, 437).
163. Livingstone's account goes back to the meeting with Stanley at Ujiji.
164. For Hadramaut.

the road to inspire respect by curving them with a well armed & superior force.[165] With 300 white soldiers, English, French, German & a force of medical men,[166] Americans or Russians, I would guarantee to do it.

[Pencil]

Com.   Ugonda – 5 hours
           Ubura – 3 "
           Myowe
           Porini[167]

Ugunda { Ugunda / Vigunda / Makekura[168]

           Porini
           Maniara
           Porini
           Porini Village
           Marefo
           Gongwe[169]

Wazavirra – Porini

Sultan Mbogo

           Mbogo
           Quicuru }
           Perro[170]
           Usense
           Perro
           Porini

Sultan Kasoonga

Country Ugongwe

20 or 21[171] days to the place where the Wazawira make the road bad.

---

165. Kirk judged the situation differently: "The Arab colony of the Interior whose centre is Unyanyembe has for sometime been led by a set of avaricious unprincipled men, whose acts of extortion both on Natives and the poorer Arabs have for sometime back been complained of to Seyd Burgash who is impotent to interfere at such a distance so long as things go well for the Arabs." Letter from J. Kirk to Lord Granville, Zanzibar, September 22, 1871, National Archives, Kew, FO 84/1344, no. 96, fol. 477–480v; received and transmitted to Sir Rawlinson, RGS, December 4, 1871, *PRGS* 16, no. 2 (1871–72): 103–4.

With the ivory trade having come to a stop, things did not go well, and Barghash sent a force of three thousand Baluchi and Hadrami soldiers to help Arabs in Unyanyembe against Mirambo in 1873.

166. 'and a force of medical men' added between lines. To be read: "With 300 white soldiers, English, French, German, American or Russians & a force of medical men, I would guarantee to do it."

167. *Porini* is a Kiwahili word meaning "in the bush."

168. Makekura, 'k[ura]' written over 'g[ura]'.

169. 'Gongwe' added on the right between 'Marefo' and 'Porini'.

170. Meaning of "Perro" unclear.

171. '25' written over '20', and '21' over '26'.

Sultan Kwasoonga place Gongwe, one day before reaching him are the Wazawira.
At Kwasoonga's is the road for Kawendi and Ufipa
Watuka is bad – this is near Unyanyembe.

[Page widthwise]
[Sketch] View before my tembe[172]

While being always liberal & courteous to the natives even to the most over bearing I never omitted the slightest precaution that would contribute to the general safety of the Expedition. Not only were all my guns loaded every night & a brace of revolvers placed[173] under my pillow but the boxes containing my cartridges were[174] unscrewed & prepared for immediate action, so that the people in case of a night alarm could get at supplies of amunition without much confusion. So also was my mind made up, and plans sketched out, so as to meet all possible contingencies. Such things as day attacks, night attacks mutiny or desertion of soldiers[175] & consequent wreck of the Expedition were always possibilities. The general skedaddling at Zimbizo gave me a series of lessons upon many subjects of which previously I was ignorant or loth to believe.
[On this page, a fine line which might be a profile]

Bott.
Balsam of Copaiba ....6 oz
Spirits of nitric ether......... ...2 oz
Sulphate of zinc............... ...2 oz
Tincture of thenbane...... ...... 1 oz
Iodide of Potassium............ ½ oz
Alum.......................... 1 oz
Quinine.......................... 3 oz
Colocynth Pills....................15 doz
1 catheter

Khamis bin Abdullah[176]
Mussoud bin Abdullah
Thani bin Abdullah
Mohuma bin Sulayman

---

172. This refers to Stanley's tembé at Tabora. The sketch was used for making an engraving (*HIFL*, 258). From this page, the notes concern Unyanyembe.
173. 'placed' added above the line.
174. 'were' added above the line.
175. 'were always possibilities' crossed out.
176. This is the list of the notable Arabs of Tabora.

Sultan bin Ali
Saleem bin Saif
Zaid bin Saleem
Hilal bin Nasur
Saleem bin Hassan
Mohammed bin Moussoud
Amram bin Moussoud
Sheikh bin Nasib
Said bin Saleem

The wood apple is about the size of a good sized plum & not unlike in outward appearance the ripe green plums, which the sight of these apples brings to my recollection. I asked the Wanguana if they were good to eat. They looked so tempting. I was told that if only a few were eaten no harm would follow, but if I ate many I should suffer pains in the abdomen and legs. I ate 5 raw & considered them not bad forest fruit, for those who had long been deprived of such things. I cooked 5 more, by boiling them and with sugar they made a first rate dessert. There is a large stone inside them. I never experienced the slightest disagreeableness from eating them, neither did Selim who to my certain knowledge ate 15 of them.

Ibis, large birds with strong beaks, with dark, glossy plumage. We saw in great numbers in the region extending from Kikoka to Simbawenni. Their queer notes heard suddenly in the silence of the jungle troubled me exceedingly when I[177] made my first sally after meat for the pot. Wa-wa-wa-wa uttered deliberately & sharply clean in the woods so unlike the note of bird,[178] made me think of lost children, of painthers & wild cats, but the author of the sound was soon discovered & brought to the ground.

Camp life. Building huts as soon as our arrival. One fetches long grass. Another seeks out forked branches.

Ibis religiosa were seen near Lake Ugombo.

snipes, herons & curlews & plovers.

The tsetse are to be found from the Western bank of the Kingani to Ujiji. Elephant oil rubbed over an animal will save him from the tsetse Chufwa, & gadfly said an Msegura. The Glanis Silurus fish are caught in the Gombe River, dried & sold in Uniyanyembe Orchella weed was seen hanging in festoon in the dense humid jungles of Msuwa & Imbiki, these passed we saw the dye-stuff no more.

---

177. 'first' crossed out.
178. 'made me' written above 'that I began to' crossed out.

The road - Small houses along the road, sometimes at cross roads, bits of manioc root, Indian corn, & a bunch of matama, offered as offerings. At other places pieces of rag &c

Wanyamuezi, very superstitious, often see heaps of sand along the road, these made by each pagazi lifting with his foot some sand.
Near the villages along the road we see the artificial hives of the natives, a stout log 4 or 5 feet long split in half, the halves scooped out laid on each other and tied together with bark cords, over which the Mganga has put medicine against thiefs, a medicine which is supposed to kill.

Wanguana put <ch…>[179] on their doors
Red ants furious things remember Selim & Omar's introduction at Kisemo
While travelling, they very often rush up the legs of your donkey. If your riding animal is a Mnyamwezi he disengages himself from these pests by vigorously stamping his feet on the ground.
On the road the women exhibited the most profound emotion when after running perhaps half a mile or so to gain a sight of the wonderful white man. They uttered just such a sound as I have heard some ladies[180] in America when they for the first time saw a magnificent painting. Phonetically the sound is spelt "Ough!"
But even the Wagogo calves & bulls seemed particularly struck with my aspect.
[asterisk] On the road. The Wanyamwezi indulge in smoking & after one or two puffs indulge in[181] a curious cough which from being at first natural, soon becomes disgustingly unnatural. Voice noisy.
A large black fly with a bluish gloss to it, about an inch and a half in length – the (P<…>) <…> e<…> amused me while lying sick in bed at Unyanyembe. See Livingstone Book P. 353
Myriapedes[182] are most common in dark places such as the neighbourhood of rivers, where their inconceivably loathsome forms may be seen crawling around you, whichever way the eyes may happen to alight
The Wanguana though black in face, and mostly bearing the stamp of the true negro are extraordinarily acute in argument.
[Inside the cover]
[Pencil] Square of Flying Horse[183]

    179. May be 'charms'.
    180. 'of the middle class' crossed out.
    181. 'coughing' crossed out.
    182. For 'millipedes'.
    183. The Flying Horse refers to a constellation named after Pegasus. Four stars delimit a square which forms the horse's body.

<u>116. 36. 30. N.</u>
S. 70. 51. 20° found[184]
[Ink]Acarnar[185]

[Pencil] Livingstone says when he gets in a four post bed, he likes to lie all sorts of ways in it – across ways – diagonally lengthways – up & down.

---

184. 'found' in pencil and crossed out in ink.
185. Achernar. Observations of Achernar by Livingstone took place on December 6, 1871 (S.A. 73).

Journey to Lake Tanganyika and Encounters

Maps Retracing Stanley's Journey to Find Livingstone

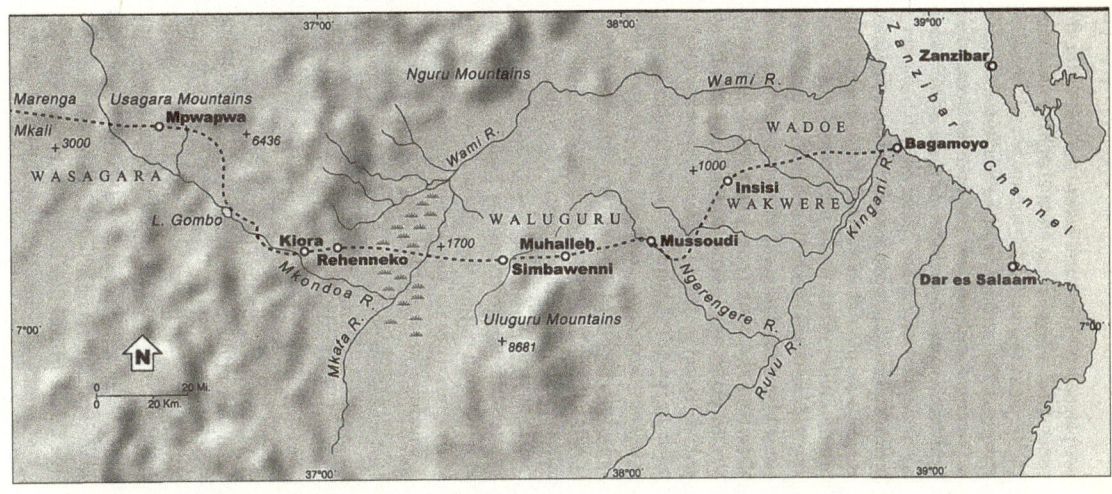

Map 2. The journey to find Livingstone, March–May 1871. Reproduced from *Imperial Footprints: Henry Morton Stanley's African Journeys* by James L. Newman by permission of the University of Nebraska Press. Copyright 2004 by Potomac Books, Inc.

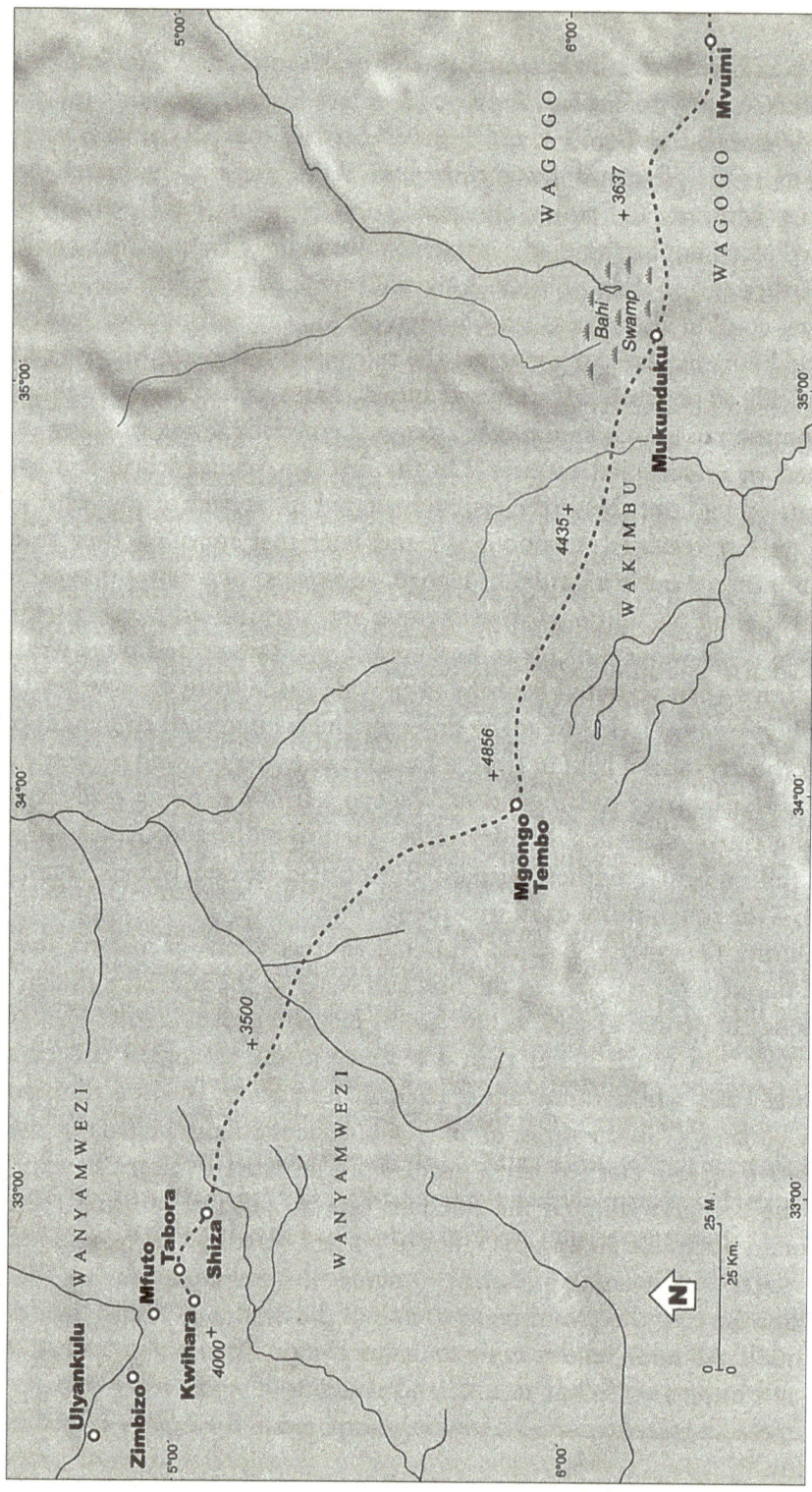

Map 3. The journey to find Livingstone, May–June 1871. Reproduced from *Imperial Footprints: Henry Morton Stanley's African Journeys* by James L. Newman by permission of the University of Nebraska Press. Copyright 2004 by Potomac Books, Inc.

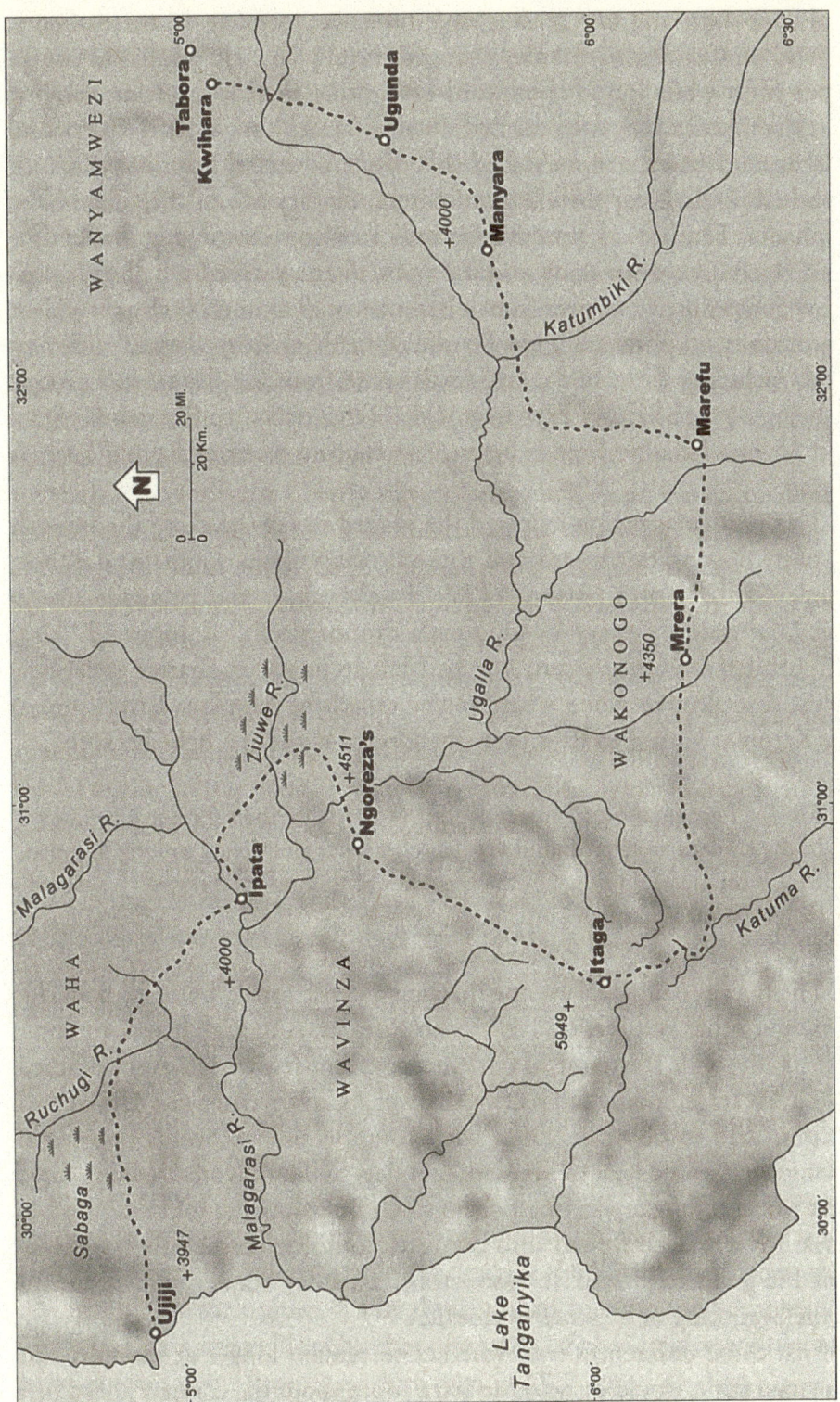

Map 4. The journey to find Livingstone, September–November 1871. Reproduced from *Imperial Footprints: Henry Morton Stanley's African Journeys* by James L. Newman by permission of the University of Nebraska Press. Copyright 2004 by Potomac Books, Inc.

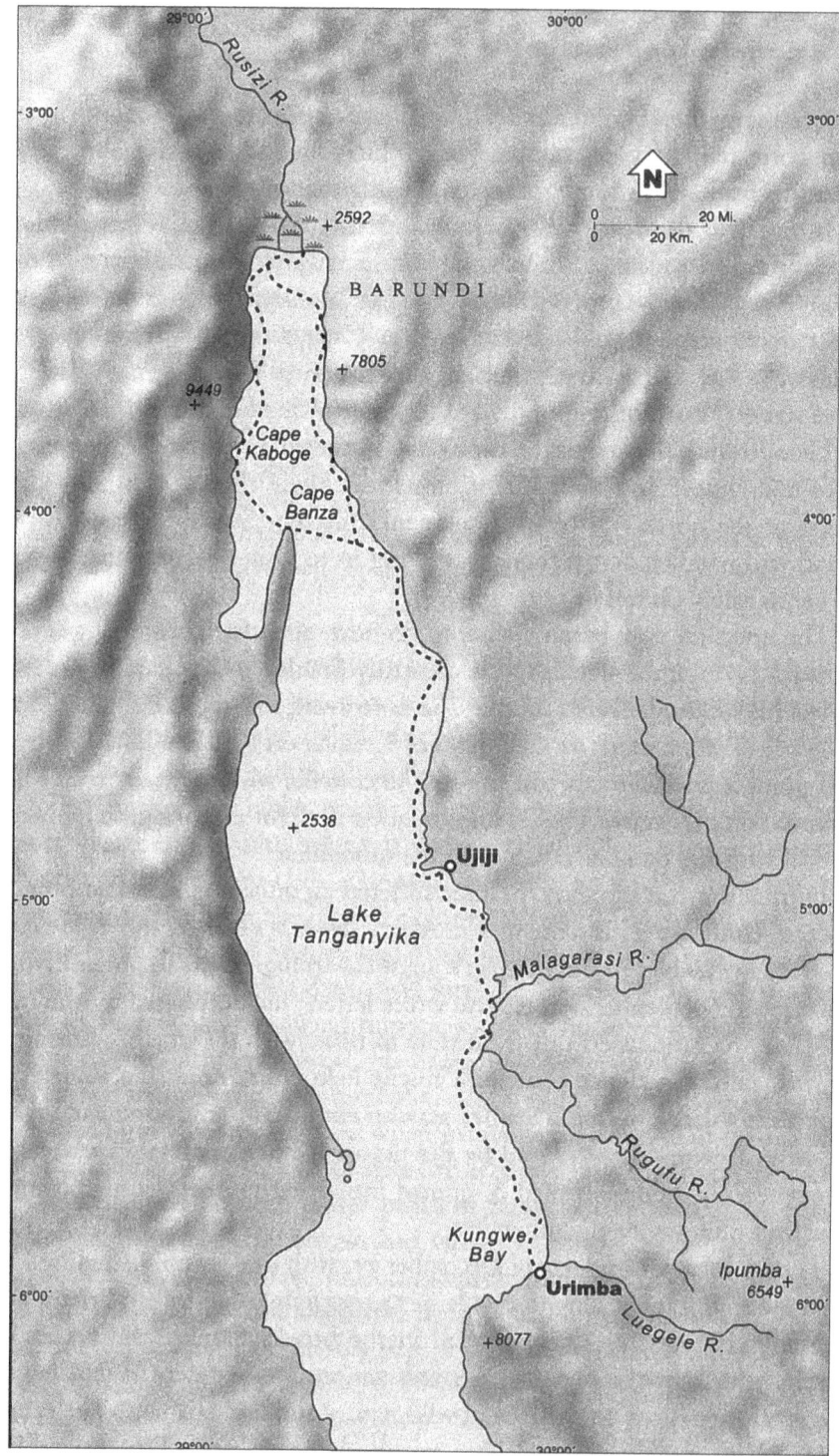

Map 5. Lake Tanganyika explorations and the start for Tabora, November 1871–January 1872. Reproduced from *Imperial Footprints: Henry Morton Stanley's African Journeys* by James L. Newman by permission of the University of Nebraska Press. Copyright 2004 by Potomac Books, Inc.

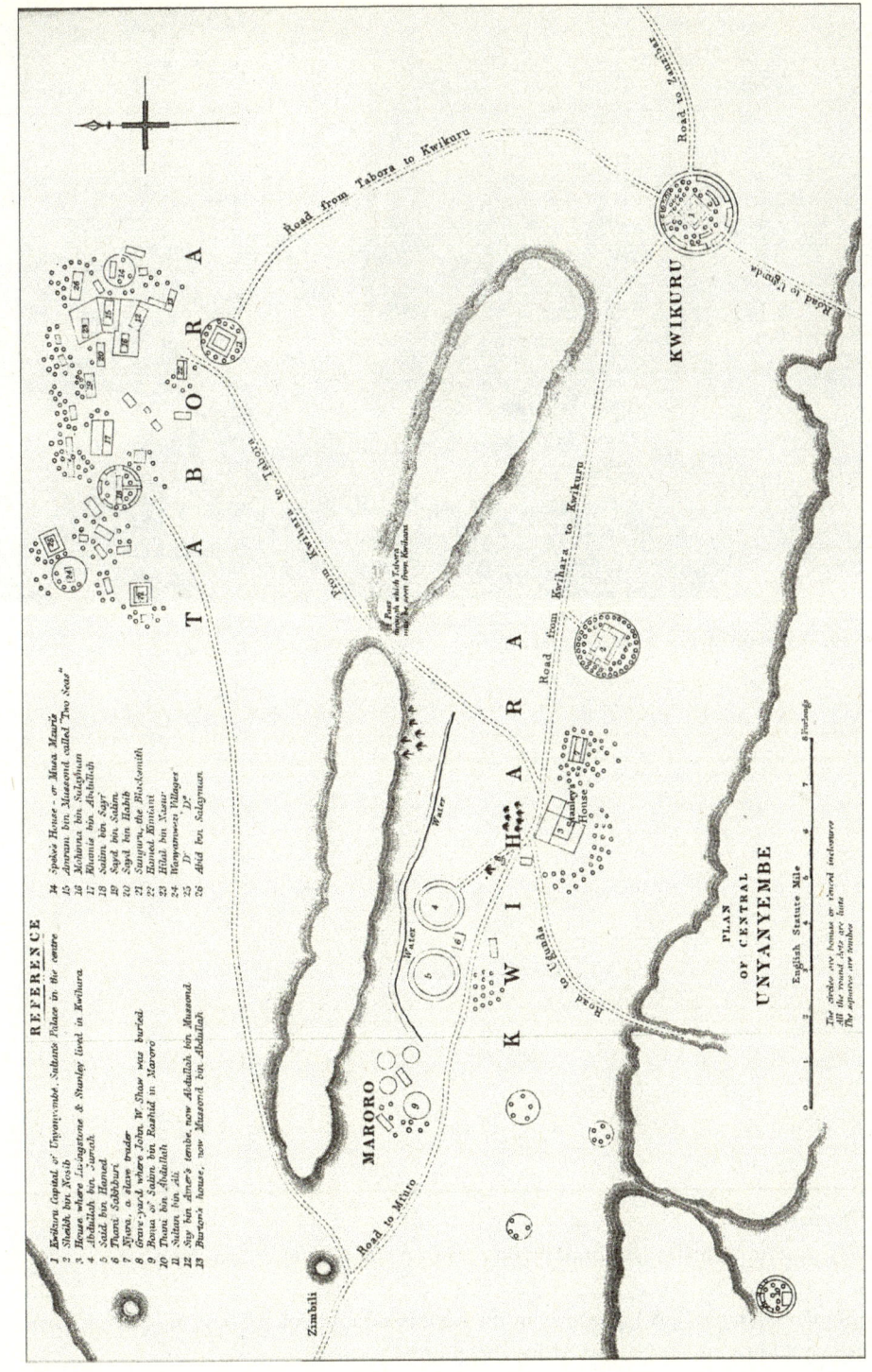

Plate 14. "Plan of Central Unyanyembe." (*HIFL*, facing 259)

Plate 29. "View of Kwihara." (*HIFL*, facing 310)

(Facing page)
Plate 15. Kalulu, carte de visite photograph, 9.5 x 5.7 cm, Gurney & Son, New York. (S.A. 5338)
The Stanley Archives (S.A.), property of the King Baudouin Foundation, are held in trust at the Royal Museum for Central Africa (Belgium).

Plate 16. Pencil sketch "Crossing the Rudewa." (Excerpt from Field Notebook S.A. 10)

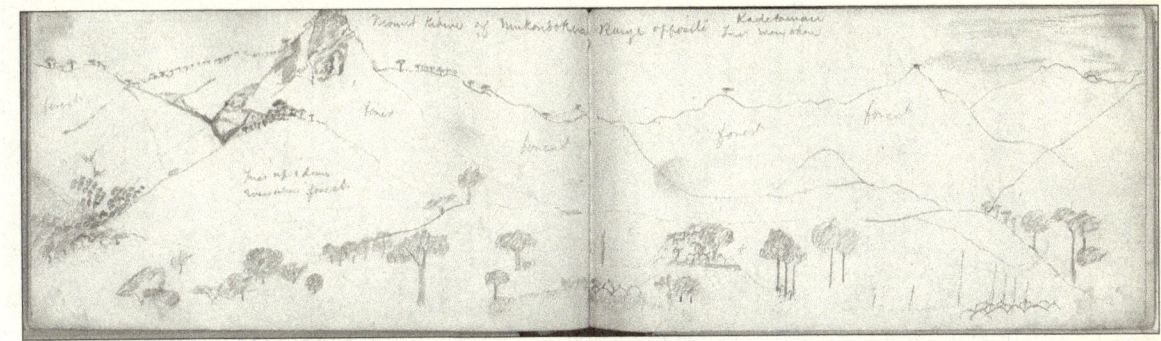

Plate 17. Pencil sketch covering a double page, "Mount Kibwe of Mukondokwa. Range opposite Kadetamari." (Excerpt from Field Notebook S.A. 10)

Plate 18. "Mount Kibwe and Valley of the Mukandokwa River." (*HIFL*, facing 244)

Plate 19. Double-page pencil and blue pencil colored sketch of Lake Ugombo, dated April 9th. (Excerpt from Field Notebook S.A. 10)

Plate 20. "Lake and Peak of Ugombo." (*HIFL*, facing 154)

Plate 21. Pencil sketch of "Unamapokera, soldier of Mayomba." (Excerpt from Field Notebook S.A. 10)

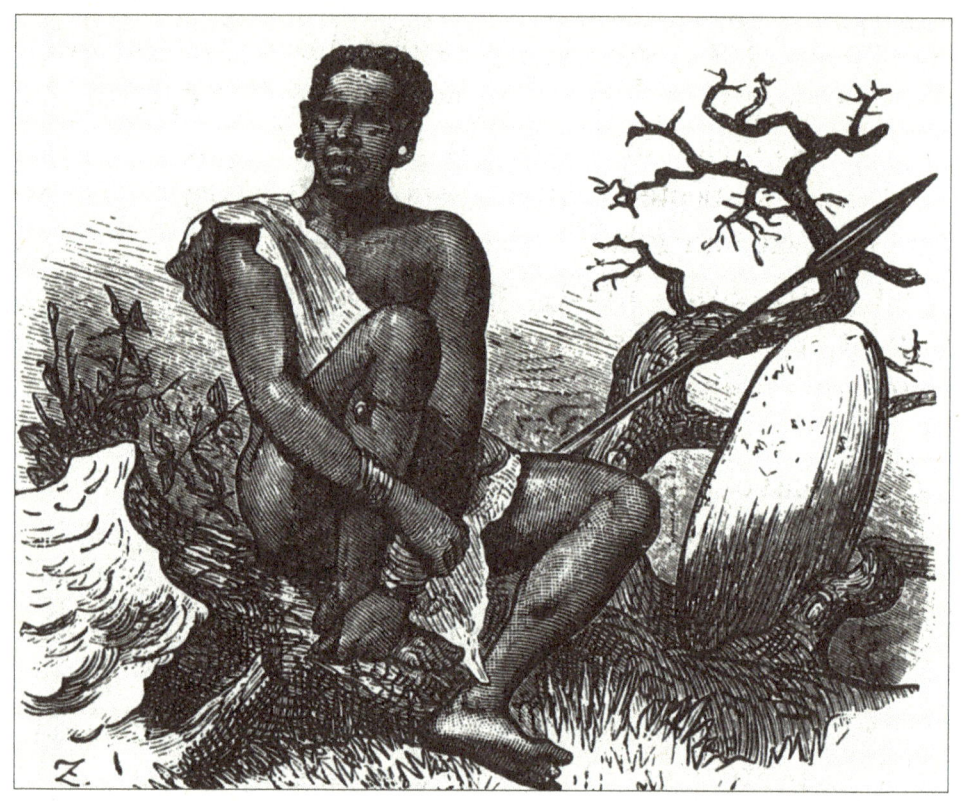

Plate 22. "Unamapokera." (*HIFL*, 635)

Plate 24. Pencil sketch of "Ugogo warrior." (Excerpt from Field Notebook S.A. 10)

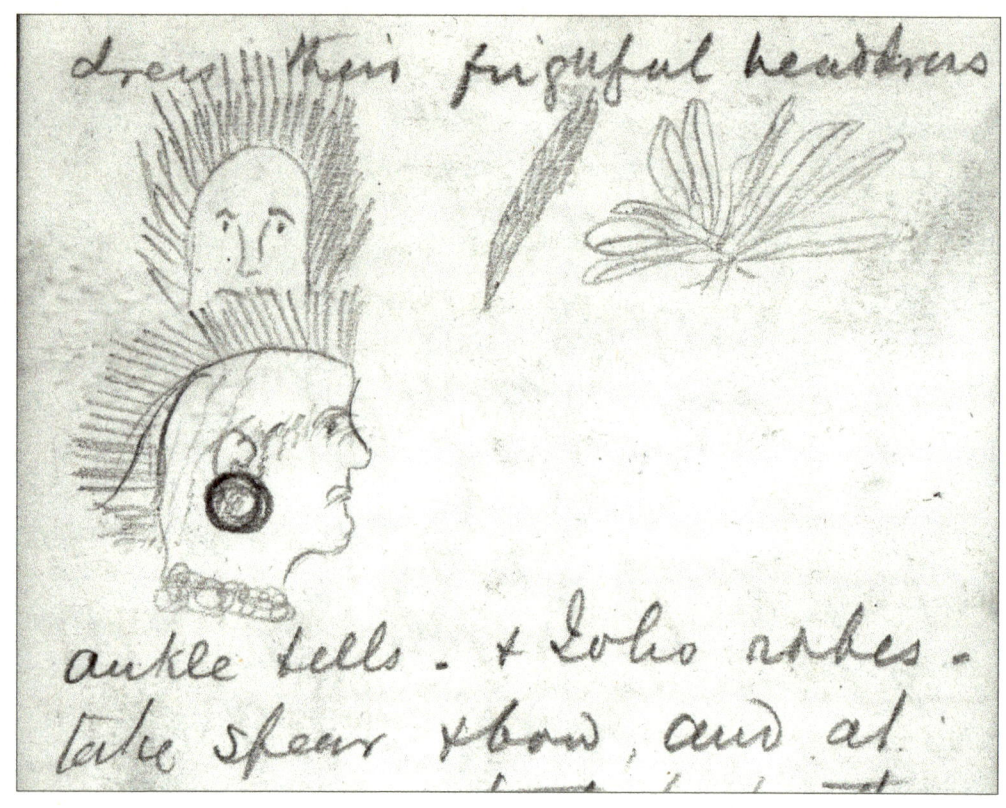

Plate 23. Pencil sketch of three headdresses. (Excerpt from Field Notebook S.A. 10)

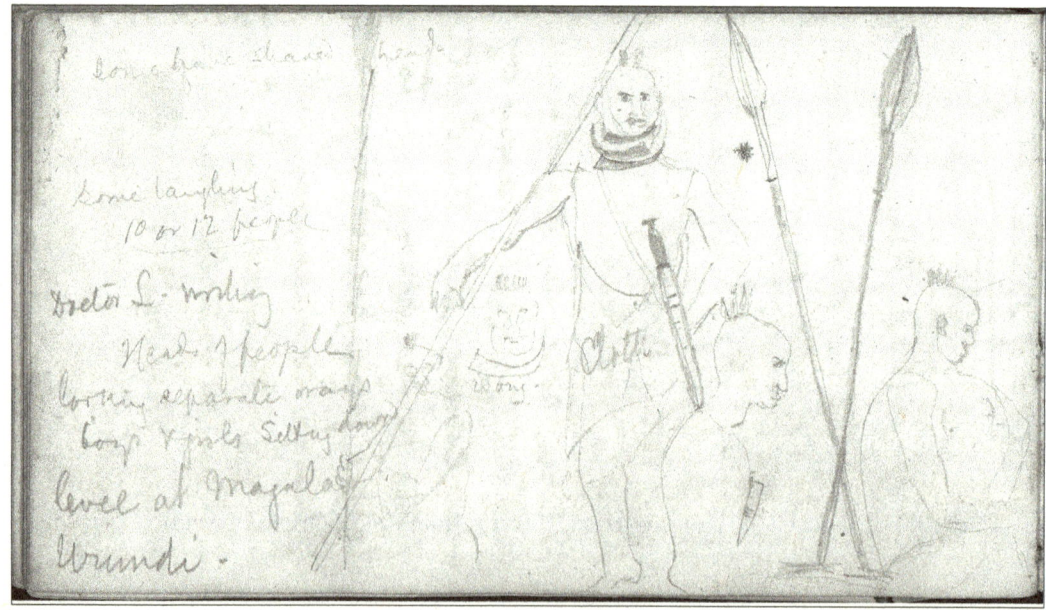

Plate 26. Pencil sketches of warriors and spears, one man in full garb, sword, feathers. (Excerpt from Field Notebook S.A. 8)

Plate 25. "Ugogo man and woman." *(HIFL,* 223)

Plate 27. Pencil sketch "View before my tembe." (Excerpt from Field Notebook S.A. 8)

Plate 28. "View in front of my tembe." (*HIFL*, 258)

Field Notebook S.A. 9, Full Transcript

[This field notebook is written in pencil, unless otherwise stated.
Inside page cover: Almanack 1868, pasted on the first page. Opposite page: additions. End of the notebook: flyleaves with an incomplete grid for bales, and many calculations.]

[This page and the following were written over other bits of notes. One may read 'Mabruk', '30 doti', 'Rehani' …]

XX Rojab[1]	5	men		30
XX Chanda XX	2	"	✓	12
XX Baraka X	3	"	✓	18
XX Mabruki Speke X	4	"	✓	24
XX Umtamani XX[2]	5[3]	"	✓	30
XX Saboori XX	2	"	✓	12
XX Ibrahim XX	1	"	✓	6
XX Ferousi XX	1	"	✓	6
XX Sadala XX	5	"	✓	30
XX Mabruk (Unyanyembe X 5 X		"	✓	30
XX Majwara XX	3		✓	18
XX Gardner XX	2[4]		✓	18
XX Selim XX	1 x		✓	6
XX Bombay X	1		-	6
XX Hamoodah	2			12
	42			
Susi	2			12

---

    1. This could be the list of the men with a higher status in the caravan, responsible for others of a lesser rank. Stanley entrusted some of his men to find porters at Zanzibar when recruiting Speke's Faithfuls, and at Kwihara when he was preparing the second leg of his journey to Lake Tanganyika. For example, Saboori, who is indicated as "2" men, was recruited at Kwihara with another Saboori as soldiers (see Appendix, Contract of Saboori Mkuba, Saboori Mdogo, and Kombo, September 17, 1871, S.A. 4748). When facing a lack of carriers for the last leg to the Lake, Stanley made his soldiers carriers for extra pay, which could account for the third column. However, this chart and the following one leave many questions unsolved.
    2. Small circle above the two crosses.
    3. '5' written over '4'.
    4. '2' written over '3', without modification of the count at the end of the line.

345

	Men	days[5]		Kubaba

[All the following names and numbers of days are checked with ✓]

~~Rojab~~	5	~~10~~ ~~75~~	~~50~~	110
~~Chanda~~	2	~~10~~ ~~30~~	~~20~~	44
~~Baraka~~	3	~~45~~	~~30~~	66
~~Mabruki Speke~~	4	~~60~~	~~40~~	88
~~Umtamani~~	5	~~75~~	~~50~~	110
~~Saboori~~	2	~~30~~	~~20~~	44
~~Ibrahim~~	1	~~15~~	~~10~~	22
~~Ferousi~~	1	~~15~~	~~10~~	22
~~Sadala~~	5	~~15~~	~~40~~	110
~~Mabruk (Unyanyembe)~~	5	~~75~~	~~50~~	110
~~Ma[jwara?]~~	3	~~45~~	~~30~~	66
~~Gardner~~	3	~~45~~	~~30~~	66
~~Seleem~~	1	~~15~~	~~10~~	22
~~Bombay~~	1	~~15~~	~~10~~	22
~~Hamoodah~~	2	~~30~~	~~20~~	44
~~Susi~~	2	~~30~~	~~20~~	44
				44

[Last line, upside down] Bill Alli[6]

[The upper part of the page has been erased. The entire page is crossed with a big X and written over. One may read 'Ulimengo', 'Kaniki', 'H[and]k[erchief]fs', 'Rehani', and some figures]

[Over it]

86.6.10

68.35

~~87.19.20~~

Canopus

87.22.10[7]

Marora

22 ½ Mericani

24 Kaniki

  4 Coombeesa

    5. This list, identical to the previous, could be the compensation due to soldiers and carriers for the rations they were deprived of during the 10 days through wilderness before reaching Imrera (January 9 to 19, 1872). Kubaba = allowance of grain.
    6. Bilali (*HIFL*).
    7. These figures could be star observations for latitude. See further under "Jan. 21, Sunday."

4 Barsati
_8_ Dabwani
62 ½

[The entire page is crossed with a big X and written over.]
Abdul Kader
22 ½ Merikani
Saboori Cuba
54 doti Merikani & Kaniki
Kombo
54 doti Merikani &Kaniki
Chanda
Wire
Kamna
~~Flour & table~~
Donkey
Kadunduguru & Merikani[8]
~~Bubu &~~ Kanyera
Samesame
Jumah
~~Table~~   Kitanda[9]
Asmani
Sungomazzi White & Yellow
Mutoonda[10]
Sadala
Mutoonda Green

[Ink] 7 ½: 528 ½ =7

[All page crossed with X]
Luwambo
Kadunduguru
Lunera
Merikani
Mwienga
Wire

---

8. About beads and cloth for trade and currency, see *HIFL*, 23–25.
9. *Kitanda* is Kiswahili for bed.
10. Mutunda in *HIFL*.

Tabuto
Wire
___

[The following words on a blank part of the same page crossed out but upside down.]

Ulimba[11]......4 days
Ngondo ...... 2 "
Pumburu…....3 "
Mpokwa ..... 1 "
       <u>22</u>
      32 days

[The following sentence is written upside down, and partly under the sketch of the map]

<u>Dr Livingstone</u>
had no tent with him. Slept on ground. When he goes again it will
[Sketch of a map with "hands" indicating directions and angular measures. Following names can be read:]
300 from Kabogo, Sigunga, Uwelasia 205, 165° Herembe,[12] 70 Tongwe, Tumba.

[Map of Livingstone and Stanley's journey from Ujiji to Sigunga, their landing point before heading to Tabora. From top to bottom, it reads:]
Sigunga, Kabogo, Misohazy, Kibwe, Kivoe, 210, Rugufu, Mviga, 233 from Kagongo, Kagongo, Malagarazi, Bangwe, Mohamed's camp, Jumah Merikani, Ruche,[13] Ujiji, Bonguru,[14] Tongwe, Urimba, Ukaranga, Tumba.[15]

[On the lower left of the page, close-up of the coast with the following names:]
Ukaranga, Liuche

<u>27th Dec 1871</u>

Started about 8 A.M. Gave farewell to everybody, and I was earnestly impressed to give salaams to everybody in Unyanyembe. Doctor in Said bin Majid's boat, and I in Moeni Kheri's boat. Large – capable of carry 40 men comfortably. The flags were up

---

    11. Urimba in *HIFL*.
    12. Herembe is spelled Nerembe in *HIFL*, 576, but the accompanying map in the book has it as Herembe. This is an example of how challenging Stanley's handwriting can sometimes be, and explains why the editor of his dispatches to the *New York Herald* often misread proper nouns.
    13. Liuche in *HIFL*, 403; and Luiché in *LJ*, 2:162.
    14. Reading uncertain.
    15. Other angular measures are given on the map of the previous page. Unlike the usual presentation on maps, North and South are inverted.

of course each over its respective owner's head. The men rowed, lots of fun & such laughing, singing, & perspiring. Quite amusing.

Our party ashore saw us, and not to be left behind ran like good fellows. Kalulu[16] himself a kid of 6 – raced the goats & kids. & Majwara & Bill alli the other boys pricked up the donkeys. About 10, we arrived at Kirindo's – an old chief who has been very kind to the Doctor – & remarkable for his dislike to the Arabs. We were at the mouth of the Ruche – very wide river oozing out among Equisitar (pith hat trees). After some trouble we lashed the donkeys 4 feet together, having tied them standing, put 15 goats in. Took us about 5 hours – all without disorder done.

28th
The same as yesterday. Our party went afoot along the lake – following the road which sometimes led within village by the water, and again emerged from the lake grass which which[17] the neighborhood of the mouth of the Ruche abounds. Everything beautifully green the effect of the rains.
Hippopotamus plenty, and in here beautifully colored with reddish rings round the base of the ears, and over the neck. One huge fellow thought we were coming towards him and took a tremendous plunge which showed the whole length of his body.

Stopped at Mohamed bin Gharib's to bid farewell nice camp overlooking lake. Cutting wood to build his Nyumba, also for Mohamed bin Sali.
Drank coffee ate vermicelli with him, has been a great friend of Livingstone, travelled with him after.

Stop at Karah tomorrow
The mass of vegetation – enormous profusion, luxuriance, is really tropical. Seen between the Liuche & the Malagarazi.
I made use of the punting pole as a flagstaff for the American flag that my people ashore who knew it might see it – or have a better chance of doing so. The doctor seeing it so lofty[18] got jealous, and declared he would have a palm tree for the English flag.
In the soft chalk stone of which most of the cliffs, bluffs -etc- seen as we near the mouth of the Malagarazi, the surf has played strange freaks with – excavates armchair like rocks – disintegrated from the main-land. In another tumble – something like that are read of – in Melvill's Omo.[19] A tale Sandwich Isles

---

16. 'the boy of 6' crossed out.
17. 'which' repeated.
18. 'so lofty' added above the line.
19. Herman Melville, *Omoo: A Narrative of Adventures in the South Seas* (London: John Murray, 1847).

29th December 1871

At mouth Malagarazi. Arrived yesterday at 2 P.M. 18 Miles from Ukaranga. P^t Kagongo bears from mouth 215 - (on southern side). Furthest Point on Western Side (Uguhha bears 223½ . Crossed today. Occupied 4 hours. Distance 3 miles.

Length of canoe 45 feet, beam widest 5 feet. Smallest canoe 33 feet long.

Bangwe bears from P^t Kagongo 342°

P^t this side of Mohammed bin Gharib's camp 350

30th Dec. 1871

Saturday[20]

Kivoe bears from Mviga 210.

Shot a crocodile at Cape Mviga. Started this morning from Cape Kagongo, then rounding Mviga. Kivoe came in sight.

Mviga 1 hour from Kagongo.

Arrived at the mouth of the Rugufu at 9. A.M.

31st Dec 1871

Sunday[21]

Sent out boat early this morning to search for food. Got 4 doti worth just sufficient for 4 days provisions. We had heard that for 6 days nothing could be obtained. We always let the children & weakly goats have passage besides lightening the people of their baggage as much as possible.

To Kivoe 230 from P^t beyond mouth of Rugufu.

To next P^t 200 from Kivoe.

Exquisitely pretty about Kivoe adapted for Mission Stations, military stations, taking health, abundance of wood into consideration.

To P^t Misohazy 200°

January 1st 1872

Monday[22]

To P^t Utongwe[23] 190°

Our people it seems had gone on ahead for they <u>did not</u> come in last night. The sea was rough, and prevented us from proceeding.

Beyond Missohaza & between it & Kabogo some very fine trees for building canoes & there are no natives about to dispute the right of cutting down.

---

20. 'Thursday' crossed out.
21. 'Sunday' written after 'Friday' crossed out.
22. 'Monday' written after 'Saturday' crossed out.
23. 'Utongwe' written under 'Kabogo' crossed out.

Three feet above the waters edge there is found everywhere the highwater mark on the reeds & rocks showing the highest rise of the Tanganyika during the rainy season

Stopped at Sigunga for lunch beautiful bay completely land locked. An island in the middle of it.

Arrived and camped at a most beautiful retired spot the mouth of the stream Uwelasia. Our party has not yet come up. We amuse ourselves with popping at hippos & crocodiles.

January 2nd 1872

Tuesday[24]

From Kabogo to P^t Herembe 340

Beyond Herembe passed a fine bay. Excellent site for a mission or a military station, but of all <....> <....> the <....> <....> of the Malagarazi.[25] The river being navigable would shorten the distance to Unyanyembe by ten days.

To Ulimba & Kivanga Kakungu[26] mountain 175°.

Arrived at Ulimba[27] found it to be a village of timid people pitched in the most uninviting swamp. Searched for two hours for a camping place. There was none in its immediate neighborhood but I found one about 3 miles South of it at the extreme South East corner of Tongwe Bay, about a mile West of Kivanga or Kibanga Mountain, in Latitude 5.54 South

Shot a goose soon after arrival with spurs on wings.

January 3rd 1872

Wednesday[28]

Went out soon after coffee, travelled close to the Lake. Seeing nothing, struck off to rear of camp came upon a herd of zebras. At 100 yds stroke a leg, I was about giving it up as a bad shot when a zebra head of the herd galloping of at the distance of 200 yds presented a fine shot I humbled[29] him at once and as our lake party was small & the land party had not yet come in, it afforded an abundance of meat.

January 4th 1872

Thursday

Went out again but was unsuccessful though I came close upon a hartebeest. In the afternoon laid down with a fever.

---

24. 'Tuesday' written after 'Sunday' crossed out.
25. Faded page with blurred writing.
26. 'Kakungu' written above 'Kivanga' is another name of this mountain.
27. An 'r' seems to be written over 'l' and crossed out.
28. 'Wednesday' crossed out.
29. Reading uncertain.

January 5th 1872

Friday[30]

Sick of the Homa.[31] Shore party arrived all safe

Rivers Lindi & Luam flow from the East to the Lualaba.

Mabruki Speke shaves his beard. Great fun to all hands for he was so proud of it & his long face bereft of beard looked feminine

Rivers Loajeri & Mogambazi

Jan 6th 1872

Saturday

Recovering from fever. Livingstone has been only twice at a theater in his life and would not care[32] six pence to see even what people call the best.

Kabogo. We must now draw our attention to the discharge of the surplus waters of the Tanganyika remarkable freak of nature hollow, cavernous – river issuing out on the other side entering into the Lualaba – 150 yds wide low down – 40 yds far up.

Jan 7th 1872

Sunday[33]

Struck Camp – marched East – through the delta of the Loajeri[34] – 1 ½ hour march. Shot buffalo with D's gun.

Jan 8th 1872

Monday

Arrived at small stream 3 hours march. East by S from Kakungu[35] Mountain. Kirangozi lost his head so I led the way & found the ford across the wild & swollen Loajeri. He was about leading us away down into a perfect labyrinth of ravines, into a roaring cataract appalling to the ear – which had we succeded in crossing we should have fatigued ourselves without making any advance - Game abundant – Country extremely grand. Our camp is between the lofty peaks of Kakungu & Kivanga

Susi the Doctor's otherwise excellent servant- was very fond of getting gloriously drunk – at Mukungu in Urundi this habit of his occasioned us severe loss - at[36] Mokamba's place in Mugere he got into the Doctor's bed, & the Doctor half asleep thinking that it was somebody else made room for him & slept on the edge of his bed but imagine his indigna[tion] when he found half naked black Susi alongside of him.

---

30. 'Wednesday' crossed out.
31. 'Homa': a Kiswahili word for fever.
32. 'Would not care' written over in ink.
33. 'Sunday' written after 'Friday' crossed out.
34. This is Livingstone's Luajeré.
35. Stanley corrected Kagungu into Kakungu.
36. 'Mugihewa' crossed out.

D^r's son – Rupert Vincent otherwise Robert Moffat Livingstone – to be inscribed
Here lies Robert Moffat Livingstone (who enlisted in – New Hampshire Volunteers under the name of Rupert Vincent) eldest son of Dr David Livingstone the great African traveller, one of the brave men who fell before Richmond in behalf of the Union.

Died at[37] a North Carolina Hospital most likely Newbern N. C. but ask Agnes.[38]

Jan 9th 1872

Tuesday

E ½ N. 3 ½ hours. Gradually rising into the Highlands. Feel very much better. Wounded a buffalo cow. She got away, had a squint at zebra, plenty of large game. Have not come to a single native since the day of departure.

Rainy all day – miserable weather – among the mountains.

Ginger, Indigo. Sarsaparilla. Hyphene & Borassus Palms & a large fruit bearing tree called Mabyah by some Natives. The fruit is about the size of a 200[39] powder cannon ball.

Jan 10th 1872

Camp in Forest, near River.[40] 3 ½ hours East. Beautiful Park land.[41]

Jan 11th 1872

Thursday

Two hours brought us to a rivulet with slippery rocks in its bed showing action of furious torrents. Mushrooms in abundance, very large. Our road leads along the base of a range running East & West on our right.

"My Kibuyu (gourd) is dead it died at the River" said one old weather-beaten pagazi in a deploring tone.

At the third hour & a half we halted for lunch, then proceeded for 2 hours to a river, running from the South West. I believed it to be at first the Mrinia Mansu. Doctor very tired.

Had a suspicion that he was being "Rowley-fied."[42]

Jan 12th 1/72

Friday

On stream from South East running N.W. March 3 hours. The Magdala Mountain is in sight that I saw to the N. W. of my road two days after leaving Imrera.[43]

37. 'Newbe' crossed out.
38. Agnes mentioned it in her letters to Stanley, August 3 and 6, 1872, S.A. 493 and 494.
39. '2' written over '6'. But Stanley kept "600 powder cannon ball" in his book (*HIFL*, 579).
40. 'near River' added above the line.
41. Identical comparison can be found in *LJ*, 2:163, January 10, 1872: "…an English gentleman's park."
42. Word coined from Rev. Rowley (see Journal S.A. 11, January 9, 1872).
43. Mrera (*HIFL*). It is unclear whether the first letter is a capital I or a loop at the beginning of capital M.

Saw an elephant – came within 40 yds of him before I was aware of his presence. As I had no confidence in my gun, settling him at once I took the precaution to retreat before it would be too late. A large river in flood is on the right of our camp coming from S. East.

Men living on mushrooms & a large flat thick root (turnip taste) – Mbembu & Matamburu out of season – scarcity of camp – Expect & hope to reach Imrera in Rusawa to morrow have gone due East from Urimba so far to 6th day.

Jan 13th 1872
Saturday
Camped by a stream with a broad belt of timber on its banks of which canoes are made. Ate mushrooms – Crossed several ridges each of which I thought would reveal Imrera village 5 hours. E.S.E.

Jan 14th 1872
Sunday
5 hours. S. East. 2 hours from last camp crossed another river 8 yds broad – quite a volume of water – continued a South East course following the curve of a ridge which like almost all the ridges, has its eastern face lofty precipitous & scraggy,[44] dips suddenly down from the bottom of which rises another lengthy slope suddenly terminating in the same manner. After 4 hours lunched – looking down upon a grand feature of Kawendi a beautiful & extensive valley watered by a perennial stream valley, well timbered & fertile.

Saw a colony of large reddish monkeys. At 4 ½ hours crossed another river perennial, all flowing to the Rugufu

To day we sighted our Magda[la][45] Mountain, it lays E. N. E. of us – by which I knew that a S. E. course would bring me to Imrera about to morrow or the next day. I think the masika is on as well. Every day it rains pouring on or about the same hour. Beautiful bewitching country Kawendi is. To go the length of it from Imrea[46] to the Malagarazi is rather uninteresting but crossing it from Urimba to Imrera reveals its exquisite manifold hidden beauties.

Lovely folds left to the elephant buffalo & zebra. Apropos of these saw ten elephants, & came suddenly across one but I deemed it prudent to retreat. Saw a herd of gnus – if not gnus – were a fine sized animal reddish brown tails like a zebra tufted at the end (8th day[47]

---

44. 'like a' crossed out.
45. 'Hill' crossed out.
46. Imrea, ms.
47. Closing parenthesis missing.

January 15th 1/72
Monday
Went up a long valley of the deserted boma – a queer secret place – ascended boldly up to the summit of another ridge

Heard four lions roaring in concert – proceeded S. E. 2 miles

Came upon a herd of hartebe[est] & zebra fired & missed being over anxious for meat got none. Came to a stream flowing to S. West. Saw sow with young ones & wild boa[r] Camped near a stream on its banks grew an abundan[ce] of Singwe fruit.[48] African jungle very kind, one day fungus, another fruit another meat – Eland, springbok.

January 16th 1872
Tuesday
My compass took us to[49] Arrived at Imrera E. S. E. 4 ½ hours. 21 <u>days</u> from Ujiji

People very tired & hungry 6 days living on forest fruit & mushrooms. Kirangozi was very much taken aback when Imrera came in sight.

17th 1872
Wednesday
Halt. Plenty of food. People eating heartily of matama or dourra. Maize. Early sweet potatoes, & beans. What a change has come over the country then it looked all gold, and auburn in Summer heat over all. Now all is springing around us spontaneously almost before our eyes.

18th
Thursday
4 hours. S. S. E. Mrinyo Mansu River flowing to Malagarazi narrow – but deep in flood. Kirangozi lost road 2[50] times. I put him right first & gained additional honor. Doctor's & my feet very sore, we cut our shoes up to guard & protect the sores.

Wild grapes in abundance of various species[51]

Our Singwe butter having given up – we have taken to day to[52] stewing wild grapes in honey.

They hang in heavy clusters on the road side & make us wish we were two weeks or a month later.

19th Friday
S. S. E Mpokwa Stream 5 hours. Gum Copal tree, Chile Sarsaparilla

---

48. Singwe fruit: a plum-like fruit (*HIFL*, 472). It could be the *Vitex mombassae*, or 'Sungwi' in Sukuma vernacular language.

49. 'My compass took us to' added above the line.

50. '2' written over '3'.

51. 'Of various species' added above the line.

52. 'cooking' [?] crossed out.

Doctor very tired – feet getting chafed with hard walking feel ashamed of myself when riding to see him walk.

20th

[In ink, facing a column of figures]

"Livingstone's figures & writing"

Zebra weight

48 lbs

48 –

28 –

79 rump

85 D°

57 –

34 foreleg

50 hindleg

56 ½ --

54 –

43 foreleg

42 D°

41 D°

13 –

8 –

--

44) 686 ½ (15 ½[53]

[Several accounts]

860 lbs of meat

141

719 lbs of fine eatable meat issued to 44 persons[54] over 16 ¼ lbs of meat issued to each person.[55]

20th Saturday

Halt. Saw giraffe a herd eleven in number crossed Mpokwa stream – got within 150 yards of them fired several times, but could not succeed in getting one down though I envied[56] one of them its skin very much. In the afternoon tried on the Eastern side of the village on a herd of six – wounded one of them but he got off despite my efforts. What remarkable creatures they are? How beautiful their large limpid eyes? Got within 50 yards of one them[57] in the evening.

---

53. '15 ½' written over 'lbs'.
54. 'equal nearly' crossed out.
55. *LJ*, 2:165, January 22, 1872, "Mr. Stanley shot two zebras yesterday, and a she-giraffe today, the meat of the giraffe was 1000 lbs. weight, the two zebras about 800 lbs."
56. 'a skin' crossed out.
57. 'of' missing.

When after my first shot one of them shewed off like a clipper about to tack, I could have declared on oath I had wounded it tried another shot – again the same ungainly dislocating movement – Wounded another – by George was my mental exclamation – as often as I shot, so often had I wounded at least I firmly believed – but it is their gait the two legs of a side move at once, & this movement seems very singular – it is a dislocating movement – somewhat like the contortion of an Egyptian dancer, a dreamy movement where the whole body from head to tail seems to share in it. The Doctor consoled me for my non-success by stating that they were very thick-skinned & that probably having no hardened bullets, my lead balls might be sticking in their hides - so thick is the skin that it makes excellent soles for the feet.

[A map or a sketch seems to be drawn under the text.]
It is[58] why <…> the Doctor is an admirable travelling companion, none knows so well how to rejoice at one good luck in hunting, none knows so well how to console. If I killed anything if it were a zebra, did not his friend Oswell[59] the South African hunter & himself long ago come to the conclusion that zebra meat was the finest meat of Africa – and if I shot a female buffalo, why she was a perfect animal the best of her kind, her horns were worthwhile carrying as very fine specimens, & was she not fat. If I returned without anything why the game was very wild or the people had made a noise, and of course the game was frightened, then how can one stalk animals already alarmed. A most considerate companion, & knowing him to be literally truthful, why I was proud of his praise when successful & easily consoled[60] even when my conscience declared I was no shot.

Arrived at Mpokwa on this day in 3 ½ hours. Old Ibrahim who had been so proud as one slave owner came in late to camp & miserable. His slave Ulimengo or the "World" has deserted & like the[61] <c…ing> owner in the Arab caravan dreams of self advancement <…> this desertion – his <te…> food & weath[62] of salt which he was taking to Unyanyembe had gone also, I asked him how could he have been so foolish as to buy such a slave and he replied tartly. Did I not earn my cloth,? Was it not then mine? Then could I not buy what I liked?

21st Sunday
Last night Doctor took observation (Canopus) found Mpokwa, to be in latitude 6°.18". 40. S. three miles further South than I had set it down from[63] compass observation. We made a halt to day & propose to make another to morrow - the Doctor's feet

---

58. Blurred writing. Words unclear, with figures written over.
59. William Cotton Oswell.
60. 'when' crossed out.
61. Several words half-erased at the end of the page indicated <…> .
62. wealth?
63. 'from' written above 'by' crossed out.

being inflamed from bad shoes – having comfortable quarters, nice houses such as Wasavira only make – good boma, plenty of fuel – & and[64] we wished to pay any people for their famine Experiences through the wilds of Kawendi.

After coffee, at instigation of Doctor melted my zinc water[65] canteens to harden leaden bullets – made ten, went out after we had finished a few[66] cups of his[67] delicious coffee - to the small plain west of Mpokwa River & visible from the boma. I had sighted several zebra there & I was resolved we should have meat. Creeping through the narrow belt of jungle which separates the plain from the river I arrived on the verge of the plain & then commenced working a painful path through the tall & thick[68] grass taking advantage of grass grown anthills until I arrived within 175 yds from them. We[69] were face to face; there was no[70] more cover[71] left for me to take advantage of. I toyed with the Doctor's O'Reilly heavy rifle, aimed steadily, altered the sights, aimed again, lifted it up & down then feeling sure & steady I fired the right & left hand barrel at two different zebras. One dropped dead shot through the heart the other[72] shot[73] in the belly with a Frazer's shell galloped off to shade – but following his spoor I soon came up with him & planting a shot low behind the ear the poor animal sprang into[74] the air, and clapped his forelegs together as if battling with an enemy, then reeling round dropped dead. And Khamisi with a fervid Allah ho Akhbar & a look at the gun drew the butchering knife across the throat.

Bombay's dream was fulfilled, the Expedition was crying for meat. Young Kalulu, my infant cannibal and Bill-Ali another young toto[75] fond of meat was hoping & wishing the "little master" (as I was called by my people to distinguish me from the "Great Master" the Doctor) would procure meat. Bombay had dreamed that I should kill plenty of meat if I took a Mgwana soldier to cut the throat of the animal after it was shot. He[76] had told his dream to his comrades, & they had induced Khamisi. According to Bombay I owed my success to having taken Khamisi & his knife with me. The kirangozi not being included spent hours in trying to kill something but returned unsuccessful though he had been promised its equivalent in cloth if he brought meat to Camp.

---

64. '& and', ms.
65. 'water' added above the line.
66. 'few' added above the line.
67. 'his' written over 'this'?
68. 'and thick' added above the line.
69. 'We' preceded by 'I lift' crossed out.
70. 'nothing' shortened into 'no'.
71. 'cover' added above the line.
72. 'another' changed into 'other'.
73. 'through' crossed out.
74. 'into' added above the line.
75. *toto*: a Swahili word for a young one.
76. 'He' preceded by 'Khami' crossed out.

The boma of Mpokwa is the most comfortable Camp between Unyanyembe & Ujiji. Castor oil plants[77] flourish in the spaces between the huts. Always plenty of game & fish at Mpokwa. Junction of several roads to Ufipa, to Usoowa to Imrera in Kawendi - to Masungu.

Teak, Cam wood (a dye plant

[Across the page, in black ink]

"Livingstone's writing and figures"
<u>Giraffe weight</u>

Hind leg	134	lbs
Foreleg	160	--
Hind leg	136	–
Ribs	108	–
Neck	74	–
Rump	87	–
Ribs	50	–
Breastbone	46	
~~Heart &~~ Liver	20	–
Heart	6	–
Lungs	12	–
Foreleg	160[78]	

[Stanley's handwriting] Skin & head 181 lbs

993

[A calculation under 993]
[At the bottom of the page, four additions in columns with names of porters under them]

25 +33= 58 +12=70 Umtamari

45+27=72 M. Speke

47 Rojab

10+10= 20 Chanda

22nd Monday

Went out and shot a giraffe, stalked him a mile across a plain behind & West of Mpokwa, 150 yds – fired followed him 400 yds up the gentle slope of a saddle found him sick – fired again. Ended, told Khamisi to stand by while I & Bill Alli the Boy

---

77. 'Castor oil plants' followed by '& the', and a blank space.
78. '6' written over '3'.

returned to the camp to send back the soldiers, Khamisi fled up a tree, vultures pecked eyes & tongue & about 5 or 6 lbs from rump.

23rd – Tuesday. Halt – sick

24 – Wednesday   "   "

25 – Thursday   "   "

26 – Friday. Mtoni Plenty of rain. Ibrahim's slave returned minus the Posho

Livingstone's Prescription for <u>Cure of Fever</u>

3 grains resin of Jalap

2 --   Calomel

Get at Apothecaries Hall, London – pure Tincture of Cardamoms put in just enough to make into a pill to prevent irritation of stomach – An hour or a little more later give cup of pure coffe[e] <u>unsugared</u> & unmilked

3 grains of Rhubarb may be added with benefit.

27th Saturday

Long march to Misonghi 6 hours – (10 ½ hours to Mpokwa)

Set by into bees. All ran. Could not help laughing though severely bitten – 2 on nose & one on finger. Doctor behind with poor Donkey. Got bit unmercifuly about head – ran – rammed his head into a bush – ran again

Chumah squeezed them them[79] out by handfuls from his head – his head very sore – Selim also always tumbling about difficulties about red black & white ants – of course got stung bad.

But poor donkey worst of all – mouth & lips much swollen[80] –

Sunday 28th

Crossed three streams (including Usense stream.

Camped on Eastern bank of 3rd stream – Distance 2 ½ hours – E ½ N. to Mossou dis[81]. Imrera 5.30 hr – long march.

Monday, 29th

Arrived at Mrera – Ukonogo by a very good path, & much shorter to the extremely bad road we had taken when going to Ujiji.

Tuesday 30th

Halt – for people to grind food for the other wilderness in front of us – 9 days – 3 wildernesses thus – one from Urimba to Mrera Rusawa – 2nd to Imrea Ukonongo – 3rd to Maniara Ugunda – Food plentiful here. Sweet potatoes good

---

79. 'them' repeated at the beginning of the page.

80. *LJ*, 2:165, January 27, 1872: "…A swarm of bees attacked a donkey Mr Stanley bought for me, and instead of galloping off, as did the other, the fool of a beast rolled down, and over and over. I did the same, then ran, dashed into a bush like an ostrich pursued, then ran whisking a bush round my head."

81. 'North' crossed out.

Rain. Rain ever since leaving Urimba – We are to day contending for comfort, Doc and I

Wednesday, 31st

Arrived at Kamirambo's Mwaru. Met a caravan under a slave of Said bin Habeeb, gave news of Shaw's death, and of the war.

Doctor said he often wished to be buried in the depth of one of the still forests of Africa, in England there was no elbow room. He had often looked at a grave thus with uch thoughts. His wife to whom he was devotedly attached lies buried at Chipanga.

Speaking of Shaw's death he attributed it to the ruin of his constitution by excessive drunkenness at Zanzibar the same cause which has caused the deaths of his own people on the Zambezi.

Thursday, Feb 1st

Forest – E–by N. 4 ½ hours. Among the blessings of this life I count wheat bread good fresh butter, molasses, hams, bacon, caviar, &c such things as out of the pale of Europe or America one cannot get. While delirious with fever I sometimes wonder at people getting sick when they have access to such luxuries as I have mentioned & are denied to me in Africa. I fear that I shall cause surprise to some when I[82] renew my acquaintance with wheaten bread, & fresh butter.

We have salted giraffe meat & pickled zebra tongues – Ugali sweet potatoes – tea – coffe & dampers, or slap-jacks, but we have had these things so often that we begin to weary of them.

The Doctor shows me a good example by his persevering attention to the welfare of his stomach.

The D. has a good knowledge of what is seen in Africa – the trees, the fruits & their virtues & the rocks are known to him. He is full of philosophic reflections upon matters of Ethnology. Camp craft he is well up in – his bed is luxurious made out of cross sticks laid over thin parallel[83]

[Number at the left upper corner] 18

We have goats with us & we have thus milk for our tea & coffee – We have four or five parrots with us & the more lightly laden of our men have invested in Salt & propose retailing it to advantage at Unyanyembe

Doctor's donkey died yesterday

Cut initials on tree at this camp L & S. Feb 1 72[84]

---

82. 'make' crossed out.

83. End of the page. The full description of Livingstone's bed appears in Journal S.A. 11, February 1, 1872, and is repeated in *HIFL*, 600.

84. This is mentioned on February 2 in *HIFL*, 600.

Friday, Feb 2nd

Forest – 5 hours – E. by N.

Numbers of elephants. We are in Ukamba which commences from the river, which is about halfway between the camps. A goat died.

Feb 3rd Saturday. Homa

Feb 4th Sunday March 3 hours. Carried.

Feb 5. 4 hours. Monday March. Carried

Feb 6th – Carried 2 hours arrived at a spot 3 miles beyond Ukamba Tuesday

Feb 7th Wednesday 4 hours. Cut the angle which we had first made when going West. Arrived at large Ziwa, on Gombe Nullah in 4 hours. Sent 2 soldiers to Unyanyembe, Chowpereh & Ferrajji, to get letters & medicines. Am a little better to day, rode after continued fever. Went up large lake of Gombe. Extremely long should say it stretches about 20 miles. Crocodiles swarm in it. Shot one dead, lashed water with its tail.

Feb 8th – Wednesday. 1 hour to old camp on Gombe. Giraffe & Eland. Went out to hunt unsuccessful. Saw a lion.

Feb 9th – Thursday. Went out again. Soon after I went came upon a group of three lions who roared in concert. They did not see me. Hunted all morning shot an eland & an hartebeest but got neither. Received a present of choroko (field peas) honey & sweet potatoes from chief of Manyara. About 1 P.M. we struck camp & marched for Manyara which place we reached about 5 P.M. The Sultan was at the gate of his village to receive us & insisted that his friend should lodge in his boma. Here was an instance of that disposition to sincere friendship with meritorious strangers which I ascribe to the chiefs in general in Central Africa where they have not been spoilt by the Arabs. I was one of the first travellers & the very first among white men who have visited Ukonongo & Kawendi & I have always found the chiefs very ready to meet me more than half way.

Feb 10th Friday. To the Ziwani under the huge Mkuyu Sycamore. Arrived about 2 P.M., having breakfasted on the road. The Doctor reads his list of small stores just arrived at Unyanyembe, and as I heard him utter -6 jars of jam -3 Tins of Biscuits, loaf Sugar, potted ham my fevered brain would dwell on these luxuries all day & on the promise of the Doctor that we would have our Christmas feast in earnest after all our disappointment.

Feb 11th. Saturday. Arrived in 5 hours at Kwikuru. Several caravans are met. The news that the white man having gone through all the country safe & is now returning to Unyanyembe has had the effect of inducing the mean souled Arabs to try their precious lives[85] on a similar venture. They have been calculating to a nicety the

---

85. 'lives' written over 'life'.

number of months I have been absent & know as well as I know myself how long I have been absent. Exaggerated reports of the progress made by the Arabs[86] in the war with Mirambo reach us daily. The fiery old Sheikh Said bin Majid angered for the loss of his eldest son Soud bin Said plunged into the war without hesitation & attacked Usagozi & the other villages under Simba the son of Moto, with considerable success.

Feb 12th Monday.
A halt to grind food for our last effort for Unyanyembe
I never fancied myself more like a newspap[er] than I did when at Ujiji with such an attentive listener as Livingstone. There we sat until late in the evening long after the sun had set long after the noise of the ramblers & loungers of the Broad way had ceased & long after the stars had appeared in the milky heaven above. I had something to say the whole time something new to relate which drew from my listener sympathetic exclamations. I never thought I had such a good memory a hundred events that I had already consigned to oblivion as things of no concern now were recalled and dressed up as my fluency allowed.

Thani bin Abdullah was a notable gaillard[87] among the noticeable Arabs who came to see me.

[Ink]

15th Forest
16th Kigandu
17th Inesuka
18th Unyanyembe
[Figures in columns]
4 + 31 + 18 = 53[88]

20th S.
10 - Sept
31 oct
30 Nov
31 Dec
<u>18</u>
100
1 Jan
31 Jan[89]

---

86. 'reach' crossed out.
87. 'gaillard': French for robust and lively.
88. This is probably the count of days to reach Unyanyembe from Ujiji: 4 days in December, 31 in January, and 18 in February.
89. This could be the count of the days Stanley traveled on his round trip to and from Ujiji: 10 days in September, 31 in October, 30 in November, 18 in February, and 31 in January.

Livingstone intends going to Ufipa crossing Rungwa River striking South & rounding the Southern head of Tanganyika 8° 4 2" S., make a southwesterly course for Chicumbis on the Luapula – crossing Luapula thence direct west to the copper mines of Katanga then[90] to a point 8 days South – about the fountains[91] mysterious & sacred, then return by Katanga to the underground houses of Rua 10 days North East – then to Lake Kamolondo[92] & by River Lufiri to Lake Lincoln thence back to Lualaba to explore the fourth Lake which he thinks will resolve the last link which is to connect this mighty Lualaba with the White Nile. He thinks it will not take more than a year & a half but I think a little over two years & we shall certainly see Livingstone himself, who will have volumes to say about the virgin Land discovered & explored. I have compared these meditated travels with those already accomplished & I fear he cannot do them in less time than two years.

[Page crossed with two lines]
Unyanyembe
Fruit, Onions Rice, holcus, sorghum, dourra or matama, maize, beans choroko - or field peas, ro..[93]–like almonds, or pistachios – peanuts – sweet potatoes, cucumbers – bananas – papaws chutney – mango, lemons citrons - a few grapes raised by Khamis bin Abdullah, milk, butter, eggs – wheat.

[Each paragraph crossed with two lines]
Visited Sheikh Sultan bin Ali – who held the rank similar to a colonel in the army of Sayed Barghash @ $ 1200 per annum – who persisted in believing that his Muscat flint-lock was superior to the Winchester repeating Rifle until 14 shots were fired in succession from it. He gave us some wheat bread, some cakes fried in ghee – and a bountiful supply of lemonade, to our men he gave an ox.
Arabs fighting or rather indulging in the usual course of slow generals. Inactivity everywhere while attempting to starve (or hoping to do so) Mirambo. They themselves having no organized transport yet made requisitions on the Arabs who remained in Unyanyembe, while they had no means to convey the provision.

[Two lines across each paragraph of the page]
A great many Wanyamwezi made application to go to the Coast, but would go nowhere that took them Westerly

---

90. 'back' crossed out.
91. 'about the fountains' written over 'then return'.
92. 'Kamolondo' with 'K' written over 'C'.
93. Word unintelligible.

At a village near Ugunda we halted, and obtained a house where I[94] suffered from fever. I noticed that a fly had gone under my pyjamas & irritated by its pertinacity to remain there I killed.

After arriving at Unyanyembe I found I had a[95] pimple on the leg, which soon assumed the appearance of an inflamed boil, which pained me excessively. The pain woke me often at night, as if a pin was being driven towards the bone. Consulting the Doctor he remembered from the description I gave of it that he had suffered the like & found worms - or that the pain was caused by the worm working itself in. Pressing upon the boil a white[96] worm very like a large maggot[97] half an inch long & thick in proportion made its appearance. On being extracted in a couple of days the sore had closed up, & the inflammation & irritating pain having ceased after extraction. This is one of the afflictions that African travellers suffer. The Doctor said he found no less than twenty one feeding on his living body.

[Three lines across the page]

Banians[98]

No supplies, mistake to suppose the Doctor gets his supplies or letters

---

Doctor's plans

Doctor don't want rest, but supplies. The Herald Cor[99] turned over to him from stor[100] of Expedition 9 Bales, 14 Bags of Beads or 28 frasillah of the beads most needed in this country -350 lbs brass wire —a small boat to cross river & a selected supply of tools beside revolvers carbines & several hundred rounds of ammunition.

Doctor's supplies always have been entrusted to the most worthless of men which was a grave fault[101]

Doctor's appearance

[Crossed with two parallel lines]

Mweni Makaya was the first that visited Manyema. Died from abscess of liver at Unyanyembe.

---

94. 'was' crossed out.
95. 'pimple on the leg' written above 'sore' crossed out.
96. 'white' added above the line.
97. 'made' crossed out.
98. A term used in Zanzibar for Hindus trading such commodities as silk, cotton cloth, glass beads, rice, and tobacco for ivory and copal. They were also active as moneylenders.
99. Correspondent.
100. Abbreviation for 'stores'?
101. This echoes Livingstone's complaint about the loss he was subjected to due to slaves employed by Dr. Kirk to convey his goods. See Appendix, Letters from Dr. Livingstone to Stanley, Unyanyembe, March 14, 1872, S.A. 477. Stanley copied this letter in his journal as "an order" given to him by Livingstone, S.A. 11.

Very neat round dishes are made of light wood by Wanguana & Wanyamuezi

[Ink]

525

459

300

350

<u>525</u>

2059

[Two lines across the two first paragraphs]
Things very dear in Unyanyembe just now 1 egg 1 khete formerly 4 eggs for 1 khete

For Mʳ Webb[102]

1 Spear with ball at end

2 Heavy Manyema Spears

3 Unyamwezi small ones

For Children Livingstone

1 Large Unyamwezi Spear

1   "   Manyema   "

1 Spear with knob at end

3[103] Unyamwezi Spears

Broken Spear to be kept for Doctor

[Not crossed out]

1 doz Pt[104] Champagne to Doctor

Dʳ Kirk will pay me £500 if he has money in that case I am to destroy draft on Ritchie Stuart & Co Bombay drawn by Livingstone. If Kirk has no money then I am to use draft.[105] [Crossed out with two lines from I am to destroy…]

[Not crossed out]

If Bennett gives anything for letter send it to Coutts & Co to be divided among his children.

---

102. W. F. Webb, big game hunter and old friend of Livingstone. "Webb and Oswell were fellow-travellers and mighty hunters … [I] admired the true Nimrod class for their great courage, truthfulness, and honour" (*LJ*, 2:66), October 4, 1870. Webb's hunting trophies and collection of weapons were displayed in his estate of Newstead Abbey (cf. Photograph of the Dining Hall in Richard Allen, *A Souvenir of Newstead Abbey*, Nottingham, 1874). Another load (a knife and leglets) for Webb is mentioned in S.A. 10, p. 9.

103. '3' written over '4'.

104. Pint.

105. Livingstone mentioned it under March 10, 1872, and expressed the sum in rupees. *LJ*, 2:173.

Gorillas plenty in Manyema[106]

The Doctor will not travel in coming home through the rain – Masika – It would be too terrible an exposure because of the Makata & other swamps & streams.[107]

1)[108]
1[109] portmanteau
✓ ~~Sadala~~ Ujiji 2 ½

2)
Box Cartridges (Tin Box)
✓ ~~Zaidi~~
5 ~~doti~~ Unyanyembe
1 doti Kwikuru

3)
Winchester & Starr Cartridges[110]
Rojab 3 doti – Ujiji
[Perpendicularly]
Powder
Buckshot
& Starr C.

4)
Powders
[On the left corner] 4 Doti
[Transversally] Unyanyembe
[On the right corner] 1 doti Imrera
✓ Saboori Mkuba

---

106. Stanley did not travel to Manyema with the *New York Herald* Expedition. He may have heard this from Livingstone who could have mistaken chimpanzees for gorillas.

107. From here most of the notebook regards the division of the goods between Stanley and Livingstone at Unyanyembe, and the preparations for Stanley's last trek to the Coast.

The reading should go backwards from the notebook's end, as it is rendered here.

108. This list or inventory of loads with carriers' names could be the balance of each carrier's account for the Ujiji–Unyanyembe leg.

109. '1' written over '2'.

110. Stanley had several rifles, and two Starr breech loading carbines, not counting revolvers. The Starr cartridges could be for his carbines or his revolvers. The Starr Company produced large quantities of both carbines and revolvers for the U.S. government during the American Civil War. It went out of business in 1867.

5)
1 Bale
~~Hamadi 5 doti – Ujiji~~

6) [The following crossed out with one line]
 2 Bale
~~Ferousi~~ 5 doti – Ujiji

7)
 3 Bale
5 Doti
Baraka
~~1 doti took at Imrera~~
[Transversally] ~~Unyanyembe~~

8)
Beads
~~Khamisi~~ (3)
~~1 shukka at Gombe Nullah~~
[Transversally] Unyanyembe

9)
~~Bed & cloths 1 doti Imrera~~
~~Chowpereh~~
~~5 doti~~
[Transversally] Unyanyembe

10)
Star.Cartridge
~~Kitanda~~
[Perpendicularly on the left] 3 Powder 3 Winchester 6 Starr
Kingaru
1 " Imrera
1 shuka Ujiji
2 ½ Unyanyembe

11)
~~1 portmanteau~~
~~Muccadum~~
~~1 doti Kwikuru~~

2 ½ doti

[Transversally] Unyanyembe

12) ~~Tent 1 doti Unyanyembe~~[111]

~~Ibrahim Kisesa~~

~~5 Doti~~

1 Doti – Ujiji

~~4　"　– Unyanyembe~~

13) ~~Pots and kettles~~

~~Ferajji~~

~~5 doti~~   Unyanyembe [written across the page]

~~Kaimna~~

~~Kitanda~~

~~1 ½ doti – Unyanyembe~~

½ doti　　Imrera

Butter

Marora 2 ½ doti. Ujiji

~~Palm Oil~~

1 doti

~~Bill Alli . Unyanyembe~~

1 doti paid to woman for mischief done in the market place at Ujiji[112]

Drive goats[113]

1 doti

Saboori Mdogo Unyanyembe

1 doti Kwikuru

Umtamani

Chain 2 ½ doti

Unyanyembe

~~Ibrahim Marora~~

~~Tin box Doctor~~

~~3 doti Ujiji~~

1 doti not to pay in Unyanyembe

Mabruk Marora

Tin Box Doctor

Doubtful

5 doti Ujiji

---

111. It is unclear whether writing was crossed out or horizontal lines were traced to divide the page.

112. Cf. Journal S.A. 11, December 13, 1871. Billali had made a row at the market in Ujiji, p. 62. 1 doti seems to be a fine taken off his salary.

113. Sketch of a map under the writing of this page.

2 doti Maganga ~~5 doti~~
~~Sundries belonging to the Doctor~~
~~Ulimengo~~
~~Salt & Box Tin [...?] & cartridges~~
29 lbs + 19 = 48

22 ………………………………..with loads
2 …………………………….2 Kirangozis
1 …………………………….Bombay
1 …………………………….Selim
1 …………………………….Susi
1 …………………………….Gardner
1 …………………………….Mabruk
1 …………………………….Hamoidach
1…………………………….~~Chandah~~
1 …………………………….Seradi
1 …………………………….Chumah
2 …………………………….2 Women

39   37
1 doti Imrera
lllllllll[114]

Kombo 1 doti Kwikuru
Kaif Halleck 1 shukka

Mabruk Unyany[embe]
  Ambari
  Mabruki Speke
Jumah
Asmani
3 boys
  Kombo

42

~~Ferajji~~
Marora   2 ½ doti
Kingaru   ½
Ferousi   5
Hamadi   5
Rojab   3
Sadala   2 ½

---

114. These nine strokes could be the fine for the nine names at right.

        18 ½
Ibrahim 5
        23 ½

Ibrahim Marora 5
Mabruk Ferous 5
Mabruk Unyanyembe
Chanda
[Same page but written upside down]
Kasagera 2 ½
Inesuka 3
Mkwekwe 2
Quihara 1 ½

Moeni-Kheri makes Moeni Makaia to bring coffee & tea with him to Ujiji.
E. M. Reilly & Co. New Oxford Street, London[115]

Lancaster Breech Loading Double Barreled Rifle
Bishop of Bond Street
Blissett 322 High Holborn London[116]
Tin Boxes wanted – Covered with Leather[117]
feet inche
  2. 6 long
  1. 1 wide
  1. 3 deep

The fever
At first you are apt to think this disease contemptible. As violent, though not quite so long you laugh at it in much the same way as you would at the other. To give a correct idea of it perhaps would be to compare, Havre to Southampton takes 5 hours. Barcelona to Marseilles 5 hours. New York to So & So 5 hours. Send a person unaccustomed to sea in a cockleshell of a boat & let him get thoroughly sick – then great prostration, & weakness. Land him in this state where is half starvation, & cheerless faces & surroundings. Before he has quite recovered, give him another dose in about a week, the third in about 2 weeks, the fourth in about 3 weeks & so on, sometimes varying these courses by crowding 4 attacks into a month he would have a pretty fair idea of

    115. This address and the following are bracketed together.
    116. 'Bissett … London' written with blue pencil.
    117. 'feet 2 1/3 long' crossed out.

the pain & anguish, of a real jungle attack without the effects. A man over 25 is apt to feel it more than a boy or a younger man. When in Arkansas State boy of 16, I used shake the fever off, much as a dog does water.

	doti		
2 Susi	9	18	✓
2 Hamoidah		18	✓
4 Chowpereh		36	✓
5 Kirangozi		45	✓
5[118] Jumah		45	-
3 Rehani		27	✓
4 Majwara		36	[blue pencil]
2 Saboori Mkuba		18	[blue pencil]
2 Ferousi			✓
~~1 Bombay~~			
3 Baraka		27	[blue pencil]
5 Ambari		45	✓
2 Chanda		18	[blue pencil]
5 Hamadi		45	✓ [blue pencil]

List of all souls[119] [Some names are preceded by a dash.]

1 Dr Livingstone
1 H. M. Stanley
1 Selim ✓
1 Bombay ✓
3 Boys ✓
~~2 Women~~
2 Kirangozis ✓
1 - Sadala ✓
1 - Zaidi ✓
~~1 - Rojab~~
1 - Saboori Mkuba ✓
1 - Hamadi ✓

---

118. '5' written over '4'.
119. This should be the list of members of the caravan when marching from Lake Tanganyika to Unyanyembe. The crossed-out individuals were part of the caravan.

1 Ferousi ✓
1 Baraka ✓
1 - Khamisi ✓
1 - Chowpereh ✓
1 - Kingaru ✓
1 - ~~Muccadum~~
1 ~~Ibrahim Kisesa~~ ✓
1 - ~~Ferajji~~
1 - Kamna ✓
1 - ~~Marora~~
1 - Bill Alli ✓
1 - Saboori Mdogo ✓
1 - Umtamani ✓
1 Ibrahim Maroro ✓
1 Mabruk ✓
1 - Maganga ✓
1 - Ulimengo ✓
1 - Mabruk Unyanyenbe ✓
1 Ambari ✓
1 - Mabruki Speke ✓
1 - Jumah ✓
1 - Asmani ✓
1 - Kombo ✓
1 Susi ✓
1 Hamoidah ✓
~~1 Gardner~~
1 Chumah ✓
1 Kaif Halleck
1 Halimah ✓ [~~left~~, in front of Halimah] 44 souls
1 Misossi ✓
Chandah ✓
2 pagazis
Sarmate
Uredi
Umgareza
~~Mabruk Saleem~~

The camp is a glorious place after all. Much better than the settled boma because more cheerful.

Tent. short side slope
Ft in
11. 8. slope length
5.   "   wall height
9.[120] "   side length

long side
Ft in
6. 10 slope length
5.   "   wall height
14. "   side length

length of pole – up to the top ring of the small tent pole

Mabruki Speke was like the man in Gurney Married[121] who sometimes blurted his thoughts out aloud.

Asked an Arab who came to visit if any[122] one had tried to raise oranges – Ujiji- Mabruki seeing that my mussulman friend
[Sentence incomplete. Rest of the page with figures and calculation related to tent]

[Page widthwise]
[Sketch of Stanley's route from North of Malagarazi to Tongwe (by canoe), and from Tongwe to Unyanyembe].

Africans
Easily to be frightened – great cowards true brothers of him who made the reply to Gen. Grant after Fort Donelson about glory.[123]
Women raise the chant upon every occasion of an arrival or a departure. If an arrival the chant is taken up as they are known to have arrived, & is soon ended for the greetings. If on departure for war

---

120. '9' written over '14'.
121. Theodore E. Hook, *Gurney Married: A Sequel to Gilbert Gurney* (London: Henry Colburn, 1838).
122. 'Any' written above 'no' crossed out.
123. This refers to Grant's victory against the Confederates at Fort Donelson, Tennessee (February 1862).

[Page widthwise]

[Sketch of the tent with D. Livingstone reading in the front of it, and Stanley on the right?]

[Left part blank]

Kinan de re re
Kinan de re re Kitunga
One of the[124] chorus used by the boatmen of the Lake

Another is
O mama re de mi ky
Mama re de mi ky

Another is   The singer is
~~O leo o leo~~   O ela par da miti
Chorus
mete mama

D[r] L.
had no tent with him when he goes again it will be with a complete new fit out.[125] He certainly relates startling things about the Missionaries who have had connection with the Makololo. Rev[d]. Fairbrother "late Missionary from China" now 30 years ago since he returned made Secretary of Funds for L. M. Society[126] said that L. was morally guilty of Helmore's death, a poor man who fell a victim to the fever at Linyanti, Sekeletu's place.[127] Price also who married his wife's sister also abused him at the Cape, & this was a man who boasted to Sir Thos. Mac Lear how if the natives bother him how[128] he would soon[129] show his revolvers & said that he had flogged several Makololo, by tying them to his wagon wheel. He seems to have been somewhat of the same nature as Stern in Abyssinia, & therefore unfortunate.

---

124. 'why' crossed out.
125. outfit.
126. London Missionary Society.
127. The Helmores, a missionary family, had planned to settle at Linyanti but did not receive the expected help from Chief Sekeletu. The whole family but two children died from malaria and hardship (1860). Livingstone was not there to welcome them and was made responsible for their tragic end.
128. 'how' added above the line.
129. 'soon' added above the line.

Hours[130]	
Mtoni Mtambu	4 ½
Camp near River	4 ½
Camp on River	3
Mpokwa	4 ¾
Mtoni	6
Misonghi	4 ½
Mtoni	4 ½
Mrera	5 ½
Mwaru	5 ½
Mtoni	4
Pori[131]	4
Pori	4
Tongoni	4
Gombe Nullah	7
Maniara	4 ¼
Ziwani	6 ½
Kwikuru	4
Benta	5
Ugunda	3 ¼
Kiganda	7
~~Kasagera~~	
Mesuka	4 ¾
Unyanyembe [132]	3 ½
	104
Shaw[133]	$100
Selim	$150
Bombay	20
Mabruki Speke	37
Zaidi	27
Baraka	27
Chowpereh	27
Bill Alli	25

---

130. Duration of daily journey.
131. *Pori* is Kiswahili for bush.
132. These are the stops from Lake Tanganyika to Unyanyembe according to the sketch of this notebook.
133. Salaries already paid? When starting the march from Lake Tanganyika, news of Shaw's death had not yet reached Stanley.

Kamna	27
Sadala	6
Rojab	6
Saboori Mkuba	6
Hamadi	6
Ferousi	6
Kingaru	12
Muccadum	6
Ferajji	27
Marora	6
Saboori Mdogo	6
Umtamari	6
Ulimengo	70
Mabruk Unyanyembe	6
Ambari	27
Jumah	27
Asmani	20
Kombo	6
Khamisi	31
	$720

Sarmine	52
Uredi Manua Sera	52
Umgareza	7
Mabruk Saleem	27
	$878

[Page widthwise]

Roof 17 feet long side[134]
Half 8 ½
Roof 8 ½ feet short side
35 feet canvass on long side
19 feet "   " short side
54:3
18 yards to make roof for long tent

---

134. Measurements for the tent.

[Figures]

To Zanzibar[135]

Honey
1 Tent
1 Box. Sundries
1 "   Necessaries
1 Bale
1 "
1 "
1 "
1 "
1 "
1 Cooking Pots
1 Doctor's Box
1 Spears & Skins
1 Skins
1 Fat & Butter
1 Bed & Clothes
1 Tea Salt & Sundries
1 Kitanda
1 Flour & ~~Rice~~
~~1 Rice~~
~~1 Tarpaulin~~
1 Choroko
1 Cartridges
~~19 loads~~
1 Tent
1 Coffee & Sugar
Writing tray for Trunk 30 inches x 14 inches wide [sketch]

N.B. Take on board Ship or Steamer

1 doz Bottles or Tins of Assorted Jam
1 Bott Pickles

---

135. List of the loads of Stanley's caravan to Zanzibar?

½ doz Sardines

½ " Anchovies

3 Pots Caviare

1 doz Tinned Fruit

1 cheese

2 Tins of Crackers

Confections

Cakes

Oranges

Potted Salmon

Raisins

Apples

1 Bott. Anchovy Sauce for fish

1st Box opened[136]

4 Shirts

2 Ps Shoes

Stockings

Shoe Strings

2nd Box opened

Candles

3rd Box opened

2 Mulligtawney Soup

10 Mutton   "

4th Box opened

12 Boxes Game Soup

5th Box

1 doz Giblet Soup

6th box

4[137]   Bott. Salt

1   "   Worcester Sauce

2[138]   "   Reading   "

---

136. An inventory of Livingstone's stores sent by Kirk to Livingstone that never made it beyond Tabora because of the war. Stanley had secured them, together with his own loads, before marching to Ujiji. (See details in Journal S.A. 11, February 19, 1872).

137. '4' written over '2'.

138. '2' written over '5'.

5	"	Harvey	"
1	"	Essence Anchovies	
2	"	Pepper	
3	"	Mustard	

7th Box
2 loafs Sugar

8th Box
3 Tins Biscuits 1 Cheese
6 Potted Hams
5 Jam
3 Curry
[Figures in ink] 459 + 450 + 300 =1209

9th Box
2 soaps. Sugar

10th Box
Candles

11th Box
10 Mulligatawny Soup
2 Mutton Soup

1 Kiweeh
2 Maguru Mafupi
3 Mapokera
4 Magomba
5 Kisewa
6 Mohanza
7 Kifukuru
8 Watikira

Wagogo Sultans [Rest of the page blank]

Mabruki Speke[139] 1
~~Kombo~~ 2
Mabruk Unyanyembe 3
Umtamani 4
~~Saboori Mkuba~~ 5
Chanda 6
~~Saboori Mdogo~~ 7
Umgareza 8
Chowpereh 9
Muccadum 10
Uredi 11
Ulimengo 12
Bombay 13
Kamma 14
Ferajji 15
Maganga 16
Jumah 17
Billalli 18
Zaidi 19
Hamadi 20
Sarmine 21
Ambari 22
Khamisi 23
Baraka 24
Kingaru 25
Asmani 26
Rojab 27

[Added on the left, without number] Sadala
[On the left, a small sketch of map of the stops] Itaga, Mrinia Mansu

Kalulu 25
Selim 26
Majwara 27

---

139. This is probably the list of soldiers who accompanied Stanley from Unyanyembe back to Zanzibar. Three names are crossed out: Kombo, Saboori Mkuba, and Saboori Mdogo. These three had been recruited at Quihara on September 17, 1871, with no mention of the length of the contract (see Contract of Saboori Mkuba, Saboori Mdogo, and Kombo, S.A. 4748). They may have remained in Unyanyembe. By giving stores to Livingstone, Stanley was less in need of soldiers.

Billalli   28
Given to the Doctor

---

38 Coils Wire

Beads

Canvas left

13   feet
 7   "
25   "
22   "
15   "
22 ½ "
24 ½ "
132 ~~cloth~~ : 3 = 44 yds
          4
       48 ½ yds

[On the right side of the page] 14 ½ / 3 = 4 ½ f

Cut Cloths

---

8 doti Kaniki

18 ½ Merikani

12 doti Cold Cloths

31 Merikani

16 ½

60

107 ½ doti

1 Bombay	✓	o	3	doti	✓	7 Rojab	✓	3 "	✓
2 Mabruk (Unyanyembe		o	3	"	✓	8 Muccadum	✓✓	3 "	
3 Sadala	✓✓		3	"	✓	9 Bill Alli	✓	3 "	✓
4 Umtamani	✓✓		3	"	✓	10 Jumah	✓	o 3 "	✓
5 Mabruk Speke	✓	o	3	"	✓	11 Chanda	✓✓	3 "	✓
6 Maganga	✓		3	"	✓	12 Ferajji	✓✓	3 "	✓

13 Asmani		✓ 3	"	✓	25 Chowpereh & wife		✓4 "	✓
14 Kamna		✓ 0 3	"	✓	26 Umgareza		0 3 "	✓
15 Saboori Mdogo		0 4	"	✓	27 Sarmine		✓25 "	✓
16 Saboori Mkuba		✓ 6	"	✓	28 Kingaru		✓✓	✓
17 Ulimengo		✓✓ 3	"	✓	~~29 Ibrahim~~			
18 Kombo		✓ 0 4	"	✓	30 Hatib		✓	
19 Hamadi		✓ 3	"	✓	31 Majwara		✓✓	
20 Khamisi		✓✓ 3	"	✓	32 Surmiti		✓✓	
21 Baraka		✓✓ 3	"	✓	33 Umbaluku		✓	
22 Zaidi		✓ 3	"	✓	34 Hamdallah		✓✓	
23 Uredi		0 25	"	✓				
24 Ambari		✓ 3	"	✓				
					Billali			
					Kalulu			
					Selim[140]			

Rojab
Bale 1   Doti
5 Gorah Merikani   37 ½
10 "   Kaniki   20
                           57 ½

Ulimengo
Bale 2
5   Merikani   37 ½
10   Kaniki   20
                           57 ½

n° 37 Chanda
Bale 3
5   Merikani   37 ½
10   Kaniki   20
                           57 ½

Maganga
Bale 4
5   Merikani   37 ½
10   Kaniki   20
                           57 ½

---

140. On the right side, names of the three boys, 'Bill Alli', 'Kalulu', and 'Selim', without numbers.

Muhongo
Bale 5
3 Merikani	22 ½
9 Doti Ulyah	9
3 " Joho	3
20 Kaniki Ulyah	20
	54 ½

Mabruk (Unyanyembe)
~~Muccadum~~[141]

Muhongo
~~Nawadi~~ Shimli [?]
Bale 6
2 Gorah Merikani	15
6[142] Black Joho	6
8 Kaniki Ulyah	6
4 Gorah Kunguru	24
10 " hkfs	20
10 " Barsati	20
	101

~~Bale 7~~
~~2 Gorah Merikani~~ }
~~Doti mixed~~   } 32

~~Hatib~~ Mabruk Kisesa
1 Black Portmanteau

~~Hamadi Mabruk Kisesa~~
Hamadi
1 Doctor's Black Box

Chowpereh
Bed & clothes ✓
Ferajji
Cooking Utensils ✓

~~Baraka~~ Kombo
5 doti
1 Tent Cover ✓

---

141. 'Muccadum' crossed out and circled.
142. '6' written over '5'.

Saboori MKuba
1 wall of tent ✓

Umbaluku
1 Bag of Rice ✓

Hamdallah
1 Bag of Rice ✓

Ambari
1 Bag of flour ✓

~~Ulimengo~~ Kingaru
Flour Coffee
1 Bag of Choroko ✓

~~Marora~~ Baraka
Butter ✓

Khamisi
Kitanda ✓

Umtamani
~~Spears~~ & Skins ✓

Sadala
1 Black Portmanteau ✓

Asmani
1 Black Portmanteau ✓

Majwara
1 New Tin Box ✓

For Pagazis
5 Gorah Merikani   37 ½
15   "   Kaniki   30
2 Red Kunguru   10
 4 Blue   "   8
13 " Dabwani   13
Barsati   23
Sohari & Ismahili   17
Hkfs   22
            Doti 160 ½
Stray   Doti 16
                  32
Total   Doti 208 ½

Bill Alli

~~1 Bundle Cartridges & Sundries~~

Salt

Soups

Cigars

Cheese

Doctor's Spears

Sarmine

1 Sugar

Cartridges

Zaidi ✓

Marora

1 Bag Curiosaties[143] ✓

For the Doctor[144]

1)

		doti
4 Gorah Merikani		30
5 "	Kaniki	10
5 "	Dabwani	10
5 "	Barsati	10
5 "	Hkfs[145]	10
5 "	Rehani	10
5 "	Ismahili	<u>10</u>
	Doti	90

2)

4 Gorah Merikani		30
5 "	Kaniki	10
5 "	Hkfs	10
5 "	Barsati	10
5 "	Ismahili	10
5 "	Rehani	10
5 "	Barsati	<u>10</u>
	Doti	90

    143. 'Curiosa' was first written, then changed into 'Curiosaties'. This was probably the bag of items that Stanley brought back to Livingstone's friends.

    144. Each bale left to the Doctor has roughly the same value and consists of a sampling of the various kinds of cloth in demand.

    145. Hkfs: handkerchiefs.

3)

4		Merikani "	30
5	"	Kaniki "	10
5	"	Hkfs "	10
4	"	Barsati "	8
5	"	Rehani "	10
5	"	Sohari "	10
		Doti	78

4)

4		Merikani -	30
5		Kaniki -	10
5	"	Hkfs -	10
5	"	Rehani -	10
5	"	Dabwani -	10
		Doti	70

5)

4 Gorah Merikani -		30
5	Kaniki -	10
5	Hkfs -	10
5	Rehani -	10
5	Sohari -	10
		70

6)

4 Gorah Merikani			30
5	"	Kaniki	10
5	"	Rehani	10
5 ½	"	Dabwani	11
5	"	Hkfs	10
		Doti	71

7)

4 Gorah Merikani			30
5	"	Kaniki Ulyah	10
3	"	" "	6
5	"	Rehani	10
5	"	Hkfs	10
2 Pieces Kunguru Red			10
		Doti	76

8)
4 Gorah Merikani	30
2 Pieces Kunguru Red	12
10 Rehani	20
4 Gorah Rehani	8
Doti	70

9)
6 Gorah Merikani 7 ½	45
18 ½ Gorah Rehani	37
Doti	82

Bale[146]

1	90
2	90
3	78
4	70
4	70
6	71
7	76
8	70
9	82
Doti	697

[Column at left]
697 doti
16[147] Bags Beads
38 Coils wire
1 Tent
1 Air Bed
1 Boat
1 Bag of Tools`
2 kegs of Tar
12 sheets Copper
3 Canvas Bags

---

146. A summing up of the bales of cloth, the total of 697 doti being half of Stanley's 1,393 doti of cloth.

147. '16' written over '14'.

[Column at right]
Clothes
2 carbines
2 revolvers
Amunition

[Pencil] 696 + 697 =1393
[Ink] 9 + 16 + 1 + 2 + 1 + 1 + 1 + 4 = 35

[Pencil]

[Figures in ink in the upper right corner] 1393: 2 = 696 ½

   1 : 1 Tent
   2 : 1 Tent
   3 : 1 Bale
   4 : 1 "
   5 : 1 "
   6 : 1 "
   7 : 1 "
   8 : 1 "
   9 : 1 Box
 10 : 1 "
 11 : 1 "
 12 : 1 "
 13 : 1 Skins
 14 : 1 Bed & Bag clothes
 15 : 1 Kitanda
 16 : 1 Butter
 17 : 1 Choroko
 18 : 1 Pots & Pans
 19 : 1 Cartridges
 20 : 1 Spears
 21 : 1 Sugar & Coffee
 22 : Flour
 23 : Rice
 24

Merikani

	4 –	30
	4 –	30
	4 –	0
	4 –	30
	4 –	30
	4 –	30
	4 –	30
	4 –	30
	6 –	45
38	doti	285

[First column crossed out with two vertical lines in ink]

Kaniki	Gorah	38	76
Dabwani		20 ½	41
Barsati		14	28
Hkfs		35	70
Rehani		63 ½	127
Ismaili		10	20
Sohari		10	20
Kunguru Red		4	22
			689
4 gorah Rehani			8
		doti	697

Field Notebook S.A. 10, Full Transcript

[This notebook is written in pencil, unless otherwise stated.]

[Sketch of the front view of a large house]

Almanach of 1868 pasted

[?] Pagazi loads or 11 donkey loads
16
1 Sungo
2 Sam
1 Bubu[1]
[?] Ka [?? of ? ea]
18 Bo[at?]
38

[Part of the text erased]
<u>Bombay accuses Burton</u>
Since Burton has said about[2] every thing that happened on the r[oa]d to Ujiji. Did he tell what he took with him from <...>? No. Why did he have not tell about the skull he picked [up?] and that he told us to put [in?] rice baskets. I think he ought to have left that out.
Said I, oh that <...> good thing, th[?] <...> [<...> the shelves in t[he ...] Royal <...> of London full of skull all parts of the world.
Bombay has <...> h[?]d.[3]

[Ink] [Upside down] 25 x 70 = 1750

---

1. *Sungo-mazzi, sami-sami,* and *bubu* are names of beads for trade (*HIFL,* 23).
2. 'about' added above the line.
3. While commenting on Bombay and the other men of the Expedition, Stanley mentions that Bombay witnessed Burton collecting human skulls (*HIFL,* 347). These lines are hardly readable.

To day this 13th
[On the left, column of names of places; on the right, calculations and numbers]
Sheesa   34 + 45 =79   14 + 32 = 46
Kigwa
Rubuga   2f   5 - - 36   (75
Mtoni
~~Tura~~
Tura   84
Madetita[4]
Mtoni

K   Doti   54
_____

[The following list is entirely crossed out name by name]

~~Hamadi————————8————————1~~   Joho   6 [not crossed out]
~~Rojab—————————10———————2~~
~~Ulimengo————————10———————3~~
~~Chanda—————————10———————4~~
~~Maganga————————10———————5~~
~~Mabruk Unyanyembe———10———————6~~
~~Sh?......————————————?~~
~~Mabruk Kisesa—————?~~
~~Kombo—————————5~~
~~Ferrajji——————————6————————7~~
~~Chompereh————————10———————8~~
~~Saboora Mkuba————————5————————9~~
~~Umbaluku————————7~~
~~Ambari——————————7~~
~~Baraka——————————5~~
~~Khamisi——————————3————————10~~
~~Umtamani————————10———————11~~
~~Sadala——————————5————————12~~
~~Asmani——————————5————————13~~
~~Bill alli——————————3————————14~~
~~Sarmine—————————5————————15~~
~~Zaidi———————————4 4 in Ugogo 16~~

---
4. Mededita (*HIFL*).

~~Muccadum   5 5 in Ugogo~~

~~Uredi Manua Sera   17~~
~~Bombay   18~~
~~Mabruki Speke   19~~
~~Jumah   20~~
~~Kamna   21~~

In cleaning dishes, the first corn-cob – or green twig or leaf answers[5] the purpose. wish a plate and you show a thumb mark on it, a wipe of a finger, and it's all right, or a corner of his loin cloth, if a tea spoon, a little[6] saliva and a wipe of a loin-cloth, nor need it surprise you if your meat eats gritty, or if you[r] teeth grind sand in eating your pancake.[7]

[Ink] [Figures of subtraction at the bottom of the page]

March 13th Wanyamwezi. Pagazis of Singiri chief of Mtesa's Caravan came to bid me a farewell.
Oh Musungu is going home
going home
To the island where there are plenty of beads.
Plenty of beads
To the sea where there are plenty of mice cloths
m- m- m- m-
While Singiri has kept us very long
From our homes, oh very long
Very long
And we have had no food
We are half starved
Bwana Singiri
Singiri
Mirambo has gone to war to fight against the Arabs
And the Arabs & Wangwana have all gone to fight Mirambo
To fight Mirambo
Oh to fight Mirambo.[8]

---

    5. From 'In cleaning' to 'answers', words are written in between the preceding lines.
    6. 'spit' crossed out.
    7. These remarks concern Ferrajji the cook (*HIFL*, 350).
    8. An expanded text is given in *HIFL*, 621–22.

Choir sat down in a semi circle. Choragus[9] knelt before a hole into which he plunged his head for a few minutes - around which he pranked[10] several tricks – such as beating his head on the ground, beat his breasts – rising up & giving beat to piercing yells – chorus best part of it, always keep time

To Mr Webb[11] Newstead Abbey
1 Knife from Box
1 Bunch of leglets of Usige Wire

To Mr Young (Paraffine)[12] Scotland
1 Knife to Mr Young
1 Bunch of Leglets
1 Spear

2 Chronometers & 1 Watch
 in Tin Box
1 with me
These to be sent to Capt Richards Admiralty House to be repaired.[13]

I have promised Livingstone to send him 1 doz Champagne teapot iron cup & saucer & plate. Carbines. Revolvers. Looking Glass. He also wants 1 dozen Envelopes. 2 Journals. Some Newspapers (late) also a telegram from London. Boat Colors to be got from Man of War.[14]
India rubber Coat. 2 pairs of pants.
[At the bottom of the page]
Ask for future correspondence with Herald

---

    9. Choragus: the leader of the choir in Greek tragedies. It is Stanley's tendency to use archaisms and foreign or precious words as a proof of his culture.
    10. 'around' crossed out.
    11. Another load of weapons was also intended for Webb. See S.A. 9.
    12. "'Paraffin' Young, one of my teachers in chemistry, raised himself to be a merchant prince by his science and art, and has shed pure white light in many lowly cottages, and in some rich palaces" (*LJ*, 2:66). Livingstone named the western Lualaba, the Lake River Young, after him.
    J. Young very generously gave "considerable sums of money at the disposal of Dr. Kirk, to provide for and relieve his long-attached friend Livingstone" (Murchison's Address, November 15, 1870, *PRGS*, 15, no. 1 (1870–71): 7. Young was Agnes Livingstone's guardian (see letter from Agnes Livingstone to Stanley, August 6, 1872, S.A. 494).
    See letter from J. Young to Stanley, August 9, 1872, S.A. 2708.
    13. These watches were delivered to Captain Richards (Admiralty). See Receipt, September 6 and 7, 1872, S.A. 2745 and 2746.
    14. Man of War, a brand of paints and varnish for boats.

1872

March 14th Leave Unyanyembe in a hurry for the coast for various reasons. The Masika is coming on fast I have but 16 days. The Doctor wants his men for a new start, I want to finish the expedition quickly, but after so many days preparation with Wanguana nothing[15] is ready until the last moment. Bombay was never ready, and he as head man set a bad example no one was ready but myself & the little gun carriers & donkey drivers. A new pagazi I had hired but the day previous for ten doti had the homa.[16] He tumbled his load off & laid down. Yet when asked if he would return his cloth & be discharged he had but since left. Bombay had left his load behind him the small box in[17] which were[18] the New York Herald Despatches & Livingstone's letters, & some watche & other valuables. He had left his load behind him though he had engaged to take it. With but twenty loads with not a superfluous atom of anything in the caravan 37 men seemed unable to convey to their island homes, the Heaven of a Mgwana's hopes where so many wished to go & but few permitted to go. The 3 hours March – was a disgraceful one the Kirangozi arrived at camp, while the last of a caravan of 37 was hardly a third of the way. Though they had been but 26 days in Unyanyembe, they travelled like raw recruits. Men just returned from Ujiji. Selim also with his usual carelessness had forgotten a few little things, but above all annoyances of that day was Bombay's neglect or forgetfulness, which might subsequently have ended in a catastrophe worse than occurred in Makata swamp.

Fancy the toil of an expedition & the vast expenditure for 15 months, the sufferings, anxieties, danger's exposure, want, fatigues, the results of which were in that box to be lost through the carelessness of this limbo-born-fool. Major Grant the associate of his former master Speke in the discovery of Victoria Nyanza, the South-Eastern feeder of the White Nile, "He is a first rate fellow for humbugging the natives."

Took 45 Arab letters from Arabs in Unyanyembe to their friends on the Coast.

Letters of Livingstone

6 for Bombay

1 " Zanzibar

20 " London[19]

2 " New York

45 " Arab

74

15. 'was' crossed out.
16. *Homa*: a Swahili word for fever.
17. 'the small box in' added above the line.
18. 'Livin[gstone]' crossed out.
19. See S.A. 11, and Appendix, "Letters carried by me from Dr Livingstone from Unyanyembe & delivered to Lord Lyons," August 1872, S.A. 4754. This list gives 19 addressees only. As Livingstone wrote to each of his children, Stanley might have written this list after having handed over his letter to Oswell Livingstone in Zanzibar.

I felt very lonely all the afternoon – as if I had but just parted with my own family. Pity[20] that parting should be necessary. I never thought while being a victim to its fever that I should leave Central Africa with a pang but it was so, and only because of a white man.

I suffered very much at evening from perspiring and a burning face after being exposed to the East wind. I expect I shall suffer to the Coast.

I cried at parting with the good Doctor – & I had to turn away rather suddenly.

This night was very uncomfortable another slight attack from the intermittent. Was fended off by 4 of Pilulas Colycinthas.[21]

March 15th Long march to Kigwira. Many laggards & much complaint. At the village engaged new ones & took the cloth already given from them. Complaints stopped. 7 hours.
Some pretty scenery about Mai Shamba (Spring watter) huge Granite & Syenite rocks – red & bare show themselves above the highest trees.

Wanyamezi chip a bit of the two front teeth & wear long ringlets

My dear Doctor,
I have parted from you too soon. I feel it, am entirely conscious of it from being so depressed. The time I have been with you has been spent in works for you & for myself. You have been writing to friends who have been daily expecting & craving a letter from you for years. I have had to work in preparing things for the different journeys we have made and for the[22] one I am about to take. The time then passed with you has been too short. I have not[23] had enough of you – this will be a cause of keen regret to me in the future, as it is now.
In writing to you – I am not writing to an idea now – but to an embodiment of warm, good fellowship, of everything that is noble & right, of sound common sense, of every thing practical & right minded. I have talked with you, your presence is almost palpable though you are absent, & I regret I have parted from you it seems as if I had left a community of friends & relations. The utter loneliness, of myself – the void that has been created – the pang at parting – the bleak aspect of the future is the same as I

---

20. 'Pity' written above 'strange' crossed out.
21. for 'Colocynthis'.
22. 'for the' added above the line.
23. 'not' added above the line.

have felt[24] before when parting from near relations & dear friends. Why should people be subjected to these partings, with the several sorrows & pangs that surely follow them? It is a consolation however after tearing myself away, that I am about to do you a service. Then[25] I have not quite parted from you, you & I are not quite separate.[26] Though I am not present to you bodily - you must think of me daily until your caravan arrives. Though you are not before me visibly - I[27] must think of you constantly until your last wish has been attended to. For a few months at least the[28] chain of remembrance will not be severed. Not yet I say to myself, are we apart and this to me Dear Doctor is consoling believe me. Had I a series of services to perform for you, why then we should never have to part.

My dear Doctor had I not turned away from you quickly at taking our farewell,[29] I should have appeared weak. Were not the Arabs present? Could they have understood my feelings? I doubt if you[30] can understand them thoroughly, but there I do you a wrong – And you will please forgive me. But by the faithful attention which I shall pay to your expressed wishes & by the readiness which I shall comply with any other or others I will prove them. Do not fear then I beg to ask, nay command whatever lies in my power. And do not I beg of you attribute these professions to interested motives, but accept them or believe in them in the spirit in[31] which they are[32] made[33] – in that true David Livingstone spirit I have happily become[34] acquainted with.

He is to be sure not to neglect the Herald, & shall not forget[35] my promise that all published letters direct from Dr Livingstone to the New York Herald shall be paid for at £20 each – Eight pages of your writing at the least on foolscap paper to be considered a letter.[36] I am certain the Herald will praise me for it. & Money to be sent to Coutts & Co., London for the benefit of your children.

Road is good – Wanguana march with a will.
Return Bag Shut. He has not told me where to send letters. Shall send care of Sheikh bin Nasib – Unyanyembe.

---

24. 'felt' added above the line.
25. 'Then' preceded by 'I wish it' crossed out.
26. 'from you' crossed out.
27. 'am' crossed out.
28. 'last' crossed out.
29. 'at taking our farewell' added above the line.
30. Preceded by 'a'.
31. 'in' added above the line.
32. 'they are' written above 'I have' crossed out.
33. 'them' crossed out.
34. 'been' changed in 'become'.
35. 'that' crossed out.
36. See this "promise" on December 16, 1871, S.A. 7. Stanley was even more precise: "8 pages of pretty close writing which will be equal to 400 lines of about 8 words each = 3200 words." Though Stanley praised Livingstone's letters to the *New York Herald* in *HIFL*, this exact deal was not recorded.

March 16th Rubuga. 6 hours. Marching excellent. Rats abound in this village – was offered a cow for 7 doti – peopled by Wasawahili – who are Shafi[37] Moslems a prayerful & fanatical sect. Kiss hands.[38]

March 17th Nyahuba– or Unyahuha.[39] 8 hours – runs North West – empties into Malagarazi – Much Silurus fish in. Water here always – now running. In dry seasons it is in pools. RAIN[40] ½ an hour during the day – and as much during the night. Came for the first time to those giant bulks – the baobab in the Rubuga forest

March 18th Arrived at Tura 7 hours. Western Tura. Tura forest prolific in thorns made tatters of my pants.
Wangwana always put green leaves in the water when they go to bring it for use. This is the Masika I have not the least doubt. It rained in earnest this afternoon with excessive thunder & lightning. The last rain stopped when but one day from Unyanyembe on our return from Ujiji - 17th February. Last Masika 1871 began 23rd March- ended 30th April

March 19th. Halt at Western Tura – a slight attack of fever & waiting for the last letters from the doctor. Much rain fell during the night

March 20th Arrive at Eastern Tura – Tura Perro[41] – the letters not yet arrived – 2.30 minutes.
Small village inhabited by Wakimbu & Wanyamwezi, who possess a small cultivated area, separated from Tura proper by a belt of jungle, where once flourished Corn & Sorghum.
In all cases when we come across the jungle proper a thick low[42] growth of shrubs & thorn-brush– we found it covering recent[43] cultivated ground. After much experience of such scenes one could almost tell the year when the wild bush replaced the grain stalk. The Wakimbu are a growing people – the Wanyamwezi I fear are dying out. The hardships of travel on the "gristle" of the race not favorable to its multiplication.

---

37. Sunni branch of Islam.
38. From 'Waswahili' to 'kiss hands' added above the line, before 'March 17th'.
39. Names given to the Kwalah River by natives of Rubuga (HIFL, 628). It is spelled 'Kwala' in this notebook.
40. Written in bold letters.
41. Tura Perro is recorded as Western Tura in HIFL, 215. But the word 'perro' remained unidentified. Could be a native word for this part of the countryside?
42. 'low' added above the line.
43. 'recent' added above the line.

Eight[44] out of ten of the bleached skulls seen on the road are those of unfortunate Wanyamwezi, died of small pox chiefly. The Wakimbu villages are multiplying rapidly & steadily advancing westward towards Rubuga.

Uyanzi might very properly be called their own. And yet it is a pity that such people as the Wanyamwezi should perish from the Earth & be no longer known as a tribe, like the interesting people the Makololu who are so closely identified with Livingstone. What a power one could build even of the remnant.

What a temptation to missionary effort.

What the Wakimbu will prove is not clear yet. They have not yet felt their power. To now they are scattered each village governed by its own sultan each village independent of the other.

Going to Unguya Unguya is the word & all are happy. Some of these lazy fellows around Unyanyembe resort to begging, with, Master, I am famished – Answer – Well, I can not help it. Who do you belong to - I am your slave Master – What[45] – I have no slave, I do not keep slaves? Ah but Master I am your slave –Your slave Master sure enough, and only your slave.

The sly fellow will not depart until he gets his fee – which may be a khete – but the most impudent hesitate[s] not at asking a cloth worth 45 khete –equal to[46] 45 days provisions. The women are not unkind to each other in distress. At this village in the next room was a female patient wandering uncloth[ed] in the delirium of fever caused by the small pox. There were two or three others present endeavoring to induce the poor thing to lie down

When a Mnyamwezi woman is pregnant, she departs into the jungle accompanied by an experienced matron who performs the kindly offices of a midwife to her.

A Mguana woman resides in her hut & a woman attends her

March 21st. Arrive at Kwala river sometimes called Tura River by Wanguana 7 hours. The river is quite formidable during the last days of the rainy season – Empties into the Gombe South[47]– as well as the Mongo[48] – the Ngwhalab – or Nyahuba[49] empties into the Northern Gombe which flows North of Tabora & through Mirambo's territory into the Malagarazi.

---

44. 'Eight' written over 'nine'. 'Eight out of ten of' added above the line.
45. Preceded by 'your slave' crossed out.
46. 'equal to' added above; 'or' crossed out.
47. 'South' added above the line.
48. For 'Mgongo'?
49. Nghwhalah River (*HIFL*, 521).

One[50] half the country separating Western Tura from the Kwala River is a true thorn jungle through the transit of which the traveller must exercise caution lest he be scarfied by the thorns.

One of my men who came with the last batch of letters from the Doctor[51] – Uredi[52]– the Wisdom Ambassador to Manua Sera in the days of Speke came near meeting with a sad accident. He fired his gun as a signal of arrival & the shoddy thing burst into half a score of pieces which went flying over our heads, & one piece of which wounded him in the head.

Several Wanguana are reported hurrying after me to the Coast that they may escape the brunt of dealing with Wagogo which must fall to my share in the transit of their country. They were sufficiently warned that the caravan would go on the 14th[53] but accustomed to Arab inexactitude they paid not much heed heed[54] to it, and now as I am marching rapidly Ugogo will be almost crossed unless they make exceeding haste before they catch us up.

My Kirangozi is a philosopher – a native of Ugomba a country near Usui –&[55] therefore a Mnyamwezi he has adopted the Island of Zanzibar as his country which he declares infinitely superior to Ugomba because of the savage manners of the people who are never at ease unless warring or raiding. Spears are bad, bullets are bad arrows are bad – even sticks are bad - surely nothing is good but eating – like we do with our Master now. Ah eating is glorious. Beef! & here he rubbed his hands at the happy memories of mastication, ox meat, buffalo meat sheep meat, goat meat. Ah who would take to fighting instead of eating – Sure nobody but a Mshensi all of which true philosophy[56] was applauded by the admiring Bombay & his brothers of the "hill land" near the sea.

I am leading Israel out of Egypt. Host of fugitive hare hearts are after us.

March 22. Kwala River near Mgongo Thembo[57] – a long march
lotus fragrant & in bloom close up at sunset

---

50. 'One' written over 'The f…'
51. It took 6 days for the two men left by Stanley with Livingstone to catch up with the caravan, and bring his last letters (*LJ*, 2:174, March 15th and 16th entries). Stanley then sent Susi back with his reply (*LJ*, 2:175, March 25th entry).
52. Uredi or Uledi, one of Speke's Faithfuls. The confusion between 'l' and 'r' in the transcription of African names is frequent (cf. infra Ugula and Ugura). See also the spelling of Lufiji River for Rufiji (January 11, 1871, Journal S.A. 7) or Rusizi River according to Stanley's spelling but the Lusize, according to Livingstone (*LJ*, 2:141).
53. 'the 14th' written above 'such a day' crossed out.
54. 'heed', last word of the preceding page, is repeated at the beginning of this one.
55. '&' written over 'he'.
56. End of the sentence from 'osophy' appears two pages later. Stanley probably skipped a sheet when turning the page to finish his sentence.
57. Mgongo Tembo (*HIFL*, 212).

[N.B. 6 lines could not be transcribed: two different texts are written, a darker one above a lighter. One is upside down over the other. Here are bits of these lines.]

Tula means resting place [.....] perils and fatigues wilderness ....
just............. find food and welcome house accomodations
Kwihara .... Cultivated ground - or the inhabited place

In camp the men pass their time often in discussing the relative merits of the countries they have traversed – one is loud in praising Uganda, another gives the preference to Karagwah – a fourth describes Ugindo as being very fine.

March 23. Sou[th] of Ngaraisu[58] at the Ziwani. A pool 100 yds long by 50 broad – during beginning of[59] rainy season – but extending to half a mile long during last days of Masika. The head of the caravan entered the boma and were forcibly ejected by the angry Wakimbu

March 24th. Tongoni, or the "Deserted Clearing". This is a clearing in the midst of a dense wood deserted like many others in this war stricken land because of a silly quarrel which culminated in a bloodshed & the forcible ejection of the Wakimbu to more northern parts. Wakimbu of Ngariswa & Kiwere were the[60] assaulted.
The Wakimbu are a timid people, and when coming amongst them the Wanguana armed with guns are not slow in domineering. This has always been the case in this land, as in the Western parts of America. The ignorant & cowardly when they obtain possession of firearms perceiving that law abiding & quiet people prefer to yield way rather than provoke people armed with deadly weapons, generally wax insolent & boastful until halted in their mischievous course by the strong arm of vengeful law. It is the same here – in this land, the Wanguana principally composed of freed slaves of all nations are armed with flintlock muskets & traverse lands where the report of a gun inspires awe. These black rowdies[61] then wax as insolent & boastful as their white brothers dwelling on the confines of civilization & spread terror everywhere until goaded beyond endurance the people combine & rise against them.

It rained last night & this morning.

Jiweh la Singa is settled now by several Wanguana & Wamrima ivory hunters.

---

58. Ngaraiso (*HIFL*, 209).
59. 'beginning of' added above the line.
60. 'others' crossed out.
61. 'These' written over 'they'; 'black rowdies' added above the line.

Uyanzi is one vast bed of Syenite, which heaves here & there into huge boulders & large disintegrated masses split by action of weather & growth of vegetation. This bed of Syenite continues as far as the Malagarazi & extends as far South as to Lutetu when hermetite[62] of iron & coarse sand stone[63] takes its place as far as the Tanganyika. The land where it is not level, or sloping towards some river, rises & subsides into broad gentle waves, and wide hollows, which are everywhere covered with a forest of dwarf trees. Except in the deeper hollows, the greater river banks, & the neighbourhood of Tanganyika large trees are scarce from the Ocean[64] to the Lake region. The largest – excepting of course the baobab is not more than a foot in diameter.

March 25. Mabunguru Nullah – End of Uyanzi on the right side – commencement of Ugogo on the left or East side. 5 hours from Tongoni to Mabunguru.

March 26th Servant of Kiwiyeh – Sultan of Mdaburu Ugogo – very amiable & quiet man.

[Sketch of a landscape] "The deserted clearing with great rocks looming above deserted
tembes"
[Legend] corn stalks, shed, rocks

[Top of the page, Sketch of a profile of a woman]
A Mgogo belle with plaited hair & beads about her neck, large copper rings on her wrists.[65]
[Below]
Camp[66]
Houses of Pagasis
Soldiers
Married folks
Master's tent
Tree with bales round it
Gate

---

62. For 'hematite'.
63. 'and coarse sand stone' added above the line.
64. 'region' crossed out.
65. This sketch was used as the basis for the head of the woman for the couple in the engraving "Ugogo Man and Woman" in *HIFL*, 223.
66. Plan of the camp with legend. This sketch was used as the basis for the engraving "Gigantic Sycamore and Camp beneath it" in *HIFL*, 328.

South of Ugogo is Ugula[67] or Ugura. South of Ugula is Urori
North of Ugogo is Usanda – Uhumba.

Wagogo when marry they send according to their means so many cows from five to 20. Sultan sends 20 or 40 or 50 goats[68] to the father of the bride. Consent of the family is to be had before completing contract of marriage – it takes many days to finish it – many family councils are held on the subject.

The Mgogo chief who gave me this, traveled with my caravan from Unyanyembe to Mvumi and at first until fully satisfied as to my intentions reluctant to impart information, but when it was explained he very readily gave it.

In Unyamwezi – in case of twins – the father takes the child's caul & travels to the frontier, and if a stream he buries it in[69] the mud – returns takes root of a certain tree & buries it at the threshold of his door, invites his friends & then follows a feast generally a couple of oxen are slain. They never kill one. If one dies, it is said the Mulungu or Miringu Kigogo & Kinyamwezi – Mniezi Mungu-Mgwana.[70]

All the Wagogo believe there is a God above whom they call Mulungu.
His idea of God is of one who when his parents have died – & there possessions are fallen to him – his spear his knife, jembe, bow & arrow his cloth, ivory or thing whatever he collects these things together into a heap & prays to them asking for more – that his riches may increase, that he may have another trade whereby he can get an increase of such things – & he believes that as God created his parents, he created him.

The[71] dead die & they die. The Sultan dies & is nothing - is finished words are finished there is no more. "True - the Sultan is no more – He who says other words is a liar."

Buried with legs & arms tied to the body - with the left hand under his head & laid on his left side with the cloth he wore during life over him put in the grave – covered over & thorns bush put over it to prevent hyaena – if a woman on her right side.[72]

---

67. Ugala (*HIFL*, 521).
68. 'or 40 or 50 goats' added above the line.
69. 'Into' changed to 'in'.
70. 'Miringu Kigogo & Kinyamwezi' added above the line. These are the names given to the Deity, according to various people, and the text is slightly different from *HIFL*, 545: "The Deity in Kinyamwezi is called Miringu; in Kigogo … Mulungu; in Kisawahili, Mienzi Mungu." Part of the sentence is missing. It should read: "It is said the Mulungu or Miringu has taken him."
71. Preceded by 'When' crossed out.
72. This line is in pencil with some letters re-written in ink.

A Sultan is buried in the middle of its village & build a[73] house over it & each time they kill an ox they kill before his grave. His[74] successor when his predecessor is dead calls for an ox[75] & slays it before his grave calling God to witness that he is to be Sultan the meat of the ox is distributed for the dead Sultan's sake.

If he has a son the son succeeds him – if childless the great chief next to him in rank. The Mzagira[76] is next to Sultan – whose business it is to hear the cause of complaint conveys it to the Sultan who through him dispenses justice – he receives the honga – carries it to the Mtemi places it before him who takes his share & leaves the other to Mzagira. The chiefs are called Maniampara,[77] or Elders & they are always giving advice.

In case of murder, 50 cows are demanded – if he has no cows the Sultan gives[78] permission to the nearest relatives to kill him with spears if the murderer is[79] a strong man he is tied spears are thrown at him, then the infuriated spring upon him cut him to pieces & scatter him broad-cast over the land.

A thief - Kuhiza – Kigogo – Msambo – if found is killed at once & nothing said.

Where did Wagogo come from.
[A blank]

Wahumba are Masai by the Washensi – they inhabit the lands of Mbogwe & Ihange a journey into their country takes 3 months

Wasanda inherit a country 5 days march from Ugogo – dress in skins of fowls.

The Mganga when the accused is brought before him cuts a fowl open - if the guts are white he is innocent – if yellow is guilty.
Witchcraft is punished with death, the chicken proves the guilt.
It sometimes occurs but unseldom, the chief catches a man & charges him with it. The people ask how he knows it. He says I will prove it by this chicken which I will cut.

---

73. 'village' crossed out.
74. 'His' rewritten in black ink.
75. 'ox' in black ink.
76. Msagira (*HIFL*, 255).
77. Manya-para (*HIFL*, 256).
78. 'no' crossed out.
79. 'is' written over 'be'.

[Sketch] "Mgogo Warrior"[80]

Bombay was neither very honest nor very dishonest – that is he did not venture to steal much – he contrived sometimes to set apart a larger share of the meat of an ox for his mess than was proper. But his dishonesty when aware of it did not trouble me much. As a servant he would have been excellent – as a superintendent – or a jemadar[81] over his fellows – he was out of his place.

Mabruki – formerly valet & tent man & handy man to Burton, was my policeman, my porter & as such he was invaluable always faithful at his post. He saw to feeding the donkeys & bringing up the stragglers, no one could have been better. Woe to the stragglers Mabruki's hand was heavy & his voice harsh. In any other capacity he did not shine.

The natives dry their grain on the roof of their houses like Rahab of old dried her flax.[82] [Sketch of an animal with horns under the writing][83]

Khamisi was a neat cleanly boy of 20, active, loud voiced a boaster of no mean powers, & the cowardliest of the cowardly. He would steal also if he had the opportunity. Clung to his gun most affectionately, was anxious if a screw got loose, or a flint would not strike fire – yet I doubt that he could fire it at any body from excessive trembling.

Belali would have been[84] good kind of a servant to have with one, for the carriage of heavy things – strong & willing – a stutterer - but as a soldier he was an arrant coward.

[A full-length profile of a native with spear][85]

March 27th Starting at dawn after a solemn warning that we were about entering Ugogo, we issued out of the camp at Kaniyaga[86] with trumpet like blasts of the hartebeest horn, & filed into the depths of cornfields which at this time, is finely ready for parching & roasting – field after field we passed – then struck into the jungle, of

---

80. This sketch was used as the basis for the engraving of the Mgogo man, side by side with the Mgogo belle, in *HIFL*, 223.
81. Supervisor of a staff of servants in India. The equivalent for Stanley is commander (of soldiers, police, gendarmes) (*HIFL*, 42).
82. "But she [Rahab] had brought them up to the roof of the house, and hid them with the stalks of flax, which had laid in order upon the roof" (Joshua 2:6).
83. This head of an animal with short horns has probably been used for the drawing of the Unyamwezi cow in *HIFL*, 516.
84. 'have been' added above the line.
85. This profile may have served to draw one of the two "Youthful Wasagara" in *HIFL*, 248.
86. 'at Kaniyaga' added above the line.

rank thorn crossing gulleys every now & then which are numerous in Uyanzi owing to the rolling nature of the country. Each ridge is crowned by heaps of disintegrated blocks of Syenite, or by a castle like rock, or by a round hill of stone, blackened slightly by sun[87] & weather. Water is almost always found near these rocks, at the base. The Eastern half is prolific of thorn bush & jasmine[88] which jasmine gave as rank an odor as the dense thorn jungles near the Coast. It is a forest of dwarf trees mostly all of which are thorn & gum which exude large quantities of gum, but amongst these trees are found several[89] delectable fruit trees – the grape & a species of fruit very like the Sultana grape – the leaf of the bush is like that of the gooseberry. The fruit hangs in clusters which though seldom ripe at this season is grateful to one hankering after an acidulous fruit. There is another about the size of an apricot bearing a stone

The central portion of Uyanzi is a fine rolling country – one forest of large fine teak & tamarind. Well watered, rich grass – an admirable country for settlements. The stones here are picturesque.

 The settlements were many after entering Ugogo – the thorn forest was rather provking owing to their long slender branches bending low over the path, catching ones cloths hat or hair very often – but it was not long the extensive fields of Mgaza[90] the subjects of Kwiyeh[91] came into view & tembe after tembe was discerned low & brown, like patch of[92] earth amongst the green expanse, flocks & herds in numbers added to the pleasantness of the scene.

 It is almost one slope to Kiwiyeh from Ngaraiso.-Soon after crossing Mabuguru Nullah it slopes rapidly. At Mukondoku – north East[93] from Kiwiyeh Uyanzi is entered by an ascent up a steep hill about 1000 feet high.

 Road leaving Kiwiyeh go to Khonko or Khokko (sleep on Road) then go to Khonse[94] then go to Macomero.

Pori – Kisimani
Msige
Mvumi Mkuba
Mvumi Mdogo

---

87. 'sun' written over 'wind'.
88. 'jasmine' added above the line.
89. 'several' written above 'many' crossed out.
90. 'Mgaza' added above the line.
91. 'Kwiyeh' rewritten over 'Kiwyeh'. Stanley kept Kiwyeh in *HIFL*.
92. 'red' crossed out.
93. 'East' added above the line.
94. Khonze (*HIFL*, 633).

The Mdaburu & Mabunguru join together & empty into the Kisigo which empties into the Ruwha[95] or Rufiji. Hippos & crocodile are in numbers in the Kisigo. 4 days march from Kiwyeh to the Kisigo one day more to Ruwha 100 miles. Unyangwira is South of Mgunda Makali – Usandewa West[96] of Unyangwira.

28th March. Halt. The population here is composed of Wakimbu & Wagogo in about equal proportions. Old Kiwyeh is dead & his young son of ten reigns instead. Though his dominion is fair to look upon & he has hundreds of dutiful subjects who number their cattle by blocks, yet his position is a precarious one, for his youth offers temptations to the Wagogo princes about him. We had barely encamped yesterday when we suddenly heard the war horns booming everywhere & messengers darting swiftly in every direction. At first when informed it was for war, I half expected it was against the Expedition, but the words "Urugu. Warugu" bandied about declared the cause. Mukondoku the populous district two days' march to the North East was coming to attack the youthful Mtemi Kiwyeh. And Kiwyeh's soldiers were runing to the fight, to meet the foe. It was Roderick Dhu[97] to the sight in alacrity. At the sound of the horns they but waited to don their war dress. Their frightful headdress[98] ankle bells, & Joho robes – take spear & bow, and at an uniform trot, go for the foe. On either flank & ahead rush the most enthusiastic exercising themselves in the mimic war, a couple of spears or so, & a sheave of arrows with the knob-stick is the arms. They kept admirable time with the ankle bells – as they went on the double quick, every tembe furnished its quota Ugogo being open & we being on the crest[99] of a landward could see them issuing from all sides – by tens by sixes form couples & singly all went on the Mukonduku road probably 300 or 400 muster.
At night they returned chanting happily – the whole had proved a false alarm. At the first outset it was believed that the Kidingo – Kidurigo or Wahehe had come & made a foray on cattle. They advance through the jungle stooping when near the cattle they are about to lift, with their shields covering of black hide – covering the back –they then make a dash switch the cattle heartily & having started them on the run – turn about & plant their shields facing the sheph[er]ds

29th Khokko.[100] 6 hours – from Kiwiyeh. Thorny jungle – dense around here. The labor has been great to cut it down. Cows are numerous, & milk for those who love it is

---

95. Ruhwha (*HIFL*, 233).
96. 'West' written over 'East'.
97. A character in Sir Walter Scott's poem "The Lady of the Lake."
98. Here are sketches of three headdresses.
99. 'crest' written above 'spine' crossed out.
100. 'Khokko' written over 'Kiwiyeh'.

cheap & good. The bullocks & bulls are fat. It is a sight to see a grown bull his hump rises above the level of his back a tower of fat.
The tsetse are few

Mchemba – Honga
Icazi
Macomero – Mwenga
Pori – Kisimani
Kididimo
Matamburu
Mvumi Mkuba

Wagogo women are remarkable for their curiosity & the pains they take to satisfy it. If we came near any of their dwellings they would race from one corner to another to have a peep then would rush out & run ahead where they planted themselves for a resolute stare to gulp down at one look all the singularities & peculiarities of white man & belongings.

The young girls are singular for their deficiency of wearing apparel, a narrow band is all they boast. This is held by one or more[101] spiral coils of brass wire wound round the loins. Others have as many as three or four fundo of beads generally of the[102] ghulabio & lunghio & Merikani or white[103] kind. The samesame encircle their necks, they have as many as 100 lbs[104] wristlets of brass wire & beads. Bits of copper are tied to the ends of their sewnet[105] ringlets. Half a dozen bright copper[106] pici of India[107] hang over their foreheads, or round their necks.[108]

The young men generally wear broad collars of fine brass chains, pieces of gourd necks are intruded through the lobes of their ears, or a rounded piece of wood of the size of a dollar. They disfigure their warm rich color of their bodies with ochrish[109] blotch[e]s which when put on the face impart a sinister cast to what would otherwise be considered as approaching to good looks. Broad wislets of ivory adorn their arms. They are also used for beating time in war.

[At the bottom of the page, and upside down]
Mpwapwa
Tubagwe
Kitangi

---

101. 'One' written over 'a, or more' added above the line.
102. 'of the' added above the line.
103. 'Merikani or white' added above the line.
104. 'they have as many as 100 lbs' added above the line.
105. 'Sewnet' [?] written above 'spunyawa' [?] crossed out.
106. 'copper' added above the line.
107. *Pici* (or *pishi*): small copper coins in use at Zanzibar.
108. 'Or' crossed out at the end of the paragraph.
109. 'ochrish' for ochre-ish

March 30th 2 ½ hours to Khonze 5 hours to Asanza – called Sanza.

A forest of Mimosa such as we saw in coming to Sanza is as singular in its beauty as that of the cypress.

Leaving the luxuriant grain fields of Khonko – or Khokko as called by the Arabs we entered a jungle of mimosa & bluish green barked thorn tree emitting a peculiar & rank odor almost sickening sloping gently to the small clearing of Khonze which is situated to the North of Usekke, a position always ascertained by a short line of rugged hills which show masses of bleached rock here & there above the crest. Khonze is remarka[ble] for the mighty globes of foliage of the sycamore which dot the clearing, and which tower above even the dome like tops of the baobab. The chief of Khonze boasts of four tembes which could turn out perhaps together about fifty armed men yet this fellow instigated by the Wanyamwezi residents at his tembe prepared to resist our advance because I sent three doti as honga. The Wagogo travellers with us who had been deputed to negotiate rushed up to me & said –Why do you sitt here –do you wish to die. These Washensi will not take the honga, but advised by the Makonongo (Wanyamwezi)[110] boast that they will eat up the Muzungu's cloth. Upon hearing this I got up & loaded my gun in their presence & informed them that the Muzungu spoke once. I would take the caravan to the jungle & since they talked of fighting, there only would I speak of them. Further more I warned Juma, the chief of the[111] Mnyamwezi that I would shoot him first if there was an outbreak. Turning to the Wangwana I said –Up men to the jungle, we will make the talk there. In a few minutes we had gained the jungle, and the Wagogo seven in number with the prime minister the Msogera[112] who turned out to be the brother of Jumma. Here[113] the Msogera said these are the words of the Mtemi. The Wazungu who have come to their country have gone to Ukonongo all roads but this. One chose the road to the South by Usekke. The other went by Pemberi N'Pereh & Mukondoku (this last was myself). None have come by this but you. Now we want to see you. We never saw a white man before. If you camp here we will take 3 doti if not you must pay five". On concluding I briefly told Bombay to give him five, as we had 5[114] hours journey before us. The Msogera was not ready for this. He sulked & left it on the ground but I had no time to bandy more words. And I urged the caravan onward which was nothing loth. The Msogera was seen to pick his cloths up & retire moodily, he & his men - being probably dubious of the effect of a strike.

We travelled the long jungle quickly though troubled much with thorns at almost every step. Mgogola was repeated often than usual this day. At 2[115] P.M. we halted on

---

110. 'are going' crossed out.
111. 'chief of the' added above the line.
112. Msagira (*HIFL*, 634).
113. 'Here' preceded by 'Though he' crossed out.
114. 'more' crossed out.
115. '2' written over '3'.

the crest of a ridge overlooking the green[116] plain of Kanyenye[117] & the clearing of Sanza. Emerging at 4[118] P.M. from the jungle having completed a troublesome descent the Asanza clearing was before us – scores of tall Palmyra, & here & there a sycamore rose above the spreading corn field &[119] tembe. A few words with the Sultan & seven doti were paid as honga. A rumor reached here of a band of Warori coming to invade Ugogo. Our appearance was hailed as bearers of good news, having heard of nothing of such things.

March 31st 2 hours march brought us to Kamyenye, to the great Mtemi Magomba who lived with his son Mutundu[120] N'Gondeh in a tembe which had nothing about it to distinguish it from the dozens around.
[Circled] Unamapokera one of the chiefs of Magomba
The Msogira as we came by his tembe - a pleasant gray-haired man was at work making a hedge of thorns round a patch of corn. He greeted the caravan with a loud Yambo, and set himself at the head of the caravan going as fast as his legs would permit him to show the caravan the camp. Being introduced to the Musungu he was very cordial – he was offered a stool & began to talk very affably remembered much about the white men who had come before me, & declared me to be[121] younger than any remembered one who[122] drank asses' milk. Heard that I was similarly fond of milk & sent his son to fetch a gourd-full. A hearty drink I took of it[123] seemed to[124] give him satisfaction. He promised the honga should be light, which promise he fulfilled – charging me 6 for Magomba, & one for himself.

[Sketch] "Unamapokera, soldier of Magomba"[125]
This man has thin wristlet of cow hide which he calls medicine.

Unamapokera a sub of the Msagira put in a claim for one doti – half of which was to be given to a brother sub. As he was a most amiable though rough in appearance his claim was admitted & a head cloth thrown in extra at which he showed his white teeth & laughed hoarsely.[126]

---

116. 'green' added above the line.
117. Kamyenyi (*HIFL*, 635).
118. '4' written over '3'.
119. 'of' crossed out.
120. Mtundu (*HIFL*, 634).
121. 'to be' added above the line.
122. 'had' crossed out.
123. 'heartily satisfied him' crossed out.
124. 'seemed to' added above the line.
125. This sketch served as a model for the picture in *HIFL*, 635.
126. Unamapokera is quite a different character in *HIFL*, 634.

Magomba's queen & daughters came near to have a look, but it was at a respectable distance. But as for Wagogo curiosity it is without compare the most prurient & unabashed of all.

April 1st 4 hours to Myumi
Mambura, soldier of Mtundu N'Gondeh was sent to escort us to Myumi – on the edge of the forest – 4 hours from Kanyenye. Leaving Myumi we struck into the jungle & thus avoided Kisewah the naughty son of Magomba. About 1 P.M. came to a small pond of water which we found in one of the water courses which crossed the dense jungle through which we labored. Resting an hour here we continued the journey until we came to a shallow[127] Ziwa which at this time of the year contains some muddy (exceedingly) water.

April 2nd The jungle now thinned considerably, and in an hour we entered the fields of Mapanga. We counted six tembes here

April 2nd Mapanga 1 hour
Nyamzaga 2 ½ hours
(continued) here altogether, & these we were passing on our way to camp preparatory to opening the honga bale when a lad rushed up from Kwikuru & asked us where we were going to. Having received his answer he hastened on ahead & presently heard him talking to some men in the field on our right. In the meantime we had come to a halt, the men were reclining on the ground near their respective packs. Bombay was getting out the honga, when suddenly out rushed about 40 or 50 men armed from the woods, the King at their head uttering such cries as only savages are accustomed to utter such as a long drawn Hhaatiih, Hhaat, Uhuh, which meant unmistakably, "You will will you, no you will not – at once defiant determined & fierce. They brandished their spears, & clubs & held their shilds up in front. Suspecting that the voices I heard[128] boded no good I had already prepared my weapons. Verily[129] what a fine chance for adventure this was. One spear flung one shot fired & the opposing bands had been dealing deathly blows on all sides.
There would have been no order – of battle – no pomp but a murderous onset & quick firing of breech loaders, aided by a volley from flint locks, the cowardly running away at once pursued by yelping Savages. And who knows how it all would have ended. 40 spears against 40 guns, but many guns would run away – perhaps all & I

---

127. 'shallow' added above the line.
128. 'away' crossed out.
129. 'Verily' added above the line.

should have been left with my gun bearer to have my throat deliberately cut like a goat if I chanced not to fall by a well thrown spear – Happy end for an Expedition! But in this land it will not do unless driven to it at the last extremity. I ordered the Kirangozi forward to ask for an explanation of all this furious hubbub & to ask them if they intended to rob us. "No, said the King we do not want to stop the road nor to rob you, we[130] want the tribute." But don't you see us halted & the bale opened to send it to you. We came here because after the honga is settled as we have only marched an hour to go on we are in a hurry to reach the Coast. You see we have no ivory nor much cloth, therefore why should we stop. The king at this burst into a loud laugh & was joined by ourselves for he was ashamed. He said, we were cutting wood to make a boma when a boy brought us news there were strange men passing through the country without stopping to explain who they were but now I have got work on hand. After I am through which will be in about two hours I will come back to you.
At 3 P. M. entered a thorny jungle & continued on our way to Nyamzaga - Sultan Mohalata,[131] reached it in 2 ½ hours. A friend I made at this place proved very stauch[132] – he belonged to Mulowa a country to the S.S.W.[133] & South of Kulabi he saved me much honga. He soon leaned to address me as Friend. Friend said he when approaching Kulabi if any Wagogo ask you where you are from Say from Ugogo, leave it to me I will take you through, & he did it well.

April 3rd Kulabi 3 hours Mvumi 3 hours. Sultan Mawala. My Ugogo friend took leave. Famine in this district. 1 doti buys one measure. Camped by a stream, water slightly brackish – brackish district. Extends from here to the Mukondokwa river.

Kiwyeh	5	doti
Khonko	5	"
Khonse	5	"
Sanza	7½	"
Kamyenye	9	"
Mapanga	4½	
Muhalata	8½	
Mvumi	8	

The country gets very naked after leaving Nyamzaga. After Kulabi of Mulowa entered Mukamwa's, then crossed[134] a broad, sandy bed of a river & entered Mvumi, wind fearful.

---

130. 'I' written over 'we' or 'we' over 'I'.
131. Muhalata (*HIFL*, 639).
132. For 'staunch'.
133. S.S.E. (*HIFL*, 638).
134. 'crossed' added above the line.

Iramba a country North of Tura - full of cattle & donkeys in great number
A naked plain, very fond of donkey meat. Speak very curiously – with mouths drawn to corners.

April 4th Eastern Mvumi 3 hours. Bombay, another Mgwana, and my friend, the young Unyamwezi merchant went with the other three doti according to request.
The Msagira remembering the beautiful supply of 18 ½ doti which I paid before strongly protested against the small honga given by the Muzungu on his return, & sized hold of the Unyamwezi merchant as a guarantee or surety for further cloth or 5 fundo of [135] beads as Honga[136] to draw plenty of caravans here. – six hours talk – the caravan being on the edge of the wilderness of Marenga Makali – the men were let go & gave a fervent Hamid el illah[137] having finished with Ugogo with honga to Mawala.[138]
Wind (Pepo) stormy blasts men shivering & Bombay put on a tarred coat as protection

Wagogo say of men dying "It is god's work, he or[139] she is lost"

Migunda field. Makali hard, strong, harsh, or bitter.

Marenga water – Makali hard or bitter

Sent Sarmine Baraka & Ambari to Coast with letters[140]
Bought ox – 12 doti

April 5th 9 hours. Desert of Marenga Makali.[141] Left Ugogo with loud hurrah. Being in the rainy season we found plenty of water.

---

135. '5 fundo of' added above the line.
136. Word difficult to read; the second letter 'g' seems having been crossed out.
137. *Hamid el illah:* "Praise God!"
138. In *HIFL* (638), Stanley mentioned the eight doti "as a farewell tribute to the Sultan" but left aside the lengthy dispute over it.
139. 'he or' added above the line.
140. The names of the porters are omitted in *HIFL*, 639, but Stanley mentioned that these letters were sent with telegraphic despatches for the *Herald* to the American Consul [John F. Webb]. The three porters arrived at Zanzibar on April 29, 1872 (see Appendix, Letter from John Webb, American Consul in Zanzibar, to Stanley, April 30, 1872, S.A. 2659). On their way back, they caught up with Stanley at Rosako (May 2), who heard of the preparations for a new "[RGS] Livingstone Expedition" from Webb's answer. The scoop of the meeting had been well kept until then, although Consul Kirk did his best to gather news for his superiors from Arab caravans. Cf. (i) Letters from J. Kirk to Earl Granville, dated Zanzibar, April 10, 1872: National Archives, Kew, F. O. 84/1357, no. 31, fol. 205–210 (received June 4, and copies dispatched to "The Queen," "Mr Gladstone," and "To Geographical Society June 5th"), and (ii) to Sir Henry [Rawlinson], Zanzibar, April 14, 1872, RGS-IBG Collections, JMS/2/127/copy 133 E. See also Lieut. Dawson's Official Report to the Secretary of the RGS, Zanzibar, May 19, 1872 (*PRGS* 16, no. 5 [1871–72]: 419–21): "On the evening of the 28th [April] three men were brought to me … who had just arrived from a white man's caravan… […] Their leader [was] Umbari … ."
141. Marenga Mkali (*HIFL*).

April 6th Chunio[142] 8 A. M. – Mpwapwa – 2 P.M. – rested 3 hours. Lost revolver on road. Rain beset us as soon as we entered Usagara

This is the 9th day of the rain since 18th March

April 7th Mpwapwa or Mpambva[143] as the Natives call it. A halt. Had a slight touch of fever. Kept me in greater part of day. Bought a gallon of milk for a shukka. Sent to Lukoleh chief of 5 tembes the first we see as we near Mpwapwa, with whom I left Farquhar. He came, gave following answers to questions given him.
"He died 5 days after you left, for Ugogo.
"Two days he could talk & get up to ease himself. Then his legs got worse & his privates swelled very bad on the night of the 5th day.
"We buried him about 100 yds South of Kisesa's Camp near the river and about 300 yds West of my tembe in a straight line.
"Jacko took possession of his things, tied them up & with two more of our soldiers carried them to the tembe of a Nyamwezi
He came to see me once only after he left to see how I was. 3 months after you left he died also. Before he died he sold your little gun for 10 doti to an Arab going to Unyamwezi
Farquhar was really thrown into a hollow under a spreading tamarind, and a little soil was hoed over his body. Such being the case the hyaenas ate the body that night. Lukole showed me the place & with my soldiers I looked sharply for a vestige of the bones, that we might make a decent grave for him but none was left.[144] Poor Farquhar a sad fate was his, and all for his lust for brandy & women.
As for Jacko there was no good in him, & he is as well dead as alive but it might otherwise have been with Farquhar.

April 8th. Matamombo 6 hours
What a difference in travel we made to day with an unloaded caravan. The spot where poor Omar my little dog died. Bought an ox yesterday for 11 doti. While Eastern Ugogo is famished Mpwapwa smiles in plenty – the rich soil thrives abundantly Wadirigo or Wahehe rob right and left. The peasants watch their gardens night and day, lest they come & steal.
Chunio, called Kunyo or Urine from its bad water by Wangwana, Marenga Makali by Wago & Wasagara. Kanya-para lord of the Hills above the saline water once owned

142. Chunyo or Kunyo, (*HIFL*, 247). Stanley explains the name of this place by the bad quality of its water (see this notebook, p. 93).
143. "Mpwapwa" is the word used by Arabs, and "Mbambwa" by the Wasagara (*HIFL*, 166).
144. From this assertion, it is unlikely that a grave was dug. Stanley gives a different story: "We collected a large quantity of stones, and managed to raise a mound near the banks of the stream to commemorate the spot where his body was laid" (*HIFL*, 640).

large herds which roamed far down into the plain forest of Marenga Makali but Wadirgo[145] came by night and attacked.

Wasgara[146] are afraid of dead bodies like the Wakhutu. Great & small are taken out & thro[w]n into the nearest pit.

Sketch of the Lake Ugombo[147]
[Legend] Trees down to the water edge, trees, rocks

Lake Ugombo – as seen on preceding page. April 9th 6 hours.

An admirable place for a settlement healthy brezes, fine rich spot.
Trees & water abundantly game of all kinds

April 10th[148] Chehu or Kehu. Sultan Kirassa. Mukondokwa. 6 hours to the second crossing. Luxuriant is the grass in the valley of the Mukondokwa truly tropical during the rains. The roads are covered with the tall grass, in tangled heaps or swathes, higher than a man's head. So different is the scene a few days after the Masika is finished.
In concentric folds of hills valley Mukondokwa

April 11th. Misonghi. Sultan Kadetamari.[149] 5 ½ hours.
Following the Mukondokwa River through its many windings, we cross several gulleys through which during this rainy season course furious torrents We pass Munyi[150] Usagara, and in half an hour pass Kiora, and arrive at the ford of the river,[151] on the left branch of which is situated the three villages over which Kadetamare rules. Kadetamare is a good old soul partial to strangers. On my arrival at the Khambi situated on a sloping hill a little below his villages he sent me about five gallons of his home-brewed, a courtesy because unexpected I returned most liberally, since I was able to do so having with me plenty of cloth. He was exalted beyond measure on seeing the fine present I sent to him and declared I was a Musungu without compare.
   The valley of the Mukondokwa is a pass, which[152] permits easy access to the table land of the interior, as the Sooroo Pass gave the Abyssinian invaders an access to the table land of Tigre. It is not by a half[153] as steep as the latter, since in this a

---

145. For 'Wadirigo'.
146. For 'Wasagara'.
147. Blue and black pencil. The sketch was used for the picture "The Lake and Peak of Ugombo" in *HIFL*, 155.
148. Chehu or Kehu. 'Sultan Kirassa' preceding 'Mukondokwa'.
149. Kadetamare (*HIFL*, 641).
150. Muniyi (*HIFL*, 151).
151. 'of the river' added above the line.
152. 'admits' crossed out.
153. 'half' written above 'quarter' crossed out.

river of some depth[154] flows through while a stream would soon empty itself in the Sooroo Pass.

It is not so sublime or rugged as the Sooroo but far more beautiful & picturesque. Every inch in this valley is covered here with the greenest verdure there with the tropical density of vegetation, the mountain's slopes with a thin forest of tamarind & the gum-copal tree, the valley with fields of tall & waving stalks of dourra maize, and millet with forests of mighty tamarind palmyra, mangrove, chenar or Plane tree, & the gigantic canoe tree rivaling in height exceeding in girth of column & inferior in the beauty of its leafage to the magnificent Mparamusi tree.

The three great sultans or[155] Mtemis of Usagara are Mbumi, Kaditamari, and Muniyi.

What a field for missionaries this Usagara presents. Health & abundance of food are assured to them & convents too I have no doubt. Except civilized[156] society nothing that the soul of man can desire is lacking here. From the village of Kadetamari I can see a score of positions & enviable sites for missionary stations, pure heath giving breezes blowing[157] over them, water in abundance at their feet fertility unsurpassed around them, with docile, & good tempered people dwelling everywhere at peace with themselves & with all the world.

As the passes of Olympus unlocked (See Gibbon Roman Empire Decline & Fall) so this pass of the Mukondokwa promises to unlock the gates of Savage Africa to the beneficent influence of the Gospel.

The Wami River might be navigated by small steam[ers] as far as this village I am almost certain. I have navigated a river of the same size more crooked more unpromising in looks than this same Mukondokwa or Wami River. I refer to the small Saline River in Arkansas, where ague is far more[158] plentiful than here. The current, except in the monsoon is not than two miles an hour. At the various fords during the dry season, I found over 30 inches, during the wet season it rises to six feet and has a current varying from 3 to five knots an hour. Its banks from its mouth are inhabited by people who would give no offence & who after the first alarm at the strange sight of a steamer, would encourage[159] than thwart the advances of such strangers. Should missions ever be established this river would furnish means of easy communication with the outside world, would do away with the fatigue of travel of seventeen hard marches of bearing to them the luxuries & encouragements of their friends.

---

154. 'of some depth' added above the line.
155. 'or' written over 'of'.
156. 'civilized' added above the line.
157. 'blowing' written over 'of'.
158. 'far more' written above 'as' crossed out.
159. 'rather' is missing.

I can fancy old Kadetamari rubbing his hands with glee at the sight of the white men coming to teach his people the words of the Mulungu,[160] how to sow and reap & build houses to cure their sick, for the missionaries must know the several duties of thorough teachers, as much as the thorough sailor, ought to know to reef, hand, & steer. What glorious grapes could not this valley grow, & what cotton, what wheat the mountain tops & what potatoes, what rice the valley & what fruit. Ah Good Providence send the good men quickly & let them not be women but men, not kid gloved dandies & journal writing polemical fellows, but thorough laborers in this garden of the Lord.[161]

Mukondokwa joins the Rufuta, Rufu,[162] Little Makata goes into the Big Makata, Big Makata into the Wami. Rudewa goes into the Wami. Mukondokwa rises in the mountains of Kayma Kaguru,[163] in the district of Mundo,[164] Usagara. 15 days off from Kadetamari.
Mount Kibwe & Peak opposite Kadetamari, 1500 feet ab[o]ve the valley.
Mdunku River runing from Kivya runs into the Munkondokwa below Kadetamari.

April 12th. Mvumi 6 hours.
This & the following day will be long remembered in the memories of the several members of this Expedition for the fatigues, & hardship incurred on these marches. The Mukondokwa serves as a drain to about 1000 square miles of mountain country. A severe rain fills this drain to overflowing and the plain below the mouth or the pass is inundated throughout its whole extent until it resembles a small sea. This was our experience – yet urgent necessity impelled us onward lest we might be compelled to camp here to the end of the monsoon rains. The valley of the Mukondokwa was a system of mountain strea[m]s overflowing their banks, and watery channels coursing furiously to their main receptacle
[Rest of the page crossed out][165]

[Double page taken widthwise]
[Sketch] "Mount Kibwe of Mukondokwa, Range opposite Kadetamari"
[Legend] Trees everywhere, trees up and down everywhere forest, forest.

to their main receptacle the river, marshy bottoms wherein we sank to the knees in mire jungly tunnels through which the Wanguana dragged their loads bent almost to

---

160. Stanley adds "the Sky Spirit" after the "Mulungu" (*HIFL*, 235).
161. This paragraph is taken up in *HIFL*, 235. It echoes criticism that Livingstone leveled at University missionaries under Bishop C. Mackenzie. See S.A. 11, January 9, 1872.
162. Rufu or Ruvu? 'f' written over 'v'?
163. Kema Kaguru (*HIFL*, 231).
164. Mundu (*HIFL*, 231).
165. "The river, marshy bottoms .... at the ford near Mvuni". This text is crossed out but is also copied on the following page.

the ground. Arriving at the ford near Mvuni, we found the water up to the armpits, and coursing through several shallow crevasses towards the plain of Makata, in all directions except upwards. The rain came down furiously, beating the surface of the river into a yellowish foam. Under such difficulties, as a rain which lashed us until we were almost breathless, an over flowing river, and mud up to our knees, we arrived at the dismal village of Mvuni. We passed the night in fighting mosquitoes, and in heroic endeavors to win sleep, in which we were partly successful owing to the utter weariness of our bodies. Sugar canes grow here in stalks as large as a <u>man's</u> wrist which is grown to be eaten here, & to earn a few shukkahs of cloth. 25 stalks sold for a shukka.

April 13th. Camp in swamp near second ford. 3 hours. It had rained the whole night, & the dawn brought no cessation. Yet, thought no one liked the appearance of the dense weather outside.

[Page widthwise]

Lo. Enclosed, hemmed in, imprisoned in a swamp
With weeping skies,
By one immense, dark & gloomy forest whose damp
And wet, do chill our blood
Tis vain to seek in[166] the dense overhanging leafage
That roofs our woeful camp with midnight gloom
For one small ray of sunshine. The dripping bocage[167]
Answers to the battering rain, as if another day of doom
Had surely come
like that[168] which Noah laid, & a world did rise
Hopeless, despairing. My thoughts are fixed upon the countless days

April 14th Rehenneko 4 hours
    "   15th Halt
    "   16th Halt
    "   17th Halt

People returned succeeded in crossing the river all safe.

Discharged 6 men with whom I was annoyed daily.

18th. Wanamgeni, Wanguana of Makuwa of Kilwa bought 115 fresh eggs in short time. 20 sold for a shukka.

---

166. 'seek in' written above 'pierce' crossed out.
167. First written 'bockage', then corrected to 'bocage'.
168. 'Which such as Noah saw' crossed out; 'Had surely come' crossed out; 'like that' written above 'a day' crossed out.

19th Rudewa River

20th. Uronga River, called Mbengerenga[169] here. Leaving Rehenneko. Crossed Ulonga or Uronga rises in Mundu then another stream & going NNE.
Came to the khambi or village of the ivory hunters -: runaways from Kilwa.

19th Crossed 2 Rivers. Water up to our armpits average depth 2 feet of water over the plain. 20th Crossed a branch of the Rudewa, and the Ulonga once again

[Sketch of a map]
[Legend] Ulonga R., G. Makata R., Little Makata, Rudewa.

[Sketch] "Crossing the Rudewa"
[Legend] Many Trees, Thick Bark[170]

[Sketch of a head of an animal]

21st Makata River
    3 days -Zungomero
        -Khetu
        -Mulaly
    Mbuni
    Simbawenni[171]

Mountains around Simbawenni famed for their goats.
Made a forced march through slush, mire, sloughs, mud, water for 7 ½ hours to Makata from Mbemgerenga.
Natives call the gadfly bungho Mkuba, tsetse bungho[172] Mdogo

22nd Chigongo – Makata.
Village nine houses. Enormous. Sultan considers himself my friend. He coveted a[173] tasseled fez of Stamboul which he saw on the head of my Arab interpreter & would not be quieted until I had made him a tassel & attached it[174] to a Zanzibar Fez. As soon as we had crossed the Makata swollen to six times its ordinary breadth and had

---

169. 'Mberenga' crossed out.
170. 'Bark' is uncertain.
171. An oblique line joins 'Mbuni' to 'Simbaweni'.
172. 'Bungho' for 'mbungo', the Kiswahili word for the tsetse.
173. 'fez' crossed out.
174. 'it' repeated.

arrived at Chigongo's village we were informed by a down[175] caravan from Usagara bound for Whinde on the Coast, that the little Makata would have to be bridged that if anything it was worse than the great Makata. A detail[176] of men was sent to bridge it & by six P. M. they had finished they said their labors. The reek & filth & deadly odor of putrefaction around this village[177] the effect of inundated waters retiring from the black mud they had deposited was such that I will never forget it.

Every moment I expected to fall down senseless. Every breath I inhaled was full of this deadly[178] poison. The horn sounding the morrow's march contrived not a little to raise my depressed spirits.

23rd. At daylight we were on our way to the L. Makata[179] now up to our armpits, then up to loins then to knees, & men up to armpits again in water for half an hour, & we arrived at the River, now about half a mile broad. In five hours we had crossed everything safely. We started again & in another half hour came to another river at this season 300 yards broad. Splash, splash, slosh, slosh all the time. This was impassable every one said. In the middle the proper bed of the river, the current was fierce surging down at 10 knots an hour. The water was very deep. To stop & look at it surrounded as we were by a waste of waters with not even a dry spot large enough to rest a bale of cloth on was out of the question The tallest men were sent at various spots to find a ford. Maganga a tall Unyamwezi found one where the waters came only to his[180] chin. After fruitless endeavor to find a better one, this ford was adopted. The tallest men followed in the wake of Maganga, and arrived at the high ground on the opposite bank, and returned to assist the others. At 3 P. M. Everything was safe on this side and the dreadful Makata was passed – 12 days of hard hard[181] fighting against water, over ground which in dry weather might easily be traversed in three marches.

24th. We all said Kwa hary[182] to the Makata and after 5 ½ hours arrived at Simbo. Here the Mnyamwezi cow becoming moribund after its hard marching & bitter experience was despatched & served as meat to the tired men.

Wangwani Jofari begging cloth. It is a custom for down caravans to beg at every good opportunity.

25th Made a long march of 7 hours & arrived at Muharreh. Arriving before Simbamwenni we saw the effects of the destructive flood that had visited here but a few days

---

175. 'down' added above the line.
176. 'detail' written over 'detachment' crossed out.
177. 'owing the' crossed out.
178. 'deadly' written over 'death'.
179. The Little Makata.
180. 'mouth' crossed out.
181. 'hard' repeated.
182. For 'kwa heri': goodbye.

ago. Kisabengo while he lived, had expended immense labor in bringing a[183] branch of the Ungerengeri close to the town which last year presented quite a civilized appearance with its stone towers & stone walls and handsome gates of Arabesque pattern. Now the branch after bursting through the dyke of Kisabengo swept the entire north-western wall, gate and tower and sweeping an entire suburb away devastated extensive cultivated tracts. The mountains at the back of the town show the traces of innumerable land slips wherein trees rocks and earth sweeping down the slopes proved fatal to hundred of Waruguru who had built their villages on the slopes.[184] In the words of the Washensi, the Waruguru are all perished their dead bodies are found every where. Further on also at Moussoudi we are told half a caravan conveying powder & guns to Unyamwezi has been swept away with almost the entire wealth of the caravan. How true this story this is we shall hear the day after to morrow. I consider our delay at Rehenneko to have saved us from much peril if not death. Every thing so far connected with this expedition has turned out to be for the best.

At Muhaweh under a large baobab I witnessed an interesting sight – a battle between the yellow ants & the whites, in which the latter suffered annihilation- the yellows destroyed a whole army of whites in half an hour.

The Waruguru sell & make flat baskets for use as trays to hold rice & food & to sift chaff from grains.

Within these days I have seen the remain of three Waganga who have suffered death by fire from necromancy (Machawi) or witchcraft. Their clothes were hung up to the nearest trees as a warning to others.

Sultana took flight during the inundation & went North.

We are 8[185] days from the coast. Mikeseh[186] – Moussoudi, Kisemo, Msuwa, Imbiki, Kingarru,[187] Hera – Rosako Kikoka Bagamoyo.[188]

26th April. Mikeseh Sultan Makungwe, Udoe. 7 hours. A long march. Birds with long tails[189] brown black about the size of a Redbreast. Red brids, with redbreasts a broad red strip on back & crimson tails. Ground stinks with the smell of the large black ants.

We heard the news confirmed of the loss sustained by a caravan which had camped too close to the river Ungerengeri at Kibrumo. It is a fault only too common with caravans & Washensi in this country. This country in appearance is very like Western

---

183. 'a' written over 'the'.
184. See *HIFL*, 646.
185. '8' written over '7'.
186. Mikiseh (*HIFL*, 113).
187. Kingaru (*HIFL*, 94).
188. Something was written '…' and erased between these two last lines.
189. Here is a sketch of this bird.

Kaiwendi. We were welcomed as old friends by the Sultan of this village, & they asked after the thing that rolled over the ground.[190]

27th April. Moussoudi on the Ungerengeri 7h 45m. A very long march. Fatiguing and painful. Descending at length from the spine of wavy range we had been travelling came in sight of the Valley of the Ungerengeri, and realized at once by what we saw the extent & nature of the[191] calamity which had destroyed nearly a "hundred" villages, one half of the inhabitants, and all the property consisting of extensive fields of standing corn, holcus[192] & other grains live stock, houses, <…> in one night (implements).[193]

The inhabitants had gone to rest as usual as they had done since they first settled in the broad & fertile valley of the Ungerengeri doubtless rejoicing at the approaching harvest, & fullness of plenty which they witnessed around them. Deep sleep was upon the valley and its hundred villages, nothing might have been heard save the monotonous cry[194] of bull frog & hiss & sound of insect life when suddenly came the flood with its loud deep roar, its raging fury & volume of waters sweeping villages, forests, cattle poultry poultry[195] debris, into one by one fell swoop into utter destruction.

The scene –six days after the flood has abated and the river[196] has subsided[197] flowing quiety enough over a broad shallow[198] bed is simply awful. Every bend of the crooked road showed the same traces, suggested the same picture of death & destruction, ruined houses, and fields of corn laid flat, & heaps upon heaps of logs & rubbish.

Caravan Unyamwezi lost
5 men & entire property, consisting of bales, kegs of powder & guns

28th April. Halt at Moussoudi.[199] The people are quite tired, complain of wearied legs, thorns in the feet & aching backs.

Only two villages are left of all the scores that were in the valley. - Moussoudi has lived here 25 years. Never saw a flood like this before. He is about to take my advice and remove his village to the range of low hills about a mile East of the river.

My people stuff themselves with roasting ears & day & night eat without intermission. Nothing but Indian corn to be had a few beans, here & there

---

190. The hand cart made to carry heavy loads proved to be too cumbersome. Stanley mentioned it for the last time at Mpwapwa, on May 17, 1871, and it was probably abandoned there (S.A. 7).
191. 'destru[ction]' crossed out.
192. *Holcus sorghum.*
193. '(implements)' written under 'in one'.
194. 'cry' written over 'roar'.
195. 'poultry' repeated.
196. 'river' written over 'water'.
197. 'running' crossed out.
198. 'chasm' crossed out.
199. Mussoudi (*HIFL*, 647).

Moussoudi has a <…>[200] is a doctor, has a son called Haruna Jina[201] "No name" because his wife was a long time bringing him forth.

People about here wear a girdle of broad leaves from Palm.

[Ink] 29th Msuwa

30th Kisemo

[On the inside cover: plan of a house[202] and over it, list of stops of Stanley's journey.]
[Several pages torn out.]

[Opposite page: Stanley's trunk mapping.]

---

200. Word undecipherable beginning with c…
201. 'Haruna Jina' probably for 'Hakuna Jina': 'there is no name'.
202. Might this be Stanley's tembe at Kwihara?

Account Book of the NEW YORK HERALD Expedition into Central Africa (S.A. 74), Full Transcript

[Exped]**ition to Central Africa**[1]

[1]

Ammunition

	Dolls	Cts
8 Kegs 6 lbs Each. Powder	10	00
2 " 8 lbs "	2	50
40 lbs Gunpowder	40	00
1 Keg 8 lb Powder	1	25
6000 Caps	3	00
1000 Cartridge Cases	18	00
2000 Winchester Cartridges	50	00
2500 Starrs "	59	00
200 " "	5	00
7 bags Shot 98 lbs	10	50
1000 Waterproof Caps		00
1 Bag Buck Shot 10 ½ lbs	2	00
245 lbs Bullets	26	00
500 Pistol Cartridges	9	00
500 Revolver Cartridges (Lepage)	15	00
15 lbs Pistol Bullets	1	80
[Total in pencil]	255	05

---

1. These pages in Stanley's handwriting were detached from a notebook and are unbound. The first left page is missing, but its content is still available in the copies of all Stanley's mission accounts from 1868 to 1879.

[2]

[From the copy of the missing left page]

Search after Livingston[e]
Expedition to Central Africa

Arms	Dolls	Cts
1 Double Breech Loading Smooth bore	115	"
1 Winchester Rifle (Present)		
1 Henry Rifle 16 Shooter (Present		
1 Elephant Rifle	50	"
2 Starrs Breech Loading Carbine	50	"
1 Jocelyn Rifle	15	"
1 Breech Loading revolver	40	"
1 " " " (Lepage	30	
22 Muskets 2.75	60	50
6 Pistol $3	18	"
1 Battle Axe 3 Napo.	12	"
2 Swords 3 "	12	"
2 Daggers 2 "	8	"
1 Spear 1 "	4	"

[3]

Necessaries			Dolls	Cts
Needles 75¢ Pins 40¢ Thread 12¢			1	27
	R.	Ann[2]		
Tape		12		
Blotting Paper		12		
Account Book	9	"		
Writing Paper	3	"		
Recapping Instrument	5	8		
Refitter[3] & Turnover	21	8		
Shot Pouch	6	0		
Powder Flask	5	0		
10 cases Tobacco	10	0		
1 Pipe	3			
1 Tea Box & Lock	4			
1 Sporting Knife	18			

    2. "R." for Rupee; "Ann or A." for Annas (currency of Zanzibar).

      3. Reading uncertain: refiller? refitter?

1 Pocket Canteen	9			
1 Nest. Glasses	1	12		
Pocket Filter	4			
2 Japanned Cups & Saucers Plates & Bowls	5	8		
3 ½ yds Waterproof Sheeting	19	4		
	126		63	00
[Total in pencil]			64	27

[4]

Necessaries			Dolls	Cts
	R.	A.		
1 Bound Sketch Block	2	4		
2 Japanned Canisters	2	0		
4 Air Cushions	42	0		
1 Air Pillow	6	4		
	62	8	26	25
1 Spring Balance 200 lbs			3	00
1 " " (Circular "			6	50
1 " " (" 500 lbs			10	00
Brass Faucet				75
2 Boxes Scented Soap			1	50
10 lbs Washing Soap			1	00
15 Chains			8	00
1 doz "			6	00
2 doz Powder Flasks			9	00
8 Locks 25ᶜ			2	00
1 doz Padlocks			2	00
6 Ring Bolts				50
1 doz Box Matches			1	50
1 Bull's Eye Lantern			1	50
1 Ink Bottle				25
2 Tin Boxes & 9 Cups			1	00
[Total in pencil]			80	75

[5]

Necessaries	Dolls	Cts
4 Carpet bags	8	00
4 Pkts Needles		40
4 doz Sail Needles	1	50

6 doz Mixed Sizes Fish Hooks	1	00
2 Baskets Cotton for Packing	1	50
12 Pads for Saddles $2	24	00
1 musquito Curtain	2	50
14 doz Candles $1.50	21	00
4 ½ Gross White Buttons	3	00
1 ½ Bundle White Thread	2	50
Thread		37 ½
2 Combs		75
Tape for Tent	3	75
7 Penknives 50ᶜ	3	50
Buckles 75ᶜ		75
Needles		12 ½
3 Bars Castile Soap	1	50
4 Note Books	2	00
8 doz Iron Rings	7	50
4 Common Note Books		40
8 Metallic Note "	3	00
[Total in pencil] $	89	05

[6]

Necessaries	Dolls	Cts
1 doz Butcher Knives	1	50
Cotton for Packing Saddles with	10	25
2 doz Hatchets	12	00
300 Iron Rings for Saddles	21	00
Iron Chain for " "	4	00
1 Chart Box 50. 1 Tea Box 1.50	2	00
1 Sugar " 1.25 1 Salt " 1.00	2	25
1 Square Tin " 1.50 1 Tin Bottle 25	1	75
2 lbs Tacks Copper 2.50 2 doz Large Needles .50	3	00
1 Clothes Box $12 1 Box with Divisions $12	24	00
1 Tea Dish Box $12 1 Soap & Candle Box $10	22	00
Cartridge " $6 4 Canteens 3.25	9	25
4 Oil Cans $6.00 Lamp 50	6	50
4 Botts Cologne $3.00 Lamp Oil 25	3	25
2 Tooth Brushes 25ᶜ 200 Flints 75ᶜ	1	"
Tooth Powder 50. Small Nails 50ᶜ	1	"
2 Frasilah of Cotton	9	00
[Total in pencil]	133	75

[7]

Necessaries	Dolls	Cts

[Rest of the page blank]

[8]

Boat	Dolls	Cts
1 Wooden Boat (Large from Mr Webb	80	00
1 " " (Small from Mr Morse	40	00
2 Blocks		75
10 Gross Screws 1.50	15	"
5 lbs Nails	1	"
Spikes	1	50
12 Bolts Canvas Nos 3 & 5	144	"
6 Bolts of Duck for Tails & Tents	36	"
3 ½ Kegs of Tar 6.50 per Keg	19	50
2 Tins White Lead 1.75	3	50
4 Botts Paint Oil	1	50
50 Ropes 20 feet Long	6	50
4 " " " "	1	00
Twine		50
3 Paint Brushes	"	60
Twine	"	75
25 pieces of Cord for repairing timbers of Boat	3	50
Rope	3	
3 Coils of Rope	4	50
12 Coils of Rope 1.50 for Halters	18	00
6 Rolls of Cotton Band 2.00	12	00
[Total in pencil]	393	10

[9]

Boat	Dolls	Cts
Twine for Sewing Boat	9	25
50 Rings	3	12 ½
12 Sheets of Ship Copper 1.50	18.00	
[Total in pencil]	30	37 ½

[10]

Cooking Pots & Dishes	Dolls	Cts
3 Knives & 3 Forks	"	75

4 Spoons		75
Copper Lids	4	00
4 Pots	4	00
2 Tin Tea Kettles 1.50	3	"
1 Copper Kettle	1	50
1 " Pot	2	00
2 Large Tin Pans	4	00
1 Coffee Pot & 4 Spoons	1	50
1 Coffee Mill	1	75
1 Tray		50
1 Silver Tea Pot	9	00
3 " " Spoons	2	25
4 Cups & Saucers	1	50
6 Plates 50.	.	50
4 Saucepans	6	00
2 Frying Pans 1.00	2	00
[Total in pencil]	45	00

[11]

Bedding & Clothing	Dolls	Cts
4 Suits of Flannel $5	20	-
6 Towels	1	50
1 Doz Pr Socks	2	25
4 Suits of Flannel Pyjamas	20	00
4 Trousers & 4 Shirts of Flannel	12	00
Sewing	5	00
3 Shirts of white Flannel	6	37 ½
4 Shirts of " " (for Selim	10	50
2 P^{rs} Canvas Shoes 2.50 6 Pr Leather $24	26	50
1 Waterproof Coat (from Mr Morse	10	00
[Total in pencil] $	114	12 ½

[12]

Tools	Dolls	Cts
1 Double Cross Cut Saw (Large Size	8	00
1 Tinmans Sodering Iron	1	50
2 Cakes of Spelter	1	00
1 set of Bitts	1	50
1 Hand Vice	3	00
1 Wire Cutter	1	"

3 Small Pincers		75
3 Augers	3	75
1 Foot Rule		25
1 Lead Melter & Ladle		50
2 Saws Hand	2	75
1 Hand Saw Large	1	25
6 Files	3	00
2 Hammers	1	25
4 Paper Tacks	2	00
2 Carpenter's Adzes	2	00
1 " Compass		75
1 Bitt, Tools, Chisels &c	6	50
1 Sett -Bitt, Augers, Files	5	00
6 Gimlets	2	00
1 Large Pincers	1	50
[Total in pencil]	49	25

[13]

Tools. Continued	Dolls	Cts

[Rest of the page blank]

[14]

Provisions	Dolls	Cts
1 Box Tea 7 lbs	7	
1 lb Coffee		62 ½
2 Botts Curry	1	00
2 " Pepper		50
6 Pt Botts Champagne	2	00
2 Botts Sauce	1	00
1 doz Brandy	27	50
2 Pots Butter	2	00
1 lb Saleratus[4]		50
4 lbs Mustard	1	40
5 lbs Tea	4	75
15 " Coffee	2	50
100" Flour	6	50
10 lbs Vegetables		37 ½

---

4. A leavening agent like baking soda.

	Dolls	Cts
20 Cans Extract of Meat	20	00
50 lbs Rice	2	50
1 Tin Pearl Barley		25
3 Botts Molasses		50
3 Botts Vinegar	1	12 ½
1 doz Sardines	2	75
20 lbs Ghee	5	00
[Total in pencil]	91	77 ½

[15]

Provisions	Dolls	Cts
5 lbs Raisins	1	00
30 lbs Sugar	2	31
15 lbs Salt	2	00
2 Gislahs[5] of Matama for Donkeys	7	56
3 lbs Sago 50. 3 Tapioca 75.	1	25
100 lbs Potatoes	7	00
4 Botts Curry	2	00
Matama for the Animals for 40 days	65	75
21 Pagazis Pice	13	12 ½
24 Soldiers "	15	00
32 Souls Rice	61	06
Europeans Marketables	42	00
Rice for the March	13	44
10 Goats " "	24	25
Matama " "	7	50
Grass for the Animals	9	40
Ferry Money	6	50
Dhows to Zanzibar 4 Times	.	50
1 Dhow Chartered	7	00
[Total in Pencil]	288	64 ½

[16]

Provisions	Dolls	Cts

[Rest of the page blank]

---

5. One Gisla of matama = 360 lbs net (source: *The Official Gazette of the East Africa and Uganda Protectorates*, 1907, no. 176, p. 70).

[17]

Medicine	R.	A.	Dolls	Cts
1 Leather Chest			20	00
1 Lancet			1	-
1 oz Quinine			3	50
5 doz Colocynth Pills			1	-
Tartaric Acid	.	12		
Tartar Emetic	.	6		
Oil Peppermint	4	.		
Ess. "	2	.		
Calomel	.	8		
Jalap	3			
Castor Oil	.	8		
Camphor	1	.		
Amonia	1	.		
Arnica	2	.		
Laudanum	1	8		
2 Botts Chlorodyne	6	.		
Ipecachuana	1	.		
Dover's Powders	3	.		
Lint	1	4		
Caustic	2	.		
Medical Book	.	14	15	37 ½
[Total in pencil]			40	87 ½

[18]

Medicine Bought at Zanzibar	Dolls	Cts
12 doz Colocynth Pills		
50 doz Catharthic "		
Epsom Salts		
Castor Oil		
3 oz Quinine		
12 ¼ Muriate Cinchonine		
Warburgh's Tincture		
Mercury ,		
Sulphate of Zinc		
Carbolic Acid		
	28	00
[Total in pencil]	28.	00

[19]

N°	Animals	Doll.	Cts
1	1 Dark Bay Horse (Present of Mr Goodhue)		
2	1 Arab Grey (from the Sultan of Zanzibar		
3	1 Donkey	26	"
4	1 "	20	
5	1 "	15	
6	1 "	20	
7	1 "	20	
8	1 "	16	
9	1 "	16	
10	1 "	15	
11	1 "	16	
12	1 "	24	
13	1 "	23	
14	1 "	18	
15	1 "	14	
16	1 "	17	
17	1. "	19	
18	1 "	23	
19	1 "	22	
20	1 "	26	
21	1 "	18	
[Total in pencil]		$368	

[20]

N°	Animals	Doll.	Cts
22	1 Donkey	16	
23	1 "	17	
24	1 "	18	
25	1 "	13	
26	1 "	10	
[Total in pencil]		74	

[21]

N°	Advances	Dolls	Cts
1	William L. Farquhar 1st Mate	50	"
2	John Smith 2nd "	50	"
	His Doby "	1	"

			Dolls	Cents
3	Abdul Kader	Tailor	10	"
4	Bunder Salaam	Cook	20	"
5	Celion	Groom	15	"
6	Jacko[6]	Carpenter	2	"
7	Aranclar[7]	Steward		
	Wanguana			
8	Bombay	Captain	40	
	For his coat	"	3	"
9	Mabruki		20	"
10	Uledi[8]		20	"
11	Ulimengo		20	"
12	Baruti Farjallah[9]		20	"
13	Ambari		20	"
14	Uredi		18	"
15	Asmani		18	"
16	Sarmine		18	"
17	Kamna		18	"
18	Zaidee		18	"

[Total in pencil]   381

[22]

N°	Advances	Dolls	Cents
19	Farajji	18	"
20	Uledi Khatalaboo[10]	18	"
21	Umgareza	18	"
22	Jooma	18	"
23	Baraka	18	"
24	Mabruk Saleem (for Drum 75¢	18	75
25	Mabruk[11]	18	"
26	Khamisi $25 per year	2	"
27	Billalli $30 " "	2[12]	90
28	Kingaroo $25 " "	2	"

6. Missing without trace after Farquhar's death.

7. Aranselar, *HIFL*, 67.

8. Died at Wilyankuru (Tabora).

9. Died of smallpox, September 5, 1871.

10. Died at Wilyankuru.

11. Died at Wilyankuru.

12. '2' written over '3'. The advance was 2.90, as it is reported in the Muster Roll.

| 29 | Chowpereh $25 per year
(cloth 1 Kitambi Ismahili   62 ½
        2 Taujiri   1.00
        Cash   2.00) | 3 | 62 ½ |

Pagazis

30	Soongooroo	4	00
31	Saboor	4	00
32	Rojab	2	50
33	Billalli	2	50
34	Jafooneh	1	00
35	Sarboko	1	00
36	Khamisi @ $25 per annum	5	00
[Total in pencil]		158	27 ½

[23]

N°	Advances		Dolls	Cts
37	Shubari 1 gun	$	2	00
38	Chumba 1 gun	$	2	00
39	Asmani 1 gun	$	2	00
[Total in pencil]			6	00

[24]

Miscellaneous	Dolls	Cts
To Ladha Damji Collector of Customs (See Receipt for 4 Dhows to transport Donkeys & Effects of the Expedition from Island of Zanzibar to the Mainland	50	25
Present to Johari Consulate Dragoman	10	00
" to 4 Hindoos for transporting Horses	5	00
To Johari's Slave for making Tents	4	25
For Belts & Leather for Halters	12	00
" Buckles	2	50
To Jetta as Commission for buying the Cloth of the Expedition	18	00
To Soor Hadji Palloo for procuring 66 pagazis, & supplying them with cloth	738	00
To Matama & Ferry for Last Caravan the 6th	9	00
To Rent for House at Bagomoyo 40 days	5	30
[Total in pencil]	854	30

[25]

1871 Jan 25th Cloth Beads & Wire for the New York Herald Expedition

Doti	Pieces	Cloth[13]	Price Per piece	Dolls	Cts
80	40	4 Hkfs[14] each Large red check	84	33	60
80	40	" " " Different color Hkfs	93 ¾	37	50
80	40	" " " " " "	81 ¼	32	50
80	40	" " " " " "	87 ½	35	00
80	40	" " " " " "	62 ½	25	00
90	18	Check- Kunguru red 20 yds each	3.00	54	00
102 ½	18	" " " 25 " "	3.06 ¼	55	12 ¼
40	2	Korjahes[15] Sohari	13.50	27	00
60	3	" "	12.00	36	00
100	5	" " (Small)	9.00	45	00
100	5	" Dabwani (Large)	12.75	63	75
100	5	" " (Small)		43	75
10	½	" Kunguru (Cutch) Large	11.00	5	50
40	2	" " " Small	7.25	14	50
100	5	" Barsati	9.25	46	25
100	5	" "	8.75	43	75
200	10	" Taujiri Burrah	8.75	87	50
200	10	" Ismahili	8.50	85	00
200	10	" Rehani	8.75	87	50
40	2	" Sohari mixed			
		" Kikoi & Dabwani		20	
[Total in pencil]				878	22 ¼

[26]

	Pieces				
40	40	Barsati		20	00
14	2	Bolts of Red & Black Joho	15.00	30	00
7	1	Bindera – Red Chintz 28 yds		3	50
25	25	Best Dabwani Ulyah		31	00
	2	Shash (Hindi (Nensu [?] (Arab Shroud Cloth 20 yds each		75 7	00 00
	2	Flowered Muslin (Jamdani		4	00

13. About cloth, see Burton, *Lake Regions of Central Africa*, vol. 2, Appendix 1, pp. 390–94; on trade goods, see Sarah Fee, "Hostage to Cloth: European Explorers in East Africa, 1850–1890" Textile Society of America Symposium Proceedings, paper 680 (2012), http://digitalcommons.unl.edu/tsaconf/680.

14. "Hkfs" for handkerchiefs.

15. *Korjah*: Unit of measure. For cloth measures, see Burton, *Lake Regions of Central Africa*, 2:388–89.

	2	doz Fezes		8	00
40	20	Pieces Barsati		20	00
2062 ½	275	11 Bales of American Sheeting Each bale consisting of 25 pieces of 30 yds each or 7 ½ doti Price per bale $	93.75	1031	25
40[16]	2	Korjahes Best Kaniki	20.00	40	00
1000	25	" Common "	13.00	325	00

[Total in pencil]   1519   75

[27]

Fundo	Frasilah	Beads[17]			Weight	Dolls	Cts
			Per Frai	Per lb ¢	lbs		
87 ½	2 ½	Hafde	5.50	15 5/7	87 ½	13	75
	½	Dudio	7.00	20	17 ½	3	50
	1	Lakhio	4.50	12 6/7	35	4	50
	½	Ghulabio	12.00	34 2/7	17 ½	3	50
	2	Sami-Sami	13.00	37 1/7	70	26	00
	6	" "	12.00	34 2/7	210	72	00
	2 ½	Hafda	5.25	15	87 ½	13	12 ½
	1	Lunghio rega	7.75	22 1/7	35	7	75
	1	" Umbamba	8.00	22 6/7	35	8	00
	2	Mutoonda	2.87 ½	8 1/5	70	5	65
	0 ¼	Bubu	3.75	10 5/7	8 ¾		93 ¼
	6	"	4.00		210	24	00
	6	Merikani	7.25		210	43	50
	1	Kadunduguru	4.75		35	4	75
	2	Sami-Sami	12.		70	24	00
	1	Lunghio	7.75		35	7	75
		1500 Sungomazzi	18. per 1000			27	00
		1200 "	12 " "			24	00

[Total in pencil]   316   20 ¾

[28]

	Wire		Dolls	Cts
No 5	5 Frasilah	$7.00	35	00
No 6	5 "	$7.75	38	75

[Total in pencil]   73   75

---

16. '8' written over '4'.
17. About beads, see Burton, *Lake Regions of Central Africa*, 2:390–94.

[29]
Livingstone Expedition
Dr.

		Dolls	Cts
Jan 17	To 1st Draft drawn in favor of John Bertram of Salem	3750	00
Feb	To 2nd Draft drawn in like manner	3000	00
March 19th	To 3rd Draft " " "	1250	00
	Total $	8000	00
	Total Expenditure	8000	00

[30]
Cr.

Recapitulation	Dolls	Cts
Arms	414	50
Amunition	255	05
Necessaries	367	82
Boats	423	47½
Cooking Pots & Dishes	45	-
Bedding & Clothing	114	12½
Tools	49	25
Provisions	380	42
Medicine	68	87½
Animals	442	-
Money Advances	545	27½
Miscellaneous	854	30
Cloth	2397	97½
Beads	316	20¾
Wire	73	75
Total $	6747	02¼
Sums already charged	460	02
	6287	00¼
Interest or Premium	1571	87½
	7858	87¾
Cash reserved	105	84
Premium on it	35	28¼
$	8000	00

Notebook S.A. 1, Excerpts for the Year 1871

[This notebook is written in ink unless otherwise stated.]

Henry M. Stanley in act with Selim Heshmesh [engaged Jan. 1870]

Selim Heshmesh — Cr

		£	s	d
1870 Jan 19	Engaged Selim as interpreter at £1 per month, Board & Clothes			
Feb 19	Wages per month	1	"	"

[The chart indicates payments up to June 19, 1871. Following page, torn out]

Selim Heshmesh — Dr

		£	s	d
1870, Jan 19	Paid Selim's Brother Jacob in presence of Selim & Am Consul John B. Hay 3 months advance	3	"	"
Mar 1	Selim lost 1 new coat for me in taking it to a tailor, price of coat £5.00. Half price	2	10	"
June 16	Selim through carelessness lost on the road near Ispahan, Persia 31 francs	1	5	10
July 17th	Selim permitted alias to steal from me 1 first class Field Glass, after I had warned him tht he would steal it. Original Price 60 francs	1	10	"
[Pencil] 1871	At Simbawenni Selim broke trigger of my 30 pound gun	1	0	0
	On the road to Unyanyembe Selim broke glass of my compass[1]		2	.

William Lawrence Farquhar ac/- with Henry M. Stanley — Cr.

		£	s	d
1870, Nov 21	Engaged W. L. F. at £5 per month at Mauritius			
	Cash of his in my charge	7	"	
		$35		

W.L. Farquhar — Dr

1870		£	s	d
Dec 10	Gave him 5 rupees		10	
" 11	" 3 "		6	
" 12	" 2 "		4	

1. These two sums are fines to be deducted from his salary.

439

" "	" " "150 Cigars		7	6
Nov 24th	1 Tin Box Tobacco		2	
Dec 12th	Postage on letter			10
1871				
Jan 13th	Washing		4	
" 14th	At night money		8	
" 16	Noon		2	
" 18	Night		4	
" 28 [Pencil]	Night		20	
		3	8	4
		£3.8.4 = $	17	10
Feb 1st	Charlies Bill for Brandy[2]		18	72
"	Tailors Bill		30	00
"	Cash		20	00
			85	82
	Premium on $50 advance		12	50
		$	98	32
			35	"
		$	63	32
[Pencil]	To 82 Doti squandered on the road		82	00
			145	32

1871 John Smith's Ac/- with Henry M. Stanley

Dr.

Feb 1st [Ink]	Cash advanced to him on account/-	$	50		
"	Premium Paid on it		12	50	
[Pencil]	To doby whom he struck		1	00	
"	Premium			25	
"	1 Pr Shoes		5	62	½
"	1 Coat		5	62	½
"	1 Girl Slave		30		
"	1 Doti Merikani for Pipe		1	00	
	1 Fundo of Beads		"	12	½
			10	12	½
			6		

[Pencil] $200 for 15 months make $13.33 1/3 per month. Up to Feb 1st his wages amount to $160.00. $160 deducted from $200 which according to contract was due him for accompanying me leaves him on Feb 1st the sum of $53. 87 ½.

1871 Feb 1   Cr

[Blank Page]

---

2. See Charlie's Bill for drinks, up to February 1, S.A. 4893.

Muster Roll of Soldiers Engaged for the NEW YORK HERALD Central African Expedition (S.A. 74), Full Transcript

(Muster roll begins on following page)

[1] Double page

[Ink, except figures in italics, in pencil]

[left corner] Discharged 15th May 1872

No	Names[1]	Wages per annum	Time of Service	When Enlisted	Wages per month
1	Bombay	$80	15 ½ mths	1st Feb 1871	$6.66 ¾
2	Mabruki Speke	$40	15 ½ mths	1st Feb 1871	$3.33 ¼
3	Ulimengo	$40	15 ½ mths	1st Feb 1871	$3.33 ¼
4	Ambari	$40	15 ½ mths	1st Feb 1/71	$3.33 ¼
5	Uredi Manua Sera	$36	15 ½ mths	1st Feb 1871	$3.00
6	Asmani[2]	$36	15 ½ mths	1st Feb 1/71	$3.00
7	Sarmine	$36	15 ½ mths	1st Feb 1/71	$3.00
8	Kamna	$36	"	"	"
9	Zaidi	$36	"	"	"

[Total in blue pencil]

---

1. See François Bontinck, "Voyageurs africains en Afrique équatoriale," *Zaïre-Afrique;* Bontinck contributed profiles of the following travelers in several issues of the periodical: Robert Ferruzi, no. 107 (1976); Mbarak Bombay, no. 110 (1976); Uledi Pangani, no. 114 (1977); Uledi Manwa Sera, no. 118 (1977); Mabruki Speke, no. 122 (1978); Ferajji le cuisinier, no. 128 (1978); Hamadi le guide, no. 138 (1979);

Amount of wages due for such time as employed	Deductions		Balance due	Fit amount of reward for good conduct
$103.33 ½	Advance 1 Coat Lost 1 tent 1 Pistol 1 axe 2 doti Kaniki Shot on Tanganyika To 1 slave girl	$40 3 6 4 3 2 10 30 $108	Overdrawn by $46.6 ½ 30	$40. 45 [pencil]
$51.65 ¼	Advance 2 doti Cloth Merikani	$20 2 $22	$29.65 ¼	$10 ✓ – 10
$51.65 ¼	Advance Run away from Mirambo	$20 3 $23	$28 65 ¼ 30	$5 ✓ 2 ½
$51.65 ¼	Advance Ran away from me	$20 3 $23	$28 65 ¼ 30	$5 ✓ – 2 ½
$46.50	Advance	$18	$28.50	$5 ✓ 5
$46.50	Advance Forfeit 2 mths pay by desertion	$18 6 24	$22.50	None
$46.50	Advance	$18	$28.50	$5 ✓ 5
"	Advance Ran away from me at Mirambo	$18 3 21	$25.50	$5 ✓ ✓1
"	Advance	$18	$28.50	
			$220.45 ¾	$80

Chowpereh, no. 140 (1979); Khamisi Stanley, no. 142 (1980); Asmani, no. 144 (1980); Majwara, no. 146 (1980); Sarmini, no. 152 (1981).

   2. Whole line crossed out with a wavy line in pencil, from "$36" to "None." It seems the fine for desertion was dropped and the advance limited at $18.

[2] Double page

Continued

All discharged 15th May 1872

No	Names	Wages per annum	When Enlisted	Time of Service	Wages per month
10	Ferajji	$20 for 6 mths $76 for 9 ½ mths	1st Feb 1/71	15 ½ mths	$3 & $8
11	Umgareza[3]	$36	"	"	$3
12	Jumah	" "	"	$3	"
13	Baraka	" "	"	"	"
14	Khamisi	$25	"	"	$2.8 ¼
15	Chowpereh	$30	"	"	$2.50
16	Kingaru	$25	"	"	$2.8 ¼

[Total in blue pencil]

---

3. Whole line crossed out with a wavy line in pencil.

Amount of wages due for such time as employed	Deductions	Balance due	Suitable amount of reward for good conduct
$94.00	Advance $18 Lost 1 gun 5 23	$71	None ✓ 5 [pencil]
$46.50	Advance $18 Lost 1 gun 5 23	$23.50	None Paid [pencil]
"	Advance $18 2 doti Kaniki 1.00 5 doti as pagazi to go to Ujiji & did not carry load 5.00 $24.00	$22.50	$5
"	Advance $18	$28.50	$5 ✓ ✓5 [pencil]

$32.24	Advance $2.00
	For repair Gun 3.00
	                    $5.00
	Left me at Mirambo 3.00
	                    $8.00
		$24.24	$5✓ ✓5 [pencil]

$38.75	Advance $2.00 1 Kitambi Ismahili .62½ 2 Taujiri 1.00 $3.62 ½	34.50 [pencil] $34.13 ½	$5 ✓ 22.50 [pencil] [or 2.50?]
$32.24	Advance $2.00 Lost 1 gun 6.00 4 doti Kaniki to his captors 4.00 1 shukkah Kaniki .50 Twice deserted 6.00 16.25	$16.07 ¾	None Paid [pencil]
		$219.95 ¼	$20

[3] Double page
Muster Roll Continued: ….
Discharged 15th May 1872

No	Names	Wages per annum	When Enlisted	Time of Service	Wages per month
17	Bill Alli	$25	1st Feb 1/71	15 ½ mths	$2.8 ¼
18	Rojab	$25	1st July 1/71	10 ½ mths	$2.8 ¼
19	Mabruk (Unyanyembe)	$25	"	"	"
20	Umtamani	$25	15th July 1/71	10 mths	$2.8 ¼
21	Chanda	$25	"	"	"
22	Sadala	"	1st Sept	8 ½ mths	"
23	Kombo	"	"	"	"
24	Saburi Mdogo	"	"	"	"
25	Saburi Mkuba	"	"	"	"
26	Marora	"	"	"	"
27	Muccadum	"	"	"	"
28	Hamadi	"	"	"	"
29	Maganga	"	"	"	"
30	Selim	$60	21 Jan. 1870 July 1st 1872	30 months	$5.00

[Total in blue pencil]

Amount of wages due for such time as employed	Deductions	Balance due	Fit amount of reward for good conduct
$32.24	Advance $1. Cloth $2.90 Desertion $3.00 $6.90	$25.34 25.50	$5 ✓ 5
$21.48 ½	Advance $6.00 Desertion 3. 9.00	$12.48 ½ 12.50 [pencil]	$5✓ ✓5
"	Advance $6.00	$15.48 ½ 15.50 [pencil]	$5✓ ✓5
$20.44 ½	Advance $6.00	14.44 ½	$5✓ ✓ 5
"	Advance $6.00 1 Doti for man 1.00 7.00	13.44 ½	$5 ✓ ✓ 8 ½
$16.66	Advance $6.00	$10.66 ½	$5
"	"	$10.66 ½	$5
"	"	$10.66 ½	$2.50
"	"	$10.66 ½	$5 ✓
"	"	$10.66 ½	none
"	"	$10.66 ½	$5.00 ✓ 5 6
"	"	$10.66 ½	$5.00 ✓ 6 12.50 [pencil]
"	"	$10.66 ½	$5 good & excellent pagazi
$150	Advance $15.00	$135.00	$45 Most excellent behavior as interpreter & servant
		$290.85 ¼	$102.50

[4] [Ink in bold letters]

Total Wages Paid to 30 soldiers, on 15th May 1872 & 1st July 1872 as per preceding pages:

	$731.26¼
Rewards:	$202.00
	$933.26 ¼

[5] [Pencil]

23.50	Kombo
16.00	Sadala
22.50	Asmani
21.	Saboori Mdogo
83.00	
10	Kingaru
5	
5	Umgareza
2.50	
105.50	

Selim 5
Majwar[a][4] 5
Billalli 5
Kalulu[5] 2

---

4. Majwara's story is narrated in Sir John Milner Gray, "Livingstone's Muganda Servant," *Uganda Journal* 13, no. 2 (September 1949): 119; see also Appendix, Contract of African Soldiers . . . , May 21, 1872, S.A. 4749.

5. Selim, Majwara, Billalli (= Belali in *HIFL*, 313), and Kalulu were Stanley's gun bearers (*HIFL*, 315). Stanley had purchased Dugum Ali (=Kalulu), a slave boy, on September 7, 1871 (S.A. 7). On that date, Stanley mentioned one slave boy only among his expedition. How and when Majwara and Billalli were recruited is not mentioned in his journal. On September 10, Stanley was still "endeavouring to purchase a boy slave to carry one of my guns, but the prices demanded for one 12 years old was, as I consider it, enormous, so I did not buy one."

Journal S.A. 12 to Zanzibar, Excerpts (May 15–29, 1872)

[This Journal is written in ink]
[Inside the cover, a note in pencil: Brown parcel in [?]]

May 15th 1872. Livingstone's draft for £500 is not needed and I tore it up. I have been busy the last few days preparing his New Expedition. What was lacking in young Livingstone's Relief Expedition – Oswell – (I find his name to be Oswell not Oswald[1] I forgot he was named after the South African hunter) Livingstone gave me money to buy. The guns 50 in number Oswell supplied as well as the amunition, the tribute[2] & provision cloth. He has assisted me most willingly & well. He also gave me Nautical Almanacs for 1872, 73, 74, also a chronometer one of Livingstone's own which was in the charge of Dr Kirk. We have also packed blank[3] journals, writing paper, & envelopes, note books canned fruits, fish, wine, tea, cutlery & table ware, newspapers & private letters in soldered tin boxes. 100 lbs Wheat flour, & biscuits have likewise been packed up.

May 16. 1872. Continuing the packing & enlistment of new men, with whom we take every precaution that they are not slaves.

May 17th Received a letter from young Livingstone wherein he asks for a[4] copy of the list of articles his father wanted & also a list of the articles which I have bought, that he may send it to the R. G. Society, with an account of expenses
He also states that he has got a dhow to take him to Bagamoyo where he proposes to go to bring over the surplus stores of his Expedition, and that Lt Dawson has agreed to give £100 to the Capt of the vessel, which is to pay for 3 persons – himself being the third in case he is ready to go.[5]

---

1. Second bracket and name "Livingstone" crossed out. Stanley noted the origin of this name in his journal on February 20, 1872 (S.A. 11), but he kept confusing 'Oswell' and 'Oswald' in the same journal (May 6, 1872).
2. 'cloth' crossed out.
3. 'blank' added above the line.
4. 'list' crossed out.
5. See Appendix, Letter from Oswell Livingstone to Stanley, May 17, 1872, S.A. 488.

May 19th Young Livingstone writes me that he is decided not to go to Unyanyembe for reasons which he thinks just & sufficient. !! This is quite extraordinary! I wrote back saying I thought it was his duty to go, but he sent a reply that Dr Kirk has advised him that it would be dangerous in his present state of health, & that as[6] there was no absolute necessity for his personal superintendence of the caravan. Of course if he suffers in health I concur that the Doctor would rather[7] that he did not go.

May 21. Engaged with Kirk's assistance[8] a young Arab Mohammed bin Khalfan to lead Livingstone's caravan to Unyanyembe instead of Oswell Livingstone, for one hundred dollars.[9] He is to be subject to dismissal on reaching, or a further engagement at $500 a year. He is recommended by Syed Barghash.[10]
Signed a contract for 57 men to act as escort, or carriers for Livingstone. Paid 56 men the sum of 20 dollars in advance and the headman Manwa Sera 30 dollars. Enlisted also 6 Nassick Boys, and a man named Salina at $5 advance.[11] The Nassick boys are Mathew Wellington, Jacob Wainwright, Benjamin Rutton, Richard Rutton, John Wainwright, Carras Farrar. They appear rather soft – but for light work they may be useful.

May 23rd Young Livingstone has dismissed his Mombasa men, as I did not think they would suit.[12]

May 25. Lieut Llewellyn Dawson left to day for the Cape of Good Hope on the barque "Mary A Way" – by which he avoids travelling to England with me.
I am negotiating with Mr Schultze[13] owner of the steamer Africa to take me to the Seychelles to catch the Mauritius mail which calls there on or about 6th of June. He asks 900 dollars. The Revd Charles New thinks he will accompany me but has not decided yet.[14]

6. 'as' added above the line.
7. Word missing?
8. 'with Kirk's assistance' added above the line.
9. On the contract signed four days later, the name is written 'Galfin'. See Appendix, Contract of Mohammed bin Galfin, May 25, 1872, S.A. 4750.
10. On Kirk's assistance and Syed Barghash's support, see Appendix, Letters from John Kirk, British Consul in Zanzibar, to Stanley, Zanzibar, May 20, 1872, S.A. 2660.
11. See Appendix, Contract of African Soldiers with Uredi Manwa Sera as Captain . . . , May 22, 1872, S.A. 4749.
12. See Appendix, Letters from W. Oswell Livingstone to Stanley, May 23, 1872, S.A. 488.
13. Probably Hans Heinrich Theodor Schultz, a representative of the German firm Oswald established 1849 at Zanzibar. Cf. Hermann Kellenbenz, "Zanzibar et Madagascar dans le commerce allemand (1840–1880)," *Omaly sy Anio* (Département d'histoire, Université d'Antananarivo), no. 17–19 (1983–84): 311–18.
14. Charles New might have had mixed feelings about Stanley, as he wrote later (1873) in his book, *Life, Wanderings, and Labours*, 518: "Of Mr Stanley's energy, determination, perseverance, endurance, tact, and pluck, I have the highest opinion; but I do not think him an angel, or a genius, or that paragon of a hero which the English people made him believe himself to be."

May 27. I sent 64 men & boys today across by Arab dhow to Bagamoyo under charge of Mohammed the Arab and escorted by Joharri –dragoman of the American Consulate, who is to go with them one march into the interior to see them well out of the town & fairly started for Livingstone.

May 28th Chartered the Str Africa for 900 dollars to take me to the Seychelles. Oswell Livingstone, Lieut William Henn, & the Revd Charles New of the late Livingstone Relief Expedition also Capt Robert Morgan whose ship was driven ashore on the beach here during the hurricane of April[15] – have agreed to accompany me to Seychelles.

May 29. We embarked for home on the Str Africa which is a vessel of about 500 tons. Her best speed seems to be between six and seven knots an hour – but it is better than staying forever at Zanzibar. Only Selim Heshmy, and young Kalulu remain of my companions of the search[16] after Livingstone.

---

15. The hurricane of April 15, 1872, ruined Zanzibar's clove tree plantations and wiped out the Sultan's fleet. Kirk gave an account of the damages and wreckages caused by the hurricane in a letter to Sir Henry Rawlinson, Zanzibar, April 20, 1872, ms. copy, RGS-IGB Collections, JMS/2/127. He mentioned Dawson and Henn's presence at the Consulate. His wife gave a lively description of the damages in a letter to her sister, published by the *Bruce Herald* 6, no. 439 (October 9, 1872): 10.

A sketch of the effects of the hurricane at Zanzibar by Lieut. Henn was published in the *Illustrated London News*, June 1, 1872.

The hurricane caused torrential rain inland, and Stanley described the devastation on his way to the coast (*HIFL*, 643–48). He heard of the hurricane having devastated Zanzibar and Bagamoyo when stopping at Kingaru Hera on May 1 (649).

16. 'of the search' added above the line.

With Livingstone

Plate 30. "'Dr. Livingstone, I presume.'" (*HIFL*, facing 412)

Plate 31. "Mr. Stanley, in the dress he wore when he met Dr. Livingstone in Africa." Stereoscopic and Photographic Co. photograph. (S.A. 5155)
The Stanley Archives (S.A.), property of the King Baudouin Foundation, are held in trust at the Royal Museum for Central Africa (Belgium).

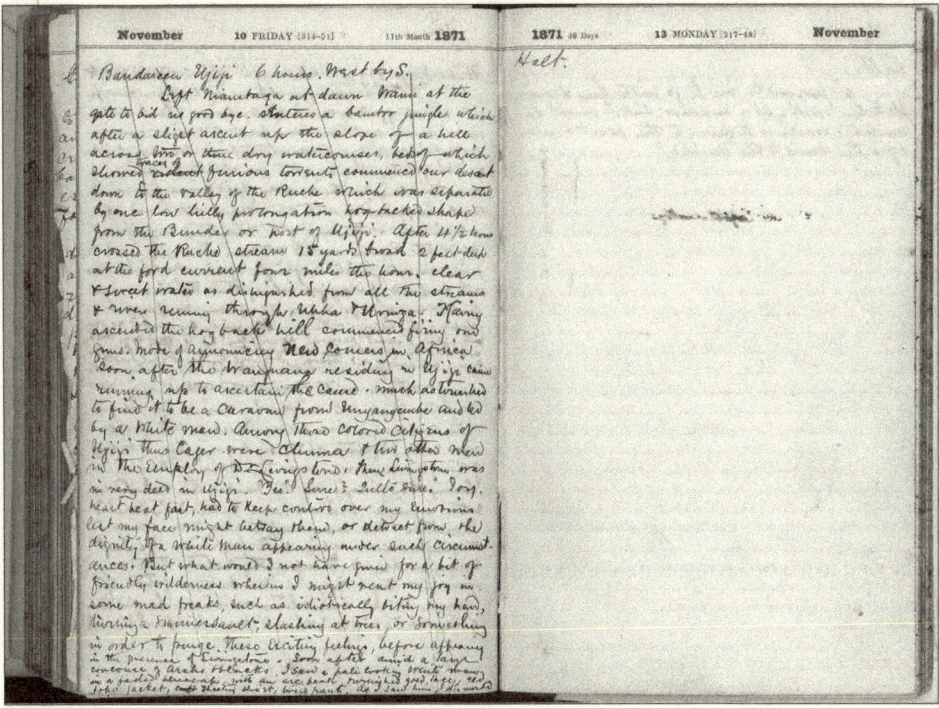

Plate 32. The page from Journal S.A. 7, November 10, Friday, 1871, when Stanley and Livingstone finally meet. The following sheet (covering November 11 and 12) is missing.

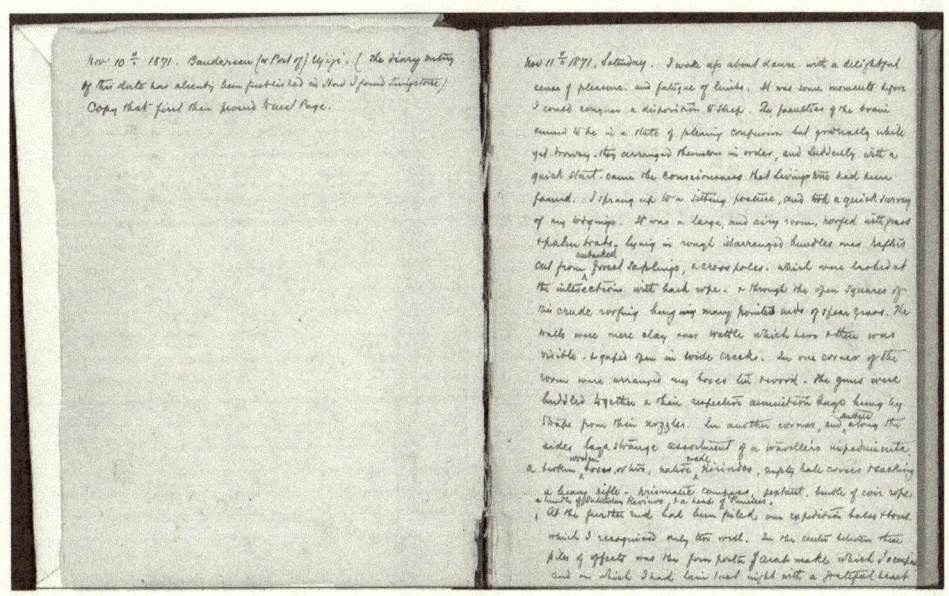

Plate 33. Entry from Journal S.A. 11 for November 11, 1871, expanding on Stanley's meeting with Livingstone.

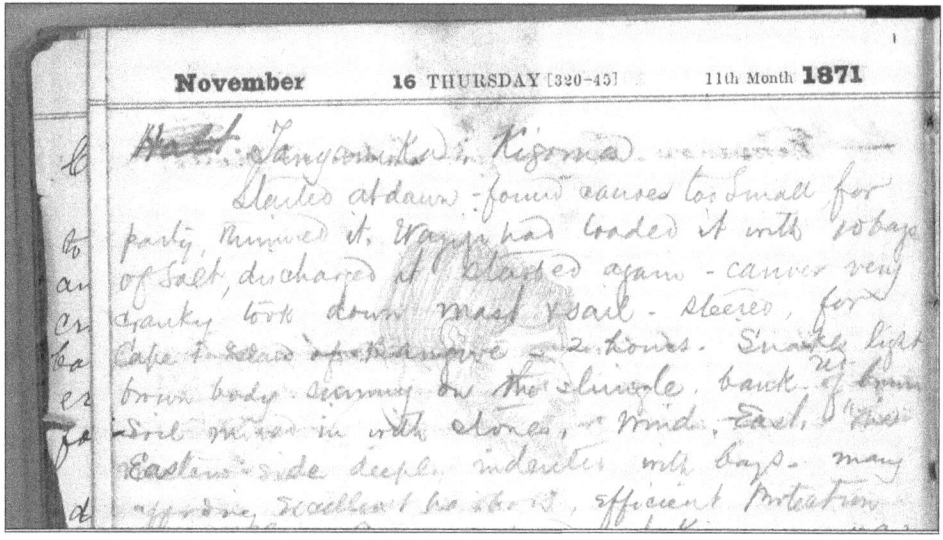

Plate 34. Sketch of Livingstone's head under lines 3 to 9, from Journal S.A. 7, November 16, Thursday, 1871.

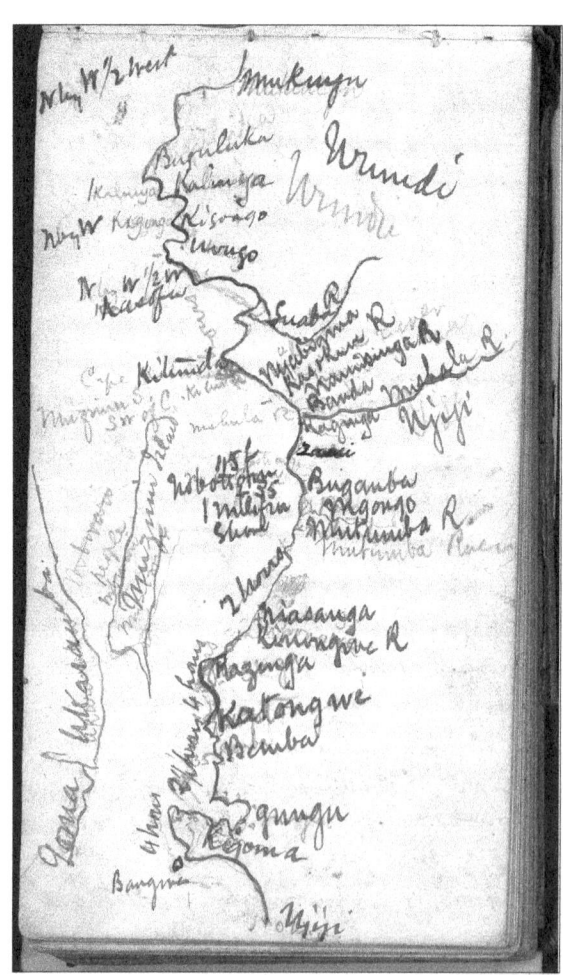

Plate 35. Ink and pencil map of Urundi. (Excerpt from Field Notebook S.A. 8)

Plate 36. Pencil sketch "View south of Cape Kazinga." (Excerpt from Field Notebook S.A. 8)

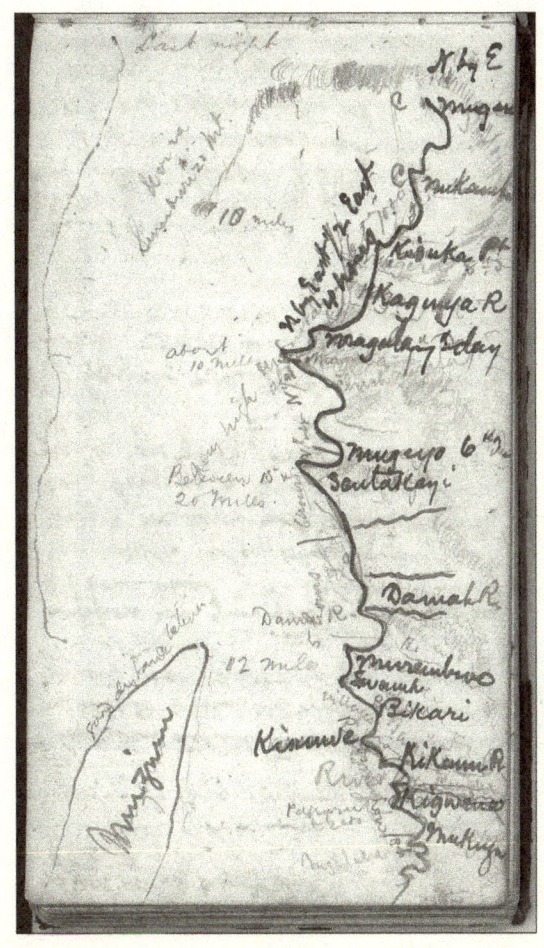

Plate 37. Ink and pencil map, facing the page "stopped at Mukungu on night of 5th day–6th day Tuesday." (Excerpt from Field Notebook S.A. 8)

Plate 38. Pencil sketch of tentative portraits of rowers. (Excerpt from Field Notebook S.A. 8)

Plate 39. Pencil sketch of "Khamis negro of 20" and "On the sand, Selim an Arab boy." (Excerpt from Field Notebook S.A. 8)

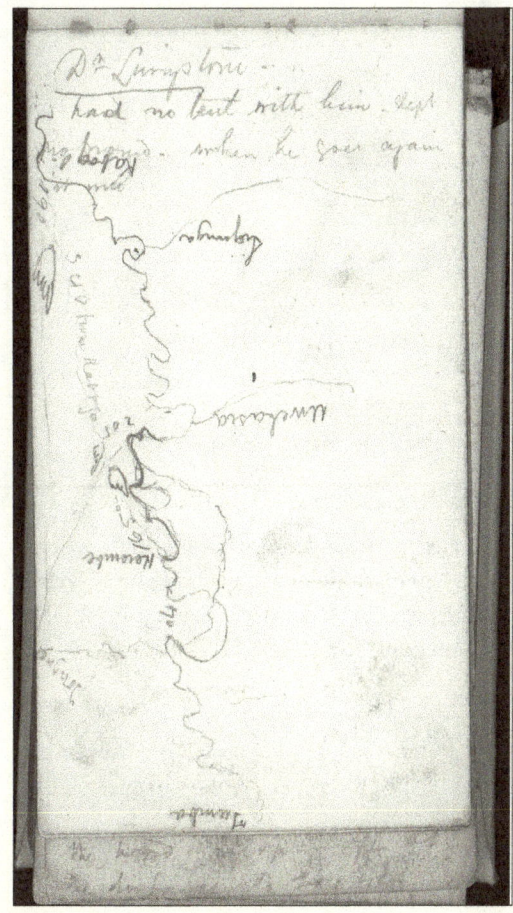

Plate 40. Pencil map on the page "Dr Livingstone had no tent with him." (Excerpt from Field Notebook S.A. 9)

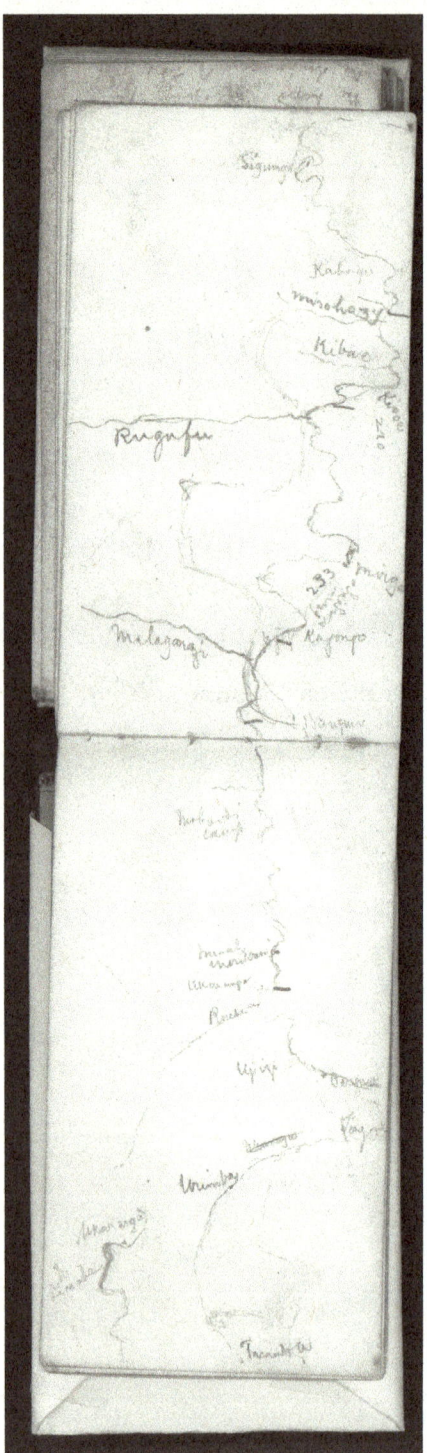

Plate 41. Pencil map (from Ujiji to Sigunga) on double page following that page. (Excerpt from Field Notebook S.A. 9)

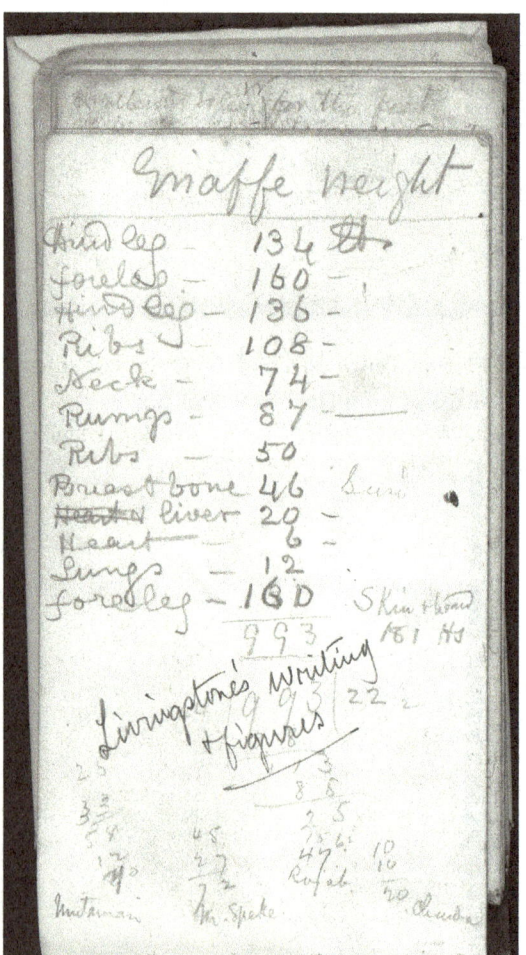

Plate 42. Notes calculating a "Giraffe weight" in "Livingstone's writing and figures" facing the page "22ⁿᵈ Monday." (Excerpt from Field Notebook S.A. 9)

Plate 43. Double page, "Livingstone's Prescription for Cure of Fever." (Excerpt from Field Notebook S.A. 9)

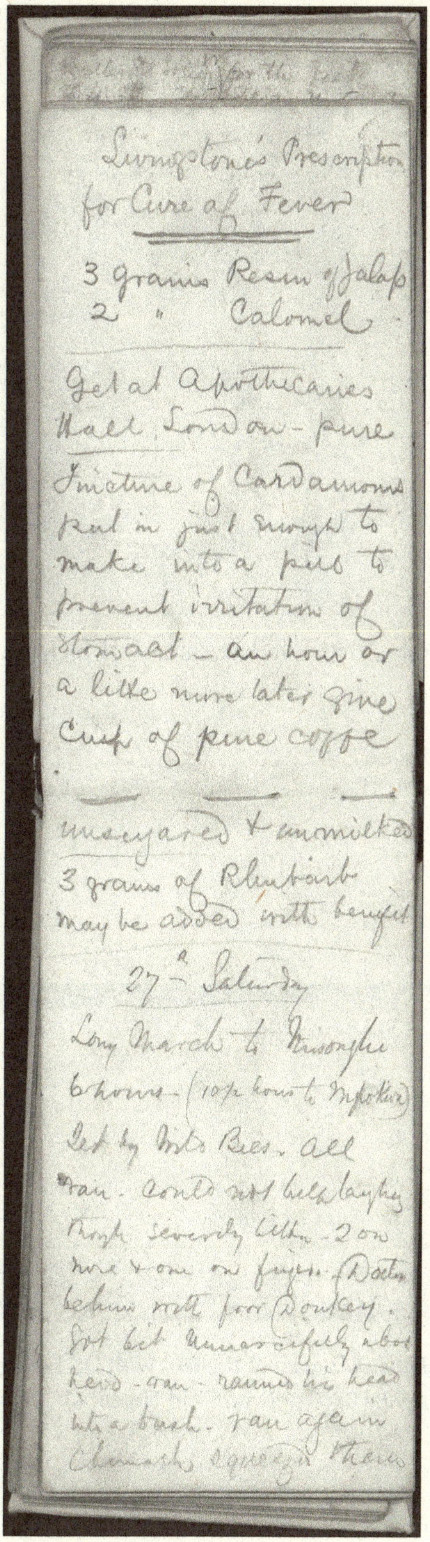

> Livingstone's Prescription
> for Cure of Fever
>
> 3 grains Resin of Jalap
> 2 "   Calomel
>
> Get at Apothecaries
> Hall, London — pure
> Tincture of Cardamoms
> put in just enough to
> make into a pill to
> prevent irritation of
> stomach — an hour or
> a little more later give
> Cup of pure coffee
> unsugared & unmilked
> 3 grains of Rhubarb
> may be added with benefit
>
> 27ᵃ Saturday
> Long march to Nusonghi
> 6 hours — (10½ hours to Mpokia)
> Led by Mrs Bees. All
> ran. Could not help laughing
> though severely bitten — 2 on
> nose + one on finger. (Dates
> behind with poor Donkey.
> Got bit unmercifully about
> head — ran — rammed his head
> into a bush. Ran again
> Chamas squeezed them

Plate 44. "Dr. Livingstone at work on his journal." (*HIFL*, facing 562)

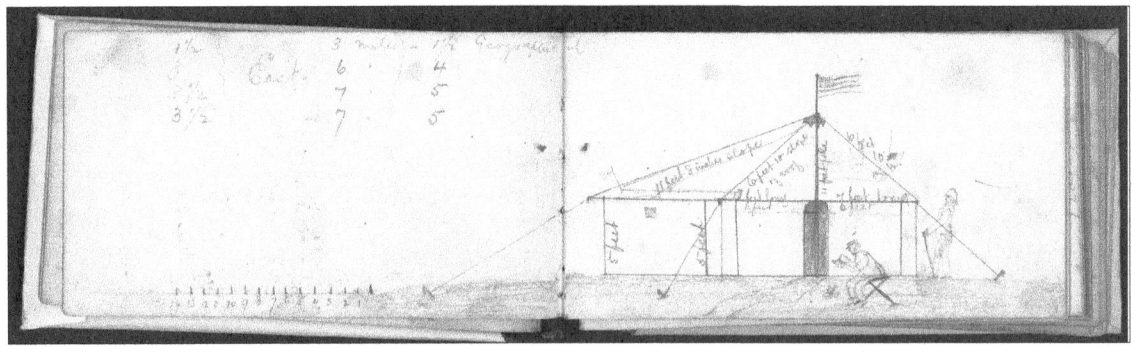

Plate 45. Sketch of the tent with Dr. Livingstone reading in front of it, and Stanley on the right. (Excerpt from Field Notebook S.A. 9)

Plate 46. "Susi, the servant of Livingstone." (*HIFL*, 499)

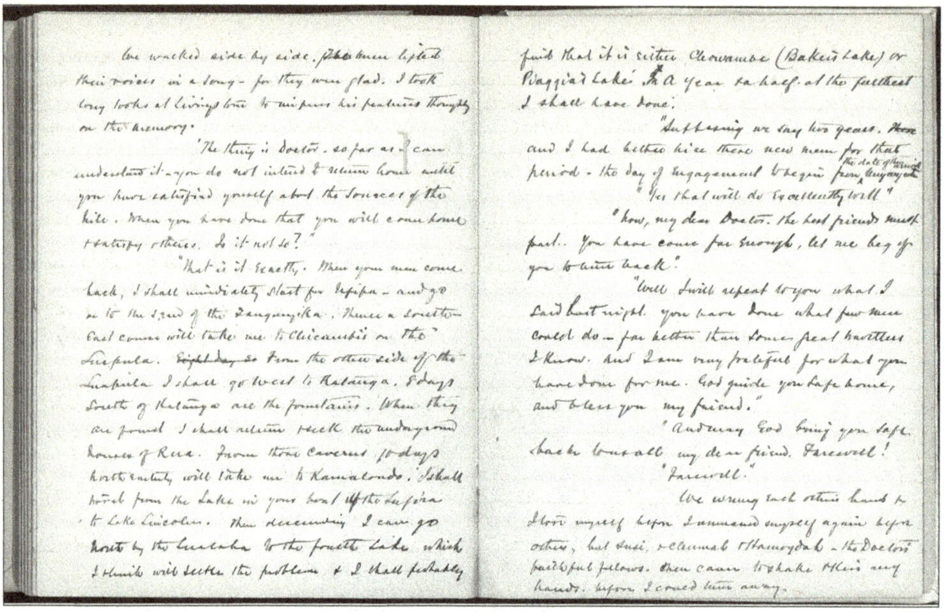

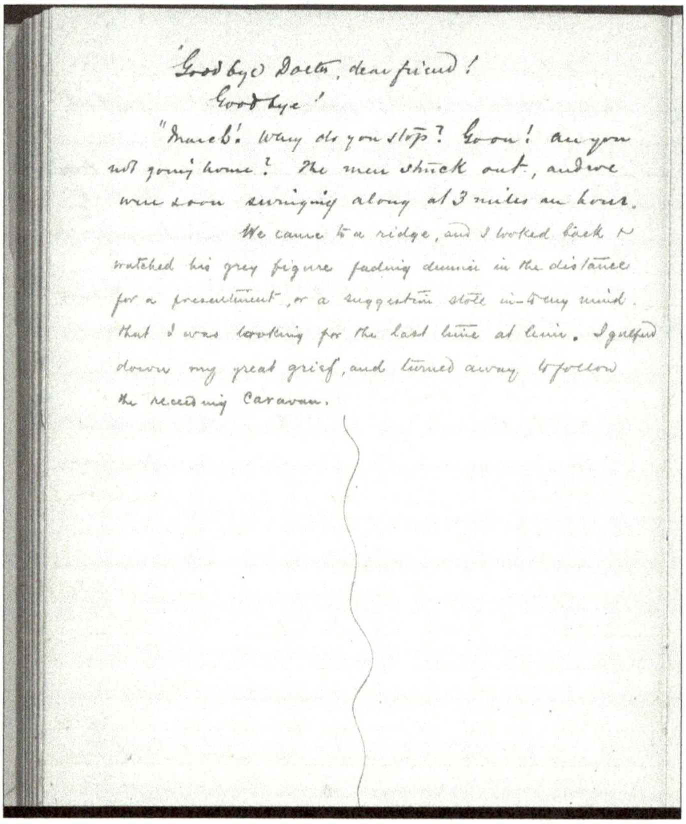

"Good bye Doctor, dear friend!"

"Good bye!"

"March! Why do you stop? Go on! Are you not going home?" The men struck out, and we were soon swinging along at 3 miles an hour.

We came to a ridge, and I looked back & watched his grey figure fading dimmer in the distance, for a presentiment, or a suggestion stole in—to my mind. that I was looking for the last time at him. I gulped down my great grief, and turned away, to follow the receding Caravan.

Plate 47. Pages covering March 13, 1872, when Stanley and Livingstone exchanged farewells and parted. (Excerpts from Journal S.A. 11)

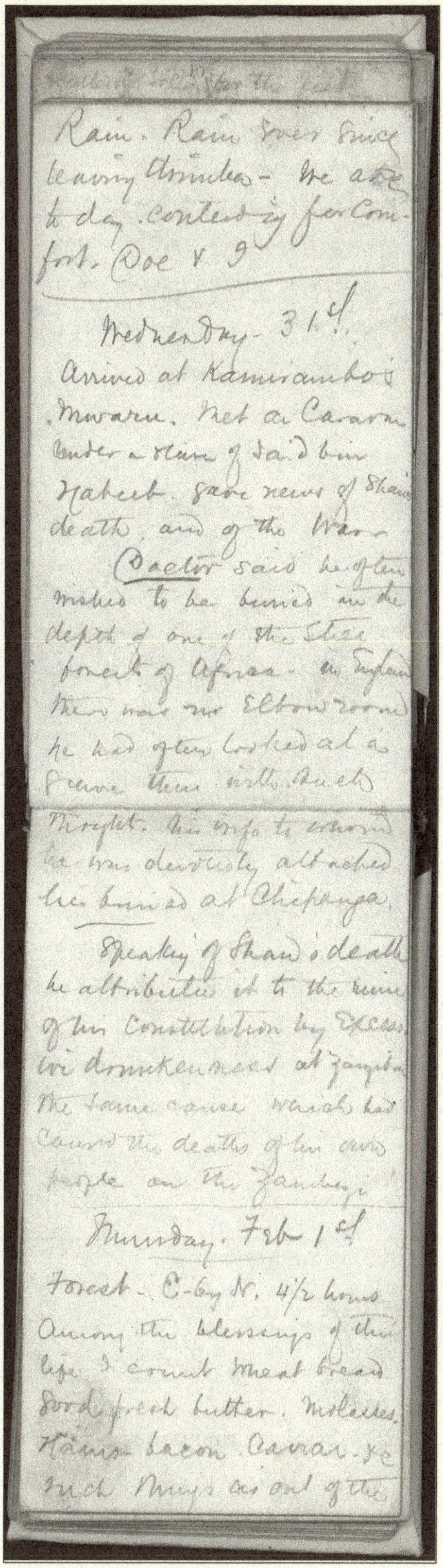

Plate 48. Double page of notes: "Rain. Rain ever since leaving [...] Wednesday [January] 31st." (Excerpt from Field Notebook S.A. 9)

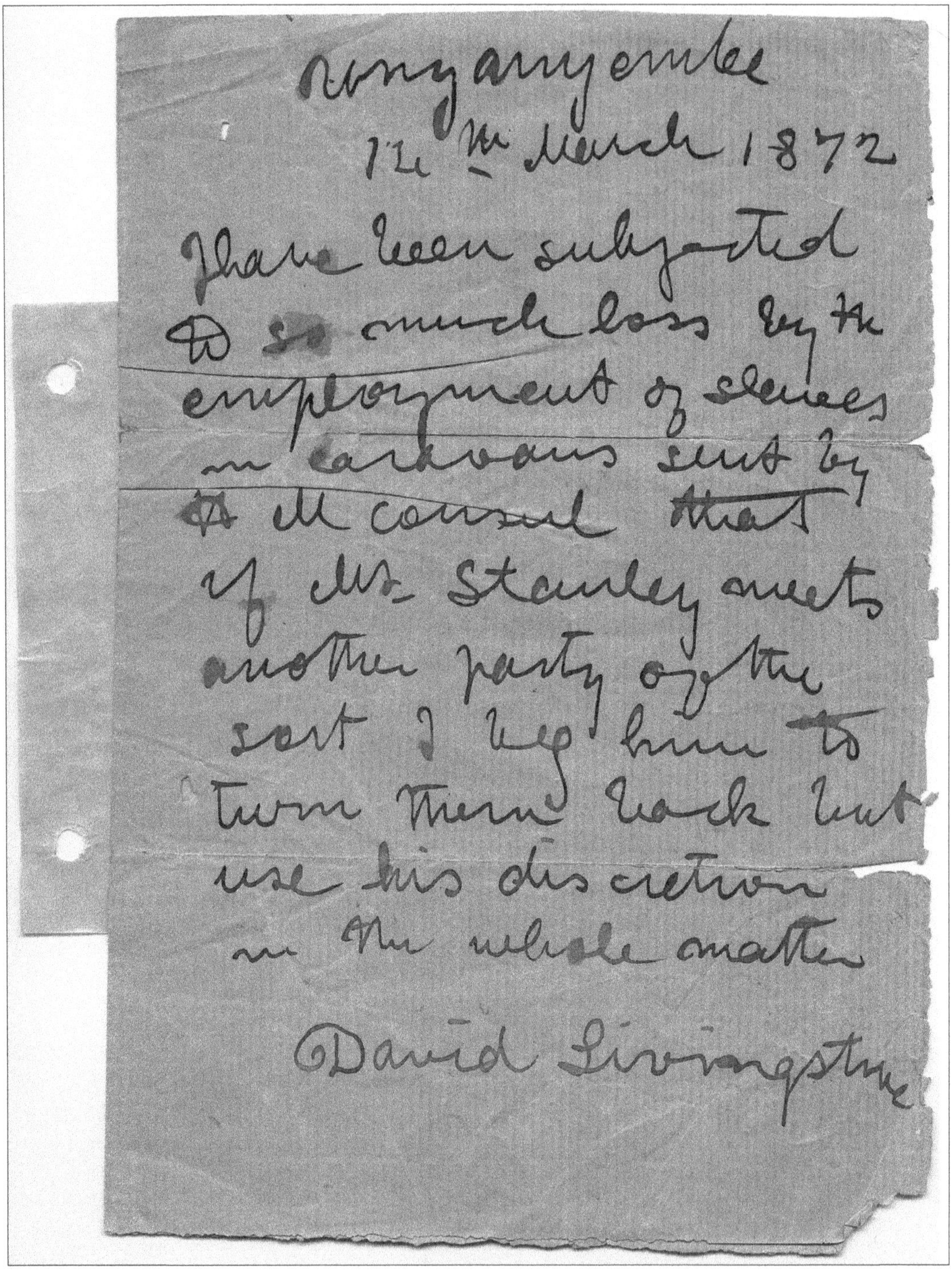

> Unyanyembe
> 14th March 1872
>
> I have been subjected to so much loss by the employment of slaves in caravans sent by H M consul that if Mr Stanley meets another party of the sort I beg him to turn them back but use his discretion in the whole matter
>
> David Livingstone

Plate 49. Letter from David Livingstone to H. M. Stanley, Unyanyembe, March 14, 1872. (S.A. 477)

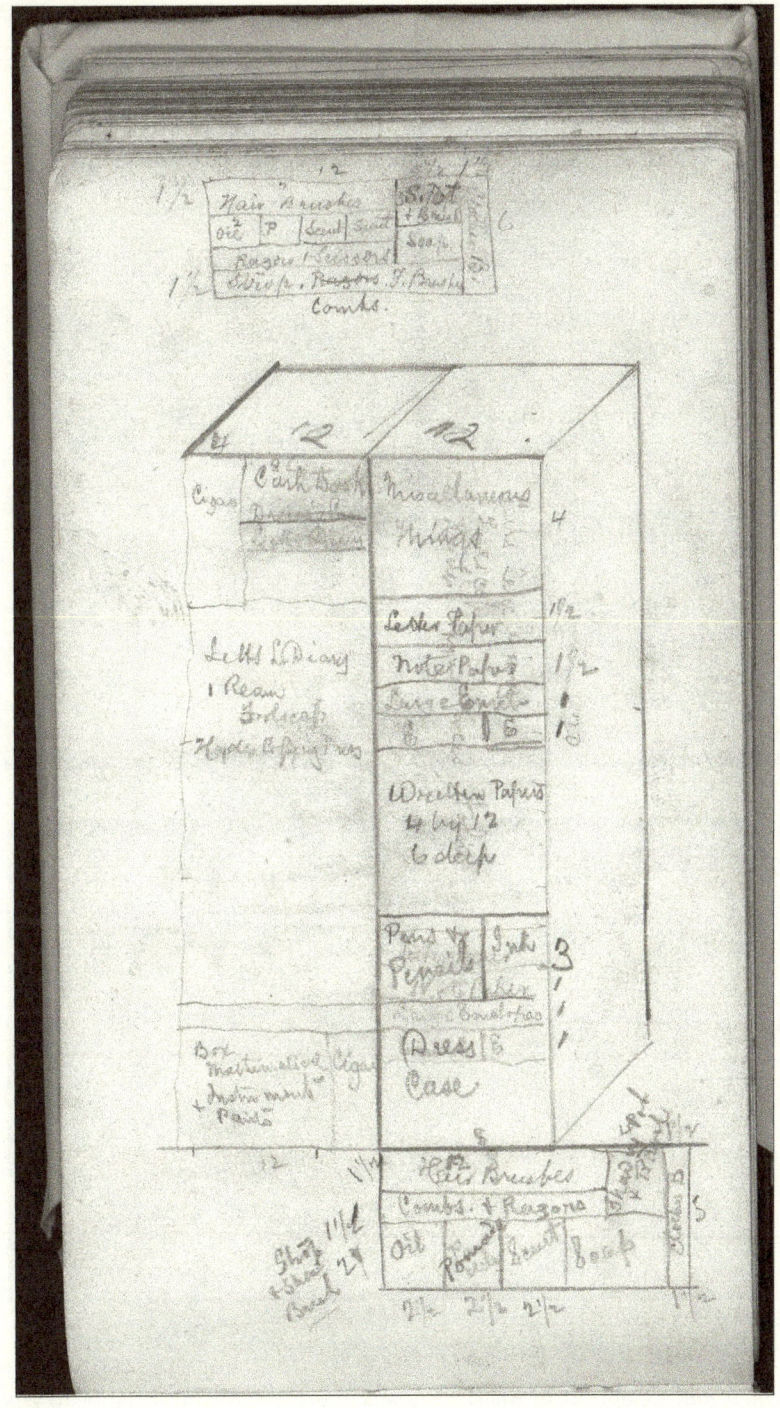

Plate 50. Pencil sketch showing how a trunk or a canteen is organized, when packed. (Excerpt from Field Notebook S.A. 10)

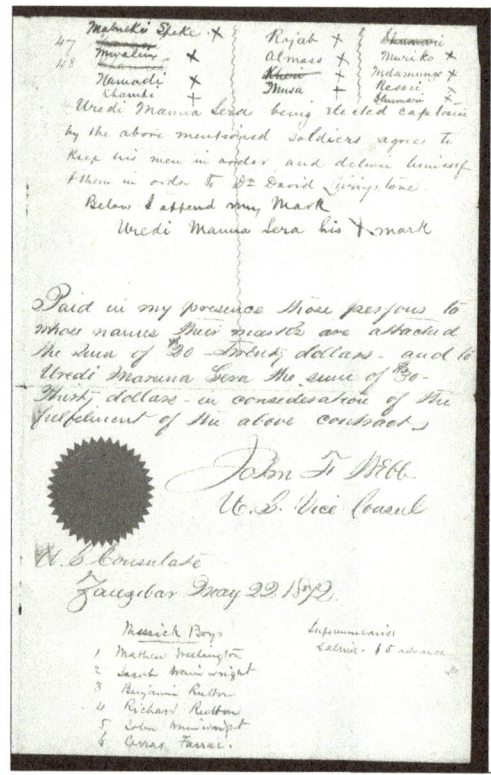

Plates 51a, b, and c. Contract of African soldiers to proceed to Unyanyembe to serve Dr. David Livingstone, with Uredi Manwa Sera as captain, U.S. Consulate, Zanzibar, May 21, 1872. (S.A. 4749)

Plate 52. "Manwa Sera. The Headman." Photograph dated November 1877, at the end of the Trans-African Expedition. (Photo Album "Congo," S.A. 5154)

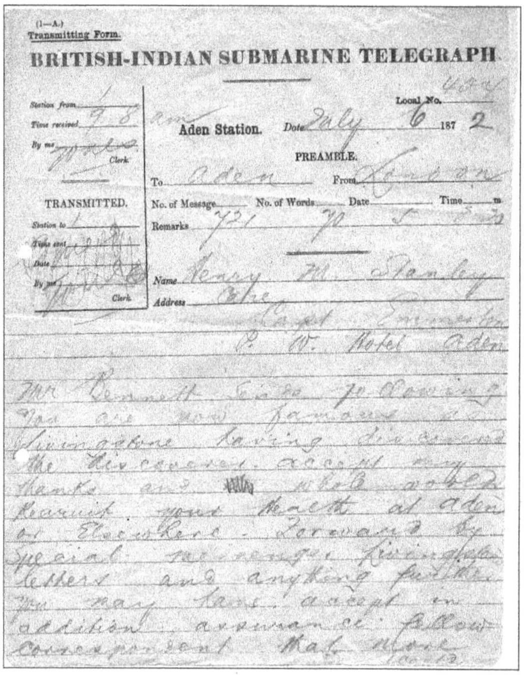

(1—A.)
Transmitting Form.

BRITISH-INDIAN SUBMARINE TELEGRAPH

Station from / Time received 9.8 am / By me / Clerk

TRANSMITTED. Station to / Time sent / Date / By me / Clerk

Local No.

Aden Station. Date July 6 1872

PREAMBLE.

To Aden From London

No. of Message No. of Words Date Time m

Remarks

Name Henry M. Stanley

Address

Capt Emmerson

P. W. Hotel Aden

Mr Bennett says following You are now famous as Livingstone having discovered the discoverer accept my thanks and whole world hearing your health at Aden or Elsewhere Forward by special messenger Livingstone letters and anything further you may have accept in addition assurance fellow correspondent that more

Plates 53a and b. Telegram of congratulation, from George Hosmer, on behalf of J. Bennett Jr., *New York Herald,* to Henry M. Stanley, Aden, July 6, 1872. (S.A. 2664)

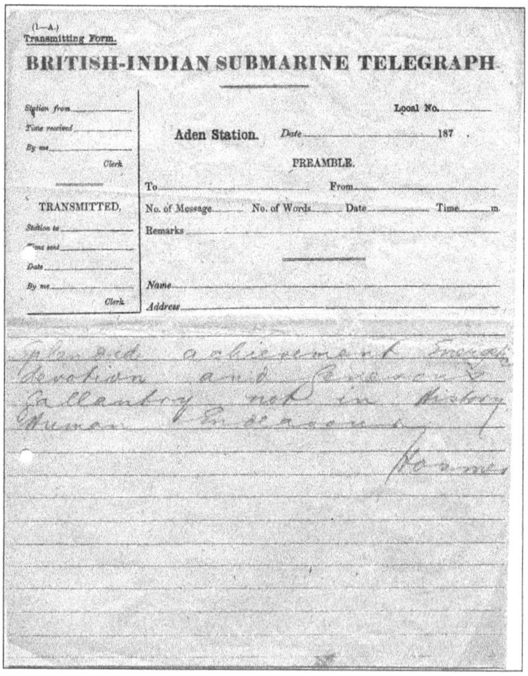

(1—A.)
Transmitting Form.

BRITISH-INDIAN SUBMARINE TELEGRAPH

Station from / Time received / By me / Clerk

TRANSMITTED. Station to / Time sent / Date / By me / Clerk

Local No.

Aden Station. Date 187

PREAMBLE.

To From

No. of Message No. of Words Date Time m.

Remarks

Name

Address

splendid achievement energy devotion and generous gallantry not in history human endeavours

Hosmer

Appendix

Contracts of Engagement of Employees for the Search for Livingstone (S.A. 4734, 4744, 4745, 4746, 4748)

Contract of Selim Heshmesh (S.A. 4734)

Selim Heshmesh, Jacob Heshmesh & H. M. Stanley.
Jan. 20, 1870

Agreement between Mr Henry M. Stanley and Selim Heshmesh and Jacob Heshmesh

Mr H. M. Stanley agrees to pay Selim Heshmesh the sum of One English pound sterling per month, and all his expenses for travelling, food and clothing in consideration for his services.
Selim Heshmesh agrees to serve Mr H. M. Stanley honestly and faithfully for the afore mentioned consideration.
Jacob Heshmesh hereby gives his consent to the present agreement.
The receipt of three English pounds sterling in payment of three months in advance from this date, is hereby acknowledged by Jacob Heshmesh1[1] in behalf of Selim Heshmesh, his brother, who is a minor.
When the services of Selim Heshmesh [2] are no longer required, Mr H. M. Stanley agrees to send him back to Jerusalem paying the necessary expenses.
Jerusalem 20th January 1870
Henry M. Stanley
Saleem Heshmesh
Jacob Hishmeh [sic]
Signed in my presence this twentieth day of January in the year of our Lord eighteen hundred and seventy.
United States Consulate at Jerusalem
John B Hay
V[ice] acting Consul
Stamp: Consulate U.S.A. Jerusalem
Two copies attested
J. B. H

---

1. 'his' crossed out.

Contract of Seedy Mubarak Bombay (S.A. 4744)

U. S. Consulate.
Zanzibar.
February 2nd 1871
I Seedy Mubarak Bombay for the sum of Eighty dollars per annum, forty dollars of which is paid in advance agree to go with Mr H. M. Stanley to Africa until such time as he shall declare my services ended.

(signed) Seedy Mubarak Bombay
his X mark

Witness A Sparhawk

Contract of Abdel Kader, Bunder Salaàm,[2] Celim (S.A. 4745)

U. S. Consulate. Zanzibar
February 1st 1871

We the undersigned agree to accompany Mr H. M. Stanley of New York during his Expedition to Africa, and to remain with him until such time as he shall declared his Expedition terminated for wages to the amount of Ten and Nine dollars respectively and promise to obey orders promptly and do all in our power to promote harmony, and the interests of the Expedition — failing which we agree to abide the consequences.

[Signature indecipherable] .... Butler

Celim his X mark   Valet or General Help

Abdel X Kadir [sic]   Cook
[Signature indecipherable]

[Green stamp of Consulate, Zanzibar]

Signed in my presence at Zanzibar
This 3rd day of February A. D. 1871
Francis R. Webb
U.S. Consul

---

2. Bunder Salaàm and Abdel Kadir were originating from the Malabar Coast. Their two signatures could be written in Tamul.

Bunder Salaàm $20
Celim   15

Witness to payment
Francis R. Webb
U. S. Consul

Contract of W. L. Farquhar (S.A. 4746)

U. S. Consulate. Zanzibar.
February 1st 1871

I, William Lawrence Farquhar[3] of Edinburgh Scotland[4] hereby agree in presence of the United States Consul[5] upon[6] the conditions that[7] if M[r] H. M. Stanley agrees to pay me $200 a year,[8] ($500 if M[r] Stanley deems his Expedition to have been successful, and my behavior excellent & duteous); that if M[r] Stanley pays me as advance $50, the premium on[9] which amounting to $12.50 is to be charged to and paid by me: <u>First</u> to accompany M[r] Stanley during his African Expedition, to obey M[r] Stanley's orders cheerfully & promptly, to do my best endeavors towards promoting harmony, and advancing the interests of the Expedition, or failing to comply, to abide all consequences[10] such as forfeit of wages etc. etc.
W. L. Farquhar

The undersigned agrees to the above conditions, & supplements it with the promise that if W. L. Farquhar's conduct has been excellent & duteous to give[11] him a free passage to England from Egypt.
Henry M Stanley

[Green stamp Consulate of United States Zanzibar]
Signed in my presence this 3rd day of February A. D. 1871
Francis R. Webb
U. S. Consul

---

    3. The name was Farquhar, as proved by his signature and his father's name (see Letter from Alexander Farquhar to HMS, Leith, July 31, 1872, KBF/RMCA, S.A. 2675).
    4. 'Scotland' added above the line.
    5. 'that' crossed out.
    6. 'upon' written over 'if'.
    7. 'that' written over 'if'.
    8. 'and' crossed out. In Stanley's estimate of the costs of the Expedition to J. G. Bennett, wages per year for Farquhar are estimated at $300 (See Appendix, Letter from Stanley to J. Gordon Bennett, January 17, 1871, RMCA, S.A. 6926, p. 9).
    9. 'on' written over 'of'.
    10. 'that' crossed out.
    11. 'give' written over 'secure'?

Contract of Saboori Mkuba, Saboori Mdogo, and Kombo (S.A. 4748)

Quihara, Unyanyembe

Sept ~~August~~ 17th 1871.

We the undersigned have voluntarily enlisted as soldiers of Mr Henry M. Stanley of New York, United States of America, and promise faithfully to pay the most implicit obedience to all his commands, to do cheerfully & promptly all the duties assigned to us in failure of which we agree to abide the consequences.

(signed)
Saboori Mkuba
his X mark
Kombo
his X mark
Saboori X Mdogo
his mark
(Witness) Bombay

Instructions to John W. Shaw (S.A. 2469)

Ujiji—November 14th 1871
To John W. Shaw of Stanley's African Expedition at Unyanyembe

This is conveyed to you by Said bin Majid, and is to inform you that we have all arrived safe. I am starting for Usige to morrow & shall return to Ujiji in 20 days after which I shall set on my return to Unyanyembe, & shall probably reach you about New Year's day. Obey implicitly the following instructions.
1st Let no one take anything of Dr Livingstone's goods out of my tembe, for any reason whatever. See that the men of Livingstone waste nothing.
2nd Finish the small boat as quickly & as efficiently as you can.
3rd Keep Sarmine and Uredi Manua Sera as well as all letters, newspapers & medicines with you until you hear from me again. Do not let them leave Unyanyembe.
I am
Yours truly
Henry M Stanley

Journal S.A. 4, Excerpts (1869)

[This journal is written in ink]

Cairo, Egypt

Feb 16 1869

It is a most miserable life in Cairo when one has nothing whatever to do but to pursue an aimless life almost or pursue some ideal that has no tangible component parts.[1] But I always feel out of place, in any town or country that has in it the least of anything approaching to French tastes. Such is the way I feel in Cairo. Here I stop at Shepherds Hotel.[2] The meals make me feel first of dissatisfied. Then the rooms awkwardly stiff French without the slightest shadow of comfort in its appearance or furniture. When I most wish to write a smartish letter, I feel uncommonly that not an idea will present itseff.[3] I am besides waiting for a telegram from London in answer to one I sent Saturday night (last). I am not certain that I am right in coming to Cairo at all.[4] But what could I do sent after Livingstone, which was in the first place a regular wild-goose chase. I went to Aden, Arabia because there was nothing definite in the instructions I received, and I imagined that the best place and I was told to do what I thought best. I stopped there three months received letter from our consul at Zanzibar that there was not the least chance of Livingstone's coming by way of Zanzibar, came back here to Egypt. Telegraph[ed] and got no answer. What the devil am I to[5] do? Now I am meandering away an Existence I know would count for something were I placed in more auspicious circumstances. I am losing valuable time I am afraid. My book has not the slightest chance of being published while I remain here, and this seeming thriftless pursuit of a man I feel positive, if in the body to be out Lake Tanganyika yet remains me because of its very thriftlessness. Though I get a salary, I feel as if I was out of a situation, & on the verge of starvation. But probably these ghosts & phantoms evil & sinisterly shaped arise from indigestion from which I suffer.
[…]

---

1. 'whether' crossed out.
2. Shepheard's Hotel, the most luxurious hotel in Cairo.
3. 'itseff' for 'itself'.
4. 'I can get to no' crossed out.
5. Continue on next page Feb. 17. Text preceded by an asterisk and an horizontal line.

Cairo, Egypt

Feb. 18, 1869

Yesterday at 2 P.M. received telegram from London "No, but come home, bring only such things you cannot sell of what I ordered." The telegram struck a cold chill into me directly. For what purpose was I ordered home was the thought instantly suggesting itself. Had I done wrong in leaving Aden, or in going there? Did not Anderson tell me to do what I thought best? Could I do otherwise? No! Come what will I have done perfectly right. They had no right to leave it to my management. In the premises, I did what was best.

It was also fortunate for me that I kept purchasing Anderson's articles till the last moment, otherwise there would have been some[6] loss. On my part or on Anderson's after reading & considering the telegram went to Hale[7]'s spent an hour with him & got a list of orders, from him. Drew £ 20, on J. S. Morgan & Co, to be told Anderson so soon as I see him.

Mr Balch came in Thomas Balch of Paris who told me wonderful stories of his son, till I was quite in a furor of enthusiasm to see him, got a letter of introduction from father to son. Went round to Taylors.

Today bid good bye to Hale & Taylor[8] & Felix Walmass vice consul. Gave 7 f. to Taylor for Walmass. Bid good bye to Hekekyan Bey,[9] took Tiffin[10] with him. Paid my bill at Shepherds, ran off to station, too late, stopped at Griffith's British Hotel. Board 10 f. per day. Three other Americans were stopping there, one a very young fellow who had travelled through Russia.

Feb. 19 1869

To day determined not be too late paid my bill at Griffith's Hotel 7.20. A.M.—10 f. Took carriage went off to station. Took ticket for Alexandria sent telegram to Chevrier, about Hale's letters. Left Cairo 8 A.M. Looked longingly on Egypt, for a long farewell. Arrived at Alexandria 12.40. Noon. Took carriage drove off to Messagerie Imperiale Office purchased ticket £18 for Marseilles. Run off to Telegraph Office Paid all claims against New York Herald. Paid Manager £1.4.4 forgot to take his receipt. Then went off to Peninsular & Oriental Hotel, got my big basket and trunk, gave backshesh to porters. Took carriage for Custom House. Gave backsheech 1 rupee to him. Took boat 1 rupee, 1 shilling to dragoman, 4^s/6^d to carriage from station to Custom House. At 3.P.M. sailed from Alexandria per Str "Peluse" for Messina & Marseilles. Probably the last time for years that I shall see Egypt. Good bye to it. Longingly I look towards the place, and bid it a loving good bye.

---

6. 'thing' crossed out.

7. Charles Hale, consul general of Egypt.

8. George C. Taylor, American consul at Cairo.

9. An Armenian gentleman, a civil engineer "who had occupied some important positions in the service of Mehemet Ali." L. Horner, "An Account of Some Recent Researches near Cairo …," *Philosophical Transactions of the RGS* 145 (1855): 120, http://www.jstor.org/stable/108512.

10. An Anglo-Indian word for 'lunch'. Before starting his search for Livingstone, Stanley spent several months in Bombay, where he most likely partook of such meals.

Journal S.A. 5, Excerpts (1870)

[This journal is written in ink.]

Bombay.
August 2 and 3, 1870. Tuesday and Wednesday
I must now content myself with stopping here at this Hotel[1] until I can finish my correspondence from Persia & the Caucasus which will amount to about 17 letters, before attempting anything, lest the "Herald "folks" deem me unworthy. But if any vessel shall leave this port for Zanzibar direct, why then I shall pull up stakes, & leave also, & finish my correspondence if possible at sea. I shall also, lest by any chance my letters be lost, take press copies of each.

Bombay.
October 4 to October 7, 1870 [entries blank]

October 8, 1870. Saturday.
Purchased my passage[2] ticket[3] to Mauritius from Captain Jabez Petherick,[4] for self & Interpreter Selim of Jerusalem.

Bombay.
October 9 and 10, 1870 [entries blank]

October 11, 1870. Tuesday.
I left 3 trunks in care of Dossabhoy, Merwanjee & Co, n°7 Parzee Bazaar St. Bombay, the receipt of which I have taken with me to Africa. Bade good by to Shepherd,[5] Dr Doo-little, Walton the Learmonth Bros. Van Reenan, &c.
Found a dog at the Byculla Hotel, a black & tan pup about 2 months old. I have called it "Omar".

---

1. Byculla Hotel. See August 1, 1870.
2. 'passage' above the line.
3. 'of passage' crossed out.
4. "Petherick, Jabez b. Fowey 1820 C81527 Plymouth 1853[;] vol.11 1855–1871; vol.23 no voyages listed," in "Index to the Captains Registers of Lloyd's of London" (Guildhall Library Ms 18567), http://www.history.ac.uk/gh/capsP.pdf.
5. Alex F. Shepherd was a journalist at the *Times of India*.

Bombay.
October 12, 1870. Wednesday.
Left Bombay per barque Polly, Capt Jabez Petherick, 362 tons. A./. by Lloyds Register paid 300 rupees for self & Interpreter, to Mauritius, sailed at 8 A.M.
Mate, Mr Farquhar[6] from Edinburgh

Mauritius. At sea to Seychelles. At sea.
November 21, 1870. Monday
Set about preparing for journey to Seychelle
En-route to Zanzibar. Engaged William Lawrence Farquahar,[7] late 1st Mate of the Barque "Polly" to be my Superintendent of Porters and 1st Man proposing to penetrate Africa in the course of my mission at £5 per month, and if successful in it to pay him at the rate of £100 a year, with board and lodging. Bade good bye to "Polly", and embarked on board the "Romp" Capt Baillou for Mahe Seychelle Islands. Spent last night on "Dunloe".

Seychelle Islands
December 10, 1870. Saturday.
At 7 A. M. Doctor Brookes came off & gave us pratique. Went ashore with Dr Brookes. While going ashore asked him for vessel going to Zanzibar. He replied "Two vessels only in port one an American whaler, "Falcon" Capt Tosiah Richmond New Bedford would probably go to Zanzibar, the other brig was going to Mauritius. The Captain was uncertain whether he could take us she being a whaler, having no accommodations for passengers.
Stopped at Hotel Royal. Fare to go ashore $4.

December 11, 1870. Sunday.
Saw Captain Richmond again this morning, and after six hours talk, during which time I had to explain my mission, as an inducement. He offered to take us, leaving the price to Charles Dupuy —Ex-American Consul. Board for 3 persons at Hotel Royal $3, a day. Had my cart fixed, and Boxes ordered to carry amunition. Population of Mahe 9000 people who mostly speak French. The Police very active, Mahe very quiet, Creoles talkative and sociable.

---

6. W. Farquhar was mate on board the *Polly*. Stanley gave the different vessels on board which Farquhar had been posted before, in notes at the beginning of this journal:
    William Lawrence Farquahar, "Polly"
    Hamilton, Scotland
    Ships "Ellen Stewart", "Widian Miles", "Mrs Mitchell", "Sir Ralph Abercrombie"
    St.s "Magdala", "Gongar Krishna"
    Ships "Barossa", "Indemnity"
7. The correct spelling is Farquhar. See S.A. 7, note 8.

Seychelle Islands.
December 12, 1870. Monday.
This morning went to Charles Dupuy's. Asked him price of passage to Zanzibar. Replied $200 for 3. Captain Richmond just then came in and after a little talk said he would take $150, provided Selim would help the Steward on board. I asked him if he would be satisfied with $125 "No I cannot, he said. Bennett is rich enough to pay what I ask, and you would find it cheaper at the end." After some hesitation, I accepted, and paid him 200R[8] = $100 on account.

December 13, 1870. Tuesday.
Cart came in from blacksmith, & boxes from carpenter. Charges Cart $6. Boxes $7.00. Advanced out of £7.00 to W. L. Farquhar. £1.00 & 7^s/6^d for cigars. Visited the cemetery. Also Capt Baillou's home, towards night. Mahe people terribly French in their proclivities.

December 14, 1870. Wednesday.
This morning at 9 A.M. we went on board myself, Head-man-Farquhar, and Selim Heshmesh Interpreter. Because of calms we had to stop in harbor all day. At 6 P.M. raised anchor & departed. "Falcon" of Salem, is a brigantine 126 tons register carries 22 inclusive of the Captain. She has been 28 months out. After cruising a little to the North West of Seychelles, she will sail for Zanzibar to get her provisions, then home.

At sea. Cruising. <u>Indian Ocean</u>
December 22, 1870. Thursday.
My man W. L. Farquhar is intensely lazy, or else he thinks himself too good to work at all for £5 per month, though when I engaged him, he seemed as if it were an excellent opportunity. I had some trouble to induce him to work at an India rubber coat for me though it is the first time since the 21st of November, that I have asked him to do anything for me.

On Board "Falcon" Whaler. At sea
December 27, 1870. Tuesday.
 N. E. trades. Start from 50 miles N. W. of Mahe for Zanzibar. We have been all busy to day upon my preparations for my journey to Central Africa. Capt Richmond of the "Falcon" made my tent pins. My tent was aired. My African carriage was boxed & set up. While trying it on board, got upset. Very amusing. The wheels of this carriage are but 15 inches apart in order to adapt it for the foot paths in Africa.

---

8. Stanley wrote "R" with two slashes, for Indian rupee.

December 28, 1870. Wednesday.
Still busy at my carriage. Mʳ Farquahar's conduct became so unbearable that I spoke to him about it, at[9] which he gave signs of being considerably astonished. Apparently he had forgotten the position in which we stood towards each other. Had I permitted his unwarrantable conduct to proceed further without comment, it would have spoiled him completely, or rendered him unfit to be my company.

December 31, 1870. Saturday.
Squally & dirty weather. Set up a new topsail.
(For further information about myself & Expedition, and daily incidents turn to Diary 1871.)
My cash in this world amounts to only £553. 11ˢ· 3ᵈ· after 13 years hard work, which averages [Rest of the page blank]

---

9. 'at' written over 'for'.

Letter of Introduction from John MacGregor to David Livingstone (S.A. 480)

Suez. Nov. 16. 68
Dear Doctor Livingstone

I have waited here to see you but now must defer that pleasure till I come back after a long voyage in my canoe in Palestine & Egypt.
God be praised that you should be safe & sound in old England.
This is kindly taken by Mr. Stanley of New York who will be highly delighted if you will allow him to have a few minutes conversation with you.
My father and sister are quite well and are living at Southsea near Portsmouth.
I hope you will pass one quiet night in a good bedroom in this hotel.
Yours truly
John MacGregor

Letters from Francis R. Webb, American Consul in Zanzibar, to Stanley (S.A. 2598, 2654, 2655, 2657)

S.A. 2598

Consulate of the U. States of America
Island of Zanzibar
December 26.1868

Henry Stanley Esq
Suez Hotel Aden
Suez Egypt[1]

My dear Sir:
I have to acknowledge receipt of your letter from Aden requesting me to assist you in obtaining information of and from Dr Livingston[2] and in reply I beg to assure I should be very happy to do so did the opportunity occur, but the probability of that great traveller's coming to Zanzibar is very slight. Dr Kirk the British Vice Consul here, and who was with Dr L. for some years during his travels in Africa thinks it more than probable that he will come out at the Nile and has not the least expectation of having the pleasure of seeing him here.
In September H.M.S. "Octavia" left here, and as I see by the Bombay papers, on her arrival at Trincomalee[3], reported that when she left Zanzibar Dr Livingston was reported within a week's march of the coast. This if you saw it probably misled you to believe he would come here, but it is hardly necessary to say that the statement was without the slightest foundation of truth and was probably written from some entire misconception by the writer of some conversation which took place between him and Dr Kirk.
Trusting you will succeed in your wishes on the exodus of the Doctor I am Dear Sir
Very Respectfully
Francis R. Webb U. S. V. Consul

---

1. Stanley received this letter on February 1, 1871 (S.A. 4; S.A. 73).
2. Livingstone written with no 'e'.
3. Port of Sri Lanka.

S.A. 2654

Zanzibar June 11th 1871

My dear Mr Stanley:

Your letter dated April 28th which left you in sore trouble of mind reached me on the 20th of May and I immediately commenced to investigate the matter. I found that the two Washenzi had arrived two or three days before and had them up for examination. They said they passed your camp and a man who called himself Abd-el-Kader told them a Mazungu had been driven away by you and asked them to look out for him which they did, but saw nothing of him. But soon after found the donkey with the gun, beads, &c strapped on him. Supposing the Cook to be on ahead they proceeded, passing thro' Simbaweni, and then their story agreed with yours, being brot. back there &c &c.

After hearing all they had to say, I decided from their appearance, that they had not hurt the Cook, but kept them in custody, and reported the whole to Syeed Bergas[4] with the request that he would send a party up to Simbaweni and bring back here the donkey &c and everything which the Sultana (who is a slave of old Syeed Silliman, uncle of Syeed Bergas) had robbed your soldiers, and also to hunt round among all the villages in the vicinity for the Cook. The party was about starting on the 3rd inst when two native soldiers came in escorting Mr Cook himself with the identical blue-flannel coat on which you say in your letter was found in possession of the two Washenzi. So you see if we had hung the two men on the evidence your soldiers gave and you reported to me we should have committed a grave mistake.

When I examined them they said on finding the donkey they hunted about for its owner, and that among the other things strapped upon the ass were two _white_ coats, which were probably what your soldiers referred to. The Cook (who was in rather a ragged condition; the blue flannel coat aforesaid and a pair of trousers which he had on the last time you saw him) was rather sore footed and said, on leaving your camp he wandered away off the road which you had come, and was overtaken by two men who took his donkey and left him (this I don't believe). He then found his way to a village a short distance from the road, where he was kept nearly a month by the head-man, and then sent with two soldiers to guard him to Zanzibar. That is all he had to say for himself except that he never stole a kernel of rice from you and that you had him whipped for nothing, which of course is all bosh. I gave the poor devil a present of five dollars as he was entirely destitute and he is I believe going back to his Doby business. The two Washenzi who belonged, it turned out, to a caravan led by a man whom I knew very well we have let go, but we shall still send on the party to Simbaweni to bring down the things of which the Sultana robbed your soldiers and the property of the Cook.

I have not kept copies of my previous letters to you and therefore forget whether I have written you that your letter dated April 11th reached me April 27th and that I wrote to Mr

---

4. For Bargash.

Bennett enclosing your letter to him April 29th. Many thanks for your kind attention to my request and your noble vindication of Syeed Majid who was my particular friend and a good friend to all Americans.

We have not much in the way of news to tell you, the Franco- German war having ended, the Frenchmen went to fighting among themselves. The Reds (Communists) got possession of Paris and some of the large Cities and started one government without law or order, and M. Thiers with his party which is the govt recognised by foreign powers is located at Versailles and very fierce battles have been fought. I send you herewith a lot of telegrams to April 30th.

The Conference at London settled the Eastern question just as Russia desired and the Black Sea is now open. The Commission for the settlement of the Alabama Claims &c is now sitting at Washington. Nothing has as yet transpired as to their decisions.

We have been very gay here for the last fortnight. An English Admiral with part of his squadron have been in port and those whose business it was to do so have been entertaining him and his staff. Dinner parties &c have been the order of the day and we are all thankful that our furious dissipation ended yesterday with the departure of the Admiral for Seychelles. We have had only one American vessel here lately which came here lately which came from, and went to New York, with Mr Morse on board.

Mrs Webb and the children desire to be most kindly remembered to you as to all your American friends here. You will undoubtedly see Dr Livingston at Ujiji, and we hope to see you back here in October.

Very sincerely, Your Friend F. R. Webb

S.A. 2655

Zanzibar July 16, 1871

My dear Mr Stanley:

I have not much time to write you as the Arab who takes this starts from Bugamoya this morning and I have to send to overtake him, nor have I much to write. A mail arrived from Seychelles yesterday and brought the enclosed letter for you and I send you the three latest Heralds that came to me. I also send you a small box of cigars as a present from the children. Should like to send you a lot of all sorts of things but you know I cannot overload the Arabs people or they would throw them away.

My latest advices from the U. S. reported that Mr Bennett had hesitated to pay your draft for $3750 and it was protested, so I was very anxious to hear from home, but got nothing by the Mail yesterday. However this morning in reading Taria's letters from London, I find that his correspondents there had received the proceeds of the draft from mine in Salem. I am hoping to hear from you soon, the last news was that you were near Ugogo, and that all your donkeys had died.

I have really nothing to write you in the way of news the Frenchman are still fighting among themselves. With kind regards and best wishes from us all.
Believe me
Very Sincerely Yours,
F. R. Webb

S.A. 2657

Zanzibar September 25, 1871

My dear Mr Stanley:

Your two soldiers came in on the evening of the 21st with your letters of June 23rd and August 14th and 15th and we were all truly glad to hear from you as we had previously heard of the fight at Wilyankuru and were afraid that you might have suffered from it. So that though we were very sorry to hear that you were so ill, were glad it was no worse. I do not like it very well that you accompanied the Arabs on the attack as I am afraid that Sultan Mirambo's people will remember you and be revenged when you come back their way. I was sorry to hear that Farquhar had died but suppose it was his own fault. Achako (the thief) has not turned up here yet and your two men say that they could hear no intelligence of him on the road. Sheik Hashid has sent off two caravans lately and I wrote you by each of them and sent papers. His son M'Selim is with the first one. I shall tell your two men, if they pass them on the road to take the packages from them. Your letter for Mr Bennett will be forwarded in a day or two.
Sarmeen and Uredi say that they lost the two five dollars pcs. you gave them on the road. So I shall give them five dollars to fit them out for the journey back. They will bring you the medicine you ordered the quantity of which however Christie[5] I believe has increased thinking you would not have enough, some briar-wood pipes as you request, some Maizena from Mrs Webb, and all the late newspapers, some of which are kindly contributed by Mr Kieck[6]. Now before I forget it I must ask you to inquire carefully of all the people around you and then judging yourself from what you see and know, write to me what effect the troubles up there and stoppage of the traffic will have on the Ivory trade for next year and the year after, and how long you think the roads will be blocked up so as to prevent Ivory Caravans from passing. It may be of great importance to us to know in season whether or no our supply of Ivory here will be materially affected by the war. Syeed Bergas sent me word yesterday that he should start 500 soldiers off at once for Unyanyembe to help his friends, but knowing how Arabs always procrastinate I expect it will be some time before they go. I expect this will be the last letter I shall write you from here as I hope to leave for the U. S. in about 20 days. Please continue to write to me however, under cover to Mr John Webb who will remain here, and he will forward them

---

5. Dr. Christie, of Zanzibar.
6. Most probably for 'Kirk'.

on to me after perusal and attend to anything you may want the same as if I was here myself. I am sorry not to be here when you return but Christie tells me that it is more than my life is worth to stay here through another hot season and as it will be six years before I get home since I left there I think it likely that I need a touch of cold weather to stir me up a little. You must come to Salem, Massachusetts when I you get back and hunt us up. In the large bundles of papers which I have sent, you will get all the news so far as we know it, and I believe there is no change here since you left that would interest you. Spalding is still here but Mr Goodhue and Mr Morse have gone. That Cook of yours presented a claim to Dr Kirk for $100, for the Donkey and Clothes which he lost after he left you, but I explained to Kirk that he had already accepted $30, from the Sultan in lieu of his sending soldiers to Simbaweni to bring the things down as I had requested him to do and so Mr Cook must be satisfied with what he has got as he should be, and thankful that he escaped with his life.
Mrs Webb and the children desire their kindest regards to you as do also Messrs. Webb, Sparhawk, and Spalding. Mrs W. regrets very much that she will not be here to see your return, as she witnessed your departure. She and the children are very well now. Accept my hearty sympathy in all your undertakings and believe me
Very Sincerely Your Friend,
F. R. Webb

P. S. to H. M. Stanley Esq
September 25, 1871

Your two soldiers will start tomorrow morning, in company with seven men going up to Sheik Nasib. They take a tin box of medicines from Dr Christie for which I have paid $25. And I have put in a bottle of Brandy, one of Stoughton's Elixir[7] and a vial of Bourbon Whiskey to put you in mind of home. I have also paid $5 for each of the men to pay for their subsistence on the road. I have cautioned them about being careful of the things to keep them dry and I trust they will all reach you safe. Dr Kirk I believe will write asking you to take charge of the property now lying at Unyanyembe for Dr Livingston, and Dr Christie also writes to you by this opportunity. I should be glad to send you all sorts of nice things to eat but knowing how important it is that your men should travel light so as to reach you as soon as possible, I refrain. We all send you instead our best wishes and hopes for your prosperity and success. May God bless and watch over you and bring you back safe.
F. R. W.

---

7. An old medicine for stomach disorders (George B. Griffenhagen and James Harvey Young, *Old English Patent Medicines in America*, Contributions from the Museum of History and Technology, Paper 10, Bull. 218 [Washington, DC: Smithsonian Institution, 1], 155–83, http://www.gutenberg.org/files/30162/30162-h/30162-h.htm).

Letters from John Webb, American Consul in Zanzibar, to Stanley (S.A. 2658, 2659)

S.A. 2658

Zanzibar Dec. 23, 1871.
H. M. Stanley Esq.
   My dear Sir,
   I avail myself of an opportunity offering today by the return to Unyanwemba of one "Zide" a slave of Said bin Salim, to forward to you a small package of the latest papers we have, and to wish you God speed in your undertaking. Enclosed please find two letters from Messrs Dossabhoy Merwanjee & Co. Bombay. Capt. Webb and family sailed for home in the Bk Glide, leaving here Nov. 13. He left with me a copy of a letter he received from London dated Sept. 25. 1871, much is as follows – "Mr Webb &c &c. I write you this to inform you that a change has been made in the N Y. Herald Office Agency here & that I am in charge while Mr Levien the former Agent has gone home. This you will understand may be of especial interest in view of matters relating to the Expedition of Mr. Stanley. Will you kindly make a note of the fact, that I am ready to cash here at any moment any draft that you or others at Zanzibar may cash for Mr Stanley or to order by telegraph, that the same be paid at Bombay or Alexandria. Will you be so good as to acknowledge receipt of this and let me know if there is any way in which I can facilitate the operations of Mr Stanley" &c &c. Geo. Hosmer.
On the arrival of this man "Zide" on the 7th inst Said Burgush sent him to me to furnish me with information regarding you. He gave what I think was reliable news of you, up to the term of your leaving Unyanwemba, which according to his judgement was between the middle of August & middle Sept. He brought us the sad intelligence that after you had left U. reports had reached there that you had been robbed of your goods by a chief Jarko [Tarko?] through whose country you passed to avoid Mirambo. This report was soon exagerated into your having been killed &c &c. I wrote Hosmer that I placed no dependence in the latter report. I should have taken no notice of it, had I not been well aware that "our own correspondent" for the Times of India would have furnished that paper with the item, and therefore felt I had better make mention of it to Mr Hosmer, being careful to impress upon that I could find no reasons to believe it true. I hope you will write us when an opportunity offers, especially since this report has been circulated – for though we may not credit it, still it tends to increase our anxiety for you.

I am sorry I have no N. Y. Heralds to send you, but Capt. Webb took them all with him to read on the passage home. I should have sent more than I have, had one of your men been sure to take the package, but I am afraid to send too heavy a bundle by these people for fear they may "lose" it. I have nothing new to write you. You will notice by the Boston Papers I send, the terrible conflagration at Chicago which surpasses anything we have ever had in our country.

Our Ivory market feels seriously the effect of the troubles in the Manuwazie country, and the receipts of the article are very small. I wish when you write, if not too much trouble you would give me your idea of the Ivory trade, that is your views as to the quantity held there &c, and what the prospects are for the troubles being settled and also what in your opinion will be the future effect upon the Ivory trade. I presume no expeditions are arriving at, or leaving Unyemwemba. Luddah, Jairam Sewjees Agent died about a month since.

All your European friends in Zanzibar are well and join with me in the expression of best wishes, and God Speed.

Yours truly

John F. Webb.

S.A. 2659

Zanzibar April 30th 1872.

My dear Mr Stanley,

Your dispatches by the hands of Salamene, Baracca & Umbare were received yesterday P.M. & I now hasten to send the bearers back to you with the articles you requested & also my congratulations on your success thus far. It is of the utmost importance that these men should leave at once, and not remain here as they would be severely "interviewed" by the correspondent of the Bombay Paper – and those interested in the "Livingstone Expedition" who have established their camp at Bugamoya preparatory to their final start.

There is a strong feeling in Zanzibar – regarding your movements – and you must be well aware that the Americans here will do all in their power to prevent your news being anticipated by other parties – although it will be difficult to do so – as parties here are very inquisitive. We heard about three weeks ago that you had met "Livingstone" – & I took the liberty of telegraphing Mr. Hosmer of London as follows, "Report considered reliable that Mr Stanley and Dr Livingstone met at Ujeejee in January".

I have got you the best Port & Champagne that I could – but I fear it is poor – and now start the boys back to you at once – for I know it will not answer to have them hanging around here – especially at the present time. I cautioned them to avoid the Englishmen in camp at Bugamoya – and to be sure and leave the place at once as soon as they arrive. I think your movements will have great effect upon the "Livingstone Expedition".

They feel ashamed now, while we Americans are delighted to think how successful you have been. You may think I have unnecessarily hurried the men back – but it is the only safeguard. Your letters will be forwarded to Bombay by vessel to sail in six or seven days. Shall send them to our Agent there to be prepaid for London.
Wishing you God speed and hopeing to see you soon
   I remain
   Yours truly
   Jo. F. Webb

Letters from John Kirk, British Consul in Zanzibar, to Stanley (S.A. 2656, 2660)

S.A. 2656

Zanzibar, 25th September 1871

Dear M[r.] Stanley

The news brought here by your couriers is very sad and I fear it has placed you in an extremely difficult position, to say nothing of the delay in a seemingly unhealthy place where you are only lessening the funds at your disposal. I hope the men will soon reach you with the few things they can carry.

Help in this way of fever from Zanzibar is impossible but I think the Arabs have brought this on themselves. I have long had complaints of the way in which the little imp called a governor behaves to both Arab & Native always ready to be bribed or to plunder as seems most suitable to the poor devil in his power, but if this be the true origin of this war it serves him and them jolly well but I pity you.

I may tell you however from my experience that these wars never extend over the area they are said to do and are more easily out marched than might at first seem possible but then will your porters follow you on a regular wild Expedition a little off the beaten track. That was just the difficulty we found when without the Makololos who certainly were fine fellows for pushing through and caring nothing for the gentiles whom they despised.

Do you not think that by coming back a little you might go South through an open country and join the Wemba and Cazembe road, Arabs do so often, but in that heat, I fear there is little new I should much rather see you if you felt strong enough going to the North East to the Ukerewe and there await some of the Pangani or Wembas Caravans and having followed them return by the back of the [Snow?] Mountains, there you will have new things to describe and some say a burning mountain.

If you go South don't forget those queer [sub …?] caverns that no doubt by this time you have been told of. There is no new geographical facts to relate I send you the résumé of the Com[man]d[er] Negri[1] the last I have a few letters I enclose for Dr Livingst[one] and I will ask you to do your best for him you can by seeing what the little Sheikh is about in not sending on the second lot of things I forwarded to his

---

1. Cristoforo Negri (1809-1896), geographer, and diplomat, one of the founder members of the Società geografica italiana. Represented Italy at the Brussels Conference (1876) and the Berlin Conference (1884–85).

care. I have written to him telling him to follow what you say and if you should see him doing away with anything please just take the whole at once out of his hands and I shall tell the new governor all about it but if a chance offers please send them on.

We are very sorry to think that Cap. Webb is about to leave but he will be represented by his namesake I am sure if I can do here anything for you I shall be only too glad as I doubt not will any other if I should be gone, but I see no prospect of that now.

With all best wishes
Ever Yrs very sin[cere]ly
John Kirk

S.A. 2660 (three letters, same date)

[1st letter]

Zanzibar, 20/5/72

My dear Sir,
In answer to my application of this morning for the Arab headman described in D. Livingstone's letter His Highness says there is no one at his disposal in whom he has sufficient confidence but that if I can arrange with or indicate a fitting man he will use his whole influence to induce him to accept and act fairly.

Considering the Sultan's small hold over his people I can fully understand his unwillingness to become responsible but I am sure he will do what he can in the matter if you or I take some one before him.

Is there any Arab you know who would go on the terms offered by Dr. Livingstone? Swahelis I could find but an honest and active Arab is rare and can do so well here on his own account that it will be difficult for the Sultan or either of us to obtain his services.

The original engagement of the Membas men was a matter of Mr New's arrangement but I like the Akida so far as I have seen him. You are however quite right in foreseeing complications through the two parties and naturally any one to command both will expect still higher pay than either of those under him, whether sent by the sultan or by us. This matter of pay or inducement must be fairly faced and settled or trouble will come in the end.

Yours v[er]y sincerely
John Kirk
H.M. Stanley Es.

[2nd letter]

British Agency
Zanzibar
20/5/72

My dear Sir,
I hardly understand from your note whether you now wish to cancel what you said on arrival relative to not wishing a head Arab to take up Dr Livingstone's men.
Dr L's own letter to Seyd Burgash has been long ago transmitted and explained to him but I then mentioned that you no longer thought of troubling him for this responsible head man described.
Under this altered circumstance Mr W. O. Livingstone having abandoned the idea of following his father I shall be only too glad to aid you with the Sultan and shall if your desire at once send and tell him to pick out the proper man whom you will of course yourself review and reject or approve as you think best.
Very truly yours
John Kirk

[3rd letter]

British Agency Consulate
20/5/72

My dear Sir,
I shall lose no time in forwarding a <u>Memo</u> to H. H. Seyd Burgash and ask him to send the man he may select without delay to you.
Of course unless the Arab seems a thoroughly trustworthy person he must be rejected for as you say there are other means at hand and his presence no absolute necessity, Unyanyembe being on the high road and the way so far quite simple and easy.
Yours very truly
John Kirk

Letters from Dr. Livingstone to Stanley (S.A. 477, 478, 479)

S.A. 477

Unyanyembe

14th March 1872
I have been subjected to so much loss by the employment of slaves in caravans sent by H[er] M[ajesty's] consul that if Mr Stanley meets another party of the sort I beg him to turn them back but use his discretion in the whole matter.

David Livingstone

S.A. 478

Kwihara 16th March 1872

My dear Stanley
I sympathize with you in the worry & vexation inflicted by the incorrigible Bombay. I saw the Portmanteau as soon as I returned and arranged to send it off but before we could well turn ourselves about Sa[r]men or Salemen made his appearance for the tent pole and he had run all the way. He is as good as Bombay is bad. I saw the "ne'er-do well" with an arm full of ropes and thought that you had ordered him and said nothing. He took away as I saw this morning all I had placed behind for the gunwale of the boat. If you don't need them please return them by Susi. But if you do I shall buy & get[1] others from the Arabs. I send a bit of blue stone for Madwara's ulcers. He knows how to apply it.
If you can telegraph on your arrival in London be particular please to say how Sir Roderick is. You put the matter exactly yesterday when you said that "I was not yet satisfied about the sources but as soon as I shall be satisfied I shall return and give reasons for satisfaction fit for other people". This is just as it stands. I wish I could give you a better word than the scotch one to "put a stout heart to a stey brae" (a steep ascent) for you will do that and I am thankful
that before going away the fever had changed into the intermittent or safe form. I could not have let you go but with great concern had you still been troubled with the contin-

---

1. 'them' crossed out.

ued form. I feel comfortable in commending you to the kind gaurdianship of the good Lord and Father of all.

I am gratefully yours

David Livingstone

I have worked as hard as I could copying observations made in one line of march from Kabuire back again to Cazembe and on to Lake Bangweolo and am quite tired of it. My large figures fill six sheets foolscap and many a day will elapse ere I take to copying again. I did my duty when ill at Ujiji in 1869 and am not to blame though they grope a little in the dark at home.

Some Arab letters have come and I forward them to you.

D. L.

Tell them at home that we are theoretical discoverers of the outlet of Tanganyika. We have dreamed about it and that ought to please them.

S.A. 478

To H. M. Stanley Esq.

List of goods to be sent from Zanzibar

Fifty freemen at $25—$30 a year to be engaged to go with me till I finish my work, and do all manner of service = to get extra pay for carrying loads, and they will be allowed to invest their wages in ivory as our goods decrease—one half year's pay in advance—also a note to say what may be due here on arrival[2]:

Muskets for each

Powder horns for each

Hatchets for each

A chain for all

1000 flints

2000 bullets

10 kegs of gunpowder

Honga cloth

Rations for the way

6 strong padlocks

A bridle

A few tins of flour

A few tins of Crackers

A few tins of Preserved fruits

Preference being made to light weight in travelling.

A few tins of Sardines

A few tins of Salmon

---

2. These men were engaged for $30 dollars per year and received $20 dollars in advance (see S.A. 4749, Contracts of African Soldiers).

10 or 15 Pounds of Tea
A little sewing thread & needles
12 large envelopes
Nautical Almanacs for 1872—3
Whittier's Poems
One blank journal of smooth paper
Two strong donkeys not to be loaded or allowed to drink water at all at Marenga M'kali
One chronometer (stopped)
David Livingstone
Unyanyembe March 1872

16th March 1872
PS. I saw your silver tea strainer only last night after I had gone to bed. I have written a note this morning to Mr Murray, 50 Albemarle St = the publisher to help you if necessary in sending the journal by Book Post or otherwise to Agnes. If you call on him you will find him frank and no "eyeglass" though he needs one I believe. A pleasant journey to you
David Livingstone

S.A. 479

Lake Bañgweolo—South Central Africa
[some misreadings or changes in the printed text]
[after Aug. 15, 1872]

My dear Stanley
I wrote hurriedly to you when on the eve of starting from Unyanyembe, and the mind being occupied by all the little worries incidental to the starting of a caravan, I felt and still feel that I had not expressed half the gratitude that welled up in my heart for all the kind and able services you rendered to me at the coast. I am also devoutly thankful to our loving Father above for helping you through all your manifold Masika toils, and bringing you safely to Zanzibar with your energies unimpaired, and your heart still willing to exert yourself to the utmost in securing all the men & goods I needed for this my concluding trip. I am perpetually reminded that I owe a great deal to your drilling of the men you sent. With one exception the party has worked like a machine. I give my orders to Manua Sera and never need to repeat them. I parted with the Arab sent without any disagreement. He lost one of the new donkeys at Bagamoio, then put two strangers[3] in the chain without fastening the free end and they wisely walked off, bridle, bits and all, then suffered a lazy Mombasian to leave the cocoa somewhere and get 5 dotis at Unyanyembe as a carrier while[4] no one either before or after that could get any

---

3. Livingstone wrote 'strangers' and not 'stragglers' as it has been printed.
4. 'well' in the printed text.

good out of him. Added to this the Arab shewed a disposition to secure a second $500 supposing that we should be one month over the year. Though he could do nothing except through my native headmen. I therefore let him go and made Manua Sera, Chaoperi and Susi heads of departments at $20 extra if they gave satisfaction. This they have tried faithfully to do and hitherto have been quite a contrast to Bombay who seemed to think that you ought to try and please him. Madjwara is about perfect but slow, slow,[5] and keeps your fine silver teapot spoons & knives as bright as if he were an English butler, gets a cup of tea or coffee ready at 5 A.M. or sooner if I don't advise him to lie down again, walks at the head of the caravan as drummer, this instrument being the African sign of peace as well as of war. He objected at first to the office because the drum had not been bought by either you or me! Some reasons are profound—this may be one of them. The Fruits Fish Pork Biscuits Flour selected far better than I could have done. No golden syrup could be found or you would have sent some, the tea very nicely secured, your wish for joy over the plumpudding was fulfilled though it would have been better had you been near the Chambeze where we spent Christmas to enjoy it. I keep most of your handsome present of champagne for a special occasion. One rifle was injured at Bagamoio, the other and your splendid Revolver all I could desire for efficiency, the 15 shooter cartridges are not satisfactory but everything else gives so much satisfaction I could not grumble though I were bilious. I thank you very much and very sincerely for all your kind generosity.

The new Zanzibar donkey came lean leg sore & stiff so I left him with Sultan bin Ali. Your two country beasts were in capital condition. Another you left died with all the symptoms of Tsetse poison fully developed. He had the run of all the patches of cultivation around us & perfect liberty, but perished the first of his species I have seen die like a Tsetse bitten ox, the larger country animal died from the same cause but had none of the symptoms except swelling of mouth & nose and above the eyes. He rallied twice but when we left the South end of the Tanganyika where all was hot & dry we suddenly mounted up in the rainy season of Urungu or Burungu where the cold and wet acted as the natives told us in former years they woud do on all our cattle that had the poison in their systems. I had found long before we had done with the excessive heats in the mountains that flank Tanganyika that riding in the sun is more trying to the system than marching on foot. The perspiration caused by tramping modifies the[6] effects of temperature somewhat as wakefulness does those of extreme cold. In the hurry of departure I neglected your advice to buy others, but I was so overjoyed by having got the men the idea being knocked up by marching found as little place in my mind as it does in that of a boy going home from school.

The Chambeze was crossed long ago by the Portuguese who have thus the merit of its discovery in modern times. The similarity of names led to its being put down in map as "Zambesi" (Eastern branch) and I rather stupidly took the error as having some sort of authority. Hence my first crossing it was as fruitless as that of the Portuguese. It took

---

5. 'but slow, slow' added above the line.
6. 'effects of' added above the line.

me full twenty two months to eliminate this error. The Cazembe who was lately killed was the first who gave me a hint that Chambeze was one of a chain of rivers & lakes which probably forms the Nile, but he did it in rather a bantering style that led me to go back to the head waters again & see that it was not the mere "chaff" of a mighty Potentate. There on an island in the middle of Bangweolo with 183° of sea horizon around the natives slowly drawing the hand around said that is Chambeze flowing round all this space & forming Bañgweolo before it winds round that headland and changes its name to Luapula. That was the moment of discovery, and not the mere crossing of a small river. The late Cazembe I found sensible & friendly – His empire has succumbed before a very small force of Arab slavers & Banyamwezi. Pereira the first Portuguese who visited the Cazembe of eighty years ago, said that he had 30,000 trained soldiers sacrificed twenty human victims every day and the streets of his capital were watered daily. I thought that my late friend had 30,0(oo) diminished by two oos, and sacrificed 5 or 6 pots of pombe daily but this may have been only a court scandal. The streets of his village were not made so I was reminded of the famous couplet about the Highlands roads, "If you had seen these roads before they were made, you would lift up your hands and bless Colonel Wade". I have been the unfortunate means of demolishing two empires in Portuguese geography, the Cazembe's and that of the Emperor Monomotapa. I found the last about 10 days above Tette. He had too few men to make the shew Cazembe did but I learned from from[7] some decent motherly looking women attached to his court "zembere" that he had one hundred wives! I have wondered ever since, and have been nearly dumfounded with the idea of what a nuisance a man with a 100 wives in England would be. It is awful to contemplate and might be chosen as a theme for a young men's debating society. I wish some one would visit Mtesa of Uganda without Bombay as an interpreter. He Bombay[8] is by no means a sound author. The King of Dahomey suffered ecclipse after a common sense visit, and we seldom hear anymore of his atrocities. The mightiest African Potentate and the most dreadful cruelties told of Africans owe a vast deal to the teller[9] = you and I passed the islet Kasenge where African mothers were said to sell their infants for a loin cloth each. This story was made to fit into an other[10] nice little story of a "mother bear" that refused to leave her[11] young. A child that cuts its upper front teeth before the under is dreaded as unlucky & likely to bring death into the family. It is called an Arab child & the first Arab who passes is asked to take it. I never saw a case nor have the Arabs I have asked seen one either, but they have heard of its occurrence. The Kasenge story is therefore exactly like of the Frenchman's who asserted that the English were so fond of hanging themselves in November you might see them swinging on trees along the road. He may have seen one. I never did. English and American mothers have been guilty of

---

7. 'from" is repeated.
8. 'Bombay' added above the line.
9. 'teller' written above 'describer' crossed out.
10. 'an other' added above the line.
11. 'her' written above 'its' crossed out.

deserting infants, but who would turn up the whites of his eyes, and say as our author at Kasenge did, these people are no better than or not so good as[12] she-bears.

Three of the Banurungu chiefs had died since my first visit and the population all turned topsy-turvey as the result of the elections = they elect a sister's son instead of the heir apparent (the heathen) because, say the sly dogs, the heir <u>apparent</u> may not be the heir <u>real</u>!! New stockades had been built on new sites, cultivation on grass & forest lands necessarily small, and food could not be got for either love or money. As I am of the old orthodox school I disapprove of the election of chief magistrates everywhere. When you found a good man like general Grant why not call him Prince as the Germans did their good man Bismark, quintuple his salary and live the rest of your days like Christians? You make the ladies think that your ranting at elections is perfect bliss, while if you caught them & forced them to vote only once, you would hear no more of women's rights = they bless their dear hearts, would take to feeding the hungry instead of palavering at public omnium gatherums.[13]

[2nd sheet]

It may be no more than a mere coincidence that the public advice through the Foreign Office was backed by the solemn assertions of the slaves that they were instructed or rather ordered by the English Consul to force me back. I cannot believe that any man with his wits about him would be fool enough to place himself in their power but they did learn from some one that it was desirable to make me retire and being in some respects like children they seem to have quite overacted their part. It is said that a little American girl asked a gentleman visitor who had been received by Mamma with great cordiality if his neighbour were a fool. "No my dear he is a very sensible man" "but why do you ask that?" "because Mamma said <u>you were next door to a fool</u>! The astute Banians with whom the Consul was notoriously confidential may have discerned his proclivities and delivering the advice undiluted, the slaves by their asseverations and persistency in naming the Consul, probably went much further than even their masters intended. Now that I am gaining the victory over all machinations I can afford to forgive though it would be foolish to forget much dearly bought experience. I have a little curiosity to know what the "other plan than a new exped[ition] was which the Government had in view when declining to end the Search & Relief Expedition. If they had an offer from one already out to take a few Arabs run in to the North end of Tanganyika & there settle the Nile problem and call me out of Manyuema where I was reported to the Foreign Office to be living (in idleness) like an Arab, this would be a feasible explanation for which I regret Sir H. Rawlinson did not enquire.

I do not wish to appear more generous in undertaking this work than I deserve. You once thought that I must have felt sure of being no loser if I succeeded. I carried a letter from Lord Russell to Sir Roderick Murchison in which His Lordship stated his intention

---

12. 'or not so good as' added above the line.
13. Omnium gatherum: a miscellaneous collection of persons, an assembly.

of giving me £500 a year if I settled with any influential chief. I might have settled with Mataka in his beautiful Highland home overlooking at 5000 feet[14] Lake Nyassa, but if I did I should abandon the task set me by my dear warm hearted Sir Roderick, and I could not bear to disappoint him. I therefore deliberately elected to please him rather than fill my purse. Don't however make too much of that, for I was then of the opinion that two years would be ample for exploring the watershed of South Central Africa, and I elected only to sacrifice two years salary or say one thousand Pounds.

Instead of being "sure of being no loser" the only thing I was certain of was that a certain Mr Murray a supernumerary clerk in the Foreign Office did stop my salary and wrote home that my services would not carry any even the smallest claim on H. M. Government. This was so insultingly nauseous from a mere Jack in office that I never could quote it = He altered it a little when Lord Clarendon pronounced it to be "both ungracious and unjust". I cannot bear to wrangle about money, and I shall prefer to strike out some new line of labour in which to spend my declining years before I sink into peaceful oblivion. I have felt sore at this Mr Murray's exhuberant impertinence the like of which never left the Foreign or any other office because the Great men above him knew nothing about it. They would have first offered me other work. Mr Murray was himself put in as a third undersecretary in order not to be thrown idle. The West coast slave trade was then rife. It ceased but this gentleman did not[15] cease to draw his own salary. Possibly he is more of an honour to his country than your servant.

[new sheet]

It sent a glow through my frame to read in the Herald the accounts of good kind-hearted souls in New York feeding the hungry on Thanksgiving day and sending portions home with love into many a house. Blessings on the donors.

This Lake[16] so far as I have seen it is surrounded by an extremely flat country though all 4000 feet above the level of the sea. When first discovered I was without paper but borrowed a little from an Arab and sent a short account home. I had so much wading and but[17] four attendants that I took only the barest necessaries. Yet no sooner was the discovery announced at the coast than an official description was forthwith sent to the Bombay Government in which it was gravely stated that the Lake is "like Nyassa-Tanganyika, and the Albert Nyanza, overhung by high mountain-slopes, which open out in bays and valleys, or leave great plains which during the rainy season become flooded, so that caravans march for days through water knee deep, seeking for higher ground on which to pass the night". The only "mountain-slopes" are anthills—some of them twenty feet high. They could scarcely be called high unless thought of as placed on the top of 4000 feet. Other statements in this official description are equally

---

14. 'at 5000 feet' added above the line.
15. 'not' added above the line.
16. It is not certain that this third sheet, not numbered by Livingstone, belongs to the same letter.
17. 'but' written over 'only'.

opposed to the truth as that "Cazembe's town is built on the banks of the Luapula". Englishmen having a crotchet for map making traced every step of the Portuguese slaving Expeditions to Cazembe and built the village in Lat. 8° 43' South—that is in deep water near the North end of Lake Moero and over fifty miles from Luapula. I found it in Lat. 9° 37' South and on the banks of a lagoon or loch having no connection with the Luapula which river however flows six or seven miles West of the village away into Moero. Now it is very unpleasant for me to expose this and other misstatements and appear contradictious, but what am I to do? I was consulted by Sir Roderick Murchison as to[18] this present expedition and recommended the writer of the above referred to description as a leader[19] = Sir Roderick afterwards told me that the offer was declined unless a good salary and a good position to fall back upon were added,[20] as Speke & Grant had in their pay and commissions. He then urged the leadership on myself. I agreed as soon as the work on which I was engaged should be published. My good warm hearted friend added in a sort of prophetic strain "You will be the real discoverer of the sources of the Nile". I don't wish to boast of my good deeds, but I need not forget them, and it was by my direct intercession solely that my friend got the[21] salary and position he now holds. Having secured the prerequisites then came a sort of self-invitation to share in the honours. "You cannot imagine how much I long to have a run with you again in the wilds. I feel as if I must have it some time". This eliciting no response next followed a public advice for me "to retire and leave the work to others as I must be tired &c." It went to the Foreign Office and was published by the Royal Geographical Society—then the official description of Bangweolo shewing possibly an eager desire to mix up his name with discoveries which he had too much regard for money to make himself.

[End of the letter?]

---

18. 'a leader for' crossed out.
19. 'as a leader' added above the line.
20. Though Kirk is not clearly named in this letter to Stanley, his name and attitude are clearly exposed in Livingstone's letter to Murchison, March 13, 1872, *PRGS* 16, no. 5 (1871–72): 435.
21. 'the' added above the line.

Letters from W. Oswell Livingstone to Stanley (S.A. 488)

My dear Stanley

I forgot to mention this morning when I saw you that I would like you to furnish me with a copy of the list of things which my father gave you & also a list of things which you have already bought for him, so that I may be able to give an exact account of the money I have expended when writing to the Royal geographical Society. I have got a dhow which starts this afternoon & which is at my disposal when she reaches Bagamoio.
Yours truly
W. Oswell Livingstone
P.S. Dawson has agreed to give $500 to the captain of the native vessel: this is for three persons myself being the third in case I may be ready to go.
W. O. L
British Consulate
17 May 1872

Dear Stanley

I have decided to dismiss these Mombas men[1] as keeping will only entail considerable expense. If I send them up to the country I shall have to furnish so many extra guns.
Yours ever
W. Oswell Livingstone
23 May 1872

Dear Stanley

I find I have only 20 doti of Sohari so I have sent some extra Dwabani & a few Jawa to make up the number
Yours truly
W. Oswell Livingstone
British Consulate
24 May 1872

---

1. These men had been recruited by Charles New on behalf of Lieut. Dawson, and transported to Zanzibar with the help of the Sultan's steamer (Letter from Dawson, Zanzibar, April 19, 1872, *PRGS* 16 (1872): 381).

Zanzibar [35 *in pencil, on the upper right corner*]
British Consulate
24 May 1872

My dear Stanley

I was just on the point of sending over the things which I promised when your note came. You are evidently annoyed at my not sending them last night, but I can't help that. I was engaged during the evening about money matters. I have no original list of things which you mention.
I find that the box labelled Sardines is full of Salt.
Yours ever
W. Oswell Livingstone

[*Adresses on the reverse*]
H. M. Stanley Esq
U. S. Consulate

Letters from the NEW YORK HERALD Staff in London to Stanley: Finley Anderson (S.A. 2588, 2589); Douglas A. Levien (S.A. 2626)

Finley Anderson (*Herald*'s London Office) to Stanley

S.A. 2588

[In blue pencil] 1st search after Livingstone
The Queen's Hotel
St Martins le Grand, London
October 20, 1868

Henry Stanley, Esq.
Special correspondent New York Herald

Dear Sir:
Having received the joyful news that Dr Livingstone is on his way home from Africa via Zanzibar, the New York Herald desires you to proceed to Suez, or if practical to Zanzibar, to meet him. The Americans are deeply interested in his personal welfare and his researches. You may assure him that the people of the United States not less than the people of Great Britain, have anxiously looked for his safe return from his perilous explorations. They are awaiting with the greatest interest the news of his actual arrival at Zanzibar, and some account of his researches. Ask him if he will have the goodness to give you an outline of his journey and discoveries. The interest we feel in the matter will warrant you in telegraphing the account either from Egypt or from India, regardless of the expense.
Very truly Yours
Finley Anderson

S.A. 2589

The Queen's Hotel
St Martin le Grand, London

Friday Oct. 23, 1868

My dear Mr Stanley,

    I have just returned from Liverpool, and find your parting letter; and also that in accordance with your telegram your trunk was sent to you this morning. I hope it will arrive in Marseilles in time for you to get it before you leave there. I enclose you the letter that I told you I would send. If you should find Dr Livingstone you might read it to him if you think proper. Of course you will bear in mind the verbal instructions you received in London. I will see the Royal Geographical people, and will probably send you a telegram about the time you reach Alexander [*sic*].
    I wish you a safe pleasant & successful trip.
    Yours very truly
    Finley Anderson

Douglas A. Levien (*Herald*'s London Office) to Stanley

S.A. 2626

14 Cambridge Square
Hyde Park, London
Nov 29, 1869

My dear Stanley,
    I enclose you a letter of credit for £600 and send with it my best wishes for your signal success in your great undertaking. I have no doubt you will carry it through in perfect style. The latest news from Livingston[1] seems to render it certain that he is alive, and that after all is the most important feature of your commission. I talked the matter over with Mr Bennett, and his idea is decidedly Napoleonic.[2] I have not received such full and frequent letters from Suez as I expected, but perhaps they have been sent direct to New York without coming to London. Mad Lebeuf Dolby writes me that she had seen you.

---

    1. Livingston is written without e.
    2. Probable reference to Gordon Bennett Sr., who called himself "the Napoleon of the newspaper press." James L. Crouthamel and Andrew Jackson, "James Gordon Bennett, the *New York Herald*, and the Development of Newspaper Sensationalism," *New York History* 54, no. 3 (July 1973): 311, http://www.jstor.org/stable/23169403.

In the expectation of hearing great things from you, I wish you all health and comfort on your extended pilgrimage.

By the way, I hear indirectly that the Canal will be a failure after all. If this is so, do not conceal the fact. It is none of our profit or glory. It is said that while it may do as a sort of transfer Canal it will never last as a passage way for vessels without transshipment of cargoes. Of course you will enquire fully with all this. Write as often as you can & always let me know personally how you are getting along. You may fully rely on my sending you supplies of money promptly & I make the present letter £100 more than you asked because I am sure you will be careful as you always have been in regard to expenditures.
With best wishes from all, believe me
Very truly your friend
Douglas A. Levien

They objected to make the letter of Credit run over 12 months, but wherever you may be at the end of a year, you will no doubt have used up the amount.

I open my letter to say that from news just received from Constantinople I should not be surprised at an outbreak between the Sultan & Khedive. If such an event should occur you would of course throw yourself into that before starting on your journey elsewhere.
D. A. L.

Letters from Stanley to J. Gordon Bennett (S.A. 6926, 6925)

H. M. Stanley to J. G. Bennett, Zanzibar, January 17, 1871
S.A. 6926

Zanzibar Town
Zanzibar Island   Jan 17, 1/71

James Gordon Bennett Esq. Jr.
New York Herald

Dear Sir,

A week ago after an incredible amount of patience such as could only be possessed by Job I arrived at this island in compliance with your request. Before proceeding further I must lay before you certain facts.

When I was in Abyssinia I felt that to make the "Herald" Expedition perfectly successful, needed a Letter of Credit upon which a tried & economical & faithful Correspondent should be allowed to draw at his discretion. When later still you telegraphed me to stay in Egypt that idea recurred to me again, when on the brink of starvation I sold my watch – yet I had a telegram in my hand stating I had done well & faithfully – and this was but three weeks after my return from Abyssinia.

When again I was[1] sent[2] on my first search after Livingstone, my instructions were so vague, so unsatisfactory suggestive of impecuniosity, that no one – that I could not at least venture to do anything – I had £200 with this I was to go down to Alexandria, perhaps Suez, perhaps Aden, where expectations were strong just then that Livingstone would pass.

---

1. 'I was' written in pencil above 'Anderson' crossed out.
2. 'me' crossed out.

<u>2</u>

Now, I think of it, I believe it would have been unsuccessful – for the man's life would have been badgered out of him by a dozen correspondents.

This last time that I have gone out it was you personally, who explicitly gave me my instructions. "Visit the Suez Canal. Go to Jerusalem then to Constantinople & the Crimea, and then the Euphrates Valley, then Zanzibar, and if you hear of Livingstone likely to come, go out to meet him."

"How much money do you allow for this?" I asked.

"Oh! As much as it will cost. Draw £500 now and when it is over, draw another – and an other" &c, you replied.

Well I have drawn but £600, that has lasted me a year.[3] I made it last all the way through Egypt, Palestine, Constantinople, Sevastopol & the Crimea, the Caucasus, Turkestan, Persia, Bagh-dad, Bombay to Zanzibar. I made it last to carry me 18,898 miles, over which no other American traveller's footsteps ever trod the most of it.

During this period I have been constantly writing to Levien, telling him where to send the next Letter of Credit. If I have written once, I have written fifteen times, and when I left London he was full of the fairest promises.

3

He would keep me supplied with money. He would write letters of encouragement.

Yet I have at last arrived at Zanzibar (85 days from Bombay, because of the cholera here) and there is no letter for me – not one word from the Agent, or the Office, – not one in a whole year.

I am not one to expect sentimental letters, nor one who takes delight in reading them but I am one who prompt himself expects every man to be prompt & correct in business.

Many a man would have believed – were he in my place – that he was a beggar. I had brought all my guns, ammunition & clothes for my African trip to dare that which Burton & Speke failed with $15.000, I intended to do it for $4000, or $5000 at the furthest. Yet upon coming to[4] this island with all this paraphernalia of African travel, I find a deadlock in my way. No money! No letter!

What was to be done? Should I go back, stay here until you sent me money – or go on? But how could I stay here, go back, or go on –without money?

I looked over what letters Mr Levien had sent me when I was in Egypt, and there I read, "You will no doubt have spent this money £600, long before the year is out (I made it last 13 months) in that case you must let me

---

3. See Appendix, letter from Douglas A. Levien (*Herald*'s London Office) to Stanley, November 29, 1869, enclosing a letter of credit of £600, S.A. 2626.

4. 'to' written above 'upon' crossed out.

4

know before you get out of reach of letters, where to send you another Credit." That was satisfactory, then Mr Levien was informed that I was to go somewhere out of reach of letters—he had received orders also to[5] supply me with money as my travels needed it. So far, so good.

I also looked over my diary of 1869, to read what verbal instructions I had received from you. "Go out to meet Livingstone if you think you can reach him, and what money you need you draw." Just so. All is satisfactory.

Well, I then went to Mr Webb, the American Consul at this place stated to him my exact position, what I had come to Zanzibar for (as he was since my visit to Aden in 1868 after Livingstone, our confidante) and asked his advice. He begged permission to see what letters I had. I showed those of Levien of December 1869. He said they were quite satisfactory, that it was evidently I was to go somewhere, & that since I had arrived at Zanzibar he had no doubt it was after Livingstone, and that any money I needed I could get by paying 20 per cent.

Not forgetful of the least part of my instructions, I went over to Dr Kirk (former companion of Livingstone up the Zambezi, and present correspondent & intimate friend of his) and questioned him as to where Livingstone was."

5

Dr Kirk replied in these words, "

Dr Livingstone is on the western side of Lake Tanganyika. He expects shortly to come to Ujiji, which is about 4 months travel from here (Zanzibar). I have sent him some fresh supplies, & boatmen, and they are on the other side, (that is on the coast at Bagomoyo, about 25 miles from here preparing to start for Ujiji.

"Oh, indeed I said. Do you think Baker will meet him?"

"Oh, no, not at all. Dr Livingstone is pretty well known to me, and I know that with all his modesty, he has the very highest idea of himself, and appreciates more than any other man what he has done. If he hears of Baker in the neighbourhood he will go further away. If Baker gets to the North side of Tanganyika he will go to the South side. If Burton & Speke were at Ujiji, he would take himself to the West side of the Lake. He hates Burton like poison. He is a man of strong likings & dislikes. He is vain, and easily annoyed. Any slights, no one would take them so much to heart as he himself."

"Indeed, I said. "Which way then do you think he will leave Central Africa?"

"Oh, this way of course, from Ujiji to Zanzibar. Perhaps, if he were not afraid of meeting Baker, he might descend the Nile, so that he could say he had been the first white man

---

5. 'get' crossed out.

6

to traverse Africa from[6] the Cape of Good Hope to Alexandria. But as Baker has such a large force with him Livingstone will be sure to hear from him & come this way, by way of Zanzibar."

"You do not think then he will try to reach Loanda?"

"No, I am certain of that, for he has once been there, and knows every foot of ground to Loanda. No. Here is the most likly [sic] spot he will try to reach."

"How far South, do you think" I then asked "Baker will reach?"

"He may try to put his steamers on the Tanganyika—from the Albert Lake, which are supposed to be joined together by a stream of water."

"Burton, never hinted to anything of that kind." I said

"No, not in his finished & late work the "Lake Regions of Central Africa". But in his earliest manuscripts, he said that the Wavira (a ferocious tribe) live on the banks of a very swift stream which flows from the Tanganyika Northwards—or to the Albert Lake—in which case Baker with his large force of men will be able to press through in any direction, supported as he is by the Viceroy of Egypt."

"What is Baker up in that country for, is it for exploration & science, or to stop the slave trade?" I asked.

7

"No Sir, neither. Baker is a man who likes adventure. Of course as Adventure leads to Exploration, it suits Baker very well, but he is not there to stop the slave trade. Baker has not any such sentiment in him. I dare say if he met a gang of slaves in the hands of a trader, he would pitch in for the love of the thing & liberate them. But Baker's purpose in Central Africa is that he is a well paid employee in the service of the Viceroy, he is to get all the trade in ivory of Central Africa into the Viceroy's hands. The Viceroy has already driven all the ivory traders from Gondokora & the Upper Nile by sheer pressure, causing some of their villages to be burnt, others to be robbed, putting a score of official difficulties in the way, until there is not a single European ivory trader left. For the Arabs & Turks, a hint is sufficient for them. If Baker succeeds in getting his steamers to Ujiji, he will ruin the ivory trade of the island of Zanzibar, for Ujiji is the great depot of ivory trade of Central Africa.

Now Sir, having heard such good news, to me – my duty was plain – this was the news I desired to hear, this is what I came for, and the conclusion arrived at is this – that arrived at Zanzibar after an expense of £650, through all that round-about route of over 18,000 miles, that having invested £200

8

of your, and my money in purchasing guns, ammunition, flannel clothes, medicines, and scores of other concomitants of travel; that as Livingstone is at Ujiji waiting for his

---

6. 'Africa from' added above the line.

supplies, that as his supplies are starting from the Coast, that it is my duty to go after him to meet him, to <u>interview</u> him, & to do something in the way of exploration myself, provided it does not take me from my express & special path of duty. Even if my mission prove unsuccessful, it will have been great glory –glory enough to last a century. For Burton & Speke with all their appliances, with their $15,000, only reached Ujiji, and when in sight of Tanganyika, did not sail round it, nor sound it. They saw it & that was all.

When I get to Ujiji, Livingstone may be on the western shore of the Lake, or the northern or the southern. Would it not be a pity if after arriving at Ujiji, I should have to halt there for want of means to cross, or sail round the Lake? To obviate this difficulty I shall take two canvas boats with oars and sails, so that I can cut off Livingstone wherever he is.

I start with confidence, knowing that if successful you will thank me, if unsuccessful that it shall not be through any fault of mine. I shall start on the 1st of February. I shall outstrip Livingstone's

9

supplies, and reach Ujiji about the 1st of June I shall take a month at the furthest to sail round the Lake to find him. I shall then return immediately if I find him back to Zanzibar which place I hope to reach about the 1st of November. If I have not found Livingstone, but have heard that he has gone down the Nile I shall then hasten after him with my canvas boats from the Victoria Lake down the Nile, and having an object in view I have no doubt I shall catch him unless he has had too long a start.

The following list will intimate the nature of the Expenses to Ujiji & back, calculated for one year.

	D. cts
1 Boat 25 feet long, 6 ½ feet beam	$80.
B. loader. 1 rifle Starrs Patent 8 Pkgs of Cartridges	31.
12 Flintlocks, & bullet moulds at $4	48.
Breechloader. 1 rifle & 4 Pkgs of Cartridges	28.20
1 Elephant Rifle, muzzle loader	50.00
2000 Metallic Cartridges for 2 Starrs Rifles	50 –
150 lbs Bar Lead	20 –
25 lbs Powder Keg	20 –
1 Boat 10 feet long, 4 ½ feet beam	40.
Balance Passage Money from Seychelles to Zanzibar	50.
Cloth	4.50
Money advance to 1 European Navigator W. L. Farquahar, wages $300 per year	75.00
4 Bolts of American Twill for Tent & Boat Sails	24.00
	520.70

	$520.70
5 Bolts of canvas No 3 to make Boat	$ 60.
Bill of Banian Merchant for Tools & Cooking Pots	62.50
4 suits of Flannel	20.00
Thread, Buttons, needles, soap, musquito net	20.00
4 Flannel shirts for self	10.00
4 " " for my interpreter	10.00
4 Suits of Pyjamas	20.00
Carpenter's Bill for Ammunition Boxes	10.00
Jirmans Bill for lamps, Sugar, & Tea &c	20.00
2 sail maker's Bills	10.00
Quinne, Warbugh's Tincture, & colocynth	5.00
Dhow to transport to main-land	50.00
1 camel	30.00
2 donkeys -$40	80.00
4 " $20	80.00
Advances in Money to 7 of Speke's Faithfuls for 1 year	160.00
6 Pack Saddles, Halters, Chains & Padlocks	40.00
Provisions	100.00
Rope, tar, Twine, Sail needles	20.00
Shoes & Boots	20.00
Flints	4.00
Fish Lines & Hooks	2.00
Beeswax	1.00
2 Bags of Buckshot	5.00
Sounding Line for the African Lakes	10.00
Hire of 12 armed slaves for 1 year	240.00
Extra wages at the end of the year to 7 of Speke's Faithfuls	200.00
Wages at the end of the year to W. L. Farquaha[r]	225.00
" " " " to Selim-Interpreter	60.00
	2105.20

Carried forward

Brot forward	$2105.20
To purchase food for 100 porters & 30 followers for 1 year, together with pay to the African porters.	
10000 yds of Merkani Cloth (American cotton)	$ 937.50
Beads 30 men's loads	$ 600.00
Wire 10 " "	$ 200
	$3842.70

I am obliged to draw $4000 on you for Actual Money received, and $1000 more, which is 20 per cent premium for $4000, making a total of $5000. By this mail you will receive a draft drawn on you in favor of John Bertram & Co of Salem to the sum of $3750, which you will please pay[7] & charge to my account. I could not draw on London, because no responsible merchant has any business with London. For several of the above items, I shall hold myself personally responsible. In another week, there will be a further draft of $1250, making a total of $5000 which you will also please pay & charge to my ac/-

I remain,
Very respectfully
Your obedient servant
Henry M Stanley

P.S. I shall communicate as often as possible with you, informing you how I am proceeding. Please send one letter containing any further instructions you may have to give me, about the transmission of my interview with Livingstone, to Zanzibar, care of M^r· R. Webb American consul, and a duplicate of it care of the American Consulate at Thebes <......>[8]

And now dear Sir, I must bid you a farewell – perhaps for ever. If I fail and die, then I shall have merited a just obituary in your [9] columns. If I live, and have been successful it will be with glowing pride that I shall receive your thanks. Fare you well and my best wishes be with the "New York Herald" and its energetic manager.
 [signed]
Stanley

---

7. 'pay' added above the line.
8. One line unreadable due to moisture, loss of paper, and/or gummed paper.
9. A blank space.

H. M. Stanley to J. G. Bennett, Zanzibar, May 18, 1872

S.A. 6925

Zanzibar
U.S. Consulate
May 18th 1872

James Gordon Bennett Jr Esq.
Dear Sir,

  I have returned from Central Africa having arrived here on the 7th inst. after 54 days forced marches from Unyanyembe. Before I left Zanzibar 13 months ago, I promised you to carry out your instructions faithfully unless death prevented me. I now write to you to inform you that I have redeemed that promise that I have obeyed your instructions to the very letter, and that success has crowned your Enterprise. Animated only with the desire to do my duty to the "New York Herald", I halted at nothing, was ever pushing on until my men cried out from sheer fatigue "Have Mercy". Whenever wars troubled the countries through which we had to pass, I put myself at the head of the column, struck off into the depths of the forest, and with compass in hand held on my way until I had left the war disturbed country far behind. Dr Livingstone can testify to this. In order to escort him safely to Unyanyembe, I had to travel through a forest 10 days, with compass in hand until I sighted my road in Kawendi. My men praised the compass, they did not praise me. I have suffered 23 fevers, but now having tasted some of the good food of Mr. Webb the American Consul I cannot say that I feel much the worse though I look 10 years older than when I started.

  When suffering a fever on the road to Unyanyembe in company with Dr. Livingstone my messengers returned from the Coast, and the only letter I got from America was from a Notary public in New York informing me briefly that one of the drafts I drew was protested.[10] My task was almost ended, Livingstone was with me – escorted by me – I had been far more successful than I could ever have expected. Yet in the presence of this grand success, the protest was in my hand. Subsequent information, however, received from Mr Webb after arrival here[11], sets the matter all right, & I am quite happy. I feel pretty tired & worn out but a few weeks good food will set me all right.

Congratulating you upon the successful termination to this arduous Enterprise – because the glory is due to the "Herald", I subscribe myself,

  As your ever ready Correspondent
  Henry M. Stanley

---

  10. See S.A. 11, February 14, 1872.
  11. In fact, Stanley received the same day, in the same batch of letters, the news that his draft had been protested, and the information from the new American consul at Zanzibar, John F. Webb, that the whole matter had been settled for the best (S.A. 11, same date).

List of Letters Carried by Stanley from Dr. Livingstone (S.A. 4754)

[List of Addressees][1]

Letters carried by me from Dr Livingstone from Unyanyembe & delivered to Lord Lyons. August 1872.[2]

John Murray[3] [S.A. 2690]
Lord Kinnaird [S.A. 2705]
Bevan Braithwaite Esq. [S.A. 2698 & 2724]
W. Black
Professor Buchanan[4]
G[?] W Bates[5]
Sir Roderick Murchison[6]
The Duke of Argyll
Miss Agnes Livingstone [S.A. 493]

W. F. Webb Esq [S.A. 2694]
Sir Bartle Frere[7] [S.A. 2688]
W. C. Oswell [S.A. 2714]
John Livingstone[8] [S.A. 485]
Thomas Steele Livingstone [S.A. 490]

---

1. Numbers between brackets refer to letters of thanks the addressees sent to Stanley.

2. This line was added later with another ink. In fact, these letters were delivered to Lord Lyons, the British ambassador in Paris, on July 31, 1872. Acknowledgments from Lord Enfield (Letter, August 1, 1872, S.A. 2678) and from Lord Granville (Letter to Stanley, August 2, 1872, S.A. 2685), published in *HIFL*, 718.

This list includes 19 names, though Stanley said he carried 20 letters (S.A.11, March 15, 1872). But this list was obviously written when the letters were delivered to Lord Lyons in Paris. If Livingstone had written to Oswell Livingstone as he did to his other children, Oswell should be the twentieth addressee, but he had received his letter in Zanzibar directly from Stanley.

3. About J. Murray and W. Cotton Oswell, see William E. Oswell, *William Cotton Oswell, Hunter and Explorer*, 2 vols. (New York: Cambridge University Press, 2011).

4. Professor Andrew Buchanan, Livingstone's teacher of medicine and lifelong friend at Glasgow University. See Andrew Ross, *David Livingstone: Mission and Empire* (London: Hambledon, 2002), 13.

5. Could be Henry Walter Bates, assistant secretary of the Royal Geographical Society.

6. Murchison had died in 1871. Livingstone's letter to Murchison was received by the Foreign Office on August 1, 1872, and by the RGS on October 22. It is a charge against Kirk. (*PRGS* 16, no. 5 [1871–72]: 433.)

7. Sir Bartle Frere supported Livingstone's explorations. See F. V. Emery, "Geography and Imperialism: The Role of Sir Bartle Frere (1815–1884)," *Geographical Journal* 150, no. 3 (November 1984): 342–50, http://www.jstor.org/stable/634329.

8. D. Livingstone's eldest brother. He left Scotland and settled in Canada.

Messrs Coutts[9]
James Young [S.A. 2708]
Miss A. Mary Livingstone [S.A. 491]
Captain Richards [S.A. 2745 et 2746]
Earl Granville (5 letters) [S.A. 2685]

---

9. Coutts & Co., banker.

Contracts of African Soldiers with Uredi Manwa Sera as Captain to Serve Dr. Livingstone (S.A. 4749) and Contract of Mohammed bin Galfin (S.A. 4750)

Contracts of African Soldiers with Uredi Manwa Sera as Captain to Serve Dr. Livingstone

S.A. 4749

Consulate of the United States of America
Zanzibar
May 21st 1872.

We the undersigned late members of the "New York Herald" Expedition and others severally and respectively agree – for the sum of Thirty dollars per annum
" Twenty dollars in advance[1]
to proceed from Zanzibar to Unyanyembe, and there serve Dr David Livingstone in the capacity of soldiers, pagazis, or servants – or for any other service he may require – cheerfully & faithfully – failing which we hereby agree to abide the consequence, for the term of two years – said term to commence from the date of our arrival in Unyanyembe.[2]
In witness whereof we append our marks:
[Listed in two columns]
1 Chowpereh X
2 Maganga X
3 Hamadi X
4 Billalli X
5 Mukkadum X
6 Saburi X
7 Zaidi X
8 Khamisi X
9 Rojab X
10 Sarmean X
11 Chanda X
12 Baraka X
13 Ulimengo X

---

1. Added between two lines above '-six months' pay in advance' crossed out.
2. The caravan reached Dr. Livingstone on August 15, 1872.

14 Mabruk Unyanyembe X
15 ~~Mabruk Speke~~ X
16 Ferajji
17 Ramadan X
18 Khamisi X
19 Anamuri X
20 ~~Shumari~~
21 Khatib X
22 Twakali X
23 Bukhet X
24 ~~Mwalim X~~
25 Hamadi X
26 Farjalla X
27 Khamis X
28 Makawa[3] X
29 Toufiki X
30 Ferous X
31 ~~Kombo~~
32 Ferahan X
33 Jumah X
34 Ferajji X
35 ~~Salim~~
36 Sunguru X
37 Sunguru X
38 Khamseen X
39 Sheban X
40 Mabruk
41 ~~Hamadi~~ Hassani X
42 Moeni Falumi X
43 Hasssani X
44 Tom[?] X
45 ~~Khamisi~~
46 Pangawassi X

[Listed in 3 columns]
[1st column]
Mabruki Speke X [no number]
47 ~~Hassani~~

---

3. Could be the name of "Majwara" mis-spelled. Majwara returned to the Coast with Stanley (See Letter from Livingstone to Stanley, S.A. 478), but figures again in the party sent by Stanley to Livingstone ("Madjwara is about perfect but slow, slow… ", S.A. 490). Majwara was present when Livingstone passed away (*LJ*, Vol. 2, p. 308).

Mwalim X [no number]
48 ~~Khamisi~~
Hamadi X [From here, names without numbers]
Khambi X
[2nd column]
Rojab X
Almass X
~~Kheni X~~
Musa X
[3rd column]
~~Shumari~~
Muriko X
Mdamungo X
Resasi X
Shumari X

Uredi Manua Sera being elected captain by the above mentioned soldiers agrees to keep his men in order and deliver himself & them to Dr David Livingstone.
Below I append my mark
Uredi Manua Sera his X mark

[In John Webb's writing]
Paid in my presence those persons to whose names their marks are attached the sum of $20 – twenty dollars – and to Uredi Maruna Sera the sum of $30—thirty dollars—in consideration of the fulfilment of the above contract.

John F. Webb
U.S. Vice Consul
[Red stamp of the Consulate]
U. S. Consulate
Zanzibar May 22, 1872

[Under, with Stanley's writing, in two columns]
Nassick Boys
1 Mathew Wellington
2 Jacob Wainwright
3 Benjamin Rutton
4 Richard Rutton
5 John Wainwright
6 Carras Farrar

Supernumeraries
Salina $5 advance

[On the back of this contract, an account in Stanley writing]
May 9th $2500
May 28th $500

Contract of Mohammed bin Galfin

S.A. 4750

Duplicate[4]
United States Consulate
May 25th 1872.

I, the undersigned, Mohammed bin Galfin, an Arab of Muscat, and resident at present of Zanzibar hereby agree to take a caravan for Dr. D. Livingstone to Unyanyembe from Zanzibar, and to deliver said caravan into the hands of Dr. D. Livingstone, in consideration of the sum of one hundred dollars, which is now paid to me; and further agree to serve Dr. D. Livingstone in the capacity of Ras Kafilah or chief of his caravan—subject to his orders at all times, to follow him whithersoever he may desire for the sum of Five hundred dollars per annum—said salary to commence from the time of my engagement with Dr. Livingstone at Unyanyembe.
Witness my hand and seal this day the 25th May 1872, or the 18th day of the 6th month of the Mohammedan Year.

[Two signatures in Arabic]
Witness
Henry M. Stanley
Augustus Sparhawk
W. Oswell Livingstone Com.der Livingstone Search Expedition

---

4. 'True copy' crossed out.

Glossary of Kiswahili Words

boma = A general term for any kind of fortified structure
choroko = vetches, field peas
frasilah = a weight measure, roughly 35 lbs.
hongo / muhongo = tribute
joho = crimson cloth
khambi/khambe = camp
kirangozi = guide of the caravan
kitambi = cloth?
kivindo = a pot in which a potter keeps his tools
mganga/maganga = a traditional doctor
mtama/matama = sorghum
matete = *tete* refers to formed but unripe grain
maweri = a cereal, millet?
mbawala = bushbuck
mbuga = A small depression of heavy clay soil supporting grassy-like vegetation
mgogo / mwungwana/ wanguana = freed person. But *Mgogo* refers to a person of the Wagogo. Also a log
mpundu = *Strychnos innocua*. Edible fruits, medicinal (http://www.fao.org/forestry/25323-096344a3de335832e8f363c3ac5184a66.pdf)
Mshenzi/Washenzi = singular/plural for an uncouth, savage person
Mtemi = Sultan, Chief
mtobwe (Shambaa): *Mimusops*, medicinal, firewood
muhallaka = beans
mukunguru = malarial fever
Musungu = white man
mvule = *Milicia excelsa*. Timber
pagazi = porter
pori = brush
porini = in the brush
posho = daily rations for porters

shukka = two yards of cloth
tembe = flat-roofed house
tembo = elephant
terekeza = a long march
yambo = salutation. A variant of "Jambo!"

Bibliography

Manuscript Sources

National Archives, Kew, FO 84/1344
RGS-IBG Collections, The David Livingstone Collection, DL4: "Documents of 1865–73 concerning Livingstone's last expedition," Royal Geographical Society (with IBG), London
Stanley Archives, Collection King Baudouin Foundation, entrusted to the Royal Museum for Central Africa, Tervuren, Belgium

Printed Sources

Allen, Richard. *A Souvenir of Newstead Abbey*. Nottingham: Allen and Son, 1874.
Anderson-Morshead, A. E. M. *The History of the Universities' Mission to Central Africa*. London: Office of the Universities' Mission to Central Africa, 1897.
Andersson, Charles J. "Explorations in South Africa, with Route from Walfisch Bay to Lake Ngami, and Ascent of the Tiogé River." *Journal of the Royal Geographical Society of London* 25 (1855): 79–107. https://archive.org/stream/jstor1798105/1798105#page/n1/mode/2up, http://www.jstor.org/stable/1796021.
Bayard, Taylor. *A Visit to India, China, and Japan in the Year 1853*. New York: Putnam; London: Sampson Low, 1855.
Belzoni, Giovanni Battista. *Narrative of the Operations and Recent Discoveries . . . in Egypt and Nubia*. 2 vols. London: Murray, 1820.
Bennett, Norman R. *Mirambo of Tanzania, ca. 1840–1884*. New York: Oxford University Press, 1971.
———, ed. *Stanley's Despatches to the* New York Herald, *1871–1872, 1874–1877*. Boston: Boston University Press, 1970.
Berclouw, Marja. "The Travels of Francis Galton." Masters advanced seminar and shorter thesis, University of Melbourne, 2010. http://dtl.unimelb.edu.au//exlibris/dtl/d3_1/apache_media/L2V4bGlicmlzL2RobC9kM18xL2FwYWNoZV9tZWRpYS8yNTQ0OTk=.pdf.
Blaikie, Wiliam G. *The Personal Life of David Livingstone*. 1880; repr., London: John Murray, 1913.
Bontinck, François. "La date de la rencontre Stanley-Livingstone." *Africa: Rivista trimestrale di studi e documentazione dell'Istituto italiano per l'Africa e l'Oriente* 34, no. 3 (September 1979). http://www.jstor.org/stable/40759179.
———. "Voyageurs africains en Afrique centrale." *Zaïre-Afrique*: Robert Ferruzi, no. 107 (1976); Mbarak Bombay, no. 110 (1976); Uledi Pangani, no. 114 (1977); Uledi Manwa Sera, no. 118 (1977); Mabruki Speke, no. 122 (1978); Ferajji le cuisinier, no. 128 (1978); Hamadi le guide, no. 138 (1979); Chowpereh, no. 140 (1979); Khamisi Stanley, no. 142 (1980); Asmani, no. 144 (1980); Majwara, no. 146 (1980); Sarmini, no. 152 (1981).
Bridges, Roy C. "Exploration and Travel outside Europe (1720–1914)." In *The Cambridge Companion to Travel Writing*, edited by Peter Hulme and Tim Youngs, 53–69. Cambridge: Cambridge University Press, 2002.
———. "The Sponsorship and Financing of Livingstone's Last Journey." *African Historical Studies* 1, no. 1 (1968): 79–104.

———. "W. D. Cooley, the RGS and African Geography in the Nineteenth Century." *Geographical Journal* 142, no. 1 (March 1976): 27–47, and no. 2 (July 1976): 274–86. http://www.jstor.org/stable/1796021.

Bruce Herald 6, no. 439 (October 9, 1872): 10. (Letter from Mrs Kirk to her sister.)

Bunyan, John. *The Pilgrim's Progress from This World to That Which Is to Come.* 1st ed., 1678.

Burns, Robert. *The Works of Robert Burns,* vol. 1. Glasgow: A. Fullarton, 1834.

Burton, Richard F. *The Lake Regions of Central Africa.* 2 vols. London: Longman, 1860.

———. *Zanzibar: City, Island, and Coast.* 2 vols. London: Tinsley Brothers, 1872.

Chrétien, Jean-Pierre. "Les premiers voyageurs étrangers au Burundi et au Rwanda: Les "compagnons obscurs" des "explorateurs." *Afrique et histoire* 4, no. 2 (2005): 37–72.

Cooley, William D. *Inner Africa Laid Open, [. . .] and the Discoveries of Messrs Oswell and Livingstone in the Heart of the Continent.* London: Longman, Brown, Green, and Longmans, 1852.

Crouthamel, James L. *Bennett's New York Herald and the Rise of the Popular Press.* Syracuse, NY: Syracuse University Press, 1989.

Crouthamel, James L., and Andrew Jackson. "James Gordon Bennett, the *New York Herald,* and the Development of Newspaper Sensationalism." *New York History* 54, no. 3 (July 1973): 294–316. http://www.jstor.org/stable/23169403.

Dicken-Garcia, Hazel. *Journalistic Standards in Nineteenth-Century America.* Madison: University of Wisconsin Press, 1989.

Dobbin, Christine E. *Asian Entrepreneurial Minorities: Conjoint Communities in the Making of the World-Economy 1570–1940.* London: Curzon, 1996.

Driver, Felix. *Geography Militant: Cultures of Exploration and Empire.* Oxford: Blackwell, 2001.

———. "Henry Morton Stanley and His Critics: Geography, Exploration and Empire." *Past and Present,* no. 133 (November 1991): 134–66.

Duignan, Peter, and L. H. Gann. *The United States and Africa: A History.* New York: Cambridge University Press, 1983.

Eliot, George. *Theophrastus Such, Jubal, and Other Poems and the Spanish Gipsy.* Chicago: Belford, Clarke, 1839.

Emery, F. V. "Geography and Imperialism: The Role of Sir Bartle Frere (1815–1884)." *Geographical Journal* 150, no. 3 (November 1984): 342–50.

Emtage, J. E. R. "The First Mission Settlement in Nyasaland." *Society of Malawi Journal* 8, no. 1 (January 1955): 16–24. http://www.jstor.org/stable/29545733.

Fee, Sarah. "Cloths with Names: Luxury Textile Imports in Eastern Africa, c. 1800–1885." *Textile History* 48, no. 1 (2017): 49–84. DOI: 10.1080/00404969.2017.1294819.

———. "Hostage to Cloth: European Explorers in East Africa, 1850–1890." *Textiles and Politics: Textile Society of America 13th Biennial Symposium Proceedings.* Washington, DC, September 2012. Paper 680. http://digitalcommons.unl.edu/tsaconf/680.

Fraser, H. A., William George Tozer, and James Christie. *The East African Slave Trade, and the Measures Proposed for Its Extinction, as Viewed by Residents in Zanzibar.* London: Harrison, 1871.

Galton, Francis. *The Art of Travel; or Shifts and Contrivances Available in Wild Countries.* London: J. Murray (1st ed. 1855; 2nd ed. 1856; 3rd ed. 1860).

Gordon-Cumming, Roualeyn George. *Five Years of a Hunter's Life in the Far Interior of South Africa.* 2 vols. London: J. Murray, 1850.

Griffenhagen, George B., and James Harvey Young. *Old English Patent Medicines in America.* Contributions from the Museum of History and Technology, Paper 10, Bull. 218, 155–83. Washington, DC: Smithsonian Institution, 1959. http://www.gutenberg.org/files/30162/30162-h/30162-h.htm.

Hall, Richard. *Stanley: An Adventurer Explored*. London: Collins, 1974.

Harder, Kelsie. "A Vocabulary of Wagon Parts." *Tennessee Folklore Society Bulletin* 28 (1962): 12–20.

Hook, Theodore E. *Gurney Married: A Sequel to Gilbert Gurney*. London: Henry Colburn, 1838.

Hore, Edward C. *Missionary to Tanganyika, 1877–1888*. Edited by James B. Wolf. London: Frank Cass, 1971.

Hughes, Thomas. *The Life of David Livingstone*. New York: A. L. Burt, 1902.

Illustrated London News, June 1, 1872. (A sketch of the effects of the hurricane at Zanzibar by Lieut. Henn.)

Kellenbenz, Hermann. "Zanzibar et Madagascar dans le commerce allemand (1840–1880)." *Omaly sy Anio* (Département d'histoire, Université d'Antananarivo), nos. 17–19 (1983–84): 311–18.

Kennedy, Dane, ed. *Reinterpreting Exploration: The West in the World*. Oxford: Oxford University Press, 2014.

Kirk, John. "Letters from Dr. Kirk, Concerning Dr. Livingstone." *Proceedings of the Royal Geographical Society* 15, no. 3 (1870–71): 206–9.

Lacerda, José de. *Portuguese African Territories. Reply to Dr Livingstone's Accusations and Misrepresentations*. London: Edward Stanford, 1865.

Lacerda e Almeida, Francisco José Maria de. *The Lands of Cazembe: Lacerda's Journey to Cazembe in 1798*. Translated and annotated by R. F. Burton. London: J. Murray, 1873.

Leduc-Grimaldi, Mathilde, and James L. Newman, eds. *Adventures of an American Traveller in Turkey*. Tervuren, Belgium: RMCA, 2013.

Livingstone's Africa: Perilous Adventures and Extensive Discoveries in the Interior of Africa, from the Personal Narrative of David Livingstone … together with the … Results of the Herald-Stanley Expedition. Philadelphia: Hubbard Bros., 1872.

Lodhi, Abdulaziz Y. "The Iranian Presence in East Africa." In *Haft kongeree wa haft murraka*, edited by M. A. Khajeh Najafi and M. Assemi, 267–74. Uppsala, 2007.

MacGregor, Duncan. *A Narrative of the Loss of the Kent East Indiaman, by Fire, in the Bay of Biscay on the 1st March, 1825*. Edinburgh: Waugh and Innes, 1825.

MacGregor, John. *The Rob Roy on the Jordan, Nile, Red Sea, & Gennesareth, &c.: A Canoe Cruise in Palestine and Egypt, and the Waters of Damascus*. London: J. Murray, 1869.

Machado, Pedro, Sarah Fee, and Gwyn Campbell, eds. *Textile Trades, Consumer Cultures, and the Material Worlds of the Indian Ocean: An Ocean of Cloth*. Palgrave Series in Indian Ocean World Studies. Cham, Switz.: Palgrave Macmillan, 2018.

McDermott, J. F. *A Glossary of Mississippi Valley French, 1673–1850*. St. Louis: Washington University Studies, 1941.

Melville, Herman. *Omoo: A Narrative of Adventures in the South Seas*. London: John Murray, 1847.

Murray, John. "Rupert Vincent, I Presume." *Crossfire*, no. 96 (August 2011). http://www.acwrt.org.uk/uk-heritage_The-Search-for-Robert-Livingstone.asp.

New, Charles. *Life, Wanderings, and Labours in Eastern Africa*. London: Hodder and Stoughton, 1873.

Newman, James L. *Imperial Footprints: Henry Morton Stanley's African Journeys*. Washington, DC: Potomac Books, 2004.

Oswell, William E. *William Cotton Oswell, Hunter and Explorer*. 2 vols. London: Heinemann, 1900.

Pallaver, Karin. "Muslim Communities, Long-Distance Trade and Wage Labour along the Central Caravan Road: Tanzania, 19th Century." *Storicamente* 8, no. 20 (2012).

———. "Nyamwezi Participation in Nineteenth Century East African Long-Distance Trade: Some Evidence from Missionary Sources." *Africa: Rivista trimestrale di studi e documentazione dell'Istituto italiano per l'Africa e l'Oriente* 61, nos. 3–4 (September–December 2006): 513–31. http://www.jstor.org/stable/40761872.

———. "A Second Zanzibar." Some notes on the history of precolonial and early colonial Tabora, Tanzania (1840–1912). Draft, ECAS 2009, Leipzig. http://aegis-eu.org/archive/ecas2009/panels_.

———. *Un'altra Zanzibar: Schiavitù, colonialismo e urbanizzazione a Tabora (1840–1916)*. Milan: Franco Angeli, 2010.

Pesek, Michael. "Ruga-Ruga: The History of an East African Profession 1820–1918." In *German Colonialism Revisited: African, Asian, and Oceanic Experiences*, edited by Nina Berman, Klaus Mühlhahn, and Patrice Nganang, 85–100. Ann Arbor: University of Michigan Press, 2014.

Prestholdt, Jeremy. "Mirroring Modernity: On Consumerism in Cosmopolitan Zanzibar." *Transforming Cultures eJournal* 4, no. 2 (November 2009). http://epress.lib.uts.edu.au/journals/TfC.

Proceedings of the Royal Geographical Society 15 (1870–71) and 16 (1871–72).

Reid, Wemyss. *Memoirs and Correspondence of Lyon Playfair*. London: Cassell, 1900.

Rockel, Stephen J. *Carriers of Culture: Labor on the Road in Nineteenth-Century East Africa*. Portsmouth, NH: Heinemann, 2006.

———. "A Nation of Porters: The Nyamwezi and the Labour Market in Nineteenth-Century Tanzania." *Journal of African History* 41, no. 2 (2000): 173–95. http://www.jstor.org/stable/183432.

Ross, Andrew. *David Livingstone: Mission and Empire*. London: Hambledon, 2002.

Rowley, Henry. *The Story of the Universities' Mission to Central Africa from Its Commencement, under Bishop Mackenzie, to Its Withdrawal from the Zambezi*. London: Saunders, Otley, 1866.

Sclater, Philip L., and Oldfield Thomas. *The Book of Antelopes*. Vol. 2. London, 1897.

Seitz, Don C. *The James Gordon Bennetts, Father and Son: Proprietors of the New York Herald*. Indianapolis: Bobbs-Merrill, 1928; repr. New York: Beekman, 1974.

Shepperson, George. "David Livingstone 1813–1873." *British Medical Journal* 2, no. 5860 (April 28, 1973): 232–34. http://www.jstor.org/stable/25425436.

Smith, George. *The Life of John Wilson, D.D. F.R.S. for Fifty Years Philanthropist and Scholar in the East*. London: J. Murray, 1878.

Srinivasan, Padma. "Indian Traders in Zanzibar with Special Reference to Jairam Shewji (19th Century)." *Proceedings of the Indian History Congress* 61, part 2 (2000–2001): 1142–48.

Stafford, Robert A. *Scientist of Empire: Sir Roderick Murchison, Scientific Exploration and Victorian Imperialism*. Cambridge: Cambridge University Press, 1989.

Stanley, Henry M. *How I Found Livingstone: Travels, Adventures, and Discoveries in Central Africa, including four months' residence with Dr Livingstone*. London: Sampson Low, Marston, Low & Searle, 1872.

Taylor, Bayard. *A Visit to India, China, and Japan in the Year 1853*. New York: Putnam; London: Sampson Low, 1855.

Waller, Horace, ed. *The Last Journals of David Livingstone in Central Africa, from 1865 to His Death*. 2 vols. London: John Murray, 1874.

Waters, Tony. "Social Organization and Social Status in Nineteenth and Twentieth Century Rukwa, Tanzania." *African Studies Quarterly* 11, no. 1 (Fall 2009): 57–93. http://africa.ufl.edu/asq/v11/v11i1a3.htm.

Withers, Charles W. J., and Innes M. Keighren. "Travels into Print: Authoring, Editing and Narratives of Travel and Exploration, c.1815–c.1857." *Transactions of the Institute of British Geographers* 36, no. 4 (October 2011): 560–73.

Electronic Sources

Bombay Africans. RGS, https://www.rgs.org/NR/rdonlyres/831B3822–2330–4773–8B53-A2E3328D2FBD/0/BombayAfricansPartTwo.pdf.

"The Date of the Livingstone-Stanley Meeting," by Justin Livingstone and Adrian S. Wisnicki. http://livingstone.library.ucla.edu/1871diary/meeting1.htm.

National Forestry Resources Monitoring and Assessment of Tanzania (NAFORMA). Species List sorted by vernacular names. http://www.fao.org/forestry/25323–096344a3de335832e8f363c3ac5184a66.pdf.

Royal Museum for Central Africa. *The Inventory of the Henry M. Stanley Archives.* https://www.africamuseum.be/research/collections_libraries/human_sciences/stanley.

Index

This index lists only names of places and persons that are directly linked to Stanley's journey to find Livingstone and their travel together.

Abdul Kader/Abdul Kadir/Abd-el-Kader, 32, 106, 107, 109, 115, 118, 132, 134, 347, 434, 476, 488, 491
Abraham, 319
Achmet, 97, 100–103
Albert Nyanza/Lake, 60, 208, 235, 273, 315, 321, 504, 514
Almass, 523
Ambari/Umbari, 142, 371, 373, 377, 381, 383, 385, 392, 413, 434, 442
Anamuri, 522
Anderson, Finley, 2, 3, 184, 189, 481, 508, 509, 529
Antari, 158, 159
Asanza, 409, 410

Babisa, 196, 318, 319
Babwar, 163
Baker, Sir Samuel, 63, 192, 198, 208, 220, 234, 235, 273, 288, 315, 513, 514
Balegga, 235
Bambarré, 197, 199
Bandareen, 160, 182
Bangwe, 161, 192, 204, 348, 350
Banurungu/Burungu. *See* Urungu
Banyamwezi. *See* Wanyamwezi
Baracca/Baraka, 108, 284, 345, 346, 368, 372, 373, 377, 381, 382, 384, 385, 392, 413, 434, 444, 493, 521
Bargash/Barghash. *See* Sultan of Zanzibar
Barundi, 164, 206, 303, 304, 305, 328
Barungu/Baulungu, 196, 319
Baruti Farjallah, 9, 27, 30, 113, 127, 128, 434
Basansi, 37, 169, 170, 215, 217
Bates, W., 271, 519
Baulungu. *See* Barungu
Belali. *See* Billalli
Bemba, Lake, 222
Bennett, James Gordon, Jr., 2, 3, 7, 12, 17, 18, 40, 60, 63, 86, 184–86, 189, 197, 200, 201, 233, 235, 242, 256, 259–61, 269, 367, 477, 484, 489, 490, 509, 511, 518
Benta, 376
Bertram, John, & Co, of Salem, 64, 176, 438, 517
Bihawana, 24, 95, 178
Bikari, 206, 307

Billalli/Bill Ali/Bill Alli/Belali, 5, 30, 31, 127, 131, 171, 219, 246, 248, 250, 346, 349, 359, 360, 369, 373, 377, 381, 382, 383, 385, 392, 405, 434, 435, 446, 448, 521
bin Abdallah/Abdulaah, Khamis. *See* bin Abdullah/Abdallah/Abdulaah, Khamis
bin Abdullah, Mohammed, 120
bin Abdullah, Mussoud, 323
bin Abdullah/Abdalla, Thani, 30, 123, 125, 126, 158, 264, 323, 364
bin Abdullah/Abdallah/Abdulaah, Khamis, 27, 29, 110, 120, 121, 122, 124, 203, 274, 323, 365
bin Abid, Said, 116
bin Ali, Sayf, 121
bin Ali, Sultan, 121, 267, 273, 324, 365, 501
bin Amir, Snay/Sny, 121
bin Asman, Khaif, 19, 73
bin Galfin/Khalfan, Mohammed, 42, 450, 451, 52
bin Ghalib/Gharib, Mohammed, 38, 70, 117, 188, 191, 232, 275, 349, 350
bin Habeeb, Said, 121, 250, 361
bin Hasheed/Hashid, Selim, 251, 490
bin Hassan, Saleem, 324
bin Jumah/Juma, Abdullah/Abdulla, 26, 27, 109, 110
bin Khalfan, Mohammed bin. *See* Galfin, Mohammed
bin Khari, Mohammed, 171
bin Magid/Majid, Said (Ujiji), 188, 191, 203, 231, 251, 348, 479
bin Mahmoud, Selim, 107
bin Majid, Said (Kwikuru), 28, 34, 70, 115, 152, 186, 255, 363, 489
bin Mohammed, Sultan, 25, 103, 104
bin Moussoud, Mohammed, 116, 324
bin Moussoud, Nasim, 116
bin Moussoud/Mussoud/Moossud/Massoud, Amram 26, 27, 73, 109, 113, 121, 324
bin Nasib, Abdullah/Abdulla, 24, 90
bin Nasib, Sheikh, 26–31, 109, 110, 114, 115, 122, 123, 126, 127, 129, 264, 274, 291, 324, 397, 491
bin Nasur, Hilal, 324
bin Omar, Said, 117

533

bin Rasheed, Mohammed, 122
bin Rasheed/Rashid, Salim, 20, 76
bin Said, Soud/Mussud, 115, 116, 191, 255, 363
bin Said/Syed, Hassan, 25, 105
bin Saif/Sayf, Salim/Saleem, 121, 324
bin Saleem, Zaid, 324
bin Sali, Mohammed (at Cazembe), 319, 320
bin Sali, Mohammed/Mwhammed, Governor, 38, 171, 188, 191, 197, 232, 349
bin Salim, Hassan, 25, 105
bin Salim/Saleem, Said/Sayed/Syed/Zaid, Governor, 18, 25, 26, 27, 28, 69, 105, 108, 109, 112–14, 122, 123, 127, 251, 261, 263, 272, 273, 324, 492, 495
bin Sulayman, Mohuma, 296, 323
bin Sultan, Amir, 26, 107
Bobemba, 196
Bombay, Mubarak Bombay (Captain porter), 19, 21, 33, 36, 67, 70, 71, 72, 83, 95, 115, 118, 134, 140, 141, 142, 151, 154, 155, 157, 164, 205, 231, 246, 248, 284, 289, 294, 306, 307, 345, 346, 359, 370, 372, 373, 377, 381, 382, 391, 393, 395, 400, 405, 409, 411, 413, 434, 442, 476, 478, 483, 487, 498, 501, 502
Bombay (City/Govt.), 4, 7, 17, 24, 38, 40, 42, 59, 60, 89, 119, 135, 175, 190, 194, 222, 225, 229, 243, 262, 270, 271, 283, 289, 367, 395, 481, 482, 483, 492, 494, 504, 512
Bombay Paper (newspaper), 487, 493
Braithwaite, Bevan, 519
Buchanan, Professor Andrew, 519
Bukhet, 522
Bunder Salaam, 21, 82, 84, 434, 476, 477
Burgash/Burghash/Bergas. See Sultan of Zanzibar
Burton, Richard, 9, 22, 37, 64, 67, 71, 94, 95, 106, 109, 121, 140, 168, 192, 202, 203, 209–11, 214, 234, 235, 256, 310, 391, 405, 436, 512–15
Burungu. See Urungu

Camirambo/Kamirambo, 33, 145, 250, 361
Cazembe/Cezembe, 192, 193, 196, 197, 233, 253, 257, 272, 289, 316, 319, 495, 499, 502, 505
Celim/Celion 82, 434, 476, 477
Cezembe. See Cazembe
Chalamaganza, 94
Chamate, 314
Chambeze/Chambezi, 196, 257, 316, 501, 502
Chanda/Chandah, 136, 345–47, 360, 370, 371, 373, 374, 381–83, 392, 446, 521
Chebungo/Lincoln Lake, 198, 284, 288, 364
Chehu/Kehu, 415
Chicumbi, 284, 288, 364
Chigoma. See Kigoma
Chigongo, 37, 168, 214, 419, 420
Chipanga, 361
Choonio/Chunio/Chunyo/Chunyu/Kunyo, 24, 92, 177, 299, 414
Chowambe/Baker's Lake, 192, 288

Chowpereh/Chaoperi/Chompereh, 23, 87, 88, 254, 276, 284, 362, 369, 372, 373, 377, 381, 383, 384, 392, 435, 443, 444, 501, 521
Christie, Dr. James, 119, 294, 490, 491
Chuma/Chumah, 160, 193, 195, 197, 200, 265, 288, 317–19, 321, 360, 370, 374
Chumba, 435
Chunio/Chunyo/Chunyu. See Choonio
Congo, 9, 67, 198, 315, 316

Dama/Damah River, 164, 205
Dawson, Lieut. Llewellyn, 41, 42, 292–95, 413, 449, 450, 451, 506
Dossabhoy Merwanjee & Co., 119, 175, 482, 492
Dugum Ali. See Kalulu
Duke of Argyll, 519

Egypt, 104, 198, 201, 211, 256, 260, 477, 480, 481, 486, 487, 508, 511, 512, 514

Farjalla, 522
Farjallah. See Baruti Farjallah
Farquahar. See Farquhar/Farquhar, William Lawrence
Farquhar/Farquhar, William Lawrence, 5, 18, 19, 23–25, 30, 59, 61, 62, 69, 86, 87, 88, 91, 104, 127, 414, 433, 439, 477, 483–85, 490, 515
Farrar, Carras, 450, 523
Ferahan, 522
Ferajji/Farajji/Feraggi, 21, 39, 75, 81, 187, 189, 230, 250, 258, 278, 362, 369, 371, 373, 377, 381, 382, 384, 392, 434, 442, 444, 522
Ferous/Ferousi, 114, 345, 346, 368, 371, 372, 373, 377, 522

Galton, 235, 236
Gardner/Garner, 193, 319, 345, 346, 370, 374
Gihawa. See Mugehawa
Gitara/Itara, 312
Goma, 192, 305
Gomba, 315
Gombe (river), 33, 140, 141, 180, 254, 324, 399
Gombe Nullah, 146, 362, 368, 376
Gondokora/Gondokoro, 117, 185, 514
Gongwe, 322, 323
Grant, Major James A., 210, 211, 289, 395, 505
Granville, Lord, 60, 70, 113, 117, 119, 186, 198, 199, 273, 322, 413, 519, 520
Gunga, 162

Habay, 38, 172, 221
Halima/Halimah, 185, 187, 189, 190, 230, 374
Hamadi, 21, 70, 229, 368, 371, 373, 377, 381, 382, 384, 392, 442, 446, 521, 522, 523, 527
Hamdallah, 141, 262, 383, 384
Hamoidah/Hamoidach/Hamoiday/Hamoodah, 193, 230, 252, 289, 345, 346, 370, 372, 374

Hashid, Sheik, 490
Hassan (Mseguhha), 143, 144
Hassani, 522
Hatib/Khatib, 383, 384, 522
Henn, Lieut. William, 41, 42, 292, 293, 294, 295, 451
Hera, 421
Herembe, 39, 233, 348, 351
Heshmesh/Heshmy, Selim. See Selim Heshmesh/Heshmy
Heshmesh, Jacob, 439, 475
Hosmer, George W., 3, 40, 262, 492, 493

Ibrahim, 247, 345, 346, 357, 360, 371, 383
Ibrahim Kisesa, 369, 373
Ibrahim Marora/Maroro, 370, 371, 373
Icazi, 408
Ihange, 404
Ihata, 34, 155
Imbiki/Mbiki, 19, 74, 134, 177, 324, 421
Imesuka/Mesuka, 180, 376
Imrea/Imrera, 34, 39, 150, 151, 173, 181, 220, 244, 245, 346, 354, 355, 359, 361, 368, 369, 371
Inesuka, 32, 134, 263, 364, 371
Iramba, 413
Isinga, 155, 156
Itaga, 34, 150, 152, 381
Itara. See Gitara

Jacko, 106, 127, 414, 434
Jafooneh, 435
James, 319
Jarko (Tarko?), 492
Jetta, 435
Jiwe la Mkoa, 25, 103
Jiwe la Singa, 25, 104, 401
Jofari, 420
Johanna Island, 18, 67, 194, 195, 317, 318
Johari (Joharri), 18, 67, 435, 451
Jooma/Jumah/Jumma, 31, 131, 155, 347, 348, 371, 372, 374, 377, 381, 382, 393, 409, 434, 444, 522

Kabirigi, 158
Kabogo, 39, 159, 232, 233, 235, 348, 351, 352
Kabongwe, 162
Kabuire, 289, 499
Kaburan, 312
Kadetamari/Kaditamari/Kadetamare (sultan), 299, 415, 416, 417, 435
Kagongo, 39, 174, 232, 348, 350
Kagunga, 164, 170, 304
Kagungu/Kakungu, 233, 239, 351, 352
Kaif Halleck, 371, 374
Kaima. See Kamna
Kaiwendi, 422
Kakumba, 37, 168, 214
Kakungu. See Kagungu

Kalulu (Dugum Ali), 30, 42, 128, 171, 219, 248, 349, 359, 381, 383, 448, 45
Kamirambo. See Camirambo
Kamna/Kamma/Kaima/Kaimna, 21, 83, 285, 347, 373, 377, 381, 382, 393, 434, 442
Kamolondo/Camolondu, 284, 315, 319, 321, 364
Kamyenye/Kanyenye/Kamyenyi, 98, 410, 411, 412
Kanengi, 158
Kaniyaga, 40
Kannena, 203
Kanya-para, 414
Kanyama, 168, 214
Kanyenye. See Kamyenye
Karagwah, 103, 117, 309, 310, 401
Karah, 232, 349
Karindwa, 312
Kasagera, 371, 376
Kasegara/Kasegala, 134
Kasenge, 502, 503
Kasokwe, 304
Kasoonga. See Kwasoonga
Katanga, 288, 312, 364
Katangara, 37, 168, 214, 284, 313
Kavimba, 37, 168, 214
Kavimvira, 313
Kavuruwé, 215
Kawanga/Kawaga, 35, 156, 157
Kawendi/Ukawendi, 28, 114, 123, 125, 137, 152, 179, 180, 244, 248, 323, 354, 358, 359, 363, 518
Kayma/Kema Kaguru, 417
Kazima, 121
Kazinga, 163, 304, 305
Kehu. See Chehu
Khamis/Khamisi (porter), 20, 21, 74, 83, 247, 248, 254, 285, 310, 359, 360, 368, 373, 378, 381, 382, 385, 392, 405, 434, 435, 443, 444, 521, 522, 523
Khamsseen, 522
Khatib. See Hatib
Kheni, 523
Khetu, 419
Khokoro, 33, 141
Khonko/Khokko, 406, 407, 409, 412
Khonse/Khonze, 406, 409, 412
Kiala, 34, 154, 155
Kibrumo, 421
Kibwe, 348, 417
Kididimo, 24, 95, 178, 408
Kidingo, 407
Kidurigo, 407
Kifukuru, 380
Kigandu/Kiganda, 32, 109, 134, 135, 144, 179, 180, 263, 364, 376
Kigogo, 403, 404
Kigoma/Chigoma, 35, 161, 162, 204, 216, 302
Kigwa, 26, 108, 178, 392
Kigwira, 396

Kikoka, 19, 70, 176, 324, 421
Kikuro, 137
Kilwa, 418, 419
Kingani, 75, 76, 78, 324
Kingaroo/Kingarru (village), 71, 72, 73, 74, 81, 177, 297, 421, 451
Kingaru/Kingarru/Kingaroo (porter), 19, 22, 79, 84, 369, 371, 373, 377, 381, 383, 385, 434, 444, 448
Kinnaird, Lord, 519
Kinyamwezi, 403
Kiora, 23, 86, 92, 177, 415
Kira, 77, 78
Kirabula/Kirubula, 168, 214, 310
Kirangawana, 78, 297
Kirassa, 163, 164, 303, 415
Kiriba, 313
Kirindo, 231, 349
Kirira, 251
Kirk, Dr. John (British consul), 17, 18, 42, 60, 66, 68, 70, 113, 117, 119, 186, 188, 200, 218, 225, 240, 241, 258, 265, 266, 270, 283, 292–95, 322, 366, 367, 379, 394, 413, 449, 450, 451, 487, 490, 491, 495–97, 505, 513, 519
Kiroka, 21, 73, 81
Kirubula. *See* Kirabula
Kirurumo, 102, 103
Kisabengo, 421
Kisemo, 20, 75, 76, 78, 177, 297, 325, 421, 423
Kisewa/Kisewah, 380, 411
Kisigo, 407
Kisimani, 406, 408
Kisokwé/Kisokweh, 24, 92, 299
Kisuka, 164, 168, 207, 309, 310
Kisunwe, 307
Kitangi, 408
Kitangule, 208
Kiti, 25, 100–102, 178
Kitunda/Kitundu, 164, 170, 304, 305
Kivanga, 239, 351, 352
Kivo, 312, 314
Kivoe, 39, 175, 208, 232, 348, 350
Kivya, 417
Kiweeh, 99
Kiwere, 401
Kiwiyeh/Kiwyeh/Kwiyeh, 380, 402, 406, 407, 412
Kolobeng, 238, 239
Kombo, 27, 113, 345, 347, 371, 374, 378, 381, 382, 384, 392, 446, 448, 478, 522
Kuddam, 136
Kulabi, 412
Kunsuli, *See* Kussouri
Kunyo. *See* Choonio
Kussouri/Kusouri/Kusuri/Kunsuli, 25, 103, 104, 178
Kwala/Kwale. *See* Nqualah
Kwala/Kwalah/Kwale/Nqualah/Nghwhalah, 25, 26, 106, 398–400

Kwansibura, 314
Kwasoonga/Kasoonga, 323, 322
Kwihara/Quihara, 10–12, 26, 29, 30, 73, 109, 113, 119, 120, 121, 122, 124, 129, 133, 136, 251, 274, 289, 345, 371, 381, 401, 423, 478, 498
Kwi Kuru (capital of Nzogera), 156
Kwikuru/Quicuru/Cwcuru, 123, 255, 257, 274, 278, 322, 363, 367, 369–71, 376, 411
Kwiyeh. *See* Kiwiyeh
Kwviru, 316

Ladha/Ludha/Ludda, Damji, 17, 19, 60, 65, 66, 70, 186, 200, 435, 493
Lafui, 315
Levien, Douglas A., 2, 3, 40, 60, 63, 184, 260–62, 492, 508–10, 512, 513
Liemba, 196, 202, 319
Lincoln Lake. *See* Chebungo
Lindi, 234, 352
Liuche/Riuche, 231, 348, 349
Livemba. *See* Luemba
Livingstone, Agnes, 184, 239, 253, 267, 276, 290, 320, 353, 394, 500, 519
Livingstone, Anna Mary, 267, 268, 320, 520
Livingstone, Robert Moffat (alias Rupert Vincent), 36, 240, 320, 353
Livingstone, Thomas Steele, 267, 320, 519
Livingstone, Tom, 184
Livingstone, W. Oswell, 184, 449, 450, 451, 497, 506, 507, 524
Livingstone's Relief Expedition, 493, 494
Loajeri river, 235, 237, 239, 352
Loanda, 235, 239, 281, 514
Locanda-Mira, 153, 154, 156, 160
Lomami, 315
Luaba, 304
Lualaba/Luaaba, 186, 197, 198, 200, 214, 257, 273, 284, 288, 315, 316, 319, 321, 352, 364, 394
Luam, 352
Luanda. *See* Ruanda
Luapula, 192, 193, 196, 197, 284, 288, 364, 502, 505
Ludda Damji. *See* Ladha Damji
Luemba/Livemba, 117
Lufiji. *See* Rufiji
Lufira/Lufiri, 197, 284, 288, 364
Luganda, 154
Luhunga/Luhanga, 309
Lukoleh, 414
Lukomo in Kimeni/Kimenyi, 35, 157
Lumani, 197
Lunda, 196
Lunera, 347
Lusize. *See* Rusizi
Lutetu, 402
Luvumba, Cape, 37, 169, 215
Luwambo, 347

Mabala, 164
Mabruk, 30, 127, 345, 434, 522
Mabruk Kisesa, 384, 392, 414
Mabruk Marora, 370
Mabruk Saleem, 32, 88, 134, 136, 374, 377, 434
Mabruk Unyanyembe, 345, 346, 371, 373, 377, 381, 382, 384, 392, 446, 522
Mabruk/Mabruki Ferous, 114, 371
Mabruk/Mabruki Speke, 9, 22, 23, 83, 87, 88, 151, 171, 219, 234, 235, 284, 345, 352, 360, 371, 374, 375, 377, 381, 382, 393, 405, 434, 442, 522
Mabunguru/Mabuguru, 25, 100, 178, 402, 406, 407
MacGregor, John, 38, 172, 222, 486
Maclear, Sir Thomas, 271, 289, 376
Macomero, 406, 408
Madedita/Mededita, 25, 26, 105, 178, 392
Madete, 23, 87, 177, 299, 300
Madjwara. *See* Majwara
Magala, 36, 164, 207, 309, 310
Maganga, 27, 113, 370, 373, 381, 383, 392, 420, 446, 521
Magdala Mountain, 244, 354
Magomba, 380, 410, 411
Maguru Mafupi, 380
Mai Shamba, 108, 396
Majwara/Madjwara/Majwar, 30, 345, 346, 349, 372, 382, 383, 385, 443, 448, 498, 501, 522
Makata (Little Makata, Big Makata) river, 22, 23, 80, 83–85, 89, 104, 115, 176, 177, 281, 367, 395, 417–20
Makekura, 322
Makolola/Makololo/Makololu, 223, 375, 376, 399, 495
Makungwe, 421
Makuwa, 418
Malagarazi, 33, 34, 39, 141, 147, 148, 150, 152–56, 158, 174, 220, 227, 232, 246, 348–51, 354, 355, 375, 398, 399, 402
Mambura, 411
Maniara, 139, 140, 141, 142, 322, 361, 376
Manieka/Munieka/Munika, 25, 99, 100
Maniema. *See* Manyema
Manwa Sera (Uledi/Uredi Manua Sera/Manua Sera), 29, 41, 119, 145, 374, 377, 381, 383, 393, 400, 434, 442, 450, 479, 490, 500, 501, 521, 522, 523
Manyara/Maniara, 32, 33, 139, 254, 363
Manyema/Maniema/Manyuema/Unyema, 20, 24–26, 70, 76, 90, 105, 107, 117, 157, 187, 188, 190, 192, 193, 197–200, 214, 220, 233–35, 253, 268, 269, 272, 274, 281, 283, 312, 319, 366, 367, 503
Manyuema. *See* Manyema
Mapanga, 411, 412
Mapokera, Unamapokera, 380, 410
Marefo, 322
Marenga Makali/Marenga Mkhali/Marega M'kali, 24, 92, 93, 143, 413, 414, 415
Marora, 123, 171, 346, 370, 369, 371, 373, 377, 385, 386, 446
Marugu, 319, 321

Marungu, 20, 26, 76, 105, 107, 275
Masai, 98, 404
Masanghi/Masonghi/Masangi, 28, 115, 118
Massoudi, 267
Masua, 299
Masungu, 359
Mataka, 504
Matamburu/Matambulu/Matômburu, 24, 94, 178, 408
Matamombo, 24, 89, 299, 414
Mateko, 307
Matumbi, 25, 102
Maungu, 248
Mawala, 412, 413
Maweni, 299
Mazitu, 195, 222, 272, 318, 319
Mbambwa. *See* Mpapaw
Mbarak/Mubarak/Bombay. *See* Bombay
Mbengerenga. *See* Uronga
Mbiki. *See* Imbiki
Mbogo, 139, 144, 145, 322,
Mbogwe, 404
Mbumi/Mbuni, 416, 419
Mchemba, 408
Mdaburu, 402, 407
Mdamungo, 523
Mdunku, 417
Mededita. *See* Madedita
Membas, 496
Mesuka. *See* Imesuka
Mfuto, 28, 29, 31, 114, 115, 117, 118, 120, 129
Mgaza, 406
Mgeta, 78, 297
Mgogo, 97, 99, 300, 402, 403, 405. *See also* Wagogo
Mgongo/Mgongo Tembo/Thembo, 25, 104, 163, 303, 400
Mgunda Makali/Mkali, 105, 143, 145, 407
Mgwana. *See* Wangwana
Mikesseh/Mikeseh, 20, 77, 78, 177, 421
Mikindyni/Minkindiny, 317
Mionvu, 157
Mirambo, 8, 10, 11, 27–31, 33, 34, 39, 73, 109, 113–16, 120-123, 116, 129–31, 133, 136, 140, 142, 147, 160, 188, 190, 191, 203, 220, 251, 255, 265, 274, 284, 322, 363, 365, 393, 399, 443, 445, 490, 492
Mishense/Mshense. *See* Washense
Misohazy, 348, 350
Misonghi, 33, 148, 249, 250, 360, 376, 415
Misossi, 374
Missohaza, 350
Mizanza, 25, 97, 98, 178
Mkasiwa, 123, 129, 130, 135, 145, 148, 251
Mkata, 24, 95
Mkuti, 160
Mkwekwe/Mkwenkwe, 32, 133, 136, 180, 371
Mnyamwezi, 135, 325, 399, 400, 409, 420

INDEX 537

Mnyamwezi. *See* Wanyamwezi
Moeni Falumi, 522
Moeni Kheri/Muini Kheri/Muniyi Kheri/Munyi Kheri/Munia Kheri/Munia Kheris, 38, 171, 173, 191, 203, 220, 222, 231, 232, 321, 349, 371, 415, 416
Moeni Makaia/Muini Mokaya/Mweni Makaya 274, 281, 371, 366
Moero, 319, 321, 505
Mogambazi, 235, 352
Mohalata/Muhalata, 412
Mokamba/Mukamba/Mokam/Mukiamba, 36, 37, 165-168, 207, 208, 212–14, 309–13, 352
Morambala, 223, 253
Morembe/Murembwe/Mwrembere, 164, 205, 206, 307
Moto, 79, 251, 255, 363
Moussoudi/Mussoudi/Mossoud, 20, 76, 77, 177, 421, 361, 421, 422
Mpanda, 312
Mpokwa, 33, 149, 180, 246–49, 348, 356–60, 376
Mponda, 195, 317
Mpwapwa/Mbambwa/Mpambva/Umpapaw/Umpopaw, 23, 24, 30, 88, 89, 104, 127, 299, 408, 414, 422
Mrera, 33, 142, 146, 147, 180, 361, 376
Mrima, 78, 143, 145, 146
Mrinia/Mrinyo Mansu, 353, 355, 381
Mruta, 310, 313
Msalalo, 25, 102, 178
Mshala, 205, 304
Msige, 406
Msowwa, 248
Msungu/Musungu/Wasungu, 72, 75, 87, 95, 97, 100, 103, 108, 140, 146, 157, 317, 393, 410, 415
Msuwa, 20, 74, 75, 177, 324, 421, 423
Mtawe, 159
Mtesa, 284, 310, 393, 502
Mtoni/Mtonee, 33, 34, 77, 89, 100, 104–6, 108, 140, 144, 145, 148, 149, 151, 177–81, 248, 296, 300, 360, 376, 392
Muccadum, 369, 373, 377, 381, 384, 393, 446, 521
Mugehawa/Mugihawa/Mugihewa, 36, 37, 165–68, 208, 213, 214, 313–15, 352
Mugera/Mugehera/Mugere, 165, 310, 312, 313, 352
Mugeyo, 36, 164, 205, 206, 207, 309
Muhalleh/Muharreh/Muhaweh, 20, 76, 78, 79, 177, 420, 421
Muhaweh. *See* Muhalleh
Muini Dugumbi/Dugumbe, 214, 321
Mukamba. *See* Mokamba
Mukamba/Mukiamba. *See* Mokamba
Mukamwa, 412
Mukanigi/Mukanyigi, 36, 37, 165, 166, 207, 212, 314, 315
Mukanyigi. *See* Mukanigi
Mukatika, 95
Mukiamba. *See* Mokamba
Mukindu, 313

Mukondoku, 25, 98, 99, 406, 407, 409
Mukondokwa (river), 23, 86, 87, 177, 299, 412, 415–17
Mukungu, 36, 164, 169, 205, 218, 306, 352
Mulaly, 419
Mulowa, 412
Mulungu/Miringu/Mniezi Mungu-Mgwana, 403, 41
Mundo/Mundu, 417, 419
Muni/Munia/Muini/Muniyi/Munyi. *See* Moeni
Munia Bwiri, 171
Munieka/Munika. *See* Manieka
Murambira, 313
Murchison, Sir Roderick, 70, 184, 202, 210, 219, 223, 225, 249, 257, 270, 271, 282, 286, 289, 394, 407, 498, 503–5, 519
Murembwe. *See* Morembe
Muriko, 523
Murray, John, 290, 500, 519
Musa, 27, 523
Musa/Mussa/Moosa ("Livingstone's man") 67, 195, 318
Musunia/Musunya, 158, 159
Mutimbi/Mutumbi, 312
Mutundu/Mtundu N'Gondeh, 410, 411
Muzimu/Muzmu, 37, 163, 170, 302, 303, 305, 307
Mvuha, 78, 297
Mvumi/Mvuni/Mvumi Mdogo/Mvumi Mkuba/Mwmi/Umvoomi, 24, 93, 177, 299, 300, 403, 406, 408, 412, 413, 417, 418
Mwalim, 522, 523
Mwaru, 33, 145, 250, 361, 376
Mwenga, 408
Mweru, 187, 192, 193, 196, 197, 273

Mwezi sultan, 309, 310
Mwienga, 348
Mwmi. *See* Mvumi
Mwrembere. *See* Morembe
Mwrembere. *See* Murembwe
Mwrinyo, 300

Namsinga, 304
Naviungo, 312
Nawadi, 384
Negri, Commander Cristoforo, 495
New York Herald Expedition, 1, 2, 4, 5, 367, 424–38, 441, 511, 521
New York Herald/Herald, 2, 3, 7, 12, 19, 26, 27, 37, 38, 40, 59, 60, 63, 69, 70, 73, 110, 111, 119, 133, 161, 168, 172, 175, 184–86, 189, 199, 214, 215, 221, 227, 259–61, 263, 269, 289, 296, 348, 366, 367, 394, 395, 397, 413, 481, 482, 489, 492, 493, 504, 508, 509, 511, 512, 517, 518, 521
New, Revd Charles, 292, 293, 450, 451, 496, 506
Ngami Lake, 227, 235, 239
Ngaraiso/Ngaraisu/Ngaraeswa/Ngraiso, 25, 102, 178, 401, 406

Ngariswa, 401
Nghwhalah. *See* Nqualah
Nghwhalah/Nqualah. *See* Kwala
Ngondo, 39, 173, 348
Ngraiso. *See* Ngaraiso
Ngwhalab. *See* Nyahuba
Niamtaga Boma, 35, 159, 160
Niasanga, 35, 38, 162, 163, 171, 204, 219, 303
Nile, White Nile, 6, 11, 63, 67, 117, 123, 189, 192, 193, 196, 198, 202, 210, 214, 225, 233, 257, 273, 284, 288, 315, 316, 319, 321, 364, 395, 487, 502, 503, 505, 513–15
Niongo, 145
Njara, 140
Nqualah/Kwale/Nghwhalah, 25, 26, 106, 399
Nyabigma, 36, 163, 164, 205, 304
Nyahuba/Unyahuha, 398, 399
Nyakagunda, 313
Nyamagana, 313
Nyambwa, 96
Nyamwezi. *See* Wanyamwezi
Nyamzaga, 411, 412
Nyangwe, 187, 193, 197, 199, 200, 214, 257
Nyassa Lake, 18, 26, 107, 117, 195, 196, 222, 253, 269, 273, 317–19, 504
Nzogera, 34, 153, 154, 156

Okami, 78
Omar (dog) 24, 60, 61, 89, 297, 325, 414, 482
Oswell, William Cotton, 227, 236, 244, 246, 320, 357, 366, 519

Pangani, 495
Pangawassi, 522
Pemba Island, 17, 63
Pembera Mperé/Pembera Pereh/Pemberi N'Pereh, 25, 96, 178, 409
Pumburu, 179, 348

Quangeregere, 312
Quicuru/Cwcuru/Kwikuru, 123, 255, 257, 274, 278, 322, 363, 367, 369, 370, 371, 376, 411Quihara. *See* Kwihara
Quitamani, 300

Ramadan, 522
Ramata, 309, 312, 314
Rasheed, Ibrahim, 120
Rawlinson, Sir H. C., 113, 322, 413, 451 503,
Rehenneko, 23, 85, 177, 418, 419, 421,
Resasi, 523
Richards, Capt, 286, 394, 520,
Ripon Falls, 210
Ritchie Stuart & Co. (bank), 283, 367
Riuche. *See* Liuche
Robeho/Rubeho, 89
Rofubu, 313

Rojab, 119, 345, 346, 360, 368, 371, 373, 377, 381, 383, 392, 435, 446, 521, 523
Rosaco/Rosako, 19, 70, 78, 176, 291, 413, 421
Rovuma/Rowuma, 194, 195, 222, 317
Royal Geographical Society, 113, 210, 236, 269–72, 282, 292, 294, 295, 413, 449, 505, 506, 519
Rua, 197, 220, 284, 288, 364
Ruanda/Luanda, 117, 165, 208, 310–12, 315
Rubeho. *See* Robeho
Rubuga, 26, 106–8, 178, 392, 398, 399
Ruche, 160, 348, 349
Rudewa, 23, 85, 176, 177, 299, 417, 419
Rufiji/Lufiji, 17, 66, 400, 407
Rufu/Ruvu, 417
Rufuta, 417
Ruga-Ruga, 33, 122, 127, 139, 142, 143, 144, 160, 188
Rugufu, 35, 159, 232, 348, 350, 354
Ruhinga/Ruhingo, 36, 165–67, 208, 209, 212, 213, 313, 314
Ruhuha, 313
Rungwa, 33, 148, 149, 283, 364
Rusawa, 34, 39, 150, 151, 173, 354, 361
Rusizi/Lusize, 6, 11, 36, 38, 165, 171, 208, 213, 231, 282, 302, 311, 312, 313, 314, 400
Rusugi, 35, 157–60
Rutton, Benjamin, 450, 523
Rutton, Richard, 450, 523
Rutwe, 314
Ruvirizi, 313
Ruviro, 313
Ruwenga. *See* Uringa
Ruwha/Ruhwha, 407

Saboor/Saboori/Saburi/Saboora Mkuba/Saburi MKuba/Saboori Cuba/Saboori Mdogo, 27, 113, 345, 347, 368, 370, 372, 373, 377, 381, 384, 392, 435, 446, 448, 478, 521
Sadala, 27, 113, 127, 345–47, 367, 371, 373, 377, 381, 385, 392, 446, 448
Said Bargash/Said Burgush/Syed Bargash/Syed Burgash/Syeed Bergas, "His Highness." *See* Sultan of Zanzibar
Salamene. *See* Sarmine
Salem (city), 40, 64, 88, 175, 176, 259, 438, 484, 489, 491, 517
Salim, 522
Salina, 41, 450, 524
Sange, 313
Sanza. *See* Asanza
Sarboko, 107, 435
Sarmate, 374
Sarmean. *See* Sarmine
Sarmine/Salamene/Salemen/Sa[r]men/Sarmean/Sarmeen, 21, 29, 69, 81, 87, 108, 119, 377, 381, 383, 385, 393, 413, 434, 442, 479, 490, 493, 498, 521
Seedy Mubarak Bombay. *See* Bombay

Seleem, 346
Selim Heshmesh/Heshmy, 10, 19, 21-23, 30, 31, 34, 37, 42, 60, 61, 71, 80, 84, 88, 91, 98, 101, 127, 129, 131, 132, 143, 144, 146, 147, 152, 169, 172, 193, 212, 213, 216, 221, 249, 289, 297, 310, 311, 324, 325, 345, 360, 370, 373, 377, 382, 383, 395, 429, 439, 446, 448, 451, 475, 482, 484, 516
Sentakeyi, 206, 309
Sepoys, 194, 195, 317
Seradi, 370
Shamba Gonera, 19, 69, 70
Shaw, William, 19, 20, 22, 23, 25, 26, 28–32, 35, 74, 75, 82–84, 87–89, 97, 98, 109, 110, 115, 119, 123–25, 127, 129, 130–32, 134, 136, 144, 186, 251, 258, 275, 287, 296, 361, 377, 479
Sheban, 522
Shereef/Sherif, 171, 186, 188, 200, 265, 321
Shirwa, 253, 273
Shisa/Shiza/Sheesa, 26, 87, 108, 178, 392
Shubari/Shumari, 435, 523, 522
Shupanga, 240, 253
Sigunga, 39, 232, 348, 351
Simba, 33, 147, 148, 149, 251, 255, 363
Simbamwenni/Simbaweni/Simbawenni, 20, 22, 73, 78, 79, 82, 83, 84, 297, 324, 419, 420, 439, 488, 491
Simbo, 21, 82, 100, 177, 420
Singiri, 284, 393
Smith, John, 19, 70, 71, 72, 433, 440
Soongooroo/Sunguru, 435, 522
Soor Hadji Palloo, 19, 70, 71, 72, 435
Soor Hadji Pallu, Sewa Haji Paroo. *See* Soor Hadji Palloo
Spalding House of Commerce, 17, 64, 66, 491
Sparhawk, Augustus, 18, 67, 476, 491, 524
Sparrowhawk. *See* Sparhawk
Speke, John H., 37, 105, 108, 117, 121, 127, 168, 202, 203, 209–12, 214, 234, 256, 262, 263, 310, 312, 395, 400, 505, 512, 513, 515, 516
Sultan of Zanzibar, 17, 22, 60, 65, 73, 113, 191, 322, 365, 433, 450, 488, 490, 492, 496, 497
Sultana, 84, 406, 421, 488
Sumburizi, 309, 310, 314
Sunuzzi, 159
Surmiti, 383
Susi, 36, 164, 193, 197, 200, 205, 208, 252, 265, 288, 289, 307, 321, 345, 346, 352, 353, 370, 372, 374, 400, 498, 501
Swarura/Swaruru, 98

Tabora, 9, 10, 27, 29, 72, 109, 111, 113, 119, 120, 121, 126, 129, 203, 216, 265, 267, 274, 287, 323, 348, 379, 399
Tagomoyo/Tagamoyo, 199, 233, 268, 321
Tanganika/Tanganyika Lake, 2, 6, 10, 11, 18, 24, 28, 34, 35, 36, 60, 66, 85, 103, 107, 117, 123, 125, 126, 128–30, 140, 145, 147, 148, 150, 159, 161, 162, 163, 165, 166, 168, 180, 193, 196, 202, 208, 209, 220, 221, 231, 250, 256, 257, 268, 282, 284, 288, 302, 303, 306, 307, 312, 314, 315, 319, 321, 345, 351, 352, 364, 373, 376, 377, 402, 443, 480, 499, 501, 503, 504, 513, 514, 515
Tarya (Taria) Topan/Topeen/Topin, 17, 19, 40, 60, 65, 68, 173, 259, 489
Thani, Sheikh, 19, 73, 75, 90, 94, 99, 100, 101, 103, 104, 300
Tom, 522
Tongoni, 33, 142, 376, 401, 402
Tongwe/Utongwe, 38, 39, 171, 172, 221, 233, 348, 350, 351, 375
Toufiki, 522
Trincomalee, 487
Tubagwe, 408
Tumba, 348
Tura, Eastern Tura, Middle Tura, Western Tura, Tura Perro, 26, 94, 105, 106, 178, 287, 289, 290, 392, 398, 399, 400, 413
Twakali, 522

Uashi, 37, 168, 214,
Ubanirama, 105
Ubari, 117
Ubura, 322
Udoe, 78, 421
Uemba, 117
Ufipa, 126, 136, 145, 248, 283, 288, 323, 359, 364
Ugali, 361
Ugallalla/Ugalalla/Ugalla/Ugala/Ulagalla, 20, 78, 122, 171, 172, 177, 298, 403
Ugogo, 9, 24, 25, 93, 95, 97, 98, 100, 145, 155, 296, 299, 300, 393, 400, 402, 403, 404, 405, 406, 407, 410, 412, 413, 414, 489
Ugomba, 400
Ugombo/Ugambo, 23, 24, 88, 89, 177, 299, 300, 324, 415
Ugongwe, 322
Ugowa, 122
Uguhha, 350
Ugula/Ugura, 400, 403
Ugunda, 32, 136, 138, 180, 251, 258, 274, 286, 322, 361, 365, 376
Ugundo, 108
Uhha, 35, 156, 157, 159, 160, 220, 303
Uhumba, 403
Uhumbo, 105
Ujiji/Ujeejee 6, 10, 11, 13, 18, 20, 24–30, 35, 38–40, 70, 72, 73, 76, 90, 105, 107, 109, 111, 113, 114, 116, 117, 120, 121, 123, 126, 127, 136, 157, 158, 160, 163, 164, 170–74, 182, 184–87, 190, 193, 197–200, 204, 205, 208, 214, 218–21, 224, 225, 229–31, 233, 234, 241, 244, 245, 247, 248, 250, 251, 255, 257–59, 263, 264, 266, 269, 272, 275, 277, 287, 289, 290, 303–5, 311, 319–21, 324, 348, 355, 359, 361, 363, 364, 367–71, 375, 379, 391, 395, 398, 445, 479, 489, 493, 499, 513–15

540 INDEX

Ukamba, 142, 180, 253, 254, 362
Ukami, 78
Ukaramba, 305
Ukaranga, 35, 39, 158, 159, 174, 231, 348, 350
Ukerewe, 495
Ukhumbu, 297
Ukonongo/Ukonogo, 107, 126, 129, 131, 136, 139, 145, 150, 220, 250, 303, 361, 363, 409
Ukwenhe/Ukwenni, 78, 297
Ukwere, 78, 81, 145, 146
Ulagalla. *See* Ugallalla
Uledi Khatalaboo, 127, 434
Uledi Pangani, 442
Uledi. *See* Uredi
Ulimba. *See* Urimba
Ulimengo, 31, 98, 117, 131, 247, 278, 279, 285, 346, 357, 370, 373, 377, 381, 382, 383, 385, 392, 434, 442, 521
Ulonga/Uronga/Mbengerenga, 419
Umanda, 28, 115
Umbaluku, 383, 384, 392
Umbare, 493
Umbari. *See* Ambari
Umgareza, 31, 127, 131, 374, 377, 381, 383, 434, 444, 448
Umpawpaw/Umpopaw. *See* Mpwapwa
Umtamani/Umtamari, 345, 346, 360, 370, 373, 377, 381, 385, 392, 446
Umvoomi. *See* Mvumi
Unamapokera. *See* Mapokera
Ungerengeri, 20, 21, 76, 77, 79, 81–83, 297, 421, 422
Uniyanyembe. *See* Unyanyembe
Unonoro, 314
Unyahuha. *See* Nyahuba
Unyambogi, 101, 178
Unyamwezi, 105, 283, 367, 403, 413, 414, 420, 421, 422
Unyangwira, 407
Unyanwemba. *See* Unyanyembe
Unyanyembe/Unyanwemba/Unyemwemba/Uniyanyembe, 18, 19, 22, 25–32, 35, 38, 39, 40, 69, 71, 73, 76, 84, 88, 104, 105, 107–11, 113, 116–18, 120, 122, 123, 127, 130, 139, 144, 157, 160, 164, 171–73, 178, 181, 186, 190, 193, 203, 207, 209, 210, 220, 221, 250, 251, 254, 255, 256, 258, 259, 261–65, 267, 272, 274, 283, 284, 286, 288, 289, 293, 303, 321, 322, 323, 324, 325, 348, 351, 358, 359, 362–70, 373, 375, 376, 381, 384, 395, 397, 399, 403, 439, 450, 478, 479, 490–93, 497, 498, 500, 518, 519, 521, 524
Unyema. *See* Manyema
Unyemwemba. *See* Unyanyembe
Unyoro, 117, 220, 315
Uredi/Uledi, 19, 119, 374, 378, 381, 383, 400, 434, 490
Uredi Manua Sera/Uredi Manua Sera/Manwa Sera. *See* Manua Sera
Urimba/Ulimba, 233, 244, 250, 348, 351, 354, 361
Uringa/Ruwenga, 36, 165, 166, 167, 314, 315
Uronga/Mbengerenga, 419
Urori, 27, 121, 403
Urua, 24, 145
Urudu. *See* Urundi
Uruguru, 78, 297, 407
Urundi, 36, 37, 117, 163, 164, 169, 205, 207, 303, 304, 309, 310, 312, 315, 352
Urungu/Banurungu/Burungu, 117, 501, 503
Uruva, 90
Usagara, 3, 78, 85, 86, 299, 414–16, 417, 420
Usagozi, 255, 363
Usanda, 403
Usandewa, 407
Usanghi/Usayengi, 122
Usegura, 73, 85, 298
Useguru, 78
Useguwa, 79
Usekke, 409
Usense, 148, 250, 322, 361
Usige/Uzige, 35, 36, 162, 164, 165, 207, 309, 310, 314, 315, 394, 479
Usoowa/Usowwa/Usowa, 149, 179, 359
Usowa/Usowwa. *See* Usoowa
Usui, 400
Usumbara/Usumbura/Uzumbara, 314, 315
Utanda, 33, 149, 179, 246
Utongwe. *See* Tongwe
Uvinza, 155, 157–60, 220, 303
Uvira, 37, 168, 214, 309, 310, 314
Uwelasia, 39, 233, 348, 351
Uyanzi, 25, 101, 399, 402, 406
Uyeow. *See* Wahiyou
Uyowa/Uyoweh, 122, 140
Uzaramo, 70, 78
Uzige. *See* Usige
Uzumbara, 314
Uzumbura. *See* Usumbara

Victoria Nyanza/Lake, 6, 26, 60, 107, 123, 209, 395, 515
Vigunda, 322

Wadirigo/Wadirgo, 414, 415
Wago, 414
Wagogo, 95, 97, 99, 100, 154, 306, 309, 321, 325, 381, 400, 403, 404, 407–9, 411–13, 525
Waguhha, 155, 157
Wahehe, 99, 407, 414
Wahha, 35, 231
Wahiyou, Uyeow, 195, 223, 317
Wahumba/Wahumbu, 99, 114, 404
Wainwright, Jacob, 450, 523
Wainwright, John, 450, 523
Wajiji/Wagigi, 37–39, 161, 164, 168, 169, 172, 206, 207, 214, 215, 231, 303
Wakami, 78
Wakaniamara, 299
Wakawendi, 151
Wakhutu, 415

Wakimbu, 102, 106, 398, 399, 401, 407
Wakotani, 317–19
Waller, Horace, 253, 265, 317
Wami, 160, 307, 416, 417
Wamrima, 298, 401
Wanamgeni, 418
Wananghombeh, 138
Wangwana. *See* Zanzibaris
Wangwana/Wanguan/Wangwani/Wangwan/Mgwana, 98, 105, 106, 113, 115, 120, 127, 129, 139, 141, 143, 151, 153, 154, 160, 170, 178, 291, 303, 308, 321, 324, 325, 366, 393, 395, 397, 398, 399, 400, 401, 409, 414, 417, 418, 420, 434, 525
Wanyamwezi/Wanyamuezi/Wamyamezi/Mnyamwezi/Nyamwezi/Banyamwezi, 21, 27, 30, 69, 72, 83, 90, 95, 102, 105, 113, 115, 123–25, 127, 129, 130, 135, 139, 142, 143, 157, 272, 283, 300, 325, 365–67, 393, 396, 398–400, 403, 409, 413, 414, 420–22, 502, 520
Warori, 113, 410
Warudi/Warundi, 169, 204, 205, 268, 306, 309
Waruguru, 421
Warumashana/Warumashania, 167, 311, 312
Warundi. *See* Warudi
Wasagara/Wasgara, 405, 414, 415
Wasanda, 404
Wasavira. *See* Wazawira
Wasawahili/Wasawahahili, 124, 398
Wasegura, 78, 81
Wasgara. *See* Wasagara
Washense/Washensi/Washenzi/Mishense/Mshense, 75, 82, 87, 127, 129, 151, 298, 404, 409, 421, 488, 525
Wasungu, 100, 140, 317
Wasungu. *See* Msungu
Watikira, 380
Watuka, 323
Watusi, 114, 130, 131, 157, 158, 274, 282
Watuta, 120, 122, 123, 143, 144
Wavinza, 231, 321
Wavira, 169, 514

Wazawira/Wasavira, 323, 322, 358
Wazungu, 409
Webb, W. F., 197, 198, 236, 271, 282, 283, 286, 321, 366, 394, 519
Webb, Capt. Francis R. (U.S. consul at Zanzibar), 2, 7, 17–20, 38, 40, 60, 64, 66–68, 76, 84, 119, 171, 184, 258, 259, 428, 476, 477, 487, 488, 489, 490, 491, 493, 496, 513, 517
Webb, John F. (U.S. consul at Zanzibar), 41, 261, 262, 291, 293, 294, 413, 490, 492, 493, 494, 518, 523
Wellington, Mathew, 450, 523
Wemba, 495
Whinde, 420
Wilyankuru, 122, 127, 132, 255, 434, 490

Young, Sir James (Paraffin), 67, 184, 237, 286, 394, 520

Zaidee/Zaidi, 22, 31, 32, 84, 131, 134, 136, 367, 373, 377, 381, 382, 386, 393, 434, 442, 521
Zambezi, 192, 196, 222–25, 228, 233, 235, 240–43, 251, 253, 255, 268, 271, 273, 276, 280, 315, 316, 318, 361, 513
Zanzibar, 2, 4, 7, 9, 17–19, 23–26, 29, 38, 40, 41, 42, 60–70, 84, 88, 90, 91, 103, 104, 107, 111, 117–19, 122–24, 128, 134, 171, 175, 184, 187–91, 194, 203, 208, 216–20, 230, 242, 243, 251, 256, 258, 259, 261, 262, 266, 267, 270, 275, 289, 291, 293, 295, 297, 298, 317, 321, 322, 345, 366, 378, 381, 395, 400, 408, 413, 419, 425, 431–33, 435, 450, 451, 476, 477, 480, 500, 483, 484, 487, 488–90, 492, 493, 495–501, 506–8, 511–15, 517–19, 521, 523, 524
Zanzibaris, 30–32, 222, 231, 248, 256, 276, 291
Zassi, 35, 37, 162, 163, 170, 171, 205, 218, 303, 305
Zide, 492
Zimbili, 28, 114, 115
Zimbizo, 28, 116, 321, 323
Zingomero/Zungomero/Zungo-Mero, 66, 73, 419
Ziwa, 142, 362, 411
Ziwani, 32, 33, 138, 139, 141, 142, 180, 254, 363, 376, 401
Zouga, 227, 239